H. P. LOVECRAFT

LETTERS TO JAMES F. MORTON

James F. Morton

H. P. LOVECRAFT

LETTERS TO
JAMES F. MORTON

EDITED BY
DAVID E. SCHULTZ AND S. T. JOSHI

Hippocampus Press

New York

Published by Hippocampus Press
P.O. Box 641, New York, NY 10156.
http://www.hippocampuspress.com

Cover design and Hippocampus Press logo by Anastasia Damianakos.
Cover production by Barbara Briggs Silbert.

First Edition
1 3 5 7 9 8 6 4 2

ISBN 978-0-9844802-3-4

Contents

Introduction

> When Howard Lovecraft was among us, his mind alone was capable of meeting Jim Morton's on the same plane, and an evening in their presence was hours with the gods.
>
> —*Edward H. Cole*

The premise seems implausible. A young man of twenty-four, still living with his mother, quite out of touch with the ways of the world, joins an organization for amateur writers. It appeals to him because, for the last decade, he had published his own little amateur science magazine, written astronomy articles for the newspapers, and even dabbled in verse and fiction. The writer quickly establishes himself, being elected first vice-president of the United Amateur Press Association (1915) and then president (1917). He publishes his own little paper, the title of which, the *Conservative*, reflects clearly not only the views of the paper but also of its publisher. His outspoken views have both admirers and detractors. And after getting his ears boxed by one of the organization's grand old men, a liberal, free-thinking anarchist, the two become staunch correspondents and lifelong friends.

It is well known that H. P. Lovecraft, writer of weird fiction and epistolarian extraordinaire, had correspondents of all ages and backgrounds scattered around the country, numbering in his later years to more than one hundred. Early in life his correspondents were primarily fellow amateur journalists, many of whom became lifelong friends. In time, as he published in circles wider than amateur journalism, they came to include fellow professional writers—Clark Ashton Smith, Robert E. Howard, Henry S. Whitehead, Henry George Weiss ("Francis Flagg"), August Derleth—and, ultimately, an ever-growing multitude of young fans of his writing. But chief among them, perhaps the most unlikely, a man who, among all Lovecraft's associates, was closest to being his intellectual equal, James Ferdinand Morton, Jr.

Lovecraft's earliest statements about Morton, whom at the time he had not yet come upon either in person or by mail, were far from favorable. To Maurice W. Moe, Lovecraft had written: "I can scarcely wait for your essay, 'Why I Am Not a Freethinker'. I understand that Mr. Morton is a man of liberal education, so that your controversy must have been a veritable Gigantomachia."[1] Lovecraft had heated differences of opinion with Moe in matters religious, but in opposition to radical freethought the two could be allies. In fact, Lovecraft first encountered Morton somewhat indirectly, and probably unexpectedly. In only the second number of his *Conservative*, Lovecraft blasted

---

1. HPL to M. W. Moe, 16 January 1915 (ms., AHT).

7

the views of Charles D. Isaacson, as expressed in Isaacson's journal *In a Minor Key*, particularly his recognition of Walt Whitman as a great American poet and also his views on race prejudice. In a piece called "In a Major Key" (following prefatory mock praise for Isaacson's journal overall), Lovecraft stated: "Great as may be the literary merit of the publication, its astonishing radicalism of thought cannot but arouse an overwhelming chorus of opposition from the saner elements in amateur journalism." The "saner elements in amateur journalism," of course, constituted Lovecraft and Lovecraft alone. Lovecraft proceeded to expound on his views of the nature of race. He observed: "Race prejudice is a gift of Nature, intended to preserve in purity the various divisions of mankind which the ages have evolved. In comparing this essential instinct of man with political, religious, and national prejudices, Mr. Isaacson commits a serious error of logic."

As one might expect, Isaacson did not receive Lovecraft's salvo idly. In response, Isaacson wrote:

> There comes a musty smell as of old books with the reading of the Conservative, although I am confident he will not be able to realize it until he is shown very carefully—
> He is against free speech.
> He is against freedom of thought.
> He is against the liberty of the press.
> He is against tolerance of color, creed and equality.
> He is in favor of monarchy.
> Despite his repeated abeisance [*sic*] to the intellectuality and spirituality of the Jew, he continually attempts to place him apart—explaining away the ideas of an individual by his religion. It is unseemly for a man who boasts of his land and his ancestry that he should still cling to the Tory notion and defy the best spirit of America by refusing to acknowledge the nationality of an American, born here of American-born parents, a citizen, loyal, broad, [*sic*] eager to serve his nation, because of opposing creeds![2]

James F. Morton, Jr., Isaacson's colleague, also took up the defense in "'Conservatism' Gone Mad." Morton's response sheds considerable light on his own personal thought and history. Despite the inflammatory title of the essay, is remarkably perceptive and shows great restraint. Yet in the end, it surely was a devastating lesson in humility:

> For the true conservative one must always have a large measure of respect. He represents the desirable and indeed necessary social influence which restrains the more radical among us from proceeding with excessive haste in our anxiety to cure that which is awry in conditions as they exist. . . .

---

2. Charles D. Isaacson, "Concerning the Conservative," *In a Minor Key* No. 2 [1915]: [10–11].

As a representative of somewhat extreme radicalism I cheerfully admit the foregoing principles, and would not abolish the sane conservative even if I could do so. The radical is necessary to insure progress and prevent stagnation, and the conservative is needed to keep the balance and to save the principle of orderliness in the midst of the necessary transition from the old to the new. The radical may become fanatical and destructive, and the conservative may become a bigot and a reactionary. I presume that Mr. H. P. Lovecraft, who chooses to label himself "The Conservative" par excellence, is a rather young man who will at some future day smile at the amusing dogmatism with which he now assumes to lay down the law. By the courtesy of Mr. Isaacson I have the opportunity to see the July issue of the Lovecraftian publication. The editor takes himself more seriously than he is fully warranted in doing. . . . Mr. Lovecraft's conservatism . . . smacks not so much of loyalty to present accepted truths or even still current habits of thought, as of reversion to the outgrown partial and restricted views of a past age. It is in large measure reaction, rather than conservatism.

One imagines Lovecraft smarting under Morton's spot-on assessment of him. But he must have found some balm in Morton's closing lines, which proved, within a decade, to be every bit as accurate as those opening the essay:

From the sample afforded in the paper under discussion it is evident that Mr. Lovecraft needs to serve a long and humble apprenticeship before he will become qualified to sit in the master's seat and to thunder forth *ex cathedra* judgments. The one thing in his favor is his evident sincerity. Let him once come to realize the value of appreciating the many points of view shared by persons as sincere as he, and better informed in certain particulars, and he will become less narrow and intolerant. His vigor of style, when wedded to clearer conceptions based on a wider comprehension, will make him a writer of power.

Lovecraft's response to Morton's stinging, but never humiliating, defense of Isaacson was the verse satire "The Isaacsonio-Mortoniad" (a nod to Alexander Pope's *Dunciad*). It grudgingly acknowledges that Morton's observations had merit and recognizes Morton as a foe to be respected. Lovecraft attacked Morton and Isaacson both, one imagines mostly to let off steam; but he never published the poem, perhaps because he recognized the essential veracity of Morton's comments—especially in the closing words—and saw that his knee-jerk response was in the end but a feeble protest. Most tellingly, Lovecraft observes: "The raging blast, sent earthward to destroy, / Is watch'd and study'd with artistic joy." Surely there was some admiration and respect for his powerful adversary.

At about the time Lovecraft composed "The Isaacsonio-Mortoniad," he expressed his thoughts about Morton in a letter:

Morton is a problem. I can feel the more wholesome nature of his work—with him I can come to grips as man to man—there is no slimy Jewry or Orientalism there—while Isaacson defies analysis with his shifty Asiatic caprices. Morton is harsh, insolent, overbearing, but not nasty. He has doubt-less been criticised very roughly himself, and thereby made bitter toward men of conservative ideas. I understand that he overstudied in Harvard, taking a Master's degree in the same time that most young men take only Bachelor's honours. He has taught too much—overreached sane human limitations. I re-spect James F. Morton, Jr., no matter how much he reviles, for his has been a life of conscientious research and unceasing mental endeavour. His "Frag-ments of a Mental Autobiography" in LIBRA justify his erratic views,[3] & im-pose kindness on his critics. He is to be tolerated gently, & his declining years must not be vexed with any more criticism than is demanded by the self-defence of his victims. I can sympathise with Morton in many ways. I am not an orthodox disciple of religion, but I deem it dangerous to tamper with any system so manifestly beneficial to morality. Whatever may be the faults of the church, it has never yet been surpassed or nearly equalled as an agent for the promotion of virtue. And the same thing applies to our present social system. It has its defects, but is evidently a natural growth, and better fitted to pre-serve an approximate civilization than any Utopian scheme conjured up over night by some artificially thinking radical. . . .

But radicals are "above" all truth & science, so let them rave on—Nature is too strong to be hurt seriously by their mistakes![4]

Lovecraft knew much of Morton's background. He knew that Morton held two degrees. (Lovecraft himself did not graduate from high school.) Morton, twenty years Lovecraft's senior, was twenty-ninth president of the National Amateur Press Association (1896–97). Early in the twentieth cen-tury, he had been involved with various radical groups. He once belonged to the colony at Home, Washington, home to anarchists, freethinkers, eugeni-cists, communists, nudists, and others who did not fit into mainstream soci-ety. He was an early editor of the *Demonstrator: A Weekly Periodical of Fact, Thought and Comment,* an English-language anarchist newspaper, and other similar publications. Morton took up many causes that Lovecraft himself ve-hemently opposed. Writing to the Kleicomolo (a round-robin letter circulated among Lovecraft, Moe, Rheinhart Kleiner, and Ira A. Cole), Lovecraft stated: "I would have him [Kleiner] remember, that I censured and satirized Mr. Jas. F. Morton, Jr., as severely as anyone, for his wanton destruction of the public faith and the publick morals."[5]

---

3. *Libra* was an amateur journal edited by JFM beginning in 1907. His "Fragments of a Mental Autobiography" ran in five installments (see Appendix).
4. HPL to Kleiner, 25 November 1915; *Letters to Rheinhart Kleiner* (New York: Hippocampus Press, 2005), 25–26. It is true that HPL did censure and satirize JFM in "The Isaacsonio-Mortoniad," but he had shown the poem only privately.
5. October 1916, *Letters to Rheinhart Kleiner* 59.

Not long thereafter, Lovecraft made a feeble attempt to get even with Morton for his devastating critique of Lovecraft. In "Concerning 'Persia—in Europe'" (January 1917) Lovecraft pounced upon a trivial slip of the pen Morton had made in an article. Lovecraft sneeringly begins, "Since Mr. James F. Morton, Jr., so conclusively demonstrated his scholastic infallibility over a year ago, in his lofty essay on 'Conservative Run Mad [*sic*]', the undersigned would like to inquire about a remarkable geographical statement contained in his clever article in your September number."[6] By stooping to such a rhetorically inflated commentary on such a trifling matter, Lovecraft merely confirmed his immaturity.

It seems improbable that Lovecraft and Morton ever could be friends. But in the next two years, Lovecraft's feelings about Morton mellowed.

> Speaking of Morton—I like him more & more as I become further acquainted with him. Despite my antipodal differences on most matters, his absolute sincerity concerning all things appeals to me strongly. Most radicals are affected poseurs, but it did not take E. H. Cole's recent article[7] to convince me that J. F. M. Jr.'s zeal is of the genuine & serious variety. He maintains an open attitude in discussing poetick imagism, & I am going to ask Mo to lend me the *Kleicomolo* instalment containing the latter's lucid discussion of this theme; as well as the inimitable burlesque; to send along with my next instalment of the argument. Mo is an old opponent of Morton's, & will no doubt be glad to help me out![8]

Somewhere along the way, when is not known, the two became engaged in epistolary exchanges, and amiable ones at that. In April 1920, Lovecraft writes the Gallomo (another round-robin letter group of Lovecraft, Moe, and Alfred Galpin) that, "At the recommendation of James F. Morton, Jr., I am perusing the works of a modern imaginative author named Algernon Blackwood . . ." Lovecraft's enthusiasm for weird literature surely played a part in his coming to be friends with Morton. The circumstances for Morton's recommendation are not known—his earliest surviving letters are dated three years later. But still, the two had not yet met. Lovecraft missed an opportunity in mid-August 1920 to meet Morton at a Hub Club Picnic, but before long the two did finally meet face to face:

> . . . Whilst I was looking at some interesting photographs of oldtime amateurs & conventions, a heavy step sounded on the piazza, & at last I succeeded in shaking hands with the elusive person I have wished so long to meet—James Ferdinand Morton, Jr.! Never have I met so thoroughly eru-

---

6. *CE* 1.137.
7. Presumably Cole's piece in the *National Amateur* (December 1918; see the Appendix).
8. HPL to Kleiner, 16 December 1918; *Letters to Rheinhart Kleiner* 154.

dite a conversationalist before, & I was quite surprised by the geniality & friendliness which overlay his unusual attainments. I could but regret the limited opportunities which I have of meeting him, for Morton is one who commands my most unreserved liking.[9]

Shortly thereafter, Lovecraft composed a speech entitled "What Amateurdom and I Have Done for Each Other" (1921), in which he confessed that amateur journalism's profoundest effect on him was not merely to provide a satisfying hobby—no, amateur journalism had give him "life itself." In describing his career thus far as an amateur journalist, Lovecraft said: "My attempts appear to be received for the most part with either coolness or distaste, though the encouragement of a few critics like W. Paul Cook, James F. Morton, Jr., and Samuel Loveman has more than compensated for the hostility of others."[10] It is not known what such encouragement from Morton might have entailed. Lovecraft had been friend and correspondent of both Cook and Loveman from the outset, but Lovecraft may have had in mind his first meeting with Morton in 1920, and even also the words of veiled support in "'Conservatism' Gone Mad." Lovecraft's earliest extant letter dates to February 1923, Morton's to Lovecraft (a fragment) to around April of that year; but when correspondence may have commenced is difficult to tell. For example, in February 1924, Lovecraft told Morton that he recalled reading Morton's poem "Haunted Houses" "w'en ya wrote it h'ars & h'ars ago!", but when might that have been? There must have been some interplay between the two in early 1922 when both Lovecraft and Morton had items published in the humor magazine *Home Brew*. Of them Lovecraft wrote: "Mine own fictions ["Herbert West—Reanimator"] are miserably mechanical, whilst the Augustan Morton here sinks to flat & pitiable commonplaces.[11]

Lovecraft called Morton "a thoroughly erudite . . . conversationalist"; but since epistolary correspondence was, to Lovecraft, the same thing as face-to-face discussion, he surely realized he had met someone with whom he could discuss intelligently virtually any subject. But interaction between the two was not limited to letters alone. There were many future opportunities for personal discussion. Over the years, the two met fairly frequently as finances and circumstances allowed, but when they could not meet, they contented themselves with fairly frequent letters. Their correspondence may have arisen primarily because they had undertaken the editing and publication of *The Poetical Works of Jonathan E. Hoag* (1923). The roles Morton and Lovecraft played in the preparation of the book are blurred because each had a hand in revising Hoag's verse, although in the end Lovecraft's was the stronger.

---

9. HPL to Kleiner, 10 September 1920; *Letters to Rheinhart Kleiner* 197.
10. *CE* 1.272–73.
11. HPL to Kleiner, 12 March 1922; *Letters to Rheinhart Kleiner* 221.

Morton was a key figure in the professional publication of Lovecraft's fiction. To be sure, he was not the only person who alerted Lovecraft in 1923 to the appearance of *Weird Tales*, a magazine that might be sympathetic to the kind of stories he was writing and which until then had been published only in amateur journals for a very small audience. It was Morton who urged Lovecraft somewhat earlier to submit stories to *Black Cat* and *Black Mask*. The latter two magazines never published Lovecraft's stories, but *Weird Tales* did, and Morton early on urged the editor to publish Lovecraft's work. At about this time, Lovecraft began sharing the burden of his revisory work for David Van Bush with Morton. Morton felt the two could establish a business for assisting aspiring writers. In December 1923, he proposed to Lovecraft the formation of The Crafton Service Bureau, offering "expert assistance of a group of highly trained and experienced specialists in the revision and typing of manuscripts of all kinds, prose or verse, at reasonable rates." The bureau was advertised in Charles A. A. Parker's little magazine, *L'Alouette* in September 1924, but it appears nothing came of the venture. Both Lovecraft and Morton had compositions in the March 1924 number of *Weird Tales*. It contained Lovecraft's "The Rats in the Walls" and also Morton's poem "Haunted Houses."

During Lovecraft's "New York exile" (March 1924–April 1926), Lovecraft saw Morton and others of the Kalem Club (a group of writers, mostly amateurs, whose last names started with the letters K, L, or M) quite regularly, meeting at the residences of the various members, and engaging in long discussions well into the night. Morton's career at the time was that of lecturer, primarily, and that skill surely came into play at many of the meetings.

The Lovecraft–Morton correspondence is every bit as genuine as their actual conversation. The reader will find ample evidence of that in the (extant) Lovecraft side. These are probably among the most comic and lighthearted of Lovecraft's letters. From time to time, Lovecraft writes in a style that apes the day's slang and, thus, is quite unlike his otherwise mostly formal letters. Early letters begin with classical sounding greetings such as "Salve, Maxime!" or "Illustrissime!" Over time, these devolved into orotund, alliterative (or assonantal) pronouncements, such as "August Antagonist of Ambulatory Answering" and "Luminous Lanthorn of Lithological Lucidity." We find, in the few surviving Morton letters, that Morton was no slouch when it came to pontificating. Compare his "Great God of Georgian Geoconstructional Grandeur" or "Incomparable Inventor of Immeasureable Imagery." And Morton signed himself "Mortonius" and "Plantagenet" as a foil to Lovecraft's own steady "Theobaldos." Many of Morton's letters, oddly enough, sound almost as though they had been written by Lovecraft himself:

> As to the question of "ae" versus "e," your position is both stronger and
> weaker than in the "our" matter. Your argument itself is much more forcible,
> but British, as well as American usage is running more rapidly against you.

The solitary "e" became long since universally received as a philological English equivalent of the Greek and Latin dipththongs [*sic*] in numberless words; and those on which you take your stand merely hold out longer than the rest. But even in England they are rapidly giving way to the simpler vowel. I do not know that even you write "oeconomics;" and if you do, you are nearly solitary in so doing. So your argument of universal usage in "the most cultivated parts of the civilization," even we humbly accept England as our permanent cultural superior (which is challengeable), does not apply with anything like the same force as with the "our" words. The "oe" and "ae" dipththongs are palpably doomed, though they will linger in slowly lessening usage for a generation or two longer. The beauty which you assign to them is largely imported into them by your early associations with them, and the pictures that they accordingly call up. But they are left-overs with no real role in the pattern of normal English speech; and to most ears they have no advantage over the clear-cut "e."[12]

There are lengthy though delightful discourses about canned beans, sweetened condensed milk, amateur affairs, genealogy, stamp collecting, and mineralogy. At times there are heated debates (of which we see only one side) on any number of topics about which the two did not agree, but from which, despite strong differences of opinion, both could walk away amicably. For example, Lovecraft wrote at length of his impatience with games and sport as nothing more than time-wasters, and also somewhat exasperatedly about Morton's need to follow a schedule, a practice Lovecraft would have found utterly stultifying. But it was not all debate or farce. There is, perhaps, no more poignant line in all Lovecraft than the simple greeting, "Dear Jim," when Lovecraft had to inform his friend that his dear Aunt Lillian had died, signaling that, for the moment, a somber mien was required.

Only 45 or so letters by Morton to Lovecraft have survived. Lovecraft seemed only to keep only the most significant letters from correspondents. He kept nearly all his letters from Robert E. Howard, E. Hoffmann Price, C. L. Moore, and E. A. Edkins. Why Lovecraft did not keep more of Morton's letters is not known. Lovecraft used the backs of some of the few surviving letters in drafting *The Dream-Quest of Unknown Kadath*, "The Whisperer in Darkness," *At the Mountains of Madness*, and "Some Repetitions on the Times," but other letters survive separately. It is fortunate that Morton's letters were put to humble use in the composition of some of Lovecraft's tales. Those letters, some only fragmentary, show both playfulness and sobriety equivalent to Lovecraft's own.

Morton was the more successful of the two in securing gainful, long-term employment. (One suspects that Lovecraft never aspired to such a goal himself, preferring, instead, to do as he pleased every day, even if that meant liv-

12. JFM to HPL, 6 January 1930 (ms., JHL).

ing very, very frugally.) In 1925, now aged fifty-five, the former anarchist became the curator of the new Paterson (NJ) Museum. On paper, Morton was not particularly qualified for the position, but he convinced the Library's Board of Trustees to hire him, and he quickly turned the museum into a significant institution, particularly through acquisition of the world's first practical submarine and through his extensive work on the museum's mineral collection. For much of 1925 and into early 1926, Lovecraft hoped, perhaps unrealistically, that Morton could persuade the museum trustees to hire Lovecraft as an assistant; the collapse of this pipe-dream augmented Lovecraft's inclination to return to Providence in April 1926. Morton held the position of curator until he retired at age seventy. The museum's mineral collection was graced not only with items from Morton's personal collection, but also with specimens that Lovecraft himself provided or helped to obtain. In "The Call of Cthulhu" (1926), Lovecraft acknowledged Morton's accomplishment shortly after he was hired:

> I had largely given over my inquiries into what Professor Angell called the "Cthulhu Cult", and was visiting a learned friend in Paterson, New Jersey; the curator of a local museum and a mineralogist of note. Examining one day the reserve specimens roughly set on the storage shelves in a rear room of the museum, my eye was caught by an odd picture in one of the old papers spread beneath the stones.

Lovecraft's later letters to Morton contain much discussion of genealogical matters, in which the two men discovered more and more familial connections between them. Perhaps the most enjoyable anecdotes Lovecraft tells about Morton are those involving visits to Maxfield's ice cream parlor in Warren, RI, during which they and others engaged in entire meals consisting of nothing but ice cream:

> Morton's visit held up my correspondence, but we had a damned good time. . . . [W]e visited the colonial seaport of Warren, down the East shore of the bay—incidentally stopping at a place (quite a rendezvous of our gang) where 28 varieties of ice cream are sold. We had six varieties apiece—my choices being grape, chocolate chip, macaroon, cherry, banana, and orange-pineapple."[13]

Morton was shattered by Lovecraft's death in 1937. Even three years afterward, he still could not bear to write more than a few short paragraphs about a man whom he felt volumes were required to capture adequately on paper. It is telling that in Lovecraft's "Instructions in Case of Decease," the first person named after Lovecraft's surviving aunt, Annie Gamwell, and his "literary executor," R. H. Barlow, was James Morton, whom Lovecraft

---

13. HPL to Robert E. Howard, 24 July–5 August 1933; *A Means to Freedom* 2.628.

wanted to have his ancestral copy of Cotton Mather's *Magnalia Christi Americana* (1702), as well as other books on Americana. Morton himself contributed *The Works of Lord Chesterfield, Including His Letters to His Son, &c.*[14] to Lovecraft's library.

Lovecraft's correspondence, late in life, became an almost unbearable burden. "I try to amputate dumbbell branches of my correspondence, but they are like the Hydra's heads."[15] Quite likely, once his most active years in amateur journalism were behind him, he sought out few, if any, new correspondents. Instead, fans, admirers, would-be writers, and others found their way to him. No query (save the letters from one Harold David Emerson, a crank who signed himself ★Harold) went unanswered, and a reply from Lovecraft merely instigated yet another letter to him. When the crush of letters became too much, he said he needed to trim the list of correspondents; but in light of his habit of polite response, it is difficult to imagine how did so. But among the lengthy roster of correspondents, James F. Morton stands out not only as among the least likely but also among the most enduring. His avuncular advice (much like Lovecraft's own to his protégés) and lively letters were part of the gift of "life itself" bestowed on Lovecraft in Lovecraft's early days as an amateur journalist.

—DAVID E. SCHULTZ
S. T. JOSHI

A Note on the Text

Lovecraft's extant letters to Morton number one hundred sixty-two. Of those, only three, owned by the John Hay Library, are original manuscripts. The balance survive only as transcripts from the original letters as prepared by Arkham House in anticipation of publishing selections from them in Lovecraft's *Selected Letters*. Many of the transcribed letters have not been previously published, and of those that were, many were heavily cut. This book, though it includes the transcribed letters in their entirety does not represent the entire universe of Lovecraft's letters to Morton. Arkham House rarely transcribed postcards, and Lovecraft surely sent many to Morton. The editors at Arkham House typically selected only text of potential interest for transcription, and so many of the letters are not complete. And some letters have been lost. Whether the original letters were returned to Morton is unknown, as is their whereabouts today. The source for all letters in this book is the Arkham House transcript, save for the three letters held by John Hay Library. Images in letters taken from the Arkham House transcripts are tracings of

---

14. First published in 1774. JFM's gift was the first complete American edition (1860).
15. HPL to JFM, p. 295.

Lovecraft's own drawings. Letter no. 43, a letter probably written to Frank Belknap Long, later typed for circulation to several correspondents, is included because it bears the notation: "To James Ferdinand Morton, Esq." It, too, is in the possession of the John Hay library.

Morton's letters to Lovecraft, housed at the John Hay Library number fewer than 45. Some are fragmentary, but there is one eleven-page letter. All are typed, save for a single postcard. Lovecraft used many of the letters or parts of them to draft various stories.

This book also contains two letters by Lovecraft to William L. Bryant, and one by Bryant to Lovecraft, all owned by the John Hay Library.

Acknowledgments

Peter Ruber was instrumental in placing in our hands the transcripts of Lovecraft's letters for this book. Susan Stravinski, Academic Librarian, Special Collections, University of Wisconsin, Vincent Golden and Jacklyn Penny of the American Antiquarian Society, and Rosemary Cullen of the John Hay Library provided copies of rare publications and manuscript material. Colleagues who lent valuable assistance in various ways to the preparation of this volume include Kenneth W. Faig, Jr., Stefan Dziemianowicz, Derrick Hussey, and Steven J. Mariconda.

Abbreviations

AHT	Arkham House transcripts of Lovecraft's letters
ALS	autograph letter, signed
AT	Lovecraft, *The Ancient Track* (2001)
CE	Lovecraft, *Collected Essays* (2004–06; 5 vols.)
D	Lovecraft, *Dagon and Other Macabre Tales* (1986)
DH	Lovecraft, *The Dunwich Horror and Others* (1984)
JHL	John Hay Library, Brown University
LL	S. T. Joshi, comp., *Lovecraft's Library: A Catalogue* (rev. ed. 2002; numbers refer to entries)
LR	Peter Cannon, ed. *Lovecraft Remembered* (1998)
MM	Lovecraft, *At the Mountains of Madness and Other Novels* (1985)
MTS	Lovecraft–Wandrei, *Mysteries of Time and Spirit* (2002)
NAPA	National Amateur Press Association
SL	Lovecraft, *Selected Letters* (1965–76; 5 vols.)
WT	*Weird Tales*

To Howard

    from James

———————————

When of great Lovecraft's merits I would write,
My Muse in vain essays the lofty flight.
But then I see his wit with kindness blend,
And straight forget the genius in the friend.

[found among Lovecraft's papers]

Letters to James Ferdinand Morton

[1]   [AHT]

Feb. 10, 1923

I have come to regard architecture and decoration as the greatest of all arts, since it is the least personal and least tainted with vulgar emotion. As I grow older, I see more and more clearly what utter damn nonsense and rubbish human ethics, aspirations, beliefs, and kindred illusions are. Nothing matters in a universe devoid of values or significance; and that art is the truest, which is *least connected with ideas or purposes or sentiments.* I am not sure but that uselessness and triviality are the basic essentials of real art—at any rate, I prefer that which is most frankly impersonal, decorative, and whimsical. Line and colour—that is all there is to life. I have ceased to admire character—all I now value in any man are his manners, accomplishments, and choice of cravats. I will admit, however, that there is a certain importance in the cut of one's hair and regularity of one's features. And so forth. The greatest historical tragedy of modern times was the fall of the periwig.

To end the suspense—this bird Cole is getting political again. At the Hub meeting[1] Feby. 8 he urgently invited me to dine with him at an inn the following eventide; & I, poor fish, fell into the trap.

Act II

Time—Feby. 9, 6:30 p.m. Place—Copley Sq. Grill

Enter some macaroni & fish. Exeunt, respectively, down gullets of Theobaldus and Edvardius. Uneasy silence, & Colic hemming & hawing. Dark clouds—& the thunderbolt!

Well—'twas a second company playing Boston in the old tragedy whose Broadway premier occurred on that pedestrian eve of 12th October.

Would I, in the sacred name of friendship (& were we not brothers & ξένοι after my December Roselanding?)[2] & of amateurical patriotism (& did I not owe much to the dear ol' cause?) take a nomination for another siege of that DAMNED PRESIDENCY!!??[3]

(Intermission for outraged gasps.)

Poor Cole—so young yet so distrest! Arguments? Migard, but 'e was full of 'em, & had one pat every time I piped out a feeble protest.

Wou'd I be so heartless as to quit just as I had things going, & thereby cause my original sacrifice to prove vain & unavailing? Wou'd I drop my pickaxe just because the whistle blew? Did I not know that I—& I alone—could

21

keep Loveman in the fold and cause him (the Hon. Edward Harold Cole) to "come back" on all fours & issue a paper? . . . . Oswald, the smelling-salts!

Anent the Fascist problem—assumedly we approach it from radically different directions.[4] Galpinius and I have been discussing democracy a lot lately, and we agree that it is a false idol—a mere catchword and illusion of inferior classes, visionaries, and dying civilizations. Life has no ultimate values, and our proximate values can be little more than what we like to see or possess. "Right" and "wrong" are primitive conceptions which cannot endure the test of cold science. Now Galpin and I maintain that, logically, a man of taste should prefer such things as favour strong and advanced men at the expense of the herd. Of what use is it to please the herd? They are simply coarse animals—for all that is admirable in man is the artificial product of special breeding. We advocate the preservation of conditions favourable to the growth of beautiful things—imposing palaces, beautiful cities, elegant literature, reposeful art and music, and a physically select human type such as only luxury and a pure racial strain can produce. Thus we oppose democracy, if only because it would retard the development of a handsome Nordic breed. We realise that all conceptions of justice and ethics are mere prejudices and illusions—there is no earthly reason why the masses should not be kept down for the benefit of the strong, since every man is for himself in the last analysis. We regard the rise of democratic ideals as a sign of cultural old age and decay,[5] and deem it a compliment to such men as Mussolini when they are said to be "XVth century types." We are proud to be definitely *reactionary*, since only by a bold repudiation of the "liberal" pose and the "progress" illusion can we get the sort of authoritative social and political control which alone produces things which make life worth living. We admire the old German Empire, for it was a force so strong that it almost conquered all the combined forces of the rest of the world. Personally, my objection to Germany in the late war was that it formed a menace to our English Empire—an Empire so lamentably split in 1775–83, and so regrettably weakened by effeminate ideas of liberty. My wish was that we English reunite into one irresistible power and establish an hegemony of the globe in true Roman fashion. Neither we nor Germany will ever be really strong till we have unified imperial control.

Our modern worship of empty ideals is ludicrous. What does the condition of the rabble matter? All we need to do is to keep it as quiet as we can. What is more important, is to perpetuate those things of beauty which are of real value because involving actual sense-impressions rather than vapid theories. "Equality" is a joke—but a great abbey or cathedral, covered with moss, is a poignant reality. It is for us to safeguard and preserve the conditions which produce great abbeys, and palaces, and picturesque walled towns, and vivid sky-lines of steeples and domes, and luxurious tapestries, and fascinating books, paintings, and statuary, and colossal organs and noble music, and dramatic deeds on embattled fields . . . *these are all there is of life;* take them away and we have nothing which a man of taste or spirit would care to live for. Take them away and our poets have nothing to sing—our dreamers have nothing to dream about. The blood of a million men is well shed in producing one glorious legend which thrills posterity . . . and it is not at all important *why* it was shed. A coat of arms won in a crusade is worth a thousand slavering compliments bandied about amongst a rabble.

Reform? Pish! We do not *want* reform! What would the world be without its scarlet and purple evil! Drama is born of conflict and violence . . . . god! shall we ever be such women as to prefer the emasculate piping of an arbitrator to the lusty battle-cry of a blue-eyed, blond-bearded warrior? The one sound power in the world is the power of a hairy, muscular right arm!

Yah! How I spit upon this rotten age with its feeble comforts and thwarted energies—its Freuds and Wilsons, Augustines and Heliogabali,—rabbles and perversions! What these swine with their scruples and problems, changes and rebellions, need, is a long draught of blood from a foeman's skull on the battlements of a mountain fortalice! We need fewer harps and viols, and more drums and brasses. The answer to jazz is the wild dance of the warlike conqueror! Don't complain of the youth's high-powered motor-car unless you can give him an horse and armour and send him to conquer the domains of the neighbouring kings! Modern life—my gawd! I don't wonder that literature is going to hell or chaos! What is there to write about now? Before we have *literature* we must have *life*—bold, colourful, primitive, and picturesque. We must change a George V for a Richard Coeur de Lion—a PLANTAGENET![6]

Of course, all talk of reviving real & vigorous life is a pipe dream. Our civilisation, like all its predecessors, is nearing the end of its rope; so that all we can sensibly do is to throw a little sand on the toboggan. And I think that the Fascisti movement is the best sand-box we have yet seen. True, it overrides technical *law*, but *not until that law has justly forfeited the tolerance of sensible men*. Democratic government is rabble whim. More important than any legalistic formality, are certain traditions woven inextricably into the finer part of the race; & these *must* be preserved, by *any* means at hand—legal or illegal. Freedom of press & speech *sound* well—but these vague principles cannot be allowed to interfere with the fight of a race for the values which are its only solid possessions. In fine—today certain nations need certain policies; & they need them so badly that we can't afford to complain of any means they use in getting them. I don't give a damn how the Fascisti got in power, but I take off my hat to them if they have preserved for Italy the life that built up her palaces & towers, bridges & monuments, arts & letters. These fruits of civilisation are all that count.

What we must do is to shake off our encumbering illusions and false values—banishing sonorous platitudes in a civilised realisation that the only things of value in the world are those which promote beauty, colour, interest, and heightened sensation. The one great crusade worthy of an enlightened man is that directed against whatever impoverishes imagination, wonder, sensation, dramatic life, and the appreciation of beauty. Nothing else matters. And not even this really matters in the great void, but it is amusing to play a little in the sun before the blind universe dispassionately pulverises us again into that primordial nothingness from whence it moulded us for a second's sport.

By the way—I saw your *Tribune* letter on the Fascisti.[7] Admirably written, though I can't agree!

My trip?[8] An intoxication of Colonial delight! I can now think of nothing save ancient New-England! O Marblehead, how many are thine antique glories! I see again thy tortuous & labyrinthine alleys, winding, winding, winding up & down, about & around; precipice & hollow; terrace & stone steps; & all clutter'd & bedeckt with the houses of immemorial antiquity rising brown & peaked, chimney'd & gabled; hoar & venerable; set here & there at every angle & every level till old Nuremburg & Whitby seem plain by contrast! O houses gabled & fabled; archaic, spectral, mythical; with your blear'd blinking window-panes & grotesque clusters of chimney-pots—O fungous growths of Colonial dream; body'd phantasms of piratical legend—I sweep down on ye from basalt pinnacles & as a wind rattle your primal sashes & whirl your century'd vanes! The lore & the madness of the sea are in ye, for are ye not the fanes of fisher-folk where under waning moons the children of Druid isles offer up nameless tributes to Dagon the Unfathomable? Mystery sleeps here, for all is as it was and will be.

Salem I "did" as with a fine-tooth comb, & in the twilight I climbed Gallows Hill. Up . . . up . . . & up . . . Damn that wind—why *can't* it sound less *articulate?* At last I was on the summit, where in the bed rock still lurk the iron clamps that held the witch gallows. A reddish light bathed the weird town below, & it was indeed a weird town as seen from that bleak hilltop where strange winds moaned from over the untenanted wastes to the westward. And I was alone on that hill in that sepulchral place, where the allies of the devil had swung, . . . & swung . . . & hurled out curses on their executioners & their descendants. I thought of certain imprecations of the dead in fact & fiction . . . . . "God shall give them blood to drink"[9] . . . . . . & at that moment, as God is my judge, I heard faintly but distinctly the clanking of chains in the wind . . . . the chains of the gibbet which had not stood since 1693 . . . . & from that accursed wind came a shriek that was more than the shrieking of wind . . . . . a malignant, daemoniac sound that left in my ears the hideous echo of a syllable . . . . "ire" . . . . which in turn brought up as if in shocking memory a crude couplet I never heard before or since:

> "We swing higher,
> You feede ye Fire."

Yes—it was some trip; & I hung around Gallows Hill till quite late. I mean to visit Salem often in future—it has a greater aesthetic appeal to me than any poem ever written in words.[10]

But I must cease—what a colossal bore I am! Now I MUST do that Hoag preface![11] Tuus in aeternitate—Tibaldus.

Notes

1. I.e., the Hub Club, a group of amateur journalists in the Boston area.

2. An allusion to visiting the amateur Edward H. Cole, who lived at 57 Roseland Street in Boston. Ξένος is any citizen of a foreign state with whom one has a treaty of hospitality.

3. HPL was at this time serving as interim president of NAPA, taking over after the resignation of William J. Dowdell. Cole was urging HPL to run for a full term for the 1923–24 official year, beginning in July.

4. Benito Mussolini's march on Rome occurred on 27–29 October 1922, thereby putting his Fascist party in power. He became a virtual dictator in early 1925.

5. This conception is derived from the work of Friedrich Nietzsche, whose thought influenced both HPL and Galpin.

6. HPL emphasizes the familial line of Richard the Lion-Hearted because JFM claimed descent from it.

7. Presumably a letter by JFM to the *New York Tribune;* not located.

8. A side-trip, on the way to Providence from New York City, through Salem and Marblehead in early January. Cf. *SL* 1.203–6.

9. A central utterance in Nathaniel Hawthorne's *The House of the Seven Gables* (1851): "God will give him blood to drink!" It is Matthew Maule's curse on the Pyncheon family after he has been wrongly convicted of witchcraft.

10. Salem was the inspiration for HPL's fictional town of Arkham.

11. HPL, co-editor with JFM of Jonathan E. Hoag's *Poetical Works,* was tasked with writing the preface to the book. The book contains six tributes to Hoag in verse by HPL.

[2]   [AHT]

Old 598

Feby. 24, 1923

Hail Odovakar,[1] Fellow-Chieftain of the Goths!

Pax vobiscum! May sleep return to thy mighty head, whence 'twas snatched by the cynical vacillations of a Theobald! As a rule, I hate firm & unequivocal utterance—it's so damnably middle-class—but since I hate rules even more, & am always eager to do a friend a good turn, I'm hastening to sit finally & tightly upon the sources of your unrest. But before you start blaming me for listening to Cole, remember that I listened to you last October! What one Harvard man can do, another has a chance of doing; & after one false step, the poor victim is always liable to flop again! And so with me!

Bah! What a mess one gets into by trying to please everybody—& my only interest in all this damned official mess is to please my friends—you, Cole, &c.! Yah! Grrrrrr!

And as to the immaturity of the divine Galpinius—doest not recall my tribute in *Tryout* to his nineteenth birthday?

> Is't true, indeed, that thou so short a Time
> Hast known the Air of our terrestrial Clime?
> Art thou not rather some experienc'd Sage
> Who hast, like Aeson, lost thy hoary Age?

I really wrote that for his seventeenth birthday, but publication was delayed.[2]

And as to the future of civilisation—pish! It doesn't matter one way or t'other. All roads lead to oblivion.

Yes—I guess Ol' New-England can give the rest of America points on historic beauty. But OLD ENGLAND! Honestly, if I once saw its venerable oaks & abbeys, manor-houses & rose gardens, lanes & hedges, meadows & mediaeval villages, I could never return to America. The only reason that I don't save like hell & get in on Dench's[3] tour is that I simply couldn't come back, once I saw the ancient glories & monuments of my race. I would jump in the Thames, the Cam, or the Isis; the Usk, the Ouse, or the Severn, first. When I see Old England at last, it must be as a son returning to his fathers, & I must be in a position to settle there for ever in peace & archaic dignity.

Thine—Tibaldus.

Notes

1. Also known as Odoacer (435–493), half Hunnish, half Scirian chieftain of the Germanic Heruli. Deposed Romulus Augustulus, the last Roman Emperor in the West (476).

2. As noted, the poem appeared as "To Alfred Galpin, Esq: President of the United Amateur Press Association, on His Nineteenth Birthday, November 8, 1920," *Tryout* 6, No. 12 (December 1920): [7–8] (as by "L. Theobald").

3. Ernest A. Dench, formerly of England, was a Brooklyn amateur and member of the United.

[3]   [AHT]

Old 598
March 1st, 1923

Salve, Maxime!

GOD DAMN SON OF A——BLAH!!! This headache will either kill me, or the bird that has to wade through the incoherent paragraphs now unfolding their labyrinthine course! I can't sit up but a few minutes at a time, & there's more ?&%#$:() beastly work here to do than a regiment could dispose of in a decade. Bah.

About the Cole mess—I'd better curl up with a bottle of cyanide & get it over with before I do any more harm to myself and others.[1] Bah. Probably I've incurred his undying coldness—he hasn't answered that definitively declinatory epistle yet—and now Mrs. Adams writes that he'll probably be peeved at her! Undertaker, put a good shot of embalming fluid in the old simp's head—it's been dead a long time. Tell Mrs. A.[2]—though I'll answer her myself in a day or two—that I'll take all the Colic blame myself & exculpate her, & you, & everybody but poor me—in toto. He might as well be damn mad at one guy as half mad at several birds.

As to the general province of amateurdom—there I disagree with you. It is not a section of all life—if it were, it would include sculpture, painting, music, mathematics, science, & what the hell not—but is in truth an organised outlet for energies of the literary sort. When a guy wants a damn good time, he can go to the banquets of the Union League Club, or the Hell's Kitchen Social & Athletic Club, according to his social status—but amacheoordom is for amachoors—an' they's s'posed to have some int'rust in writin'. Bah. If the National wants to be a catchall for the mob of grammar-school journalists & mail-order hounds, it can do so with my blessing after the first week in July— but that wasn't the way of the Old United. I now question whether such a society as that can permanently exist; & believe the only hope for amateur letters lies with a totally informal & unofficer'd group to be formed within any or all of the boy's-clubbish associations. And that is probably a vain hope. I hope Campbell & Daas[3] will lead a movement for the revival of the United, but shall not do any more leading myself. I'm through with starting things— henceforward I'm merely a follower. They have my blessing & co-operation to a reasonable degree, but I can't make over an association single-handed. The United I knew doesn't exist today.

Honestly, my hatred of the human animal mounts by leaps & bounds the more I see of the damned vermin, & the more I see exemplified the workings of their spiteful, shabby, & sadistic psychological processes. Blessed is the plague, which with its divine & health-giving breath removes these putrescent superfluities by the thousand! Yah!

And damn this headache.

With renew'd assurances of that consideration which is warranted by the sincerest amity & respect, Believe me, Sir, ever

    Yr most oblig'd
      Most obt: Servt:
        Theobaldus

Notes

1. HPL presumably told Cole that he was not interested in running for president of the NAPA for 1923–24.
2. Hazel Pratt Adams (the subject of HPL's "The Absent Leader"). Adams ran for and was elected president of the NAPA for the 1923–24 term.
3. I.e., Paul J. Campbell and Edward F. Daas.

[4]   [AHT]

> The Old Dump—
> 8th March—
> gawd knows whither!
> 1923

Monarch of gods and daemons & all spirits!

Ouf! So the opus Hoagianum draweth at last to its close! Hath he sent you the praefatio? Since he ain't sent it 598ward, I hope to gawd he has—it's the only copy, & if it's lost I absolutely won't write another. Let Fr. Rierstead[1] do it & be damned! I shall certainly heave a sigh of relief when I have the finish'd volume in my hands . . . . . . & off my hands! Yes—more than one goof will be darned glad when the final gold lettering goes on the blue binding.

And that headache! Oh, bebby! It was the beginning of a full-sized spell of nervous collapse, or exhaustion, or whatever in hell ya call it, during which I simply couldn't do a g. d. thing but sit around in easy chairs like a dumbbell with the pip, whilst my aunt put hot cloths on me classick (accent on the *sick*) brow. Mail piled up, but it meant naught to the Old Gentleman. There I sat, too beastly lethargick & neuralgick to move, & told the world to go to hell.

As to my temperament—why gawd love yer, of course I got red blood! Red blood, an' guts, an everythin'! If ya wanna see what a human egg I am, jest lead me to a good arena or amphitheatrum or sumpun of the sort, & bring on yer gladiators & animles, & all that! Grrrr! Yah!! gimme the sight of a meat-fed Numidian lion & a coupla tough bimboes arm'd as bestiarii!! Watch em roar & snort as they pink the old cat in the nose whilst he claws 'em up & rips the guts outa the both of 'em! Yah! Habet! habet![2] Attaboy! Now drag 'em off & put fresh sand in the arena whilst the light-arm'd meridiani come on & spatter things up with raw blood! But hold! Who in the name of Hecate is this? The crowd roars, shrieks, gurgles, pants, snorts, yells . . . . . "Ave, Pale, Hercules Romane!"[3] It is the golden-hair'd god, the invincible archer for whose lethal arrows the forest & the desert have been scour'd for wild living targets . . . . it is Caesar—L. Commodus, beloved son of our beloved Antoninus! Twang! Ædepol, what clamour! Ululations . . . . death . . . . nausea . . . . blood . . . . human stuff!

Y'know, I'd love to attend prize-fights if the crowds at our R. I. mills weren't so beastly common. 'Twas different in London when the Regent used to attend performances of the fancy,[4] & watch Tom Crib pelt Bob Gregson in the smellers till he (Gregson—not Crib . . . . or the Regent) was uncorked & red-snouted.[5] Ah, me, but H. R. H. has been dead these many years. Poor young rascal . . . such a disappointment to his father, George III, whom God Save!

Oh, yes . . . I'm really frightfully human and love all mankind, and all that sort of thing. Mankind is truly amusing, when kept at the proper distance. And common men, if well-behaved, are really quite useful. One is a cynick only when one thinks. At such times the herd seems a bit disgusting because each member of it is always trying to hurt somebody else, or gloating because somebody else is hurt. Inflicting pain seems to be the chief sport of persons whose tastes and interests run to the ordinary events and direct pleasures and rewards of life—the animalistic or (if one may use a term so polluted with homiletick associations) *worldly* people of our absurd civilisation. Amateurs shew this vulgar trait most offensively. The Hub upheavals are a sardonically good example, & another one is the unfeigned *gusto* & *delight* with which most of the small-minded rabble greeted the news of Dowdell's decline & fall. I shall never forget the anticipatory lip-licking with which Mrs. Miniter began the savoury revelation to an avid audience last November . . . . how they all revelled in that morsel! Faugh! And then how they crowded around to gloat over the latest arrest of poor Mrs. Ellis's wayward son![6] A moralist would have sighed to see such "evil" minds . . . but Theobald the Cynick merely repressed a tendency to vomit, well knowing that these people were not at all "evil", but merely average specimens of the rotten human herd whose chief pastime is mutual befouling. As for me . . . . I am a tough egg. I may be human, all right, but not quite human enough to be glad at the misfortune of Dowdell or of anybody else. I am rather sorry (not outwardly but genuinely so) when disaster befalls a person— sorry because it gives the filthy herd so much pleasure. To be a real hater, one must hate *en masse*. I hate animals like the Haughton[7] rhinoceros mildly and temperately, but for mankind as mankind I have a most artistically fiery abhorrence and execration, I spit upon them!

The natural hatefulness and loathsomeness of the human beast may be overcome only in a few specimens of fine heredity and breeding, by a transference of interests to abstract spheres and a consequent sublimation of the universal sadistic fury. All that is good in man is artificial; and even that good is very slight and unstable, since nine out of ten non-primitive people proceed at once to capitalise their asceticism and vent their sadism by a Victorian brutality and scorn toward all who do not emulate their pose. Puritans are probably more contemptible than primitive beasts, though neither class deserves much respect. In fact, we find very little in human character to command our respect. That is why, since I like to respect people for my own quaint amusement, I invariably judge a man by his cravat. Cravats, I sometimes think, are the only true realities of life. And life is so earnest and serious!

Now let's laugh in the manner of Ciceronian augurs . . . . haw!

This afternoon, just to polish up for the Hub meeting, I'm going to accompany my aunts to see Mr. Sheridan's "School for Scandal", which I have not seen since I went to Drury Lane in 1777. The present production is by an excellent stock company, & Sir Peter will be play'd by Prof. Crosby of Brown University, an amateur Thespian who occasionally condescends to lend his art to professional stock ventures. I've seen this bozo as Darlington in "Lady Windermere's Fan",[8] & as . . . . oh, what's his name . . . . . that noble-friend-of-the-family gink in "The Second Mrs. Tanqueray".[9] I wish they'd play "The Heir at Law"[10] nowadays. I read most of that classick in the B R T subway betwixt Parkside & Times, & I R T betwixt Times & Ninety-sixth.

And after the S for S, I'm gonna drag my aunts to a cinema joint to see "Java Head"—because it's said to be full of ancient *Salem* scenery.[11] This'll be my first trip outa the house since the day I was actually at Salem—except for the time I hauled Haggerty[12] up here from the Narragansett Hotel. But Gaw-damighty! I sure gotta get this damn hair cut before I hit Bostonium!

Well—I gotta beat it for the' Op'ry House. May the gawds attend thee!
Thine hble and obt Servt
Θεοβάλδος

Notes

1. Unidentified.

2. "He has him! He has him!"

3. "Hail, Palus, a Roman Hercules!"

4. George IV (1762–1830), king of England (1820–30), was appointed Prince Regent in 1811 upon the insanity of King George III. The period 1811–20 is therefore called the Regency period.

5. Thomas (Tom) Cribb (1781–1848), the pugilist, was the Champion of England during the early 1800s. Bob Gregson, the "Lancashire Giant," was 6 feet 2 inches and weighed 217 pounds for his 1808 battle with Tom Cribb, won by Cribb.

6. Annie Cross Ellis (1873–?), professional newspaper woman at the Boston *Post* and Hub Club member. Her son, Willard T. Ellis (1896–?), also was an amateur.

7. Ida C. Haughton, about whom HPL wrote the satiric poem "Medusa: A Portrait" (1921). See letter 6.

8. By Oscar Wilde.

9. A play (1898) by Sir Arthur Wing Pinero (1855–1934).

10. A play (1808) by George Colman the Younger (1762–1836).

11. *Java Head* (Famous Players/Paramount, 1923; silent), directed by George Melford; starring Leatrice Joy, Jacqueline Logan, and Frederick Strong. Based on the novel by Joseph Hergesheimer. HPL refers to his elder aunt, Lillian D. Clark.

12. Vincent B. Haggerty.

[5]   [AHT]

Old 598
March 25, 1923

Rain, Snow and hail, your Mightiness!

All is received—& congrats on thine industry! That Bush stuff'll pull you down $23.38 if my arithmetic ain't forgotten; & you shall presently behold the aureate reward.[1] I'd forward it now if I had that much.

Have been having a damned gloomy time. My aunt (not the one you saw, but the elder & 598-governing one)[2] became prostrate with grippe the very day after I wrote you—I guess the two shows were two or too much for her—& Fortune depressed the dignity of a Theobaldus to the ignominy of domestick exertion. In fine, I had to serve as a sort of composite nurse & housekeeper, even descending to the depths of preparing food & cleansing & dehydrating china & silver . . . . but let us not think of such demeaning practicalities. The nervous strain damn near laid me out, & I am only now recovering my wonted poise—or pose. Amateur work & correspondence languished in neglect, so that today I owe about forty epistles. But now my aunt is up, about, & in charge again; so that I can again speak of the usual boredom instead of the unusual boredom. Bah.

Say—who the hell was George W. M. Reynolds?[3] Galpinius hath made me read two books of his—"Faust & the Demon", & "Wagner the Wehr-Wolf"—which bear the earmarks of the 1820–1830 period of childish extravagance, simplicity, & bombast . . . . degenerate posterity of "The Castle of Otranto". And oh, Boy! the dialogue is simply plutocratick! . . . . . . "execrable being, receive at last the reward of thy turpitude!" And the rapier darted like lightning to its hilt in the base breast of the varlet. And Galpin hasn't the least idea of who Reynolds was.

Sunday afternoon Bimbo Al shew'd up at 57 Roseland, & the wise cracks flew hot & heavy.[4] If Wycherly, Vanbrugh, Farquhar, Etherege, Sheridan, Wilde,[5] or any of them bozos from the accession of Charles II down to Dunsany's "Lost Silk Hat" ever pulled any snappier line of patter & comebacks than that same little egg Sandy, I sure gotta hand it to 'em . . . . I gotta hand it to 'em. Take it from me, kid, that gink is a whole comedy of manners in himself, except that he ain't got the manners. But he's right there wit' de comedy stuff . . . you tell 'em, Oswald! I wish I could remember all the dialogue . . . . . that's the hell of making up your stuff as you go—it doesn't stick. But it went something like this:

COLE "So you think you're a live one, Albert?"

SANDUSKY "Sure—ain't I used Lifebuoy Soap all my life?"

THEOBALD "But, my dear Sandusky, what have you used *since*"?

Well—we kept it up—or tried to—till eleven p.m., when I beat it for my usual eleven-forty-five. Back to the demnition grind—& I ain't been outa the beastly house since. Ho, hum! It's a great life if ya kin forget it.

The human race? Oh, dear! Why discuss trifles! But I had quite a fling at the poor fishes in last week's *Haldeman-Julius Weekly*—the editor printed not only the *paragraph I sent for publication, but my eight-page letter besides.*[6]

After all, mankind is mildly amusing—if only as a topic for controversy. Some gazabo[7]—who had incidentally slammed a former contribution of mine—started a symposium on "What is the paramount end, aim, & object of *life*"? & this is what I pulled—the longest single sentence on record . . . . . a *life* sentence, as it were. Ow!

> The paramount end, aim, and object of life is contentment or tranquil pleasure; such as can be gained only by the worship and creation of beauty, and by the adoption of an imaginative and detached life which may enable us to appreciate the world as a beautiful object (as Schopenhauer tells us it is) without feeling too keenly the pain which inevitably results from reflecting on its relation to ourselves.

Sage Stuff, Oswald—sage stuff! Now let's have a drink!

Well—get after me if I try to hold that $23.38 out on ya too long!

Thine ignominious helot—

ΘΕΟΒΑΛΔΟΣ

Notes

1. HPL refers to revisory work done for David Van Bush by him and JFM.

2. Annie E. P. Gamwell and Lillian D. Clark, respectively.

3. G. W. M. Reynolds (1814–1879), prolific British journalist and prolific author of popular fiction.

4. "Bimbo Al" is Albert A. Sandusky, who was paying a visit at the home of Edward H. Cole.

5. HPL refers to the British dramatists William Wycherley (c. 1640–1715), Sir John Vanbrugh (1664?–1726), George Farquhar (1677/78–1707), Sir George Etherege (1635?–1692), Richard Brinsley Sheridan (1751–1816), and Oscar Wilde (1854–1900).

6. To the Editor of the *Haldeman-Julius Weekly*, [c. February 1923?], *Haldeman-Julius Weekly* No. 1424 (17 March 1923): 1. Rpt. in *Letters to Samuel Loveman and Vincent Starrett* (West Warwick, RI: Necronomicon Press, 1994), 38–40.

7. John Mason of Oklahoma had called HPL an "intellectual snob" for comments voiced by HPL as quoted in the *Haldeman-Julius Weekly*, 20 January 1923.

[6]   [AHT]

Old Dump
March 29, 1923

Monarch Still Mightier!

Well for the love of almighty gawd! 234 lines more, bringing that dumbbell's indebtedness to you up to a cool 38—count 'em—38 bones! Oh, boy! And to think how my ragged nerves are hesitating on the brink of some junk for Bush's mag[1] what ain't 'arf so bad as 'is own slobbering! I must learn a lesson in fortitude, tell *National* piled-up correspondence to go to hell, & wade in for the con! That's the only way I'll ever get out another *Conservative*[2] . . . . & as for Cleveland in July—well, I won't fret myself about the impossible.

G. W. M. Reynolds eighteenth century? Nothing of the sort! The eighteenth couldn't possibly cook up such addled junk as the early nineteenth got away with. Reynolds has one trick that gives away his post-eighteenthness—he makes that peculiarly irritating William-Fourthism which to me is the most silly of inversions . . . when he wants to say—as any good Addisonian would say—"I beheld a most magnificent vista" or "I beheld a vista of the greatest magnificence", that bimbo pulls something like this—"I beheld a vista the most magnificent." That places him as definitely after my own age as "intriguing" places the modern saphead in his corresponding period. Reynolds is a King-George-IV-ite, King-Williamite, or Early Victorian . . . . . if he ever wore a periwig, he'd stowed it away in mothballs long before he dished out "Faust" & "Wagner"! I guess I'll never place the geezer, since you, Galpin, Long, & Loveman are equally benighted as regards his life & deeds! But he sure was an amoosin' cuss.

Machen's "Hieroglyphicks"? Down in me notebook she goes! I'm nuts on that Machen guy anyhow—I guess I told you how I lapped up the "House of Souls" & am meanin' to bite off the "Hill of Dreams" whenever I can clamp me lunch-hooks on it. But I ain't ben outa the house since I got home from the Hub feed, & gawd knows when I'll pound the pave again. I just nachally ain't got ambition enough to do nuthin'—I don't want anything at the liberry quite enough to hike out after it—& I'm supposed to be the same bozo what hoofed it up from Twenty-third to one hundred thirty-eighth after a six-mile jaunt & Palisade Climb! Gawd, but how environment does get a guy!

McNeil tipped me off to that *Weird Stories*[3] thing, which he says is published out in Chi, but I ain't saw it yet. I'll tip it a wink the next time I lamp a news stand. Maybe some of my worst stuff is bad enough to earn me a pois'nal toin-down instead of the printed rejection slip that Dagon got.[4] But a guy's gotta sling a mean line of Socony[5] to put anything over on them magazine bimboes. They're hard eggs, Archie!

I consider'd with interest the printed circular which you theoretically enclosed, & would feel an even more acute interest had the enclosure been a material reality. I always was a materialistic oilcan. Inference, deduction, & conclusion lead me to imagine that the document may not be unconnected with a certain reluctant willingness to translate impossible into merely improbable verse—*more Tibaldico*—though this assumption may prove my intuitive processes somewhat rushy. At any rate, my curiosity is awake, & I should relish an objective glimpse of the pronunciamento at such a date as its transmission may prove practical.

Hub stuff? Gawd, I can colour up the banquet any way to suit my audience. You being a BPCer,[6] I naturally made it seem comic, so that you would rejoice in BPC superiority. Same with Gaurge J.[7] & his gang. But when I tell the Boston folks about it, I crack & wisecrack it up to the skies! That's practical cynicism—ya learns it in amateurdom. There is art in being a perfect hypocrite & two-faced person . . . . my model is Mr. Snake in "The School for Scandal". (Not that he was original—but I like his name.) Well—I just gotta line from me fren Al, askin' me to shoot 'im some guff on de big eats. So I ups & pulls a spasm of voise, called "The Feast",[8] w'ich I dedicates to 'im, & fits out wit' 2 Latin mottoes 'n' everyt'ing. Complimentary? Say, Oswald, if sugar was as sticky as de Socony I spilled, it ud be woit' wot dey's charging for it! Watch me, kid! Dis is de way I starts 'er off—

> Lud, Sir! What's this you ask me to relate?
> The Boston Feast, & all I heard & ate?
> Sure, that were hard, since Comus was so free
> That sheer Profusion clogs my Memory!
> Dazzled with Art, & drugg'd with splendid Fare,
> My rustick Pencil falters in Despair,
> And Scarce commands the Talent to set down
> The modish Revels of a learned Town!

I only gets nasty twict—once when I says of de harmonique:

> With Melody ne'er eager to desist

(subtle stuff). An' anudder time w'en I hints where de Boston orators come from:

> For Boston Eloquence no Peer hath known
> Since the first Founders kiss'd the Blarney-Stone.

I winds up real modest—

> So on the Scene the Curtain's Folds descend,
> And the gay Feast draws pensive to its End;
> Joyn'd to the Ages, planted in the Sky
> To wake the Songs of better Bards than I.
> Pozz—now I'm done! And you, Sir, I entreat
> To hide my Couplets well within your Sheet;
> That the kind Folk who heard my speaking through,
> May have less Cause to curse my Name anew!

Shall be glad to see *The Old Timer*,[9] & hope Old Medusa gets hers unshielded by Adamic censorship. But don't fancy the old rhino is really a human being—she simply ain't! That cow-mountain is nothing but a festering tumour of ectopic tissue, produced by fatty degeneration & morbid cell-sprouting—a senile & purulent excrescence on the race, wholly acraniate or at best microcephalic, & with muscular reactions—which produce written articles—caused by neuro-ganglial maladjustments induced by a gall-bladder dislocated by malignant elephantiasis into a position corresponding to the seat of the rudimentary brain in that species of primitive organism of which she is a noisomely decadent variant. She—or it—is a mere octopus of ugliness, nightmare, stupidity, & snarling malevolence . . . . a pitiful object that ought to be buried.

But I gotta beat it for the Bush.

Abasedly Thine,

Theobaldus.

Notes

1. *Mind Power Plus.*

2. The *Conservative* No. 12 is dated March 1923, but presumably came out a bit later.

3. I.e., *WT*, the magazine that published more of HPL's work than any other. Its first issue is dated March 1923, but it was probably for sale a month or so earlier.

4. "Dagon" was rejected by *Black Mask,* as HPL pointedly noted in one of his early letters to Edwin Baird, editor of *WT*.

5. I.e., oil. The term is an acronym for Standard Oil Company of New York.

6. The Blue Pencil Club, an amateur group in Brooklyn.

7. George J. Houtain.

8. The poem was for a meeting of the Hub Journalist Club (10 March 1923).

9. Published by Hazel Pratt Adams.

[7]   [AHT]

April 5, 1923

Auguste:

I gotta jot down an humiliating admission before pride or forgetfulness choak it off! Ya recall that line of Socony I pulled about the essential nineteenth-centuryism of that damned inversion—"Scenery the most magnificent"—& such. Well—I believed it when I said it; but in perusing Mrs. Radcliffe's "The Italian," (1797) I've just come across the following: "Do not leave me", said she, *"in accents the most supplicating"*. Which shews that this especial form of decadence beat the most decadent of centuries by at least four years! Of course, my general contention that this form does not belong in the dominant eighteenth century tradition still holds—for by 1797 the truly classical school was thoroughly played out; but I'll concede the technical error & let it go at that!

I've been eating up Gothick stuff lately—all the posterity of "Otranto". Miss Reeves' "Old English Baron" (1777) is infernally tame, but in damned good Georgian English. Radcliffe stuff is vastly—immeasurably—superior in interest & atmosphere, though the language is more stilted. (And yet it beats Reynolds by a mile!) I'm reading that volume of selections which Little Belknap picked up right under his Old Grandpa's nose at the shop in Vesey-Street, & which he magnanimously gave the poor old gentleman as a Christmas gift.[1] Ahead of me lie "Monk" Lewis & Maturin selections.[2]

Shantih! Shantih! Shantih![3]

Θεοβάλδος

Notes

1. George Saintsbury, ed., *Tales of Mystery.*
2. HPL began to write his own modern Gothic tale "The Rats in the Walls" in August.
3. HPL quotes the closing line of T. S. Eliot's *The Waste Land* (*Dial,* November 1922; *LL* 238). HPL wrote unfavorably about the poem in "Rudis Indigestaque Moles" (*Conservative* 12, March 1923; rpt. *CE* 2).

[8]   [AHT]

The Old Dump
22 April, 1923

Ave Maxime!

Hell! Work is my Nemesis! Having accumulated over *fifty* unanswer'd epistles, I'm trying to dispose of 'em at the rate of fifteen per diem, but am falling down on it. I could have done it once, but ten average specimens seems to be my limit now.

The Hoag book came—& oh, bebby! didn't it gladden me soul! It looks so damn professional—& to think of my preface stuck in large as life—in a real book! But why the hell did Balch[1] crowd matters so? I was hoping for a fat, spread-out thing, with never more than one poem on a page—like Bush's stuff. Oh, well—n'importe! And the portrait—say, it's great! And all the index stuff . . . . snappy work, I'll radio the empyrean! Too bad there are some Try-outisms[2]—but as was said of misplaced milk . . . . Some of this may have been my fault in supplying bum copy—I wish now I had read the proofs. Note the metrical intrusions in the "Celtic's Dream"—

ˊ ˇ ˊ ˇ ˊ ˇ ˊ ˇ

A bauld Oirish Tip was (me) father

ˊ ˇ ˊ ˇ ˊ ˇ ˊ

And me mother was the same;

ˊ ˇ ˊ ˇ ˊ ˇ ˊ

How he'd (he cud) twirrl his shtick av black thorn

ˊ ˇ ˊ ˇ ˊ ˇ ˊ

Phwin an orange man there came!

And then in my preface to the "Inspiring Scenes" Thing,[3] we find "Dillon's pleasing heights" (good Georgianism) debased to "Dillon's pleasant heights". (Nondescript banality.)

Also in my 1922 tribute—

"Gorgeous *be* thy brother sun".[4]

sinks to "Gorgeous *by* thy brother sun". The way of the world! But I wish when they misprint they'd be truly incoherent, & not make a sort of feeble half-sense. I'd rather have *the* appear as *thx* or *yhe,* than have *inane* appear as *insane,* or anything of that sort. This reminds me of what they did to poor Kleiner and me in the Dowe memorial. Kleiner had a line

<blockquote>"Beauty & joy *in* everything",</blockquote>

and they rendered it

<blockquote>"Beauty & joy *and* everything".</blockquote>

'n everything! Blah! Such is life! I had a line

<blockquote>"Unfeign'd the grief with which *the* gen'ral heart"</blockquote>

and they gave it

<blockquote>"Unfeign'd the grief with which *each* gen'eral heart"[5]</blockquote>

yah! Grrr! Mrs. Sawyer[6] read that proof . . . that's why I'm on the Miniterian side of the Hub Hen feud!

Oh, well! mere nugae! But say! That book will look swell when bound in splendid blue with golden lettering! I'll wager Hoag & his family will go nuts over it! Hoag says I can have all the copies I want, so (since I ain't chargin' nothin' for editorial labours) I'm gonna be damn greedy, & ask you to slip me *fifteen, besides* supplying the following local N.Y. ams, who are likely to be interested: Kleiner, Belknap, Mrs. Green,[7] Houtain . . . . but I'll leave the rest to you. I know good ol' McNeil would be grateful for one. And of course, supply by mail all the gazinks what have tributes published. Hoag'll give you such addresses as you don't know.

Bush has just shot me three of his new books of pomes, containing work by you & me.[8] It's interesting to see in retrospect the things o'er which one hath suffer'd. My old work—1917–18–19—&c.—interests me because of its obvious inferiority to the revision I grind out nowadays—which ain't sayin' anything in particular for the latter! The inference is, that I'm improving by slow degrees—for there's a knack to this sort of thing. I only hope it won't make a hack outa me & put my own style on the blink.

Tatler? Of course religion was fashionable in the Augustan age, though few intelligent men believed much of it. It was a very pretty affectation, & had I been alive I should doubtless have found amusement in pretending belief. Even now I am occasionally tempted to join the Catholic Church—it is so picturesquely pagan, & means so deliciously little. As for #163, that's one of my favourites—dost recall my frequent pseudonym of "Edward Softly"?[9]

The basic verity of that fact. All I want now is to settle down in a comfortable middle-aged way with my reading and authorship, revision when necessary, and the correspondence of a few particularly congenial friends. The turmoil and technicality of associational machinations have become so disgusting and irksome to me, that I shall never again come into contact with them save as an especial favour now and then to some more than ordinarily valued friend. The 1914–1922 chapter of spontaneous activity is closed. I'm now too thoroughly cynical to expect much of amateurdom, or to give many damns about it; save as a perpetually chaotic mess from which a few odd souls can get some impetus toward literary development . . . or at least toward a fairly comfortable literary disillusion.

But hell, I gotta quit!

With appropriate congratulations, commiserations, &c. I am

Ever yr most oblig'd, most obt Servt.

Tibaldus

Notes

1. Evidently a reference to Allan C. Balch (1864–1943), a wealthy hydroelectric entrepreneur and patron of the arts. He was born in upstate New York and attended Cornell University. He may therefore have known Hoag and appears to have funded the publication of his *Poetical Works*.

2. Charles W. ("Tryout") Smith's amateur journal, the *Tryout*, was notorious for its numerous typographical errors.

3. HPL wrote a poetic preface of 18 lines to Hoag's poem "Fragments from an Hour of Inspiration."

4. Ironically, the word *thy* was rendered *they* when published in *SL*.

5. "In Memoriam: J. E. T. D."

6. Laurie A. Sawyer of the Hub Club.

7. Sonia H. Greene, the future Mrs. Lovecraft.

8. Presumably *Inspirational Poems* (St. Louis: Hicks Almanac & Publishing Co., [1921]), *Grit and Gumption* ([St. Louis: David Van Bush, 1921]), and *Poems of Mastery and Love Verse* ([St. Louis: David Van Bush, 1922]).

9. In the *Tatler* No. 163 (25 April 1710), Addison (under the pseudonym "Isaac Bickerstaffe") pretends to praise a poem, "To Mira on Her Incomparable Poems," by "Ned Softly," calling it "a little nosegay of conceits, a very lump of salt: every verse has something in it that piques . . ."

[9]   [AHT]

The Old Roost
Thursday the Third, [May] 1923

Most Sovran Citizen:—

Ecce! Grandpa Theobald is articulate, though damn near all in with a sort of beastly near-grippe which has made me nearly *stone deaf* for a week and a half, & play'd gawd's own deuce with my digestion. The only faculty left unimpair'd is my profane contempt for all creation. Bah.

Meanwhile, my small child Alfredus has come finely out of the appendicitis operation, with fourteen stitches & a cheerful serenity of temper.

De Tryoutismis libri Hoagici[1]—I hope I ain't did no harm! All I said to Jonathan before your admonition came, was that although some trivial slips had occurred,—one or two of the slips inevitable in books, & mostly in my own tributes rather than in the text proper—there were no major errors. The reason I mentioned this at all, was that I wanted to smooth it off easily—for Hoag has been rather quick to notice defects in the *Greenwich Journal* & *Troy Times* versions of his poems.[2] If I've actually put my foot in it, kindly kick me with appropriate gusto—gawd knows I'm the most tactlessly blundering cuss under the accursed & daemoniac sun! And tell Hoag—if he has anything to say—that the mistakes are all due to my bum copy anyway—that, & my careless waiving of the proof-reading privilege. Give it to me—that's sound business policy, for it's you who are going to collect the cash—& I don't give a damn how keenly he realises my carelessness—I wasn't gonna get no money no-ways! But I doubt if he thinks about it at all—the whole thing is such a triumph that it'll knock him dizzy when he lamps it . . . . & the same goes for Allan the Plute.[3] My copy was certainly bum—you'll recall how "Dionondawa"[4] had me worried till I asked you which of two versions I'd sent. The real fault is Millionaire Al's—for being in so deodamnate much of a hurry & preventing the deliberate sort of work which makes for scrupulous accuracy. Tell the bimbo so if he gets fretful.

About mailing books—you might slip me *twenty* instead of *fifteen* . . . . I decided to strike JEH for that number, & with five hundred copies & me not chargin' 'im nothin', he hadn't orta howl! My aunts want one each, & so many amateurs have shewn eagerness that I'll be short if I don't lay in a good supply. It ain't every day that I get my name on the title page of a reg'lar eighteen-karat gilt-topp'd cross-my-heart-an'-hope-to-die **book.** Oh—by the way—this childish pride business reminds me of a good one on poor Goodenough! I wrote him 'that his tribute looked well in the appendix'; & he, assuming that mere *appendix* was a sort of tail-end caboose of ignominy, came back with an injured sob that he hadn't expected me to tuck his deathless lyric away off in small type in some obscure place after the way I'd praised it a couple years ago when I asked him for it.[5] Nice ol' Arthur! I hasten'd to relieve him, & assured him that the appendix was a thoroughly respectable & even slightly aristocratic appendix, in which all the tributes were assembled with a refined impartiality . . . . & that he had a whole half-page in as large type as anybody had . . . . . & that his lyrick came fourth among the eight tributes whilst my own junk came last . . . . good li'l Artha, now he can sleep blissfully, & with untroubled mind! I'm damnably eager to see the bound books . . . . . & by the way . . . . in mailing copies to the bozos who have tributes in the appendix, put the postage in your bill to Balch. Hoag takes the financial responsibility of supplying these goofs. Don't worry about the Hoosack Vale—your revision is probably far better than mine, which was hasty stuff.[6] Yes—ye'll have to get out a second or centennial volume—I wonder if I shall live to write the preface? Hope not—life is such a grind. Wilde said life was Grecian while death was Gothick, but I think he exaggerated. I find life so tediously Alexandrian! . . . or even Byzantine . . . .

Say—are you a sportin' guy? If either of us were other than broke, I'd propose a bet! Once again I've followed a Mortonian tip, as I did when sending "Dagon" to the *Black Cat* and "The Tomb" to the *Black Mask*,[7] and have slipped *Weird Tales* five of my hell-beaters . . . "Dagon", "Randolph Carter", "Cats of Ulthar", "Hound", and "Arthur Jermyn". And what I'm betting is that the editor (like those of the tenebrous feline & falseface) doesn't bother to write a personal letter to accompany the returning manuscripts. I've gave *Weird Tales* the onct-over, & find it rather dumb. Most of the authors is the kind of eggs what think Jordan Marsh is a swamp.[8] Stereotyped language & methods of presentation—second-hand thrills—weak shivers—but hell! I can't get a real shiver out of any living geezer except Art Machen. In the April *Weird Tales*—the only issue I've saw—there's just one spiel worth reading; & that's "Beyond the Door", by Paul Suter. I've heard of the bimbo that edits *Weird Tales*—Edwin Baird—he used to write mediocre serials for the old *All-Story*.

"Fause Murdoch?"[9] . . . . . Deal with it as thou likest after 'tis out. Far be it from me to urge its entry anywhere, *auctore nolente* . . . . . though it looks like a winner with any judge but the kind that's so dumb they thinks Merrimack is a laughing Irishman.

When I took the N.A.P.A. executiveship, it was when the blamed thing was down . . . . I didn't wait till George had done it . . . . (either way!) But as I've more recently said—I shan't do anything in the *United* myself, or ask anybody else to, until I see more evidence of a *real* movement to smoke out these damned wood lice. It's up to Paul Jonas[10] to start things.

As my term of servitude draws to a close, I begin to feel the exhilaration of approaching fossildom . . . long nights of uninterrupted reading, when I shall slither & wallow in all the diseased & unnatural horrors of nether hells with the putrid & sadistic authors of my choosing—or when, these tame literateurs proving as insipid as a mere Huysmans or Baudelaire, I shall seize a pen made of a condor's wing & dipped in carbonaceous putrescence, & leave on yellow pages a trail of ideographick foetor which shall be to their superficial dabblings as Poe is to Frances Hodgson Burnett.[11] Idyllic small hours of care-free mornings—when they ain't no presidential messages to weigh down the soaring soul—& by the way, I've just got the May bull off to Henricus Martinus.[12]

Speaking of authorship—lamp the enclosed panegyrick delivered on the coming-of-age of our tiny pal Belnapius![13] 'Ittle-Sonny says he likes it, & is glad his old grandpa did it in a Poe-esque rather than Papal style.[14] Incidentally—Sonny's coming to Providence to see the Old Gentlemen this month or next—we've both been urging each other to visit each other; & since my brokeness proved the more absolute, Grandpa's Pet said he'd give in & do the choo-choo work himself. The arrangement will have advantages—for I can shew the child our old Athenaeum, where Poe spent many an hour, & wrote his name at the bottom of one of his unsigned poems in a magazine, & the house of Mrs. Whitman, where he spouted enough cheap sentimentality to make up for the amount he mercifully omitted from his tales.[15] Yes—small Belknap will like Providence—& I may take him to Boston to show him off to the Hub Club, (some of whom think he's a myth, & that I wrote the White critique myself)[16] & give him a peek at those twin abodes of my spirit—Salem & Marblehead. Better come along yourself if you can—& make up the good old trio of Sept–Oct–Nov days! We could even climb Durfee Hill[17]—or climb it as far as the snow line, for Sonny can't exercise violently.

Speaking of hikes—sorry as hell I can't be with you Memorial Day! This Stiles bimbo sounds distinctly interesting, & if I had even a shadow of the coin, I'd be there with bells on! Trouble is I'm invited so damn cordially to Cleveland, that if I go anywhere else (except around near New England spots) the gang will be offen me for life! Expenses are the limit this year—I owe Parker[18] a helluva lot on that Conservative, & have plunged to the limit on a new summer suit which I absolutely had to have, since the family wouldn't let me be seen on the streets of Providence in that azure rag-bag I sported last year. This new outfit—which is very sedate & grey—set me back forty-two plunks . . . . . which sure is spendin' until it hurts! And I remember the time a guy could grab a real nifty set of rags for twenty-five berries . . . . gawd, but things has changed since good ol' 1914!

Well, I gotta ring off . . . the deaf ear is ringing already, like the H$_2$O of a young Niagara!

S'long—

Θεοβάλδος

Notes

1. "On the Tryoutisms [i.e., typos] in the Hoag book ."

2. The *Greenwich Journal* and *Troy Times* were local papers in upstate New York that published Hoag's poems (he lived in Troy). The *Troy Times* also published several of HPL's tributes to Hoag.

3. I.e., the plutocrat. The reference is to Allan G. Balch (see letter 8n1).

4. Referring to the poem, "An Ode to the Falls of Dionondawa." The name is more properly rendered "Dionondehowa," referring to a region in upstate New York.

5. Goodenough's "A Tribute," *The Poetical Works of Jonathan E. Hoag* 59.

6. "Hoosac Mountains" are mentioned stanza four of "Pad and Pencil on the Mohawk Trail," which mentions a "vale" in the second. But apparently Hoag had submitted a poem titled "Hoosac Valley," which "came much too late to be included" in his book, to both HPL and JFM, and both revised the poem independently (JFM to HPL, before 20 May 1927 [ms., JHL]).

7. HPL is confused; he sent "Dagon" to *Black Mask* and "The Tomb" to the *Black Cat*.

8. Jordan Marsh & Company was a department store in Boston that grew to be a major regional chain in New England.

9. By JFM. Published in HPL's *Conservative*.

10. Paul J. Campbell.

11. Frances Hodgson Burnett (1849–1924), British playwright and author best known for her children's stories, in particular *The Secret Garden* and *Little Lord Fauntleroy*.

12. Harry E. Martin, Official Editor of the NAPA (1922–23) and therefore the editor of the *National Amateur*. The "May bull" was HPL's "President's Message" for May 1923.

13. "To Endymion: (Frank Belknap Long, Jr.): Upon His Coming of Age, April 27, 1923." Long was in fact born in 1901, therefore his coming of age had occurred the previous year.

14. I.e., the style of Alexander Pope.

15. See HPL to C. F. Strauch, 16 February 1932 (ms., JHL): "the historic Athenaeum [at 251 Benefit Street] where Poe & Mrs. Whitman used to ramble through the book alcoves. At this latter place I had an attendant show Brobst the pencil signature which Poe affixed at Mrs. W's request to the anonymous text of 'Ulalume' in the American Whig Review [December 1847]. Mrs. Whitman, ignorant of the authorship, had been praising the poem—when Poe very proudly announced that it was his. Mrs. W. then declared that he ought to sign the copy in the library, which he did casually on the spot. This anecdote floated about orally in Providence folklore for 60 years, though no one had even bothered to verify it. Then—in 1909, at the time of the Poe centenary—Dr. H. L. Koopman, head of the John Hay Library of Brown University, determined to track it down. Going through the old Athenaeum files, he found the issue of the review containing 'Ulalume' —& there, surely enough, was the faint pencil signature 'Edgar A. Poe' beneath the printed verses." On this matter see *Collected Works of Edgar Allan Poe: Volume I, Poems,* ed. Thomas Ollive Mabbott (Cambridge, MA: Harvard University Press, 1969), 413, 423. Cf. Will Murray's interview of Harry K. Brobst, *Lovecraft Studies* Nos. 22/23 (Fall 1990): 40–41.

16. Frank Belknap Long, Jr., "An Amateur Humorist," *Conservative* No. 12 (March 1923): 2–5, a defense of Samuel Loveman's poetry against the attack made upon it by Michael Oscar White. Edward H. Cole criticized Long in the "Bureau of Critics" column in the *National Amateur* for March 1923. HPL discusses the controversy in "In the Editor's Study," *Conservative* No. 13 (July 1923): 21–24.

17. Durfee Hill, a mountain summit in Providence County, climbs to 801 feet above sea level.

18. Charles A. A. Parker printed the final issue of HPL's *Conservative*.

[10]   [AHT]

The Ol' Shack
May 17, 1923

Ave, Illustrissime!

Hell, what a week! Grippe has me for fair, and I'm three-fourths deaf, one-eighth paralysed, one sixteenth febrile . . . . . but gawd!

As my card no doubt indicated, the Bush matter duly arrove, & was forwarded instanter to the illustrious inspirer. I'm looking for the $10.94 any day now—& you'll see it the day after. My utter brokeness forced me into Bushic activity this last week-end, & I cleaned up 724 lines of contributed *Mind Power Plus* material (not as technically bad as DVB's own drool) at one dollar per twenty-four lines. This hauls me in thirty dollars and seventeen cents, but XX bones of that has gotta be passed on to Parker as final payment on the coming twenty-eight page *Conservative*. This contributed stuff, as I say, isn't as metrically & grammatically hashed as Bush's own—but gawd! in silliness it's even worse, if that be possible! One pair of "New Thought" rhapsodies is so damn rich that I'm giving you a peek at the stuff—just pipe the enclosed! This Evelyn Whitell sure is the prize Dumb Dora of the Bush menagerie! Get that "Boy's Truth Prayer"—oh, Clarence! He doesn't say who carried the stretcher after the fight, who took him in when it rained, what morgue got him when he had the flu, or what mantelpiece he et off when Pa got through with him! Gawd is my all! And that "Swanee River" parody is priceless, too!

As for *Weird Tales*—Bro. Baird handed me a bit of a novelty by sending a personal spiel when he socked back my junk. He says that if I'll re-type the stuff in *double-spaced* form he'll consider acceptance . . . . . but that's too indefinite to get me enthusiastic. Yah! how I hate typing! But I'm so damn hard up I may try *one* as a gamble . . . "Dagon," I guess. . . . And if he doesn't accept that he knows where he can go!

Yes—Grandpa's little Belknap sure is a properly ethereal object for semi-classick versification! Sure his ma's all right—so's his pa—damn pleasant, cordial, & hospitable folks, for whom I have the sincerest respect—but when it comes to actual congeniality & community of interest I naturally find more delight in their one tiny chick, whose thoughts run to those matters which absorb my own. I'm enclosing some of the child's epistles, which reveal him perhaps better than his conversation—for he's a shy young faunlet. Please return 'em. I wish you could be here when I shew him the Providence Athenaeum where Poe & Mrs. Whitman used to stroll, & the various other links with the past which make this city habitable in spite of its impossibly dull bourgeois population.

And speaking of my grandchildren—did I tell you that the one & only Alfredus has won a graduate scholarship in the University of Chicago, where he will both study & *teach* during the year 1923–4? I always knew that pert little divvle had the goods!

Oh, boy! How could you have the heart to tell me of all them comin' metropolitan doin's w'en I ain't got the price to take 'em in! It makes me homesick for the sight of the Woolworth Tower, & the B. R. T. subway, & Riverside Drive in the sunset, & the old Dutch churchyard beneath the 1796 spire, 'n' everything! But an empty purse is a stern master, so I guess I gotta content myself with the neighb'ring reedy streams & rustic groves, just as I'll have to at Convention Time, when I would fain loiter by Erie's flow'ry marge or wander to the woods of Wade Park along Euclid's leafy windings. Bah. Eheu.

The new *Wolverine* hath just arriven, & I find therein a monstrous fine critique of the work of one Randolph St. John Clyner, Gent.[1] Am I right in assuming the author to be a resident of 211 W. 138th?[2] If not, I'm wasting a perfectly good compliment . . . . . but you can take it as a compliment anyhow that I should quickly associate you with a particularly fine review, no matter by whom. So that's that.

May gawd be with ya till we meets again—in hell or before. Thine obt:

Theobaldus

Notes

1. I.e., Rheinhart Kleiner.
2. The article—"The Vivisector," by "Zoilus," *Wolverine* No. 14 (Spring 1923): [11–13]—has mistakenly been thought to be by HPL himself.

[11]   [AHT]

Down on the Farm
26 May, 1923

Doctissime et Oratissime:—

Hell! I've gotta go to an ear specialist today—me aunt's gonna drag me, because I've been dodging it a coupla weeks already. If there's anything I hate, it's medical puttering—makes me think of my harrass'd youth, when life was one g. d. doc after another. But that stuff gets us all in the end—even Tryout says he's gonna see a medico for the first time in his seventy-one years! I gotta idee that this deef stuff of mine may be permanent—move over, Smithy, Grandpa's gonna set on the ear-trumpeter's bench!

Hain't heard from the little Bairdie yet, but betcha a plugged 1804 dollar he shies at "Dagon" now it's put up to 'im straight without no chanct of dodging. Yah—how I hate typing! I dunno whether or not I'll try anything else—a goof don't hafta yell at me twict to fade, as a general thing, & I hates to stick around where I ain't popular. I considers a #13 boot a more or less delicate hint anent the beauties of a varying environment. So I guess if Bairdie tweet-tweets agin "Dagon", he won't see any of its little brothers any more!

Congrats on the luck! Esperanto seems to be spreading—squeeze the old dames good—that is, to the last copper denarius![1] And here's hoping the younger generation learns enough English by next season to soak in your LB of B of E course! Since Davy's watchin' his step a bit, I guess I gotta pay more attention to other work—I gotta bum novel & a hell of a book-length narrative poem on the shelf, but I have ben goin' easy because I don't think I kin milk the authors for as much as I gypped outa Dave. Ish Kabibble![2]

As for amachoor choinalism—what is it anyway? The name sounds familiar, but I can't quite place it. Must be one of the things I was interested in when I went to grammar school & collected stamps & bugs and played the harmonica at recess & walked on the top of the stone wall on Angell Street & Arlington Avenue . . . . . . yes, I'm sure I've heard of it!

And as to my scrap with the bean-balancers—my dear fellow, you don't suppose I really care for the moderns! Bless me—I'm merely defending my children Sam & 'Ittle Belknap . . . if ya wanna get a slant at my other personality, jest lamp my rhymed tribute to Sir Randolph Clyner in the recent *Try-out!*[3] I have no opinions—I believe in nothing—but assume for the time whatever opinion amuses me or is opposite to that of the person or persons present. Ho, hum! My cynicism & scepticism are increasing, & from an entirely new cause—the Einstein theory. The latest eclipse observations seem to place this system among the facts which cannot be dismissed, & assumedly it removes the last hold which reality or the universe can have on the independent mind.[4] All is chance, accident, & ephemeral illusion—a fly may be greater than Arcturus, & Durfee Hill may surpass Mount Everest—assuming them to be removed from the present planet & differently environed in the continuum of space-time. There are no values in all infinity—the least idea that there are is the supreme mockery of all. All the cosmos is a jest, & fit to be treated only as a jest, & one thing is as true as another. I believe everything & nothing—for all is chaos, always has been, & always will be. Ease, amusement—these are the only relative qualities fit to be classed as values. Sure, I can be a meliorist—the present civilisation is declining, & I'm glad! glad! glad! because I can adopt a new system of values in which that civilisation is an evil or disease . . . . better & better . . . . like my damned ear ain't gettin'!

The trouble with these Malden Louisa-Alcott-hounds[5] is that they don't know beauty when they see it. The poor dubs are blind to the delicate radiance of glowing & bejewelled phrase & atmosphere. For aesthetic insight, & knowledge of the background of art, they can be herded with the bozo what sued the railway for shippin' him a Venus de Milo wit' the arms broke off. They're so dumb they think Benedetto Croce is a new kind of knitting![6] Oh, well! Let 'em paddle in the water! Parker gave away something of his future line of attack in a letter to me—he's gonna pick up what he considers unconsciously comic phrases in Loveman's & Sonny-Boy's work—so I'm slipping into the new *Conservative* the enclosed counter-crack on the simpering question.[7]

Yess—Grandpa's chilluns sure is great boys! And now young Davis[8]— our little Merrimac pal—hath just written the Old Gentleman an epistle *ninety* pages long—forty-five reg'lar Dodge Report sheets! Watch that li'l rascal—if he isn't a second Galpinius, I'm a bum judge of babes! As for tiny Belknap— he's the greatest *aesthete* of 'em all. His seclusion (lately broken by two agreeably argumentative sessions with Kleiner & good ol' McNeil at the latter's dump) is possibly as much of an asset as a liability—it promotes individuality & imaginative vividness. Such things *can* happen in our day—I ain't no parlour-snake nor corner lamp-post myself, & it looks as though I were dropping gradually back in the even more perfect hermitage of earlier years—a process which deafness will promote. Then look at Tryout, too! But I suppose me an' Smithy ain't in Sonny-Boy's aesthetic class, so we don't cash in very strong w'en it comes to a philosophical presentation of the anchorite question! Incidentally, I sure will be glad to see the child when he hits the eastbound side-door pullman & slaps his dawgs over the Providential pave!

No, my dear Watson, you didn't tell me you were the Zoilus![9] I discovered it by my own masterful methods—massive eye, eagle brain—with not a single clue except Lawson's statement! [10]

Thy resp. & obt.

Θεοβάλδος

P.S. Did I tell you *High Life* is barred in Providence?[11] I saw the City Solicitor at Gawge Joolian's request—but nothin' doin'.

Notes

1. JFM later became vice president of the Esperanto Association of North America.
2. "Isch ga-bibble" (Yiddish for "I should worry") was a novelty song released in 1913. A cartoon postcard issued in 1915 rendered the phrase as Ish Ka Bibble.
3. "To Rheinhart Kleiner, Esq., upon His Town Fables and Elegies."
4. Einstein's theory of relativity was believed to be confirmed by observations of a solar eclipse on 21 September 1922. The subject was discussed in a front-page article in the *New York Times* (12 April 1923) and probably other papers.
5. HPL alludes to the members of the Hub Club, especially Edith Miniter, Charles A. A. Parker, and others living in Malden, MA. He suggests that their appreciation of art and literature does not extend beyond the Victorian work of Louisa May Alcott.
6. Benedetto Croce (1866–1952), Italian literary theorist, idealist philosopher, and politician. HPL puns on the term *crochet*.
7. See letter 9, n. 12.
8. Edgar J. Davis.
9. Zoilus was a Greek critic (fl. 4th century B.C.E.) who gained notoriety by sharply criticizing the Homeric poems. HPL himself was author of several "Vivisector" columns in the *Wolverine* that appeared under the Zoilus pseudonym.
10. Horace L. Lawson, editor/publisher of the *Wolverine*. The clue is unknown.
11. Formerly *Home Brew*, which had previously published two stories by HPL.

[12]   [AHT]

Headquarters Unchanged
29 May, 1923

Ecce!

Well, the leetle Bairdie took "Dagon" after all, & wants more from his Grandpa Theobald's pen! Attaboy, Ed! "Dagon" will appear in the July *Weird*

Tales,[1] & a cheque will amble hitherward about that time. Baird doesn't let on how much it is—but I guess not much. Still—every little bit helps, & I guess I'll type another yarn before long. I'd orta slip youse a commission, since it was your encouragement which made me hawk "Dagon" around!

Oh—I went to the specialist—& lo! I can hear once more! He found a lump of hardened wax below the vision & beyond the conjecture of the simp that gave it the onct-over early this month, & after its removal the ol' receivin' set made a quick curve back to normalcy! But if it hadn't of went w'en it did, there'd a ben hell to pay—it was poundin' th' ol' drum like a jazz-band bone-juggler! Ho, hum! But it is a frightful bore to hear again—the world sounds so beastly commonplace! I miss the detachment & exoticism of deafness . . . . . . in my ears there sounded the surge of strange tides lapping the golden shores of unimagin'd worlds, & the shrill cries of grotesque parraqueets whose scarlet & orange plumes flashed weirdly through the tropic forests of luxuriant fancy. And now the bally clocks, & tram-cars, & wagons, & motors, and all that sort of thing. Bah!

I read Machen's "Hill of Dreams" last night at one sitting. It's a deuced clever account of a somewhat dippy John whose imagination is O.K. but whose blood is healthier than his brains. One of these intense, moony, neurotic, emotional yaps, but bright at that. It may be subtly autobiographical, but not literally so—for the hero ends it all in Chapter VII, whilst Arty M. is still punchin' his meal ticket. In imagination & colour, this performance sure is the poodle's sport-shirt, & I gotta han' it to Arty for pullin' a pretty nifty line! He done it in 1897, but couldn't get nobody to print it till 1907. Then he couldn't get nobody to buy it, so it's comin' up in this scintillant year of 1923, nicely reprinted—with a maddening raft of tryoutisms—all by Al Knopf. (advt.)

But hell! All this is damn small Irish bananas! For real, 190-proof class, ya gotta hand the silk-lined cuspidor to me snappy li'l grandchild Al Galpin! Oh, bebby, shoot me w'ile I'm happy! Some time ago Profs. Giese & Ernst of the University of Wisconsin got a commission of some sort to translate Bre'r Poquelin's "Le Misanthrope" & "L'Avare", & Ed Rostand's posthumous play "La Dernière Nuit de Don Juan"—& they're slipping the Rostand job to The Boy![2] Hip! Hip! Hip-pocket!! Who says my precious chee-ild ain't the canary's wrist-watch? The play is just nasty enough, no doubt, to be popular with the modern rabble of Freudian mock-highbrows; so will land Alfredus on all fours in the literary world . . . . whoopee! Twenty-one years old, & a full-fledg'd younger Intellectual! You can lay big money that I'm feelin' pretty damn cocky about this impending triumph of The Kid's—especially since most of that dumb amateur drove have been persistently blind to his supreme worth & mountainous superiority. Mike White—hee, haw! Pull down your vest, bo!

Well, that's that!

I am, Sir, ever yr most obt &c.

Theobaldus

P.S. Bairdie took to the Clark Ashton Smith stuff as a duck to water! He hadn't intended to use any verse in *Weird Tales,* but fell for C A S so hard he's gonna write him & cop all the turribul pomes he kin!

Notes

1. "Dagon" did not appear until the October 1923 issue.
2. HPL refers to Molière (stage name of Jean-Baptiste Poquelin, 1622–1673). *Le Misanthrope* was translated by William F. Giese in 1928 as *The Misanthrope.* Neither Giese nor Professor Ernst (unidentified) appears to have published a translation of *L'Avare* (*The Miser*) or of *La Dernière Nuit de Don Juan* (*The Last Night of Don Juan*) by Edmond Eugène Alexis Rostand (1868–1918), and no translation of the latter by Galpin is known to have been published.

[13]   [AHT]

June 24, 1923

Augustissime:—

             At last a moment to breathe! My trip—a glorious exploration of Colonial marvels—wore me out altogether, so that I couldn't touch a pen for damn near a week; but now I'm able to resume the aspect if not the substance of correspondence. Meanwhile National matters have opprest me— laureate junk, & a silly mess about getting the names of Recorder & Custodian of Ballots to that poor fool Howard Jeffreys—who himself printed my announcement of the appointments—a matter urged by that equally dumb simp Juliette Haas, who could have read the beastly names herself & sent 'em to Jeffreys without bothering me[1] . . . . . Hell, but these amachoors are a soft lotta cuckoos! I guess my boy Alfredus is right when he reflects—as he does in his latest letter—

> "Reflect, O mon sage pere, upon the stench & ignominy of professional journalism, & how far removed its pitiful pen-p____s [?] are from any degree of civilisation, intelligence, honour, or elementary honesty, then remove all that this vile trade has of enterprise & shrewdness, contract its ambitions so that the pitiful exercise it permits has no excuse except *causa sua,* then define for me the term "amateur journalist", studiously avoiding all references to animal excrement!"

And this is what the child wrote after I had sent him *The Conservative!* I hope your own opinion of my humble sheet will be less critical—& that you will pardon the literary ineptitudes of those who sought vainly to achieve the "Fause Murdoch" level! By the way—if you have any use for extra copies, I'll be delighted to shower you with such articles.

             Damn! That was the last I could write with pen & ink—simply couldn't push the beastly outfit. Now let's see if the text will get any less stupid—a matter depending on whether my present exhaustion & lassitude are merely physical or both mental & physical. Pardon the pencil—but it's the privilege of feebleness. Smithy has also sunk to that level. We old guys sure is a pathetic lot. (Yeh—I guess it's both mental & physical—I don't seem to get any brighter).

Say—I wish that stamp request had come a day earlier! I threw away a twelve-center just too soon—but that's life! That old collection of mine hasn't been mine since 1916, when I gave it to my cousin Phillips Gamwell. He died on the last day of that same year—from other causes—& the collection is now stored among his mother's things in some obscure place—either in Providence or Cambridge. She treasures his effects so much, that I'm damned if I know whether it would be in good taste to ask for the things back again—one must be aesthetic, even if cynical & unsentimental—so I couldn't possibly predict the future of these varicolour'd scraps of paper. But if I do get hold of 'em—look for a windfall! My cousin was a great kid—a Belknap and Alfredus rolled into one. They remind me of him—he was my best & earliest grandson! I can still see myself training him when he was three & I was eleven!

As to cynicism—it's what we all have to come to, & for my part it matches my eyes & complexion to a T. It's damn good stuff, too—honestly, it's unbelievably cheering as compared with the lugubrious teleology & febrile ethics of such hapless neurotics as Cook & Loveman. Poor Loveman is in a frightful state of melancholy—I have to cheer him up with twenty-page sermons in favour of nonchalant cynicism.

Weird Tales? Yeh, it's kinda amusing to get a profesh aquarium for "Dagon". But I've no idea that leetle Bairdie'll ever take another. "Dagon" was a luck shot, & Ed probably asked about the others to be polite. I've fixed up "The Picture in the House" for him, & am bettin' heavy it'll come back with or without thanks. Hell! Don't congratulate me on havin' a lotta stuff done! It's the TYPING that's the devil's own torment, & that bolognee wants everything double-spaced! damn him. It's fun to write 'em—but hell to copy 'em. When I chuck this _____ _____ son of a _____ of a National presidency—& get a little strength above my collar & beyond my right cuff—I want to grind out a deuce of a lot of shocking monstrosities—& the chances are I'll try 'em on Bairdie before I ever have the patience to copy the old line TEXACO. I'm now sic'ing other amachoors onto *Weird Tales.*[2]

Deafness? Gawd, how I miss it! Hearing is so common. But I don't see many people nowadays, so it doesn't matter much—nothing does, for that matter. I shall always remember—as a precious, sacred memory—that I have been deaf—

Yeh—I gotta cop Art Machen's "Hieros." Must get busy trailin' it at the libe. And this bimbo Marsh—"The Beetle" sounds damn good—& I see there's a new edition of Stoker's "Jewel of Seven Stars"—dished up for the current Tut craze, no doubt. And I await with interest the final culinary procedure on the 3d Vath ep.[3] [. . .?]

Later we did Brattle Street—Cantabridgia—a Tory Row where I felt on familiar ground—& afterward Sandy dumped Ed at 36 Tower & me on a tram line to Sullivan Square. I panhandled a night's lodging off Parker—with two free meals—& on Saturday went on a lone jaunt to eternally magical MARBLEHEAD. Oh, baby! I'm dreaming of it yet!! The Lee Mansion![4] Sweet spirits of ammonia! Boy, that BRITISH carving & wainscotting! Solid mahogany, & a premium coupon in every package! And the old couple there tipped me off to a whole section of *pricelessly quaint streets that I'd never seen before*—the hill betwixt Abbot Hall & the harbour. Man, man! What a delirium of Colonial antiquity! Daedalian convolutions of antediluvian byways, courts, doorways—yes, enthusiasm is delightfully suited to occasional use. And I saw a swell RIOT—O citizen sovereignty! Three Boston Mick bootleggers in an auto truck—all fighting soused—bumped into a telegraph pole & beat up a young fellow who gave 'em the ha-ha. They were so fiendishly brutal that a mob gather'd, & nearly got the bozos away from the one nervy bull (say— that boy gets my hat off every trip! He was a whole constabulary & refrigerating plant in one! Old Marblehead fishing stock, I'll say!) who was running 'em in. It was deliciously uncivilised, & I could trace the resemblance to the rebel hordes who in 1775 defied His Majesty's rightful authority. Nobody was killed or maimed—which greatly disappointed me. After that frost I found the old houses an exciting relief.

Well, that's that! Thine obt tho' languid

Tibaldvs

Notes

1. See "President's Message," March 1923: "Miss Juliette Haas, originally Historian, has accepted appointment as Secretary, and is prepared to receive applications or furnish blanks" (*CE* 1.323).

2. Among the amateur writers who, with HPL's aid, appeared in early issues of *WT* were Frank Belknap Long, Sonia H. Greene, and Clark Ashton Smith.

3. HPL refers to the third of the *Episodes of Vathek* (1912) by William Beckford, but it is not clear what HPL means by "culinary [i.e., W. Paul Cook] procedure." Possibly Cook was to lend the book to HPL, as in 1925 he refers to rereading it (see *SL* 2.36).

4. At 161 Washington St. "Built in 1768 by the leading citizen Maj. Jeremiah Lee, it is still perfect today, having been sold in 1804 to the Marblehead Bank and carefully kept till 1909, when its present owners—the M'head Historical Society—bought it" (HPL to Frank Belknap Long, 23 June 1923; AHT).

[14]   [AHT]

Foothills of the Durfee Range
Friday the 13th
1923

[13 July 1923]

Domine:—

Still brandishing th' ol' pencil, & for a double reason—as my Marblehead card must have hinted. To think that the pen I have cherished since 1906 should so basely desert me![1] Helas! I'm waiting now for Sandusky to get back—he gets lots of fountain pens free in connexion with ad work, & not long ago gave Cole a veritable pippin with a barrel as capacious as a camel's stomach. Maybe he'll find me something cheap—gawd knows I need cheapness if anybody does.

Yeh—th' ol' job's over, & amachewerdom looks pretty distant in the background. I had a jolt from your friend Landon,[2] who passed over "Hypnos" as ambiguous, & handed Laur. & Hon. Men. respectively to Dudley Carroll ("An Inhibition") & Edna Hyde. ("Sadie Lustig"). I'm through with fiction, I guess—just as I got through with serious verse three years ago—& will henceforward do no writing except in defence of people who really have ability. What little I shall write in 1923–4 will be strictly pro-Loveman and anti-White; which reminds me that Laureateship returns in the *Essay* class are pretty tough on the bean-shooters. My new *Conservative* dope copped the frosting, & Little Belknap's "An Amateur Humorist" pulled down next best. This way out, Michael! Speaking of Laureate stuff—I suppose you know you have the history title whilst E. Miniter enjoys the leavings. In the poetry class Nix Waterman pulled a bonehead stunt by handing the laureateship to John Ravenor Bullen & giving Samuelus a mere Honorable Mention.[3] Luckily SL dodged this insult by having made an eleventh-hour withdrawal of his entry—which was shoved in without his knowledge or consent. Now Nix has gotta name another Honorable Mention.

As for politics—go to it, boys, & may the shrewdest bimbo confiscate the hawg-meat! Grandpa's out of it all—I'd have asked to be excused even from that director sinecure if the thought had traversed my cerebrum. I'm neither for nor against Gawge Joolian—that is, if he pays Clark Ashton Smith what he owes him[4]—& will smile benignly on any sort of a government that minds its own business & leaves real amateurs free for literary activity. Heigho! Now for the wide, open spaces, as the barber said five years ago when he trimmed Sam Loveman's dome. As to the whole amateur field—I'm not entirely agreeing with Alfredus, but I sure can see what he means. For further details, consult what the printer left of my July message, & what the delegates recall of my annual shot of blah as read at the convention.[5] Moe said only one bird left the room—but I guess most of the others would have if the dope hadn't paralysed them. White Mule,[6] ol' chap!

So you are now a broadcaster? Last thing I heard, you were in the cinema—Montreal-Esperanto conclave—but I suppose one must be up to date. Let us hope that WOOF or whatever it is[7] has a liberal purse, & that the general wireless telephonick publick are susceptible to intellectual cultivation. If you keep it up, I'll have to get one o' them radio contraptions myself! And so the Morons want to know about "Love in Literature"—only eight months after you told the Sunrise bunch all about what love is? This love stuff sure is the fad of the age—or was until the publication of "Yes, We Have No Bananas."[8] Every man his own sheik, & gawd help the censors & the sensible! T'other day the new *Citsov*[9] blew in, & I perused its contents with interest. Ya got some job, brother, tryin' to wake up a nation in the late Byzantine period!

Hell, but I *can't* keep awake! I'll johnhancock this before I start the dreamland trombone, slippin' in a full quota of good wishes, writesoons, & hopetoseeyas.

No bananas!

Θεοβάλδος

P.S. Who won—Willard or Firpo?[10] I've had no news as yet, but am all on aidge.

Notes

1. HPL lost his Waterman pen, which he had since 1906, on his most recent trip to Marblehead.

2. Herman Landon (1882–1960), a pulp fiction writer chiefly known for a 1920s detective series called the "Gray Phantom," was the NAPA's laureate judge for fiction.

3. Nixon Waterman (1859–1944), journalist and poet, was the NAPA's laureate judge of poetry.

4. George J. Houtain had not paid Clark Ashton Smith for his illustrations of HPL's "The Lurking Fear" for *Home Brew*.

5. HPL refers to his "President's Message" (*National Amateur*, July 1923), the last of his interim presidency. "The President's Annual Report," which was apparently read at the NAPA convention in Cleveland, was published in the *National Amateur* for September 1923.

6. I.e., moonshine.

7. Actually station WEAF (which JFM had called "great"; JFM to HPL, 3 July 1923; ms., JHL).

8. "Yes! We Have No Bananas" was a novelty song by Frank Silver and Irving Cohn from the Broadway revue *Make It Snappy* (1922). It became a major hit in 1923 (number 1 for five weeks).

9. JFM's little paper, *Loyal Citizen Sovereignty*.

10. On 12 July 1923, 42-year-old Jess Willard attempted a comeback when he fought the Argentinean Luis Firpo at Boyles Thirty Acres in Jersey City before a crowd of 100,000. Firpo won.

[15]   [AHT]

6 August, 1923

O More Than Mightiest:—

Heigho! Gawd pity the polar bears on a night like this! Well, here's Grandpa again, with the first stamps over four cents (ain't that what ya wanted?) which has blew in hither since your request. Pardon the excessive cancellation—I didn't do it. And I dassent use a ink eraser for fear I'll spoil Benny Leonard's—I mean Franklin's—complexion & coiffure.[1] Oh, yes—& here's a couple 5's I forgot about. One of 'em ain't inked up so damn bad, & ya kin lamp me ol' pard Teddy pretty nifty. Hell, but I admired that bimbo.[2] He had some petty illusions, like most guys; but he sure knew where to tell the world to get off! I like a strong gink—you tell 'em, Onions—& I wish like hades this baby had made himself Emperor. Republics are getting to be so cliché.

About this egg Landon—don't worry! I shall start spillin' the Socony when I feels like it! I guess I'll just lay off a few years like I done betwixt 1908 & 1917—the rest done me good. A guy wants to take a rest onct in a w'ile, to lay aroun' & soak up atmosphere & colour & all that from readin' & rubber-neckin'. But at that I don't think I'll publish nothin' more—unless that slow-motion Bairdie decides to release his mag after all, & to loosen up wit' de heavy sugar. I'm fed up on the literary dope, anyhow—gettin' damn monotonous. Me for Colonial architecture & antiques these days. And I ain't sure but what authorship's a bit vulgar anyway. A gentleman shouldn't write all his images down for a plebeian rabble to stare at. If he writes at all, it shou'd be in private letters to other gentleman of sensitiveness & discrimination. Μεν-τοι, σεμερον ευδεμιαν βανάναν εχομεν![3]

Yeh—I guess for laureatic inclusiveness you cop the lace-edged steam roller! The extra-Nation realms now await you—& you're welcome to anything you can find in 'em. Say, compared to the present United, King Tut is live enough to walk the dawg! Convention—my gawd, I dunno as they held it! I ain't heard a word outa that buncha stiffs for near haff a year. Only thing to do is to let 'em enjoy the chutes in their own naive way, & then have somebody salvage the disjecta membra when Leo's gang gets fed up & rings off.[4] For beautiful dumbness them bozos is sure the ornithorhynchus'[5] pocket-flask! But I should worry! I'm a fossil this trip all right all right, & other heads can bother about the beastly politics stuff.

As for window displays—gawd knows what you & Dench do with 'em, but I guess you'll find that Providence has its share. The truth is, that for a small town Providence ain't half bad. They's a lotta jack in circulation, & the shops & everything seems pretty lively & nifty. The ol' burg has some 250,000 insects of its own, & is the natural centre of a metropolitan district which can't include less than 500,000. I think you'll like the place—if ya don't hafta vegetate here all the year round. I can't say as I know any burg quite so pretty within a fairly small land area—the approach from the station is the horses' dancing-pumps, whilst the residential east side gives a panorama absolutely unequalled by any other full-sized city for pure Colonial antiquity.

I'll take ya on one long serpentine walk which will make a Georgian of ya or kill ya! Atmosphere? Bo, it's so thick they cut it like dey cuts ice on ponds, wit' a saw! Benefit Street (laid out 1752, built up 1770) & the narrow intersecting streets, all on the side of one of the steepest hills in New England—oh, Clarence, but ain't it the humming-bird's rubber boots! And for the old Providence of the later days—the Poe & Sarah Helen Whitman days—man, it fairly rises up & taps ya on the shoulder, & says "look me over, kid!" I'll show ya the dump where Sadie hung out, & the sick looking back-yard that Poe called a moonlit garden & all that sort of rot[6]—& the *Athenaeum,* where the pair of 'em used to spoon in the alcoves. Boy! It ain't changed a jot, & fairly reeks of the forties. Ast A. M. Adams.[7]

This Ursimontane stuff[8] certainly is the wyvern's inner tube!

And pray gawd we can each hook enough jack by mid-September to put the programme through! Oh, leetle Bairdie, why in gawd's name dontcha come acrost with de price o' "Dagon"? May lectures flourish & may trials fade, till a half decent stack of fish be made! Yeh—I sure will slip ya, subsequently, any extra berry pastures I stumble on—but they's damn lean pickin' just now, as my flat wallet mutely proclaims! Hell, but life is a bore—& mostly so on account of the vulgar necessity of financial striving. I wisht some guy would croak & leave me about £1000 per year—damn modest wish, but I could be moderately cheerful on it!

Slip me all the latest low-down, & prepare to be converted to Georgianism.

Thine obt Servt.

Θεοβάλδος

Notes

1. HPL refers to Leonard E. Tilden, an amateur journalist a veteran amateur journalist of New Hampshire, and later Washington, DC., who was attempting to secure second-class postage rates for amateur journals. At the time, Benjamin Franklin's image appeared on the one cent stamp.

2. See HPL's poem "Theodore Roosevelt: 1858–1919."

3. I.e., "Yes! We Have No Bananas."

4. HPL's "literary" faction was voted out in the UAPA election in July 1922, with Leo Fritter beating HPL for Official Editor. But in the election of July 1923, HPL's faction was reelected: he won back the position of Official Editor, and Sonia H. Greene was elected President, even though she was not aware that she was even on the ballot. In revenge, the previous administration withheld funds and failed to answer letters, so that only a single issue of the *United Amateur* (May 1924) was published in that official year.

5. *Ornithorhynchus anatinus* is the platypus.

6. The John Reynolds House (c. 1785) at 88 Benefit Street. Sarah Helen Whitman (1803–1878) lived at the house when it was owned by Samuel Hamlin, a Providence

pewterer. HPL mentions Poe's romance with Mrs. Whitman in "The Shunned House."

7. A. M. Adams was an amateur journalist and the husband of Hazel Pratt Adams.

8. HPL appears to refer to Bear Mountain State Park, a large park on the New Jersey side of the Hudson River that had become a popular area for hiking, skiing, etc.

[16]   [AHT]

South of Pascoag
23d Septr., 1923

Illustrissime!

Ha! I fooled ya! You thought all that pedestrianism had killed me off, yet here I am alive & everything, & with my usual smile of cynical placidity on my coarse features![1] After getting home Wednesday I slept 21 hours without a break, & after six hours of subsequent consciousness I slept 11 more; then came more consciousness & a sleep of 13 hours, after which was more consciousness, which still persists into Sunday morning. Am I rested? Well, I would be if it weren't for this damned *cold*, which keeps me wheezing like a one-lunged Ford. But that is getting better at last, so I may well sing of sunshine & happiness & all that damned rot.

Mrs. Gamwell—who came over & ate up one of our left-over eggs—expressed regret at not seeing you, whilst Mrs. Clark—who tried to eat up the other but saw a green spot in it which she didn't like—expressed pleasure that she had better fortune in that respect. Heigho! The favours of fate are bestow'd with blandly ironick injustice!

There's a Harding stamp on the outside of this envelope, but none have come in lately. However, I've asked my more obliging correspondents to turn in those they get on any envelopes, so unless they're forgetful I'll have at least a few for you. I like these stamps—such a relief from that vulgar red, & those eternal drowsy features of poor Genl. Washington. Harding was a handsome bimbo—I'm sure sorry he had the good luck to get clear of this beastly planet.[2]

Sept. 23–24.

Oho! Another sleep—this one twelve hours long! Consciousness & I sure do hate each other! But I guess I've slept off the worst of my cold.

Well—I ben stirrin' folks up about the United situation, & if the ol' hulk doesn't get floated again it won't be my bally fault! I got a note from Mrs. Greene asking to be relieved of the unexpected & cataclysmic presidential burden, but have written back urging her to hang on for dear life until Daas, P. J. C., & I get the matter thrashed out. If she resigns, the office will automatically fall on that impossible creature Mazurewicz[3]—1st Vice-Pres.—which of course means utter chaos. You see we have a definite presidential succession, unlike The National with its need for directorial action. *But*—I shall not try to do anything, or to ask S. H. G. to serve, *unless* I am absolutely assured of the active & strenuous cooperation of Daas & Campbell.

Well, I gotta ring off & see what I can do with the accumulated mail before me. It's a tough job, as you know from personal experience!

Yours for progress, patriotism, & pedestrianism,

Theobaldus Ambulans,

Grand Titan, K.K.K.

Notes

1. JFM had visited HPL earlier in September. The two of them explored Marblehead extensively on foot on the 15th and also made a trip to the small towns of Chepachet and Pascoag, in northwestern RI, on the 19th.
2. President Warren G. Harding died of pneumonia on 2 August 1923.
3. HPL refers to Edward T. Mazurewicz, the vice president of the UAPA during the 1922–23 term, re-elected for 1923–24, and hostile to HPL's faction. In "The Dreams in the Witch House" (1932), one Joe Mazurewicz is "a superstitious loomfixer."

[17]   [AHT]

Same Ol' Joint
28 October, 1923

Reverend and Philatelic Sir:—

The scene now became wildly beautiful by reason of one of the most gorgeous sunsets in the history of the province. The whole west flam'd forth as if—to quote poor Lucian Taylor in Mr. Machen's book—the door of some Cyclopean furnace had been thrown wide;[1] & the old mansion stood out black against a veritable iridescent tumult. The spectacle was an holocaust polychrome & unearthly, nearly every colour having its place—even a vivid & sinister *green* which seem'd to typify the poisonous corrosion & putrefaction of the decaying elder America. It was like the phrensy of hysterical cymbals & trumpets translated into light & colour; a screaming, terrible thing whilst it lasted. And because it was violent & terrible, it was very beautiful. Before it faded—as everything fades—we had pass'd the Simmons mansion & come upon a still older house—a mighty farmhouse of 1740 or so, with severe Colonial doorway with Dorick pilasters & triangular pediment. Back . . . . back . . . . down the years. . . . .[2]

Scarce less is my envy at perusing your account of the new quincuncial lozenge of wits, which holds forth at the abode of my small child Belknap.[3] I shou'd in truth relish a share in the deliberation of this agreeable body, since New-England offers no conversation fit for a true-born cynic & despiser of mankind. I am indeed sensible why the late Henry Adams Esq. found the air of his native provinces so oppressive to the reason, & repugnant to the taste.[4] There has, I vow, been no sprightly or civilis'd discourse in the region, since

the late evacuation of Boston by His Majesty's forces, & the going away of
the loyal gentry.

I am grateful, as before, of the charity you shew in your opinion of
"Dagon"; & vastly in your debt for the epistle you writ to Mr. Baird. This
worthy man not long ago writ me in a manner which elevates my inherent
vanity to unbearable altitudes. He says, 'my work makes a peculiar appeal to
his readers', as attested by numerous letters from them; & he desires I shou'd
address my mail to his home in Evanston hereafter, & he may be certain of
early perusing it. He solicits my tales in unbroken succession, designing to
publish the following in his next three issues: "The Picture in the House",
"The Hound", and "Arthur Jermyn". Were it not for an awkward delay in
monetary remittance, I shou'd account my self very well off; & assume
forthwith the airs and impertinences of an acknowledg'd author. I have, I
may remark, been able to secure Mr. Baird's acceptance of two tales by my
adopted son Eddy, which he had before rejected. Upon my correcting them,
he profest himself willing to print them in early issues; they being intitul'd
respectively "Ashes", and "The Ghost-Eater". In exchange for my revisory
service, Eddy types my own manuscripts in the approv'd double-spac'd form;
this labour being particularly abhorrent to my sensibilities.

But I must give over these my remarks, for I must take a nap against the
afternoon; when (tho' 'tis devilish cold) I am pledg'd to visit my son Eddy in
East-Providence, & help him with his newest fiction, a pleasing & morbid
study in hysterical necrophily, intitul'd "The Lov'd Dead". I have just finisht a
wretched novel of the romantick sort, "Midwinter", by one John Buchan,
which my aunt got for me at the library because it deals with my eighteenth
century & brings in Sam Johnson as a character. Dash me, Sir, if I comprehend why grown men write puling romance. If they draw not life, like Mr.
Fielding, why the pox can't they be downright phantastical, & avoid that
mawkishness which ever attends the depiction of fallacy in familiar scenes?

Ever yr mo resp & obt Servt
Theobaldus

Notes

1. HPL alludes to the first line of Machen's *The Hill of Dreams:* "There was a glow in
the sky as if great furnace doors were opened."
2. This passage is largely repeated in HPL's letter to Frank Belknap Long, 8 November 1923 (*SL* 1.263–64).
3. HPL evidently refers to a gathering of five colleagues ultimately known as the
Kalem Club.
4. Henry Adams's scorn of the cultural failings of his native New England (and of the
United States as a whole) is recorded in *The Education of Henry Adams* (1918) and other
works.

[18]　　[AHT]

5 December, 1923

Hail, hail! The gang's all here!

Labour? Vile string attach'd to the fish which it is alone empower'd to draw! Infamous necessity! But at that I'm glad you've got a whack at it, if it helps enhance the tranquillity of your spirit. As for me—I'm neck deep—& without hooking any particular carload of the jack! Tough luck. The latest nuisance is the trade paper game. Harry E. Martin wants me to write up some local department stores for his *supply buyer*, but I'm gawdamned if I've the least notion of how the hell to go about it. And Lynch is panhandling for copy for his alleged magazine on beauty-culture—after doing me dirt by printing my name on a line of sickly texaco that I slung him out of pity last month, on the sole condition that he keep my identity out of it. "Meditations of a Manicurist"—kin ya beat it as a line for a 200-lb. middle-aged he-man?[1] And that dub wants me to get my claws manicured at his expense at a local beauty-parlour, in order to collect atmosphere. This way out! But say! Speaking of trade papers, it's damn funny Providence had so few window displays to show you when you were here. Since that time my aunts are constantly telling me about new & nifty layouts in every window in town—department stores, gas-stove emporia, hardware joints, & what the hell not. If I thought I could cash in on occasional speils of that sort, I'd rustle up some infor from Dench, but I guess it wouldn't pay. Too damn much bother. My gawd, but all life is a beastly bother!

I suppose you were properly surprised at receiving a Chepachet card from my adopted son & me, & being thus reminded of Durfeian futilities.[2] Well, kid, that locality sure has gotta jinx hung onto it; for d'ya know, me & Eddy was likewise too late to get at what we were aimin' fer! We were on a still hunt for the grotesque & the terrible—the ghoulish & the macabre—in the form of a hideous locality which Eddy had heard certain rusticks whispering about . . . . . *Dark Swamp*. The peasants had mutter'd that it is very remote & very strange, & that no one hath ever been completely across it because of the treacherous & fathomless potholes, & the antient trees whose thick boles grow so closely together that passage is difficult & darkness omnipresent even at noon,[3] & *other* things, of which bobcats—whose half-human cries are heard in the night by cotters near the edge—are the very least. It is a very peculiar place, & no house was ever built within two miles of it. The rural swains refer to it with much evasiveness, & not one of them can be induc'd to guide a traveller thro' it. It lies near where we were lost south of the pike— there & westward—& probably brushes the foot of Old Durf himself. Very few know . . . . or admit they know . . . . of it. Eddy discover'd its rumour at the tavern in Chepachet one bleak autumn evening when huntsmen gather'd about the fire & told tales. One very ancient man said that IT dwells in the swamp . . . . & that IT was alive even before the white man came.

Well, anyway, we took the nine-twenty-five for Chepachet on Nov. 4, & wasted all the noon period getting shunted from one villager to another for directions. One bimbo—a bearded chap named Sprague, who lives in a colonial house—was especially valuable, & gave some extra tips on Durf. We must stop at his house next fall, for he'll show us a back road—the Sand Dam Road— which will take us more directly than the Putnam Pike, no matter what the geological survey dopes out. Eddy & I generally follow'd the route we took in September, but this time we didn't turn in the blind road south toward that pond. Instead, we kept on the pike past Cady's Tavern, (1683) where we saw a brush fire, & ate lunch, & past the big reservoir which you'll recall on the map; finally turning south toward the swamp, & continuing to be referred from one farmer to another. The last swain we were directed to was Ernest Law, who owns Dark Swamp, & who was reached by a rutted road that climbs upward betwixt woods & stone walls. As we ascended toward his agrestic seat we were transfigured & exalted by the magnificence of the landskip—a landskip that culminated in a crest mysteriously limned against the fire & gold of a late afternoon sky. Another moment & we had spy'd what stretcht beyond the crest: to the right the antient farmhouse of Mr. Law, & to the left the most gorgeous & spectacular rustick panorama that either of us had ever beheld or indeed conceiv'd to exist. It sent me into poetick numbers:

> Far as the Eye can see, behold outspread
> The serried Hills that own no Traveller's Tread:
> Dome beyond Dome, & on each flaming Side
> The hanging Forests in their virgin Pride.
> Here dips a Vale, & here a Mead extends,
> Whilst thro' the piny Strath a Brooklet bends:
> Yon farther Slopes to violet Aether fade,
> And sunset Splendour gilds the nearer Glade:
> Rude walls of Stone in pleasing zig-zag run
> Where well-plac'd Trees salute the parting Sun:
> Vext with the Arts that puny Men proclaim,
> Nature speaks once, & puts them all to Shame![4]

Only the inaccessible nature of this prodigious prospect preserves it from the pollution of common visitation by the cits & Mohocks of the town. As it is, I doubt if ten men in Providence are sensible it is on the globe. We found Mr. Law to be a pleasing fellow of the middle sizc, whose venerable farmhouse is uncommon, curious, & engaging. He told us how to reach Dark Swamp, & inform'd us it is a very odd place, tho' the peasantry have a little exaggerated its fearful singularities. We thank'd him for the civilities he shew'd us, & having congratulated him on the fine location of his seat, set out to return to town with the information we shall use upon our next trip. We walked back to Chepachet under the ebony & powder'd gold of a rural night sky, having cover'd full seventeen miles afoot, in all. I, of course, scarce felt so slight a jaunt, & was ready to snicker buoyantly when the village idiot started a clog-dance in the tap-room of the tavern, where we had paus'd to drop you a card. Then the stage-coach for Providence came, & the trip was over.

Eddy & I have since then explor'd much of Providence—more, in fact, than I had ever thought to exist. There are, as I told you last September, whole sections in which I had never set foot; & some of these we have begun to investigate. One southwesterly section I discover'd from the 1777 powder-horn map, & set out to explore it on 22nd Nov., in the hope of finding colonial doorways. Did I find 'em? BOY! Not a stone's throw from that 1809 "Round-Top" church[5] that I shew'd you, lies the beginning of a squalid colonial labyrinth in which I mov'd as an utter stranger, each moment wondering whether I were indeed in my native town or in some leprous, distorted witch-Salem of fever or nightmare. Ugh! This ancient & pestilential network of crumbling cottages & decaying doorways was like nothing I had ever beheld save in dream . . . . . Goya . . . . . Hogarth . . . . . Hills where rotting Dorick columns rest on worn stone steps out of which rusted footscrapers protrude like malignant fungi. . . . Dirty small-paned windows leering malevolently on all sides, sometimes glasslessly, from gorged sockets. . . . . . . There was a fog, & out of it & into it again mov'd dark monstrous diseas'd shapes. They may have been people, or what once were, or might have been people. . . . . On thro' the fog we went, threading our way thro' narrow exotick streets & unbelievable courts & alleys, sometimes having the ancient houses almost meet above our heads, but often emerging into unwholesome little squares or grassless parks where five or six tangled streets or lanes open out in expanses as loathsome as Victor Hugo's "Cour des Miracles"[6] . . . . Then, when we wou'd reach the crest of some eminence in this uneven ground, we wou'd see on every hand the strange streets stretching down silent & sinister to the unknown elder mysteries that gave them birth. . . . . . grotesque lines of gambrel roofs with drunken eaves & idiotick tottering chimneys, & rows of Georgian doorways with shatter'd pillars & worm-eaten pediments . . . . . streets, lines, rows; bent & broken, wan & wither'd, twisted & mysterious . . . claws of gargoyles obscurely beckoning to witch-sabbaths of cannibal horror in shadow'd alleys that are black at noon . . . . . long, long hills up which daemon winds sweep & daemon riders clatter over cobblestones . . . . & toward the southeast, a stark silhouette of hoary, unhallow'd black chimneys & bleak ridgepoles against a mist that is white & black & slanting—the venerable, the immemorial sea; the antient harbour where pirate barques once rode unquietly at anchor. No, I had not thought that Providence held such places as this. We came out silently.

Weird Tales? Well, they've accepted "The Rats in the Walls", *twilit* & all.[7] Cheques? Faith is a noble Christian virtue. The only trouble with S.H.G.'s story was that they changed the title to "The Invisible Monster"—flat & literal—when it was sent as "The Horror at St. Martin's Beach". This same Leetle Bairdie wants to call "Arthur Jermyn" "The White Ape". Blah!!!! Did 'ittle Sonny read you "The Festival" & "The Unnamable" at the weekly meetings of your gang? This same gang makes me damn impatient at my absence from its radius. Hell, but I'd like to horn in some Thursday! Literary stuff is damn tame here—just now my aunts want me to read "Alice Adams" by Booth Tarkington, to discuss with them. Heigho!

Loveman has finished the Herm, but has suffered a renewed lapse of melancholy—"been through hell", as he says. Cleveland oppresses & lacerates his spirit, & he is thinking of a move to *Providence,* where he can bask in Georgian tranquillity & Theobaldian cynicism. It may materialise no more than other proposed Lovemanick moves, but you can bet I'm giving some tall tips on industrial advantages & all that!

Well—I mustn't keep a busy scholar from his tasks any longer.

Pax Vobiscum!

Theobaldus Avus.

(Awaiting Dec. 27.)

Notes

1. This obscure bit of Lovecraftiana has not been found.

2. HPL and C. M. Eddy, Jr., visited Chepachet on 4 November and also sought unsuccessfully to find a sinister area called "Dark Swamp," failing in the endeavor. The reference to "Durfeian futilities" alludes to an attempt by JFM and HPL to visit Durfee Hill on 19 September; but Morton took a wrong turn and they never reached the area.

3. Many years later, Eddy wrote a fragmentary story based on the visit to Dark Swamp, entitled "Black Noon."

4. Published posthumously as "[On a Scene in Rural Rhode Island]."

5. The Beneficent Congregational Church at 300 Weybosset Street, built in 1809 and remodeled in 1836 by James C. Bucklin.

6. The "Cour des Miracles" (court of miracles) is a locale in Paris described by Victor Hugo in *Nôtre-Dame de Paris* (1831; *The Hunchback of Notre Dame*).

7. The comment may refer to Baird's objection to the use of the adjective "twilit" (at the time, "twilight" was also used as an adjective, perhaps more commonly than "twilit"). See also letter 25, regarding Everett McNeil's complaint about the scene of the twilit grotto.

[19]   [AHT]

23 Dec. 1923

Auguste:—

Well, I'll be damned! You're just too late to catch the card—& the cuttings, & the Harding stamps, & everything.

Thursday, 27th December, 11:04 a.m., Union Station, Providence, Rhode-Island, at the central information booth in the main concourse. Will I be there? Listen for the attached curfews, kid! And by the way—I hope you won't mind if my protege Eddy trails along. He may look a bit plebeian—wizened and pathetick & all that sort of thing—but he means so damn well, & is so bright to catch at ideas once they're presented to him! And he's keen for literary & cultural improvement, & phlogistically avid to worship at the shrine of Mortonian erudition. He seems to come from a decayed branch of a really good old Rhode-Island family; but has acquired, through lifelong poverty, something of the subtle external aspect of the lesser yeomanry. I'm sure he'll prove a docile subject for a Plantagenet monarch!

Unaffected Brumalian benevolence from
Theobaldus Antiquus

[20]   [AHT]

2nd January, 1924

O Thou Who Art Super-Mighty:—

Heigho! Craft salutes On, & expresses his complete approval of the document, which by this post goes properly created to Carolus Parcerus.[1] Most of the ability in this game is yours, but in case some guy wants his bum verse touched up, there's no harm hanging grampa's name onto it. Here's to luck, & may we both spend with philosophick moderation the darby we rake in! Really, one ought to be able to hook a little jack if connected up with the right bozos. Eddy was spieling off a plan to me a month or so ago, which provided for all sorts of revision down to the crude attention which plebeian criticks give even more plebeian "song-poems".[2] He wanted me to think up a very distinctive & perfectly original sort of name for the damn thing, & after about ten minutes' profound cogitation I cooked up the crisp monicker "Associated Secretaries". If yuh wanna make a merger, & enlarge your bureau to cover the raw junk Eddy handles, just drop the boy a line—he hangs out at 61 Furnace St., Providence. Helluva name . . . Helluva place. He & his wife cop a number of dissociated pence by doing this sort of minus-grade revision—he showed me some of the scelerous, slithering unnamabilities they handle . . . O gawd & montreal,[3] give us Bush for a relief! Well, anyhow, this is to say I'm with you in whatever you like, & the devil take the hindmost. I hope Parker'll make a go of his paper, but I don't believe it . . . though don't tell him I said so. The woods are full of 'em—that's the damn trouble. And here's hoping the best for CITSOV—just get the Ku Klux back of you, & we'll hit the high spots!

I hadn't been walking five minutes after leaving the boat when I thought of that name I wanted to tell you in the museum—the name for the line separating the shaft & capital of a column. It's "hypotrachelium"—a forty-dollar word, as Sandusky would say, & I'm clicking it off now without having look'd it up on

me shelves, although I'll verify before putting the seal of conclusiveness on this
labour'd paragraph. . . . . . . I WIN. . . . . got it right the first time, & Webster
backs me up. Ain't I always right, even when I don't say anything? You tell 'em!
Thine in the most complaisant & commercial of moods,
Theobaldus

Notes

1. In the September 1924 issue of *L'Alouette* (ed. Charles A. A. Parker), an ad by HPL
and James F. Morton appeared on p. 132: "THE CRAFTON SERVICE BUREAU
offers the expert assistance of a group of highly trained and experienced specialists in
the revision and typing of manuscripts of all kinds, prose or verse, at reasonable rates.
. . ." For the full text, see "[Advertisement of Revisory Services]," *CE* 5.283.
2. "Song poem" usually refers to song *lyrics* that have been set to music for a fee.
3. The expression "O God! O Montreal!" is a refrain found in the poem "A Psalm of
Montreal" by Samuel Butler (1835–1902), first published in the *Spectator* (18 May 1878).

[21]   [AHT]
8 January, 1924
O most Unsurpassable and Scenically Unimpressionable:
CAAP sent me a sample cover & title page for his semi-pro lark, & it certainly does look like a pretty snappy li'l' bird! [1] I'll try to shoot him whatever
top-hole poetry blows my way—especially the necrorrhaeal slitherings &
macrophobic unnamabilities of *Clark Ashton Smith,* who has not only joined
the United, but give me unlimited liberty to pirate any damn thing I like from
any of his published books.[2] Hoopla!
Hell, but I envy you them Belknap sessions! But say! it's a new one on
me that his mamma lets him stay up till 2 a.m.! Imprudent Child! Sorry about
Kleiner's throat—here's hoping it's on the mend. And say! Have you seen
that precious sissy Gordon Hatfield, that I met in Cleveland?[3] Belknap says
he's hit the big town, & that he's had some conversation with him. When I
saw that marcelled what is it I didn't know whether to kiss it or kill it! It used
to sit cross-legged on the floor at Elgin's & gaze soulfully upward at Loveman. It didn't like me & Galpin—we was too horrid, rough & mannish for it!
Well-zassat! Yr obt & obsequious
Theobaldus

Notes

1. A clever pun, for *l'alouette* is the skylark.
2. Two of Clark Ashton Smith's poems appeared in *L'Alouette:* "Plum-Flowers"
(March 1924) and "The Refuge of Beauty" (May 1924), the latter a reprint from *Ebony
and Crystal.*

3. HPL had met the minor composer Gordon Hatfield, an associate of Hart Crane, when he was in Cleveland in the summer of 1922.

[22]   [AHT]

25 Jan., 1924

Cheerio, yer 'Ighness!

And now, O stolid Contemner of Colourful Cathedrals & Sinuous Alley Parlieus of Amorphous Necrophagi, incline a shell-like crystal detector whilst Grandpa broadcasts the dope on the Really Appreciative Egg what's been trailin' around the' ol' village here! The name uh this guy is Edward Lloyd Sechrist, & he's a United top-notcher of the last Renshaw bunch before the bustup.

Sechrist, like me, thinks Ed Poe is just about the diatom's anemometer; & doesn't want to miss out on any patter that touches him. This was the first time I ever seen this guy, & kid, it was worth the money! We spotted each other for an arcade of foliated Byzantine bicycle handlebars the second we telescoped in the Biltmore lobby, though we'd only saw one another in head-&-shoulder halftones before. He's a goof about your age, but with less thatch on the ridgepole—tho' not wot yuh'd call too-late-for-Herpicide by 3 to 7 hairs. Ree-fined centsative face, dinky li'l' iron-grey soup-strainer, zippy dresser, & all that. Comes from interesting old stock—Germans settled in Maryland & Virginia's eastern peninsula in 17th century. I been writin' this bob three years runnin', & it sure was the aepyornis' alembic to get a retinal range on him. Talks just as good the same like he writes—nice cultivated pipes & all that. He's some top-hole sphere-scrambler, & has parked his puppies in Africa & the South Sea Islands durin' the course of his rounds. His classiest line is Polynesian folklore, & the way he punishes them yakahula bedtime tales in syncopated prose sure does wake Waikiki & put the ha in aloha![1] Some bird! An' I'll say he's the boy to help raise the United de profundis ad caelum.[2]

As for the United—be of stout heart! We ainta gonna hoit the National! We goes in for the strickly littery polished stuff—did I tell ya we got CLARK ASHTON SMITH for a reg'lar, with permission to reprint anything in his books?[3]

Tho you didn't thee dear Gawdon! How perfectly too bad, for he'th thuch a nithe boy! And so Grandpa's poor 'Ittle Sonny goned & forgotted Gordon's name! But I guess it came out O.K., for when Sonny dropped me his card, he had the name right enough. Some dilemma—should he go down & tell the clerk that he wanted a man who was a friend of Samuel Loveman in Cleveland & had just telephoned to F. B. Long Jr.? Bless the miracle of Mnemosyne[4] that saved the Situation! Damn it all, but Grandpa is sorry his littlest boy is so bally delicate! I hope he'll be as careful as he can in diet, regimen, & everything else, so that he can gradually get around to be Grandpa's big strong man! I'm afraid 2 a.m. is pretty late for lambkins to be up—but I guess his mamma knows best. Precious child! There's more in that busy little head than you'll find in any hundred usual amateur crania.

Oh, yes! And I just got a gushing letter from Leetle Bairdie! At his request I'd written him what I thought of his new book,[5] & he sure did take to the Ol' Gent's dope as a flapper to chocolate creams! He want to know why I don't do professional reviewing for real money . . . O Roscoe, where is thy kick![6] But he calls for more copy, & says that THIS TIME his deflated pneumatic treasurer is gonna loosen up with gallazhro-Sheanic absoposilutitude. I'm shootin' him "Festival" & "Unnamable" . . . . . with no extra charge because he calls me one of his two star writers, the other guy being that Quinn baby what pulled "The Phantom Farmhouse". Oy yes—& the Feby. issue kennels my "Hound"-dawg with three bad misprints & a picture so dumb it thinks Giorgionë is the guy that O(l)neyville was named after.[7]

I thank you.

Θεοβάλδος

Notes

1. HPL refers to Edward Lloyd Sechrist, "(the ex-Washingtonian bee expert) [who] lived in Tahiti for years—close to the natives—& studied their folklore in detail" (HPL to Elizabeth Toldridge, 29 May 1929; ms., JHL).
2. "From the depths to the heavens."
3. Four of Smith's poems appeared in the *United Amateur:* "To the Chimera" (May 1924), "Apologia" (July 1925), and "Loss" and "Query" (May 1926).
4. The Titaness who was goddess of memory, mother of the Muses.
5. Edwin Baird, *Fay* (New York: E. J. Clode, 1923), a novel.
6. Cf. 1 Cor. 15:5: "O death, where is thy sting? O grave, where is thy victory?"
7. Giorgione (born Giorgio Barbarelli da Castelfranco; c. 1477/8–1510[1]), an Italian painter of the High Renaissance in Venice. In his rendering of *Olneyville*, HPL alludes to the fact that the locals do not pronounce the initial *l*.

[23]   [AHT]

9th Feby., 1924

Great Spieler of the Lighter Arts:—

Crowded spell? My gawd, that's my favourite university degree. A onearmed* paperhanger* with fleas is a man of leisure alongside o' me, Kid! I'm tryin' to mop up my letterfiles*, & it sure is a merry round, I'll susurrate to the circumambient slences. May Ahrimanes chaw up the hindmost![1]

Yeh—I dissolve yuh of all stolid indiff'runce to wot is big & fine & noble in colonial & sinister architecture! It's the nacherl-grown brand for these parts, & if we don't put it back on the map to stay, yuh kin deflect me south

---

*Get the nonhyphenated, neomortonian effeck!

for a syzygy of twilit parallelopipedons! But I gotta train youse literal guys to lamp mor'n what ya gets in vulgar line & shadow. Ya wanna edicate yer glims to projeck a kinda aesthetic mem'ry onta all the dope around youse, so as the most commonplace dump or gangway'll take on a weird slipp'ry glamour from the light inside yer coco. That's what this here baby Art Machen learns ya to do—he pulled a swell line on just that in the 1st spiel in his "House O' Souls".[2] O say though—I seen a new book of Artie's—it's call'd "The Terror" & it's about war time. Kinda swell, but wit' a little 2 mutch diagram tacked onta de end. Well well & wot kinda dump yuh got in Sout' Brooklyn? Yes yes go on yuh int'rust me strangely. Here's hopin' to gawd I get on de spot before they croaks the ol' hangout—I'm all for the cold shimmy joints!

"The Hound" was my own title—as you'd orta remember, you havin' heerd it the day or 2 after it was wrote, & handin' me de tips what made me change it on bot' ends! But "Artie Jermyn's" playin' in hard luck, seein' as Leetle Bairdie's hell bent to call it "The White Ape" . . . . BLAH! I give the proofs of dis de onct-over yesterday, them bein' sent becos of 3 miss prints in the Houn-Dawg. Glad this bozo Leeds sees some percentage in my texaco. From wot I seen & read of this bird, I think he's a reg'lar guy—a 100% he-man, & the gemsbok's snowplough at that.

But oh, Clarence! Wot a inside corneal circumnavigation I'm gettin' on *Weird Tales!* I want you should tell 'em, Ignatz! The baby what owns the whole damn outfit—a bolognee called Henneberger—has wrote me a long line of dope about how much fish ($51,000) he has lost on his 2 mags, & how he's gonna change de contents of *W.T.*—gettin' the big-timer Houdini in—& how (pipe dis, boy!) I'm the best writer what he's got, & how he wants a novel from me, of 25,000 words or over, & how he ain't satisfied wit' de mama's boy dope other bimboes slips 'im—& how he means damn well & is gonna come acrost wit' a cheque LATER . . . . get the stretcher, boys!

Well well, if you don't know the whole Tut outfit! You sure are right there wit' de Little Egypt stuff, as I recall from you tellin' them Boston flats about that 1st poet in the world! For me, I goes more inta dis Rome dope—Caius J. Caesar, Cnaeus P. Magnus-Johnson, & them. As for wot you don't know about women. . . . bee-have! Say, Kid, I guess 1 Harding stamp would carry all you ain't wise to about the nifty sweet mammas! First class male, at that. O you Sheik! But wait till us Ku Kluxes come stalking after youse! De woild is your harem, boy, but look out or the Kleagles & grand goblins'll get youse! Well, I gotta lay off & attend a secrut initiation of a Klan local what I am Kleagle of.[3]

Yures for citizen soverenty,

Theobaldus

Notes

1. Ahriman was the devil in the Zoroastrian religion.

2. The first story in Machen's *The House of Souls* was the novella "A Fragment of Life," an attempt to depict the beauty of "ordinary" life.

3. A kleagle is an officer of the Ku Klux Klan whose main role is to recruit new members.

[24]   [AHT]

19 Feby., 1924

O Fountain of Felicity in a Desert of Monotony:

Well—the Ardinii[1] continue to flock in—even more profusely than when you were hard up for 'em. That's life—little when you want much, much when you want little. But theh ain't no more bein' made, so I guess yuh kin stow 'em all away to some sort of advantage. Smithy was damn grateful for the precancelleds—damn fine old chap! He wants the high denoms especially—& I'll bet that Youngstown baby titillated his most esoteric psyche!

Weird Tales? Boy—what I told yuh afore was only the beginnin'! I'm hearin' damn near every day from Henneberger—the owner of the outfit—& just had a special delivery order to collaborate on an Egyptian horror with this bimbo Houdini.[2] It seems this boob was (as he relates) thrown into an antient subterraneous temple at Gizeh (whose location corresponds with the so-called "Campbell's Tomb" (not Paul J.'s) betwixt the Sphinx & 2nd pyramid) by two treacherous Arab guides—all bound & gagged as on the circuit—(him, not the guides) & left to get out as best he might. Now Henneberger (who is beginning to do some personal directing over Bairdie's head) wants me to put this into vivid narrative form—it having merely been told orally by Hoodie. I've shot back a query as to how much sheer imagination Houdini'll stand for—since I gotta idea he tries to put over his Munchausens as straight dope, in which he figures most heroically. But if Henny & Hoodie give me a free hand—then b'gawd I'll pull a knockout! I'll have them guides dress up as mummies to scare the bound Houdini—yet have Hoody escape without encountering 'em. And then, when Hoodie takes the police to the scene, I'll have the guides found dead—strangled—chok'd lifeless in that antient necropolis of the regal stiffs—*with marks of claws on their throats . . .* claws . . . claws . . . principal & subordinate clawses . . . *which could not by any stretch of the imagination belong either to their own hands or to the hands of Houdini!!!* Brrr . . . I hope them guys gives me leave to plaster it on as it should be plastered! Henny says that Houdini wants to get in touch with me about some books or other when he gets back from a lecture tour. Well—here I am, & it's all jake with me if dey's any jack wit'in reach o' me lunch-hooks! I'm a practical man, & ya kin get anyt'ing outa me if ya flashes a fat enough roll! Oh gawd—I forgot to tell ya that Henny has *come acrost* wit' a cheque for ONE HUNDRED BERRIES! (No spoofin'—100—count 'em—100—Not a misprint. Sweared to before J. Flatt Tyre, Not'ry Publick, my commission expires July 52, B.C.

1066.) But I'm still sportin' a 7⅛ Kelly. That sort of blah is a flash in the pan, and w'en *W.T.* goes blooey yuh kin' find Old Theobald hangin' out at the same ol' blind pig on the corner. Sure I seen yer pome—& a good un it is, as I told ya w'en ya wrote it h'ars & h'ars ago![3] Bairdie turned down one by our 'Ittle Belknap—for which I appropriately curse him. *Don't spread this in advance,* because the victim han't been tipped off yet, but (*whisper*) Leetle Bairdie is gonna be unhooked from *W.T.* in May, Farnsworth Wright reigning in his place. He'll continue with *Detective Tales,* though. I'm kinda sorry if it cuts into his incomin' heavy metal, for I like the guy—but Fate is Fate. "The Transparent Ghost"[4] nearly killed Henny. He froths at the mouth if ya speak of it, since he thinks it's the cheapest kind of cheap joke. Say, why not write up about that Brooklyn ghost joint for *W.T.?*[5] I betcha ten of my new-caught fish it'd make the *Eyrie!* I gotta see that place—gawd preserve it till I raise the price of a ticket . . . which same I hopes the NYNHSH won't do.

Sonny-Boy just writed his Old Grandpa a letter, & sent a lot of nice enclosures. Bless the child! But I wish he could get to be Grandpa's big strong man! He may, at that—for when I was his age I was just as frail . . . & gawd, lookit wot a fat healthy ol' hawg I am now! I sure am longin' to connect up wit' your gang, & mebbe I'll do it yet! With Hell's Kitchen for a stampin' ground, we'd orta be do amphioxus' license-plate as real rough babies wit' stiletto & automatic! Not but what the B. P. C. is O.K. in its way—that must of bin a nifty li'l feed, & I'm glad yuh copped the Wilde dope.

Well—cheerio, ol' timer!

Tibaldus

Notes

1. I.e., Warren G. Harding postage stamps (later as Ardinii Varini, or Harding Warren).
2. "Under the Pyramids" (published as "Imprisoned with the Pharaohs").
3. "The Eyrie" in the March 1924 *Weird Tales* contains a letter from JFM, in which he states that he is glad the magazine is accepting submissions of poetry and offers "Haunted Houses" for publication. The poem appears with the letter. (A typescript of the poem survives at JHL.)
4. A three-part serial by Isa-Belle Manzer (February, March, and April 1924).
5. The *Brooklyn Daily Eagle* of 8 November 1885 contains a story about a haunted house in South Brooklyn on Amity Street. See http://www.bklyn-genealogy-info.com/Cemetery/ghosts/1885amity.html

[25]   [AHT]

259 Parkside Ave., Bklyn, N. Y., March 12, 1924

Bismillah, O Sheik ul Islam!

Well, Kid, having thought up all the ordinary, regular ways of giving you a jolt, but finding you impervious to the shafts of my strange & violent personality, I'm herewith springing on you the posolutely latest, patent-applied-for device for the infinitesimal splintering of an ingrained and well-nourished phlegmaticism. Give me credit for being tolerably original, at least!

You will gather from the above date line that I am at this writing considerably nearer that South Brooklyn haunted house than I was at last reports. You will also gather, if you go in for detective stuff, that the old Remington is along with me—most unusual suggestion of permanency for a mere visitor. My gawd, the plot thickens!

Well, to make a short-story long, it appears that Grandfather Theobald is camped out here for good. How come? Oh, just the capriciousness of old age! Yuh see, this sheik stuff of yours is damned catching, & I thought I'd try a bit of it—since I'll try anything once—in that more conservative fashion which befits a staid elderly person of Colonial tastes & Novanglian background but imperfectly shed.

In other words, Old Theobald is hitting the high spots on a partnership basis, the superior nine-tenths of the outfit being the nymph whose former name has just been canned in favour of mine own on the doorplate at the above address.

Yes, my boy, you got it the first time. Eager to put Colonial architecture to all of its possible uses, I hit the ties hither last week; & on Monday, March the Third, seized by the hair of the head the President of the United—S. H. G.—and dragged her to Saint Paul's Chapel, (1766) at Broadway & Vesey Streets, where after considerable assorted genuflection, & with the aid of the honest curate, Father George Benson Cox, & of two less betitled ecclesiastical hangers-on, I succeeded in affixing to her series of patronymics the not unpretentious one of Lovecraft. Damned quaint of me, is it not? You never can tell what a guy like me is gonna do next!

No—I'm not puttin' over any spoof! It's the real stuff, & if you could lamp the nifty little certificate George slipped us you'd believe it. It's straight goods—the inhabitants of this dump are H. P. & Sonia H. Lovecraft—& if you're from the Ozarks now, you'll migrate away from there in something less than a week, when you get the swell engraved announcement (really engraved—you can feel of it & everything) that Dutton's is soaking me 62 bucks for. (No—not 62 for yours alone, but for 200).

And now get this, Archibald! DON'T FOR THE HOLY REGARD OF PETE & PEGĀNA LET OUT THIS NEWS UNTIL YOU GET THE ENGRAVED CARD! Be a true Son of the Sphinx, & forget I ever told you a word! I want to spring this bomb on the amateurs artistically—else I wouldn't have paid that 62 fish. If The Boys meet Thursday, don't breathe a hint that you think me any nearer than the corner of Angell Street & Butler Avenue. It's barely possible that I may not be able to keep from telling my ownest 'Ittle-Child Belknap, but I may not do even that.[1] I'd like to see what the blessed little divvle would say on receiving one of the cards! And by the way—my daughter Mrs. Gamwell is around these parts also—in Hohokus, N J. (yes, there is such a place)—& if you come over here to dinner Sunday at about one p.m., as S. H. & I hope you will, you may possibly behold her.

All of which is what. Harrowing details? Oh, yes—the inevitable melilunar hegira![2] For this rubber-stamp institution we (good stuff, that WE, when Old Theobald does the bossing!) chose a trip to antique & Colonial Philadelphia, famed as the metropolis of these colonies in the eighteenth century, & yet replete with architectural memorials of that felicitous aera. I had, as you will recall from our museum conversation in Providence, never been there before; & it was therefore with no little antiquarian eagerness that I turned my steps thither. No—I didn't leave the bride behind. I had a rush job of typing to get done, & I needed someone to dictate to me when I mixed exploration with patronage of a public stenographick office. You can bet she did dictate to me, & is still doing it . . . . as much as a haughty, cynical personality can be dictated to.[3] Well, anyway, we seen Philly & we seen it good—& gawd, what a picturesque mess it is! Of all shopworn, Victorian, ill-lighted barnyards—lissen, Oswald, if the Main Street of Marblehead was so dim as the theatre hours, they'd petition the town watchman to hang up two whole lanthorns more! But all ragging aside, the town has a nifty personality. Its architecture as a whole, whether due to Quaker influence or German designs, is utterly unique as compared with all other Colonial architecture I have seen; & leaves an unforgettable picture of arched, marble-faced doorways, keystoned windows, & little flights of steps all alike down long vistas of street. If them Archibalds down there is wise to themselves, they'll play up that style for all it's worth in future building—but hell—they got one swell handicap in the way the burg got built up in the middle nineteenth century. That place has more baroque stuff on its main street than any other I ever gave the retinal review to. But I won't knock. It's got some darned classy stuff, & the interior of the rebel "Independence Hall" is sure the titanotherium's operaglasses when it comes to slick & elegant design. After a little independent investigation, we rubbernecked on the Royal Blue Line, which ain't nearly so bad as it's painted. Fairmount Park ain't by any means so worse—& the tropical junk in Horticultural Hall sure is enough to furnish out a dozen South Sea travelogues in the finest Traprock manner.[4] Do I ramble? Well, that's what we did in Philly. But anyway, I'll chuck in a few enclosures which will say more than this transplanted boiler-factory. After a return to 259, we broke the news to the family back in Providence—who took it heroically, no doubt actuated by an eminently justifiable relief at getting rid of the Old Man. As coincidence would have it, Mrs. Gamwell was just about to depart on a visit to Hohokus, N. Joisey; so that already yet I have saw her after the execution—assisting her in meandering from the Grand Central to the Erie Dee-po via an Hudson Tube which I had never before seen or explored, but to which my vast attainments in theoretical geography made me the most competent of guides.

And so it goes. Never thought you'd see Grandpa settled uxoriously down to placid domesticity, did you? But O is K, & the ball-&-chain keeps me finely regulated chronologically, so that I actually got to three places on time last week—just as when my daughter Mrs. Gamwell gets behind and pushes. That's the kind of guy I am.

As for the industrial stuff—Mah Stars, Mah Lawdy, Mah Jong! That century knockout is the real goods,[5] whether or not Friend Everett believes it; but just as he says, Henneberger undoubtedly forked it over in a lively expectation of favours to come. BOY, that Houdini job! It strained me to the limit, & I didn't get it off till after we got back from Philly. I went the limit in descriptive realism in the first part, then when I buckled down to the under-the-pyramid stuff I let myself loose & coughed up some of the most nameless, slithering, unmentionable HORROR that ever stalked cloven-hooved through the tenebrous & necrophagous abysses of elder night. To square it with the character of a popular showman, I tacked on the "it-was-all-a-dream" bromide—& we'll see what Houdie thinks of it. I have an idea Henny will have to stand for it, because it came in so late that there won't be a damn second to change it—and it's already announced. Houdini, I guess, is a pretty good chap in a flashy plebeian way. The amateur Charles G. Kidney met him personally a couple of weeks ago after one of his anti-spiritualistic lectures in Cleveland, & was captivated to the gurgling-point. Also, Houdie has dropped me a note full of his circulars & cuttings, duly annotated, & calling attention to his home address, where he would some time like to see me. He hangs out at 278 West 113th, & is said to have the best collection of dark & weird volumes in America. I guess I'll run up & lamp him some day—for Henny said he had some sort of book proposition to spill. If he's another D. V. B.—a bigger & better Bush, as it were—I'll freeze onto him.

But that ain't all the industrial stuff. I may or may not have told you about that review I did for THE READING LAMP, after S. H. had looked up the editor & found the latter favourably disposed.[6] This editor, a shrewd palaeoparthenoid[7] person yclept Gertrude E. Tucker, took mightily to S. H., & has become a frequent visitor at 259. Having seen some of my junk—both stories & letters which are virtually essays—she has begun to evolve plans for their remunerative employment; so that contracts, placings, & even BOOKS have been hinted at in more than equivocal terms. All of which lissens pretty swell to me, who am ever out for the jack. Gertie wants me to start off three trial chapters of a book of essays on antique New-England & its background of the supernatural . . . . stuff like I've wrote Sonny Belknap in my travelogues, if he's ever shewn 'em to you—& she also wants to see my unpublished stories with a possible view to book publication . . . . though far be it from me to pull the Alnaschar stuff prematurely.[8]

Further speakin' of industrialism—slip my congrats to good ol' McNeil for his run of luck! I'll slip 'em myself a week from tomorrow, when I formally join The Boys for good, (unless they blackball me as Dr. Johnson's Literary Club blackballed my good friend Gen. John Burgoyne, the minor playwright, who was defeated by the rebels at Saratoga, in the Colonies)[9] but meanwhile my felicitations are as sincere as if already spoke. I like Fren Ev'rett—he may not understand why bleached bones bestrew twilit grottoes, but he's a damn good fellow & model of kindly virtue for all that—added to which, he knows how to interest the young—no mean accomplishment, I swear.

About the Ardinii Varini—o gawd and montreal! This blow after both S. H. & I have been stuffing an envelope just for you! And I even picked up a beharding'd envelope in Central Park t'other morning as I was taking my constitutional prior to delving into antique Aegyptus at the Met. Mus. Well—here they are as a lawst farewell—& you'll find some of your precious men higher up amongst 'em if you search with sufficient diligence. I'm damned if I'll stop now to sift 'em! Lud, Sir, but I fear the profusion of the memorial issue will impair that scarcity which is the measure of value amongst virtuosi of distinction, so that all your pains will have been expended for an incommensurate reward! Good luck with the collection as an whole—& don't forget to send the precancell'ds to Smiffkins.[10]

Glad you like the Hoagic dope.[11] Jonathan is still alive & kicking the old Spencerian—he's just sent me a new pome to doctor up, which same I'll do with that conscientiousness ever characteristick of me. What if he doesn't tumble to all the Graeco-Romanisms in my tribute—they look pretty, don't they . . . . . . & who cou'd reasonably ask more? As your old cell-mate Oscar opined: "All art is at once surface & symbol".[12]

Speaking of Oscar—I pine to contemplate the want of taste reveal'd in the paragraph you quote, wherein he fails to recognise the severe beauty of Georgian design.[13] But why shou'd I marvel, when in that strange character there was ever something tawdry, & savouring of the rococo? His very praise of the heterogeneous taste of the artist-poisoner Wainwright shews the limitations which affectation impos'd upon his aesthetick judgment.[14] Then, too, it shou'd perhaps be admitted, that Georgian design flower'd most perfectly in these Colonies, where it had something of the freshness of a first growth. (For the previous growth of Gothick houses was of no great elegance or pretentiousness). Aside from certain publick edifices such as those design'd by Sir Ch: Wren, the houses of Great-Britain had by no means the freedom & lavishness of external detail which marked those of America, & tho' the taste of the interiors was more conservatively classical, it had an heaviness inseparable from black oak, which is infinitely less beautiful than the fictile white pine which gave birth to the panels & pilasters of these Colonies. However, even at that, bimboes like Grinling Gibbons[15] (a genuine mantel by whom I saw in Portsmouth N. H.) could certainly brandish a nefarious carving knife; & I'd stake any one of them against a baker's dozen of sloppy sissies like Oscar.

I see by a card to the wiff that you & some other amateurs have been to Washington. Attaboy! That's a burg I wanna take in some day if I can hook the berries to do it on, for there must be a hades of a lot of near-Colonial stuff tucked around the odd corners—maybe even the gaol & patent office which our naval forces under Sir George Cockburn spared when we razed that harbour of Yankee democracy in 1814.[16] GOD SAVE THE KING! Now that I seen Philly, I wanna work down the coast & take in Baltimore, Wash, Alexandria, Richmond, & all that sort of thing. Nor would New Orleans be a bad field for the explorer if time & sestertii permitted!

The *United* is gonna make a last stand as soon as the household at 259 is well settled down. No use bothering with the enemy—we'll issue an UNITED AMATEUR whether there's anything to put in it or not, & give them Columbus eggs such a vacuum-cleaning that they won't be able to stand on end. Both the big offices are in one family now—a straight Theobald outfit; & if we don't shew 'em what concentrated bossism can do, then your old Grandpa has clean forgotten the art.

Well—one can't spiel for ever! Come over Sunday if you can, & we'll give yuh an earful—an' incidentally I'll read yuh my new hellish Houdini dope, which makes even the "Rats" tame by comparison.

Wit' best ree-gards from me an' the missus,
Believe me, Sir, ever Yr most hble,
Most obt Servt,
Theobaldus

Remember—MUM till you get the engrav'd announcement!

Notes

1. HPL did not in fact tell Long in advance of the sending out of cards announcing his marriage. He acknowledges Long's congratulations in a letter of 21 March 1924 (ms., JHL).
2. A false coinage, being a Greek-Latin hybrid (meli = honey, lunar = moon).
3. HPL had lost the typescript of "Under the Pyramids" at or near Union Station and advertised for its return (it is from this advertisement, in the *Providence Journal,* that we know the correct title of the story). When it was not recovered, Sonia dictated the story to him from his handwritten draft while he typed it on a borrowed typewriter.
4. George Shepard Chappell (1877–1946), American architect, journalist (with *Vanity Fair*), and author, wrote several humorous books during the 1920s and early 1930s, including travel parodies under the pseudonym Walter E. Traprock, such as *The Cruise of the Kawa: Wanderings in the South Seas* (New York: Putnam, 1921).
5. HPL refers to the $100 he was paid for "Under the Pyramids."
6. Frank Belknap Long to HPL, [20 Dec. 1928] (ms., JHL) mentions that HPL had reviewed *What Is Man* by J. Arthur Thomson for the *Reading Lamp* several years previous.
7. I.e., old maid (literally, old virgin).
8. In the *Spectator* No. 525 (13 November 1712), Joseph Addison tells a tale (which he found in Antoine Galland's French translation of the *Arabian Nights*) of Alnaschar, a

petty merchant who deals in glassware. One day Alnaschar became so involved in a daydream about attaining fantastic wealth from his business that he inadvertently kicked over his glassware, shattering it.

9. Gen. John Burgoyne (1722–1792) was a British army officer, politician, and dramatist, whose works included *The Maid of the Oaks* and *The Heiress*. His forces were defeated at Saratoga by the American troops on 17 October 1777. Cf. "A Reminiscence of Dr. Samuel Johnson" (1917): "I remember how John Burgoyne, Esq., the General, whose Dramatick and Poetical Works were printed after his Death, was blackballed by three Votes; probably because of his unfortunate Defeat in the American War, at Saratoga."

10. I.e., Tryout Smith.

11. Presumably information relating to Jonathan E. Hoag. HPL had just written another birthday poem to Hoag, "To Mr. Hoag upon His 93rd Birthday, February 10, 1924."

12. Oscar Wilde, "Preface," *The Picture of Dorian Gray* (1891).

13. Oscar Wilde spoke disparagingly of Georgian domestic architecture in the essay "More Radical Ideas upon Dress Reform" (*Pall Mall Gazette*, 11 November 1884).

14. Thomas Griffiths Wainewright (1794–1847), artist, writer, and infamous poisoner of his sister-in-law, his uncle, his mother-in-law, and a friend. Oscar Wilde wrote of him in "Pen, Pencil and Poison" (*Fortnightly Review*, January 1889).

15. Grinling Gibbons (1648–1721), Dutch-born wood carver known particularly for his work in England, including Blenheim Palace, Hampton Court Palace, and St Paul's Cathedral.

16. Rear Admiral George Cockburn (1772–1853) played an important role in the War of 1812; he captured and burned Washington DC, on 24 August 1814.

[26]   [AHT]

259 [Parkside Avenue]
March 14, MDCCCCXXIV

Arise, Sir James!

About spreadin' the glad tidings—well, Kid, I suppose it'd be a rather rum go to rob you of a scoop, so here's slingin' ya permission to spill matters to whatever bunch you hook up with Sunday. Far be it from me to spoil anybody's whole day! The envelopes to them cards has blew in from Dutton, but the contents thereof have yet to appear. Being promised Monday, I trust in gawd & the parcel post—& the LXII fish. But DON'T LET IT LEAK TO SONNY BELKNAP! Grandpa's nice boy must have the full benefit of a copper-plate thunderbolt, be it soon or late. That's wot both the storm-&-stress[1] & my aunt tell me, although I was all for knocking him out over the telephone.

As to the fitness of a Church-of-England ceremony—gawd, boy, but you do take your religion serious if you think that side of the question had anything to do with it! Background, Kid—background! Don't you see the aesthetic impressiveness of investing a momentous decision with all the quaint & picturesque beauty of gesture & ritual that nearly two thousand years' practice has gently woven into the inmost texture of our civilisation! Do you give the hook to Greek myth merely because you don't believe literally in the anthropomorphic existence of the twelve Olympians? Religion, my son, is a pleasing fiction associated inextricably with the artistic progress of our culture; & deserves just as much recognition as any other ornament. Did I not imply as much last December when I admired the First Baptist Church, & sought reverently to play "Yes, We Have No Bananas" on the venerable organ? You tell 'em, Alexander! As to my re-TI-cence (cf. Heins' Dictionary)[2] about posting the banns & other advance bulletins—sure, it was to avoid promiscuous bride-sheiking. Yuh never can tell with some o' these slick li'l' love-pirates cruisin' about, & I hadda be on my guard after seein' a certain Valentino pettin' Mary Crossey Kennedy's[3] hand on the back seat of an auto whilst her meal ticket on the front seat was drivin' so reckless that poor li'l' Sandy sure thought the whole outfit was steering for a watery grave in the Charles! Oh, you!

B. P. C.—sure I'll join 'em if the waitin' list doesn't keep me on the outside for the next few years! And as for The Boys of a Thursday evenin'—why, Kid, I consider myself a charter member by correspondence! Yuh couldn't keep me away with a crowbar! I don't believe I can make the Sunrise Monday, but it's fifty-fifty about the Writers Chewsday.[4] I know their dump, & if I can get there you'll know it. Later on, if I can annex ten spare green-berries, I may put in an application for membership; though no doubt I care too little about the selling side of the profession to fit in perfectly—that is, if Br'er Uzzell's estimate of a year & a half ago still applies.[5] Tough luck you can't get over Sunday, but I ain't a guy to butt into a gempmun's previous engagements!

And then for the exploring stuff! Maybe some day we'll get to Durf—but meanwhile I guess there's plenty to lamp in this decadent sink of Babylonish hetrogeneity. Among the stuff I wanna soak up are all the things you've mention'd, plus such sights as the Billopp house on Staten Island,[6] & that archaic Schenck van Something affair on the outskirts of mine own new village of Flatbush—that dump that the old seafarin' bird built with the timbers of his ship,[7] & which is now (if memory deludeth not) the only edifice within the corporate limits of Hilanopolis[8] which dates actually from the sovereignty of the Holland States-General. The year is 1656, I believe. As for Philly—of course there's a certain monotony in the repetitious nature of its domestick architecture, but at that it's a quaint burg for a bimbo what ain't never saw it afore. As to its Sabbatarian restrictions—I didn't run up against none the week days I was there, & even so, I guess they can't keep a guy offen the streets where the quaint houses are—which same is all they is to Philly anyhow! Ho, hum! Vita brevis, ars longa![9] Sure I mean to give Wash the corneal circumnavigation some day. I've heard of this Lincoln memorial thing, & if it's truly classick in conception I won't raise no kick about including it in the caoutchouc-cervical[10] catalogue.

As to Henneberger—well, kid, if you don't take my word, just give the enclosed the optical solitaire. (Please return). Gawd knows what the bozo is really after, but as I says, why come to me if nameless phobic convulsions ain't wanted? It's clear the guy looks for some zippy dream stuff—dead Pharaohs doin' sinister shimmies by the light of pale torches—so what was an egg like me to do but take the cue? I ast ya, Ethelbert! I dunno whether I told ya or not, but I got a note & some printed stuff from Houdini himself, who may have some jobs for me to do. If I can get together with him, maybe I'll convert him to my way of thinking, & extract permission to put him through worse terrors than ever he imagined before! But time will tell. The aeons & the worlds are my sport, & I watch with calm & amused aloofness the anticks of planets & the mutations of universes. As to other business stuff, I gotta contract here ready to sign from that READING LAMP bunch, for the handling of my work outside the WEIRD TALES stuff. This I'm gonna analyse with a microscope before jazzing the old Conklin over the dotted line, because I don't propose to be bound & gagged whenever I wanna pull something casual-like. However, I guess the major features are O. K., because it provides for publicity & marketing that I'd never get in hell's own aeternity on my own hook. And after all it may all come to nothing—I ain't one o' them optimistic saps.

Say, I just thought—if you got any Ardinii Varini what you don't want, ship 'em to Old Pal Smithy! That baby is keen about 'em, & refused to return those on the envelopes I sent him. Hereafter I'm gonna send him all I get . . . . . for it would break my heart to depart from the fine old custom, hallowed by generations of usage, of saving & sending Harding stamps. But here are some threes. What a hell of a shame you didn't get to savin' them in war time, when they was so thick that a guy began to see violet where he used to see red. Tough luck about the shipwrecked Hun—here's hopin' he recoups to the value of at least a few hundred vigintillion marks. You pulled suthin' new on me with the Walloon dope—but rely on me to be up & looking! . . . . . . Well what the hell! How's this for appropriateness? Bell just rang—parcel post—book from Sechrist, with a fine black or brown or whatever you call it seven-center—old style. Here you are, & with an old man's blessing.

That book from Sechrist, by the way, is on architecture.[11] I shall peruse it with interest, & pass it along to you if it is sufficiently loud in its praise of Georgian designs. What you say about other brands lissens reel well to speak it—but I'd make a helluva lotta exceptions. I ain't got nothing against straight classick—that is, Graeco-Roman, or on the other hand against straight Gothick. But what gets me is this damn hybrid stuff they pulled in the Victorian age. If that wasn't the chromosome's air-rifle for sheer spifflocated ugliness, you can knock me sou' sou' west for an atrium of indented Pekinese motor-trucks! I've no use for Renaissance piddling or Byzantine or Romanesque pish-posh. I takes mine neat. I will say, though, a good word for Moorish at its best.

T. Babington? Yeh—I've read that dope. Tom had his good points, but I ain't takin' him 100% any more'n I'm takin' Oscar. He pulled sumpun good, though, in them "Lays of Anc. Rome".[12]—o—o—o—Well, Here's how. Spill what you like, & may the lawd watch over thee. Regards from the better nine-tenths, & sincere wishes for an early get-together.

Yr Obt

Θεοβάλδος

Notes

1. Typically "storm and strife," Cockney rhyming slang for *wife*.

2. Apparently a reference to longtime amateur Charles W. Heins.

3. Another member of the Hub Club.

4. HPL refers to a meeting of the Writers, evidently a professional organization, of which JFM was a member.

5. Thomas H. Uzzell (1884–?) writer, editor, and teacher in New York City during the 1920s and '30s. He was fiction editor at *Collier's*, taught seminars on fiction writing at New York University, and published several books on the craft of writing, including *Narrative Technique: A Practical Course in Literary Psychology* (1934), *Writing as a Career* (1938), and *The Technique of the Novel* (1947).

6. The Conference House (also known as Bentley Manor and the Captain Christopher Billop House) was built before 1680 and located near the southernmost tip of New York State on Staten Island. It is the only pre-Revolutionary manor house still surviving in New York City. The Staten Island Peace Conference (11 September 1776), held there, unsuccessfully attempted to end the American Revolutionary War.

7. HPL apparently refers to the Jan Martense Schenk (or Schenk-Crooke) House at East 63rd Street and Mill Avenue, Brooklyn, built in 1656 by the Schenk family. Although the Schenks were a shipping family, and the house does contain curved timbers and an archlike inverted frame, it is not clear whether any part of the house was actually constructed out of ship timber.

8. A reference to the mayor of New York City, John J. Hylan (1918–25).

9. Part of a Latin translation of an aphorism by the Greek physician Hippocrates, usually truncated to its first two statements and usually rendered "Ars longa, vita brevis" (art is long, life is short). The full text in Latin is: "Ars longa, / vita brevis, / occasio praeceps, / experimentum periculosum, / iudicium difficile." See letter 47 for a humorous alternate.

10. HPL's comic expression for "rubberneck" (sightseeing).

11. Possibly Harold Donaldson Eberlein, *The Architecture of Colonial America* (Boston: Little, Brown, 1921; *LL* 290).

12. Thomas Babington Macaulay (1800–1859), *Lays of Ancient Rome* (1842; *LL* 560).

[27]   [AHT]

259 [Parkside Avenue]
May 6, 1924

Cheerio!

Tough luck—but anyway, I'm glad youse guys hadda swell time! The wiff didn't feel equal to a full-size hike Sunday, & I decided not to go myself in order to conduct her on a mild trip in the afternoon, so that she wouldn't have to lose all the outing spirit of so fine a day. Result—we visited the Lefferts cottage & Jumel mansion,[1] rode down from the latter to Washington-Square atop an omnibus, explored the Colonial streets of Greenwich, (making a special study of doorways) & ended up by having dinner at an odd tavern call'd "The Pepper Pot", where eccentrick persons sing & otherwise make themselves conspicuous . . . . but where some finely panelled Colonial window embrasures furnish'd a note in common with my self.

Yesterday the wiff & me takes another trip—this time pullin' the bum stunt again, & ridin' clean up to Fort George[2] on roofs, (durin' the which ride we seen your hangout—tho' we didn't stop off to buy no ol' Virginny yams), arter which we slides down the hill to Dyckman Street, laps up the Dyckman cottage, & sets sail for the Van Cortlandt mansion.[3] This latter havin' been soaked in, we beats it for home, where I still are.

Today I'm due at Sonny's for lunch at twelve-thirty, tho' I'm gonna sandwich a session at the barber's if I can hook the time. Then at five-thirty I meets the wiff down town, & we does some more explorin'—this trip, Colonial houses aroun' the tip of Manhattan, of which same quite a bunch is mention'd in a little guide book what I got. Then—but it all depends on the ball-&-chain. If she feels equal to a wild night, we'll show up at The Writers. But if she doesn't, I'm afeard I'll have to be listed among those absent. She generally has to hit the hay early, & I have to get home in proportionate time, since she can't get to sleep till I do. Otherwise, I keep her awake waiting, & she feels like hell the next day. Alas for the old days of Aug.–Sept.–Octr. 1922, when as a mere guest I could stay out as late as I damn pleased, & she never knew when I came back—or whether I came back at all, at all! However—I think I can get her used to my being out *one* night a week—the night of The Boys—so you can expect to lamp me with bells on the evening you gets this spiel—Wednesday, May 7—up at Small Sonny's. On this occasion my new pal La Touche Hancock—the seedy Lloyd-George—may be on hand to promote the merriment.[4] I have an idea this bimbo would make a damn good member for our gang—but judge for yourself when you gives him de onct-over.

As I say—I just got a rush job from BUSH—who also wants me to be associate editor of his beastly magazine. MY GAWD, Oswald, the ambulance!!!

Well, ta ta!

Theobáldos

P.S. Our friend Eddy is thinking of suing Henneberger for the price of two *Weird Tales*.

Notes

1. The Lefferts Farm Cottage (c. 1890), originally at Jamaica Avenue and 115th Street,

Brooklyn, and subsequently moved to 115th Street between Jamaica Avenue and 86th Avenue. The Morris-Jumel Mansion (1765), at 65 Jumel Terrace in upper Manhattan.

2. There are or were five forts named Fort George in New York State. HPL probably refers to the one built in 1776 in upper Manhattan, at 192nd Street and Audubon Avenue.

3. The Dyckman House (1783), at Broadway and 204th Street, Manhattan; the Van Cortlandt House (1748–49), at Broadway and West 246th Street in the Bronx.

4. Ernest La Touche Hancock (1859–?,) a minor poet, journalist, and short story writer, and author of *Desultory Verse* (1912). HPL called him "old-time wit & columnist La Touche Hancock (once a shining light on the old N.Y. Sun), who eventually drank himself to death" (HPL to J. Vernon Shea, 14 February 1934; ms., JHL).

[28]   [AHT][1]

July 11, 1724

Illustrissime:—

        Did you sell Esperanto to the air last night? Our gang couldn't listen in, because Belknap's radio isn't powerful enough to pick up Philly. All mourned your absence—& McNeil *was* there. Later we walked down town along Riverside Drive, & finally Kleiner, Leeds, & Theobald bummed around cheap lunch rooms till after three a.m.—observe the gradual disintegration of a once choice spirit amidst the corrupting contamination of a tawdry & plebeian metropolis!

        Well, anyhow, this is to tip yuh off to the next meeting of the gang—which same is next Thursday, July 17th, at 8 p.m. or so, *right here at 259 Parkside*. Don't fail to shew up, for *we* want a wild time. Belknap hits the Maine trail Chewsday, & wants to be remembered to you.

        Oh yes—& here's some stamps! Best I could round up this time—hope for better luck later.

        Attaboy! And be sure to be here the 17th.
                Yr most obt Servt
                Theobaldus

Notes

1. Written on the stationery of the Robert Morris Hotel, Philadelphia, Pa.

[29]   [AHT]

Novr. 18, 1724

Mortonius Ol' Grind:—

        Say—how's this for noive? You busy as hell, & the Old Man astin' a favour!
        Can you get Friday—Nov. 21—free? It's this-a-way. The frau has gotta go down to the Taown Hall or somew'eres to wind up all the red tape on her naturalisation papyri, & needs two—count 'em—two res-sponsible parties to

swear they've know'd 'er five—count 'em—five years, & testify that she ain't bent on overturninin' the respublica. Now our far from tongue-tied neighbour Dame Moran is gonna be one—count it—one, but she needs another to complete the effeck of Georgian symmetry.

Can you be it? Like ya done recent-like fer Dench's ball-&-chain? If so drop us a line casual-like on a card, or from Audubon 4295 to Flatbush 3586, sayin' that yuh're game, & that yuh kin drop in at this joint at *twelve-thirty* sharp to share our humble midday meal (brekfuss fer me & lunch for the sturm und drang) preparatory to the obsequies of the arternoon.

How about it? I know I gotta helluva noive—but I'll do as much fer yous some day—when yuh need naturalissation as one of His Majesty's subjects after our reconquest of these seceded colonies. Count on me to say you're the real Planta-genista stuff, whose heart was allus in the right place despite the wanderings of your soul in unorthodox desert places!

So zassat. Here—Friday—twelve-thirty noon—& we're your sempiternal debtors. And grandpa'll tell you—or thee—or thou—all about his Philadelphian maeanderings. Hell, but I gotta crush on Philly—I'm damn'd if I know whether I'm a Friend, Dunkard, or Mennonite—but anyway I have Pennsylvania vaccinated on the tissues of my spirit!

Attaboy—& try to be a good sport. Luck with your doctor dope—I'll write a coupla pages for ya if it'll help any!

Hoping to see ya Friday—

Yr Obt

Θεοβάλδος

[30]   [AHT]

Via Clintonia

2/16/25

To His Serene High Mightiness, Ferdinand II, Commander of the Antique, Curious, & Exotick, Sire:—

Hitherto awed to silence by the dignity of your newly empurpled state, I now breathe batedly those respectful congratulations upon your accession, which it becomes a simple & unpolisht country-gentleman to proffer. Ave, Maxime! Hath not merit receiv'd its due, & true greatness reacht that pinnacle of recognition for which it was ever fitted by bounteous Nature? Io, Io, Evoë, Evoë!

Meanwhile, Sire, must not Royalty be amus'd? In such a belief I have not remitted the custom of supplying you with those piquant crosswordiana which delighted your humble days as heir-apparent, & am here enclosing several specimens of presumably acute transvertian ingenuity. I am profoundly sensible, & I felicitate their creator on having achiev'd an audience so august.

And now, Sir, if you have not wholly put behind you your antient custom of sometimes journeying incognito among commoners, may we of this wretched abod[e]—Sir George Willard-Kirke, Bt., & Lewis, 23ᵈ Viscount Theobald—not look forward to the felicity of a Royal visit on the evening of Wednesday next—18th February—when at this castle will assemble the regular conclave of feudal baronage, including Lord Francis de Long, of Belknap Manor, Sir Arthur Leeds, K. C. B.,[1] Cardinal Samuel Loveman, Bishop St. John of Bushwick, and your miserable hosts? Suitable verses will be compos'd in your honour, singing the praises of vested rank both vertically & horizontally.

And so it goes! Here, Sir, is our esteem the most profound, (colloq. Late XVIII cent.) which in all humility do we proffer, soliciting that, unworthy tho' it be, you do for some brief space preserve it in the Musaeum of your heart!

Shantih, Shantih, Shantih!

Council of Peers,

per. L. Theobald,

Exalted Secretary.

Notes

1. Knight Commander of the Most Honourable Order of the Bath, a British order of Chivalry.

[31]   [AHT]

Friday, [late May] 1925

Iacobe Maxime:—

Thou wert mourn'd night afore last—but hope sustains our desolated residue. Just now I'm keeping up by the artificial excitement of clothes-buying—oh, baby, but yo' orta set yo' ah's awn de volupshus rags dis chile am a-hangin' awn he carcass! In sober fact, I'm indulging in one very sedate creation of the cruelly spoof'd Monroe Clothes system—grandfatherly in conservatism of cut, & dignified in sombreness of fabrick. Happy thought—I'll enclose a sample, since I have all the extra trouser-bottoms for future mending purposes. (After the first fifteen years I may need a patch or so.) It set me back only twenty-five tin soldiers, & I've blown in on a $2.35 straw lid to set it off. Some village dandy? Boy, dey doan' come no sweller up in Seventh Avenue and 140th Street! Better tustle back from your migrations & attend one of the meetings at which I expect to strut around in naively childlike vanity! I had a hard time picking an outfit, & this one come sudden't like. I was dinin' with the ball-&-chain at John's, in Willoughby Street, when I seen the Monroe sign in a winder opposite. One of the price statements— 21.50—lured me on in & up—& before I reeled out I had fallen for the aforementioned scenery. Since then I have been fussing about alterations, & when I finally get the thing—today—I expect to sport the most acceptable false facade that I've sported for some little while. And if any —— ———— thief touches *this* outfit; why, by ————, I'll smash his ——— ————— ——————— for him with one fist whilst I pulverise his ———— ————

————————— ———— with the other, meanwhile kicking him posteriorly with both feet in their most pointed shoes & manner! I.E., if I catch him.[1]

Well—back to the ———— ———— envelope addressing! A patriarch's new-suited blessing on thy head! Pax vobixcum!

Theobaldus

Notes

1. HPL refers to the fact that, in late May 1925, his apartment in Brooklyn was broken into and three of his suits were stolen. Over the next several weeks, HPL went to great efforts to secure three new suits at bargain prices.

[32]   [AHT]

Tuesday
[30 June 1925]

Mortoni Rex:—

I was sorry not to be able to get to the B. P. C. meeting, but my amiable consort felt like some fresh air during the day, so we went to Inwood[1]—accompanied by Belknap, who brought Grandpa a fine cloth-bound Bookfellow Anthology with one of his sonnets in it![2] And when the afternoon was over, the good vrouw felt too tired for vespertine revelry. Sunday was so dubious that I didn't know whether you'd go or not. When it cleared up in the afternoon we went out to the semi-rural region beyond Yonkers—toting all the while an umbrella we didn't have to use.

Kirk finally moved out of this dump yesterday, & insisted on presenting me with enough of his old printed stationery to last me the rest of my days. Some boon for a pauper! Well—if I get that museum job I'll surcharge the Kirk printing with a rubber-stamp device of my own!

Enclosed is the usual quota. That Norse stamp came from Kirk—& I'll let you have any which I may chance upon.

Which being so, permit me, Sir, to subscribe my self yr most oblig'd, most obt: Servt

Theobaldus

Notes

1. Cf. HPL to F. Lee Baldwin, 27 March 1934 (ms., JHL): "Up in the Bronx the Zoölogical Garden is interesting & well-stocked—& in one place on Manhattan Island there is a remaining bit of primitive forest—at Inwood, near the northwest tip."

2. George Steele Seymour, ed., *A Bookfellow Anthology* (Chicago: The Bookfellows, 12 vols., 1925–36; *LL* 786). HPL had only Vol. 1 (1925), which contains Frank Belknap Long's "A Sonnet for Seamen," p. 93; this copy is Long's autographed presentation copy to HPL.

[33]   [AHT]

Friday Evening
[17 July 1925]

Sapientissime:—

Tough luck! Wednesday's meeting, lacking its supreme lumi-
nary, was as dull as hell—sinking, in fact, to the abysmal cesspool of inanity
where it welcomed such mental teething-ring exercises as the question of how
to get the fox, the goose, & the corn across the river one at a time . . . & other
kindred reminiscences of rural childhood cogitations as resurrected by our genial host. Try like the devil to get there next time—a Leeds meeting,[1] Wednesday, July the 22nd, at **Kleiner's.** We haven't fully decided on the seat of the
McNeil meeting of July 29th, but it'll probably be the Circo-Caminian Eyrie at
the Earl of Rochester's country-seat in Bloomingdale, near King's-College.[2]

By this time you are cursing Pegāna's high ones because of the absence
from this missive of the usual supply of the drug. Cheer up! It's coming third
class under separate cover, companion'd by an item I've been trying for years
to dig up for your private collection of Aonian curiosa . . . the immortal "Poet
& Philosopher",[3] which surely belongs nowhere save by the side of "The
Bride of Gettysburg",[4] P. J. Pendergast's "Selected Gems", D. V. Bush's out-
pouring, & other choice bits which you have. I meant to send it when I sent
the Pendergast jewellery, but couldn't find it. Now it's turned up in a cabinet
which I'm cleaning out for the first time in aeons—which I moved from Angell to Parkside & Parkside to Clinton without subjecting to analysis & classification. My blessing accompanies the document.

Of your trip I indeed heard much last Wednesday from Kleinerian lips.
Boys, Grandpa envies you-all! I hear you stood in three states at once—a feat
surpassable, I seem to recall without consulting the map, only by going S.W.
& planting one's hoof simultaneously in Utah, Colorado, Arizona, & New
Mexico.

As for the B. P. C. meeting—look heah, boy, w'at kindah place yo' done
pick for dat suspicious conjunction? Ah gets de kyard 'nouncin' ob it a couple
weeks ago, & on de strenth of dat (seein' as how Ah ain't nebber ben up Pel-
ham Park ways befo') Ah takes de wife out dar one afternoon fo' a outin! She
ain't nebber ben dar befo' nudder. Well, sah, w'en we gits off de train we looks
arou', & sniffs de air, & hol's ouah noses, & gets right awn agin! Gawdy laws,
man, de crowds we done conserve! Day may hab ben dolichocephalic, but dey
sho' was pungently brunet!! Harlem out in fo'ce, boy, wid Alexander's Ragtime
Ban' a-playin' de 138th Street blues! Yassuh, it may be a fine place wiv a great
rocky sho', but Ah hates to fink ob de chromatick aberration whut's likely to
circumfase obah de landscape on dat bright & sunny Sabbath mo'nin'!

Glad you voted—I did the same for you & saved the day, since Townsend
won by a single vote. Ain't counted *United* votes yet, but guess there was no

contest. Conover of Cincinnati will take Secretaryship.[5] Yes—I've earned a vacation, & mean to spend the rest of my life bumming around in my new suit!

Yr most obt
Theobaldus

Notes

1. "Leeds meeting" refers to meetings of the Kalem Club at which Arthur Leeds would be present, but not Everett McNeil; the converse applied to "McNeil meetings." This arrangement was necessitated by the fact that Leeds had been unable or unwilling to repay McNeil $8.00, causing McNeil to sever relations with Leeds.
2. HPL to Donald Wandrei, 1 July 1927: "This cycle—Hempstead, Flushing, Jamaica, Flatbush, & Williamsburg—really shows very clearly the way N.Y. devours an adjacent town. You can omit *Williamsburg* if you like, since Greenwich Village is just as good a sample of the last stage of the process. Other former villages are Chelsea, Bowery Village, Bloomingdale, (where Belknap lives) Yorkville, &c. Another good suburb to visit is *Yonkers,* a city on the north rim of N.Y., beyond Van Cortlandt Park" (*MTS* 126). The "Circo-Caminian Eyrie" refers to the apartment jointly occupied by George Kirk and his colleague Martin Kamin.
3. *The Poet and Philosopher: A Quarterly Magazine Devoted to Poetry and Philosophy* (New York: F. L. Schmidt, 1913f.), edited by Fritz Leopold Schmidt.
4. By J[ohn] Dunbar Hylton.
5. Clyde G. Townsend was elected president of the NAPA for 1924–25 and 1925–26. Howard R. Conover was an amateur journalist, part of the faction in the UAPA hostile to HPL's "literary" faction.

[34]   [AHT]

Thursday, [15July 1925]

Illustrissime:—

Damn sorry not to have you here last night—I had on the new scenery & quite knocked out my *two*—only two—guests, Kleinerus & McNeil. Poor old Mac will have to take back his strictures on me as host, for I loaded him with enough appletarts & cake to give him a week of nightmares, & topped it off with enough coffee to keep off the sleep that engenders nightmares. Three cups apiece, & one left over for Kleiner! I got it at a corner cafeteria in a nice forty-nine cent aluminum pail with a handle which I purchased to replace the stannic jetsam of last Sunday, so disastrously lost en route to Babylon & the Far East. Our discourse, mild & proper, was mainly of poor old Bryan—whose dramatick decease formed the Dayton bedtime story which so 'intrigued' you as you saw it in semi-headline form.

Hoping to see yuh Wednesday—I am, Sir,

Ever yr most oblig'd & obt Servt
Theobaldus.

P.S. Yesterday me & wiff had a hike on the Palisades—ascending by Dyckman St. ferry. Great scenery! I'd never been up there before save in the Englewood omnibus.

[35]   [AHT]

Sextilis the Second, 1925
[2 August 1925]

Most grave & reverend Seignor:—

Wednesday? Hot stuff! I'll have a new horror tale to read to you—something based on the latent terror in the Brooklyn slums right near here. It's called "The Horror At Red Hook", but it isn't very good. Kinda rambling & long-winded. Also I hope to have another & better attraction on exhibition, which same you'll see when the time comes. Nifty scenery & coffee guaranteed—unless I'm too damn broke for the latter. But I'll shew you the new shiny pail anyhow!

Well—I guess I gotta lay off & polish my new horror—let's see if I can make a real story out of it! Don't back out of Wednesday night—& expect me to bob up in Paterson whenever you & the men higher up press the button.

Believe me, Sir, at all times

Yr most oblig'd, most obt Servt:
Theobaldus

[36]   [AHT]

Saturday-Sunday Midnight, 1925
[November 1925]

O Sage:—

Peste! Sacrebleu! Nom d'um cochon vert![1] O Saint Dieu et Notre Dame de Montreal! THIS GAWD-DAMN COLD!!!! I can't navigate a pen, although my present attire consists of the following strata:

(a) Suit
(b) Winter Overcoat
(c) Heavy Blanket
(d) Waves from the electrick heater one foot away.

But maybe I'll survive through the night, since I see a fire has just been started in the furnace.

Howsumever—even if I don't get frozen stiff I sure am bored stiff, & your fellow-Iacobus of Boomer is the cause. I've put in damn near a whole day on the —— ———— thing, & have drawn up the accompanying body of verdicts & revisions. Maybe I'm blunted by the allopathic dose of 400 pages of quasi-goodenoughery, but I didn't see much that could be notably asterisked as high spots . . . . . although you may take all of my Class A selections as the equivalents. These are really very good poems, & do Jacobus Larcinius genuine credit. The B. items aren't at all bad for amateur work, & where they most conspicuously sag I've tried to tried to tighten 'em up a bit. But most of the residual truck does The Fool-Killer as credit, & I wouldn't advise its inclusion in any future volume. I'm curious to see how well my lists coincide with what you drew up & what Kleiner will draw up. If Pearson doesn't pay us for this Bushwhacking I move we all go on strike—indeed, Loveman flatly refused to bind himself to the toil, as Sonny also probably will. But I always was a facile goat. I'll take the book to the meeting Wednesday & heave a sigh of relief—if I don't freeze to death in the damned interim.[2]

Oh, yes—& here's a 28-grain pill of the drug—plus a particularly exotick & potent essence of it distill'd by Clark Ashton Smith, Esq., the poet. Try to do it without looking at the key—I'll wager you're stumped for once in your life, & on the shortest, demurest little divvles of words at that! Please return it ultimately, as Smith wants it back. He says it's by far the *simplest* of all that he has made, but unfortunately the others were lost in the mails.[3]

So thash thash. I can't form a bally letter more—hands simply paralysed unless I hold 'em over the heater & thaw 'em out afresh for every beastly word. Gawd help your hike de luxe if the weather doesn't turn!!

Yr most obt

Theobaldus

Notes

1. "Name of a green pig!"
2. James Larkin Pearson (1879–?), *Pearson's Poems* (Boomer, NC: Published by the Author, 1924). A volume of this title had been published in 1906.
3. Clark Ashton Smith, at this time, was designing exotically worded crossword puzzles. See HPL to CAS, 4 November and 24 November 1925, where HPL reports on JFM's reactions to the puzzles.

[37]   [AHT]

Sunday Novr. 22, 1925

Sire:—

Incidentally, Belknap has three questions to ask you about his coming book and its contents—questions to which he'd profoundly appreciate an early written answer if you can't get to see him at the Kirk birthday orgy. They are these:

(1) Is the following phrase grammatically permissible?

"The golden roofs were throng'd with *heads* of *ev'ry lad* alive"[1]

Does this imply hydra-like qualities in Everylad, or is the expression ev'ry lad sufficiently plural in significance to justify its coupling with the plural noun *heads*?

(2) Is the following phrase too rococo, & too suggestive of the expletives

that their feeble aid *do* join, to be permissible?

> *Thy sons* . . . . *did praise thee*[2]

This is in a stately sonnet to the city of Florence.

(3) Is it good form to add to the signature of the writer of the *introduction* of a hook (in this case Loveman) a list of his literary achievements? (As— Editor of 21 Letters of Ambrose Bierce. A Round Table in Poictesme,[3] &c.) Sonny thinks it will add to the prestige of his work it is introduced by a man who has edited items connected with Bierce & Cabell. Bierce—Cabell— Long—a logical triad. . . . . . . The title-page would read thus.

A
MAN FROM GENOA,
and other poems;
by
Frank Belknap Long, Jr.

———— —— ————

introduction
by
Samuel Loveman,

Editor, Twenty-One Letters of
Ambrose Bierce, A Round Table
in Poictesme, &c.

————

New York
1926

Is this disproportionate, topheavy, steatopygous, or otherwise gibbous & mal- form'd? Let the child know & he'll be your debtor aeternally.[4]

Loveman, in his introduction, speaks of Belknap as *drugged & duped* with beauty. Honest old McNeil, in reading this, quaveringly expressed the fear 'that Mr. Loveman will make the average reader think that Mr. Long takes drugs if he says he is *drugged & doped*'. (As he read it!) Rare old boy! Will heaven ever coin another literalist like him? But speaking of drugs—here's your hebdomadal supply.

Well—such is which. Hope to see you Wednesday night, & guess I'll see you Thursday anyhow, since I've accepted a Thanksgiving invitation from Dench on the strength of your predicted presence. Till then, au revoir—& may Heav'n attend thy labours.

I am, Sir, ever yr most oblig'd, most obt Humble Servt—
Theobaldus

Notes

1. "The Marriage of Sir John de Mandeville."
2. "Florence": "For thy great sons did praise thee when they died."
3. *A Round-Table in Poictesme* (coedited with Don Bregenzer), an anthology of essays about James Branch Cabell.
4. The title page of *A Man from Genoa* reads as follows: "A MAN FROM GENOA / AND OTHER POEMS / BY FRANK BELKNAP LONG, JR. / WITH A PREFACE BY SAMUEL LOVEMAN / ATHOL, MASS. / PUBLISHED BY W. PAUL COOK / The Recluse Press [in Old English type] / 1926."

[38]   [AHT]

Decr. 27, 1925

Welcome back from Paradise,
O Commander of the Faithful!

The next meeting—Wednesday, December 30th—will be held at honest old McNeil's; & I certainly hope you can be present, since the sensitive old codger has a sort of notion that we shun his roost. We had a great time up at Belknap's Christmas, & I came home absolutely bulging with gifts. To start with, the Child gave Grandpa a nice conservative dark blue cravat & a piece of rock from Spitzbergen. Then we all had silk handkerchiefs from the pack of the Santa-Claus on the dining table. Then—having trooped back to the parlour—we were treated to a grab-bag session—a huge red stocking being passed around among the five recipients—Loveman, McNeil, Pa Long, Sonny Belknap, & Grandpa—until its bounteous store of Woolworth utilities was exhausted. It made nine trips, & I lugged off the following items—

1 stick shaving soap	1 reel tape measure
1 tin talcum powder	1 penholder
1 toothbrush	1 pair sleeve garters
1 ivory-handled nail file	1 pkg. large envelopes—in one of which I
1 card shirt studs	enclose this epistle & its precious enclosures.

But Gawd 'elp us, this wa'n't all! There was a game of identifying advertising pictures in which—despite a bland ignorance of all contemporary magazines & their posterior pages which caused me to tag only *six* out of *twenty-five*—I won because the others were even worse than I. Sonny could only spot *three*, & Loveman & honest old McNeil *five* apiece. Thus I walked off with still more merchandise—the prize consisting of a fine circular tin of chocolates with a golden peacock & crescent moon on the cover. After a collective trip to the cinema we all returned to supper & found at each place a "lollypop" on a wooden base & enclosed in a Janus-bodied cardboard Santa Claus. This further added to my load, & when I got home I certainly had a festive little dump to heap around my submarine tower—which, by the way, I keep on my desk in plain sight, mounted on a miniature cedar chest labelled "Providence, R. I.", which formed part of my home Christmas Box.

I hope you Surbury'd yourself with a maximum of enjoyment, & that the prosaick resurrection is not proving too painful. Whilst you were in New-England, I had a bit of its forests sent to cheer my lovely rock at Toais [?]—a calendar of birchbark, with leaves, red berries, evergreens, fungi, moss, & miniature pine cones glued & sewed on—from Mrs. Miniter, who is spending the holidays in her ancestral North Wilbraham. In response to so graceful a gift, I indited the following lines:

> MADAM, what thankful Raptures rouse my Breast,
> Out from the native Shades I love the best;
> I pine for Greens & Groves I cannot see,
> And lo! Novanglia's Woodlands come to me!

Oh, before I forget it—do you know anything about a British amateur or ex-amateur named Nigel Van Biene? He wants me to act as American agent for a literary bureau he's conducting, & I'm asking advice before signing the contract he has submitted. Honest old McNeil, of course, is agin' it—& promises to tell me in detail Wednesday night why he'd advise me to have nothing to do with it. On that occasion I'll shew you Van B's epistle & see what your impartial, curatorial, & catalytick opinion is.[1]

Meanwhile I am, Sir, ever yr most oblig'd, obt Servt

Theobaldus

Notes

1. See HPL to Lillian D. Clark, 26 December 1925 (ms., JHL): "Among my mail on this day was a letter from an ex-amateur in London—Nigel Van Biene—who wants me to act as American agent for a literary bureau which he established last August & which he says is succeeding finely. The work would mainly involve the placing of MSS. in professional magazines, & would be on a commission basis. Before I commit myself either toward acceptance or declination I shall seek a variety of opinions from those whom I deem competent—in fact, I have already begun to do so, with conflicting results so far. McNeil advises against, Loveman is rather neutral, & Sonny is mildly in favour." It does not appear as if anything came of this venture.

[39]   [AH 24.39; *SL* 204]

Tuesday the 5th [5 January 1926]

O Caelestial Omnipotence:—

I am drowned in the fountains of my weeping, & sunk into the caverns of my sorrow! Counting the golden dinars in my shabby purse after the latest extortions of the launderer, I abase myself at discovering that my stomach & intellectuals are at war, so that if I starve not the one I must needs starve the other! In other words—a survey of my unwontedly depleted coffers reveals the embarrassing circumstance that if I attempt the scholarly Paterson pilgrimage tomorrow night (.62 plus .62 equals $1.24) I shan't have pence enough left to finance my meals (& very narrowly computed feasts, at that!) till the next cargo of gold, ivory, apes & peacocks ambles along from down Ophir way! This is tragedy indeed, & I touch my forehead thrice to the dust in recognition thereof! Of course, if any miracle comes to my aid at the final moment, I'll be with you to belie this lugubrious bulletin—but if not, then I must lachrymosely solicit a vigintillion pardons, & ask you to transmit my most melancholy regrets to all such sages as may add to the illumination of your already genius-illumined palace on this joyous occasion. Misery is mine, & I grovel appropriately!

But for the Blessed Vargin's sake, repay me not in evil kind by getting too broke to shew up here at the McNeiler on Jany. 13th! My felicity depends upon the adornment of my wretched feast with the most refulgent of gems! Possess, O Flambeau of Patersonic Tenebrosity, a cardiac organ; & heap upon my valueless cranium the carbonaceous symbols of Eblis' aeternal conflagrations! Be here as much before VIII as fancy & circumstance determine to allow, & rest assured that—salutarily warned by the horrible example of this week's fiasco—I shall have parked enough jack aside to make certain (I add, absolutely certain!) of the refreshments!

I herewith enclose a supply of the drug to date, & shall have another for you to claim here on Wednesday the 13th. My own favourite pastime lately has been writing that weird-tale article for Cook, & doing the incidental reading essential thereto.[1]

With my rotten memory I lose the details of half the stuff I read in six months' or a year's time, so that in order to give any kind of intelligent comment on the high spots I selected, I had to give said spots a thorough re-reading. Thus I'd get as far as "Otranto", and then have to rake the damn thing out & see what the plot really was. Ditto the "Old English Baron". And when I came to "Melmoth" I carefully went over the two anthology fragments which constitute all I can get of it—it's a joke to consider the rhapsodies I've indulged in without having ever perused the opus as a whole! "Vathek" & the "Episodes" came in for another once-over, & night before last I did "Wuthering Heights"* again from kiver to kiver.[2] Ere long—as soon as I can get a fresh batch of correspondence out of the way—I'm going to give your Bulwer-Lytton favourites another chance to amuse & instruct me. Yes—all told, Grandpa's a pretty busy old gen-

---

*Say—if you want to cast a live subject for debate into the meeting, why not start a controversy as to whether Wuthering Heights was really written by Emily B. or by her ne'er do well brother, Bramwell. I see by an editorial in a Providence Journal that this old debate has broken out afresh!

tleman—though at that I'm only on page twenty of the bally manuscript. It'll be a young book when I'm through with it—& Culinarius will greatly lament that sentence of his—"there is absolutely no limit as to length."

But to return to our mourning—it's a damn shame that fracture thus over-takes my financial essence at this inapropos hour—but the allotments of the Immortal Ones are not to be questioned. One must be a philosopher, & be sur-prised or dismay'd at nothing. So slip my most cordial compliments to all my fellow-guests—I say fellow-guests because I shall be present in spirit—and don't fail to be at the McNeil meeting here on Wednesday the 13th. Tip the others off to the locale if you get a chance—tho' I s'pose I'll shoot 'em cards anyhow.

And so it goes. If any fortunate windfall breezes in betwixt now & seven p.m. tomorrow, I'll be amongst youse guys at 211 Carroll,³ but chances loom demnition bleak just at this moment. Now I gotta clean up some correspon-dence & hit the hay—me not havin' did which latter since night afore last.

With recrudescent saline rivers blinding my soulful gaze, & splashing mu-sically on the sheets before me, I remain, Sir,

Your high mightness's most despicable Servant
Theobaldus the Tearful

Notes

1. HPL was researching and writing "Supernatural Horror in Literature."
2. HPL refers to Horace Walpole's *The Castle of Otranto*, Clara Reeve's *The Old English Baron*, Charles Robert Maturin's *Melmoth the Wanderer*, William Beckford's *Vathek* and *The Episodes of Vathek*, Emily Brontë's *Wuthering Heights*, and probably Edward Bul-wer-Lytton's *A Strange Story; The Haunted House [sic]; Zanoni.*
3. Morton's address at the time.

[40]   [AHT]

Jany. 12, 1926

Sire:—

As for me—my current diversion is still the writing of that Culinary arti-cle on the weird tale, & the reading & re-reading appertaining thereto. I want to know, to a slight extent, what I'm talking about—though I shall doubtless mention scores of things I never even glanced at. I wonder if William Harri-son Ainsworth¹ is worth reading?

Well—such is which. Again the ocean of my tears drowns the flow of my rhetorick. Yr sorrowful & obt Servt.

Θεοβάλδος

Notes

1. Apparently HPL never read the work of William Harrison Ainsworth (1805–1882),

British historical novelist. Among his novels most clearly related to the weird are *The Tower of London* (1840), *Guy Fawkes* (1841), *Windsor Castle* (1843), *The Lancashire Witches* (1849), and *Auriol; or, The Elixir of Life* (1865).

[41]   [AHT]

Friday, [March] 1926

Lux Mundi:—

    And here's your dollar back! Nothing any good for so little at the Met. You could have gotten a measly little Greek or Roman lamp like mine,—& still can, if you wish—but I didn't fancy that had much appeal, since you didn't altogether rave when told about them last year at that 6th Ave. shop. The only Cyprus glass you could have obtain'd for a dollar consists of *broken bits*—this way to the elevator going down!

    But gawdamighty! The sale as a whole is an infinite tantalisation! *Piles* of stuff if a guy can cough up anywhere from five bucks toward the sky. Little terra-cotta *heads* of excellent Graeco-Roman design, but even the worst of 'em sets yuh back four berries. However—get this—the sale is a *semi-permanent* affair; since there's enough truck to last years at the present buying rate, & they mean to clean it all out if it takes till Mexico freezes over! I certainly expect to rake in an item or two during its course—preferably a Roman head of fairly decent grade. During the summer, with rigid oeconomy, I might feel justified in taking even a ten or fifteen fish plunge, if I knew I could get a really good piece of Roman workmanship to stare at me for the rest of my life. I advise you, also, to visit the place & give your trustees a red-hot picture of the chance of their lifetime. Hell! now that they've got a real curator, why the devil don't they set to work to get a real museum? This Met sale certainly is a windfall for any bimbo with the jack!

    Well—thash thash. See yuh Wednesday night at Kirk's. Been soaking up more Blackwood at the libe—but find most of him a bit wearying. May soak more today.

                    Insignificantly thine—
                        Θεοβάλδος

[42]   [AHT]

10 Barnes Street
Providence, R. I.
May 16, 1926

O Illimitable Potency:—

    I trust the first two instalments of the drug duly reached you—the first thro' Little Belknap, & the second bewixt the leaves of the returning *World Lore*. For the latter I was very grateful, having perus'd it with interest & appreciation. I kept *Hobhouse*¹ out to read on the train during my journey home; but was so engrossed by the emotions of reawakening life at sight of New England, that I could not, after all, do aught but gaze out the window at stone walls, rolling pastures, & white church steeples—imagining them when none were in sight. But—my room being now finally arrang'd—permit me to assure you that Leonard T. is still on top of his pile on my library table! Well—here is the third instalment of the drug, plus a letter of resignation from the B. P. C. which I trust you will guide into the official hands. The Missus wishes to make sure that our affiliation closes honourably & without residual debts; so pray bid the treasurer let us know the worst at once, & a suitable cheque will be forthcoming. I should probably have let the matter go—like the boarder who lowers his trunk from the window & decamps with unpaid board. (N.B. Of course there's nothing personal in this allusion—but don't quote the metaphor—or simile, rather—around 365 West 15th St.)[2]

Well—I suppose Sonny shew'd you my travelogue of the return to civilisation,[3] so that little save details remains to be added. It is astonishing how much better the old head works since its restoration to those native scenes amidst which it belongs. As my exile progressed, even reading & writing became relatively slow & formidable processes; so that my epistles were exceedingly brief & labour'd efforts. Now I find something of my antique Providence fluency returning by degrees, & have been able to keep my correspondence in manageable shape without more than a fraction of the effort which I was forc'd to expend when ingulph'd in the nightmare of Brooklyn's mongrel slums. That experience has already become the merest vague dream—& it is with difficulty that I can make myself realise, in any really convincing or subjective way—that I have ever been away for any length of time. I am Providence, & Providence is myself—together, indissolubly as one, we stand thro' the ages; a fixt monument set aeternally in the shadow of Durfee's ice-clad peak!

With every distinguisht consideration, I am, Sir,

Ever yr most obt. &c.

Θεοβάλδος

Notes

1. *World Lore* is unidentified; possibly a mistranscription of the well-known poetry magazine *Poet Lore* (1889–1963). Leonard Trelawny Hobhouse (1864–1929) was a British liberal politician and one of the leading theorists of social liberalism. It is not clear what book by or about Hobhouse HPL was reading.

2. Kirk's address.

3. HPL's celebrated letter to Long of 1 May 1926 (*Letters from New York* 308–15).

[43] [TLS, JHL][1]

Providence, Rhode-Island,
June 9, 1926.

My dear Son:—

I am very much flatter'd by your choice of me as informant regarding the antiquities and points of interest in Philadelphia, insomuch as this request implies a sanguine confidence alike in my powers of observation as a traveller, and in my tenaciousness of memory as a recaller of events long past. 'Tis a source of regret to me, that I have lost that sett of exhaustive notes on old streets and buildings which I compil'd with so much effort at the Philadelphia Publick Library; but in the absence of this I will draw copiously upon my mnemonick resources, aided whenever possible by such guide-books of the town as I still have by me.

Philadelphia, the metropolis of these colonies in their best days, was founded in 1683 by William Penn, Esq., a Quaker, upon the banks of the Delaware River, in territory given him by a royal charter of His late Majesty Charles the Second in 1680, and having thin previous settlements of Low-Dutch and Swedes. This date is very late for a colonial town; Portsmouth, Salem, Newburyport, Marblehead, Boston, Plymouth, Providence, Newport, New-Haven, and all my favourite spots being by that time well-establisht and prosperous. Since Mr. Penn was a Quaker and a holder of theories, his city was lay'd out with much greater regularity than was the case with towns of more natural and spontaneous growth—indeed, there was from the first a certain artificiality comparable to that of the new Federal City of Washington, or other modern centres of population. This design was aided by the even surface of the ground, and the absence of multitudinous streams and other topographical features which usually prompt picturesque irregularity in antient settlements. Even the most venerable parts are of chessboard precision; so that although many narrow and alluring courts and alleys are found, there are scarcely any of the steep, curving, and boldly fantastical effect which the traveller encounters in Providence, Old Boston, Marblehead, or East-Greenwich. With the growth of the city, the settled area extended westward from the Delaware to the parallel tributary Schuylkill, so that the entire inter-river peninsula is now thickly built up, with generous overlappings even beyond the Schuylkill. On both sides of that stream, and united by several bridges, is the wild natural expanse of Fairmount-Park, containing the 1876 Centennial grounds and having an undulating surface which contrasts agreeably with the plainness of Philadelphia in general. It is in this district, on the bold bluffs above the convolutions of the river, that the finest country-seats of the colonial gentry were built. Near a bend where the river turns westward, there flows into it a sub-tributary call'd the Wissahickon, from the north, whose deep and finely forested gorge is perhaps the most pleasing bit of natural scenery I have ever beheld. Here are few houses, but arboreal solitudes of a sort to tempt the choicest Dryads from their Dorick and Ionian groves! Germantown, north of Old Philadelphia but now part of the greater city, was founded by Quakers, Dunkards, and Kennonites from Germany; and tho' later augmented by the country-seats of many Philadelphia gentlemen, retains to this day a character and aspect widely different from that of the larger town. Mr. Penn's original home, the first brick edifice in the region, was built in 1682 before the formal laying out of the town. It is still standing, tho' removed from its original location to Fairmount Park. One may add, that the pre-Revolutionary portion of Philada. is that lying betwixt the Delaware River on the east and Seventh Street on the west, and betwixt Poplar Street on the north and Christian Street on the south. By late Georgian times—the beginning of the nineteenth century—the compact district had advanced as far west as about Thirteenth Street. In former times the whole region was divided up into many small jurisdictions, but all are now merg'd into one vast municipality of Greater Philadelphia.

The central position of Philadelphia in the area of the colonies, the solid and enterprising character of the Quaker inhabitants, and the personal genius of the celebrated Dr. Franklin, who had early migrated thither from your own Province of the Massachusetts-Bay, all combin'd to impart to the town a prosperity of phaenomenal swiftness and magnitude; so that before the middle of the eighteenth century it was the recognis'd metropolis of the English part of America, and the seat of numerous publick institutions both learned and philanthropick, saecular and religious. Dr. Franklin, whose immortal experiments in the capture of electrical fire were here conducted, succeeded in divesting the people of much of their Quaker primness and narrowness; and little by little a gay and wholesome social life sprang up, whilst architectural skill rear'd to the sky a pleasing array of rich and tasteful structures. In 1731 the Library Company of Philadelphia founded the first publick library in these colonies, thus setting an example which other towns were all too slow to follow. Ours in Providence came not till 1754, when Stephen Hopkins, Esq. took steps to remedy a deficiency of which he was very heartily asham'd.

By the time of the late unfortunate rebellion against His Majesty's lawful government, Philadelphia had become built up in an extreamly definite and distinct fashion, wherein the Quaker spirit of the founders blended very agreeably with the newer atmosphere of progress and prosperity. Some of the houses were of the general American urban type of the period—small brick facades, backward-sloping roofs, and one or more dormer windows overlooking the street. Of this style is the celebrated abode of Mrs. Betsey Ross, still standing, where the permanent colonial flag is reputed to have been first design'd and fashion'd. More, however, had a peculiar form and tone of their own; being arrang'd in long solid blocks of red brick, with white marble steps, arched doors fac'd with marble, and windows with marble lintels and keystones. There were no porches, but merely flat facades with low flights of steps rail'd on one side, as the sole jutting feature. To glimpse a typical street of these houses, a ravine with solid red cliff walls and innumerable white flights of steps projecting out from the flat marble-fac'd doors, was to feel oneself unmistakably in Philadelphia—tho' the town of Baltimore is said to have effects not altogether dissimilar. A singular local uniquity is the optical *spy*—a reflector attached to the front window of a house to shew the inhabitants of the second storey who is standing on the low porchless steps before the front door. Occasional mansions in the suburbs were of more ambitious type, and excelled in their general design even the best houses of New-England; tho' their doorways never quite attain'd the inspired and classick delicacy of our own. Stone rather than wood was the favour'd building material for rural manors of this sort. The publick buildings of the town were rich to the point of lavishness; their survivors yet furnishing some of the finest models of colonial architecture in America. Philadelphia, having matured so early, received a prodigious building-up of durable brick in Georgian times; and still contains in all probability more colonial houses than any other city in the Union. Block on block they stretch in crumbling rows; sometimes sunk to nigger slums, and sometimes reclaim'd with praiseworthy diligence. A great number of them have been demolisht in clearing space for the new Delaware River Bridge in Camden, in New-Jersey, but even with these removals the remaining number is past all calculation. They are not, as a general thing, readily visible to the casual observer of the town; for they are more or less tuckt away into obscure quarters. A first impression, in truth, wou'd proclaim Philadelphia a thoroughly Victorian city, with certain still newer buildings which are beginning to oust the nineteenth-century horrors in the most central business parts. I scarcely wonder at the indifference with which George Willard Kirk, Esq., after the most cursory of glances, now regards the place. It wou'd take a truly discriminating walk under suitable guidance to demonstrate to him his error.

My best trip to Philadelphia began on the evening of November 10, 1924, when I arriv'd in town about nine o'clock and register'd at the Y.M.C.A. for an indefinite sojourn. Being as much accustom'd to explore by night as by day, and having already a little familiarity with the place, I did not wait till morning before commencing my observations; but sally'd forth at once for a preliminary survey in the light of the corner lanthorns—guided by a map knowledge which took me at once into the Georgian labyrinths toward the Delaware.

The first plunge into the colonial part was singularly dramatick. Having gone south to the corner of Broad and Walnut Streets through the prosaick centre of the city, I dodged round behind the Ritz-Carlton Hotel—sloughing off, as I did so, every vestige of modern times! One turn, two turns—and I was in a compleat colonial world of tangling alleys, with peaked gables, small-paned dormers, and ancient bricks dominating every vista and filling every thought. What a piquant world of vanisht yesterdays! Streets hardly wide enough for two to pass—brick walls separated from the roadway by iron posts in prim rows—prospect on prospect of antediluvian roofs—pillared doorways with shining knockers—but what's the use? Lud, Sir, but I can't describe it as it suddenly burst upon me when I rounded that obscure corner behind the Ritz-Carlton that night nigh two years ago! This section, as I later learnt, is the "Greenwich Village" of Philadelphia; and has been restor'd to magnificence with great cost and labour. Its principal highways are Chancellor, Camac, and St. James' Streets; and it is here that is situate the bookshop and publishing-house whose dealings with Saml: Loveman, Esq. prov'd so dishonourable. Emerging from this particular district on the south, I observ'd the antique lengths of Locust, Spruce and Pine Streets, and the innumerable colonial alleys thereto adjacent; together with some of the archaick churches and their ghoulish yards. My soul was lifted incredibly into the atmosphere of the Georgian past, and on the following day I resolv'd to begin a canvass which might leave no vestige of this elder wealth untasted by me.

The morrow was dull and grey, but the spirit of colonial exploration brighten'd all things. Resolv'd to explore more intelligently, I repair'd to the publick library, where I was greatly help'd by the books, and by the advice of one of the attendants—an old lady descended from the best local families. This library is hous'd in a building of about the Civil War period—quite in contrast to the modern structures in Providence, Boston, and Paterson—but the architecture is very conservative, and lacks the bad taste of most Victorian designs.*

Having now a little expert knowledge, I plung'd again into colonial labyrinths, and revell'd in an intoxication of antiquity. One by one I lookt up the notable houses and doorways recommended by the best authorities; (how I wish I had not lost that list I compil'd!) and tho' some of them had been torn down, a vast proportion were still there to reward my pious pilgrimage. I return'd to St. Peter's Church (S. Third & Pine Sts—built 1761), which I had seen by sinister moonlight the night before, and meditated long in the grassy churchyard where the willows weep and rustick flagstones lead among the antient gravestones. Then I enter'd the fane, noted the colonial high pews and turret-like pulpit, and finally succumb'd to the charm of the stately organ musick—reminiscent peals which awak'd a thousand ancestral memories of OLD ENGLAND. God Save the King!

I now proceeded still further east—to Second Street and the old Market (cor. of Pine), where my breath was fairly taken away by the sight which greeted me. Imagine an antient street rising toward the south, with colonial gables and dormers on both sides silhouetted against a grey sky, and spreading abruptly to accomodate a large building in its very centre. That building— a trim brick bit of colonialism with massive white cupola, white lintels, and a white string course betwixt upper and lower storeys—is the old Market

---

*A magnificent new library in the classick manner is now building on the parkway which leads from the City Hall to the Schuylkill.

House itself; and vary'd indeed is its long history. During the War of 1812 it was used as a recruiting station and known as Commissioners' Hall. Meer words cannot describe the peculiar effect of this singular scene upon me—and the passage of two years hath not diminisht its force. The region is squalid, but a strange charm inheres. Perhaps it is because *every* structure in sight is colonial; because these structures are all larger and more elaborate than the colonial survivals in other cities; because the quaint spire and gilded cross of St. Peter's towers up majestically at the extream right; or because the rising ground limns the line of roofs and chimneys against the blank sky and thus adds a dramatick unity to the picture. Be all this as it may, there is a glamour profound and inescapable; and I felt queer impressions of previous familiarity steal over me—impressions involving visions of colonial farmers' wains, and the clatter of hooves as periwigg'd horsemen push'd their way thro' knee-breech'd crouds.

Pausing in this vicinity only long enough to observe certain fine old houses and doorways in Second Street recommended by the books I had consulted, I struck out for the north, and was soon at the corner of Dock Street, before the splendid old Maritime Exchange with its semicircle of giant Corinthian columns above the first storey, and its crowning skyward monument—a free adaptation of the famous Choragick Monument of Lysicrates in Athens. This is the work of Strickland, and I was very much imprest long ago by an etching of it in the Shepley Library in Providence.

Not a stone's throw away is one of the earliest classick revival buildings in America—the old bank in Third Street, with its Grecian temple facade, erected in 1795. It is still a bank, and still in fine preservation, for which I am profoundly thankful. The only false note is a use of the popular American Eagle motif in the frieze—a thing which clashes with the Hellenism of the conception as a whole.

I now proceeded to the corner of Fifth and Chestnut Streets, where I was confronted by as magnificent a row of Georgian publick buildings as any antiquary's soul cou'd ask for—Congress Hall, built in 1790 and housing the Federal government when Philadelphia was the nation's capital; Independence Hall, or the old Colony-House, famous for its part in the regrettable insurrection of 1775–1783; and the U.S. Supreme Court House, built in 1791 and now housing a notable collection of relicks. To circumnavigate this splendid colonial array, viewing it from all angles and especially from the square to the south, whence many other colonial buildings may be seen, is to live again in that subtle atmosphere of the urban 18th century, of which so few perfect specimens now survive. The effect is marvellous—elsewhere one may find the spirit of the colonial village and small town, but only here may one grasp to the fullest extent the soul of the colonial *city*—mature and populous when the third George sate upon our throne.

Independence Hall is the largest and by far the finest of this group of buildings. At present it is tripartite, with a great central structure and two wings; the latter built shortly after the revolution, and the former, or Independence Hall proper, erected by Andrew Hamilton, Esq. (a famous lawyer and amateur architect) for the provincial Assembly of Pennsylvania in 1734. The belfry and steeple were completed in 1751—being now restor'd after removal in 1781. The interior of this edifice is without doubt the finest example of colonial carving and panelling I have ever beheld. It were futile to try to describe, save in prose-poetry, the mass'd effect of the exquisite cornices, pilasters, wainscots, doorways, staircases, mantels, columns, and other decorative details; all of the purest middle Georgian tradition, and gleaming whitely as a perfect background for the delicate furniture and absorbing relicks with which the place abounds. Amongst these latter things are the desk of the President of the Congress, the well-known Liberty Bell, formerly hung in the belfry but now especially display'd on the ground floor in a hall, a sofa of Genl. Washington's and a chair of Chief Justice Jay's, the silver inkstand and sand-shaker used in preparing the seditious so-called Declaration of Independence, and many notable paintings, amongst them works of the Philadelphian Benjamin West, and of his still greater pupil, the Rhode-Islander Gilbert Stuart, Esq. The rear doorway of Independence Hall, surmounted by a mightily tasteful Palladian window, is a delightful specimen of Dorick art as employ'd in early colonial design.

Nearby is that still more faithful representative of the Dorick order—the old pillar'd Custom-House (1824); and some distance east of the Independence Hall row of buildings, set back from Chestnut Street at the end of a little colonial court like Harding's Alley in Providence, (which I shew'd you in 1923) is Carpenter's Hall, an edifice of considerable historick importance. This structure, commenc'd in 1770 but not finish'd till much later, hous'd the first treasonable Continental Congress in 1774; at which event Genl. Washington and other rebels knelt and pray'd, under the false impression that Boston had been destroy'd by bombardment. The interior hath many historical relicks, and the exterior is very fine, including a red brick facade, classick doorway, and gleaming white belfry.

I now turn'd north to the old Quaker Meeting-House (4th & Arch Sts.) and Christ Church Cemetery (5th and Arch), where I ponder'd long by the grave of the estimable Dr. Franklin—whose parents' graves I know of old in Boston's Granary Burying Ground. Fired by the name of Franklin, I presently turn'd northwest to find the venerable square that bears it; and at length arriv'd at a fine expanse of greenery surrounded by early 19th century mansions in a manner reminiscent of Washington-Square in New-York. These mansions are now sunk to the state of lodging-houses, and the park and fountain are not unknown to the shabby herd of bench-loafers; but little physical deterioration has set in, so that reclamation would be easy. In the region just east of this, there was in progress a wholesale demolition of colonial houses to provide for the titanick new bridge; but by now the completed feat of engineering must be visible in all its grandeur.

I travers'd this region on my way to the northern reaches of Second Street, where books had led me to expect several colonial inn-yards with brick and stone archways. I found only one of them—the ancient Black Horse—and even this was abandon'd and boarded up. However, the walk well repay'd me, since it led me through streets and alleys so solidly colonial that at times I had a dazed doubt of the reality of the scene—or of my own existence in this prosaick and decadent XXth century!

Next came Arch Street and the Betsey Ross house—which is a shop for souvenirs, with several rooms open to display the neat and tasteful panelling. Here I found one of those garrulous old antiquarians of whose species I am so fond—a quaint fellow like honest George Fuller of the Royall House at Medford, if you know what I mean—and he gave me some invaluable hints on local antiquities, including a sloping and particularly colourful colonial alley which I lost no time in visiting. That alley—once called Elfrot's Alley but now forming part of the legal line of Cherry Street—is a marvel which, once seen, can never be forgotten. It is astonishingly narrow, and lined solidly with unchanged colonial doorways in old brick houses. The cobblestones are of immemorial age, and slant downward toward the centre where a channel for drainage exists as in Georgian times. This alley runs east from Second Street, just north of Arch.

Dusk had now fallen, so that I could take only the most cursory exterior glance at Christ Church and the neighbouring alleys. Accordingly I boarded a southbound car in quest of Old Swedes' Church (1750) and the gruesome churchyard in front of it. This fane was built by those Swedish settlers who establisht themselves here before Mr. Penn, and with whom the Dutch under Petrus Stuyvesant had such incessant warfare on account of the neighbouring Dutch settlements in Delaware. It is situate in the midst of a district as colonial as the rest of eastern Philadelphia, high on a banked terrace overlooking the railway yards and the waterfront. In the pallid light of feeble lamps the antique and curious spire loom'd up impressively, whilst the ghoulish headstones leer'd on every side. It was a cheering sight, and I wish I might have had time to revisit the spot by day.

Resuming explorations on the following morning, I made direct tracks for old Christ Church (2nd St. N. of Market), which I found prodigiously enchanting both outside and inside, and in whose fascinating churchyard I paus'd long enough to ponder upon the mortality of mankind and the general decay of this age. This edifice is of much vaster grandeur than St. Peter's, with a lofty, snow-white, carv'd interior, and ornate stain'd glass in the great Palladian window of the apse which looks on Second St. The exterior is in splendid taste, and exhibits on a large scale that alternation of black (ends) and red (sides) bricks so frequently seen in colonial construction.

From Christ Church I proceeded north amongst endless colonial alleys, finally taking to Front St. in quest of an house at 111 Spring which Dr. Franklin used to inhabit. Failing to find it, (I think it is torn down for the bridge) I took the elevated north, and soon arriv'd at Penn Treaty Park, a green waterfront space hedg'd in by ugly factories, where in 1682, under a great elm which blew down in 1810, Mr. Penn sign'd his celebrated treaty with the Indians, that gave him the land by native sanction as well as Royal grant. There is a wharf here, and I obtain'd some fine views of the river, the Camden waterfront, and the adjacent shipping. After this I took the car in quest of the house where Poe lived during his editorship of Graham's Magazine—520 N. 7th St.—but found it mov'd far back in a yard whose gate was securely lockt. The large-scale widening of Spring Garden Street some time ago hath caused great changes in this locality.

My next step—after a call at the inevitable Leary's bookshop—was at the superb neo-colonial building at 13th and Locust Sts.—pure Georgian in every detail both inside and out—which houses the collection of the Penn. Historical Society. Here I was long detain'd in a state of the keenest interest and excitement, for there spread around me in lavish array some of the most captivating relicks of elder times which I have ever seen. The whole life of the 18th and late 17th centuries surges back into existence amidst this multiplicity of intimate memorials—Mr. Penn's razor (not a Gillette)—the original wampum treaty with the Indians—Robert Morris' strong-box—a ticket to the fashionable Meschianza—the architect's original plan of Independence Hall—a 1710 Bradford prayer-book—the sword presented by Louis XVI to John Paul Jones—but who cou'd catalogue it all? You must see it, if you have to cut the whole amateur convention to do it! It was after four when I broke away, but I still had time to visit the bits of modern quaintness near Rittenhouse Square. Just off Ludlow St.—which runs west from 19th St. immediately below Market—is a green alley of tiny new cottages of multifarious colouration and self-consciously bizarre design—something like Washington Mews in New-York—call'd Lantern Lane. Farther south and west the quaint ideal has been followed with greater success; one small alley having sidewalk posts like those of the ancient Philadelphia alleys, and a court running east from 22nd St. below Walnut being develop'd into a typical English village. This village extends back through lanthorn-topt gates to a rear wall of brick, where an house surmounts an arch thro' which vehicles may pass. The effect is certainly redolent of British semi-rusticity—especially since the houses along the court are mostly of the peaked, gabled, plaster'd Tudor sort, with one Georgian brick building to add the needed touch of variety and organick vitality.

I now took the car for Mr. Penn's house in Fairmount Park, which I wish'd to see more thoroughly than on a former visit. This is, as formerly mention'd, the oldest brick house in Philadelphia; and has the alternating red and black bricks so frequently seen in that town. Only the large front room is open to the publick, but this gives a fair idea of the proportioning, wood-work, and fireplace. The house formerly stood in Letitia Street, in the old part of the town near the Delaware, but was moved to the park in the 'eighties.

Twilight had now set in, and I saw that it would be necessary to post-pone my tour of other houses in the park. Walking back over the Girard Avenue bridge and up the eastern shore a bit, I visualised the lay of the land and plann'd my itinerary for the following day.

When that day came, however, I decided to cover another suburban region of country-seats and villages before exploring Fairmount Park; so that mid-morning found me on a trolley bound for the eccentrick Bartram House in the Kingsessing district to the southwest beyond the Schuylkill. The route led through the Rittenhouse Square district which I had travers'd afoot the day before, and thence to the city's rim—where, on a high bank above the river and now surrounded by a cemetery, I saw the fine colonial mansion Woodlands, built by Wm. Hamilton, Esq., in 1770, and forming one of the earliest American examples of the third and most delicate phase of Georgian architecture. In some respects this splendid house foreshadows the classical revival of the early 19th century, for on its south front is a lofty pillar'd portico of the Grecian temple variety. But the car sped on, and I was soon at the Bartram house—a whimsical, home-made stone mansion constructed by John Bartram, the bota-nist, with his own hands in 1731. It lies back some distance from the road, and is reacht through the fine botanick gardens lay'd out by the builder. The north facade is plain, but on the south side above the river there is a profusion of rococo ornament in stone, and three two-storey Ionick columns—made of thinnish concentrick discs pil'd up, and surmounted by huge and uncouth vo-lutes. Bartram was quaintly peculiar, and his nature is reflected in the crudity and heterogeneity of his house. Ornamental stone panels are set here and there—both in house and outbuildings—and around the windows are curious German mouldings of carved stone. The doors are double—vertically so—and over one of the windows is the following pious inscription, placed there in panel form thirty-nine years after the building of the house:

> 'TIS GOD ALONE, ALMYTY LORD,
> THE HOLY ONE, BY ME ADOR'D
> JOHN BARTRAM 1770

The interior not then being open for inspection (tho' it may be now) I walkt north a brief space and took a car for the adjacent small city of Chester, where stands a famous 1724 court and town house, the oldest building of its kind in the country. The ride led thro' a highly interesting region, and at one turn of the road I saw a fine old deserted stone mansion of the Middle Colonies type—with cornice extending round the gable ends—bearing a panel with the date 1760.

Chester I found very interesting. The Town Hall is in many ways unique; and bears traces of the Welsh influence paramount in this region. Opposite it—across the street—is a wooden inn where Genl. Washington writ his midnight report of the battle of Brandywine, and where he later received congratulations as first president of the new republick. Around a stone-paved court behind the Town House, are grouped the newer city hall and office of the Chester Times, both of pure Georgian design, and built of grey stone to match the 1724 edifice. Nearby are many colonial houses, and altogether the scene is one to delight the antiquarian eye.

Returning to Philadelphia, I next set out for Fairmount Park, determin'd to observe before nightfall such colonial country-seats as lie on the eastern bank of the Schuylkill—reserving the rest for the morrow, when I wish'd to greet the dawn from the majestick hills of the western park. All these old mansions, as imply'd at the beginning of this epistle, rise on or near the towering slopes beside the river; commanding the most agreeable prospects, and presenting the most engaging aspect. Beginning at the south I observ'd Lemon Hill, the residence of the celebrated Robt Morris, Esq., the Fisher place, built in 1743, and Mount Pleasant—the ornate and magnificent structure of second-phase Georgian architecture, built in 1761 by Capt. John Macpherson and bought during the revolution by the traitor Genl. Arnold. I have seen few houses more genuinely splendid and baronial than Mount Pleasant. It has a thorough sumptuousness, elegance, and majesty seldom attain'd save in mansions of the Middle Colonies. The hipped roof, doorway pediments, brick quoins, Palladian window mouldings, quadruple and arch-connected chimneys, and massive cornices all bespeak an heaviness which sacrifices nothing of grace, but which turns itself to advantage by creating an atmosphere of unparallell'd dignity. Smaller outbuildings of similar ornamentation, design'd for servants' quarters, give the estate a profoundly manorial, and almost southern cast; whilst the lawn down to the river (tragically broken by a railway track) adds the final touch of substantial elegance.*

Going north, I observ'd and appreciated two more mansions of later date—Rockland, built in 1810, and Armiston, whose valley prospect is unique and majestick. Beyond these lies Edgely, a middle Georgian specimen much defac'd with additions, Woodford, a magnificently rambling structure in the later colonial manner, and Strawberry Mansion—a wooden farmhouse rais'd to seignioral dignity by the addition of two huge square wings at the ends. These last three houses I explored in the twilight, guided by an intelligent man of middle age of whom I had askt directions, and who—as a matter of amazing

---

*Genl. Arnold never actually dwelt in this house. In Sept. 1926, when I revisited it, it had been open'd as a publick museum; and I was overcome by the magnificence of the interior woodwork & the splendour of the furniture (Georgian) there install'd.

coincidence—turn'd out to be a greater and more fully inform'd architectural enthusiast than I! He furnisht me with many pointers on Philadelphian antiquities, and explain'd to me the meaning of a peculiar metal device I had found on the front of many colonial buildings—an oval panel of the following nature: (see Fig.) I had speculated long upon its possible significance, and was now inform'd that it was the sign of a house which had subscrib'd to the Fire Association of the period—an organisation sponsor'd by Dr. Franklin—and which was therefore intitul'd to the protection of the then newly-introduced fire-engines. The notion of an universal free fire department was unheard-of.*

That evening I paid a call on the local amateur Washington Van Dusen, who is a pleasant elderly person residing (tho' in a modern house) in historick Germantown. He writes poetry and paints in oils, and is descended from the most ancient Philadelphia families. In historical matters he is quite an authority, and I gain'd from him many useful hints to guide my morrow's exploration of his antient section. It was so dark when I call'd, that I really had no sight of Germantown that night; but cou'd look forward to it as fresh territory to be tapp'd on the succeeding day.

Friday morning I was up before the sun, for I wish'd not only to observe the gold and rose dawn from the hills beyond the Schuylkill, but also to have as long a day as possible, since my departure from Philadelphia that night was financially imperative. Before taking the car for Fairmount Park I strolled in the gloom to the ancient Christ Church region, where in a network of ancient alleys I found the oldest house still standing in the town†—a 17th century brick relick with steep slate roof and flat dormers. The pitch of the gambrel—as here illustrated—is a Swedish feature; this influence coming from the Swedes who had built farms along the Delaware before the coming of Mr. Penn with his English and German colonists.

Now taking a westbound car and depositing my 8¢ token (almost as in Providence) with the sleepy conductor, I set sail for the Schuylkill and Fairmount Park. The waning moon was bright as I debark'd near Mr. Penn's transplanted house and proceeded up Lansdowne Drive, and it shone beautifully on the white wood of Sweet Brier Mansion, a late colonial and very New-Englandish country-seat whose lawn sweeps majestically down to the river.

---

*There were at least two other fire associations, I find, with house-plates of similar size but different design.

†In Sept. 1926 I found that this house did not deserve its former distinction; the *really* oldest house (1691) being a brick gambrel-roofer not far away in the same tangle of alleys at the corner of American & Ionick Sts.

I now walkt across the park and through the Cyclopean gates of the old 1876 Centennial grounds—grey dawn overtaking the moonlight as I pass'd famous Horticultural Hall. It was definitely daylight when I climb'd George's Hill, and great bars of fire streakt the sky as I surmounted the crest and beheld the old estate of Belmont with its 1750 manor-house and sweeping terraces descending toward the Schuylkill—beyond which the distant spires of Philadelphia stood out in an impressive panorama. This was, in more senses than one, the "high spot" of the pilgrimage. Sitting down at a table near the house, I began to write a letter home, during the course of which the flaming disc of the sun burst forth in a flood of glory.

I now cross'd a ravine, beheld a cottage which the poet Moore inhabited during his American trip of 1802, and proceeded to the northern limit of the park, where the Georgian mansion of Chamounix looks down from a pointed bluff upon limitless village-dotted valleys and the glimmering silken thread of the Schuylkill. Then taking a car, I proceeded with several changes to Germantown, the destin'd seat of my most exhaustive explorations. I stopt at the very border in order to observe the early Georgian mansion of Stenton (1727) and its delectable old-fashion'd gardens which the Indian summer had kept still in bloom.* This particular sub-district is known as Wayne Junction.

Germantown itself is an antient village, once wholly distinct from Philadelphia, but overtaken as Providence has overtaken Olneyville, or Boston Roxbury. It was founded in 1683 by Germans whose peculiar religious sects (Dunkards, Mennonites, etc.) evoked the hostility of the Lutheran majority in Germany, and at first its sole language was the German. Architecturally it copied English influences at a very early date, so that few traces of a continental heritage are apparent. It did not, however, emulate its neighbour Philadelphia; and its houses remind one rather of New-England save that they are of stone and that the larger mansions have cornices carried round the gable ends—a Pennsylvania feature of Welsh origin. The life of Germantown is still its own; and tho' Philadelphia has ingulph'd it, it continues to have its own newspapers, libraries, customs, and styles of building. It is now a very fashionable suburb; but tho' the new residents are Philadelphians, they have deferr'd to the local tradition and built stone mansions of the Germantown type instead of following the brick and marble-trimming tradition of Philadelphia. Some of these new mansions lie on splendid hilly estates, and are so closely modelled on the old Georgian lines that one can hardly distinguish them from the many really old mansions which survive on every hand. The oldest part of Germantown is its main street, now call'd Germantown Avenue. Here are endless rows of colonial houses—many with a striking history, since the place has seen vary'd and stirring events, including a prominent battle of the revolution—of every sort of architectural

---

*In Septr. 1926 I gain'd admission to Stenton & was pleas'd with the fine proportions of its simple interior. Its thick brick walls are honeycomb'd by secret passages.

pattern; the whole having occasional suggestions of New-England, and certain corners boasting a veritably Marbleheadish aspect. One goes north up a steep hill, and sees it before one—a great stone mansion atop a bluff to the left, and little white East-Greenwich-like houses on the curving slope to the right. Then the procession begins, broken by a square, a park, and a white marble town hall (in process of construction when I was there) whose curving lines suggest the old Philadelphia Maritime Exchange, and the Greek monument which in turn suggested that. In Vernon Park, where the Site and Relic Society maintains a fine historical museum in a colonial mansion, I obtain'd folders of the principal old houses; a copy of which I will endeavour to enclose with this epistle. Of the objects there describ'd, I view'd all save the Rittenhouse homestead,* Roset house, and Rock house. Particularly interesting were the Wister house, where the ends of the wooden beams project through the stonework of one of the gable ends, the Green Tree Tavern, the old German pre-Georgian manor-house of Wyck, oldest building in Germantown, the Mennonite meeting-house and churchyard, Keyser house, Washington Tavern, (a *wooden* house of perfect *New-England* gambrel outlines) the Concord School, the Peter Keyser house, the Chew mansion, (which bears revolutionary bullet marks and has statues in the yard with heads knockt off by revolutionary cannon-fire) the Lutheran school, (1740) the Academy, and so on . . . . . . but space forbids a catalogue!

At last I struck off abruptly westward, with the intention of obtaining a glance at that famous beauty-spot, the Wissahickon valley, which extends north from the east side of Fairmount Park and passes somewhat near Germantown. It is a deep, wooded gorge of prodigious scenick magnificence, at the bottom of which flows the narrow, limpid Wissahickon on its way to join the Schuylkill. Legend has woven many beautiful tales around this piny paradise with its pre-cipitous walls, and even our own Rhode-Island Quinsnicket Park must look to its laurels in comparison. A bridle-path runs close to the water, whilst half-way up the eastern bank runs a footpath—the delight of the imaginative and beauty-loving pedestrian. The whole valley is part of Philadelphia's park system.

Traversing some luxurious avenues in the Mount Airy district north of Germantown, I eventually hit upon a descending path which at once sub-merg'd me in a sea of perfumed pines. Down, down, down . . . . . interminably down past old farmhouses and bits of abandon'd stone buildings . . . . . dizzying descent like that of Ulysses, Aeneas, or Dante into Hades . . . . . then ahead a glimpse of further abysses sudden and profound—poignant green, macabre brown, and distances vast and vertiginous, with a glint and a ripple in the far depths where sight faintly merges into imagination.

I clamber'd down the whole distance, and stood beside some bubbling rapids that diversified the generally placid stream. Above me on either side

---

*In Sept. 1926 I found the Rittenhouse homestead—a captivating little mill in a deep wooded ravine tributary to the Wissahickon Valley.

were precipices reaching into the sky, and arcades of green that shut out heaven and the world alike. Down there in the hush'd verdant twilight I paus'd to ponder, and finally set out along the foot-path, whose insecure footings were now and then supplemented by steps, bridges, and railings. Midway in air—alone with the forest and the river-gods! Fancy the riot of classical memories and fantastical notions that ingulph'd a born pagan and mythologist! I am not sure yet whether it was a dream or a reality—but in any case it was ecstatically vivid, and has remain'd so thro' all the intervening two years. The part I saw was the merest fraction—yet advancing time forbade further lingering.* Regretfully I climb'd up the slope at my left and enter'd the world again—plodding back to Germantown, getting a lunch, and consoling myself with a glimpse of the old village in the twilight, with evening's first candles gently shining thro' the antient fanlights and small-paned windows.

Such was the end. With dusk at hand and cash at an end, only the railway remain'd; so boarding a car and winding up my affairs, I was soon in the Broad Street station for final farewells.

I regretted the departure, for Philadelphia has an atmosphere peculiarly suited to old gentlemen like me. A city of real American background—an integral and continuous outgrowth of a definite and aristocratick past. What a poise—what a mellowness—what a character! Yet it has a real prosperity as well as a history, and is enjoying a building wave in which the uglier Victorian structures are gradually succumbing to new houses cast in judicious reproductions of the old Georgian manner. A great old town—shall I ever forget it? Those mazes of colonial brick alleys, that red and black brickwork, those projecting eaves and corniced gables, those slanting cellar-doors and lateral footscrapers, those iron sidewalk posts, those panell'd double doors and semicircular fanlights, those zigzag brick sidewalks, those ancient needle-like steeples, those "F.A." house plates, those queer window reflectors—all these urban things, with the glamour of quiet squares and venerable churchyards where the ghost of Dr. Franklin wanders, and besides them the glorious countryside of Fairmount and the Schuylkill, where ancient manor-houses rest on their high terraces and immemorial lawns whose feet the silver waters bathe. These, and quaint Germantown, and the vale of the Wissahickon . . . .

Eheu—and now it is all miles away and two years in the past! But I shall revisit it in spirit with you, and revel in whatever account of its marvels you may please to give me afterward. Some day I, too, may see it again†—but I am old,

---

*In Sept. 1926 I explored the entire length of the Wissahickon Valley & its tributary Cresheim Creek, beholding the most magnificent scenery I ever glimpsed in my lifetime. My stock of imagination is permanently enlarged by this awesome revelation of beauty.

†I did see it again for four days in the middle of September, 1926. Stopping at the Y.M.C.A. as before, I visited the Sesquicentennial Exposition (whose reproduc-

and snugly at home in my own native region, which is more to me than any other ever cou'd be, and even more beautiful intrinsically than the Pennsylvanian realm of which I have just spoken. For me again are New-England's hilly streets and classick doorways, her Georgian steeples and her wood-fring'd plains. Yes, my son, it is without envy that I can bid you godspeed on your journey—and may the coach be good, and the roads smooth and open!

Yr obt: parent,
L. THEOBALD, JUN.

Notes

1. This letter apparently was intended for circulation to many correspondents; at the top left-hand corner HPL has written in pen: "(To James Ferdinand Morton, Esq.")" All footnotes by HPL were added after the letter was initially written.

[44]   [AHT]

10 Barnes St.,
Providence, R.I.,
June 10, 1926

O Fountain of all Wisdom:—

As for me—fricasseed Fido! but ain't me & Æsculapius ben burnin' the taller dip at both ends in some hecktick team work! On May 16 my elder aunt—Mrs. Clark—got tooken with a spasm of intercostal neuralgia; & although at no time in any danger, was confined absolutely to her bed until a day or two ago. At first, before a good nurse could be obtain'd, I had to stay over at her place day & night; going home only to collect my mail; but eventually we got a competent daughter of Hygeia[1]—a h'elderly Cockney lydy nymed Missus 'Arrrison, oo's 'ad mooch h'experience a-treatin' of sech cyses—so that all I have to do now is bring in meals, run grocery & pharmacy errands, & stick around for three hours in the h'arfternoon, w'en Mrs. 'Arrison tykes 'er h'outin'. A coupla days ago my aunt sat up for the first time, & yesterday she staged a pedestrian experiment which might be called quite successful if you don't judge it by your Pat. Ramblers. Within a month I hope she will be able to move over here.

To be continued—

Θεοβάλδος

Notes

1. The Greek goddess of health, cleanliness, and sanitation.

---

tion of an old Philadelphia street more than atoned for its general mediocrity) & observed whatever of the antiquities of the region I had overlook'd before.

[45]   [AHT]

10 Barnes St., Providence, R.I.

June 24, 1926

Magister:—

As to the rival sciences of planet-probing & pebble-picking—
pray accept my apologies for confusing you high-toned mineralogists with
that lowdown bunch of strata-sharks & fossil fans who degrade their talents
in the service of geology! I getcha, kid, & 'twon't never happen again! Never
will I trust no cheap geologist to slip me the inside stuff on quartz-heaps &
orichalcum-caches—a decision in which I am confirm'd by the strange &
inconsiderate silence of the Park Musaeum goof what I wrote to a coupla
weeks ago. Really, I'd advocate your making a motion for his expulsion from
the curator's equity association on charges of unfraternal conduct! Now I'm
gonna write the Sunday Journal question & answer department & the Pub.
Libe—& if I don't get no service out nobody, why, I'll get real mad, so there!

The only good in religion is Gothick architecture & those forms & cere-
monies which a picturesque paganism has bequeathed to us through its popish & high-church successors. Pax vobiscum! In hoc signo vinces! E pluribus
unum! Certe, nullas bananas habemus! Ita est tuus senex![1]

Hee, haw! I knew you wouldn't find Grandpa's Bad Boy[2] quite so bad!
This is the first news I've had of the little rascal's N.Y. visit, & I'm glad to
hear that he drew a full house. Your estimate of him accords with that which
many other learned & cultivated observers have expressed, & is undoubtedly
correct in essentials—though increased contact with the child & close observation of the lightning manner in which his brain grasps & digests ideas,
will probably increase your admiration for his phenomenal capacity. Rate of
reading, as you may have heard, is by some consider'd a good general index
of a man's mental calibre; & in this connexion I wou'd remind you that Alfredus Magnus is the only person of our especial "gang" who can rival yourself in that field. Of course he has his affectations (how did he wear his
hair?) & foibles; but I fancy increased age will appropriately modify these
things, leaving behind a permanent residuum of solid achievement & stable
brilliancy. I only wonder *what* the little divvle will be—musician or philosopher, artist or critic, creator or commentator? His view of the universe is, so
far as I know, very like my own; but it is engrafted upon a set of emotions &
associations so antithetical to mine, that our practical reactions to life are
virtually opposite & unrelated. I can well imagine his liking New York, &
fancy he will ultimately drift there unless Chicago develops enough premature decadence & metallic sophistication to satisfy his Gallic & artistic soul.
But there is no need to worry about him—he will never be backward in performing that modern & disillusioned Whole Duty of Man—the enjoyment
of a good time in his own sweet way. Speaking of scintillant children—I
can't resist enclosing some letters (for ultimate return) from that still more

infantine phenomenon, our newborn fellow–New Englander, Edgar Davis, who has known the air of this globe only since 1908. This child is developing most precociously, but along lines infinitely more conservative, so that whilst he does not achieve the irresponsibly brilliant flights of an Alfredus, he is more securely anchored & guided. I really think he can be definitely classed among the very few genuine super-babes of the amateur circle—filling out a shining triangle of which only Galpinius & Little Belknap are authentick fellows. I am glad to find such an incandescent specimen in good old New England—& with the old colonial blood flowing unmixed in his Yankee veins. Talman isn't quite such a soaring comet as these young marvels; but he's a damned fine boy, & will make a thoroughly pleasing companion. I've told him to drop in on you at the Paterson library. Glad China is still mitigating the sordidness of 4th Ave., & that the Dench outfit is so happily transplanted. But for gawd's sake, what malign fate hath caused the amiable Did-he-Was to live (or die down) with such melancholy literalism to the pasttense implications of his name? Eheu! But no doubt Sir Thomas Tryout (obiit MDCCCCXXI) will mitigate that loneliness which such an old-time amateur would doubtless experience if uncompanion'd in the Elysian groves. R. I. P.![3] If Samuelus hath already forgotten the current feud, let us hope that T. Ortonius Vraestus[4] will soon follow suit. That circumstance, coupled with the restoration of an undivided McNeilism through the Passing of Arthur to Ft. Dearborn, would quite unify (for the nonce) the rifted convocations of our cholerick & temperamental circle![5]

Well—that's that. Better & worser halves unite in cordial greetings & the latter has the honour to subscribe himself as

Yr oblig'd & obt Servt

Θεοβάλδος

Notes

1. The series starts with the Christ's greeting to the apostles from the gospel of John, "Peace be with you," and is followed by the phrase Constantine I adopted as a motto ("with this sign you shall conquer") after his vision of a chi rho on the sky just before the Battle of Milvian Bridge against Maxentius on 12 October 312. *E pluribus unum* ("Out of the many, one") is from the Seal of the United States; *Certe . . .* means "Yes, we have no bananas!"; *Ita est tuus senex!* means "So's your old man!" Each Latin expression becomes increasingly less ecclesiastical and more mocking.

2. Alfred Galpin.

3. See HPL's elegy "Sir Thomas Tryout: Died Nov. 15, 1921" (*Tryout*, December 1921; *AT* 147–49).

4. HPL's Latinized rendering of Vrest Orton's name.

5. For the schism in the Kalem Club, see letter 33n1.

[46]   [AHT]

10 Barnes St., Providence, R. I., June 28, 1926

Clarissime:—

Oscar—et tu! Gawd, but what is left to me in life! That's the darn trouble of growing old—all one's old pals start croaking one after the other, till the only place a bimbo can feel at home is in the cemetery. This very second I'm dropping a black-border'd card to the bereaved neighbour; asking for the SL & RK Elegies, & adding a less ambitious but equally sincere tribute worded thus:

> Damn'd be this harsh mechanick age
> That whirls us fast & faster,
> And swallows with Sabazian rage
> Nine lives in one disaster.

> I take my quill with sadden'd thought,
> Tho' falt'ringly I do it;
> And, having curst the Juggernaut,
> Inscribe: OSCARVS FVIT![1]

Give me best to Philad[a.]—'twas a gay old burg in my day, when occupied by His Majesty's troops. Oh, boy, will I ever forget that *Meschianza?* Yuh kin see one of the tickets up in the Hist. Society at the cor. of XIII & Locust.

Yr. oblig'd obt Servt

Θεοβάλδος

Notes

1. Loveman's elegy on Oscar (a cat owned by a neighbor of George Kirk) was "Oscar Redivivus" (in *Out of the Immortal Night* 111); Kleiner's was "On a Favorite Cat: Killed by an Automobile" (in Hart and Joshi, *Lovecraft's New York Circle: The Kalem Club: 1924–1927* 131). HPL's poem, untitled here, is titled "In Memoriam: Oscar Incoul Verelst of Manhattan: 1920–1926" in a postcard by HPL to Kirk (2 August 1926).

[47]   [AHT]

10 Barnes Street, Providence, R. I.,
August 18, 1926

Sapientissime:—

Incidentally, I have two elucidations of recent problems to offer. Firstly—that house in Newport *was* Solomon Southwick's! I got it from a book whose recency & authenticity are not to be impugned. What is more, there are strange legends about it—in connexion with the hidden gold of Captain Kidd, notwithstanding the fact that it was not built till 35 years after the bozo in question performed his aërial minuet.[1] Antient houses on the water's edge are ever subject to the inventions of a pleasing legendry. Secondly—I've found out what that motto on the street-car advertising signs means—"No yellow tickets". It ain't, as we thought, a nawsty little fling at the omnibus industry, but a cynical & sophisticated warning directed toward the motorist who rolls his own Royce. In this burg, a yaller ticket is the official notification to appear in court which a bull slips a guy w'en he's been leavin' his Detroit roller-skate hitched up to the curbstone too long; & since lex is longa whilst memoria is brevis,[2] it stands to reason that most goofs what habitually do their Christmas shoppin' in the fambly Lizzie are apt to get shot the saffron more more'n once in an epoch. Moral, cut the Socony combustion & yuh'll cut the expense account in Judge Rueckert's tastefully rococo reception-room—& the logical way to do this is to invest in the United Electrick Railway Co.'s modestly designed tokens—this way, gents, only 35¢ fer five of 'em!

And so it goes. Pardon the garrulity of old age. Just now one of life's big decisions is before me—shall I begin typing my article with this ribbon (in fair shape, but likely to fade afore I'm t'roo) or shall I be wasteful & insert a fresh one? I hate to have an abrupt change midway through my text. Well, I'll lay off an' start decidin'.

> Yr. oblig'd & obt Servt,
> Θεοβάλδος

Notes

1. Solomon Southwick (1731–1797) published the *Newport Mercury*, which championed the cause of the Revolution. HPL presumably refers to the house at 77 Third Street, built about 1760. Captain William Kidd (1645–1701) was a Scottish sailor remembered for his trial and execution (by hanging) for piracy after returning from a voyage to the Indian Ocean, believed by some to have been only a privateer.

2. The law is long, whilst memory is short. See letter 26n7.

[48]   [AHT]

Theobald Manor, Friday, Aug. 20, 1926

Magister:—

And now accept my sympathy anent moving! I've been through the mill myself four times, (1904, 1924a, 1924b, 1926) hence can speak out of a comprehending heart. And of course I realise the added labour of settling the collections. Gawd be wi' ye!

By the way—were you one of the guys whom I've questioned from time to time regarding the source of the Beacon Hill custom of having panes of *purple glass* scattered about in house windows? If so, you'll be interested to know that I've apparently tracked it down. The explanation now offer'd me is this: at the time of the erection of most of the mansions—1795–1820 or thereabouts—the finest Boston window glass was made by a firm using a new & (as it turned out) imperfect formula; so that the panes turned purple after exposure to the suns of many years. Old Beaconites, however, took kindly to the change; & accepted purple panes as a symbol of the antiquity of their abodes, so that they replaced only such as suffered breakage. There are several objections to this theory, notable among which is that which would inquire why the erroneous glass formula was used over so long a period, when its consequences must have become visible before long. But it is the only hypothesis I have seen offer'd, hence I shall accept it until I encounter a better one. Incidentally—I'd like to drag you around Old Boston some time, & see which of us can tell the other the most about the richly historick terrain cover'd. Just as a sample, here's a question: *is or is not the King's Chapel burying ground a true churchyard?* (This has a triple catch to it, so lookout!)[1]

Well—it'll be dawn soon, so that I can tell whether or not I'm going to Newport. This'll be a birthday trip for it was at nine a.m. of Aug. 20, 1890 that I swooped down like a curse upon this already accursed world. Thirty-six today! My gawd, how the years fly. Stolidly middle-aged—when only yesterday I was young & eager & awed by the mystery of an unfolding world—in the midst of the golden 'nineties, with free silver & Cuba libre & the new state house & the new station & the electrification of the cable-cars stirring up the atmosphere. 'Rah for McKinley & Hobart, (even if the latter has balled up your museum!) & the full dinner-pail![2] How I recall the old newspaper headlines, & the magazines & comick weeklies! Things aren't so piquant now. 1926! I can't believe it!

　　　Yr hble and obt Servt.

　　　　Θεοβάλδος

Notes

1. The burying ground, founded in 1630, was the first cemetery in the city of Boston. In 1686, the local Anglican congregation was allotted land in the cemetery to build a church after being unable to locate land elsewhere. See JFM to HPL, 11 September 1926; ms., JHL: "There may be a play on the difference between a 'chapel' and a church, and dispute as to whether a graveyard near or adjacent to a church is literally a churchyard, a possible question as to whether the chapel was built *after* the ground was already in use as a burying place, a question whether there was any connection between the two except an accidental juxtaposition, a question of 'consecration' of the ground or the lack of it, or God knows what else; all of which is out of my ken. I should naturally look upon it as a churchyard in the old sense of the term; but I am ignorant of the historic date or of the possible catch or the technicalities in the case."

2. Garret Augustus Hobart (1844–1899) was the 24th Vice President of the U.S., serving under William McKinley. He died in Paterson, NJ.

[49]   [AHT]

10 Barnes St., Providence, R. I.,
Septr. 27, 1926

O Unsurpassable:—

Reaching Providence at six p.m., my first act was to purchase the two varieties of Friend's Beans which you order'd. These I have now done up in a fashion I deem durable, & will upon my next excursion to the post office forward them to you: by whom I trust they may be eat with pleasure & profit.

And anyhow, so far as practical application to national policy is concern'd, these matters are wholly secondary to the one vital matter of preserving an atmosphere in which the established population can live comfortably. Really, the great question in any immigration policy is not so much the effect on the remote future as the maintenance of enough congeniality of population to save the legitimate natives of a place from feeling like strangers on their own hereditary sod. Only a damn fool can expect the people of one tradition to feel at ease when their country is flooded with hordes of foreigners who—whether equal, superior, or inferior biologically—are so antipodal in physical, emotional, & intellectual makeup that harmonious coalescence is virtually impossible. Such an immigration is death to all endurable existence, & pollution & decay to all art & culture. To permit or encourage it is suicide—as you can clearly see in that hell called New York, where a chaos of god-damned whipped Mongoloid Jew-scum has raised a stench intolerable to any self-respecting white man. Biologically, the Nordic is probably not superior to the best Mediterranean stock, or the unbroken and now almost extinct Semitic white stock; but just as the Chinese culture ought to be preserved where it is once entrenched, where the Nordic culture is once entrenched, it must be preserved.

Yours for blond Aryanism—
Θεοβάλδος

[50]   [AHT]

Monday, 1926
[late October 1926]

Incomparable Exaltation:—

Having at last attacked the long-deferr'd task—& ensconsing them in neat & identifiable files, I am imprest with the need of getting rid of the accompanying junk before I get it mixed up with something important. Accordingly I am herewith doling out the usual narcotic supply with my customary condescension. This job of classifying is something of a relief as compared with the stuff I've been doing—for know ye, I have a new David V. Bush on my hands in the person of the redoubtable wizard Houdini. This guy was in town early in the month, & rushed me to hell preparing an anti-astrological article[1] to be finished before his departure—a matter of five days; for which I received the not wholly despicable remuneration of seventy-five (yes, LXXV!!!) bucks in tangible (tho' not very crisp) greenbacks—three twenties, one ten, a two, & three ones. He says he has a devilish lot more for me to do; but just now I'm holding him up for a certainty of decent pay, so in the end he may back out. (He wants me to come to Detroit a week—where he is playing—& talk things over, but I'm sidestepping that the best I can.—Later still—I see in the paper that the poor guy has just had a collapse.)[2] At present I'm loaded down with a lot of books he's lent me for research, & a weighty list of subjects—beginning with witchcraft—which he wants tackled. Once I receive orders to go ahead on the witchcraft article, it's goodbye to the sunny world outside my scholastic cell—for it sure does take digging to satisfy that bozo! Meanwhile I am breathing while breathing is good, & am also helping honest C. M. Eddy Jr. a bit on some work he's doing for our magical taskmaster. The necromantic neo-Bush is inclined to be dissatisfied with Eddy's unaided performances, yet poor E. can't afford to lose so important a client.

As for my real recreation—oh, Boy! I took a trip last Wednesday which eclipses even our Durfeian achievement of August! You'll recall how much that western R. I. terrain reminded me of my own ancestral Foster–Coventry region. Well, Kid, this time I hit the *real thing*—taking with my younger aunt (Mrs. Gamwell) a tour intended to be the first of several through the *actual scenes* from which we are sprung, & whose spirit & atmosphere are ineffaceably stamped on the germ-plasm bequeathed to us down a long line of rustic progenitors.[3] I had previously been in that region but twice in my life; in 1896, when I spent two weeks at the colonial farmhouse of my great-uncle James Phillips, & in 1908, when I took a very casual single day's jaunt with my mother; this infrequent visiting being due to difficulties of transportation only just solved by means of one of those new-fangled motor stage-coach lines.

On this occasion we started at nine a.m. from the Eddy Street coach terminal (whar you 'n' me got the Chepachet stage) over the antient Plainfield Pike, noting in due time the historick Fenner farmhouse (1677)—homestead of one of Rhode-Island's greatest old families—& later on the region devastated to create the new Scituate reservoir. In less than an hour we reach'd the general section associated with our lineage, & were delighted with some of the doorways (simple late Georgian) around Clayville. At length we disembarked at the quaint hilltop village (with a *gorgeous* view!) oddly known as "Rice City",[4] & struck northward along a back road across the town line from Coventry into Foster, & toward the brookside hamlet of Moosup Valley, "metropolis" of our Phillips-Place-Rathbone-Tyler-&c. country.

Here I was destined to be surprised by the loveliness of the countryside. I had known before that it was pretty, but having seen it only twice,—once thirty & once eighteen years ago—I had never properly appreciated it. Now, in my old age, I was forcibly struck with its incomparably graceful lines of rolling hill

& stone-walled meadow, distant vale & hanging woodland, curving roadway & nestling farmstead, & all along the route the crystal convolutions of the upper Moosup River, crossed here & there by some pleasing rustick bridge. At one bend in the stream I paused with proper pensiveness; for there in 1848 my great-grandfather Capt. Jeremiah Phillips met an untimely end in his own mill, (now demolished) being dragged into the machinery by the skirts of his voluminous frock coat as a malign wind blew them against some wheel or belt. Whenever we enquired the way we found that our names were well known to the inhabitants, & I doubt if any person we saw was not related to us in some more or less distant fashion—such being the universal consanguinity of an antient pastoral community. Finally we beheld across the meadows at our left the distant roofs & white church belfry of Moosup Valley, & were soon descending to it past the idyllick farmhouse at the bend of the road—once the seat of Aunt 'Rushy—Jerusha Foster—who used to give candy to my mother & aunt when they came to see her back in the early 'sixties—but now occupy'd by a fashionable Providence man—one of the Nicholsons, whose mother my younger aunt knows—who has married into an old local family.

Crossing the rushing Moosup by another of those deliciously Arcadian bridges, we were soon in the pine-shaded village cemetery, where for some time the colonial slate slabs kept us busy. There were scores of our kindred there—Tylers, Howards, Fryes, Hopkinses, Rathbones, & Places—although our closest relatives all rest in private burying grounds near their respective homesteads. We now walked through the "civick centre" of the village, noting the church, schoolhouse, grange, & publick library—all of which is family 'property' through association. A distant relative—the Rev. George Kennedy—built the church & was its first pastor, whilst my grandmother's cousin Casey B. Tyler (a local writer & historian, also notary publick, town clerk, & State Senator 1850–51) left his private library to the village to form the present Tyler Free Library—which has some 5000 volumes & is annually aided by the state. The village formerly contain'd a smithy, two stores, a slaughter house, & a tannery; but commerce declin'd when the old stage route left, & the omnipresent Ford has driven out all that could support a blacksmith. Beyond the "civick centre" we climbed the hill to the old Casey Tyler house (called the "Red Store" in the 'fifties because of its colour & because of a commercial enterprise of its literary owner's) where my aunt Mrs. Clark was born, & here we were literally enchanted with the beauty of the landscape. Across the road a wooded valley dips magnificently to the lower meadows, while to the east & north are incredibly lovely vistas of stone-walled rolling pastures, clumps of forest, bits of stream, & purple ranges of hills beyond hills. The house itself, a large three-story structure, is of early nineteenth century origin; but beside it is the still intact colonial homestead of a story & a half which housed James Tyler (Casey's* father) before he built it. I told my aunt upon reaching home that she had certainly chosen an ideal spot to be born in! From there we retraced our steps to the village, this time stopping to see a cousin, Mrs. Nabby (Abigail) Tyler Kennedy, whom Mrs. Clark asked us to look up, & who lives in the oldest homestead of all—the antient Judge Tyler† Tavern whose oldest parts date back to 1729, (according to some, 1728) when William Tyler, Gent., made the region his family seat, & took up most of the land in sight. That land, call'd the "Tyler Purchase", was later divided amongst other colonial proprietors; & a hearteningly large part of it still remains in the hands of blood descendants. The region is the most truly American & wholesomely colonial I have ever seen; for there seems to be no break or alteration in the steady stream of hereditary habits & traditions which dates back to the times when Col. Thomas Parker married 'Squire Tyler's daughter & knocked the local raw recruits for the French & Indian Wars into shape on the training-field back of the old Tavern. Much of the Tavern, by the way, was blown down in the great gale of 1815; so that the house at which we stopt is really a composite, with its final form dating from 1816. The room in which we sat, however, was part of the original house; & had the immense floor-boards, exposed corner-posts, & panelled overmantel which told authentically of the early Georgian period. Our cousin, tho' only 72 years of age, is now the oldest inhabitant; & I was astonish'd at the amount of family lore she has preserv'd. She has much better genealogical records than ours, & will be a mine of information if ever I start the close research I have long plann'd. She reaches the time of William the Conqueror direct through two lines, Tyler & Foster; & believes she could do so through others with a little additional compiling. Her mother was my grandmother's closest confidante & associate in the 1840's, so that she knows as much about my particular branch as about her own. All in all, I was very glad to run across this manorial family Sibyl, with whom my immediate kindred had been wholly out of touch since the 'seventies, when she attended a seminary with my elder aunt. She was, indeed, able to unlock the present as well as the past; being custodian by right of seniority & ancestral position of all the keys in the village. Kindly enough, she took us through the old church,—where her husband's father had preach'd sulphureous damnation—the grange in which she is an active worker, & the Tyler Free Library, which her kinsman founded & of which her daughter (who now lives in my grand-uncle James

---

*The House of Casey was established in the patriarchal Narragansett Country, where large slave holding was the rule, & was connected with the great Newport house of Wanton, which gave the Province three Royal Governors & some spectacular privateersmen. The marriage of James Tyler to a Casey gives us an interesting link with the Newport Tories.
†The 'Squire Tyler of Revolutionary times was a magistrate, & in his day a formidably businesslike whipping post stood in front of the house!

Phillips' homestead where I visited in 1896) is the present librarian. The latter building is simple, but the collection is astonishingly good. I have a new respect for the taste of my bygone cousin,* whose old desk occupies a place of honour at the end of the main room. The recent library accessions are as well chosen as Casey Tyler's original private stock, & if the natives read many of them, they will be in no danger of retrograding toward a state of yokelry.

Now leaving Moosup Valley, we "clumb" another hill past "Aunt 'Rushy's" homestead (which them city folks a-stayin' thar dew keep up in right pert shape!) & enter'd the especial territory of the Places—encountering on our right the well-beloved homestead whose crayon picture by my mother you may have noticed on my wall. I had seen this twice before—in 1896 & 1908— but had really never given it the appreciation it deserves. Now, in my sunset years, I can accord greater credit to that vanish'd Place who built it—or its predecessor—, for truly, I never saw an house so intelligently adjusted to make the most of all the aesthetick features of the landscape. In front, acrost the rud, ye kin see on th' right the ascent of rocky meadow extending to the James Phillips house & later to the Job Place estate atop the hill; this slope balanc'd by a breathlessly lovely valley panorama on the left, in which the stone-wall'd meadows descend in terraces to the gleaming bends of the river, whilst the white village belfry peeps alluringly thro' embowering verdure (now turn'd to the riotous red & gold of autumn) & sets off the endless undulations of purple hills beyond. Behind the house & its attendant orchard a sparsely wooded ravine winds gently down to lower pastures, & forms a background worthy of any artist's brush. Altogether, I was prodigiously imprest with the beauty of the whole picture; & wished ardently that I might buy back the place, which pass'd from the family some half-century ago. The Vale of Tempë here finds its reincarnation, & the very birds pipe Theocritus & the Eclogues & Georgicks of Maro.[5] The house, in which my own mother & her mother & mother's father before her were born, is of the prettiest New-England farm type; & dates from a late colonial period when the larger homestead on the same site was burn'd down. It is now tenanted by the parvenu newcomers who took it fifty years ago, (anyone around Moosup Valley is a stranger & newcomer unless his family has a good two centuries of settlement there!) & has quite sadly deteriorated since our forbears had it. I can even see a marked falling-off since 1908, when I was last there. We paus'd at length in the family burying-ground, separated by a bank wall & iron gate from the roadside, & admir'd several comely skulls & cheerful cherubs—to say nothing of urns, fountains, & weeping willows—on the many slabs of slate & marble. No fragments, unfortunately, were *conveniently loose;* (I *do* want a paperweight of New-England slate instead of New-Jersey red sandstone!) tho' I was strongly

---

*Whose historical & antiquarian articles in the papers, "cutely" signed "*K. C.*" & preserved in our old family scrap books, never impressed me heavily.

tempted by an entire slab of the 1840 period, remov'd from the grave of Stephen Place, Jr. in 1903, when a Western relative erected a finer stone, & now lying against the wall at the rear of the enclosure. It would look delightful against the background of my room—say under the picture of the house—& if ever I'm around there at night with a vehicle. . . . .

Epitaphs were abundant, but I found nothing really quaint or grotesque. The rural 'squires of that region were too much in town, & too well train'd in taste at the village academies, to blossom forth with the engaging illiteracy found in other parts of New-England. Time has not been kind to the antient slate, & moss has play'd its obscuring part; so that the earliest epitaph I could read was that of my great-great-grandfather, Stephen Place, (there were endless Stephens) who died in 1817. His stone (topt by a willow weeping over an urn) reads thus:

> "The dust must to the dust return,
> And dearest friends must part & mourn;
> The gospel faith alone can give
> A cheering hope, the dead shall live."

Inane, but hardly *quaint* in the truest sense. His wife Martha, who departed this life in 1822, revels in equal inanity:

> "Hail, sweet repose, now shall I rest,
> No more with sickness be distress'd;
> Here from all sorrows find release,
> My soul shall dwell in endless peace."

We now proceeded to the old James Phillips place, scene of my 1896 visit, & here again I was astonisht by the beauty of the landscape. The antient white house nestles against a side hill whose picturesque rocks & greenery almost overhang the north gable end, while across the road is a delicious combination of hill & vale—hill to the left, with the Job Place estate & its burying ground at the top, (James Phillips, having married Job Place's daughter Jane, lies there) & to the right the exquisite "lower meadow" with its musical winding brook. The only flaw in the picture is a recent social-ethnic one—for FINNS, eternally confound 'em, have bought the old Job Place house! This Finnish plague has afflicted North Foster for a decade, but has hardly secured a real foothold in Moosup Valley, only two families marring the otherwise solid colonialism. They are seldom seen or heard—but it does make me crawl to think of these accurst peasants in the house where my great-uncle's wife was born—& tramping about an antient Place graveyard! Maybe a *hand* will reach up thro' the rocky mould some day. . . . . . . Well—after this I fancy people will be careful about how they dispose of their real estate! Entering the James Phillips house—which has not alter'd since 1896—we were welcom'd by its present inhabitants—a distant kinsman (whose mother was Christopher Place's daughter) named Bennis, & his wife, daughter of Nabby Tyler Kennedy & librarian of the Tyler Free Library. News of our presence in the region had travelled ahead of us; & I was greeted with two bygone letters of my mother's, which Mrs. Bennis had found among Uncle James' old papers in the attick! This pastoral "grapevine telegraph" (or rather, Bell Telephone) is really quite amusing—for we were heralded in advance wherever we went. Even our first casual inquiry at Moosup Valley caused us to be overtaken at the Tyler Tavern by an honest housewife bearing a newspaper cutting of my grandfather's obituary, which the village thought might be of interest! At Uncle James's place I continued some observations on the feline part of the population which I had begun in Moosup Valley, & decided that the prevalence of tailless Manx Cats was mark'd enough to constitute a distinct local feature. Evidently the breed secured a strong foothold at an early date, diffusing its blood throughout the continuously settled territory adjacent, but stopping when the distances became extreme. These uncaudal creatures are lively & graceful, & one soon forgets the handicap impos'd upon them by Nature—an handicap, indeed, which we poor featherless bipeds are not asham'd to share! The house pleas'd me as much as it did in 1896, & I envy'd afresh the rag carpets & the wealth of colonial furniture. The Dyckman cottage in New-York will illustrate the atmosphere of the place better than anything else in your immediate reach—allowing of course for the difference betwixt Dutch & New-England designs. I was permitted to revisit the corner room where I slept thirty years ago, & where I used to see the green side hill thro' the archaick small-paned windows as I awoke in the dewy dawn. Certainly, I was drawn back to ancestral sources more vividly than at any other time I can recall; & have since thought about little else! I am infused & saturated with the vital forces of my inherited being, and rebaptised in the mood, atmosphere, & personality of sturdy bucolick forbears. A pox on thy taowns & decadent modern notions—one sight of the mossy walls & white gables of true agrestick America can flout 'em all! An health to His Majesty's Province of Rhode-Island & Providence-Plantations! God Save the King!!

Later in the afternoon my good 33 1/3d cousin Bennis took us in his car to another scene of our family history—the village of Greene, in the taown of Coventry, where my grandfather establish'd himself & his enterprises in early manhood, & where his last two children (including Mrs. Gamwell) were born. He found the place a tiny crossroads hamlet call'd Coffin's Corner, but at once proceeded to build a mill, a house, an assembly hall, & several cottages for employees—finally renaming the village after Rhode Island's arch-rebel. All his edifices are still standing, (that's how we build things, Kid!) tho' some of them are diverted from their original uses. The house—a capacious Victorian affair of sixteen rooms—remains in the hands of those distant kinsfolk (the Tillinghasts, descendants of old Pardon Tillinghast who founded the Providence sea-trade in 1681) to whom it passed when my grandfather came to Providence for good in the 'seventies; whilst the mill is broken up into shops & tenements. The hall retains its pristine impressiveness; its lofty rooms forming the present home of

Ionick Lodge, the Masonick branch founded by my grandfather, & of which he was the first Grand Master. It did me good to see his picture there, enshrin'd in proper state. All the population speak of him with affection, & I was especially pleas'd to talk with those who knew him in person—the old folks like 'Squire Gardner Wood & Col. Brown, & the antient cracker-box senate in the gen'ral store, many of whose white-bearded or stubbly patriarchs worked for him some sixty year' gone. One old boy named George Scott shed actual tears of sentimental reminiscence at being confronted with Whipple Phillips' darter & gran'son!

Well, by that time it was night, and we had to take the six-twelve stagecoach home. We had had a great day, but even so had hardly scratched the surface of what we wanted to see. The territory cover'd was more Place & Tyler than Phillips or Rathbone country, & a first sight of the antient Phillips homestead (home of 'Squire Asaph Phillips (built 1750) whose marriage to Esther Whipple of Providence brought us the blood of that damn'd prophane ruffian who burn'd His Majesty's arm'd schooner Gaspee in 1772) and burying ground at Mount Vernon (near the Plainfield Pike) still lies ahead of me.* I hope to take it in before winter—but if I don't, I shall have something to live till next summer for. Anyway, I have definitely adopted the bucolick squirearchical ideal, & am already acquiring a distinctly provincial accent—such as Foster folks ought to use, although they don't seem to. Had I not renounc'd literature, I shou'd compose a pastoral poem in the heroick couplet, intitul'd "Moosup-Valley; an Eclogue."

And so it goes. Hope the gang hangs together well. Sonny tells me that honest old Mac (a rural soul after my own simple Foster heart!) reached the point of tears the other night in his defence of naive virtue against Dionysiack Lovemanism! Attaboy! The traditional picture forever! To hell with sophistication!

Yr Arcadian & agriculatural Servt—

Θεοβάλδος

Notes

1. Non-extant.

2. When Houdini took the stage at the Garrick Theater in Detroit on 24 October 1926 (his last performance), he had a fever of 104° and a case of acute appendicitis. He reportedly passed out during the show, but was revived and continued. He died at Detroit's Grace Hospital of peritonitis from a ruptured appendix on 31 October.

3. This trip inspired "The Silver Key" (1926).

4. An historic district in Coventry, RI, established in 1732.

5. The Vale of Tempe is the ancient name of a gorge in northern Thessaly, Greece, between Olympus to the north and Ossa to the south, celebrated by Greek poets as a favorite haunt of Apollo and the Muses.

---

*GOD DAMN!!! My aunt has just telephoned a relative, & finds that the place BURNED DOWN only FIVE YEARS AGO!

[51]   [AHT]

Novr. 17, 1926

Empyrean Apotheosis:—

I haven't yet attempted the task of convincing the Houdini heirs that the world needs his posthumous collected works in the best Georgian manner, but honest Eddy has gone the length of trying to collect the jack on an article for which the departed did *not* give his final & conclusive authorization, & which I consequently advised him not to write at the time! Well—I hope he gets it, for otherwise I shan't feel justified in collecting the price—in typing labour—of my aid on the text in question. Eddy is starting a typing & revising service, but he is going after such an incredibly low-grade clientele—advertising in cheap farm papers & landing a type of bucolic cretin which I never realised existed—that I can't do much to help him. The very best stuff he gets is too frankly ridiculous for any treatment at all except consolation & disillusion. Them guys is so dumb that they think the Farm Bloc is a semaphore on the Boston & Maine!

Glad to hear news of the Kalem galaxy, & hope that nice old Mac will find a proper spot to dream his naive boyhood dreams & listen to the Mikado in. Why doesn't he advertise in the *Paterson Call?* I'm sure he ought to land something half decent in the end. This slum game is something a guy can stand just so long & then no more. One year, three months, & seventeen days of Clinton street fed me up plumb & plenty, & I see by the papers that even a bum like Harry Kemp the pote has had to pass up the ratteries of Manhattan's exotick eastside.[1] How Kirk manages to hold out in that XV st dump is beyond me—but maybe the cats thereabouts form a redeeming & domesticating influence. Too bad Talman doesn't take universally—he has his limitations, but is withal a very pleasing youth with excellent background & breeding. Some of his tales are very clever, & I think his new witch yarn (which you may or may not have heard) is quite distinctive with the New-Netherland colour.[2] Glad to hear that everybody—or almost everybody—is hiking, & hope that on some short & slow jaunt you can get even Mac & Sonny. "When I take a walk I want to go just as slowly as I please, & enjoy the scenery . . . I don't see any use in just hurrying along so's to see how fast you can go, & that's what some people apparently do!"

As to Lazarus—he's still got to shew me that he's Dives in poetick genius![3] But I s'pose yuh never can tell. The Herm book is all right—but god damn James Joseph Moloney of the Culinary type force for working his ancestral brogue into the word *blasphemies* on page 23. Get this, 'bo—

Bow pale-checked to their blashphemies

Sink me, Sir, does he want me to get a light check'd suit to perform my genuflections in, or does he refer to the anaemic nature of the remittances secured by my toil? And to think I read them ———— ———— proofs *five* —

—— —— times! That line was O.K. in the last set except that the compound epithet was given in the good old-fashion'd way—with elision—which Samuelus went back on at the last moment. I mark'd this one thing for alteration—& see what they done to the whole —— —— line!

As to eyeshades and reversed caps—you can't convince me that either or both is or are (a) worth getting indignant or critical about, or (b) any more foolish than dozens of other accepted customs. Everything in the world outside primitive needs is the chance result of inessential causes & random associations, and there's no real or solid criterion by which one can condemn any particular manifestation of human restlessness. Only a hyper-rational or hyper-aesthetick standard of classicism could demand a direct & absolute use for everything—architects frown on needless ornament, yet the triglyphs of the very simplest order are merely fake representations of the ends of beams no longer used. None of this damn detail is worth bothering about—the only thing in the cosmos approaching a value is pleasant traditional association. Association is the real test—the degree of a thing's absorption into the imaginative life of a given race-stock or cultural stream. But of course there are mildly amusing differences in degree in the extravagance or far-fetchedness of sundry associative innovations. Taste is the sole criterion, & gentlemen don't bother with extreme crudities like the skeleton or reversed caps. However— the rabble may all go to hell uniformly crowned in such regalia for all it matters to anybody who is anybody!

Good luck with your trip—& thank heaven you can get at least the edge of God's Country in, even if it's not farther than Stamford. I never entered New England territory during my entire exile, since I couldn't have left it again after once setting foot on its hallowed soil. Sorry you can't get here till summer, but I'll rub the landscape into you then! And meanwhile whenever you say the word I'll shoot ya some more beans nourished on civilised air & soil. Thanks profusely for the ailurophilic matter—but why'n Montreal's name didn't ya send the whole thing instead of just the first page? To Gotham with it! I'm just tantalised, not fed! But anyhow, I agree with that psycho-analyst—first time I ever did agree with one of the breed, but I can't help it if they *will* be truthful now & then.

Yrs with purrs—
Theobaldvs Thomafelis

Notes

1. Harry Hibbard Kemp (1883–1960), American poet and prose writer, known (and self-promoted) as the Vagabond Poet, the Villon of America, the Hobo Poet.
2. "Two Black Bottles," revised slightly by HPL.
3. The reference is apparently to an amateur poet named Lazarus. HPL makes a pun on the biblical reference to Dives and Lazarus (Luke 16:19f.).

[52]   [AHT]

Novr. 23, 1926

Uneclipsed Right Eye on Māna-Yood-Sushāī:—

Damn! I *haven't* most of that article because the ——— ——— picture took up most of the ——— ——— page—but anyhow I don't need it, since I've known all my life a million reasons why cats are above all comparison with dogs. As for the other article—that gets a polite Kleinerian Yes? out of me, & that's about that. Very interesting, very interesting. What a coincidence that the B. P. C. has this topick just now—or did the Tribune symposium suggest it?[1] I hope you're on my side. Wonder where Kleiner stands? I have ominous fears, since he used to assume a particularly heavy aura of genteel boredom when Kirk & I would stop in some areaway about three or four a.m. & devote a couple of hours to the naive cultivation of some pleasing grimalkin's acquaintance. (Y'all 'members de cat we done interrogate up bah yo' place in Wes' 138th one mo'nin' befo' de dawn's early laht?) As for a remark or two from Grandpa on the subject—o gawd! but howja think I could ever keep down to that compass when I get started on my especial side-pardners? I aims to please, so dutifully took my pen in hand; but Pegāna love yer, the first thing I knew I'd ruined the better part of ten pages, so's I had to change the thing from a club speech to a pers'nal Providence-Paterson epistle. Well, in two pages more I wore out my mind on a poignant peroration & called it a diurnal interval in the grand style; but I'll still have to leave the abridgment question to you, & let you employ your Bushovical discrimination in picking out paragraphs for the Huns-at-Verdun act. It hadn't oughta be hard for you, since your gang runs under the trade mark of the azure crayon. All I know is that you could never give 'em that dreary dozen—they'd walk out on ya.

And so honest old Every Heverett has fell for Brookalyn & jurned the great silent majority of Erster-stewers in that undiscover'd desert of deserts wherein 169 Clinton broods ominous & repellent! Pore ole geezer![2] Unless I have succeeded better than I hope in purging my naive soul of metropolitan memories, his present cell of hibernation is somewhere on the high ground west of Prospect Park—the shabbier than genteel tract of neutral & nondescript landskip through which the Smith St. cars rattle Coneyward along 9th. Well—if he would have it so, that doesn't take me any farther from the First Baptist steeple! But it's my idea of grotesque perspective for a bozo to be in such a damn hurry that he can't wait to dig up a real dump, when he's been roosting in the same place for five years previously!

Speaking of geography—did Kirk & Loveman tell you that they are coming on a week-end trip to Providence in about three Saturdays? Gawd, but won't I put 'em through the mill! This'll be Samuelus' first peek at a real town, & Georgius hasn't seen it any too thoroughly at that. I'm doping out quite a programme for them, with the colonial hill & a trip westward for a hilltop view of the whole city on the first day, & a series of little trips to suburbs—Pawtuxet & Quinsnicket—or Bristol in place of any one of these—on the second. Or else day #2 can be given up to one resplendent exploration of colonial Newport. Too bad neither of 'em is an ice cream hound, or else I'd give 'em the revelation of their lives at Maxfield's emporium in Warren![3]

As to the capital question—after all, individualism isn't much to worry about among the majority. So long as they keep decently quiet & don't get in people's way it's best to let 'em do whatever contents 'em the most. Just kill off the demagogues, officially or informally, & let the sheep flock comfortably. So far as the sensitive few are concerned, I think that a reasonable compromise betwixt the dominant modes of the race-stock culture & the original manifestations of the individual may be held to form the most artistic course. A broad adherence to the ethnic-cultural scheme is absolutely necessary as a source of that background which furnishes points of reference, apparent interest & significance, & the illusion of values to the deeds of men, but of course an utterly literal & universal identity of opinions & perspectives would create monotony & fail to utilise the diverse temperaments with which various persons are endowed. Some individuality, then, is a keen desideratum; though taste always sets limits beyond which conduct or decoration instinctively offends. One must not be extravagant or conspicuous in one's relation to the inherited set of illusions & preferences, else harmony be violated. In general one can afford to be freer in thoughts than in deeds or decorative fruition, whilst deeds & ornaments are ever-present realities for or against a perfect aestheticism.

Now about them beans, about which I trust you will not deem my tactics too fabian. (ow!)[4] I'll get 'em, in all probability tomorrow; but may not have 'em on the trail into the desert till the end of the week. Incidentally—a careful search of your envelope & contents has so far failed to reveal any of the defraying medium alluded to in the text. Has the envelope been held up by yeggs, or did you find a significant omission on your desk after the mailing? The latter, I devoutly hope!

Glad to hear the room & Eden Musee[5] are coming along. Speaking of household woik & turl—I cleaned the brass of my telescope yesterday for the first time in twenty years. Gehenna, what a green mess! And I couldn't get it very brilliant even in the end. That's what neglect does!

Well—toodle-oo! Yr feline & obt Servt

Θεοβάλδος

Notes

1. The Blue Pencil Club was planning to conduct a discussion of the relative merits of cats and dogs, and JFM wished HPL to participate at long distance. He had sent HPL a discussion in the *New York Tribune* (unlocated), evidently featuring Carl Van Doren advocating the superiority of cats over dogs, and Albert Payson Terhune (the creator

of Lassie) vaunting dogs over cats. HPL wrote his essay, "Cats and Dogs," on the day he wrote this letter.

2. HPL refers to Everett McNeil, who had moved from Hell's Kitchen (a district on the west side of Manhattan) to Brooklyn.

3. Maxfield's was an ice cream shop in Warren, RI, where HPL enjoyed taking his friends (including JFM) for ice cream eating contests.

4. A delicious pun. *Fabian* means to use cautious, slow strategy to wear down opposition, avoiding direct confrontation; but HPL also alludes to the Latin word for bean, *faba.*

5. An allusion to JFM's museum in Paterson.

[53]   [AHT]

Sunday Night, 1926
[26 November 1926]

Incomparabilissime:—

Well—I suppose you *think* you've had a hike today, but Boy! Yuh'd orta see the one *I've* had! Yes—it's the good old Wissahickon, & I'll give yuh a shiny penny (when I get one) if you can pull a scenic stunt in New Jersey to beat it! Spoofing aside, I've never seen its equal during all the weary years of a long & disillusioned life. It's *gorge*ous—stupefying— hypnotising—but why attempt description? You'll have to see it for yourself. I did the whole thing—devoted a whole day to it—& don't think a moment wasted. What precipices—what primaeval forest—what giant monarchs of the grove—what limpid waters, singing cascades, and bubbling tributaries— what rocks and eaves—what ledges & bridges—!!!! In the more southerly portions the very earth sparkles with some shining powder that the fanciful would call star dust—but which I, as a veteran mineralogist, (I didn't say ge- ologist—but had I orta had sez petrologist?) know must come from the oxy- dising up of the neighbouring rocks—which have mica or something. Being exceedingly charitable where expense is not involved, I herewith enclose a very modest specimen as a nucleus of the Theobald Collection of American Rocks, for which I shall expect a special wing to be built at the museum.

Well—such is which. Here's hoping you get an early whack at Philadᵃ again—& don't for Pete's sake miss the Wissahickon!

Yr obt

Θεοβάλδος

[54]   [AHT]

Saturday, [December] 1926

O Voice Omniscient of Pegāna's Central Fountain:—

As to the remarks of Mr. O'Higgins *de catis canibusque*,[1] I may rejoin that they are no more or less beside the point than most remarks based upon such false arts as phrenology, psycho-analysis, palmistry, & the like. As a matter of fact, most attempts to classify cat & dog lovers exactly according to social & philosophick standing must necessarily fail because of the essential complexity of the human mind. All we may say is, that the more purely an aesthete a man is, the more likely he is to prefer cats; since the superior grace, beauty, manners & neatness of the cat cannot but conquer the fancy of any impartial observer emancipated from mundane & ethical illusions. In reality the purely aesthetick factors far outweigh the philosophick; so that although a gentleman *respects* a cat for its independence, aloofness, sufficiency, & coolness, he really *likes* the cat principally because of its peerless beauty & the superior gentleness & cleanness of its habits as compared with those of the noisy, smelly, pawing, slobbering, messy dog. It has a charm & a poise & a classic restraint which dogs totally lack, & its appeal to the imagination is tremendous—all this wholly apart from any question of affection, devotion, dependence, aloofness, superiority or inferiority. Really, no cat-lover of sound sense need appeal at all to the treacherous catch words of psychology. All that is required is to establish a standard of pure beauty without subsidiary encumbrances, & the cats have it in a walk! We love kitties, gawd bless their little whiskers, & we don't give a damn whether they or we are superior or inferior! They're confounded pretty, & that's all we know & all we need to know! But of course one must rationalise & philosophise & draw ponderous inferences for publick perusal in a world of heavy mental superfluities, so articles like mine & Mr. Van Doren's will continue to be written. With regards to Felis Long & Jeanette Kirk & Littlest Oscar when you see them, I am, Sir, Ever yr most resp & obt

Θεοβάλδος

Notes

1. Harve O'Higgins appears to be an amateur, possibly a member of the Blue Pencil Club. The term *catis* is, of course, a false Latin ablative plural for cat (more properly *felibus*).

[55]   [AHT]

Sat., Feby. 26, 1727

Magister Magistrorum:—

I shall invest your fortune with discretion & discrimination, seeing to it that nutriment of civilisation fails not to penetrate into the darkest desarts of foreign lands. It is unfortunate that the adventurous traders of the Novangli do not establish commercial posts & colonies amongst the barbarians, for the sake of such of their sons as thro' necessity dwell in the outer night. And this reminds me that there are now *two* more brands of fabae Bostonienses on the market, cook'd in what purports to be the authentick manner, which you might enjoy sampling at some period or other. One you may be able to get in the New-Netherlands, since it is a product of that Dutch merchant Van Camp. The name of this delicacy is the "Bean-Hole" bean, & it is alleg'd to be bak'd in a brick oven underground, in the fashion of the wood-cutters of the District of Maine, Province of the Massachusetts-Bay. The other is an Hatchet product, put up by the Twitchell-Champlin Co. of Maine & Boston, & I am coming to prefer this even to Friend's. The beans are darker & more brown'd, & they appear to have a good quota of molasses in them. I love molasses, for it reminds me of the old sea-trading days when the Providence docks along the Town Street (mod. S. Main) used to groan with casks & barrels from Martinique, St. Eustatius, Surinam, & Havana. In these times the little boys used to hang about the wharves to lick the casks or catch the drippings in their mouths, & many a child in that way learned enough to serve him in good stead as a judge of qualities & varieties when he went to sea or took a clerkship in one of the warehouses of the Browns, Tillinghasts, Crawfords, or Carringtons. When anyone asked the old captains & traders of about 1760 which cargo had the best molasses, they would generally point to a small figure nearby & say, "Ask that little molasses-faced Moses, he knows more than any of us!" Moses was indeed a good judge, for he was the youngest of the famous Brown brothers, John, (merchant) Joseph, (architect & scientist) Nicholas, (merchant) and Moses, (philanthropist) & later became not only a successful trader but a Quaker of prominence & the greatest philanthropist in the colony. He founded a school which survives as the leading preparatory institution in town, & in general prov'd to be one of the most useful & agreeable of our local gentry.

This reminds me that I last month visited the Ladd Observatory for the first time in twenty years, & observ'd there many things which were not present in my day. Amongst these was the telescope of Joseph Brown, made by Watkins of Charing Cross, London, & imported for use during the transit of Venus in 1769. It is a small Cassegrainian reflector, & as good today as when Brown purchas'd it.

Returning to gastronomick matters by the prefixing of a guttural consonant—did you know that there is a Friend's *brownbread* to match the beans? Whenever you like I'll get you some—it's fifteen cents per can, & pretty good. But I like *Hatchet* brownbread still better. That's twenty cents, & well worth the difference. All this discriminating knowledge of groceries is really an essential part of the accomplishments of a gentleman in this colony, where so much of the local tradition revolves around a shipping in which such commodities extensively figured. I am sure it is my South-County ancestry which makes me such a cheese-lover, for the planters of that region (who liv'd in true Virginia style with many slaves, unlike the rural gentry in other parts of New-England) did their prime business in cheese & horses. Narragansett cheeses & Narragansett pacers were known the world over till that accursed revolt of 1775 ruined everything decent in the province. I also ought to know rum, niggers, sugar, & molasses, since these were the great staples of

Providence & Newport trade. As it is, I know sugar & molasses pretty well, but fight a bit shy of the other two for reasons largely olfactory.

Enclos'd is a folder of an art exhibition which I visited (in that Colonial house on the hill in front of which I photograph'd you in 1923) on account of the local subject matter. The original of the view reproduc'd on the cover is very impressive—State House & St. John's belfry shewing very finely thro' the framework of the vernal bower—& if I had the 300 ducats demanded by the canny limner, I'd surely add to my rep as an art connoisseur by giving it a place of honour in my gallery. A still more enjoyable outing of mine was the lecture on early R. I. houses lately deliver'd at the School of Design hall by that eminent Rhode-Island architect, Norman M. Isham,[1] who superintended the installation of the panelled rooms of the American Wing of the N. Y. Metropolitan Musaeum. Isham shares with George Francis Dow (of Ipswich & Boston) of the Society for the Preservation of New-England Antiquities the distinction of being the greatest living authority on Colonial houses.[2] Well, Sir, Isham had some monstrous fine lanthorn-slides of Newport houses, & I learned from his address just about half as much again about old R. I. architecture as I ever knew before! Incidentally, he shed a great white light on something you may recall my mentioning at Newport last August. You know how *colonial* & *provincial* old Trinity is, & how different in tone & atmosphere from the other work attributed to Harrison[3]—the classic & sophisticated Redwood Library, Old City Hall, King's Chapel in Boston &c.—& how I wondered that such a polished artist (he study'd under Vanbrugh & had a hand in the building of the Duke of Marlborough's Blenheim House)[4] cou'd have produced such a locally *vernacular* work as the old meeting-house. I explain'd it by its date—1726—& remark'd that Pete must have made progress before his Redwood period (1750). Well, Sir, do you know, *Peter Harrison did not design Trinity!* All the books are wrong, & Isham got the straight dope last summer when studying the church's antecedents. *Richard Munday,* they guy who did the frankly provincial Colony House, (which we were so courteously shown over) is the real architect of Trinity, so that its rusticity stands amply explain'd.[5] And my eye for classick forms stands (or looks) vindicated. God Save the King!

You may recall that when we visited Trinity we were told of Isham's visit to London to find archetypes of the steeple. Well, he didn't find anything; & his present conclusion is that no British originals were consulted. The one probable source of the church's general plan is Christ Church in Boston, (the pseudo Old North) near where your hymnological sons won a bronze tablet by beginning to breathe, which was built in 1723 & a novel object of admiration when the raising of Trinity was undertaken. Munday (*not* Harrison—get that straight!) was a Bostonian by birth, & stood by the old home town when choosing his plan. Really, this matter of architectural authorship ought to be straightened out as much for Munday's credit as for Harrison's; for whilst Trinity is not a classick building, it is certainly a splendid example of its sort; & will add sensibly to the reputation of a man hitherto credited with only the Colony-house. But Harrison was the real artist. We simply must get into that old Jew synagogue which he built, & which Isham says possesses the finest Colonial interior in New England if not in all America—rather on the order of King's Chapel. I tried again last year, but did not succeed, although a shopkeeper said that one David, the Sexton, can be found on Long Wharf where he keeps a ship-chandlery. The new Jews of Newport are by no means so good as the old ones—Dutch & Portugese—that the Revolution drove out. Those old Levis & Mordecais had a monopoly on the local candle & spermaceti trade, introduced whaling to the colony, & contributed freely to the Newport library & learned institutions. But I guess even the new ones aren't as bad as the Mongoloid scum of New York—at least, one doesn't see so many hellish caricature faces on the streets. Peter Harrison, says Isham, is also responsible for many private mansions in Newport, probably (from internal architectural evidence) including the Vernon house (Rochambeau's Headquarters) in Clarke street, which we beheld. This latter is Isham's own discovery—but after studying the perfect British symmetry of the design, as distinguished from the more naive products of local architects, he is dispos'd to exclaim, *aut Petrus aut diabolus!*[6]

Another outing of mine was a week ago Thursday, when I heard a lecture on contemporary poetry at Eagles Hall by the Irish bard & critick Padraic Colum.[7] Paddy largely agreed with me, & is inclin'd to believe that industrial-ised & mechanised modern life with its wild notions can never find perfect expression in art—a state of decadence is to be deplor'd, & to be endur'd thro' archaistic vision & antiquarian inspiration—the way (although he didn't mention it) the barren later years of the Hellenistick aera were enliven'd by an imitative return to the archaick Greek style. Vive la decadence! "And fellow-guestship with the glutless worm!"[8]

Since last taking my Patersonic pen in hand, I am become a novelist—tho' rather in miniature, since my first product hath only 110 pages, & my second (still unfinisht) is not like to go beyond 150. The exercise in the tech-nique of the longer tale, with its more complex structure & more rigorous interconnexion of elements, is damn'd valuable practice even if (as I suspect) the present & immediate fruits of my labour incline toward the condition of n. g.-ness. Not that it matters much one way or the other![9]

And so it goes. Don't let the Flatbush vandals break up your minerals! With usual amenities, I am, Sir, Ever yr most &c.

Θεοβάλδος

Notes

1. Norman Morrison Isham (1864–1943), prominent architectural author, historian, restorationist, and professor at Brown University and the Rhode Island School of De-sign. HPL owned his *The Meeting House of the First Baptist Church in Providence: A History of*

the Fabric (Providence: [Printed at the Akerman-Standard Co.,] 1925; *LL* 465).

2. George Francis Dow (1868–1936), a leading antiquarian of his period and a member of the American Antiquarian Society and the Society for the Preservation of New England Antiquities (now Historic New England).

3. Peter Harrison (1716–1775), colonial American architect. He was born in York, England, and emigrated to Rhode Island in 1740.

4. Blenheim Palace, near Woodstock, Oxfordshire, is the seat of the Duke of Marlborough. Built from 1705 to 1725 and designed by Sir John Vanbrugh (1664?–1726), British architect and dramatist, it exemplifies Vanbrugh's heroic style of architecture.

5. Richard Munday (1685?–1739), prominent colonial American architect and builder in Newport, RI. He built several notable public buildings in Newport between 1720 and 1739, helping to modernize the city. He designed the current building of Trinity Church (1725–26).

6. "Either Peter or the Devil"—a parody of *aut diabolus aut nihil* (either the devil or nothing).

7. HPL heard Colum (1881–1972) speak on 17 February 1927.

8. Clark Ashton Smith, "The Refuge of Beauty" (1918), l. 14.

9. HPL refers to the composition of *The Dream-Quest of Unknown Kadath* and *The Case of Charles Dexter Ward*, both unpublished in his lifetime.

[56]   [AHT]

All-Fool's Day
April 1, 1927

Fabiane Maxime:—

Heighho! I laid in your four cans of ochreous-optic'd last Saturday, & will try to get the rest tomorrow. I'll apportion this final purchase amongst Friend's normal, Van Camp Bean Hole, & Hatchet beans & brownbread. I suppose you know about Friend's brownbread. It astonishes me that the Van Camp product is not sold in the provinces, for the company is a nation-wide one of very different scope from the Friend & Hatchet outfits. However, I suppose the uncivilised palate can't appreciate the real stuff; so that no doubt the Bean Hole brand is made by the Van Camps for exclusive Novanglian consumption. I must apologise for my tardiness in attending to the matter, & can only say in defence that I warn'd you good an' proper. I have been out but once since writing you, & on that occasion—as befits an Old Providence merchant prince—obtain'd the shipment of edible gold above mention'd; the four cans being all that I cou'd conveniently bring home at once in a coach with only two horses. Tomorrow I hope to complete the assembling of the shipment, Sunday I will spend in meditation upon ways & means of safe transportational encasement, & Monday I may possibly be able to entrust the consignment to a fast sloop bound for the Jerseys—but do not hope too wistfully, since all manner of delays are liable to occur in warehouses & counting-houses as busily crowded as are those of the Providence marine interests along South Water street. And speaking of the antient water-front—has Belknap shewn you the Old Providence calendar I sent him? He was so interested in an article on South Main street that I chose him to start with, but if I can get others I shall supply the rest of the gang.

As to my susceptibility to the Arctic influence—ya can't laff that wit' no Christian Science applesass, kid! It's de straight goods, as many a chance incident hath proved. For example—I went to an astronomical lecture last December on an evening that was merely moderate, but whilst I was within, the weather began doing things. I emerged under the full psychological impression that it was *not* cold, but before I'd walked five blocks I was g. d. near knockt out—breath choak'd off, eyes & nose running like Nurmi,[1] headache & nausea, & a sense of *obstruction* impeding all my muscular motions & neural coördinations. I staggered like honest old Mac before he took the pledge, (no—I *hadn't* been consuming any colonial rum made from Martineco molasses at Mr. Abbot's distil-house over against the Great Bridge)[2] & had to plunge against some intangible opposing barrier as if it had been a physical wind—& only *after* these symptoms had for some time plagu'd me, did my slow old head realise what the actual trouble was. I was mentally prepared to walk home briskly—wholly free from unfavourable or restraining anticipations—& ya see what I got! It took me about an hour to get my balance again after I reeled into the house—& I was mighty darned careful the next time I reeled out! But it ain't altogether the cold which has dictated my recent indoor programme. I've been abnormally rushed with various tasks at my desk.

As to Frederick Bligh Bond, Esq.—I thought I sub-lent you that book (lent me by Æmilius Paullus Culinarius Atholicus) when you were here—together with another crazy mess about Atlantis & Lemuria—asking you to pass it on to Little Belknap.[3] Odd error—but I suppose I must have sent the stuff directly to the child. Anyway, the book I mean was merely a wild, rambling mess telling in detail what the cutting you lately sent me told in brief—about the spirit voices of old monks which guided Bond in his discovery of the Henry VII chapel amongst the Glastonbury ruins. The book is all right now—Sonny returned it to Cook long ago—but I was curiously sure I had lent it to you last August.

About this weird tale article—I wish you'd jot down a few of the undeserved omissions you think I made, for gawd knows that additional items is sumpun what I don't want nothin' more than! I'm ludicrously unfit for handling any encyclopaedic theme, & I so warned Culinarius in the first place; but he *would* have me do the damn thing, so he's gotta stick by the results. I've just read proofs of the first two chapters—don't know yet what sort of an instalment plan he's gonna adopt for publication. I have a sort of vague & nebulous idea of expanding the thing for some mythical second edition—& in preparation for that fabulous event I'm laying by all such hints, tips, & suggestions as conveniently come in this direction without effort on my part. So shew your stuff, Kid—in 1926 I followed up the reading suggestions you gave me in 1921, hence you may expect action by 1932 or so on anything you may condescend to hand out now. It may interest you to know that in an XIth hour codicil I amplified my F. Marion Crawford paragraph by including some tolerant comments on "For the Blood is the Life" (which Leeds used to praise) and "The Dead Smile" as well as "The Upper Berth"; this enlarged horizon resulting from the perusal of a collection called "Wandering Ghosts", lent me by my newest prodigy great-grandchild, Donald Wandrei of St. Paul, Minn. This infant, by the by, is himself planning a history of weird fiction of much ampler scope than mine, for which purpose he is slowly accumulating an enormous bibliography of the Gothick & the bizarre.[4] Wandrei is a great boy—about to graduate from the University of Minnesota at the age of nineteen. You will see him this summer, for he plans to come East—at least to visit, & perhaps to settle permanently—& I have of course told him that the gang will be glad to assist in his welcoming. He says—"New York is my destiny"—but I have sought to disillusion him regarding that obnoxious fungous growth.[*] He is a genuinely weird genius who has had terrible glimpses of the black shapes & haunted void *outside.*

As to my two novelettes—O gawd! If the seventy-two pages of that article damn near done me in, whatell ya think I'd make out of the 150 odd whereof each elongated fiction consists? When I shuffle off, I wanna use KCN & not a Remington![5] Just writing this allusion to them 150 odd pages gives th' ol' head a twinge! But I done a short story lately, which is now going the rounds of the gang. Samuelus hath it now, & if ya asts him for it I fancy he won't hold out on ya. Don't be too harsh with it—it's an atmospheric episode of the Arkham cycle.[6]

As to my Theobaldic predecessor—ohell! that bimbo Lounsbury would have to spoil a perfectly good pseudonym![7] If he makes a great man outa Lewis I, it will become a mark of egotism to assume the papal title of Lewis II, so that I'll have to find another dunce to tie my antiquarian personality to! I can't use Cibber, for he was a great adapter & made Shakespeare safe for democracy.[8] Who in thunder shall I be, anyhow? I guess I'll be Lawrence Eusden II,[9] for although he was a pote-laureate (which I ain't never ben in neither *United* nor *National!*) he writ the following in his translation of the Pyramus & Thisbe incident from P. Ovidii Nasonis Metamorphoseon, & I think that lets him into Boeotia by a thumping plurality:

(Pyramus has just pulled a hara-kiri act)

"As out again the Blade he dying drew,
    Out spun the Blood, & streaming upwards flew.

---

*N. Y.—not the destiny!

So if a Conduit-Pipe e'er burst you saw,
Swift spring the gushing Waters thro' the Flaw;
Then spouting in a Bow they rise on high,
And a new Fountain plays amid the Sky."[10]

I've heard of this rehabilitation of the Elder Theobald, & have wondered just how much there was in it. I hate to think of Mr. Pope as displaying traits unbecoming in a good Catholick & well-descended (I say *descended*, for his own father was a linen-draper, so I can't say well-born) English gentleman. Perhaps Prof. Lounsbury is mistaken—one hears such terrible things about everybody these days! But I think I must read the book. One can't afford to be ignorant of one's own time! The passage you quote is an amusing example of the distorted perspective of a decadent aera. Poor Lounsbury! But at that the Elizabethan period wasn't so bad. Fact is, I freely concede that it represents the absolute high-tide of our race and culture. It hurts like hell to say it, but it seems scientifically true beyond dispute. The amount of vital energy— aesthetic, political, & military, intellectual & physical—liberated by the English people in the latter half of the sixteenth century is surely a thing of over-awing magnitude—our truest Renaissance—& I doubt if any later increase in diffusive refinement—of decorative taste in the eighteenth century & of life & manners in the middle nineteenth—can make up for the decline in sheer daemonic force of racial & national genius. God Save the Queen! My own Georgian period lacked in poetry & sublimity what it gained in clearer reason & finer sense of form, & the Victorian age lacked in force, sincerity, & decorative perception what it gained in manners & conceptions of life as a fine art. If I could create an ideal world, it would be an England with the fire of the Elizabethans, the correct taste of the Georgians, & the refinement & pure ideals of the Victorians. For the post-Victorian age I see little hope. There is indeed a return to Georgian decorative conceptions, but it is an imitative one based upon a mere pedantick appreciation. The human soul is sterile—we are weary, bored, impatient, & well on the toboggan.

I've heard—through graven heralding & Belknapic report—of the Circian plunge, & wish the fond groom a plenitude of felicity. I was wondering what the dame thought of that Augean Stable at 365 W. 15th when Sonny informed me that her lord & master had shifted operations from quiet Chelsea to the still more archaic & idyllic Greenwich; at which spot I wish him renew'd success. What does he call his joint now that he's quit Chelsea cold?[11] I'll have to get his new address, although I suppose the P. O. duly forwarded my congrats. Sonny spoke of the new SL–GK frigidity—poor old Herm, he simply can't stand the atmosphere of matrimonium! And Ortonius again! Boys, boys! Well, I'm damn glad I ain't no sensitive pote! Does Talman come around much? He looked to me like good gang material, but yuh never kin tell just who is or ain't gonna take.

Yes—Belknapius Parvulus spoke of them anthologies, & I extended the proper congratulations. If they're any good I shall ask him for the loan of 'em. They had good sense in keeping my junk out—& I think Little Farnsworth is taking a tip from them, for he don't cotton to Gran-Paw's yarns like he used tuh.[12] The latest *Weird Tales* is weird by courtesy only—nothing boosts circulation like plain, understandable, matter-of-fact weirdness that reg'lar guys can get de foist time—the least good for the greatest number, as it were. By the way—young Sandy tells me that he's thinking of breaking into the fiction game. Not that he's started, but that he feels the urge. Ring Lardner & Jawn V. A. Weaver[13] also ran.

Yours for the testimony of the rocks & the fruit of the twining legume.

Θεοβάλδος —'ε' Ευσδενς

P.S. Our young friend Scriba[14] is honour'd. A paper has written up his book as a feature & reproduced the title-page as an illustration. Thus MY name (as prefatory writer) goes down to posterity. Don't you wish you'd signed as Ed-in-chief?

Notes

1. Paavo Johannes Nurmi (1897–1973), Finnish runner, known as one of the "Flying Finns." During the 1920s, he was the best middle and long distance runner in the world, setting world records at distances between 1500 m and 20 km.

2. See Thomas W. Bicknell (1834–1925), *The History of the State of Rhode Island and Providence Plantations* (New York: American Historical Society, 1920), p. 929: "Distilling had reached Providence and stills were running on the Town Street at Abbotts on the southeast corner of Market square; Angells near Thomas street and Antrims at Smith street. Providence commerce started on the products of the stills." Cf. *The Case of Charles Dexter Ward*: "The next morning, however, a giant, muscular body, stark naked, was found on the jams of ice around the southern piers of the Great Bridge, where the Long Dock stretched out beside Abbott's distil-house, and the identity of this object became a theme for endless speculation and whispering" (*MM* 137).

3. Frederick Bligh Bond (1864–1945), British architect, archaeologist, and psychical researcher. HPL refers to his book, *The Gate of Remembrance: The Story of the Psychological Experiment Which Resulted in the Discovery of the Edgar Chapel at Glastonbury* (Oxford: Blackwell, 1918). Cf. HPL to Frank Belknap Long, [21 August 1926] (ms., JHL): "What it is is just this: the alleged report of a series of planchette seances conducted by two men, one of whom is an actual archaeologist of repute, though known to be an occultist—Frederick Bligh Bond, Director of Excavations at the highly important ruins of Glastonbury Abbey. Bond held these seances before & during his work on the Abbey, & declares that there spoke to him the spirits of certain monks who had anciently dwelt therein; (using a *mind*-language which took its outward words from his own brain, so that the archaisms were admittedly unsystematic & imperfect) directing his discoveries & leading him to find a wholly unsuspected chapel where something much

different had been looked for." The book about Atlantis and Lemuria is probably W. Scott-Elliott, *The Story of Atlantis and the Lost Lemuria* (London: Theosophical Publishing Society, 1925), which he had read c. June 1926.

4. The bibliography was never completed. The bibliography contained in *MTS* lists many of the titles in Wandrei's library.

5. Potassium cyanide. The Remington is HPL's typewriter.

6. "The Colour out of Space."

7. Thomas R. Lounsbury (1838–1915), American literary historian and critic. HPL owned his *History of the English Language* (New York: Henry Holt & Co., 1879; *LL* 546). HPL may be referring to Lounsbury's treatise *The First Editors of Shakespeare: Pope and Theobald* (1906), which rightly praises Theobald for his edition of Shakespeare. HPL chose the name for a pseudonym because Alexander Pope had satirized Theobald as a dunce in the first version of *The Dunciad* (1728). In fact, Pope was envious that Theobald's edition of Shakespeare was widely regarded as superior to Pope's own.

8. Colley Cibber (1671–1757), British actor-manager, playwright, and Poet Laureate. Pope had also skewered Cibber in the first version of *The Dunciad.*

9. Laurence Eusden (1688–1730), British poet who became Poet Laureate in 1718.

10. The passage is from Eusden's contribution to "Garth's Ovid"—a translation of Ovid's *Metamorphoses* edited by Sir Samuel Garth, to which many illustrious poets contributed. It was first published in 1717.

11. I.e., George Kirk's address. Kirk married Lucile Dvorak, to whom he had been engaged since 1924, on 5 March 1927. Even though he moved his bookshop out of the Chelsea district, he continued to call it the Chelsea Bookshop.

12. Frank Belknap Long had suggested to HPL *Not at Night,* which contained Long's "Death Waters," and *More Not at Night,* which contained his "The Sea-Thing." Both volumes were edited by Christine Campbell Thomson. Despite HPL's disparaging comment, several of his stories appeared later in the series.

13. Ringgold Wilmer Lardner (1885–1933) was an American sports columnist and short story writer best known for his satirical writings on the sports world, marriage, and the theatre. John V[an] A[lstyn] Weaver (1893–1938) was assistant book editor of the *Chicago Daily News,* author of five volumes of verse, two novels, and a play before going to Hollywood to write dialogue for the movies.

14. A pseudonym of Jonathan E. Hoag.

[57]　　[AHT]

Thursday, May 19, 1927

O Titan Anatomist of Our Planet's Skeleton:—

It hath gone! Peace flutters on columbine pinions over a mansion purg'd of profanity! But O Gawdnmontreal! You had ought to of saw my face the day after I writ you! I had the damn thing plugged, but that didn't turn the trick—& not till the next day was the infection or ulceration cleaned out. Then came surcease! But it ain't all jake yet, for I'm letting the D. D. S. give other osteological parts of my mug the once-over they've needed for the past few years, hence considerable mining & ploughing are still in progress. My next appointment is Tuesday the 24ᵗʰ . . . . . O Māna-Yood-Sushāī, do what you can to slow up the earth's rotation a bit!

Junius the VII—hot dawg! I slipped Br'er Bill a note yesterday—which was three weeks lacking a day before the important occasion, so him & Fisher ought to be able to dope out their availability in plenty good season for you.[1] I'll letcha know when & what Bill says—but why thell do you let that make any diff? I can steer ya to enough rock-patches myself—by foot & trolley—in any case to keep ya out of mischief! One of those items was pretty damn amusing to me—directing us as it did to something which is almost my own real estate! Yuh notice that dope about the Violet Hill, Manton Ave. quarry, on the land of the Providence Crushed Stone & Sand Co.? Well, said Co. is a dago named Mariano de Magistris, on whose land I've had a pathetic drop-in-the-bucket mortgage for the past twenty years! Every Feb. & Aug. the guy sends a small cheque, but never pays up—so I've come to regard him as something of an institution, & feel a very proprietary interest in his rocky freehold. It's in a bum neighbourhood—a coming wop nest—& the land'll probably be n. g. when Mariano gets all the mineralogical specimens outa it, so I'd stand a good chance of losing my modest thou if I ever had to foreclose. But it's good whilst it lasts, & I'm glad that Fate's whirligig has enabled the region to be of value to a reg'lar white man & scientist! When I lead the party thither I shall have the assured air of an old squire making the rounds of the tenantry—I've never been near the damn place as yet, & haven't the remotest idea of what it's like except that I know all that region has gone Guinea.

But before quitting the subject of Bostonium, let me express my gratification at your safe receipt of them beans. So you prefer Friend's to Bean Hole, eh? I must do some more comparative testing myself. The Hatchets cut considerable ice with me—I shall be interested to hear your report on 'em. How's the brownbread? And do you like Friend's brownbread? Of the two breads, I distinctly favour the Hatchet—us warlike Nordicks is allus strong for cold sharp steel as agin flabby & acquiescent amity. Yhaaah! Blood an' beans!

As to cold & colds—sink me, Sir, but I never said that post-lecture freezing slipped me no coryza! What it done was merely to exert on my nervous system the same effect that low temperatures always exert—jazzing things up so that muscular reactions, respiration, circulation, &c. got a bit tangled. Dizziness & headache, not sneezing & blowing, were the pleasing fruits. All this ain't nothin' *unhealthy*, I'll freely grant—but like my late dental disturbance, *I don't like it!!* I might live just as long in Labrador as in Brazil—but hell! what would I get out of it? Give me the mild equator's zone, where ice-fiends ne'er may harrow; better fifty hours of Tampa than a cycle of Point Barrow! No, kid, the infection gag won't work . . . . I ain't never yet seen the germ that can tie my breathing & moving & thinking up in warm weather with such a jinx as it can sport in zero weather. The graph of actual evidence ain't on your side, 'bo! And just as a sidelight on *hot* weather conditions—don't lay it onto mere external architecture, 'bo! Where's your memory? But three short years ago I was very emphatically of your build—yet I didn't miss any of my customary July airiness of spirit, for all the un-aërial beef & suet on my bones! Moreover—that eclipse morning occurred whilst I was still a problem for Sheraton chair-makers, yet scant comfort did my proteid integuments afford me![2] No, 'bo, I've seen the world from every avoirdupois angle, but fat or lean, it's about the same. January doesn't make a hit with my cellular tissue—be it abundant or infrequent—& July does. That's simply that, without sequel, residue, or refutation. However—the enclosed articles are all right enough. I'm with them, & always have been—in fact, I've always terrified my conservative kinsfolk by the indifference which I display toward wetness when a fifty cent pressing of my garments is not thereby involved. I slop around gaily without any rubbers, & never even pause to dry my feet. I return this medical data, since you may be able to use it in starting a good fight with somebody or other.

Well—don't let the rocks get moth-eaten, & snatch as much time off as the men higher up will let yuh! And don't forget June 6–7th.

Yours till I get further data—

Ρυμερ-Θεοβάλδος

Notes

1. William Bryant, curator of the Park Museum in Providence, and Lloyd W. Fisher of Brown University. See Appendix.

2. HPL refers to a time in the not too distant past when he weighed nearly 200 pounds.

[58]   [AHT]

May 23, 1927

Fabiane Maxime:—

Dunno whether this'll get around afore I sees ya or not—I'll take a chanct anyhow. Expect a bowed & broken man to do the honours as municipal claviger—for that damned dentist's BILL has come, & a far less welcome Bill than Bryant it is. 36 BUCKS! O GORD!

And the light diversion wherewith I'm paying it off is the most deodamnate piece of unending Bushwork I've ever tackled since the apogee of the immortal Davidius himself—the sappy, half-baked Woman's Home Companion stuff of a female denizen of once illustrious Cleveland whose pencil has hopelessly outdistanc'd her imagination.[1] Gawd bless the money-orders, but Pete sink the manuscripts!

Ah—but here's the *real* news. In a burst of unaccustomed sportmanship (before I got that 36-fish knockout from Lewis Howe Kalloch, D.D.S.) I put a shilling into a can of Friend's Yaller-Eyes *without* any preliminary assurances from curato-fabal headquarters; the concomitant pork being thus raised to the dignity of a pig in a poke. I took, as I say, this doubtful & delicious hazard, laying down my shilling with almost Brodeian unconcern. And O, BABY! Wot a kick I got! Kid, I'M SOLD! I hereby adopt Friend's Yaller as my FAVOURITE, my officially favourite bean! Man, they knock to hell anything else short of Peary & Byrd & Scott & Amundsen that ever climbed a pole! Texture! Cooking! Say, who the hell are Van Camp & Hatchet? Ast me anudder, bo! Now I wonder if the still untasted renal residue will go & eclipse this discovery? I ain't getting' none o' them till you reports, but have laid in another can of the ochreoptical.

Well—we're all set for Chewsdy. I shan't be in physical training because this Abaddon-stricken revision keeps me tied desperately to my desk, but the very force of bounding away from the damn junk will supply whatever motive enthusiasm my lack of hiking-practice will have tended to subtract. Now, rocks & weather, do you stuff!

Yours for better minerals & shorter manuscripts,

ΘΕΟΒΑΛΔΟΣ

Notes

1. Zealia Brown Reed Bishop, for whom HPL ghost-wrote several stories. The story he cites here does not appear to survive.

[59]   [AHT]

May 24, 1927

Sage Soldan of the Sev'n & Seventy Strata:—

De rebus fabalibus[1]—I have lately been conducting an exhaustive three-corner'd test of Friend, Bean Hole, & Hatchet, & believe I shall have, after all, to award the palm to your Melrose staple. The Hatchet—which I had before sampled only in conjunction with its proper (& indisputably superior) brownbread—prov'd a disappointment when consum'd independently, whilst the Van Camp product lacked a certain precision in traditional flavour. This left the field clear for Friend's, a final sampling of which confirm'd the verdict at which I had so conscientiously been arriving. Certainly, no other stannically circumscribed bean so faithfully approximates the hereditary delicacy of these colonies in all its nuances of palatal tone. I am converted. And now—my research having hitherto extended through only the standard variety—I must experiment with the Yellow Eye & Kidney modifications. What are they like? Are they baked in the ordinary fashion like their less voluminous compeers? Behold the depth of my ignorance, which seeks light from the lamp of experienced sophistication before sinking 48¢ in a can apiece of the two eíbá incognita. (They ain't got no 15¢ cans of these like they got of the reg'lar kind.)

Well—be good till p.m. of June 6th!
Yours for a populous safari of Rhodinsular erudition—
Θεοβάλδος

Notes

1. Latin for "on the matter of beans."

[60] [ALS]

June XVIII [1927]

O Cerebral Culmination:—

This won't meet thine eye for some time, since the present week marks your tantalising so-near-&-yet-so-far stunt, but I might as well go on record while the going's good. I've been meaning to plead for mercy regarding my non-transmission of the minerals (them trustees will begin to suspect you went on a lark if you can't produce the goods soon!)—& lo! 'ere's me chawnce! The fact is, O Ratiocinative Apex, that I ain't ben outa the dam house senct ya see me a week ago las' Chewsday! A fact, Kid—I walks 'ome from the King's arms at midnight after seein' ya safe within—& I doesn't step outa me door thereafter! Whyfore? *Work*—gordam it! Labour! Exertion! Toil! Travail! Application! Grinding! Chores! And then some! Yes, 'bo, it all sums itself up in one succinct & despicable word—*revision!* Just now an oasis heaves into sight, & I'm about to break gaol for the first time—payin' me younger daughter a call at the old Truman Beckwith house[1] with its glamorous yard & terraced gardens. So, Sire, you can appreciate as how I ain't had much time to hunt up wooden boxes & express offices & all that sort of rot! I shall get to all that next week—& meanwhile your pretty silicic posies are safely treasured, with plenty of care & mothballs to keep them from decaying, rusting, or evaporating. But I got some reel bad news for yuh, at that! Prepare yourself—think of my sartorial annihilation on May 24, 1925—& then buckle down to know the worst. Yes—that's it. You *have had* a grey cloth cap! I reached your immaculately plus-foured fellow-curator as soon as I could, but that wa'n't soon enough. All was over. A battered helmet, not for a moment associated with the Titan dome it once enclosed, was found in the curatorial chariot—& lo! was ruthlessly abandoned to external Nature in a totally unidentified part of Rhodinsula's undulant countryside. Eheu! I mourn with thee. I would of helpt ya ef I cud of!

Well—now that's offen me chest! Only one thing more in the way of tragedies. And that is—your voting instructions didn't get to me quick enough to make me scratch Brooklyn as con seat. Bein' a United man with a wholesome hatred of the National, I thought I'd shove the outfit into the gordamdest place I know, & so I wrote Brooklyn. If Moidel[2] brings on his Warren gang I hope the reception committee steers 'em to 169 Clinton St., where hell-fire aeternally Burns.[3] At that, though, I don't believe yuh'd ever have collected much of a crowd at the aqueous dripping. Just a few vacation-ists—but no convention. Which, incidentally, would a ben much less bore-some than a convention. Howsumever, mea alea est jacta[4]—straight Bacon ticket without even thinking up vice-prezzes—so they ain't nothin' to be done. I voted early & offen to get the dam ballots outa the way. Incidentally, I'm rather glad to hear that my Erford views are shared.[5] Not that I think the plan will ever work—but it sort of brought back my days of middle-age to dabble in controversy again as I used to do a decade or more ago. It's a hel-luva while senct I've had a reel good fight—nowadays a guy has to be above the ordinary as a damliar or damfool to get a rise outa my senescent mellow-ness; but Erford is all that, I'll ululate to the conjoinèd hemispheres! I hope he answers back—I'd kinda enjoy callin' somebody names in the antient way again, like I done in the still unpublisht Isaacsonio-Mortoniad:

> See fumbling ERFORD in confusion flit,
> And mask with Billingsgate his want of wit;
> Loud o'er the rest in raucous falsehood bray,
> Whilst grinning foes applaud the antick fray.
> Health to his goose, whose mind & quill combine
> To wake our mirth, & kill his dull design:
> Thrice-gen'rous clown, whose prattle works alone
> Against his purpose, to promote our own!

As to the early history of the United—whatnell do care? The society cannot be said to have existed until it became suitable for a gentleman's affiliation, hence everything antecedent to the familiar literary period need not be regarded! Like the funeral orators of the Roman republick, who cre-ated heroick legends to embellish the glories of the antient families they cele-brated, I shall weave a past for the United of which no gentleman need be asham'd!

Now as for Melmoth—O GAWD! O MONTREAL!! *MELMOTH!!!!* I wander————

There—that open window & that whiff of sal volatile helps matters. Let us change the subject whilst yet there is time. I trust that your recent minera-logical excursion was productive of pleasure, & that your Cantabrigian voyage will be uniformly attended by success & honours.

I peruse with interest & attention your citation concerning Messrs. Ry-mer,[6] Theobald, & Pope, & am indeed sorry that I did not adopt the patro-nymick of the learned Thomas as my standard pseudonym! What a man after mine own heart, to expose the melodramatick pretensions of that mounte-bank Bacon—or Breakspear—or whatever he called himself—& to point out so acutely the prosaick aridity of that long-winded desart of didacticism, the "Paradise Lost" of Mr. Milton![7] Ah, me, the nomenclatural opportunities which I lost in my thoughtless & ignorant days of middle age! And fancy Theobald I. degraded into dull respectability & brainfulness! Gord! Lemme hide my abashed visage amidst the frontal curls of my full-bottom'd Monmouth Cock[8]—to think that I—even I—shou'd have done aught to identify myself with the sound & the commonplace!

And so that's that. 'Ere's 'opin' for July—if ya make it around the 20th we may have a regular convention, with Little Belknap & young Wandrei from the west. ¶ Well—nex' week I'll play the poltergeist & treat yuh to a fusilade of rocks! Meanwhile riot well in Cantab! Yr obt Θεοβάλδος

Notes

1. The Truman Beckwith House (1826, John Holden Greene, architect; now the Providence Handicraft Club) at 42 College Street, only a few doors west of the final residence of HPL and his aunt Annie Gamwell at 66 College Street.

2. Jacob Moidel, Official Editor of NAPA (1926–27).

3. HPL makes a pun on the name of his landlady at 169 Clinton Street, Mrs. Burns. The joke is augmented by the fact that, for much of the period of HPL's residence there, a coal strike caused Mrs. Burns to be very stingy with the heat.

4. "My die has been cast," a reference to the Latin phrase attributed by Suetonius (as *iacta alea est*) to Julius Caesar on 10 January 49 B.C.E. as he led his army across the Rubicon in northern Italy, thereby initiating the civil war that ended the Roman Republic.

5. J. F. Roy Erford, head of the United Amateur Press Association of America, the faction of the UAPA that split with HPL's faction in 1913 over a disputed election. It is possible that Erford was now suggesting a reunification of the two factions, although by this time HPL's faction was all but defunct.

6. Thomas Rymer (1643–1713), British poet, critic, and translator, and Historiographer Royal (1692–1713).

7. Rymer harshly criticized Shakespeare in his treatise *A Short View of Tragedy* (1693). In the same work Rymer made a brief and dismissive comment on *Paradise Lost* ("which some are pleas'd to call a Poem"), but otherwise he did not discuss Milton in detail in any of his critical works.

8. The Monmouth Cock was a three-cornered hat of the 1670s and 1680s.

[61]   [AHT]

Holy (not Witches) Sabbath, 1927
[30 July 1927]

Magister Magistrorum:—

Well, here's the first of a new series of excuses for not shootin' along that quarry-plunder. Busy? O gord, send down a vacation from thy cerulean altitudes! Nothing but hell-blasted revision ever since the last of the history-making convention faded into the vista of morning—plus some weary attempts at editing those posthumous Bullen poems & some data-digging for good old Moe, who is writing a treatise on poetry & wants Grandpa's help in rounding up some odds & ends of erudition.[1] Mocrates is at the Madison Y. M. C. A. for the summer, helping Prof. S. A. Leonard edit a new series of high school classicks. He is getting to be a great authority on the finer points of educational examination, & this fall will publish the Moe Book Tests covering 100 titles common in H. S. outside reading—at three-fifty per set. Moe wanted to make the statement that the heroick dactylick hexameter was the dominant poetick measure of classical antiquity, but I'm telling him to go slow. It was the dominant epick, didactick, & satirical measure, when we consider the fact that all the great body of dramatick poesy was in iambick trimeter, (plus choral lyricks) & that the fields of the elegiack couplet & other measures included such titans as Archilochus, Theognis, Tyrtaeus, Anacreon, Alcaeus, Sappho, Alcman, Stesichorus, Simonides, Pindar, Callimachus, Catullus, Propertius, Tibullus, Horace, Ovid, Martial, & so on, we must concede that the dominance of the heroick dactyl was by no means so great as that of the heroick iambick pentameter in our own literature. Another thing Moe wanted me to do was to construct him a pentameter line all in spondees. I'm not sure it can be done, but I hammer'd out the following on a long chance—

$$\overline{}\ \underline{}\quad\overline{}\ \underline{}\quad\overline{}\ \underline{}\quad\overline{}\ \underline{}\quad\overline{}\ \underline{}$$

Thus with / weak wings / that thrush / seeks out / far lands

But that wasn't all—hell, no! The bozo wanted me to dig him up some false—& some plural—rhymes in the great poets; which same I done, although I couldn't find more than one of the *quadruple* rhymes he was so keen after—that one being *eligible* & *intelligible* in Byron's "Don Juan".[2] Another thing he wanted was a collection of ridiculously bad verse culled from the files of the amateur press—to illustrate amorphous metre, untrue statement, padding, & sentimentality. Amidst such an embarrassment of riches I scarcely knew what to select—but it occurred to me that you may have some especially juicy items in your chamber of horrors. Could you lend Moe P. J. Pendergast's "Selected Gems", or any issue of *Poet & Philosopher* which may be on hand? He'd be sure to return anything safely. And by the way—the name of his street changed, so you'd better get it down on your books as 2303 *Highland Avenue*, Milwaukee. Just now, of course, he is to be reached at the University Y. M. C. A., Madison, Wis. Of course he'll have to have "The Ballade of the City of New London"![3]

Well—the grand conclave moved at a slower pace after the sun of your presence set upon it. From Monday till Friday Wandrei & I took things rather easy, visiting the art museum & going the bookstall rounds—during which latter process I fell for a volume of Mrs. Whitman's poems at $1.50, & Scott's "Demonology & Witchcraft" (in better shape than yourn, so there!) for a single berry. Friday morning I set the kid on the right northward trial, & settled down to the beastly grind.

He had good luck on the road,[4] meeting Culinarius on time in Worcester & spending Friday eve, Saturday, & Sunday in Athol. Monday morning he set out for West Shokan, N. Y., & had some magnificent luck—including a free dinner & cigar from an affable Jew drummer in a Ford who carried him clear to the door of his destination—the farmhouse of the weird artist Bernard Dwyer. Dwyer he found to be a splendid chap—equal in every way to epistolary impression, & a logical member of our marvellously cohesive albeit geographically scatter'd gang. The Doré of West Shokan is a fascinatingly attractive giant six feet four inches tall, & of such massive build that he weighs over 200 without an ounce of fat on his hard, athletic frame. He is a renowned swimmer, strongman, & amateur woodchopper, & lives on a farm with his parents. He is twenty-nine years of age, but naive, boyish, & unspoiled—with an effervescent smile & deep, booming voice of musical mellowness. His work, as I may have said, is remarkably like Clark Ashton Smith's; & I shall be prodigiously glad to see him when he comes hither, as he means to do soon. Wandrei meant to stay a week with Dwyer, but got word from home recalling him. He is therefore on the road once more—his latest letter to me being from Albany.

Well—be good to the local rocks, & get around New England way when yuh can! Here's the usual supply of the drug—may it never pall!

Yr oblig'd & obt

Θεοβάλδος

P.S. Oh, yes—"The Colour Out of Space" appears in the new September *Amazing Stories,* just on the stands.

Just heard from Galpinius the Incomparable. He's won a prize with a musical composition of his—a s[c]herzo for string quartette, whatever that means. And Clark Ashton Smith is at last receiving favourable newpaper comment on his exhibited paintings.

Notes

1. HPL was editing John Ravenor Bullen's *White Fire* and assisting Maurice W. Moe with treatise of poetic appreciation, *Doorways to Poetry* (never published).
2. The rhyme *eligible/unintelligible* (not *intelligible*) appears in Byron's *Don Juan,* Canto I, stanza 90.
3. Presumably an amateur poem; unlocated.
4. Wandrei was hitchhiking back to St. Paul, MN.

[62]   [AHT]

Septr. 13, 1927

Focus & Pivot of the Ultimate Cosmos:—

I'll ask little Farnie what other *Weird Tales* hacks endure the filth & miasma of the neo-Babylonish area, though I don't fancy he'd answer me any more readily than he would Sonny. Grandpa doesn't stand in very thick with that outfit now that "The Dark Lore" & "The Bride of Osiris"[1] are the kind of stuff they cultivate. And they cut about thirty-six lines out of Wandrei's "Red Brain."[2] But I'll write—& will of course make the hieratick secrecy of the matter a paramount consideration. No overrunning of the ranks with penny-a-line trash! Bairdie's letter sounds very interesting & promising, but I don't know as it does much good to interfere with the vices & vulgarities of plebeians. The sooner they go to the devil, the sooner they'll die off, gordam 'em . . . . I used to believe in censorship, but now think that purity & asceticism are only for gentlefolk. Sensuality & physical living & all that assort well with the thoughtless peasantry & working classes . . . . let 'em rot! The kitty-cat article absorbed me intensely—multifarious thanks! You ought to see the tiny black fellow I had playing with me one night at Cook's last month—just old enough to be playful—a furry single handful of pep who raced with my pen as I wrote at the desk, & made delicious footprints over all my unfinished letters. Subsequently he grew drowsy, & contracted to a small sable sphere in Grandpa's lap. He wasn't Cook's property, but a neighbour imported from next door.

Why do we run to accentual iambicks, whilst the Graeco-Romans ran to quantitative dactylicks? Ast me anudder, 'bo—I weren't consulted when things was knocked into shape! Chance undoubtedly played a big part, & the nature of our speech—its different phonetic cast, emphasis on accent & ignoring of quantity—doubtless did the rest. I think we (through Norman-French) may possibly have inheriteed the iambus from the classic *drama*, whose dominant measure was (in quantitative language) a dipodic trimeter needing only a mediaeval or modern accentual scansion to become the classic iambic hexameter or 12-syllable Alexandrine of the French. Kick off an odd foot, & you have the good old British heroick—God Save the King! Them Sabbath puzzles comes from the *Prov. Sunday Journal*—the long solving times being due to our superior aesthetic evolution, which has raised us above the level of the crudely intellectual, with its gamin-like quickness of apprehension. We live deliberately & beautifully.

Congrats on the crocodiles of Franklin—undoubtedly inferior to the real Rhodinsular product.

Yrs for civick uplift—
Θεοβάλδος

Notes

1. By Nictzin Dyalhis (*WT*, October 1927) and Otis Adelbert Kline (*WT*, August–October 1927), respectively.

2. *WT*, October 1927.

[63] [ALS JHL]

Lud's Day
[October 1927?]

Minaret of Magnificence:—

Gawd be glorify'd! The Prov Pub Mark makes distant shipments itself, so one packing job is properly dodg'd! And after all, they *did* have a lower rate per dozen—20¢ lower—so the 24 came to just 8 bucks. The postage & packing were 81¢, making a grand total of $8.81. I am adding the residual 59¢ to the 2 bucks already filed for mineral packing & expressing . . . . . . but let us change the subject . . . . . . I've had too many headaches lately to want to invite another! By the way—since the Publick Market does its own packing, don't hesitate to order anything you like through me. See what a generous & accomodating guy I am when I don't have to do any work! Have you tried Friends' & Hatchet Brownbread yet? No life is complete without.

Well—I wonder how Doc Long took the returns! I recall that he was glad to see Manassa Jack come out on top last July, but maybe the different opponent changed matters this trip. I see Dempsey is trying to stage an alibi which would retroactively nullify his Firpo victory of four years ago, but guess it won't get 'im nowheres. Looks like Gene was gonna hang on a few years like Dempsey, & Willard & the Smoke done afore 'im[1]—but some younger bozo'll tell anybody from Chi that 'this-to-thatting' is easy! If you think it is, try to change *opium* to *fiend*. That stuck me, & I don't give a damn who knows it—though the R. M. Line o' Type says it can be done.[2] OPIUM—ODIUM . . . . . you do the rest. But if yuh wanna reel defence of the art, write to good old Moe. He invented it independently ten or fifteen years ago & tried it on his Appleton pupils, hence is vastly interested in the progress of this independent parallel growth.

As for almanacks—whoopee!!! I got 1859 last night, thus filling up my file *complete to date from 1839!* Now my wants are as follows:

Anything before 1805 *in any condition*

1805 if perfect*	1821 if perfect
1806	1822 " "
1807	1825
1808	1829 if perfect
1809	1831
1810 if perfect	1832
1811 " "	1833
1812 " "	1834
1813 " "	1835
1814 " "	1836
1816	1838

*this means that I have a more or less bum copy

1817
1818
1819
1820

Why you aren't interested in old almanacks is more than I can fathom. They are fascinating symbols of national continuity, & delicious bits of informal rural folklore. I suppose ya know that Prof. Kittredge of Harvard has written a book of old New England lore based on the Farmer's Almanack—its contents & history. I have this volume—you really ought to read it! It's as much a part of a New England education as Friends' Beans! It sure did give me a kick to find Dudley Leavitt's Farmer's Almanack still going after all these years. The last previous copy I had seen was of the Civil War period. But of course my main standby is Robt. B. Thomas's old reliable.[3]

Well—I s'pose you got the card from hereabouts proclaiming the sojourn of that supreme artist & heraldick authority, Wilfred Blanch Talman of Spring Valley, New-Netherlands. He blowed in Friday morning, & has since been engaged in the noble task of getting Grandpa interested in heraldry. Never before was I so conscious of my humiliating ignorance of a subject of which every armigerous gentleman ought to possess at least a smattering; & I have now resolved to make a study of the subject, employing the famous & standard treatise of Fox-Davies.[4] Friday afternoon Talman took me to the genealogical department of the publick library & shewed me how to look up the arms of various lines which converge in me, & he also was kind enough to draw several different coats of which I have possessed verbal descriptions only. This is a late date at which to rectify my ignorance, but better late than never. My god! To think that I *never before saw the coat-of-arms of the Allgoods* (my father's mother's family) *pictorially blazoned,* (though I've always had the description, which I was too ignorant to interpret) & *never had even an accurate description of the Place & Rathbone arms,* notwithstanding that the former are of my mother's mother's family, & the latter of that family—one generation farther back—of which I have a *double* strain because my two maternal grandparents were first cousins—the children of the sisters Sarah & Rhoby Rathbone, who married a Place & a Phillips, respectively. And, oh, boy! what a wallop of a kick I got out of the *Phillips* data. It seems that the British branch of the same line—the line of Rev. George Philips, who came to Salem & Watertown in 1630 on the ship *Lion*—now sports a *baronetcy!* Hot dawg! My present British cousin is *Sir* James Philipps, & he has a couple of suitable supporters to set off the familiar azure shield with the sable lion.* The way the spelling has changed is queer. It was

---

*this colour-on-colour arrangement is bad heraldry, Talman says; but the Philips grant is an ancient one, & can't be complained of at this late date. Scott describes

originally PHILIPS—one *l* & one *p*—& the Rev. George so spelt it. But George's son Samuel put in an extra *l*, & all the American branch have done so ever since. Meanwhile back home somebody stuck in an extra *p* instead, creating an amusingly wide divergence betwixt the consobrine patrynymicks.

$$\text{PHILIPS} \diagdown\diagup \begin{matrix} \text{PHILLIPS (Am.)} \\ \\ \text{PHILIPPS (Br.)} \end{matrix}$$

Well—here's my quarterings to date—as far as Talman has interpreted the various verbal directions in my records. And to think that of the whole lot I had only the Lovecraft & Phillips ones blazoned out before! But Cato learn'd Greek at 80! Now for Tyler, Perkins, Wilcox, Whipple, Hazard, Howard, Hill, Fuller, Morris, Field, Mathewson, Casey, [*not* a Mick! He was a Protestant & his name was Samuel. Came to Newport—probably from Ulster—1680.] Stanton, Garton, Tillinghast . . . . help! help! My god, here is a lifetime's work ahead of me! I guess I'll get Talman to do the work, & pay him in revision! Incidentally, he's gonna make me a swell bookplate with the 1st Baptist steeple in it![5] ¶ Glad the mineral classification is progressing well. I won't complicate the job by sending the R.I. consignment *too* soon! ¶ Yr obt
ΘΕΟΒΑΛΔΟΣ

P.S. Belknap tells me that Loveman has been in the hospital for a couple of weeks after being hit by a motor in Cleveland. Tough luck to have his whole vacation spoilt! I've just dropped him a card of sympathy, but Sonny says he's getting better now & will be in N.Y. in a week. ¶ And I s'pose you've received the names of W.T. contributors that Wright sent.

Note the *fasces* in the Rathbone arms. Viva Mussolini!

Notes

1. Jack Dempsey (1895–1983), nicknamed the "Manassa Mauler" (he was born in Manassa, Colorado), held the world heavyweight title from 1919 to 1926. He had beaten the huge Argentinean boxer Luis Angel Firpo in a match in September 1923.

a similar combination in "The Lady of the Lake["]. Of all my arms I think the *Place* one is the most artistic—simple & effective, with good contrast of colours.

He lost his title on points to Gene Tunney in September 1926. In July 1927 he beat Jack Sharkey in a bout at Yankee Stadium, setting up a rematch with Tunney on 22 September 1927. Tunney won the controversial fight, during which he was given an unusual amount of time to get up from a punch after Dempsey refused to retreat to a neutral corner. Tunney (1897–1978) held the heavyweight title from 1926 to 1928. Previously, Jess Willard (1881–1968) held the title from 1915 to 1919, when he was defeated by Dempsey. "The Smoke" is unidentified.

2. "A Line O' Type or Two" was a popular column in the *Chicago Tribune*, edited by Bert Leston Taylor until his death in 1921, followed by Richard Henry Little.

3. Robert Bailey Thomas (1766–1846) edited *The Farmer's Almanack* (sometimes titled *The Old Farmer's Almanack*) from 1793 to 1847. It continued publication until 1940.

4. Arthur Charles Fox-Davies (1871–1928), *The Art of Heraldry: An Encyclopædia of Armory* (London: T. C. & E. C. Jack, 1904).

5. The bookplate Talman designed instead had a typical Georgian doorway with fanlight.

[64]   [AHT]

Thursday
[20 October 1927]

Vertex of Valhallan Vicegerency:—

Well, Sir, I am grateful for the reputed site of New-York, in Neopalaesti-nobabylonia, & wou'd surely take advantage thereof were my finances in less tenuous condition. As it is, however, I fear I must attend the Kalem opening with my ethereal aura only, & gnash my teeth in impotence at thought of the rich colonial exhibit at the Musaeum. Thanks, incidentally, for the cutting. As for "Dracula"—bless my soul, but I never thought that anybody'd ever make a stage-play of it![1] I observe that there seem to be no *castle* scenes, & fear that Mr. Stoker would feel himself somewhat curtailed were he to mingle in the sophisticated throng of dramatick presentation. I shou'd bewail with much profundity my inability to witness this enactment; but as it is, I seem to have outlived all my response to the theatre—finding in it no imaginative nour-ishment, & never feeling really satisfied till I get the subject in visualisable form on the printed page. Therefore my periwig-rendings are less Sabazian than they might otherwise prove. If the play were in town and cost less than two bucks for a decent seat, I'd surely sop it up—but since it ain't, I feel that I can deny myself a glimpse & still live unshadowed by any cloud likely to affect the major part of my after years. Incidentally—it will be interesting to watch the developments of the shew, & see how well your predictions regard-ing its vitality are verify'd.

I was indeed apprised of the loss of our good old friend last Tuesday. It seems impossible that I shall not again behold his familiar script in my mail, nor write another of the birthday odes which had come to seem such a Feb-ruary fixture. On October 9th he sustained a fall whilst alone in his room in the morning, fracturing his hip and receiving a very considerable nervous shock. He was taken at once to the Mary McClellan Hospital in the neighbouring town of Cambridge, where for a week he bore intense pain with the greatest fortitude. So robust was his constitution that the end was a surprise to his physicians when it came—but come it did, & on the morning of Monday the 17th another well-lov'd link with the past was broken. The funeral occurred yesterday from that quiet Vista Buena, close to Dionondawa's singing spray, which he cherished so warmly in life. I yet feel confident that, but for the accident & its consequent demands on his physique, he would have rounded out a century & gone far beyond it. Upon learning of the melancholy event, I could not restrain myself from preparing some elegiack stanzas, which I have sent in triplicate to honest *Tryout*, the *Greenwich Journal*, & the Hoag family. I will append a transcript of them here, tho' sensible of the many deficiencies they possess, & conscious how inadequate they are to the utterance of profound & sincere lamentation:

AVE ATQUE VALE

— · —

To Jonathan E. Hoag, Esq.,
February 10, 1931–October 17, 1927.

Wild on the autumn Wind there comes a Crying
    As from some mountain Spirit, griev'd and lone,
And thro' the Woods resounds a deeper Sighing
    Than throbb'd last Night for Summer overthrown.

Vapours of Grief the waning Moonbeams deaden
    That glint upon Dionondawa's Spray,
And in the Steeple all the Chimes are leaden
    That toll o'er village Square and hillside Way.

The old farm Home and rustic School seem blended
    With Phantoms strange and wistful, Wave on Wave,
While on a spectral Peak there fades untended
    The last weird Campfire of the fabled Brave.

Legend and Song, and Mem'ry's ancient Treasures
    Slip half away, and glimmer more remote,
Robb'd of the Life that SCRIBA'S magick Measures
    Breath'd in their Soul, and echoed in each Note.

For he has paus'd amidst his crystal Singing,
    Melting into the Sunset's mystic Gold;

He, who with Dorick Accents sweetly ringing,
    So long had charm'd us with his Tales of old.

Poet whose Annals were themselves a Poem;
    Legate to us from brighter Years than ours;
Beacon to all who had the Boon to know him;
    Silver of Head, but wreath'd in Springtime's Flow'rs.

Gentle and kindly, blest with upright Vision,
    Valiant for Truth and Loveliness and Right;
Learned and wise with active Mind's Precision,
    And radiant with the Artist's lyric Light.

Lib'ral, yet stern when Sternness was a Duty;
    Mellow with Humour's quaint enliv'ning Glow;
Eager and tender with the Love of Beauty,
    And courtly with the Grace of long ago.

Honour's own self, whom many an Honour garnish'd;
    Scion of proud Columbia's staunchest Line;
Thrill'd with the wonder of a Youth untarnish'd;
    Aw'd by the Works of Nature's vast Design.

Minstrel of cottage Hearth and cloud-capt Mountain;
    Fond, sprightly Laureate of Days long gone;
Teller of Secrets of the woodland Fountain,
    And hopeful Prophet of a future Dawn.

Ninety-and-six the Years he bore so lightly,
    Close to the cherisht Fields that gave him Birth;
Think him not old, whose Spirit burn'd so brightly,
    One with the ageless Things of Heav'n and Earth.

Think him not old, nor think him even vanisht,
    Tho' now his well-lov'd Form be laid to rest;
Can deathless song by Azraël's Hand be banish'd,
    Or lifelong Vision cease its starward Quest?

Then let the mountain Wind bewail no longer,
    Nor lasting Gloom shroud any scene he knew;
He is still here, his olden Song but stronger,
    Fix'd in the fulgent World his Fancy drew!

Well—I suppose Grandpa Theobald will be the next! There isn't much left in
the world to interest a naive old gentleman of homely, simple tastes; & we old
folks shall quit the scene without regret.

Hot dawg! Hope I can work in another hike before my enemy the frost-soviet gets in its dirty propaganda!

Well—slip my comps to the Colem!

Yr obt

Θεοβάλδος

Notes

1. Bram Stoker's novel *Dracula* was adapted into a stage play in 1924 by Hamilton Deane. A revised version by Deane and John Balderston opened in New York on 5 October 1927.

[65]   [AHT]

Thursday, 1927
[13 November 1927]

Lightning-Rod of Lucretian Luminescence:—

Hot dawg! Add to file of memorable coincidences of history—*today*—when your bulletin breezed in—is the *exact day* set aside by advance arrangements for the grand packing orgy on *them min'ruls!* I couldn't find any decent box at the groceries—merchants run to cardboard cartons these days—so planted down ¾ of a bean for a first-class coffin at a movin'-an'-storage joint. The pallbearers delivered same only las' Saturday—& here we are, boys, all on the job! It's been my idea to put the books right in with the ites, but if it gets to S. R. O. I'll make a separate parcel of 'em.

Oh gawd—let's not talk of min'ruls & packin' till after I gits me breath! We'll advert to the matter later in these pages.

As to this 'n' thatin'[1]—I s'pose you could beat me any day when you're really in earnest, senct your fancy readin' & crossword practice has gave ya a lotta trick words what a plain, simple guy with austerely Dorick stylistic ideals can't never hope to complete wit'. But here goes, in my blunt, rustick fashion:

ARK–art–ort*–oat–hat–HAM. In five. Nex' station, Kingsport!

DARE–tare–tire–tile–till–KILL. In five. And say I sent thee thither!

AXE–are–arm–aim–him–hem–HEW. In six. . . . to the line, let the quips fall where they may!

TOWN–torn–tore–core–cote–cite–CITY. In six, & gawd save the colonial houses!

TANK–sank–sand–said–slid–sled–fled–flew–FLOW. In sight. Boy, page Vermont

Now give us sumpun hard! As to your argyments on the eddicational value of a synthetick vocab to order—well, 'bo, it's all a matter of opinion. But if yuh asts me what I call the *right* way to pick up the websterian molecules, I'll say that it's

---

*Gord bless the crossword!

to be confronted by the word in its context first, & then to look it up. That's the natural way to come on 'em—the way we do in infancy when getting the automatic dope on circumambient events. Only in this way do we get the complex sets of mental associations get fixed in our heads in the proper order—for whether yuh believe it or not, the *net effect* of our education depends a hell of a lot on the *order* in which we soak up the various component impressions. When we gain words by comin' on 'em in reading & lookin' 'em up, we've got the element of *meaning*—full meaning, with all associations, specifically & concretely illustrated in the living usage of a competent artist (that is, if we're readin' the right kinda dope) foremost & uppermost in mind; & the words in question get fixed in our mental life a thousandfold more vitally than do the miscellaneous jawbreakers hauled pompously out of Roget during our pedantick 'teens. No, 'bo, I sticks by me ground. A vocabulary's gotta *grow,* not be hand-picked, else it ain't no real vocab at all. Not, of course, but what there are *degrees* in flagrancy in the artificial practice of ashtonsmithing; but the principle's bad at best. That's the kinda ethical guy I am! I can say for sure that I not only ain't never used no new crossword acquisition noways except in crosswordin' & this 'n' thattin', but that I ain't done a bit of thesauring senct 1919 or 1920 at the latest! I've swore completely off & perched right on toppa the wagon—& I guess I've gave the gate to most of the sesquipedalians what I took in tow in less mature & classically austere ages. As for the proud & beautifully modulated intellectual indolence of Rhode-Island persons of quality—why Sir, you put me at disadvantage of raising absurd objections to my dogmata; since to refute them would require a greater amount of intellectual subtlety than it is becoming for a high-spirited & beauty-loving flaveur to exhibit! Sir, I refuse to fall into your adroit trap! I simply say—with a delicate wave of a perfectly manicured & correctly gloved hand—that you are wrong & I am right. Why? Because I say so! And that is all a gentleman can add to the matter!

Well—if I keep on writin' I won't do no packin' . . . . note how feverishly I spar for time by multiplyin' my eloquence! But here's the end of the page, & paper is costly, & I'm a poor man . . . . . so I guess your stones may get boxed, at that.

Yrs for fewer & better words—

Θεοβάλδος

Notes

1. The object of the game is to transform an *n*-letter English word to another of equal length, changing only one letter at a time. Each word must be a valid English word.

[66]   [AHT]

Monday, 1927
[17? November 1927]

Cupola of Caelestial Cerebration:—

Glad that Manhattan still offers you so many attractions. I suppose it would seem more important to me if I continued to take interest in dramatick representations; but somehow with the years I've lost all power of imbibing illusion from the stage or from oral sources generally. It's gotta be down on paper in a vivid narrative style, or I don't get it! Wandrei, incidentally, has always been that way.

In a way, crosswords do harm by cluttering up the mind with an aimless heap of unusual words selected purely for mechanical exigencies & having no well-proportioned relation to the needs of graceful discourse. Words ought to represent ideas, images, moods, & impressions with all their associations & overtones—growing naturally out of a study of the best speech & writing, & never being considered in an isolated, geometrical way. One ought to be on familiar using terms with only such as are truly expressive of his thoughts—& thoughts can't be enlarged by dictionary-scouring. Effective language springs spontaneously from one's inmost mental life & habits of perspective & expression, & ought to be a supremely unconscious phenomenon. That is why I can't bear a professed *man of letters*, who employs language as something artificial & external, apart from his daily relation to enjoyment of the universe. It's all right to know what one is about in speaking or writing—to exercise a rational censorship over one's vocabulary, syntax, & rhythm—but this oversight must be purely negative, superficial, & disciplinary; never striking at the foundations of natural association which mould one's basic vocabulary and prose manner. You can spot an *artificial* use of words any day—witness Clark Ashton Smith's extravagant & essentially devitalised polysyllables, & Loveman's groping & uncertain use of "elegant" & recherché phrases in his attempts at non-poetical prose. ("nervous engagement of the flagellated climax" . . . . . O Mung! O Ohawa!)[1] These artists overshoot the mark because they try to express themselves on Sunday in a series of symbols which has not been naturalised by week-day usage in their minds. The exquisites of the 'nineties did the same thing—& so did my old pal Sam Johnson . . . "It has not wit enough to keep it sweet . . . . It has not sufficient vitality to preserve it from putrefaction."[2] Well, Sir, that's the sort of thing a crossword vocabulary—superficially & externally acquired—tends to give an illiterate person. Better by far, say I, that he remain openly & harmoniously illiterate—the honest peasant with his quaint & time-mellowed dialect was a thousandfold less repulsive than the vulgar modern mongrel with his Hearst-&-radio fluency in stereotyped & imaginationless journalese. No, by St. Paul, I am through with all toleration of rococo jigsaw rhetorick that comes overnight from outside. I am for the honest old tradition of Swift & Steele & Addison—for the plain downright English that a man speaks every day, employ'd in its usual fashion. That, sir, is the only speech pervaded with sufficient animation with guts enough to afford any iconography of dramatick convincingness & enduring vigour to breed any picture of moving force & lasting strength!

As to Providential celerity in transverbal solution—fie, Sir, upon your modernistick & ultra-analytical cynicism! Ah, could you but grasp the inner life of the purely aesthetick & anti-intellectual mind, as cultivated throughout these Plantations from the drawing-room to the very street-corner! And where? Intellect . . . . speed . . . . gad's wounds, me dear boy, but what gentleman of a civilised colony would display such street-arab accomplishments unasham'd? Lud, Sir, but any cheap swine has these things—look at the way three-fourths of New-York is gobbled up by steerage sewage & mongoloid ghetto-spawn with ratlike sharpness & concentration! Beautiful & hereditarily disciplined emotions, Sir, are the only personal qualities which any well-born county family of Rhode-Island is willing to have its members display in publick—wherefore the veriest editor or merest reporter would scorn to affix to a speed test any figure less than double that published by the oily Orientals of Times Square & Park Row. Remember that we blond Nordicks are men of guileless strength & resistless battle-fury—blunt, simple dominance & childlike love of myth & beauty—the slow, straightforward, conquering, fighting, hunting tramplers of subtlety & calculation & gamin-like shrewdness. We thirst not for speed or cunning, but for blood, power, & beauty! That's us, 'bo! And as for the word "fan"—scrape me raw, Sir, but you must be sensible that what is call'd "fan" in Providence wou'd be accounted the meerest elegant dawdler in a decadent vortex like Manhattan! What Manhattan calls a "fan" we have only in our gaols & madhouses. Conversely, what *we* would call an elegant dawdler would in New-York be buried or placed in the morgue; the perverted sensibilities of the Manhattanese being unable to recognise signs of life in the normal reposefulness of a cultivated aristocracy.

Oh, well—nothing matters. We're all bound for the devil anyhow!

Yrs. for evangelical optimism—

Θεοβάλδος

Later

Nov. 18, 1927

Hee, haw! Howzis for a lordly disclaimer of intellectual subtlety? I stand vindicated—I'm so dumb I think an asteroid is a typographical foot-note-marker!

I suppose ya seen a'ready wot I'm talkin' about—that first thistothat in which I took five to get from the west end to the east side of Arkham. Warm collie! An' t'ree minutes after that letter had went to de box I seen de grate wite lite I had orta of saw in de first plase. ARK to HAM? Man! Ef it ain't a quartet, neat and trim, then dey ain't no briedge at all!

ARK–arm–aim–him–HAM

Just four blocks on the one-man trolley!
And min'rul transportation will be saw about presently. PROVIDENCE to PATERSON N. J. in how many?

Yrs for long shots—
Θεοβάλδος

Notes

1. Loveman, "A Note" [to *Twenty-one Letters of Ambrose Bierce*]: "In Poe one finds it a *tour de force*, in Maupassant a nervous engagement of the flagellated climax."
2. See James Boswell, *Life of Johnson* (1791), s.d. 1784: "Talking of the Comedy of The Rehearsal, he said, 'It has not wit enough to keep it sweet.' This was easy; he therefore caught himself, and pronounced a more round sentence; 'It has not vitality enough to preserve it from putrefaction.'"

[67]   [AHT]

Chewsdy
[January 1928]

Lord of Heaven, Lord of the Earth, Sun, Life of the World, Lord of Time, Creator of the Harvest, Dispenser of Breath to All Men, Animator of the Gods, Pillar of Heaven, Threshold of the Earth, Weigher of the Balance of the Two Worlds,

Greeting:—
Hallelujah! Whoopee! 'Rah! Rah! Siss, Boom, Bah!
They're off—they're off, Kid, they're off!
Two husky guys from Adams' Express have just stagger'd outen the house with the coffin, & it's comin' *collect* to your learned precincts. I done this to save bother all around. Your advance remittances have totalled $2.59 in all, whereof 75¢ hath been spent on the casket. The rest of the tariff you'll pay at the Paterson end, so that makes me owe you *$1.84* at the present writing. BUT—I'm not the kind of a guy as will bother with small change, & I'm damned if I'll go down town & get a money-order. So—not havin' no chequin' account nowheres—the best thing to do is to call it two bucks even—a bill for which same amount I hereby slips in alongside of the usual reticulated narcotick. Keep the change, 'bo—youse has earned it a-waitin—& either tip the express-man or get yourself a cigar & a coupla beers. Ouf! I grow light-beaded with relief to hev them damn stones on their way!
Well—play with your pretty marbles & thank gawd (= zeus) you got 'em at last!

Relievedly thine
Θεοβάλδος

[68]   [AHT]

Wednesday
[___ January 1928]

Colleague & Conpeer of Odin:—

Now as for this-to-thatting . . . . . . I swear with superior scorn at the short cuts adopted by our imitators! It ain't good taste, as I says now & agin, to employ such recherché words . . . . words what ain't assimilated to the vital body of our langage by ample traditional association & classical usage! I don't know what the hell an *aam* is, but I feel with all my finer instincts that it ain't nothin' no gentleman cain't hev nothin' to do with! It simply isn't in Stormonth.[1] And neither is *kile*. And I don't consider that no gentleman ain't called upon to know what ain't in Stormonth. I thanks gord I ain't one of them superficial chronic puzzle-hounds what sports a mere mechanical trick vocabulerry as ain't got no lit'ry ideas behind of it! And so the B P C is getting the craze? Keep up the good work! We'll make good Chicagoans of 'em yet! Long live the Boul Mich[2] & the Loop! I can still love dear old Chi because I ain't never ben there. That's the one way to be sure of your affection for a modern quasi-American cosmopolis. Yeh—keep it up, & you'll have even Mowry rolling his rrr. . .'s in mid-western style yet!

As to your new ones—shucks! What time has a busy man to trifle with diversions like this? Still as a trivial antidote to eternal ennui it may not be undignified to glance casually at the list, without making any serious pretensions to competitive solution.

WIT–fit–fin–FUN. In three. Haw, haw! A mathematical minimum!

SICK–pick–peck–peak–weak–weal–WELL. Cured in six.

SLOW–slot–soot–moot–most–mast–FAST. In six. Kin ya step on it still more?

POOR–boor–book–look–lock–lick–lich–RICH. Fortune made in seven.

SCAMP–scarp–scars–spars–spans–spins–shins–thins–think–thick–TRICK.

In ten—are you a subtler rascal than I am, 'bo?

Now ast me summore!

And thank Pegāna all the waste ore is dumped!

Petrifically & petrifiedly thine

Θεοβάλδος

Notes

1. James Stormonth, *A Dictionary of the English Language*. HPL preferred this dictionary to Webster's because Stormonth was an Englishman.

2. HPL uses the slang name *Boul'Mich* (for the Boulevard Saint-Michel in Paris) to refer to Michigan Avenue in Chicago.

[69]   [AHT]

May [10,] 1928

Fabiane Maxime

Well, Sir, domestick Pressure bath wrought what nothing else cou'd—& I am again in the ———— ———— metropolitan region for a brief space! The wife had to camp out here for quite a spell on account of business, & thought it only fair that I drop around for a while. Not having any snappy comeback, & wishing to avoid any domestick civil war, I played the pacifist . . . . . & here I am. The g. d. burg looks about the same to me—no novelty or kick to it. I can stand it better now that I have a real home back in the States.

Hope to see you—but of course I shall get out to Paterson (probably by 'bus) before I go back. How's the U-23[1] & the minerals?

See you later.

Yr obt servt

Θεοβάλδος

Notes

1. HPL refers facetiously to the submarine at the Paterson museum. See letter 70n5.

[70]   [AHT]

Feb. 28, 1928
City Hall, Newburyport, Mass.,
Office of Ld Timothy Dexter II[1]

To Bossy's Brawn the lofty Lid we doff:
He tells the cock-ey'd World where it gets off!

Big Boy:—

Say, have I hear about me fellow-roughnick Bossy Gillis?[2] Be yourself! Wut corner of de poorhouse boulyard d'youse t'ink I'm planted in? Yankee individuality, Kid! Tim Dexter in long pants . . . . Thoreau wit' a gasoline pump . . . . Emerson translated inter quick action & Sanduskese. Are we the reel t'ing in Brahmins? I shann't hol' nuttin' out on de well-lamped primum mobile! Lissen, bozo! Bossy was down to Rhode-Islan' las' week, speilin' some hooey at a Vet'runs-of-Furren-Wars theayter benefit at Pawtucket, & he's comin' to Prov. next Monday to shoot off his mout' somew'eres. I t'ink I'll take in de show, for I feels me culture gettin' damn rusty from hibernation. W'en he was here las' week he bawls out a newspaper guy about de small signs on our one-way strreets, w'ich same he was trundlin' his 'bus de wrong way along; but I says to'm, s'z I, "Wut t'ell! Wut kina eyes has youse birds up to Joppy* got? D'youse expeck us to print the gordam lousy signs in

———————————————

*Colloquial name for pre-Revolutionary "Shantytown" on southern rim of Newbury-

Braille? No wonder youse has gotta sport big signs up to your burg—sufferin' Chrise, if ya diden', dey woulden' nobody know dey was no burg dere!" But at dat, I'll say Bossy has gotta quitea town—cuttin' all comedy. It ain't every tank on de line what kin sport a whole business section built about 1812, nor rake uppa couple swell Jawjun steeples like the Unitarian (1800) in Pleasant street & de Presbyterian (1756) in Fed'rul street.[3] Wut's more—day got dat colonial Billy Sunday—George Whitefield—pickled in a vault under de las' named of dese two. De nearby shack w'ere he croaked is still pointed out—as is also de shebang where dat nigger-houn' Billy Lloyd Garrison set up his first abolitionist howl at de age of zero hours. I spen' a hakes of a time in Joppy las' Augus', & seen ev'ryt'ing dey was to see exceptin' future Mayor Gillis. I'm gonna go again next summer & pay my ree'specks at de Hotel-de-Ville. I noticed by de cuttin's Belknap slipt me dat Bossy was a swell hit durin' his recent visit to N'Yawk. Very nachrel, s'z' I, sect he repersents that elemut of New Englan' life what comes closest to de cultural tone of what's leff of Manhattan. I moves dat after he's t'roo wit' de mayoralty we elecks him American ambassador to N' Yawk—jus' like we appints a back nigger as Liberian minister.

As for my hibernation—I ain't ben outa the shanty senct Jany. 2, on which date I was damn near knocked out by de cold after payin' honest C. M. Eddy a call. I hadda come home in a cab, & couldn't relish my vittles for a week afterward. Cold gets at my belly as well as me breath. Just now I got so many errands dat I'm tinkin' of goin' out again. Do I need a hair-cut? Lay off, big boy! Say—have youse got any museum winder-seat cushions what needs stuffin'? Or d'youse wanna live Wild Man of Borneo for your sideshow? If I ain't de real Neanderthal-Piltdown-Java-Pithecanthropus this month, I'll smash me gilt-framed mirror! I had orta sprout whiskers to match & charge a dime admission! Speakin' of dimes, though, I wonder of honest Fernando King'll charge me extry when I patronises his emporium? He'll t'ink I'm trying to repeat history, w'en he cut off me Lord Fauntleroy curls in 1894![4]

Well, 'bo, I'm glad youse is gettin' de pebbles gradually shuffled right & proper. An' say—congrats on de archetypal U-boat![5] Wow! You slipt one over on de Smithsonian & all of dem boboes fer fair! Pilgrums'll be pourin' in from all over de civilised world, & you'll be besieged by tabloid fotygraffers ever time de anniversury of de inwention comes aroun'. How d' hell did youse manage to cop this juicy plum from de dredgers? I'll bet me brass knuckles yuh had some competition from dc othcr big bugs of mooseeum-dom! Was it because the old brine-bus heppun'd to hit de ooze in your geographick radius? Anyways, here's are congrats agen! Crank 'er up & take a joy ride under de Sound & Narragansett Bay some free afternoon. An' say, is dey any min'rul storage compartment in dat aqauatick flivver? Glad to hear

---

port, applied humorously to whole city. Derived from Joppa Flats, in N'b'p't harbour.

yuh started a snappy shell game. Hell, won't it be fun to scoop up all the chamber'd Nautili from the Passaic to the Penobscot as you scoot along the weedy sea-bottom in your 1879 model touring car! As fer voluntary contributions from distant friends & well-wishers of the enterprise—yuh gotta t'row out some tips afore us lay bimboes kin git hep to de kina mollusca youse is after. To a common guy a beach is just a beach, & that's that—pebbles is pebbles & shells is shells. Shell out on de infor, Archie, & den I'll know wot to keep peeled for w'en I meditates on de secrets of Poseidon, Shaker of Earth, from de cliffs uh Newport or Marblehead. But speakin' uh congrats— pardon a commercial guy who's a bit slow workin' up to de gran' climax. A raise! Hot dawg! Attababy! Youse deserved it years ago, but better late than never. But don't blow in your excess kale too reckluss-like. Ef ya gotta endow anything, slip a few stray grands to de institushun of amachoor jurnilsum, which they tells me is so shaky it makes a aspen leaf look like a Pillar of Hercules.

As for your comin' wanderin's—hell! you ain't got much mapped out, have youse? Here's hopin' you samves Francony—which I wanna get t'see meself nex' summer. I seen the Presidential Range from Bretton Woods, & gone up to de top of Gen. Wash's periwig on de cogwheel, but I ain't never ben to the Francony region nor saw the w. k. old party what Nat Hawthorne writ up.[6] I'd give youse a buck myself & have a tree all me own ef it wa'nt so damn near broke. I jus' let myself be wep' outa five fish by the poor old *National,* which same give a tale of woe no old-time amachoor could resist. I was agin the N. A. P. A. w'en it was proud & predatory, but now dat it's down & out I pities the damn wreck. Me, I'm a Roman guy—de kin' of a egg wut Pablius Maro shot off his mout' about in de "Æneid", we'n he says as Mussolini loves to

Parcere subjectis, et debellare superbos.[7]

Give me ree-gards to Katahdin,[8] although arter scalin' Durf I don't never get het up about dese minor foothills. After all, de big event on your program is Prov.—& here I pays ya de complimunt of givin' youse free access to all the local rock piles fer de sake of prolongin' your sojourn. Stay the limit, Kid, & gawd bless yuh. An' if he doesn't help ya back wit' your booty, I will! There! Ef dat ain't horspittality, den de ol' Virginny planters was noted for deir repulses of well-born visitors! An' uh course we gotta see ef Ma Julia's got any more flavours down Warren way.

Oy, by de way! We got this-to-thats in de *Sunday Journal* now, oney dey calls 'em "laddergrams". I knew t'would hit de East some time—but at dat it don' seem tuh be taking big like it done in Chi & Milwaukee. Youse down-Easterrrrs dunno wut's wut'—wastin' yourrrr time over dem crossworrrrd foolin's! Glad ol' Dick has saw de light—or at leas' a few of de bands of de spectrum. Keep it up, Kid! You'll get 'im trained! I recall of youse tellin' me a helluva while ago dat the *Prov. Sun. Journ* puzzles was de same like de *N' Yawk Trib's,* so I didn't send 'em for a helluva time. Den I t'ought I'd see ef dey'd changed any, so tried a sample on ya; & ya seemed to t'ink it wasn't like nuttin' else. After dat I shoots 'em along reg'lar—but if yuh says dey've got like de *Trib's* again, I'll lay off. Dese syndicates is hell. I wonder what other papers handles Tingley's bull? I won't quarrel wit' youse over de elumunt of time dis trip. Ev'ry guy has got a perfeck libbuty to hol' uppinions!

Sorry Samuelus ain't bustin' no sales records yet, but hope he hangs on & pulls t'roo good in de end. 'Cordin' to Mac de Kalem's all shot ta hell. Mr. Kirk appearantly doesn't keer to hev no meetin's at his dump, & 'taint fair to push all de assemblages on Mr. Long & his parents. And of course nobydy keers to come to Brooklyn & see Mac himself. Ev'rybuddy's down on a man as has principles & writes nothin' but children's books. . . . .

Yeah, Fall River shore did do a Trojan las' act—& I shore did imitate my fellow-decadent L. Claudius Nero Caesar Imp. Aug. Cos. &c., as I cavorted about the balconies of the Golden House, hoofin' de Charleston wit' one hand & renderin' soulful jazz on de saxaphone wit' do other, whilst I recited propper lines from Virgil his Second Book, render'd thus by Mr. Dryden:

". . . . . the cracklin Flames appear on high,
And driving Sparkles dance along the Sky;
With Vulcan's Rage the rising Winds conspire,
And near our Palace roll the Flood of Fire."[9]

Hot dawg! Now fer a reel town! Who knows but dey may be a Georgian Fall-River wort' lampin' yet! De station w'ere our coach stopp'd so long is now a matter of vapour, cinder, & ash, as is most of de circumambient landskip w'ich done so much to reconsile us to de dee-lay. Dey's publishin' books uh views of de rooins—I'll hafta get youse one. Dear ol' Fall River! Incidentally—what's de mos' inflammable part of Brookalyn, N. Y.? And how much do dey soak youse for kerosene dese days? I votes for beginnin' near de corner uh Clinton & State Streets.

Ben busier'n hell wit' bushwork from various damn simps, includin' a slick ol' bozo varously called "Danziger" & "de Castro", who claims to of did mos' of de work on dat Bierce composite, "The Monk & the Hangman's Daughter." He's got so het up over provin' his claim dat he's gave me free of charge a copy of that same book, wit' Amby's original preffus tore out & a statement of his own pasted in.[10] Good work! I'd like to fin' some guy who claims to of wrote Algernon Blackwood's dope, so's he'd slip me a free set wit' only prefatory defacements!

Ho, hum! 's a gra' life. I just tore off de calendars for March. A day early, but it seems more nearer like spring to get ridda dat gordam word "February" starin' me in de face from six surfaces in dis vicinity. Oh, hell, & I gotta break hibernation soon! It does seem kinda futile to doll up & go out even w'en it's warm enough—but day's always Jawjun houses to see! An' haircuts to get!

Yrs for the U-23—

Θεοβάλδος

Notes

1. "Lord" Timothy Dexter (1747–1806), as he was known to his contemporaries, was an eccentric American businessman and author of *A Pickle for the Knowing Ones* (1805), who dubbed himself "first in the East, the first in the West, and the greatest philosopher in the known world." He was a source for the character Obed Marsh in "The Shadow over Innsmouth."

2. Andrew Jackson ("Bossy") Gillis (1896–1965) was inducted mayor of Newburyport in January 1928. A former sailor, Gillis had several minor troubles with the police, including parking in a restricted area. In general, Gillis conducted himself in a flamboyant and undignified manner. He served six two-year terms as mayor between 1927 and 1960.

3. The First Religious Society (Unitarian) of Newburyport, founded in 1725, built its new meetinghouse (26 Pleasant Street) in 1801. The First Old South Church, 29 Federal Street, first erected in 1743, giving way in 1756 to the structure still in use today. George Whitefield (1714–1770) was an Anglican itinerant minister who helped to spread the Great Awakening in Great Britain and, especially, in the British North American colonies. Note that JFM was co-author with Franklin Steiner of *The Case of Billy Sunday* (Truth Seeker Co., 1915).

4. HPL's barber (1914 city directory) was Fernando King, at 171 Westminster.

5. The Paterson Museum had acquired *Fenian Ram* (launched in 1881), the first practical submarine, built by John Philip Holland (1840–1914), an Irish engineer who had emigrated to the U.S. The vessel had been commissioned by the Irish Fenian Brotherhood.

6. Nathaniel Hawthorne wrote about the rock formation near Franconia, NH—the Old Man of the Mountain on Franconia Notch—in "The Great Stone Face," "The Ambitious Guest," and other stories. JFM sent HPL a picture postcard from the site in August 1928. The formation collapsed 3 May 2003.

7. The full statement is: "Hae tibi erunt artes, pacisque imponere morem / Parcere subjectis et debellare superbos." (This shall be your work: to improve conditions of peace, to spare the lowly and to overthrow the proud.) Virgil, *Aeneid* 6.851–52.

8. Mount Katahdin is the highest mountain in Maine (el. 5,267 feet).

9. The worst fire in the history of Fall River, MA, occurred on 2 February 1928. It was not put out until the following day. HPL quotes from Dryden's translation of Book II of Virgil's *Aeneid,* depicting the destruction of Troy. Earlier in the paragraph he suggested that he had imitated the Emperor Nero, who was reputed to have played a lyre and sung while Rome burned in 64 C.E.

10. *The Monk and the Hangman's Daughter* was written by Richard Voss, translated into English by Adolph Danziger (Adolphe de Castro), and revised by Ambrose Bierce.

[71]   [AHT]

Nones of Sextilis
[5 June 1928]

Cloud-Cleaving Citadel of Caelestial Competence:—

Don't let your hiking togs deter you if you *do* happen to find yourself near archaick Providentium. You, Sir, look better in the roughest apparel, than I do in the most polisht & fastidious of raiment! As to outing tastes—you surely *emphasise* the element of wildness more, though I wouldn't say I don't take a keen delight in it when it comes in proper proportion. Nobody likes a good landskip better than I, & I wouldn't think of keeping my eyes shut on the top of a vista-commanding mountain. While as for deep woods & sinister ravines & rock waterfalls & intimations of caves—why, Sir, I doat upon them! But I certainly don't care for the process of walking, per se. What I am out for is *a series of visual impressions,* & the more mechanicks of locomotion is a matter of the utmost indifference to me. So far as physical sensation goes, hiking gives me none, whilst climbing produces only fatigue, ennui, & occasional dizziness. I like a trip which leaves me free for imaginative activity, & which permits me to preserve my attire in a state of approximate neatness. But gordamighty, how I envy you that fly!! How much did they soak you? I've never seen a chance for ascent less than five bucks, but have always been waiting for the price to come down. When I can get a decent ride as low as $2.50 I shall certainly go to it. They charge *ten* fish at the nearest flying field to Providence,—but then, it's *worth* twice as much as to fly over gawd's country as it is to fly over N. Y. and vicinity.

I'll look up the cawfee question at the Prov. Pub. Market as soon as possible—here's hoping I have a favourable report to make! If so, how much d'ya want? one dozen—two dozen—? I may get a can or two myself if it's still available, for now that my aunt is ill, she can't make my coffee, & I'm gordamd if I'll gother with regular coffee & coffee-grounds myself. Just now I'm cutting it out except at the Waldorf Lunches downtown. I have to be up & dressed each day to do the shopping, so I can't re-achieve my magnificent indolence & hermitage of last winter. Being down town is no event at all any more!

Oh, yes—& I'm at work on the first new story I've written in a year & a half. It is to be called "The Dunwich Horror", and is so fiendish that Wright may not dare to print it. The scene is in the upper Miskatonic Valley—far, far west of Arkham.

Well—good luck, & don't deface the scenery
Yr obt
Θεοβάλδος

[72]　　[AHT]

Tuesday, June the 26th, 1928

Clarissime:—

But all this information is not the prime purpose of my epistle. The main thing is, that my employer Mr. Cook desires me to make a request of you upon his behalf. Being a bibliophile past reclaiming, & being sensible of your nice knowledge & concern regarding the subject of reading books for the young, Mr. Cook is exceeding wishful for an essay from your pen, for the coming *Recluse,* touching on the subject of old *American readers* from any point of view you may chuse—literary, academic, sociological, antiquarian, typographical, bibliophilical or whatever else your superior scholarship & ingenuity may suggest to you. Pray do not fail him in this regard, for the literary tone of the issue depends upon yr participation.[1] I do not conceive the haste in this matter to be extreme, tho' I believe it wou'd be well to have the completed essay in the editor's hands before y[e] end of the month of July. Length is unlimited, & extended expatiation will here find a welcome deny'd those whose base instincts lead them to the remunerative doorways of Grub-Street. Preliminary inquiries & correspondence will not be discourag'd, notwithstanding that pressure of business which forces Mr. Cook to employ y[e] services of an amanuensis.

We have now upon the press that sinister book, "The Shunn'd House", whose author is said to have been driven lately to a wandering life by the black spirits which haunt him. A preface is due to arrive from a precocious child in the village of Bloomingdale, some miles north of New-York; but if the said child be not quick, the volume will be issued without his patronage & approval! We are also issuing a second edition of that Bullen book—may Jehovah have mercy upon us all![2]

With manifold assurances of my distinguisht considration,

I am, Sir,

Ever yr most oblig'd, most obt Servt,

Θεοβάλδος

Notes

1. A second issue of the *Recluse* never appeared, though HPL and others had submitted contributions for it.

2. *The Shunned House* was set in type and printed in 1928 by W. Paul Cook of the Recluse Press, but the sheets were not bound. In 1933, Walter J. Coates of the Driftwind Press was going to bind the sheets but never did so. R. H. Barlow acquired 115 copies in 1934 and 150 more in 1935, but bound only a few copies. The sheets Barlow obtained eventually were bound and distributed by Arkham House in the 1960s. Frank Belknap Long did in fact provide a preface for the book. A second edition of *White Fire* was also printed but not bound.

[73]   [AHT]

Written August 9,
Read (probably) [1] Sept. 8, 1928

Compendium of Cosmick Completeness:—

Yes—I can see where our diversities of structure, as related to the reception of impressions from the circumambient world, would naturally produce considerable diversities of taste. I like to be a spectator & have things shewn me—to be, as it were, a point tranquilly at rest whist the kinetic part of the universe flies past, unfolding its phaenomena to me with more or less of interest & variety. As for the feel of one's foot on the earth—all I can say is that I *don't* like the feel of my *left* foot on the earth or pavement or floor or any damn thing else! The g.d. thing gives me twinges when I least expect it, & some time I may let a medico see what's wrong with it—though these birds soak ya so g.d. much that I'm hoping the d. hoof will come right of itself (as the right one did a coupla years ago after similar twinges) before I get to the consultation point.

O hell! So aviation ain't come down in price even yet! Why the Pete do they wanna advertise it so much if they's gonna keep it out of the poor woikingman's reach! I'll have to hook a ride on one of these transatlantick planes. If it doesn't get across, I'll have just as good a time exploring Atlantis's weedy pinnacles & barnacled temples.

Four dozen cawfee! Gord, wot a sport! I'll look up the Pub. Mark & ask 'em to reserve ya as much, if any, as is left. But you're only posponin' the agony, like the bird with a well stocked cellar in 1919.

Finished the new story yesterday, & am now trying to type it. Ugh. Show me the goof that invented typewriters & I'll paste 'im one in the beezer that'll make Tunney's fist seem like a piece of confetti, not Irish!

Well—see ya at the '29 Convention!

Θεοβάλδος

Notes

1. Notation written at a later date either by HPL or JFM.

[74]   [AHT]

Pridie Kal. Septr. 1928
[31 August 1928]

Altitude of Achievement:—

Welcome back to the decadent world of mankind! I have appreciated all the bulletins from Nature's inaccessible fastnesses, & truly envy you a large fraction of your scenick experiences.

But oh, wot a wallop of disappointment I gotta han' youse! I lookt up Borden's Cawfee at the Pub. Mark, & lo! They ain't no more to be had. They wa'n't no reserve stock at all, & I guess your shipment of las' year was about the final gasp of the stricken industry. It sure is hell! The guy what tipped me off said that the Borden factory wrote the Prov. Pub. Market that they formed the *only* large customers for the product in all the length & breadth of this terraqueous globe, & that the manufacture could hardly be kept up to supply a single retailer. Rather an odd coincidence that Prov. should furnish the last major outlet for your favourite tipple! But anyway, the lid is on at last, & naught remains but to view your pathetically dwindling stock & mourn.

Oh, by the way—here's some *reading-book* news for a specialist in that line. *I* am about to join the immortals through the inclusion of a brief paragraph of *mine*—fully signed—in a real, honest-to-gawd reader! How's that, Kid? I don't merely *colleck* readers, 'bo—I *makes* 'em! If ya don't believe me, wait till the new series of Macmillan readers comes out in the spring, & see if I ain't got sumpun in de 7th grade one!

The secret of this incident is good old Moe—who has been busy this summer, as you may be aware, collaborating with Profs. Moffett & S. A. Leonard on a new series of Macmillan readers. When I wrote Moe of my spring & summer wanderings—in my usual travelogue style—he kinda took a fancy to my description of Sleepy Hollow, & got the idee o' using the paragraph in the reader, as a local-colour note to ol' Wash Irving's celebrated tale, as there printed. Somewhat to his surprise, both his eminent colleagues consented with some enthusiasm—so in Grandpa goes![1] This, then, is true fame. I shall live upon the tongues of babes yet unborn—*exegi monumentum aere perennius*,[2] & so on.

Oh—& I have wrote another hell-raiser. It is forty-eight pages long, & is called "The Dunwich Horror". Little Belknap & Dwyer have seen it & express approval, but I have yet to try it on *W.T.* Sonny's reaction was so pyrotechnical that he had to *draw* instead of *write* his reply—a string of grotesque pictures & exclamation-points being followed by the statement that he would write more sanely on the morrow. That is no doubt the Child's idea of stuttering on paper, bless his little heart! By the way—Sonny has *bought* Spengler's "Decline of the West", so I expect you & he will have some delicious battles when you get back to the metropolitan plague zone. Of course, Spengler is unquestionably right.

Well—I gotta quit & get back to work. Just now I'm shaping some impassion'd prose that tells the world how great is its need to get back to the pure, simple precepts of a primitive Christianity unsully'd by austere Paulinism or corrupted by pharisaical theology. Some spiel! The author for whom I am performing this amusing task is a bozo in Chicago who tacks a "Doctor" to his name.[3] I don't know whether he's a medico or a sky-pilot or a Bush! Probably the latter.

Well—regards to Garrett's Mountain!⁴
                    Yr obt
                              Θεοβάλδος

Notes

1. Harold Y. Moffett and Sterling A. Leonard, textbook writers, included "Sleepy Hollow To-day," an extract from "Observations on Several Parts of America," in a book they were preparing at the suggestion of Maurice W. Moe.
2. "I have reared a monument more lasting than brass." (Horace's prophetic assessment of the value of his poems, *Odes* 3.30.1.)
3. Possibly Lee Alexander Stone, M.D., whom HPL later chastised for not paying his revision bill. The article mentioned here is non-extant. See letter 98.
4. I.e., the Garrett Mountain Reservation, West Paterson, NJ. See HPL to Lillian D. Clark, 14 May 1928 (ms., JHL): "Afterward [Morton and I] visited some of the wild & rugged scenery of the region—a rocky, daemoniack gorge which is a waterfall at high water, & the lofty eminence of Garrett's Mountain, whence we had an unparallelled view of all the neighbouring countryside. This precipitous crag—of which you'll find a picture in the folder we sent you—is really a magnificent thing; & quite outdoes our Neutaconkanut in intrinsic grandeur. I still prefer Neutaconkanut, though; since the spectacle of outspread Providence infinitely surpasses that of outspread Paterson. Atop Garrett's Mountain is a sinister & deserted stone tower, built years ago by an eccentric & now deceased millionaire. Lower on the slope is a spreading & ambitious Norman castle constructed by the same lavish person & now used as a sanitarium."

[75]   [AHT]

Monday
[September 1928]

Culminatory Concentration of Caelestial Calosophistication:—

Even so—Borden's cawfee hath went to join its fathers. Them Bordens allus was hell for killing off their own best relations, from Lizzie down. But anyhow, Providence was the last place to form a market! We know what's what, to the very last! Here's hoping your stock will tide you over till somebody starts making a good condensed caffeine product again. As for me—I've switched to *cocoa* when I have to make the damn stuff myself, since there's a new brand (Rich's) which requires only the addition of hot water. (And for me, of course, a pound of granulated $C_2H_{22}O_{11}$) Yes—it's a helluva world!

Oh, say—before I forget it—Little Belknap wants to know if it's all right to use your name as a reference regarding our integrity in revisory matters. He thinks your curatorial dignity ought to prove a good overawing agent. For my part, I'm too haughty ever to name anybody as a reference. I am I—an English gentleman—& if anybody doesn't care to deal with me he jolly well needn't—but Sonny is slightly tainted with American democracy or Manhattan practicality, hence he wants a noble name to back up our emendatory enterprise. Not that he means to print it in our advertisements—but that he wants to quote it to prospective clients in answer to their first inquiries. I trust it's all right with you. You know we're fairly honest, at least in small matters.

And so it goes. Damn dull weather lately—how I hate the coming of autumn chill!—but before it set in I did a lot of my reading & writing amidst the sylvan & agrestick shades of Quinsnicket.

Well—mind your stones & hope for next spring!

Yr obt

Θεοβάλδος

[76] [ALS JHL]

Wednesday

[October 1928]

Heav'n-hailing Height of Hieratick Hegemony:—

I've heard tell of them Steero things,[1] but ain't never got the habit. When I take a hot drink I kinda don't want a *meat-course* effect, hence I fancy I'll stick to Rich's Cocoa in the absence of Borden's Cawfee. But tonight my aunt (who is convalescing & has just dispensed with her nurse) has insisted on making me some regular, old-fashion'd 18th century coffee with grounds & steamy odour & everything! At other times I patronise the one-arms. Only a short time ago I discovered that the Waldorf chain is owned by a real old Foster, R.I. boy—one of the ancient Blanchards who have lived in my own maternal-ancestral region for 200 years & more! Henceforward I shall give him the bulk of my gastronomick custom. Yes, Sir, even in this day of Dago barbers & Greek hash-house proprietors I have my hair cut by a 100% Scituate R.I. Yankee & get my dinners at the joint of a 100% Foster, R.I. Yankee. God Save His Majesty's Colony of Rhode-Island & Providence-Plantations!

Glad you're willing to back up the honesty of the Double-L revision service—the Child will be immensely relieved to hear of your magnanimity in this direction![2] As for me—I expect any gentleman to recognise another gentleman by his intangible psychic aura of superiority. If he doesn't, it's his own fault—& I don't care to do revision for persons outside the landed gentry. I think I shall henceforward demand references from prospective clients, together with a sketch of their coats-of-arms & a brief summary of their genealogy. I shall accept only such persons as possess six or more armigerous ancestors out of the eight in the third generation back. One must be discriminating in these days of damn'd upstarts!

Glad you called on honest old Mac—the poor soul hears all too little from the outside world these days, & anyone who will drop in on him is performing a genuine act of kindness—hackneyed & commonplace though the illusion of kindness is. I've just recommended his latest book to the Provpublic for acquisition.[3] Did he shew you the writeup in the Times that young Talman gave him?[4]

I hope Sonny's meeting will come off successfully next Wednesday. Have you seen his new black hell-hound—the Scottish warlock-beastie? The child has just written a new story containing blasphemous & unmentionable horrors from other dimensions—a tale that reduced me, hardened to morbid monstrosities tho' I am, to a quivering mass of nerveless protoplasm.[5] I've told him to call up Ortonius on the telephone—the latter complains that all the gang are slighting him, except yourself, & that Kirk was coldly inhospitable the last time he called in at the Chelsea. And a sort of Wandrei-Orton feud is brewing. Boys, boys! Why can't children keep their tempers!

As for this cold weather—my opinion of it must be reserved, since it is unmailable under U.S. postal regulations. I'll begin thinking again next April or May. But even so, I'm trying to drag a little scenick sport out of the goddam autumn, & have been to good old Quinsnicket many times during the past month. I've also taken many sunset walks of urban exploration, discovering many strange & ancient labyrinths of streets quite near this house that I never saw or heard of before in my life. One of them is the greatest *AND-***WHERE**[6] that the human imagination can conceive. It is called *Bark Street*, & is a country lane running along the side of the ancient hill near that steep street between factories that I took you & honest Eddy down in 1923. Hideous, sinister houses of the 1750 period line it, & from one point along it can be obtained the finest

perspective of the Smith's Hill citadel (State House & St. Pat's) which the entire city can produce. Here's what it looks like. I first glimpsed it in the sunset & it took my breath away! ¶ Glad The Patmu flourishes. Work in all the scenick trips you can! ¶ Yr most oblig'd obt Servt ΘΕΟΒΑΛΔΟΣ

P.S. Just had a line from ol' Art Goodenough—first I've heard from him since the big Sunday blowout at his dump June 17th.[7]

Notes

1. A brand of bouillon cubes.

2. HPL and Frank Belknap Long had placed an advertisement in the August 1928 issue of *Weird Tales*, offering "Critical and revisory service for writers of prose and verse; literary revision in all degrees of extensiveness," although their enterprise was not named as HPL jocosely suggests here.

3. *The Shadow of the Iroquois* (New York: E. P. Dutton, 1928).

4. The only mention of McNeil in the *New York Times* during this period occurred in an unsigned article, "Books and Authors," *New York Times Book Review* (2 December 1928):

73, discussing McNeil's completion of the historical novel *The Shores of Adventure* (1929).

5. In "The Space-Eaters" (*WT*, July 1928), Long kills off a character based on HPL by having a shaft of animate light pour into his brain.

6. See W. Paul Cook, *In Memoriam: Howard Phillips Lovecraft* (1941), who notes that "and where" was "one of Howard's favorite phrases when showing visitors around the city. He would stop at a spot where the view would be comparable to that of a country village. 'Where, except in Providence,' he would ask, 'in the midst of a large city, will you find a view like that?' The next view would be a sylvan scene. 'Where save in Providence, in the midst of a large city . . .' he would say. The next step it would be, 'Where, save in Providence. . . .' And after that the single word 'Where . . .,' with an expressive gesture embracing the scene before him" (*LR* 137).

7. See HPL to Zealia Bishop (28 July 1928; ms. AHT): "On Sunday, June 17, a whole crowd of literati (both actual and would-be) assembled at the ancient Goodenough farm for a session of general discussion and fraternising—the event being written up quite extensively in the local Brattleboro press." HPL alludes to an unsigned article, "Literary Persons Meet in Guilford," *Brattleboro* [VT] *Reformer* (18 June 1928): 1.

[77]   [AHT]

Nov. 3, 1928

Dizzying Dome of Discernment:—

Just got your paper, & was almost paralysed by the epoch-making realisation that *we actually agree on something!* My gord, am I dreaming? Yea, 'bo, you & I are as one regarding the identity of the greatest living American administrator.[1] And as one in our happy confidence, that March 4 will find him where such an one ought to be. No person with the defective sartorial taste & atrocious pronunciation of his distinguished opponent has a right to the endorsement of a gentleman.

By the way—Neddy O'Brien gave my "Colour Out of Space" a three star listing & place on his Roll of Honour in the *Transcript* for two weeks ago. I am properly pompous & inflated over it.[2]

Well—here's hoping our loyalty to the right man will pull us down a good cabinet job apiece next year! Yrs for early & often ballots

Θεοβάλδος Πάππος

Notes

1. HPL refers to Herbert Hoover, who on 6 November would defeat Al Smith to become the thirty-first president of the United States; he would be inaugurated on 4 March 1929. HPL had reported that he planned to vote for Hoover (HPL to August Derleth, 5 October 1928; *Essential Solitude* 1.160).

2. Edward J. O'Brien's Roll of Honor (best short stories of the year) was published in the *Boston Transcript* for 20 October. O'Brien requested a brief autobiography from HPL for the annual yearbook, and although the note was published, the story was not reprinted.

[78]   [AHT]

The Morning After—Dec. 26, 1928

Apotheosised Aërial of All-Amazing Astuteness:—

Hey, bo'! pipe me swell new stationery! Me aunt give it to me fer Crismus, & I'm writin' everybody just to show as how I've got it. Then, when I've created me impression, I shall save it for Sunday go-to-meetin' use, & resume my diurnal inroads upon cheap junk & Kirk charity envelopes.[1]

Glad to hear the minruls is getting' whipped into form, & hope yuh put extra-size placards on the RHODE-ISLAND cases. As for the specimen enclosed—sorry, Kid, but I gotta give it up! Why don't ya get some bimbo at the American Museum to identify it for youse, & then look in your list of quarries to see where that particular form of inorganic blossom chiefly sprouts? It might all come back to ya with some such mnemonick pinch. And say—didja ever find out what that *extra-heavy* substance was that ya got off the quarry of my vassal, goodman Mariano de Magistris? You'll recall that I promised the excellent fellow to tell him what it was when you found out, & I'd hate to fail in the duties of an indulgent country 'squire. Intelligent curiosity is so rare a virtue in the peasantry, that it ought to be encouraged whenever it does not lend to insurrection. It is one's duty to bring one's honest tenantry closer to the great heart of Nature. You must certainly—after the perfection of your shipping system—pay the quarries of Rhode Island another visit, for I know they teem with treasure which would enrapture your increasingly expert eye. Remember there's a nice new mineralogist's hammer awaiting you here, & that the Theobald Guide Service is always on deck where places of scenick interest are concern'd. We ain't ben to the Harris Quarry at Lime Rock yet, yuh know.[2] Oh, boy—it makes me homesick for the summer to talk of such things!

Gawd! so you keep on quarryin' right t'roo de winter! Oh, no—pardon me—I didn't see the "except" the first time! Well, I'm getting' toward hibernation myself, though of course it's in *January* that I really dig down into the nethermost recesses of my burrow. Yesterday, for example, was the mildest & most genial Christmas I can recall since 1903, when I wore a summer weight coat (& short trousers!) as I rode my bicycle from home (454 Angell street) over to see my aunt, (Mrs. Clark) who then lived not far from where I am—& she is—now. Good old days! But as I say, yesterday was all right, & I went outdoors quite willingly, accompanying my aunt Mrs. Gamwell (the donor of this paper) down to that sterling Nordic Chin Lee's for a Christmas dinner in the antient English manner. Afterward we took quite a walk through quaint colonial byways, discovering several fine new "and-WHERES" which I gotta spring on youse next summer, & witnessing some of the most poignantly beautiful sunset & twilight effects (with a great round moon rising east of the venerable chimneys & cryptical elm-boughs) on record. Then we brung in a swell turkey feed from Brennan's hash-joint for Mrs. Clark—who, despite convalescence, doesn't get outdoors much yet.

Yeah—that Asbury goof sure gives a dirty dig in his praefatio. And then, after jeerin' at bum scholarship, he goes & retains the misprinted punctuation in my Delrio quote![3]

Hope you're havin' a swell time with your new clubs. Some class! Well, if the Kalem flickers, a guy's gotta join something!!

Happy New Year!

Θεοβάλδος

Notes

1. HPL had received from George Kirk a generous stack of envelopes no longer of use to Kirk. HPL used them for many years, crossing out Kirk's preprinted address, and writing his own on the back flap of the envelopes.

2. Cf. HPL to Wilfred Blanch Talman, Wednesday [April 1926]: "Rhode Island rusticity at its best, around Lime Rock, just north of the Quinsnicket reservation" (ms., JHL).

3. Herbert Asbury (1891–1963), ed., *Not at Night!* (New York: Macy-Masius [The Vanguard Press], 1928; *LL* 46), which pirated many stories from Christine Campbell Thomson's anthologies for Selwyn & Blount. It included HPL's "The Horror at Red Hook." In his introduction Asbury wrote: "Most of the authors represented in this collection appear to be comparatively unknown in this country . . ., and scholars and critics will look in vain for evidence of the skill and erudition displayed by such masters of the horror story as Edgar Allan Poe, Ambrose Bierce and Algernon Blackwood" (p. 11). In HPL's citation of a Latin quotation from Martin Delrio, Asbury retained the erroneous comma after *tali* as printed in *WT* (see *D* 264). The book was soon withdrawn from publication.

[79]   [AHT]

Jan. 1, 1929

Mineralogical greetings! Look at the bimbo I'm guiding around the Georgian architectural quarries of Providence & Boston![1] We seen some fine calcium carbonate rocks in the museum, all shaped up pretty by Grecian sculptors a coupla t'ousan' years ago. Also we seen yore Gran'paw's natal site in select Sheafe St.[2] Tomorrow Salem & Marblehead. Oh, Boy! But Providence really leads on the and-WHERES. Now I'll let the guest of honour use up some himself.

Arrogantly thine,

Θεοβάλδος

Dear James,

Our friend has been putting me thro the paces—so to speak. I saw enough this afternoon to supply me with a dozen epics and at least 300 lyrics.

Affect.

Sam

Notes

1. Samuel Loveman was visiting HPL in Providence. The two had then gone up to Boston.

2. See HPL to Frank Belknap Long and Alfred Galpin ([early February 1923]): "From Christ-Church I went to Sheafe-Street [in Boston], where was born the grandfather of our good friend and companion Mortonius; the Rev. S. F. Smith, author of the Yankee version of 'God Save the King' [i.e., 'My Country, 'Tis of Thee']. A tablet marks the house where he saw the light in 1808." *Letters to Alfred Galpin* 123.

[80]   [AHT]

June 9, 1929

Multi-Metred Mainmast of Muse-Mother'd Meliorism:—

Now about Dacosta Coffee—to think that it's only a reincarnation when I thought surely it was a bran new creation! Well—what t'ell *is* original anyhow? But it's no slouch, at that! Of course, it would be better if the milk were in it; (I don't speak of sugar, since the amount in Borden's was so slight that an extra quota was necessary) but even as it is, it's a lot better than making regular coffee & disposing of the damn grounds. You got Borden's *Condens'd* Milk all wrong, Kid! The kind what don't keep is Borden's *Evaporated,* (the unsweeten'd kind) betwixt which & the *condens'd* there is an infinitely more than verbal difference. The *Condens'd* milk is a very thick yellowish fluid with sugar in it, (so much that my aunt adds no other sweetening to her coffee, tho' I add 2½ teaspoons of $C12H22O11$) prepared by a process very different from that used in making the *Evaporated,* and *keeping almost indefinitely when open.* I've kept it almost *a month* without any deterioration. It *can't* sour, & it can't even decompose like *Evap.* All that ever happens to it—after long ages in the hottest weather—is the appearance of a little *mould* on the top; & even this can be skimmed off without affecting the lower portions. Nor could this form in less than three weeks or so if the can is properly cover'd. I cover my can by inverting over it in bell-glass fashion a large tin—one which formerly contain'd Hatchet Brown Bread, & which because of a patent opening-key retains a perfectly smooth edge. The appended diagram illustrates my eminently scientifick method—or I will shew you the actual apparatus next week. If you wish, I'll give you a brownbread tin to use in this fashion, since I have a constantly increasing supply of duplicates. With this device, you need have no hesitancy about keeping Borden's Challenge Brand Condens'd Milk as long as you like after opening the can. One 15¢ can would probably last you about two weeks if you use it only for breakfast, (I assume you dine at Roback's, successor to Westerman's) since with me a can goes about a week, used for both meals and sometimes for extra cocoa.

large empty brownbread tin

small can Borden's Challenge Brand condens'd milk.

As for Dryco—the *principle* of powder'd milk is no more original than the principle of Dacosta cawfee, since such things have been in use since I was a middle-aged man. There used to be a milk powder call'd "Klim", (reverse orthography) which may or may not be sold nowadays—but I dare say Dryco is purer & more palatable. However, these desiccated substitutes are too modern & sophisticated in atmosphere to suit my blunt rural tastes. Borden's Challenge is the stuff for a rugged county 'squire of the ancient Puritan temperament—for with its conservative stannic envelope & comfortably viscous fluidity it is almost as naive & pastoral as a cow & a quart measure. The lowing herd . . . . tinkle of bells & call of the neatsherd at evening . . . . . rolling, stone-wall'd pastures . . . . orchard-embower'd white farmhouse gables . . . . . distant steeple in the vale . . . . . God Save His Majesty's New-England plantations—& Borden's Challenge Milk! Tell ya what—I'll fix ya up a cuppa Dacosta with Challenge whitening when you're here, & see what yuh think of it. I don't use it reg'lar myself, because my aunt makes bona fide coffee for me—though I do use the Challenge regularly in the latter.

When I get yuh orally corner'd, I shall tell yuh about my exploration of the Dutch region up the Hudson—Kingston, Hurley, & New Paltz. Here I found antique manners unspoilt, & old stone houses whose date averages about 1700. Also—I met our corresponding gang member Bernard Dwyer in person, & found him a person of the utmost delightfulness; perhaps the most richly sensitive & gorgeously imaginative dreamer I have ever encounter'd.

Well, Sir, for the nonce I will leave you to your pebbles, trusting you will not forget to shew up heareabouts on the morning of Sunday the 16th.

   Yrs. for efficient coffee & conservative milk,

     Πάππος Θεοβάλδος

[81] [AHT]

                July 30, 1929

Culminating Cog-Wheel of Chautauquan Conformity:—

Hail & farewell—before I blow up with brain-fever or get carted off to the nut-factory as a result of this gord damn vortex of lousy revision—ol' Dolph de Castro & his simp yarns, coupled with our good ol' pal Maurice W. Moe, who has gave me the "perfesh" job of rounding out his forthcoming text book on poetick appreciation . . . . a marvellous volume, ef ya asts me—even before I condescended to offer coöperation.[1] Incidentally, I'm not going to take pay from Moe, even though he insists. It goes against the grain for a gentleman to charge money for a favour extended a friend. But the job does take time, confound it!

My aunt is better than at the time of my former bulletin; but has to have the landlady help her dress, & can't get downstairs. My services are now narrow'd to the routine of toting up dinner things & carting 'em down again some time in the late afternoon. When I go out for the aft—as I occasionally do on warm & sunny days when the woods & fields beckon to me & my writing-case—I shift responsibilities to one or another of the kindly old souls inhabiting this shadowy Victorian backwater.

About Brown rioting—yes, I did take a genuine pride in the virile energy & healthy antinomianism displayed on Memorial Day. We're not quite decay'd yet, when unbroken Nordick spirits can take a fling of that sort at the stultifying oppressiveness of routine & deadening discipline! 'Rah for the young Mohocks . . . . Lineal heirs of the fashionable bloods who upset sedan-chairs & roll'd excessively serious folk down hill in barrels in my day! It makes me sad to reflect that I've grown too old & grey to mix into inspiring rough-&-tumbles like this. I'd love to crack skulls in the name of free individualism, & smash office-appliance-shop windows as a symbolic nose-thumbing at the age of commerce, machines, time-tables, & aëroplane-speeded cosmic tail-chasing. Whoopee! I'll wager Dean Mason was damn'd sorry he had to go through the gesture of expelling those virile young bucks as a sop to the curst tyrants of convention & uniformity![2] Here's hoping the boys do better next year—ploughing up the new airport,[3] burning the Rotary Club, & ducking a score of mill-owners & efficiency experts in the most oil-polluted spot in the Providence river! Sing ho for simplicity, strength, lusty freedom, gentlemen's privilege, agriculture, leisure, & the square-rigg'd India trade! Narragansett cheese & pacers, Cumberland copper, Newport spermaceti, & Cranston iron. Rum, niggers, & molasses! God Save the King!

By the way—some recent heroicks of mine, on the departed glories of 1904, are about to be seen by every member of the U. of Wis. class of '04! How come? This way. Moe told me he was going to prepare a festive booklet to give each member of the class—commemorating the twenty-fifth anniversary—& the idea of '04 memories mov'd me to write him a reminiscent letter about old days & ways. It happen'd to be composed entirely in heroicks, & Moe liked it—so he took all the impersonal couplets & put 'em in his booklet![4] More anon—

            Yr obt Servt
                Θεοβάλδος

Notes

1. Adolphe de Castro, "The Electric Executioner" (*WT*, August 1930); Maurice W. Moe, *Doorways to Poetry* (unpublished).
2. HPL refers to the "tunnel riot" of 1929, when the freshmen of the Class of 1932 intended to burn the black ties they had been made to wear that year. The event was to take place at Thayer Field after a march downtown, followed by an illegal return through the East Side Tunnel. After a skirmish with police at the Arcadia ballroom, the men proceeded to the tunnel. They were blocked from entering it by policemen at both ends. The arrival of Dean Kenneth O. Mason precluded the tie-burning.

3. In 1929, the site selected for the new airport, State Airport Terminal at Hillsgrove, now Theodore Francis Green State Airport, was the first state-owned airport in the United States. It opened for business in 1933.

4. For the occasion, HPL wrote the humorous poem "An Epistle to the Rt. Honble Maurice Winter Moe, Esq. of Zythopolis, in the Northwest Territory of HIS MAJ-ESTY'S American Dominion" (1929), recounting his memories of 1904. Zythopolis is HPL's coined name for Milwaukee, meaning "Beer-town" (from the Greek ζῦθος). The printed booklet has not been located.

[82]   [AHT]

Novr. 8, 1929

Mountaintop of Mandevillian Mile-Munching:

Gawdamighty! Can it be me what is anserrin' a epistle dated Oct. 13th on the 8th of November? So much for my rep as the guy who taught C. Plinius Caecilius Secundus & Harry Walpole how to use the P. O.![1] But hell! If you seen the mess of junk I jest finish'd for old de Castro, you'd be wonderin' that I'm alive at all, instead of that I'm givin' the railway mail clarks a easy time of it! Hell! I don't believe I *am* alive, at that! There's certainly a decomposed, charnel look about the claw that convulsively scrawls these hideous last words.

Well, anyway, this here is to say I've went t'roo yore travelogue wit' de keenest interest & admiration, & that I hereby doff me laurel wreath as prime Herodotus of the gang. Yuh beat me, 'bo! I shore do hope you've gave Bre'r Marlow[2] a carbon of the dope yuh send me—it's too damn good for a limited audience—as both of me aunts unite wit' me in sayin'. And oh, wot a trip! Am I green wi' envy? Well—jest drain the blue outa me & see how yaller I looks! You shore seen Richmon' from de insahd—ah take off mah hat to yo', suh, although ah *did* see Windsor Farms, with Agecroft Hall & Warwick Priory, but jes nachelly forgot to put it in the travelogue on account of haste. And boy—how I envy you your conversation with Edw. Valentine, Esq. . . . for do you know, Sir, *he met Poe in 1849 as a small boy, & well recalls him.*[3] He has furnished material to all Poe biographers from Ingram downward;[4] being, as you doubtless realise, a kinsman of the first Mrs. Allan, Poe's beloved foster-mother. Man—wouldn't I have pump'd him dry if I'd had a conversational whack at him!!! A great old town, Richmond! I can see E. A. P. there now, as a small boy in the house at 13th street & Tobacco Alley, or as a youth in the later 5th street mansion overlooking the river. And even the squalid house where his mother died still stands—in Main street beyond the "shrine". Hades, but I must manage to take another trip there. Richmond comes the closest to being really civilised of any sizeable town I've ever seen—although I think I'd rather live in purely colonial Fredericksburg. If ever I leave Providence because of the tearing-down of its antient houses, you can bet your boots it's in ol' tidewater Virginia I'm going to live! Incidentally, though, I don't think I'll choose this bird J. E. Barrow (writer of the Providence letter) as a bosom pal. He may be a Virginian in body, but only the soul of a decadent modern cou'd sport that "live town with much business" reaction every time a cluster of houses heaves in sight! And when he does drop the "progressive" pose he gets sentimental—dewdrops & birdies & roses & all that. No—this guy is pore white trash—not the real stuff. My idea of a contemporary Virginian is somebody like James Branch Cabell. As for Charlottesville— what right has anybody but me got to go there, where Eddie Poe once scann'd the studious page, drain'd the genial glass & cast the fateful card? Ogawd! Didja lamp his room at #13 West Range? I b'lieve it's all fixt up like it was w'en he hung out there.[5] And say—if any bozo tries to tell ya that he was kickt out, or that he didn't have a damn good reason for getting into debt, just tell him to sidetrack his palate a second or two until he reads the evidence dug up from the Poe-Allan correspondence made publick by the Valentine Museum in 1925! The one guy what needs a good hairy fist poked into where his nose used to be is that tightwad hypocrite from Ayrshire, who didn't have a drop of real Virginia blood in his veins—that swivelling, sneaking, wending, canting tradesman John Allan! Faugh! I don't wonder Eddie hated the middle name he tacked onto him. Up at Fordham a guy wanted Eddie to stand godfather to his kid, which same Eddie done—with the proviso that the babe be nam'd *Edgar **Alfred**.* Yeh—I gotta see the U. of V. sometime; not only because of E. A. P. but because of its architecture. I wanna see sumpun worth sumpun what Mr. Jefferson done. Which same applies to Monticello.

No question, kid, I gotta see more of antient Virginia. It's my kind of a place. I could tell the minute I got down there that I'd passed through an alien belt into another region of regular home stuff. Old England's heritage— God Save the King! And Virginia is keeping it better than New England. We are about ready to sink for the third time, but the old Dominion has hardly begun to be waterlogged. I fear it's doomed, though, along with the rest of this continent. Even now there's altogether too much blather about progress & money & industry in the South, & another generation or two will do the mischief—introduce a speed-quantity-cash standard & substitute machine-age barbarism for one of the only two real civilisations Anglo-America ever produced. It'll get at the *parvenu* south first—Georgia & Alabama, & then the Carolinas. Virginia, where American civilisation began, will be the last place to sink. God Save the King!

I can't say that I envy you Pittsburgh—for neither industrial centres nor single-tax theories titillate my fancy very acutely or insistently. But I *do* envy you that aëroplane jaunt—for the rudimentary $3.50 taste I got at Onset in August has given me quite a taste for super-nubian soaring; a taste which I ain't yet had the opportunity to reindulge. I'd hate to see aëroplanes come into common commercial use, since they merely add to the goddam useless speeding up of an already overspeeded life; but as devices for the amusement of a gentleman, they're oke!

I did, however, manage to improve the warmer, summer days of September & October, & on many afternoons took my books & writing out to the pastoral meads & groves of Quinsnicket, or to the Arcadian slopes that tower above the antient Seekonk. In Quinsnicket I chiefly haunted a region quite newly open'd up—a deep wooded ravine, on whose banks one may spy the picturesque ivy'd ruin of a forgotten mill. Ah, me! I well recall that mill when it was standing—but it hath gone the way of all simple, beauteous things. I also haunted a roadside terrace whence I obtain'd one of the finest landskip vistas in the world—the steepled, sunset-gilded town of Saylesville in the distance, rising above a lake-carpeted valley to which the road beside me spirall'd down. On my right was the edge of the wooded ravine; on my left a rocky upland with stone walls, rows of harvest-sheaves, & gnarled orchards thro' which peep'd the trim gables of antient farmhouses. Hell, but I'd have given anything for the skill to draw such a scene! And at evening when the Hunter's Moon came out!!! Oh, baby! Now I know what Jim Flecker meant when he pulled that one about "burning moonlight" in the last act of "Hassan"!

> Each distant mountain glows with faery grace,
>   The flame-lit lakelet laps the level strand;
> Lur'd by dim vistas beck'ning out of space,
>   We take the Golden Road to Samarcand![6]

And now the skies they are ashen & sober, & the leaves they are crisped & sere.[7] Eheu! Done are the outings, & Grandpa's hibernation's on! But I hope to gawd I can get this damn revision cleaned up & start some stories pretty soon. That's the way to spend an hibernation-period!

And so it goes. I enclose an odd item or two, whereof only the travelogue needs to be returned. The account of Fredericksburg ought to tempt you down to old Virginia again—hades, but I'm positively homesick for that place. God Save the King!

Yours for cheaper niggers—
Valentine Bolling Fitz-Randolph Byrd,
of Virginia.

Notes

1. C. Plinius Caecilius Secundus (61–ca. 112), better known as Pliny the Younger, and Horatio Walpole, 4th Earl of Orford (1717–1797), more commonly known as Horace Walpole, were prodigious letter writers.
2. Harry R. Marlowe, Official Editor of the NAPA (1929–30).
3. Edward Virginius Valentine (1838–1930), American sculptor.

4. John H. Ingram (1842–1916), *Edgar Allan Poe: His Life, Letters, and Opinions* (London: J. Hogg, 1880; 2 vols.; *LL* 457).

5. The Raven Society first opened Poe's preserved room at 13 West Range at the University of Virginia, furnished with a settee from the Allan home in Richmond and a real raven (stuffed).

6. The phrase "burning moonlight" does not occur in James Elroy Flecker's *Hassan* (1915), but the phrase "blazing moonlight" is found in a scene description in Act 5, sc. 2.

7. The opening lines of Poe's "Ulalume" (1847): "The skies they were ashen and sober; / The leaves they were crispèd and sere . . ."

[83]   [AHT]

Tuesday the 19th
[19 November 1929]

Parallel-less Paramount-point of Petrifica-Pierian Peripateticism:—

A caught-up correspondence! My gord—do such things exist? But for a fact, my own ain't in such bad shape right now as it was a coupla weeks ago. But turnin' down any revision rackets that may come along in the next month or two, I had orta get a chanct at last to do some fictional hell-raisers of my own—which same I ben aimin' at for the last year & more. For a fact, I ain't wrote nothin' in the story line senct "The Dunwich Horror" in August 1928!

Ogawd, & to think ya could forget de monicker of our ol' time side kick Dave Bush!!! Well—you ain't suffered all what I suffer'd from dat bozo, or else he'd be burn'd into your recollection wit' letters of hydrofluorick acid! But how come yore choice freak-shelf hath lost its chiefest glories? Next thing you'll be tellin' me you've lost "The Bride of Gettysburg" & the "Collected Gems" of P. J. Pendergast! But as coincidence wou'd have it I've lost my own Bush junk, too. I didn't mean to, but the books got into a section of my less-needed household stuff that I left in a warehouse in Flatbush long after my return home, & the gawd dam fools hashed the whole shipment up when I finally sent for it—losing haffa dozen things including some of my early writings ("The Adventures of Ulysses; or, the New Odyssey", 1897; "Poemata Minora", 1901; &c. &c.) *and* the immortal tomes of David V. Bush! *Requiescat in pace!* And to think that pore ol' Pearson almost fell for Davy! Hot dawg! But then, he always did have an eye for freak movements. I recall that back in 1915 or so he was one of those millennium or advent cranks, of the brand that—through mystical anthropological sources unknown to such tyrocs as Huxley, Darwin, Weigall, & Sir Arthur Keith—fondly believe our Saxon stock to be descended from the twelve lost tribes of Israel!

Glad the dope on my rural-ancestral pilgrimage prov'd fairly interesting. Nothing like the good ol' past to give ya a sense of placement & reason for existence! Take my advice & get a full transcript of the dope your late aunt collected! I'm goin' after three possible data-sources myself when the weather & my energy permit. I do like to have myself down on paper & know just where I stand in relation to the stone-wall'd rolling meads & white farmhouse gables of the Arcadian realm of Western Rhode-Island. The visible beauty & dignity of a settled, aesthetically integrated region take on a fresh degree of poignancy & motivating stimulation when one can feel one's own hereditary blood-stream coursing through the scene as through the veins of some vast & exquisite organism. One can say not only, "I love these waving grasses & towering elms & brook-threaded valleys & stone-wall'd farmsteads & white village steeples", but "these waving grasses & towering elms & brook-threaded valleys & stone-wall'd farmsteads & white village steeples *are ME, MYSELF, I, THE CONSCIOUS EGO*"! And what more can any guy ask than that? Isn't all art an effort of the artist to *identify himself* with the burning beauty & strangeness he depicts? Why, then, reject such identification as Nature provides?

The past is *real*—it is *all there is*. The present is only a trivial & momentary boundary-line—whilst the future, though wholly determinate, is too essentially unknown & landmarkless to possess any hold upon our sense of concrete aesthetic imagery. It is, too, liable to involve shifts & contrasts repugnant to our emotions & fancy; since we cannot study it as a unified whole & become accustomed to its internal variations as we can study & grow accustomed to the vary'd past. There is nothing in the future to tie one's loyalties & affections to—it can mean nothing to us, because it involves none of those mnemonic association-links upon which the illusion of meaning is based. So I, for one, prefer Old New England & Old Virginia to the unknown mechanised barbarism that stretches out ahead of us—as meaningless & alien to men of our heritage & memories as the cultures of China or Abyssinia or ancient Carthage or the planet Saturn. There's no use pretending that a standardised, time-tabled machine-culture has any point in common—any area of contact—with a culture involving human freedom, individualism, & personality; so that it seems to me all one can do at present is to fight the future as best he can. Anybody who thinks that men live by *reason*, or that they are able consciously to mould the effect & influences of the devices they create, is behind the times psychologically. Men can use machines for a while, but after a while the psychology of machine-habituation & machine-dependence becomes such that the machines will be using the men—modelling them to their essentially efficient & absolutely valueless precision of action & thought . . . . . . perfect functioning, without any reason or reward for functioning at all. One can't dodge this issue in glittering generalities, or through an habitual hopefulness of attitude which after all springs merely from a certain type of gland-functioning. Certain causes produce certain results, & a look ahead is not reassuring from what we know of the laws of human action and reaction. Read "The Modern Temper", by Joseph Wood Krutch, & "The Dance of the Machines", by Edward J. O'Brien. One almost certain outcome of America's accepted system of plutocratic despotism & democracy of opportunity will be rather ironic from the point of view of your own democratic wishes. That will be the crystallisation of *an absolutely unbreakable caste system* based on *fixed mental & biological capacity*, as democracy opens the upward path to competent individuals & leaves the menial places to the naturally incompetent. With this system operating, a thousand years will see a wholly new social-political-industrial order composed of a highly intelligent ruling & administrative stratum on top, (descended from the intelligent elements of *all* classes of today) plus a vast residue of mentally inferior material (drained steadily, through opportunity to rise, of all the naturally capable material it has ever produced) wholly at the mercy of the superior class—well-fed, well-housed, well-clothed, well-treated, well-leisured, well-amused, & all that—but essentially brainless & relegated to a position of virtual parity with the well-oiled & well-treated machines with which it will share its burthen-bearing. The effect of machine-standardisation on *literature* is well shewn by O'Brien in his "Dance of the Machines". Quantity-production devoid of individualities & subtleties, or of genuine personal vision, is an inevitable result. The *Saturday Evening Post* with its bland, superficial callousness & lack of true appraisals or analyses, is a good symbol of future writing & publishing. The standards of uniformity, quantity, & monetary reward overshadow everything else. Did Belknap tell you about his recent blustering visitor—the popular magazine hack-writer who stayed till four a.m. denouncing the follies & futilities of aesthetic effort[1] & boasting of how he makes 15,000 a year writing for "the pulp"? (i.e., the grade of periodicals printed on wood-pulp paper). This creature, as vividly described in a letter from the Child, moved me to heroick expression:

> In former Times our letter'd Brethren fought
> To starve their Bodies while they fed their Thought;
> Unaw'd by Wealth, unbought by Luxury,
> They own'd their Brains, & scorn'd the Slaver's Fee.
> Poor, modest, proud, they held the princely Pen.
> Masters & Peers, & conscious Gentlemen;
> And who, unbow'd, wou'd not their Place prefer
> To the rich Tradesman's—harness'd, fawning Cur?
> But Time, the Goth, each pleasing Virtue blights
> As his curst Legions storm our guarded Heights;
> Behold! where Bards free Musick once outpour'd,
> A Crowd of Lackeys cringe around their Lord;
> From gold-stain'd Pockets beg their tawdry Doles,
> And stuff their Bellies as they sell their Souls.
> What shall they write? 'Tis not for them to say—
> King Mob will give them Orders for the Day!
> Scrawling what's bid, they woo the unwasht Throng
> In chap-book Prose, & loud illit'rate Song;
> Themselves in Boasting, not in Art, express,

And reckon Worth in Terms of Gainfulness.
See! see! where once the honest Dreamer try'd
To scale the Slopes of Loveliness & Pride,
To cast off Earth, & reach th' aetherial Mead
High o'er the Slough were wallowing Porkers feed,
Our newer Band opposing Ways pursue,
And lose the Freeman in the griping Jew.
'Tis theirs to shine in Tests of haggling Skill,
Their bulging Purses, not their Heads, to fill;
To drown their Yearnings & their Freeman's Bent
In stick Swamps of servile Excrement.
Hail to the Carcass, fed tho' bound in chains;
Pox on your Dreamer's or your Poet's Pains!
We drink to Flesh in one black Stygian Gulp,
And sink our Spirits in a Grave of Pulp![2]

Make no mistake—this is what lies ahead of us! All the national standards are shifting toward it—in the fields of politics, science, & even art. Values today are not humanistic—i.e., not based on the standard of human personality & emotion, & of the rewards inherent in self-realisation—but *mathematical & quantitative;* based on *measurement as applied to material function,* without regard for the significance of that function in producing the emotional-imaginative state of adjustment which philosophers call "the good life". The modern standard of a man is not his whole, rounded personality as expressed in his individual angle of vision, balance of emotions, background-acquirements, & the like; but merely the mechanical speed & precision of his calculative intellect alone, as coolly measured & plotted out in "graphs" & tables by standardised wielders of the Binet-Simon intelligence test. In other words, we no longer measure men as human beings, but as effective fractions of a vast mathematical machine which has no goal or purpose save to increase the precision & economy of its own useless & rewardless motions. That is why the inevitable coming of the new machine-age aristocracy of mentally-superior rulers gives me no hope of a renewed civilisation. This future aristocracy—whose pioneers are already among us in the persons of such industrialists as Ford, Firestone, Rockefeller, Stinnes,[3] Lever,[4] &c. &c.—will be one of wealth, splendour, power, speed, quantity & responsibility alone; for, having been erected on the basis of acquisition & industry, it will naturally draw all its streams of feeling from the empty ideal of size, measurement, precision, & activity-for-its-own-sake . . . . the crude ideal of *doing* as opposed to the civilised ideal of *being.* Upon this foundation will arise such art as it will possess—the hard, unsatisfying, geometrical aesthetic whose pictorial manifestations you can see in the massed planes & cubes & angles of "modernistic" & expressionistic painting. Of course it will be a kind of "civilisation", in the loosest sense of the term; but it will be *no civilisation of ours.* We can't look forward to it with any more sense of personal pride or pleasure than we could look forward to the triumph of any other alien civilisation on territory which has known our own. Wouldn't we fight an attempt of the Japanese—cultured though they are—to occupy & flourish on New England & Virginia soil? Didn't our forefathers fight the French to keep them from spreading over us from Canada & the Ohio-Mississippi valley? Shades of Sir William Phipps, Governor Shirley, Sir Wm. Pepperrell, Gen. Wolfe & Capt. Daniel Fones of the Rhode-Island arm'd sloop *Tartar!* For what did the bells in the Georgian steeples of Salem & Boston & Providence ring out when Louisburg fell in 1745? God Save the King! No, damn it! If we fought the menacing culture of the French, which was undoubtedly *superior* to our own, shall we not fight this even more alien & immeasurably inferior barbarism of the machine?

Ah sholy hope you get daown to Virginia nex' summer; an' when yo do, Suh, yo don' want to miss Fredericksburg! Ah'd give ten paounds if ah could be there raght naow—to say nothing of getting down to good ol' Richmond—& hitherto untasted *Charleston* . . . . goal of my dreams & foreordain'd home of my spirit. And New Orleans, too—& St. Augustine, Florida! Only poverty keeps me north of the Potomac from November to April!

I am desolated that you & Talman miss'd seeing good old Mac because of that date slip-up. It is possible that Mac's general shakiness caused him to give Sonny the wrong figures—just as he wrote his future address "South Dakoma" instead of "South Tacoma". But if that little Belknap-rascal made mistake himself, & told his Grandpa a wrong date to pass on to the gang . . . . . well, there'll be some stern grandpaternal chastisement in the house of Theobald! Talman went all the way to Astoria on the 18th, & found that the bird had flown on the 14th—& of course my "bon voyage" letter, timed to arrive on the 19th, found empty windows staring out over the waters of Hell Gate & the fading greenery of Ward's & Randall's Islands. I surely hope Mac reached his destination in safety & comfort, & that the combined influence of the Pacific climate & a reposeful household will give his health a sharp upward curve. Let us trust that his sister is of the conscientious sort who will see that he sticks to his diet! I told him—in writing to his new habitat—that he needn't spend energy in answering my letter; but hope he'll drop me a card with the most general news & reassurances.

As for bookplates—I certainly don't think that Talman would soak you an hundred fish for a good pachydermatous torchbearer. He's no organised professional, & is not the sort to be a Shylock amongst the gang. He gave me my plate as a sort of recognition of the help I've given him with his short stories—although I told him at the time that he was more than welcome to whatever assistance I could extend. Ask him about his rates some time, for I'm hang'd if his best work isn't good enough for anybody—be he profesh or not! The printing from a plate like mine, on stock like that of the sample you have, is only *$3.75 for 500 copies*—at a firm in Montague St., Brooklyn. Of course, if anybody wants something sweller & doggier—engraved plate, old Japanese vellum, & all that—one must pay in proportion; but for a plain, democratick guy like me, this ordinary kind of cut & stock is plenty good. I've got five hundred copies—but I shan't plaster the more tatter'd & less important items in my modest library.

Sorry a gang meeting can't be rounded up, & hope you'll get around to Little Belknap's oftener. They enjoy your calls immensely—in fact, they remarked last August that they wished your programme allowed you to get around oftener. It certainly is a delightful household—including my friend Felis, & even the usurping Canis! But one young member of that household is going to be paddled very shortly with a grandpaternal slipper if he's lost pages 25 & 26 of his Grandpa's travelogue of last spring—the one lent to you during your trip, & re-lent to him upon its return from Richmond.[5] I take it for granted that Mortonian efficiency couldn't have permitted the loss to have occurred on the first trip, so fancy the second viewer is the young person who needs a posterior touch of shoe-leather! I've no remaining copy of the missing text—but am going to ask Moe to return the corresponding pages of the original. Then I shall make the trembling culprit do penance by typing them for Grandpa on his little Corona! Haven't had a word out of Samuelus since his transfer of commercial affiliations—I'll bet he let somebody else get that pile of Farmer's Almanacks that he was saving for me until the owner quoted a price, & that he's ashamed to write the Old Gentleman after such a lapse! But hell—he needn't worry about that! Grandpa is a cynical & moderately forgiving old goof, with too low an opinion of the human will & intelligence to be disappointed or disillusion'd by small lapses. Glad Georgiocircus still flourishes. He hasn't written me since his passage thro' Providentium,[6] but I hope he saw and enjoy'd WICKFORD, as he meant to do when I bade him adieu in East-Greenwich. Orton, as I think I said, is getting out a Dreiser bibliography—which you'll no doubt see in time. But after all, it's a denatured sort of gang-skeleton with nice old Mac off the scene!

Our friend Clark Ashton Smith—Klarkash-Ton, Emperor of Dreams, whom you appreciate *so keenly*—has turned to short story writing of late, & is producing a surprising quantity of good items—several of which Wright has accepted. See what you think of them when they appear in *Weird Tales*—especially "A Night in Malneant", & "The End of the Story". Still better ones are due to follow.

Very shortly the daily literary column of the *Providence Journal*—"The Sideshow"—may feature a discussion bringing in the names of myself & of my small grandsons Belknap & August W. Derleth of Wisconsin! A coupla weeks ago the literary editor—Bertrand K. Hart—had some dope about what the best horror story in all literature is, & his suggestions were so tame & mechanical that I couldn't resist sending him a copy of my *Recluse* article, plus transcripts of lists of "best weird tales" (with my own omitted in decent modesty) which Sonny & Derleth had prepared—as a matter of pure coincidence—not long before. Hart came back with a very pleasant letter; expressing his intention of discussing the subject further in his "colyum", & asking permission to refer to my grandsons & myself by our real names. Assuming that nobody was especially keen on secrecy, I extended the desiderate imprimatur—hence expect to see the annals of the gang perpetuated in the cultivated press of a *real town*. If you have any ideal list of best weird tales to send along, come ahead & send it! I'm sure Hart would welcome any augmentations to the genial melee.[7]

And so it goes. Best wishes, regards to the daemon falls of the Passaick, & get around to Providence in the U-23 when you can!

      Yr Oblig'd obt hble Servt

          Θεοβάλδος

Notes

1. This was Armitage Trail, the pseudonym of Maurice Coons (1902–1930), author of *Scarface* (1930).

2. "Lines upon the Magnates of the Pulp."

3. Hugo Stinnes (1870–1924), German industrialist and politician. He had interests in steel, shipping, newspapers, and other industries. By 1923 he had become so powerful that *Time* magazine named him the "New Emperor of Germany."

4. William Lever, 1st Viscount Leverhulme (1851–1925), British industrialist and founder of the soap manufacturer named Lever Brothers.

5. "Travels in the Provinces of America" (1929).

6. George Kirk and his wife visited HPL in Providence in September 1929.

7. B[ertrand] K[elton] Hart (1892–1941) mentioned HPL several times in his column, "The Sideshow," in the *Providence Journal*: 101, No. 280 (23 November 1929): 2; No. 281 (25 November): 2; No. 286 (30 November): 10. See Kenneth W. Faig, Jr., "Lovecraft's Own Book of Weird Fiction," *The HPL Supplement* No. 2 (July 1973): 4–14.

[84]   [AHT]

                               Harvest-Home Day, [30 November] 1929

Apotheosis'd Aërial of Anthropological Aspiration:—

The more I think of good ol' Dave, the more I regret the loss of all his priceless works. I had a splendid set—all the original howlers bound in blue—"Soul Poems", "Pike's Peak or Bust", "Peace Poems & Sausages", &c. &c.—plus three or four of the relatively sedate results of our joint labour, bound in a sedate dark red. When I discover'd the loss three years ago, I was not inclin'd to worry unduly—being more concern'd about the loss of my own immortal juvenilia . . . . my sole fruits as a genuine Victorian (chronologically speaking) poet—but as time piles up, & Bushing days work more & more into the sentiment-wreath'd "good old" class, I feel the bereavement more & more poignantly. To think that I can nevermore banish melancholy with a glance at the incorrupted text—in the Codex Tomaculensis—of "Just Suppose"!!![1]

As for the future of Western Civilisation—& of any other cultures which the planet may preserve or develop—far be it from me to be dogmatick. All I deal in is probabilities. In the last analysis, nobody don't know nothin' about nothin'. Contrary to what you may assume, I am *not a pessimist* but an *indifferentist*—that is, I don't make the mistake of thinking that the resultant of the natural forces surrounding & governing organic life will have any connexion with the wishes or tastes of any part of that organic life-process. Pessimists are just as illogical as optimists; insomuch as both envisage the aims of mankind as unified, and as having a direct relationship (either of frustration or of fulfilment) to the inevitable flow of terrestrial motivation and events. That is—both schools retain in a vestigial way the primitive concept of a conscious teleology—of a cosmos which gives a damn one way or the other about the especial wants & ultimate welfare of mosquitoes, rats, lice, dogs, men, horses, pterodactyls, trees, fungi, dodos, or other forms of biological energy. And I fear the meliorist is not altogether free from this illusion, either. But the *indifferentist* is. He alone of all thinkers is willing to view the future of the planet *impartially*—without assigning (as indeed there is absolutely no ground for assigning) any preponderance of evidential value to such factors as appear to argue a course pleasant to himself. Not that he is especially looking for anti-human outcomes, or that he has any pleasure in contemplating such. It is merely that, in judging evidence, *he does not regard the quality of favourableness to man as any intrinsic mark of probability*. Neither does he regard it as any intrinsic mark of *improbability*—he simply knows that this quality has nothing to do with the case; that the interplay of forces which govern climate, behaviour, biological growth & decay, & so on, is too purely universal, cosmic, & eternal a phenomenon to have any relationship to the immediate wishing-phenomena of one minute organic species on our transient & insignificant planet. At times parts of this species may like the way things are going, and at times they may not—but that has nothing to do with the cosmically fixed march of the events themselves. Human liking or welfare is no probability-factor at all—& no person has a right to express an opinion on the future of the world, so long as he has the least tendency to consider a man-favouring course as *intrinsically* more likely to be probable than any other course. If he lets the quality of man-favouringness serve in lieu of real evidence to predispose him toward belief in any direction, then his opinion is null & void as a serious philosophic factor. The real philosopher knows that, *other* evidence being equal, favourableness or unfavourableness to mankind means absolutely nothing as an index of likelihood—that is, that a future hostile to man is precisely as probable as one favourable to him. And of course this works the other way around as well—so that no one is justified in thinking a theory probable *merely because it opposes man*. The indifferentist laughs as much at irresponsible calamity-howlers & temperamental melancholiacs as he does at smirking idealists & unctuous woodrowilsonians. For example—nothing makes me more amused than the hypersensitive people who consider life as essentially an *agony* instead of merely a cursed bore, punctuated by occasional agony & still rarer pleasure. Life is rather depressing because pain & ennui outweigh pleasure; but the pleasure exists, none the less, & can be enjoyed now & then while it lasts. And too—many can build up a crustacean insensitiveness against the subtler forms of pain, so that many lucky individuals have their pain-quota measurably reduced. Uniform melancholy is as illogical as uniform cheer. Another thing—it is quite absurd to think that the decline of civilisation means instant savagery & suffering. *On the contrary*, (to use my favourite forensick phrase) these letdowns are nearly always gradual & partial— so that it took Rome fully four-hundred years to slip from the Antonine peak to the utter cultural disintegration of—say—600 A.D. And even then, of course, there were rudimentary fragments of mental & aesthetic life left— together with the prospects of another civilisation around the corner. The only element of real *calamitousness* is for the member of the declining civilisation as an individual or for his generation as a group. He, & his kind, know that the near future will not be such as to call forth so much of man's imaginative & emotional resources as the present & immediate past have called forth—that life, while not necessarily a matter of complete misery & sterility, will be conducted on a lower potential, with less rich rewards for the ordeal of remaining conscious—& that the resurgent civilisation of the remoter future, beyond the slack period, will—while its height cannot be predetermined—be so completely alien to him, that—high or low—it will mean no more to him than an hypothetical civilisation on Saturn's third satellite. It's no civilisation of his— so that nothing connected with it can compensate for the sense of loss inherent in the realisation that his own set of conditions & values & secondary instincts is not going ahead unimpededly. Naturally there are many unimaginative people whose emotional adjustment depends so little on their orientation in time & space that matters like this mean relatively little to them so long as they can have their chosen conditions during their own lifetimes. Indeed, there are even people of greater sensitiveness who—while foreseeing the changes— manage to dramatise themselves in such a way as to avoid pain at the thought of their culture's ending. There may be some—such as the 19th century decadents in France—who can derive a sort of pleasurable tragic exaltation from the picture of themselves as the crew of a sinking ship—a ship which is sinking, no matter how many other ships may later put to sea from other ports. To be a Psamettichus in a dying Egypt, a Lucian in a fading Hellenistic world, a Boëthius or a Venantius Fortunatus[2] in a doomed Rome—there is quite a kick in the idea for those who like that kind of thing. In fact, we may say quite certainly that anyone's emotional attitude toward the future is essentially a matter of chance and of taste. The only thing about which any representative array of clear thinkers—an array involving the temperamental heterogeneities inevitable among individuals—can be expected to approximate similarity, is the impersonal & objective matter of calculating what the future is likely to be, whether one hates or relishes it. And even here the similarity can be only approximate, since different emotions give different individuals different habits of perception, appraisal, & reasoning—habits which importantly affect all conclusions save those depending on the very simplest, clearest, & most concrete data. One really ought to think of the future apart from all likes, dislikes, & personal perspectives. He would then see a transformation in process; likely to invalidate most of our present standards, thought-habits, & pleasure-sources, & to substitute another set of these things which—though no doubt satisfying to those born under its aegis—will call forth less of the varied pleasure-&-thought-potentialities of mankind than the systems of the past & present have called forth. He needn't call this a tragedy if he doesn't wish to— for of course he will not live to reap its worst effects, while his great-grandchildren will be too steeped in the newer order to miss any other. But it would be hardly scientific of him to deny that a decline in the intrinsic level of civilisation is involved. We know well enough that different civilisations have different levels as judged by the amount of mental & emotional energy they draw forth from their component individuals—scale Greece against Persia, Egypt against Assyria, Rome against Carthage, France against India, & so on— & we likewise know that low-potential cultures often supplant cultures of higher potential. Hellenism gave way to Romano-Alexandrianism, Mayan culture to Nahuatlan-Aztec culture, & so on. The illusion of steady collective "progress" toward any desirable end is of relatively recent origin, & becomes absurd when we reflect that Periclean Greece lies some 2400 years behind our own essentially mediocre age. So far as we can see, there lies ahead of the western world a period of great material comfort & ostentation; amidst which a real culture will come to exist as a leisure class develops, but which will find its satisfactions on a less complex & poignant plane than that of the dying Renaissance culture. Then will come a Dark Age—precipitated either through ennui, collapse or external conquest—& after that an entirely different mongrel world beginning over again; though perhaps with intermediate stages involving the decreasingly vital use of various elements of the existing culture. And after the overthrow of all these fragments, there will be another building up from the nomad-pastoral state—with priest-king-war-chief, council of nobles, & all the other familiar anthropological forms which spring from the basic species-instincts against the background of unartificialised Nature. These people will gape at the legends which their old women and medicine-men will weave about the ruins of concrete bridges, subways, and building-foundations—& about the Sphinx & the pyramids & the rock-temples of Petra. How many times this patterned drama will be repeated, we cannot tell. It does not really matter, since quantity is really a very insignificant thing. Possibly the level of the highest previous civilisation will be surpassed—especially if a return to the primitive ever sets biologically evolutionary factors into motion again, producing types superior to any of the past & present. But all this means nothing to us—no more than as if the events took place on another planet—& if evolution does resume sway over us, the resultant beings will not be *men* in the strictest sense, any more than we are the apes who preceded us ancestrally. More—if the sun gives heat long enough, there will certainly come a time when the mammal will have to go down to subordination as the reptilia went before him. We are not nearly so well equipped for combating a varied environment as are the articulata; & some climatic revulsion will almost certainly wipe us out some day as the dinosaurs were wiped out—leaving the field free for the rise & dominance of some hardy & persistent insect species[3]—which will in time, no doubt, develop a high specialisation of certain functions of instinct & perception, thus creating a kind of civilisation, albeit one of wholly different perceptions, (when other species view a given object, their ocular image of it differs sometimes widely from ours) emphases, feelings, & goals. Probably the period of human supremacy is only the prologue to the whole drama of life on this planet—though of course some cosmic collision is always capable of smashing up the theatre before the prologue is done. All this sort of thing has undoubtedly happened an infinity of times in the past—planets being born & spawning a varied life; evolution & culture ensuing; & death & oblivion eventually overtaking all. Probably there are one or two other cases existent even at this moment; for although the newer conceptions of the cosmos have destroyed the old-time notion of "a plurality of worlds," it is always likely that the tidal accident which produced the solar system had counterparts sufficiently near in time to make probable the survival of their living results. If not in our galactic universe, these survivals may exist in remoter units of the Einsteinian space-time continuum.

As for your aesthetic conception of the history of all human branches as a single pattern or continuous process in which you can take a citizenlike pleasure & pride—of course, the picture is a pretty one, & was much cited in the naive & non-analytical Victorian days when sentimental over-extensions of the evolutionary idea took the place of the disinterested anthropology of the XXth century. It is, as an emotional attitude, perfectly sound & historically interesting—& is even comprehensible to me, since it bears analogies with my own sense of the whole cosmos rather than the earth as a working unit. But unfortunately it deals too much in unrealities, & in subjective illusions based on primitive & obsolete value-conceptions, to have a vital relationship to the problem of environment for the individual in real life. The actual individual—apart from a small group of theorists who specialise in this kind of feeling & derive certain artificial emotional-imaginative satisfactions from it as I do from my "infinite-cosmicism"—can form no more of a satisfying conception of himself as a member of an hypothetical biology-stream than a hen-louse can form satisfying conceptions of himself as a proud unit in the whole pedicular pageant of cat, dog, man, goat, & sand parasites. It all may be theoretically so—all men certainly have a vague common origin in one or two earlier primate species, while a few isolated culture-ideas are occasionally passed along—or taken over in a more or less garbled & fragmentary way—from one group to another—but, from the point of view of the normal member of any existing human group, what the hell of it? It simply doesn't *mean* anything. All our feelings & loyalties are based on the special instincts & inherited values of our immediate racial & cultural group—take these away, & absolutely nothing remains for any average person to anchor his sense of direction, interest, or standards to. What do you care about the mean annual temperature of Jupiter? Or I about the welfare of some lousy Chink or god damn nigger? Nothing but *artificial sentiment*, of a thin, unreal sort insufficient to hold any but a few imaginative individuals like you or me, could make any normal terrestrial Aryan care a hang about either Jupiter & Saturn's Ring on the one hand, or Chinks & niggers on the other hand. Nothing means anything vitally to us except something which we can interpret in the light of conditions we know. Empty words & their similarities mean very little—& we are very much mistaken if we think, upon reading the precepts of some ancient & exotic sage, that these words mean the same to us that they did to the people whose minds & feelings were fed from the same background as the Sage's. Spengler points this out with tremendous force—though it was highly apparent to me long before I ever heard of Bre'r Oswald. We live, always, by two codes—the external & professed code based on an artificially cosmopolitan culture; & the inner, real, & motivating code, based on the true response of our instincts to their habitual stimuli. It is all very well to theorise decoratively from the outer code—but we must apply the inner code when we wish to calculate actual results. Stripping off the mask of nineteenth century euphemism & decorum, we know damn well that the human race is divided into many groups whose whole instinctive conceptions of what is desirable & what is undesirable are so antipodally apart in half to three-quarters of the affairs of life, that they cannot possibly be thought of as having any goal or complete set of standards in common. And to *pretend* that such a community can exist, is to complicate the matter all the worse. We misunderstand all the more, when we feign to understand what we do not understand. Half the tragedies of history are the result of expecting one group to conform to the instinctive reactions of another, or to cherish its values. One of the worst examples of this is the cringing Semitic slave-cult of Christianity which became thrust upon our virile, ebullient Western stock through a series of grotesque historic accidents. Obviously, we whose instinctive ideas of excellence centre in bravery, mastery, & unbrokenness, & whose ultimate fury of contempt is for the passive, non-resistent, sad-eyed cringer & schemer & haggler, are the least fitted of all races for the harbourage of a Judaeo-Syriac faith &

standards—& so the whole course of history proved; with Christianity always a burden, handicap, misfit, & unfulfilled mockery upon our assertive, Thor-squared, Woden-driven shoulders. We have mouthed lying tributes to meekness & brotherhood under Gothic roofs whose very pinnacled audacity bespeaks our detestation of lowliness & our love for power & strength & beauty, & have spouted hogsheadfuls of hot air about "principle" & ethics, & restraint at the same time that our hobnailed boots have kicked around in utter loathing the broken Jews whose existence is based upon these principles. That is the hypocrisy of the altruistic & humanitarian tradition—talking & theorising against Nature as she actually works within us. From our attempt to assimilate Semitism we have gained nothing but misery—& the attempt itself has not succeeded, because it was based upon impossibility. Far more sensible is it to recognise that such an alien tradition has nothing for people of our blood & inheritance—that it presupposes goals & instincts which we do not & cannot possess; exalting that which we must always despise, & condemning that which we must always cherish as the supreme criterion of respect-worthiness. It is found by experience that Aryan & Semitic individuals & groups cannot get on side by side until one of the two has thoroughly obliterated its heritage & instincts & value-sense—& yet some idealists still think that an Aryan culture can really feel the Semitic ethics it outwardly professes; or that, more absurd still, it can have understanding & sympathy with still remoter racial & cultural streams. The question of relative status among different cultures is of wholly minor importance—it is the *difference* which makes cultural amalgamation a joke. China of the old tradition was probably as great a civilisation as ours—perhaps greater, as Bertrand Russell thinks[4]—but to fancy that more than a tenth of the emotional life of China has any meaning for us, is as foolish as to think that more than a tenth of our emotional life has any meaning for a Chinaman. Each can take over isolated points from the culture of the other; but these are always subtly altered in the process of naturalisation—never meaning the same thing in the adopting civilisation that they meant in the one which developed them. And when such adoptions exceed a certain limit of safety the result is always culturally disastrous to the nation attempting them. More is bitten off than can be chewed—& the outcome is a slackening or dispersal of the feelings & creative imagination which can lead only to sterility, unrest, & dissatisfaction. China & Japan are in the midst of this danger now—happy the one which knows how to beat a retreat! Even those people who maintain the gesture of universalism & cosmopolitanisn would—ironically enough—suffer as much loss & bewilderment as the rest if such a chaos were actually to exist. Every one of them is, unknown to himself, a holder of an illusion *fashioned wholly in the manner of his own especial culture;* so that when he talks with a cosmopolitan from another culture he is only exchanging *words, not deep feelings & image-perceptions genuinely shared.* If the especial culture of any one of these idealists were to vanish, he would find himself just as lost as anybody else—& would realise at last—too late—just how much of his emotional life & sense of comfortable placement really was due to the existence of his own background as a setting for his life & thoughts; however much he may have verbally repudiated that background in favour of a theoretic, meaningless hash made up of fragments of that & everybody else's backgrounds. There is no more *reality* in anybody's primary attachment to a mythical world-stream of all mankind, than there is in my primary loyalty to the whole cosmos as distinguished from our galaxy & solar system & planet. It sounds all right as an abstract principle—but there is no ponderable & authentic instinct to back it up so that it means nothing in the real alignment of groups. The doctrine can be admirably interesting to the one who decoratively holds it, so long as he keeps it free from application to the real world of events—just as a doctrine of cosmic feeling can be admirably interesting though of comparatively slight terrestrial significance. But it all belongs to aesthetics rather than to history or sociology. Its unreality is always manifested in the retinue of sentimental illusions & bursts of artistic expansiveness found around it. You can't pick a case that isn't cluttered up with grandiose emotion & naive beliefs in such illusions as good, evil, unified human nature & goal, justice, &c. &c. This delusion is the nineteenth century's expression of the same feelings that the seventeenth expressed in the delusion of religious faith, the eighteenth century in the delusion of ethical rights, & the twentieth in the delusions of mysticism (on the part of aesthetes) & industrial democracy. It is all part of an eternal comedy, at which the gods would laugh uproariously if they existed. Meanwhile each of the old cultures flickers along in its decadent way—each reacting in its individual & separate fashion to the common experience of mechanisation & easy transportation so suddenly encountered by all. And may god save New England, Virginia, & Old England from a total loss of their familiar motivating-springs & standard-moulding reference-points till Grandpa Theobald is safely fed to the worms of Swan Point Cemetery! As to whether the past transmits anything continuously to the future—whether one can believe that a slow collective stream is being formed from drops contributed by Akhnaton's Egypt & Confucius' China & Zoroaster's Persia[5]—that all depends on how practical a view one takes. In theory, later civilisations often trace certain conceptions of theirs to the influence of certain historic cultures & individuals of the past—whom they rediscover—but in practice it is doubtful how much the majority of this alleged influence amounts to; or whether the later civilisation wouldn't have been just as well off without what it received in this manner. Of the material we inherit or adopt in this way, as much is obstructive as is helpful. And as a matter of fact, the things we really do inherit are seldom the things we like to think we inherit—seldom the pompous generalities & ostentatiously sententious platitudes of articulate figureheads & stuffed shirts like Akky & Kong, Gautama J. Buddha & Schopenhauer, Lincoln, T. Woodrow Wilson, Zarathustra, Jesus H. Christ & George B. Mahomet, Rousseau, Kant, & so on. These people talk—but what they sum up is merely the undercurrent of collective thought & feeling & illusion in their respective groups, so that personally they don't do much harm or good, as the case may be. They say nothing that those around them have not said before, & start nothing that wouldn't have started just the same without them. What is more—when the inflated words of these sententious mouthpieces are analysed, we generally see that they are by no means so profound as they appear. A certain amount of their stuff is sound enough, because it deals with primitive reactions as noted by transmitted experience; but the majority is more or less local & immediate in its application—based on temporary standards & illusions, on arbitrary goals, & on definite social-racial-industrial-geographical milieux—so that it is an utter piece of hokum to apply half the dope of some simple-minded, half-epileptic Oriental mystic or prince or fisherman or tent maker of the agricultural, half-nomadic age, to the utterly antipodal life & problems of an increasingly mechanised western world. We forget that, although human nature itself is unchanging, all codes & reaction-formulae governing human beings involve not human nature alone, but human nature in relation to the immediate objective background of facilities & folkways, needs, occupations, previous fund of intellectual ideas & emotional habits, & prevailing customs of mental & emotional discipline. Half of what Buddha or Christus or Mahomet said is either simple idiocy or downright destructiveness, as applied to the western world of the twentieth century; whilst virtually *all* of the emotional-imaginative background of assumptions from which they spoke, is now proved to be sheer childish primitiveness. Most of their sonorous blah was based on certain ideas of the "dignity" (whaddyamean, dignity?) of human personality, & the "cosmic significance" of emotional experience & objective conduct, which the psychology of today shews to have been rooted altogether in illusion & unreality. None of this truck has any value for us, *except so far as* **the habit of listening to it** *has become natural to us through personal & ancestral associations immediate enough to form parts of our genuine heritage & motivating & value-breeding environment.* Thus Christ is worthless to us except as his myth is mixed up in our childhood memories—infantile prayers, Christmas-trees, shiny pennies at Sunday-School—& our elder aesthetic appreciations—Georgian steeples & Gothick apses, organ litanies, incense, emotional mysticism, &c. &c. He is of value only as the half-Italian, half-Flemish thin man whom we see in pictures, or the little blond English boy on Christmas cards. This is the contribution of the myth to our own vital heritage. Actually, we don't know yet whether or not any such one person really existed—& in his Coptic or Nestorian or Byzantine form he is a total loss to us westerners. This, then, is the only real value of the past beyond what a few remembered experiences have taught—that it forms a set of emotional sugar-plums & landmarks for us, by choosing a few special things out of infinity's conflicting chaos & setting them up for our immediate attention & preference. But heaven knows *that's value enough & to spare*—since without this subtle & unconscious guidance our emotional dilemma amidst the rival claims of an ungraspable bedlam of crowding, unrelated, & opposite sense-impressions, perception-foci, emotional thrills, & lines of logic would be desperate beyond description. In the blurred field of aimless ideas, images, & feelings offered by the external world past & present, there is no way of getting any kind of clear image save by applying the clarifying diaphragm of *traditional feeling*—the especially selected & coloured view of the past given us as a legacy by those who have gone before us—people whose blood & milieu were like ours, & whose choice of images and prejudices is more likely to fit us than anybody else's choice. Tradition can change & grow with time, of course; & it must occasionally admit new elements or discard certain old elements when they are proved contrary to fact. But the mutation & substitution must be gradual. It must not be so rapid or radical as to pry the individual loose from everything which gives him a sense of placement, interest, motivation, & direction—not so rapid or radical as to *destroy* tradition instead of properly *modifying* it. Once *destroy* a tradition, & what becomes of those who have held it? The only *absolute* value of any precept or belief is the part it plays in our emotional life. In bald truth, there is not any goal or idol of mankind which can be said to be intrinsically & collectively good—or bad, either—for the species. Goals shift slowly—just now we have *physical comfort* & *safety* as prime illusions; but it is almost certain that life would offer more & richer gratifications to imaginatively developed men if we could have a little less of these modern idols, & a little more of that divine *freedom, adventure, & vivifying sense of uncertainty & irregularity* which the virile individual enjoyed in less plumbered & policed days. What we have chosen as a goal is just as empty as what any former age chose—we shall have another goal tomorrow, & still another the next day—but meanwhile our good rotarians will think in terms of bathrooms & bodyguards; tobacco, trials, & time-tables. I refuse to be hoodwinked by temporary fashions in belief & feeling & aspiration—& see more healthy vitality in an outlaw who kicks over the traces in the blind protest of personality against the herd, than in the tame, social-minded conformer who bows to the will of the mass & helps that mass put across its milk-toast ideal of regularity, safety, comfort, justice, democracy, & big sales & dividends. I spit upon any man who cringes to the herd because of the herd's will. The only reason for a gentleman to do anything except what his fancy dictates, is that he can best sustain his illusions of beauty & purpose in life by falling harmoniously into the pattern of his ancestral feelings. The *individual*—feudal, proud, aloof, unfetter'd, & dominant—that is all that matters, & society is of use to him only so far as it enlarges the pleasures he might enjoy without it. He owes it only enough to make it capable of forming a suitable background for him—& to societies other than that from which he has sprung, he owes absolutely nothing. By the way—don't make the mistake of fancying that I recommend the Georgian age as a single period for all men's emulation. I never do so—but always try to make it clear that my own mental-emotional kinship to it is purely an individual accident, of significance to nobody but myself. I happen to belong to the eighteenth century—probably because of the effect of colonial doorways & long-s'd books upon me during my earliest & most impressionable years—but only the other day I caution'd a would-be poet against Georgian mannerisms. The eighteenth century is my illusion, as all mankind is yours—but I don't believe in mine any more than I do in yours! I don't believe in any! What the eighteenth century really was, was the *final* phase of that perfectly unmechanised aera which as a whole gave us our most satisfying life. It was not so aesthetically great as the Elizabethan age, & in no way comparable to Periclean Greece & Augustan Rome. Its hold upon moderns is due mostly to its *proximity*, & to the presence in it of certain kinds of taste which former & succeeding ages of modern history have lacked. *Proximity* is its main lure—for it is the *nearest* to us of all the purely pre-mechanical periods; the only one with which we have any semblance of a *personal* contact, (surviving houses & household effects in large quantity; association (for Americans) with high historic tension; fact that we can still talk with old men who in their youth talked with living survivors; vestigial customs & speech-forms in greater number than from earlier periods, &c. &c.) & whose ways are in any manner familiar to us save through sheer archaeological reconstruction. Moreover—it is brought still closer to us through the fact that the intervening nineteenth century was largely a blank in general civilisation—bequeathing us only a vast bulk of exact science & a few lone names in some of the arts. To all intents and purposes, we are chucking out the nineteenth century as an accidental grotesque; so that the eighteenth is a hundred years culturally nearer to us than it would ordinarily be. It is the eighteenth century, not the nineteenth, whose tradition we are now continuing—whether toward destruction or amplification history will later say. Naturally, in looking back over the Victorian desert of illusions, pomposities, & hypocrisies, we are pretty damn glad to strike the shores of a real culture—*any* real & rational culture. And since the eighteenth century (or very early nineteenth) is the *first* sound thing we hit in this backward quest, we are naturally rather predisposed in its favour! In cutting loose from 1890, we find 1790 the most convenient thing to re-hitch to in order to make a fresh start—but of course, it is really 1790 *&* 1690 *&* 1590 *&* 1490 *&* 1390 as well, that we are continuing. We're merely cutting out a bad piece in the rope & making a new splice. But all this is aside from my personal linkage. I, indeed, have special affinities with Georgian times—but these affinities in no way involve any claims of intrinsic superiority for those times. It is merely that I am more at home then than at any other period. Probably I'd be better off, aesthetically, if my natural inclinations were Elizabethan—but I'm as gawd (i.e., accident & temperament) made me. Might as well let it go at that, for I'll be dead soon, & then it won't matter a damn what age I belong'd to! As for the really important sources of our civilisation— I think we can spot most of 'em by including Teutonic & Celto-Druidic cultures for deep blood impulses, & Greece & Rome, relay'd by France, for intellectual & emotional surfaces. Syria gave us our mockery of a religion, & produced certain types of character among us, especially in the seventeenth century; so we'll have to count in the Hebraic stream as a spasmodic influence. Back of Greece & Rome the streams get damn thin, & there isn't one whose absence would change us much. Greece got more from the Minoan or Cretan culture than from anywhere else, though fragments from Egypt, Assyria, & Phoenicia are not absent. Rome got a damn lot from Etruria but still more from its central Italic tribes, & picked up many dubious acquirements—among them the conception of the non-racial political empire upheld by mercenary troops—from that goddam bunch of pawnbrokers & tradesmen call'd Carthage. Then in the Middle Ages the Arabs kicked in with a couple of useful tricks—& that about fixes us up. What China or India or the Aztecs gave us wouldn't keep anybody up nights computing. And what is more, it is only *as collocated parts* of our own English stream that the contributions of the earlier or alien streams have any meaning for us. We owe seven-eighths of all our civilisation to Greece—yet for all that we'd be fishes out of water in Periclean Athens. What we cherish is not Hellenism but Anglo-Hellenism. That natural culture-lines are based upon the soundest & most profoundly essential elements in every civilisation, is well shewn by analysing the types most prone & least prone to override them into the nebula of cosmopolitanism. Who are the instinctive cosmopolitans? Clearly, the artificially cultivated social elite & the specialty-engrossed artistic-scientific class at one end of the scale, & the purely animal workman-peasant rabble at the other end—in every case, persons wholly removed from the massed humanistic life of their group; by artificial manners & interests on the one hand, & by sheer lack of any mental-imaginative life on the other hand. And who are the instinctive provincials and nationalists? Always those who are most deeply absorbed in the normal general activities and interests of their region, and in the currents of thought and feeling engendered by real associations and tangible objects—the devotees, that is, of reality and of real perception, as opposed to those with artificialised or specialised perceptions, or with no perceptions at all. For my part, I'm no more ashamed to be a provincial *in time* than to be one *in space*—hence I hate & oppose the encroaching machine-barbarism as much as I'd hate & oppose any other alien civilisation that tried to find a foothold on the English soil of Rhode Island or Massachusetts or Maryland or Virginia. I don't expect to keep it off—but at least I don't pretend to like it. I defy, abhor, & repudiate it—as many a Frenchman in Alsace & Lorraine defied, abhorred, & repudiated the new culture that the Prussians brought in 1870.

I'm not the only one to see a really serious problem ahead for the sensitive aesthete who would keep alive amidst the ruins of the traditional civilisation. In fact, an attitude of alarm, pain, disgust, retreat, & defensive strategy is so general among virtually all modern men of creative interests, that I'm sometimes tempted to keep quiet for fear my personal feeling may be mistaken for affected imitativeness! God, man—look at the list . . . Ralph Adams Cram, Joseph Wood Krutch, James Truslow Adams, John Crowe Ransom, T. S. Eliot, Aldous Huxley, &c. &c. &c. &c. . . . . Each has a different plan of escape, yet each concedes the same thing to be escaped from. Cram favours mediaevalism & the ivory tower, Krutch the grim & gritted bicuspids, Adams the resigned superiority of contemplation, Ransom the return to the older spirit where it *can* be saved, Eliot the wholesale readoption of tradition—blindly, desperately undertaken in a mad escape from the Waste Land he so terribly depicted, (he says he is now a classicist, royalist, & Anglo-Catholic), Huxley in a kind of belatedly 1890-ish New Hedonism or neo-Hellenism, & so on, & so on. And still more tragic are the ostrich-heads who shut off their reason altogether at a certain point—beyond which they prattle in the artificial twilight of a pretended mental infancy . . . . G. K. Chesterton with his synthetic popery, Prof. Eddington with his observation-contradicting slush, Dr. Henri Bergson with his popular metaphysical pap, & so on, & so on. And Woodiwilsonites . . . . O gawd! These fools, when a real man like old Georges Clemenceau, who knew how to face the blank infinite unflinching, had to be snuffed out! About the only trained leaders of thought who pretend to retain the "da-da-da—all's right with the world" illusion without some degree of ostrichry are the old boys like Wells & Shaw, whose minds are petrified in the Utopian woods of the exploded XIX century—though even G. Bernardus is waking up a bit, to judge from some of his recent utterances. He no longer fancies that man's only foes are stupidity & capital . . . . deadwood of a temporary Fabian perfectionism. No question—the vital contemporary thought of the twentieth century's third decade will be almost one hundred percent anti-future—differing only in its prescriptions for circumventing or evading or annihilating or denying that future as doped out by commercial & industrial determinism. And the damn funny thing is that this retreat will probably breed a grotesque form of mental hypocrisy more offensive than mechanicalism itself, & almost as bad a type of intellectual illusion as Victorianism was of moral-aesthetic illusion. This hypocrisy, of course, has to do with the new mysticism or neo-metaphysics bred of the advertised uncertainties of recent science—Einstein, the quantum theory, & the resolution of matter into force. Although these new turns of science don't really mean a thing in relation to the myth of cosmic consciousness & teleology, a new brood of despairing & horrified moderns is seizing on the doubt of all positive knowledge which they imply; & is deducing therefrom that, *since nothing is true*, therefore *anything can be true* . . . . . whence one may invent or revive any sort of mythology that fancy or nostalgia or desperation may dictate, & defy anyone to prove that it isn't *emotionally* true—whatever that means. This sickly, decadent neo-mysticism—a protest not only against machine material- ism but against pure science with its destruction of the mystery & dignity of human emotion and experience—will be the dominant creed of middle twen- tieth century aesthetes, as the Eliot & Huxley penumbra well prognosticate. Little Belknap is already falling for it. And it will exist only because life has become unbearable through its increasing traditionlessness. As for me—I won't indulge in silly metaphysical "let's-pretend-ism", but I'll take tradition at face value as a purely emotional bulwark.

And so I've rambled on to page fifteen! Gord 'elp ya! Well—what I started out to shew was that it's a mistake to accept the element of human- favourableness as a balance-swinging factor in judging between rival theories of future developments. What will come, will come—& wishes & sentimental values & grandiose conceptions of a theoretical unity haven't anything to do with the likelihood or unlikelihood of any particular course. I don't foresee an instant age of anguish & barbarism—but neither do I foresee anything suffi- ciently favourable to Anglo-Saxon culture to justify any attitude but one of hostility in the real friends of high-potential human life and expression in our civilisation. I'm not one of "those sad young men" like Joseph Wood Krutch & Aldous Huxley, but neither am I one of those opaque-goggled, blandly unctuous dodderers like the Reverend William Herbert Perry Faunce, D.D.[6] . . . . . . of Providence, gawd help us! I simply draw the hard, cold, inevitable conclusions from a visible world undergoing certain definite phenomena, & from a cosmos in which there is not the slightest shred of probability that a governing consciousness, set of absolute values, or "spiritual" side exists. Of course, I respect equally the opinions of anyone who, from the same realistic data, builds up different conclusions. I'm nothing much as an intellectual heavyweight, & you've perhaps a rather better chance to be right than I have. But I won't pretend to see what I don't see—& the opinions I hold are the honest ones which, be they right or wrong, I get directly from the facts. My only *boast* is that I keep my line of reasoning free from certain *extraneous* ele- ments such as emotional predisposition. Of my *acuteness* in reasoning I make no claims & hold no high notions. All I am proud of is that I keep my facts straight *at the start*. Now sail in & give me hell—as you undoubtedly can! The only thing I insist on is that separate elements be kept separate, & that man's course be invested with no mystical & mythical "larger drift" which only *anal- ogy* & *wishfulness* could conceive, & against rather than toward which all the facts of observed reality point. We must not confuse the ceaseless course of the cosmos, with its alternate building-up & breaking-down of worlds & suns & galaxies, with the momentary individual course of any of the transient manifestations which break out accidentally once in an age upon the surface of one or two dust-grains. The natural course of any one of these transient manifestations—such as organic life on the earth—has about the same relationship to the course of the whole galactic system that a pimple's course has to the whole career of the man on whose nose it breaks out.

I certainly hope that nice old Mac got to Tacoma all right, & that he's resting up profitably at present. Neither Belknap nor I has heard from him yet—Belknap's report to that effect being as recent as last Monday. I dropped him a card regretting the mistake in dates—but I fancy that was his own slip rather than Sonny's. The Child called on him *Octr. 6,* & understood him to say that he was going to leave *in fourteen days,* which naturally would bring the date to the twentieth, as reported to me. However, the fact that the real departure-date was the *fourteenth of the month* leads me to suspect that the patient *thought* he told Sonny just that, but that he somehow gave his phraseology the misleading twist above cited. In the same way, he gave his new address to Belknap as *Dakoma* instead of *Tacoma.* The mistake cost him Belknap's bonvoyage visit as well as yours & Talman's—for the Child went out on Thursday the seventeenth & found the bird flown. It is provoking to reflect that he left wholly uncheered by calls, when at least three were guaranteed him under the supposed date-arrangement. I hope he doesn't take this circumstance as a sign that the gang has deserted him!

I don't blame you for not bein' able to swing a bookplate bill at present—damn'd if I could have consider'd such a thing myself! But when you do it, Talman's the boy to fix yuh up. He'll certainly give A #1 service at rock-bottom rates—my plate is no fortunate accident or luck shot—I've seen three others he did, & they're all absolutely oke! Gad, but I envy that boy his handy pen! If there's anything that makes me see red, it's inability to draw— for dozens of times a day I see dream-vistas of strange landscapes & curious architectural effects that I'd give ten bucks to be able to pin down on paper in good black & white line form. I bought a book on drawin' in Boston last January, but ain't had the goddam time to open it senct I brung it home![7]

No—I knew 'twarnt you as lost them pages outa my Baedecker. The little culprit has as good as confest—so I'm gonna borrow the original from ol' Mocrates & make Sonny type the missing pages for Grandpa on his Corona. That's a more practical & fruitful punishment than spanking the Child or making him stand in the corner! The carelessness of the younger generation is absolutely beyond tolerance! Young people didn't lose things like that in my day!

Yes—I hope them comin' tales awake your proper appreciation of Klarkash-Ton, Emperor of Dreams. Talman & Orton need education in that line also! Meanwhile some malign influence—prob'ly revising that Moe text book on poetick appreciation—has got me invadin' one of Klarkash-Ton's provinces & relapsin' back into my antient weakness of attempted prosody. Here's a piece a tripe I pull'd off the other day in Little Belknap's favourite medium of the irregular sonnet that scorns the abba-abba dope in its finer details. I'm tryin' this on Bre'r Farnsworth—it'll pull down three berries if he falls for it.

Recapture

The way led down a dark, half-wooded heath
Where moss-grey boulders hump'd above the mould,
And curious drops, disquieting and cold,
Spray'd up from unseen streams in gulphs beneath.
There was no wind, nor any trace of sound
In puzzling shrub, or alien-featur'd tree,
Nor any view before—till suddenly,
Straight in my path, I saw a monstrous mound.

Half to the sky those steep sides loom'd upspread,
Rank-grass'd, and clutter'd by a crumbling flight
Of lava stairs that scaled the fear-topt height
In steps too vast for any human tread.
I shrieked—and *knew* what primal star and year
Had suck'd me back from man's dream-transient sphere!

Cheerful li'l trifle! Then one day afore yestiddy I crack'd off another one—about the way a guy dreams about a place he thinks he knows, only to have the dream leave him flat with the conviction that the whole damn contents of his beezer is illusion & unrelated disjecta membra—but here goes. Nifty octosyllabicks—& note how I'm gettin' rid of the archaisms of diction. No more inversions, contractions, or typically & artificially "poetic" words excep' when I'm off me guard. Lissen, bozo:

THE ANCIENT TRACK

There was no hand to hold me back
That night I found the ancient track
Over the hill, and strain'd to see
The fields that teas'd my memory.
This tree, that wall—I knew them well,
And all the roofs and orchards fell
Familiarly upon my mind
As from a past not far behind.
I knew what shadows would be cast
When the late moon came up at last
From back of Zaman's Hill, and how
The vale would shine three hours from now.
And when the path grew steep and high,
And seemed to end against the sky,
I had no fear of what might rest
Beyond that silhouetted crest.

Straight on I walk'd, while all the night
Grew pale with phosphorescent light,
And wall and farmhouse gable glow'd
Unearthly by the climbing road.
There was the milestone that I knew—
"Two miles to Dunwich"—now the view
Of distant spire and roofs would dawn
With ten more upward paces gone. . . . . .

There was no hand to hold me back
That night I found the ancient track,
And reached the crest to see outspread
A valley of the lost and dead:
And over Zaman's Hill the horn
Of a malignant moon was born,
To light the weeds and vines that grew
On ruin'd walls I never knew.
The fox-fire glow'd in field and bog,
And unknown waters spew'd a fog
Whose curling talons mock'd the thought
That I had ever known this spot.
Too well I saw from the mad scene
That my lov'd past had never been—
Nor was I now upon the trail
Descending to that long-dead vale.
Around was fog—ahead, the spray
Of star-streams in the Milky Way. . . .
There was no hand to hold me back
That night I found the ancient track.

Yeh—now we gettin' kina warmed up! Well—here's another one . . . . typed all legible-like & carefully enclos'd . . . . which I'm gonna ast ya to shoot back like ya done the travelogue—so's I kin lend it to some other bozo & have 'im lose haff of it. The title of this beautiful lil' bullet is "The Outpost", & the scene is the celebrated continent of Africa—in the days when great cities dotted the eastern coast, & smart Arab & Phoenician Kings reign'd within the walls of the great Zimbabwe—now a mass of cryptic ruins overrun by apes & blacks & antelope—& work'd the illimitable mines of Ophir. But far, far in the interior . . . . . on the never-glimps'd plain beyond the serpent-shunn'd swamp . . . . . rumour hinted that a frightful & unmentionable outpost of THEM brooded blasphemously—& so K'nath-Hothar the Great King,[8] who fear'd nothing, stole thither in secret one night . . . . . though whether he did so in body or in his dreams, not even he can certainly tell.

Anyhow—lamp the doggerel & see wot it done to the poor fish! N.B.
K'nath-Hothar was *not* oulothrix—& he had *thin lips*, a *very large* aquiline nose,
& a *light* complexion inherited from his *Nordick* stream. And P.S.—his father's
hair was *straight*, & the paternal nose *long* & the paternal lips *thin*. This father,
the late great King Zothar-Nin, was born in Sidon of pure Phoenician stock.
As for *prose*—just wait, 'bo, till I get one final revish job off me hands! You'd
be surpris'd . . . . . yuh ain't seen nuttin' yet!

Oh—by the way—as for prophets honour'd in their own country for the
first time . . . . get the cuttings from the lit'ry colyum of the *Prov. Journal* enclosed heare! And see how Grandpa rung in two of his small boys![9] Yuh kin
keep this dope if the subject is of enuff intrust to warrant it—otherwise
shooter back for subsequent loans. I also enclose a zippy editorial on a leading and-*where*. Oh, yes—here's a New Zealand stamp'd envelope from a
young amachure publisher that may take your eye. Wishta gord I was where
he is right now—their *November*, damn it, is equiv to our *May!* And I gotta
wait & hibernate VI mo.!

So yore min'rul collectin' is lay'd off for the winter, eh? Come & visit
Providence! This is the BEST season of *all* for visitin' here! But I suppose
your rearranging has gotta go on—hell, & after yuh got all them stones fixt
up so swell before! Don't forget Bill Bryant w'en ya ships yore dupes & oxes.

Well—here's where I give ya some peace after eighteen pages! Not because I'm especially kind-hearted, but because it's time to drag me aunt out to
Bennan's Restaurant for a turkey feed—first time she'll have et out in a year
'n' a half!

I am, Sir, ever yr most oblig'd, most obt Servt—

Θεοβάλδος

Notes

1. The Latin means a book regarding a kind of sausage—thus, *Peace Poems and Sausages*.

2. Psammetichus (Psamtik I), the first of the three kings in the 26th Dynasty of Egypt
(r. 664–610 B.C.E.); he ruled at a time when Egypt was constantly battling the king-
doms of Assyria and Babylonia. Lucian of Samosata (125?–180? C.E.), Greek satirist
and author of the satirical fantasy *True History* and many other works. Anicius Manlius
Severinus Boethius (480?–525?), Christian philosopher and author of the *Consolation of
Philosophy*. Venantius Honorius Clementianus Fortunatus (530?–609?), Latin poet and
bishop of the Roman Catholic church.

3. The idea is taken up in "The Shadow out of Time" (1934–35), where it is suggested
that beetles will supplant humanity as the dominant species on the planet.

4. See Bertrand Russell, *The Problem of China* (1922). HPL probably read an extract
from this book in *Selected Papers of Bertrand Russell* (1927).

5. Akhnaton (more properly Akhenaten, also known as Amenhotep IV), pharaoh of
Egypt (1353–36 B.C.E.); Confucius (551–479 B.C.E.), Chinese philosopher; Zoroaster
(or Zarathustra, 628?–551? B.C.E.), Persian prophet and founder of Zoroastrianism.

6. William Herbert Perry Faunce (1859–1930), American educator, theologian, and president of Brown University (1899–1929).

7. Charles Lederer, *Drawing Made Easy* (1927).

8. Not mentioned by name in the poem.

9. See letter 83n7. B. K. Hart ran lists of best weird tales as selected by Frank Belknap Long and August Derleth in his column for 23 November.

[85]   [AHT]

Saturday, 1929 [7 December]

Titanick Top of Terrestrial Tremendousness:

Sire! Despotes! Master! Your slave grovels, cringes, implores, pleads, begs, curries favour . . . . . Aië! Aië! Aië!

You may recall, Sir, that last July, when I told you of my desperate campaign to save the old brick warehouses in S. Water street, you offer'd in a spirit of divine generosity to assist in the hopeless fight to the extent of signing a letter of protest to the *Sunday Journal,* & thus lending the weight of discriminating curatorialism to the cause so sorely in need of succour. Well—months have went by, & now a salaaming helot weeps for the promis'd aid!

What hath started me up afresh is the renew'd report of the brick row's doom—plus the enclos'd article in *The Netopian,* (house organ of Providence's most influential bank)[1] which brings up the tears of nostalgia & melancholy, & rubs salt in the wounds of bereavement. Aië! Aië! Aië!

To let this priceless heritage go without the most extreme resistive measures, were almost as grave a vandalism as the active vandalism of the nameless barbarians responsible for the impending outrage; hence at last I am putting forth my final despairing wail, & calling upon the most potent of my allies. Succour, Great King! Fail not a kneeling vassal!

So here is the thing to sign! Pray put the official Jawn Hancock just above the printed signature—that's the way high-power officials end up their letters nowadays, so that they can both register their personality, & have the reader know who's talking. And don't fail to send it in a printed, return-address envelope with the academick museum aroma clinging about it. The more ponderously Savantish, the more influential![2]

As for me—I have cooked up twelve elegiack pentameter stanzas of melancholy & sent them to the *Journal* on the slender chance that some charitable editor will slip 'em in.[3] I'll let you see 'em shortly—in manuscript if they don't get as far as print. But the big thing is to have the important Mortonian letter sent! I can't imagine that yᵉ ed won't print it—if he doesn't, he's a cursed traitor to the traditional beauty of his home burg!

Have just laid in four little bookcases to stack on top of the lower bookcases in the room, & relieve the prevailing bibliothecal pressure. They don't look half bad—but they hardly do more than accomodate the already-accumulated surplus on floor & in odd corners. Not a bit of spare shelf space left!

More anon—& thanx in advance for the letter business.

With renew'd obeisances—

Θεοβάλδος

Notes

1. The *Netopian* (1920–31) was published by the Rhode Island Hospital Trust Company.
2. See Appendix for HPL's letter, written on Morton's behalf.
3. "The East India Brick Row" (written December 7).

[86]   [AHT]

Freyr's Day, Dec. [6,] 1929

Kuchinjunga[1] of Knife-Keen Kultur:—

Couldn't resist slipping you the accompanying (over)[2] dope on bookplate prices before it gets lost amidst the chaos of my table. File it away till you're ready to take advantage of the offer, & then remember our young friend!

And incidentally—here's some more zippy "Sideshow" dope. Hell, but I'm gettin' to be a well-known guy aroun' Providence! Anybody'd think I'd lived here some time! Return this—as well as the earlier slips—strictly at your own convenience. Not a damn bit of hurry. Curious how B. K. H. stumbled on this "Cthulhu" stuff just when he did—I never told him a word about writing original fiction.[3]

One kick about that "Sideshow" socony was that it gave me my first inkling of the fact that I've made Neddy O'Brien's "Best Short Story" annual & Roll of Honour for a *second* consecutive year—this time with "The Dunwich Horror". Hell, but it makes a bozo feel kinda lit'ry to become a reg'lar O'Brien standby! And when I came to track this honour stuff down, I found two minor items as well—just to make Dunwich stand out with great prominence. The full list of medals for 1929 which adorn my bespangled buzzum is as follows:

"The Dunwich Horror"——	O'Brien 3-star Roll of Honour
"The Silver Key" ————	O'Brien 1-star 3d rate mention
"The Silver Key" ————	3d rate mention in O. Henry Memorial Prize Short Story Annual—the one that gave "Pickman's Model" a 3d-class place last year.

The O'Brien mention kinda tickles the old man's vanity, since Neddy reely knows what's what in life & litrachoor, as you'll know when you've read his "Dance of the Machines". But the O. Henry pat doesn't get me xited a-tall, since the standard of that annual is largely popular magazine hokum—Saddypost slop.

By the way—of the doggerel I slipt into your last epistle, Wright has accepted "The Ancient Track" for eleven bucks, & "Recapture" for $3.50. He turned down "The Outpost" on the alleged ground of excessive length, but I'm sure the real reason is because he wouldn't believe in the thin-lipp'd non-oulothrixitude of the Great King!

Klarkash-Ton has just writ a masterful tale call'd "Satampra Zeiros". One glance at it will open your eyes at last!

Thine grovellingly—

Θεοβάλδος

P.S. That Thanksgiving feast was a success, but the goddam *cold* about knockt me out! The next evening, not knowing how cold it was, I foolishly went outdoors, & nearly perisht on the return trip—lost my dinner (glad it wasn't the day before!) & most of my balance, & have felt kinda sore & run-through-a-wringer-like ever since! I sure gotta getta plantation in Jamaica!

Notes

1. Kangchenjunga (Nepal) is the third highest mountain in the world (after Mount Everest and K2), with an elevation of 28,169 feet.
2. [From a letter by Wilfred B. Talman, on reverse of letter:] Thanks for all the things regarding bookplates. I trust you don't want those Silver Art (?) samples back, as I'd like to have them in the morgue as a genesis for ideas. They seem to be a bit high priced ordered from there. You can tell Morton that I would design him a plate for an amount not to exceed $20 (minimum $10) depending upon the amount of work & revision that I would have to do after submitting sketches to him once or twice. For this amount I would draw the picture, have the cut made (price does not include cost of cut, which would be about $2.50) and see that the thing was printed in proper shape on the right kind of stock. In other words, he would merely have to pay me for the designing and for my trouble in attending to the matters and foot bills for cut and printing. If he was satisfied with the first sketch, thus doing away with the trouble of arguing about the thing by correspondence, he should be able to get 500 plates for about $20, maybe a dollar to two less. This is a trifle higher than I would have charged a year or two ago, but I figure my time is more valuable, and less of it available, now.
3. When reading HPL's "The Call of Cthulhu" in *Beware After Dark!*, B. K. Hart was astonished to read that the residence of sculptor Henry Anthony Wilcox at 7 Thomas Street was one he himself had once occupied. B. K. Hart, "The Sideshow," *Providence Journal* 101, No. 285 (29 November 1929): 12.

[87]   [AHT]

Thor's Day, Dec. [12,] 1929

Florescent Finial of Fonetik Filosofy:—

My gord—so I didn't hit your style even tho' I try'd rather hard to eliminate Theobaldian individualisms! And as for the *spelling*—what the hell! After all my efforts to duplicate your provincial Websterian orthography, leaving the *u* out of honour, and so forth! I thought I'd caught your system to perfection—indeed, I really don't think the Yankee destroyers leave the *u* out of *glamour*, any more than they leave it out of *amour*. Look it up in some of your new-fangled alleged dictionaries & see! About *aesthetic*—help! help! help! O Māna-Yood-Sushāī in Pegāna! Are *you* one of those middle-Western diphthong-choppers,—*you*, James Ferdinand Plantagenet-Morton, of Novanglia's noblest line? ¡O Dios! ¡O Monterey! I knew that Farnsworth Wright & Maurice Winter Moe did that sort of thing—Chicago-Milwaukee brashness—& that the country editors west of the Mississippi sometimes go in for *thru, thot, altho, center,* & all that damned nonsense. But east of the Alleghenies—the erudite curator of a large city's museum—O, take me out & shoot me at sunrise! How in gawd's name do you spell *aesthetic*—"*esthetik*"—"*'s-thet-yk*"??? Boy, this is a knockout! *"Honor"* & *"la-bor"* are bad enough, but all the provincials do that. One can become harden'd, if not reconcil'd, to such things. But *thru* & *thot* & *esthetik* & *sulfur* & *fotografi* . . . . blah, yah! I guess we'd better take up Esperanto before the Keokuk & Dubuque school of pidgin-English turns our mother-tongue into a chaos of demotic hieroglyphs that a gentleman can't decipher! I have waded through it in *Weird Tales,* & the Valparaiso, Ind., *Unafraid Republican*—but thou too, O Brutus! Funny part is, I never noticed such perversions in your manuscripts—probably because I read *currente oculo,*[1] & with a naive trust that eminent Harvardians never do such things! I'll vow the better grade of Eastern papers & periodicals don't . . . . . . test a page of the *Transcript* or *Prov. Journal* or *Times* & see! Well—the fact that such *further* insidious corruptions are undermining our spelling, forms all the better argument for a standpatter like me. Once a set of idealists begin tampering with a language, there's no telling where they'll end. All standards & homogeneity of usage disappear for want of an anchor in tradition. Kat, dorg, haurse, kou, bool, howss, boi, skul, ... & so on down the scale to the utter nadir of shifting usage typical of certain Amazon-valley tribes, whose language shifts so rapidly that the young men can scarcely understand the conversation of their grandfathers. I take a reasonable middle course—dropping (in publickly display'd manuscripts) the final *k* on words like *comick* & *musick,* & writing *shore, landscape, smoke,* &., instead of *shoar, landskip, smoak,* &c., but not following individual cliques or detached sections of the Anglo-Saxon world into personal or local perversions of the widely accepted norm. There is no use dragging up theoretical arguments about phonetics—the language is far too full of traps & paradoxes to make any attempt at an Utopian eye-sound scheme more than a joke or a nuisance. It is altogether a matter of arbitrary usage & aesthetic association—& sound conservatism, for lack of any tangible value attached to any other course, sticks to the normal forms we are used to—the forms which connect up with our sense of inconspicuous rightness & easy, unconscious habituation. Doctrinaires & victims of the barbarian business-efficiency complex can write in any kind of Choctaw they like. It doesn't matter much what sort of gibberish is employ'd by the decadent world of mechanised & time-tabled Babbittry. But, by gad, Sir, gentlemen will continue, on the whole, to spell as gentlemen! It isn't so bad to write *honor* & *color*—for that vice has a full century of usage behind it in a region as reasonably civilised as the American Atlantick Coast. But when it comes to *thru, tho, thoro, brot, Etna, Esculapius,* &c. &c.—well, count me out! I have such things to the leader-writers of the Abilene, Texas, *Daily Clarion,* or the Wakookoo, Kansas, *Weekly Winding-Sheet.* Hell!!

Incidentally, though, you missed the one real bum spelling in the manuscript. *Eurythmy* had a redundant *h,* due to stenographick haste! Also—our joint pangs & anxieties are render'd purely abstract by the fact that the *Journal* used its own style-code anyhow, & would change your forms & mine alike to its own!!

Yrs. in architectural rapport but orthographical rapping
—Πάππος Θεοβάλδος

Notes

1. Literally, "with a running eye," or rapidly.

[88]   [AHT]

Wednesday, Dec. [18], 1929

Sky-Saluting Spire of Super-Sacramental Sagacity:—

Alas, that I should have to begin this epistle with an answer to your Mac-question which is worse than merely ominous! I had fancied that I would not have to break a piece of bad news which I gained from a newspaper item—*Associated Press*—presumably read by everybody; but both you & Little Belknap seem to have skimmed through last Sunday's papers with an all-too-merciful lightness—hence my melancholy task of becoming the gang's informant in a matter where I wish there were something less depressing to inform.

For our good old friend found his illness too formidable a foe to resist, & passed away on Saturday, December 14, at his sister's home in Tacoma. It gave me a devilish jolt to read it, for I certainly thought the rest & the Pacific climate would do him good; but it seems that he suffered a relapse shortly after his arrival, & was somehow unable to shake it off. It is, as you say, odd that his sister communicated with none of us despite our inquiries. According to the *Times* item (which you'll find in Sec. 2 of Sunday's paper) she did write "friends at his former residence, 457 Fifth St., Bklyn."—to me a quite inexplicable proceeding; since so far as I recall, the only person he knew there was his crabbed German landlord Muck, whom he did not at all like. But the item tells us the outcome as sadly well as any letter could. It does seem accursedly strange & dismal to try to realise that nice old Mac is no more—& to reflect that he had so short a period of emergence from the utter squalor amidst which so many of his days were spent. I had hoped tremendously that he might have a long & restful evening of life to compensate for the trials he had endured—though, as I have just written Sonny, it is at least something that he had a brief spell of better surroundings toward the close, instead of meeting the dark gulf amidst the pandaemoniac filth of Hell's Kitchen. One can't help wondering whether the long transcontinental trip was, after all, advisable in view of Mac's enfeebled condition. Both Belknap & I thought he ought to take a rest at an hospital before attempting it—& we so told him, by tongue & pen, respectively—but apparently he found the idea unpractical or uncongenial. And perhaps, of course, it would have done no good. One cannot predict exactly in such matters—as witness the optimistic report of the young doctor at St. John's last spring. I hope Mac received all our letters, & was sufficiently conscious to realise the good-will & unbroken solicitude which they contained. I wrote him two letters & several cards at the Tacoma address— the last card, though, may not have found him living. I had a Christmas card, too, all ready to mail in time to reach Tacoma before the holiday. It is almost impossible to feel, even yet, that such a card now has no destination! As for gang notifications—I suppose Talman must know; because he is on the *Times,* & reporters generally read their own papers. I don't think he wrote the item, though; (i.e., the "local angle" appended to the brief AP report) because it isn't as ample as he would have made it—or as Mac deserved. The B. P. C. ought to hear about it—especially Kleiner & Dench—& I presume you are the logical one to let each of this group know when the opportunity presents itself. I have written Little Belknap—& also Orton, to whom I happened to be writing at the time—& believe I'll drop cards to Wandrei & Bernard Dwyer. You might let Kirk & Loveman know when you drop around to their respective habitats. Would that there were less dismal tidings to spread!

It does seem hard to imagine the gang without good old Mac somewhere in the background as a high spot of its general setting—for he was one of the founders; & his naive, individual note formed one of the most characteristic contributions to the entire symphony. At any rate, he will have a kind of modest & affectionate immortality in our reminiscent folklore—as well as in the memory of the thousands of boys who have read his tales. I can hardly think of the N. Y. terrain without his quaint, likeable figure somewhere about—indeed, he is an inextricable part of that earlier & more favourable image of the metropolis which I acquired before familiarity bred disgust & ennui . . . . the exotic, glamourous, expectant, fantastic, adventurous image of strangeness, magnitude, & complex mystery springing from a first sight of Dunsanian pinnacles, labyrinthine tangles of unknown streets, seething alien-daemoniac vitality, surprising vistas of cryptic terraces & balustrades, unlimited museum-wealth, weird diversity of landscape-impressions, glittering twilights that turned to phantom-haunted nights when the dusk pressed down like a low roof on aisles & halls of supernatural phosphorescence, & the vast, level reaches of the old Dutch marsh country around Sheepshead Bay, brooding with elder mystery in the autumn gloaming, & with the winds of old Holland's canals blowing the sedges that waved & beckoned along strange, salty inlets. That vague, far-off imagery, already pushed back into a kind of dreamland by the lapse of more than seven years, would be a lot less glamourous if deprived of Mac's little plodding figure. I recall the first time I saw him—at Dench's, by the old, curious wharves of Sheepshead Bay. He used to like to go there—& you & he used to have subway races back to town on the old B. R. T.—not B. M. T. in those days. Hare-&-Tortoise stuff, if I recall aright . . . . . you, the dashing meliorist, would change at DeKalb for a bridge train, but honest old Mac would plod along on his tunnel local past Borough Hall, (there wasn't any Lawrence St. station then) Whitehall St., Rector St., Cortlandt St., City Hall, Canal St., Prince St., Eighth St., Fourteenth St., Twenty-third St., Twenty-eight St., Thirty-fourth St. . . . . & finally meet you at Times Square to prove that you hadn't outdistanced him by more than eight minutes at best! And I recall how he shewed Sonny & me Hell's Kitchen—the first time either the Child or I ever saw it. Chasms of Hogarthian nightmare & odorous abomination—Baudelairian Satanism & cosmic terror—twisted, fantastic Nordic faces leering & grimacing beside night-lapping beacon-fires set to signal unholy planets—death brooding & gibbering in crypts & oozing out of the windows & cracks of unending bulging brick walls—sinister pigeon-breeders on filth-choked roofs sending birds of space out into black unknown gulfs with unrepeatable messages to the obscene, amorphous serpent-gods thereof[1]—Forty-ninth St., Eleventh Ave.—Forty-seventh St.—Tenth Ave.—black eyes painted—police in pairs—filth—odours—fantastic faces in bonfire-flares—swarming & morbid vitality—Ninth Ave. elevated—& through it all the little white-haired guide plodding along with his simple, idyllic dreams of sunny Wisconsin farm-worlds, & green, beckoning, boy-adventure worlds, & wholesome, Utopian worlds of fixed values which never were & never can be. No that strange, Dunsanian, expansive, mysterious vision-metropolis of 1922—that metropolis so unlike any that one may find around N. Y. in 1929—wouldn't be much without honest old Mac! And because it *is* a vision-metropolis; "out of space, out of time",[2] & without linkage to the mundane, the material, & the perishable; it indeed never need be without him. Through those fantastic streets, along those fantastic terraces, & over those fantastic salt marshes with the waving sedges & sparse Dutch gables, the quaint, likeable little figure may continue to plod . . . . . phantom among phantoms, though perhaps not less real in a cosmic sense than the phantoms of electronic patterning which we call matter. Perhaps not less real, & surely more beautiful & exalted, as all things of dream are more beautiful & exalted than things of substance and waking.

As for the argumentative strain into which I inadvertently burst last month—you are indeed eminently right in saying that the best form of reply is an equally full statement of your own position from the ground up. That is really the best way in any case—to establish territory, define terms, visualise standards, & in every way anticipate & abolish the ambiguity & misunderstanding inevitable in a debate which consists merely of point-by-point attack & defence. I fancy that this is really the principle back of my own voluminously verbal plan of discussion, although I never paused to envisage & classify & approach my method. Thus I shall await with eagerness your philosophick volume or volumes, looking forward to some absorbing analysis when I get at your array of data & your interpretations thereof. Meanwhile I can but reaffirm my previously stated point—that in judging evidence, absolute impartiality must be observed. When the object of an argument is to establish *whether or not* the natural trend of the cosmos at this particular instant (for we *know* it isn't in the long run, since we can physically, chemically, & astronomically foresee the end of the solar system) be favourable to the wishes of a large part of the human species, we cannot adopt *the quality of such favourableness* as a factor in weighing the evidence, since that would constitute the logical flaw called *petitio principii*, or "begging the question". It would be, in effect, to say "that the cosmos is favourable to man, *because* the opposite conclusion is made improbable by its unfavourableness to man"—just such a flaw as appears in the proposition that "parallel lines will never meet *because* they are parallel". If we really wish to establish the favourableness of the cosmos to man, we must build up the conclusion from uncoloured & impartially selected evidence—evidence weighed with no spirit other than the cool, disinterested, *is-or-isn't* spirit. If *then* we find a favourable cosmos indicated, well & good. But no conclusion of any sort can be authentic when derived from ulteriorly influenced thinking, or from evidence chosen & coloured by wishes, preconceptions, & hereditary myths & traditions. We must face the infinite cosmos starkly & alone—mind in contact with evidence & nothing but evidence. History & formal philosophy must step aside, for only *pure science* is of value in determining *what is & what isn't*.

No hurry about the Talman bookplate business, I fancy—his rates are stable & modest! But what's the harm of plastering your library in instalments, class by class? For my part, I wouldn't waste a plate on half the tattered junk that crowds my shelves. Best books first—then down the aesthetic scale. And when I run out of plates I can have some more done from the cut at $3.75 per 500. Speaking of books—I told you of my new (cheap unpainted) cases. Four of 'em—the two larger atop the lower members of my

south-wall triptych, one of the smaller atop the door-neighbouring case beneath the golden Gothick panel, & the other smaller one on my table as a
secretary-like background against the never-used west window. The effect
isn't quite as bad & crowded as I feared it would be—but damn it all, the new
cases do no more than sop up the worst of the pre-existing surplus! Not an
inch of spare shelfage, & the two glass-door'd cases still as jammed as hell!
It's damn lucky that I'm a slow collector—but anyhow, I gotta get s'more
cases soon!

Yeh—I fear it's gonna be a helluva winter! I envy you your next summer
Southerning—which I may try to emulate to the extent of a trip to Charleston
. . . . . by the way of His Majesty's Virginia Dominion. I'll see you in Novanglia, of course—especially when you collect & pack & ship your R. I. minerals!

And so it goes. Wish this epistle didn't have to have such a melancholy
burthen—but things must be so now & then.

Yr oblig'd & obt

Θεοβάλδος

Notes

1. Within weeks, HPL wrote "The Pigeon-Flyers" (originally titled "Hell's Kitchen"),
sonnet X of *Fungi from Yuggoth*, describing this scene. Other images described here are
also found in *Fungi from Yuggoth*, written shortly after this letter.
2. Poe, "Dream-Land" (1844), l. 8.

[89]   [AHT]

Friday
[27 December 1929]

Era-Excelling Epitome of Erudition, Earthly and Ethereal:—

Your two notes at hand—but I'm ahead of you in the crossing game if that
envelope of cuttings counts as one qualified move! I envy you your trip to
Washington and Philadelphia—both favourite towns of mine—and only regret
that you can't get still farther South this time. As for the New Year rites of the
excitable New York natives—can't you get to Paterson without going to the
barbarick island at all? I'm sure all trains stop at Manhattan Transfer, where a
civilised New-Jerseyman can somehow edge toward Newark and Paterson by
means of local conveyances. Or perhaps it is to Paterson orgies that you refer—though I didn't know the Manhattan infection had spread that far.

By the way—Moe lately presented me with one of the most magnificently lyrical protests against time-table slavery and sodden submission to the
predicted and the predictable that I have ever seen—a funny thing for a ma-
chine-bound routine soul like ol' Mocrates to do, but motivated by his peda-
gogical admiration for the utter splendour of the prose style. It is "Sirenica"

by one W. Compton Leith—who is said to be one of the attaches of the British Museum. For continuous royal purple of phraseology, plus noble revolt against the ignominy of the usual and the catalogued and the expected, this piece of work comes near to taking all the first prizes in sight! Don't miss it— if you can't get it at the bibliotheca publica, wire the publisher for a dozen copies! Try it over on your piano . . . . . give it away to all your friends who shew either danger of machine-slavery or appreciation of fine prose . . . or both. Published by Tho. Bird Mosher, in Falmouth, in yᵉ District of Maine, Province of yᵉ Massachusetts-Bay—vulgarly and latterly known as Portland, Maine. Rather de luxe, though marr'd by at least one misprint—*Laertes* for *Laërtes*. It is, all told, a plea for the amplification of the too-orderly Hellenick spirit by a touch of the Gothick—the proud lawlessness of the mystical, warlike, unbroken, and imaginative North.

As for the winter—thank gawd for gas, oil, & electricity in addition to the furnace! I have my schedule now arranged so that I don't have to go out more than twice a week for supplies—Tuesdays & Fridays, usually. If it's under twenty-five degrees, I can usually manage to shift my trip to a more civilised sort of day. Christmas, thank Pegāna, was decently mild—& I succeeded in dragging my elder aunt down town for the first time in a year & a half—to partake of an old-time Christmas feast with plum pudding and all, at the hospitable refectory of that staunch upholder of ancient English tradition—Chin Lee, Esq., (a *very* distant eastern connexion—phonetically at least—of the main Virginia line of Stratford & Arlington!)[1] who so liberally stocked you with chow mein at our little pre-Maxfield supper last June. Downtown seemed rather changed to my aunt—though the front side, at least, of the doomed brick row still stands. May misfortune, leprosy, radium-poisoning, remorse, time-table slavery, sudden death, & everything else pursue the criminals who are destroying this loveliest legacy of old days—pursue them, & all their posterity even unto the time of the great Spenglerian collapse!

De re orthographica—I am the last to maintain the existence of an inflexible standard, but I think the collective usage of the most civilised part of the Anglo-Saxon world for the past hundred years is uniform, homogeneous, & continuous enough to serve as a proximate standard in the absence of any other logical basis for rule-making. I am not defending the eighteenth century— although it is then that uniform usage first began to develop—so much as the collective custom of late eighteenth, nineteenth, & early twentieth centuries. Spelling is so wholly a matter of custom, taste, & ocular appeal, that we cannot well adopt any criterion other than that of harmonious naturalness as determined by the group practice of the most cultivated & articulate minds in the most cultivated parts of the civilisation. I don't let etymology bother me at all— it means nothing to me that colour & neighbour have different histories. But it means much that these forms are the spontaneous & natural ones in constant & uniform use in the most enlightened & mature portions of our culture-area.

To my mind a barren vowel does not convey the delicate imaginative overtones of association that a diphthong does in places where a diphthong traditionally belongs. No Enceladus stirs beneath an "Etna", & no Promethean grandeur was ever evoked for Golden-Age Athens by an "Eschylus". "Medieval" darkness lacks the sublimity of Gothick towers & the fascination of hellish Sabbats. You can't tell me that an "Eolian" harp plays anything but jazzy blues, & if Paris's early girl-friend spell'd her name "Enone", I don't wonder he quit her cold for a new Jane! It would take an "eon" to cram "Edipus" down my "esophagus", complex & all; nor would I believe that any emasculate "Lestrigonian" could chew me up! No, by gad, Sir, during the few years left to me, I'll spell as gentlemen spell'd in my time! Of course I knew that some Elizabethans used the -or termination. Honor occurs in W. S.'s first Folio. But as I said, my criterion is good, civilised eighteenth, nineteenth, twentieth century usage!

> Yrs for civilisation & conservatism—
> Θεοβάλδος

Notes

1. HPL humorously associates the proprietor of a local Chinese restaurant with Robert E. Lee and his lineage.

[90]   [AHT]

Wednesday, Jan. [8,] 1930

Summation of Saxiscient Seigneury:—

Well, this is a season of melancholy news! Just had word from Cook that this wife died on Jany. 1st.—interred at Norwich, Conn., Jany 4th. She sustained a shock early in October—falling against a stove & adding burns to the malady itself. For a time she was in the hospital, but was later home with a nurse. Two weeks ago Cook wrote that there was no hope—& now I see that the apprehension was justified. Poor old soul! Though unlettered & frankly plebeian, she was always kindly & generous; & her affection for Cook was naive & touching. He will miss her as he might miss a mother—& those who, like Wandrei & me, have enjoyed the hospitality of the Cook home, must feel a pensiveness upon reflecting that their wholesome & spontaneously open-hearted hostess is no more. I've just dropped Cook a note of sympathy, & fancy he would appreciate such things from the rest of the gang.

I also heard from Mac's niece—& have sent the note to Sonny with instructions to shew it to you & Talman. All that mine adds to yours in the way of information is that Mac arrived in Tacoma very much prostrated; so that he had to be carried to his sister's home & was never able to walk again, except a trifle around the house. He had a nurse & the best of care—indeed, I imagine his final surroundings left nothing to be desired either as regards skill or solicitude. The one big mistake, I can't help feeling, was the actual transcontinental journey. He must have had to change cars at Chicago—& fancy such a sick man buffetted about the labyrinthine stations of such a civic bedlam! If he could only have rested up at some hospital for a couple of weeks before trying the trip—& if he could only have arranged with someone else going to Tacoma (some salesman or something) to accompany him & see him over the hard places! But it would have been a tough job persuading him—indeed, he did embark against advice which Belknap & I both gave him—by word of mouth & letter, respectively, as permitted by our respective geographical situations.

As for orthography—I can't see where *logic* enters a matter based wholly on custom and emotional associations. The "millions of years of potential civilisation" ahead don't register very big with me, because they have nothing to do with any civilisation which is *ours*. Those millions of years will have many civilisations—but only the first two or three will ever know that an English race & tongue ever existed, while only the first ten or twelve will be likely to involve human or quasi-human creatures at all—you know damn well that the articulata will inevitably supplant us mammalia even as we supplanted the reptilia. Thus the whole planetary drama has nothing to do with this especial case. English orthography is a limited matter connected only with the brief life of our one civilisation, just as Latin orthography concerned only the single Roman civilisation of—say—B.C. 700–A.D. 700. As measured by the span of our cultural existence, we are not near the dawn of things but damn well along—too cursedly well along to suit anybody who loves our race & folkways. English probably won't exist as a spoken tongue for more years than it has existed already. Our heyday of vitality was the Elizabethan age; & we have since been running down & losing motive force even while we have gained in finesse & delicacy. This present age is our Antonine Period—or our Alexandrian Æra, to use an Hellenistic rather than Roman parallel. Creative days are over, & for the rest of our collective life we must seek excellence in taste & precision. The nineteenth century, sterile though it was after its first quarter, was a great age for settling down & codifying & fact-digging; & it certainly gave our linguistic forms a gratifying & dependable finish & maturity they never had before. I for one am content to let well enough alone & call it a day. I resign my Georgian claims to *oeconomic* & *landskip*, but have no inclination to tolerate the neo-chaoticist usage which imperceptibly verges from *eons* & *medieval* through *thot* & *brot* to such already half-tolerated (by that vulgar herd whose jargon later works upward) abortions as *nite* and *naborhood*. I feel much as the later Romans felt when they set to work in the fourth & fifth centuries A.D., trying to clean up their debased language & cut out the African (not oulothrix but half-Carthaginian) extravagances which had nearly swamped it since the age of Severus. You can see this tendency in bimboes like Claudianus & Rutilius Namatianus. Of course, they couldn't help much—

and very likely we can't help English much. But it is faintly amusing to adhere to a sound & dying standard oneself whilst the masses wallow in chaos. *Honourable* is the customary form, though the *u* is dropped in *honorary.* The *u* of *vapour* is dropped in *vaporise.* Of course I know that usage is fairly flexible, & shall enter no protest if the civilisation as a whole gradually adopts further modifications along the lines of previous ones. That is the *natural* evolution which nobody objects to. But I'll be shot if I'll follow any arrogant provincials in their freaks of the moment—curst money-minded provincials who are doing their vilest to corrupt our civilisation on this continent & substitute a damn'd bastard machine-&-speed worship which has no more to do with us & our heritage than the *mores* & philosophy of Angkor & Indo-China, Bactria & Sogdiana! I stick to the civilisation my blood & people belong to—the Old English civilisation of Great Britain, New England, & Virginia. To that, & to the language & manners characteristic of it. If the Japanese or French or Germans or machine mongrels capture this continent & impose an alien culture on it, that means nothing to me. The alien culture may be better or worse—I don't give a damn, because it isn't mine! Just as the French in Canada (& their kin in Rhode Island as well!) refuse to adopt our encroaching civilisation, so do I refuse to adopt the encroaching civilisation of mongrel Mechanamerika. I was born a Rhode-Island Englishman, by gad, and I'll die just that. Or if the pox-rotted mongrels turn my civilisation out of Rhode Island, then by St. Paul, I'll go home to England where my line came from! An Englishman, no matter where he is, never 'goes native' unless something is the matter with his self-respect! As for my regard for classic diphthongs being based on old associations—why, Sir, *what is anybody's regard for anything based on, if not on just that? What the hell are* values, anyway? *What is anything?* (My old, perennial question!) Amidst the cosmic chaos the only things we have to cherish are the transient shapes of illusion woven from the chance scraps our memories hold. Apart from these, we are lost in the meaningless void! So I guess Grandpa'll keep on bungling along as usual, in the old way!

Your trip-report excites my envy—& as for the *New Orleans* prospect . . . . . . oh, boy! I am choak'd with jealous spleen! Gord knows that all I live for is to see (a) Quebec, (b) Charleston, (c) St. Augustine, & (d) New Orleans. When I've seen them, I shall bump myself off before the memory wears faint.

Commiserations on the musaeum servitude—& O GAWD, O MONT-REAL . . . THAT **PACKING!** Thank Pegāna I never picked a curator's life! But just the same, I'll wager you have THE mineral exhibit of the country when you're through!

Some fine weather lately—I'm going out today before it chills up!

Yrs for genial ease—

Θεοβάλδος

P.S. My lines on "Brick Row" are in this morning's *Journal*—BUT the horror of vandalism has already begun.

Just now am bowed beneath a hellish *typing* job—de Castro stuff.[1]

Notes

1. Possibly "The Electric Executioner," which HPL described to a correspondent in February as a tale he had been revising that was recently accepted.

[91]   [AHT]

Jany. 14, 1930

Fulgurant Fujiyama of Fathomless Fluorescence:—

As for poor old Mrs. Cook—I recall the days of disharmony that you mention, but imagine that they were hardly representative. Of course the culinary alliance was a very disparate & ill-founded one—even more so than most weddings—& could hardly, in view of relative ages, have had any romantic glamour so far as W. P. C.'s side was concerned. However, the habitude of long joint residence, plus the pathetic & tenacious affection on the distaff side, (of which, naturally, jealousy was merely a potent proof) could not help creating a sense of secure accustomedness & family solidarity amidst which Mrs. C. would come to seem like a devoted mother or aunt or faithful old nurse; whose nervous irrationality & anile densities must be excused, & whose loss must involve a poignant sense of strangeness & vacancy. No doubt a decade ago, when outside freedoms seemed more glittering, Culinarius would have been glad of that quiet legal liberation which a more enlightened spouse would have been still more eager to seek upon a recognition of basic incompatibility. But the very fact that poor Mrs. C. was incapable of such enlightened thought must have created an additional claim upon his pity—a pity each day sharpened by the shadow of her approaching death, as predicted by all her physicians. This shadow probably had a moderating effect upon her own temperamental violence—of which I used to hear third-or-fourth-hand reports, but of which I never directly observed any trace. She seemed to regard W. P. C. with the wistful & solicitous affection of a mother about to take leave of a fragile son—& the artist in him very plainly responded to this mood. I was impressed with the pathos of a bit of naive, crude, dialogue which they exchanged the very last time I saw them together. Mrs. Cook, jesting in her uncouth way about "how glad Paul would be to get rid of her", ended up by adding in a sorry kind of mock-archness, "but you'll miss me, old man, when I *am* gone!" And Cook, with an emphasis & gravity which backed up every word that he uttered, responded very slowly, "I surely will, Cooky, (his whimsical pet name for her) & that's no joke." One could not help glimpsing profound currents of genuine emotion—an emotion of long companionship through vicissitudes, & of vague, shared memories, that defied all consistency & all common ideas of temperamental balance—in these inept & pitifully grotesque banalities. It is, of course, a melancholy thing that Cook ever became enmeshed in so incongruous a marriage; or that, being so enmeshed, he could not have secured the early legal escape upon which a wife of greater cultivation & intelligence would have insisted. But things having developed as they did, there is no doubt but that the years created a sincere bond—remote indeed from any romantic attraction, but none the less poignant on both sides. Mrs. Cook was honest, generous, & warmhearted in her ignorant, frankly plebeian way—nervous, excitable, & unreasonable, but brave in the face of illness & pain, & capable of a profound, almost canine, devotion. The one tragic note was her union to a sensitive, highly intelligent, well-informed, & acutely imaginative man twenty years her junior & a thousand miles her superior in mental capacity & cultural potentiality—& it's hard to say on which side the tragedy bore more heavily. There's a theme for some conscientious, realistic, & un-sensational novelist—a tragedy without a villain, without lasting blame or bitterness, & with nothing but affection (albeit an affection without joy or glamour or satisfaction) in the end. Fate is the only malignant one—& even that malignancy is a blind, unconscious, & impersonal business. The individual human characters are merely puppets helplessly dashed about by complex & adverse circumstance, weakness of will, & aesthetic scruples. Most domestic misery amongst honourable people is like that—but it isn't sensational enough for popular novelists to write about, hence fails to be recognised as the major tragic pattern. Fancy as eventless a woe as this in the cinema or the *Cosmopolitan!* It is thus that the artificial conventions of the American credo are born; thus that we lose sight of actual human motivations & situations amidst a welter of ready-made tags & sensational suppositions, motivations, & situations. And the motto for honest philosophers therefore ought to be 'shun light "literature" & study life at first hand'! Cook is now feeling the strain of the autumn & winter—the long illness & eventual loss—so keenly that he says he must get away to a different milieu for a few days, & is planning a motor trip through the icy waste of Northern Vermont to visit steady, consoling old Walter J. Coates. He has asked me to come to Athol & accompany him, but I have had to refuse as a matter of sheer physiological imperativeness. Another accidental experience with the cold (+14) on Nov. 30th last—when I lost breathing-power, dinner, balance, & three-fourths of my consciousness in an attempt to walk home from my younger aunt's before I learned how the mercury had dropped—has conclusively shewed me that I can never hope to buck up against temperatures much under +20; so that a venture into the nameless Arcticities of Vermont-in-January would be the sheerest foolhardiness, & perhaps the cause of saddling Cook with the responsibility of getting a sick man to an hospital or shipping a corpse back to Providence. He indeed partly realises this, as the tentativeness of his invitation shews. Hence I don't feel that I am boorish or delinquent in declining, much as Cook hates to drive his car alone. If snow makes the roads impassable, he will abandon the Vermont venture & substitute a railway trip to Boston & Providence, in which case I shall meet him in the Hub (regardless of temperature, for in a city one can always dodge in warm doorways to regain balance & give tortured lungs & forehead & stomach a rest) & pilot him around to such museums, antiquities & historic spots as may seem suited to his mood. I rather hope he does get switched to this southerly route, for I think the varied sights of a city would be better for him than would the bleak waste & desolation of a frozen countryside. He'll come out all right in the end—& I suppose that, speaking cold-bloodedly & with an eye to futurity, his bereavement is the best thing for him. He is now an independent unit—self-sufficient & chained to no class incompatible with his intellect & inclinations. Let us hope that he still has the resilience to start his mental life afresh & live up to the great capacities which no one can fail to recognise in him. He's a great chap, is W. P. C.—in many respects one of the most remarkable & admirable characters I have ever known. Here's hoping he strides onward toward a maximum of happiness & self-realisation despite the long years of stagnation & side-tracking!

No—I hardly fancied our orthographical views would chime to the extent of either party's changing his accustomed practice! It is amusing to reflect how many apparently trivial habits are determined—among people who think at all—by what one thinks about the constitution of the universe! I'd damn well like to come out with a book some day, even though I might never win a place beside Schopenhauer, Nietzsche, or Bertrand Russell. I think I'd call it "What Is Anything?"—in spite of the popular catchpenny sound of such a title. I'd like to see your book, too—that's the way to fight, with really heavy artillery! Letters are mere BB shot beside whole books! Oh, by the way—that most perfectly disillusioned of Americans, Joseph Wood Krutch, is to give a lecture at Brown University on the 5th of March. Ordinarily I'm no lecture-hound, but I'll hear this bird if it kills me! If the mercury's under 20 I'll hire a hack.

As for yo' trip, Suh, ah hope the whole programme will come off in the most expansive & piquant possible way. Right now ah'd lahk to be daown in Alexandria or Fredericksburg or Richmond or Williamsburg—to cite the places ah know—or better still, in Charleston, St. Augustine, or N'Awleens or Bermuda or Jamaica. If I ever had the heart to leave Providence—or if those cursed Vandals ever tear the old town down before my eyes—I think I shall live in Bermuda or Jamaica. Mexico or Cuba or South America don't lure me—what I want is the tropicks plus my own Anglo-Saxon civilisation. Both Bermuda & Jamaica have Georgian houses. God Save the King!

I duly received the envelope which you forwarded from Mrs. McDonald,[1] & which contained a cutting from the *N. Y. World* in which the celebrated William Bolitho, discussing the cheap "pulp" magazines, chanced to allude to my *W.T.* effusions in not too patronising a manner. It was kind of

Mrs. M. to send the thing—but I can't resist enclosing the note which accompanied it, & which wound up with the perfect Hydeian touch of brooding hostility! Bolitho's commendation loses weight with me through his coupling of my name with that of Otis Adelbert Kline of all mechanical hacks![2]
Well—don't work *too* hard!

Yrs for fewer & lighter rocks—
Θεοβάλδος

Notes

1. Edna (Hyde) McDonald (1893–1962).
2. In his article "Pulp Magazines," *New York World* (4 January 1930): 11, William Bolitho remarks: "In this world [of pulp writing] there are chiefs, evidently. I am inclined to think they must be pretty good. There is Otis Adelbert Kline and H. P. Lovecraft, whom I am sure I would rather read than many fashionable lady novelists they give teas to; and poets too."

[92]   [AHT]

Tiw's Day
[4 March 1930]

Aërial of Apotheosised Ability:—

Goddam winter's got me about all in, but thank Cthulhu it's March now—seventeen days to the aequinox! Tomorrow night I'm gonna hear Joseph Wood Krutch (a real philosopher, ef ya ast me, 'bo!) lecture on my ol' pal Ed Poe at Brown University.

Yrs for heat & leisure—
Πάππος Θεοβάλδος

[93]   [AHT]

The Ides of Martinus, 1930
[12 March 1930]

Crudent Crown of Cerebro-Chronological Coördination:—

Well, I'll be damn'd! So Megalopolis doesn't know its own caffeine-liquefiers! Well—try your luck, & if your inquiry doesn't land anything Grandpa'll shoot ya a bottle from a real town. No question, it's about twice as hard to get any unusual nutritive material in N' Yawk as it is in any civilised burg. I suppose the resident fauna are so damn standardised that they only eat certain things dictated by such fashions as caprice & commercialism may create! You'll prob'ly want Borden's Challenge Milk for the reason that it contains a modicum of sucrose—not as much as *I* need for a cuppa cawfee, but as much as the average bimbo usually calls for. The lack of need for using a tertium quid—i.e., actual lump or granulated $C_{12}H_{22}O_{11}$—will undoubtedly appeal to your sense of efficiency. Only *one* thing to add besides hot water! I

assume that the peerless Dryco lacks the saccharine element—tho' here again
I may be wrong. Anyhow, old Chal is good enough for me—& a 15¢ can'll
last ya damn near a coupla weeks. Another thing—it'll keep ya in touch with
the old *Borden* name & remind ya of ol' times!

How the hell you manage to exist on a chain-gang schedule is beyond my
comprehension—it would drive me to suicide in a fortnight! Bondage to the
known, the *expected*, & the *predictable* removes, so far as I am concerned, every
particle of redeeming value, lure, piquancy, & significance from the fatiguing
& burthensome ordeal of prolonging life & consciousness. With these things
gone, there is left in the existence-process an insufficient array of pleasurable
stimuli to make the troublesome experience worth going through. There's no
use in claiming that time-table slavery would "give me time to enjoy more
things"—because there is nothing I could enjoy if purchased on such soul-
annihilating terms. *It is never any definite experience which gives me pleasure, but always
the* **quality** *of mystic adventurous expectancy itself—the* **indefiniteness** *which permits
me to foster the momentary illusion that almost any vista of wonder & beauty might open
up, or almost any law of time or space or matter or energy be marvellously defeated or reversed or modified or transcended.* That is the central keynote of my character &
personality, & of the character & personality of all men of the symbolic or
poetic as distinguished from the intellect type. It is a matter of *what forms a
basic life-value for me.* Obviously, nothing in objective life has any real "value"
for anybody. Dry & empty physical-intellectual experience soon becomes an
unmeaning repetition of kindred and boresome sensations unless one's
imaginative horizon be mercifully limited. What makes anything valuable or
significant in the life of *any* person is **not** any quality intrinsic in the thing itself. It is simply *what that thing has the power to symbolise for the person in question*—
how keenly that thing is able to stir in the especial individual *that sense of expansion, freedom, adventure, power, expectancy, symmetry, drama, beauty-absorption, surprise,
and cosmic wonder* (i.e., the illusory promise of a majestic revelation which shall
gratify man's ever-flaming, ever-tormenting curiosity about the outer voids
and ultimate gulfs of entity) **which alone means pleasure to humanity,**
save for the low-grade & soon-exhausted animal pleasures, & the too-soon-
monotonous & wearying pleasures of mental exertion as apart from mental
adventure. This complex expansion-freedom-adventure-power-expectancy-
drama-beauty-wonder-sense is all that makes any sensitively organised man
remain alive. What gratifies it is of value. What fails to gratify it is valueless.
True, the means to gratification for every different man must necessarily be
different; because the symbols evolving this complex sense are in each individual dependent upon his personal heredity, mental-physical organisation,
individual history, general background, & education. It is a matter of more or
less capricious *association*. Some objective experiences evoke the right symbols
for some men, other experiences for others. Apart from this evocative power,
no objective experience has any value for anyone. One man's meat is another

man's poison. That is why it is silly to call any person's course of action *wise or foolish* until we find out just *what that person is aiming for*, anyway. Only a naively unphilosophic observer laughs at a given individual for adopting a course which stints him on some specific thing commonly regarded as a desideratum. How can such an observer know whether the individual is really suffering any net loss, or whether the "desideratum" would not be wholly worthless to the individual if disjoined from the special course which he refuses to abandon? That is, how can any outsider properly weigh the relative values, for another, of a certain fixed course on the one hand, & of a certain objective thing or condition on the other hand? May not the course easily be worth more to the man who follows it, than any other possible desideratum could be? This gets us back to the fundamental truth that *nothing has any intrinsic value*. The only human values are sensations—& what the wise man will seek are simply the objects & conditions which may *for him* serve as symbols to evoke the especial sensations—the complex exaltation of spaciousness, liberation, adventurous expectancy, power, drama, pageantry, symmetry, mystery, curiosity-lure, &c, &c, &c.—whose function it is to make existence seem worth prolonging. Of course the particular objects & conditions will be different for every man, since each of us has a different nature & therefore a different symbolising apparatus. That is why I don't think you're actually *unwise* in accepting a ruled, regimented life, although I personally don't understand how such a life can give you the sensations of expansion, freedom, & wonder which you surely need in order to keep going. I couldn't get the needed sensations out of any *predicted or predictable* course of events, because such events would lack the glamorous *indefiniteness* & *uncertainty* essential to the fostering of the drama-&-pageantry illusion; the illusion of being poised on the edge of the infinite amidst a *vast cosmic unfolding* which *might* reveal *almost anything*. This illusion, I have discovered through long experiment & through a close analysis of every experience classifiable as *pleasant* or *joyful* that I have ever had, is *absolutely necessary* to an even tolerable happiness on my part. It is the sole & complete key to that elusive & evanescent quality of **interest** which I have such prodigious difficulty in summoning up toward anything not involving the elements of *surprise, discovery, strangeness, & the impingement of the cosmic, lawless, & mystical upon the prosaic sphere of the known. Facts* as such mean *nothing* to me. Not because I have the maniac's or religious mystic's tendency to *confuse* reality with unreality, but because I have the cynic's & the analyst's inability to recognise any difference in *value* between the two types of consciousness-impacts, *real* & *unreal*. I know which are which, but cannot have any prejudice in favour of either class. Even my *seeming* preference for the *unreal* is only a chance circumstance—arising from the fact that the especial sensations I need are mainly supplied by that element. Actually, I am just as willing to welcome impressions from the real (such as historic pageantry, astronomical mystery, archaeologial darkness & terror) as from the unreal, if they will give me equally poignant expansion-freedom-adventure-beauty-drama-mystery sensations. But it is the sensations only which count. Reality or unreality in themselves—as such—are to me only academic & sterile terms. I am too cynical & analytical to retain the illusion that their actually vast physical difference gives them any difference *in value* as psychological agents impinging on man's consciousness. My one standard of value is imaginative suggesting-power or symbolising-quality. Some people derive pleasure from an empty intellectual operation—from the mere registering & recognition that such a thing is so or that such a thing isn't so. This to me is the tamest & most easily exhausted of all the pleasures—except of course the sensuous pleasures of the primal clod. No sooner does my feeble interest get half-aroused, than the flicker is snuffed out by the query *"what of it?"* And so it goes. What do I get out of travel? Why, simply a more intense & poignant sense of expansion, surprise, & the imminence of unknown wonders, than I could get without such a swift & varied pageantry of physical locale. It is not the objective scenery or things which I encounter that please me, but simply *the mood & circumstances under which they strike my senses.* In themselves they are nothing. Carcassonne or the Acropolis itself would be deadwood to me if I knew weeks ahead just *when* I was going to see it, just *how* I was going to see it, & just *how long* I was going to see it. Only in connexion with the gesture of *liberation* & the aura of quivering mystery is beauty of any significance to me. There must be *uncertainty, suddenness, surprise* . . . . . God! Shall I ever forget my first stupefying glimpse of MARBLEHEAD'S huddled & archaic roofs under the snow in the delirious sunset glory of four p.m., Dec. 17, 1922!!! I did not know until an hour before that I should ever behold such a place as Marblehead, & I did not know *until that moment itself* the full extent of the wonder I was to behold. I account that instant—about 4:05 to 4:10 p.m., Dec. 17, 1922—the most powerful single emotional climax experienced during my nearly forty years of existence. In a flash all the past of New England—all the past of Old England—all the past of Anglo-Saxondom & the Western World—swept over me & identified me with the stupendous totality of all things in such a way as it never did before & never will again. That was the high tide of my life. I was thirty-two then—& since that hour there has been merely a recession to senile tameness; merely a striving to recapture the wonders of revelation & intimation & cosmic identification which that sight brought. I can capture traces of the last glimpse when I see certain *unexpected* ancient-urban vistas under certain *novel & unexpected* conditions. *Philadelphia* has vistas which stir such cosmic memories & promises. *Annapolis* has, too. *Fredericksburg* has the power to a supreme degree. *Marblehead* itself never fails to give but vivid repetitions of its first impression. I think *Charleston* will pack a similar kick—& I *know Quebec* & *New Orleans* will if I can ever get at 'em in the right way. And *Europe* would be one continuous joy . . . . . oh, boy! But there must always be the aura of freedom & surprise & indefiniteness &

wonder about the impression-absorbing process. I wouldn't pay a half-dollar
to see even London or Paris or Rome on a Cook's tour schedule! There must
always be a sense of *soaring outward* from all temporal, spatial, & material limitations along broad vistas of slanting yellow radiance from unimagined gulfs
beyond the chrysoberyl gates of sunset . . . . . . soaring outward toward the
discovery of stupendous, cosmic, inconceivable things, & toward the envis-
agement & comprehension of awesome rhythms & patterns & symmetries
too Titanic, too unparticled, too trans-galactic, & too overpowering for the
relatively flat, tame, & local name of "beauty". When a city or landscape or
experience can give me this sense of untrammelled & starward *soaring*, I account it worth my while to go after it. What doesn't give it, I don't consider
worth going after. Energy flags so damnably when such a reward is not in
sight. Why be alive? What is anything? When I first saw strange & pinnacled
New York rising mystic & violet out of its waters in April, 1922, I got this
kick to a stupendous degree—as you doubtless recall from the way I rhapso-
dised around with you & Little Sonny & Loveman & Kleiner & everybody
. . . . . darting up steps to strange sunward vistas, taking in exotic contrasts &
outspread seas of alien roofs & spires, hurtling through interstellar blackness
in cryptic subways, never knowing on just what planet or within just what
universe I would next emerge to overwhelming light . . . . beholding
monstrous inversions of the natural order—lovely white cottages & Georgian
mansions of the known, sane, world side by side with pouring tides of
swarthy slave-life from the obscene & unimaginable East & beyond the East .
. . . . . squinting faces & jabbering tongues from Antioch, Alexandria Palmyra,
Petra, Hierosolyma, Nineveh, Tyre, Sidon, Ur, Memphis, Thebes, Heliopolis
. . . . sinister hierophants & mysteriarchs from Babylon & Bactria, Sogdiana &
Scythia . . . . fabulous Samarcand & the whisper'd of Irem, City of Pillars, in
the forbidden Red Desert of Araby where the daemons dwell & whereof Ab-
dul Alhazred dreamed when he writ his *Necronomicon*. Persepolis, Parsagidae
. . . . Ophir and Cambaluc . . . . Prester John . . . Zimbabwe . . . . . Bethmoora,
Merimna . . . Sardathrion, wherefor Pegāna's gods weep . . . . . . The mongrel
sculptor in his dusty den . . . . . the mystic bookstalls with their hellish
bearded guardians . . . . . monstrous books from nightmare lands for sale at a
song if one might chance to pick the right one from mouldering, ceiling-high
piles . . . . rattle of the elevated through unknown labyrinths of accursed life . . .
sweep of red-gold sun over a luring balustraded hill-crest—and the Home of
Poe! Pressure of insane blackness on the insane lights of Times Square at
night—like a low, evil ceiling over a monstrously brazier'd and doom-
hieroglyphed secret temple of inner Ægyptus . . . . Museums with all the
evocative symbols of Greece, Rome, and nighted Khem . . . . that *Pantheon*
model! Alala! S. P. Q. R. . . . . CONSUL ROMANUS . . . brazen notes of the
tubicen . . . . tramp of the legions . . . . AVE.SCIPIO.TRIUMPHATOR . . . .
Gad, what a kick! What a sense of new, exotic worlds opening up before a

one-time (&, unknown to me, some-day-to-be again!) recluse as horizons take form from purple mystery, & marching aeons deposit strange freight before unjaded eyes! That, boy, was what I call a travel-experience! . . . . . but as soon as the sights of New York became *well-known* to me; as soon as the exotick strangeness lost its *distant mystery;* then all was changed. The very cleavage from the known, sane, world became hideous and ingulphing menace, and the very splendour and lure turned to a sense of exile and of loneliness. What gave the original scene its kick was its *freshness, strangeness,* & *utter remoteness.* It was because I did *not* live there that I found it wonderful. With familiarity, all became garishness & squalor & dead-sea fruit. As the years go by, the sense of remoteness from such abnormal exoticism of course returns; so that next month I shall probably feel a few faint echoes of the glamour & exploration-sense of 1922. The *Palisades* especially have a vague, cosmic, recapturable charm. But there will be no such kick as I got before. To get such a kick again I shall have to go to Quebec or London or Paris or Rome. Strangeness, light, colour, motion, beauty, & a sense of the past hovering near. That is what gives me the supreme urban kick. And even at that I believe that now—with my older, less astonishable personality—I could never get the kick from any large city that I could from a smaller, older, quainter place where hereditary glamour is thicker. It was because I was not past early middle age in 1922 that I got the Manhattan kick I did. Nowadays it is the still stronger *Marblehead* kick that I am more likely to repeat when I come unexpectedly upon some ancient town of equal beauty, unchangedness, & relation to the Anglo-Saxon stream of history.

All this no doubt sounds damned odd to you—and just to make it amazingly odder I'm going to slip in some doggerel reflections of my inner moods which were squeezed out of me by the provocation of revising good ol' Moe's poetry textbook last fall. I had sworn to cut out rhyming—but that bird got me doing jingles for metrically illustrative purposes, and now—confound it—I can't stop! Of this series of "Fungi from Yuggoth" I've sold fifteen—ten to *Weird Tales* and five to the *Providence Journal*—at $3.50 each; (25¢ a line) which makes my net profit on 'em exactly $52.50 to date. Not so bad for spontaneous mooning! Others I'm giving gratis to Cook & Coates—& the residue I suppose I'll dump on honest Tryout. But anyhow—the items which illustrate my moods & indicate why no mapped out programme could ever be of any value to me are (I should judge) V, (?) XIII, XIV, XVIII, XIX, XXIII, XXVIII, XXX, & XXXIII . . . . . though all the others no doubt reflect various phases, ramifications, & corollaries of the central mood-nucleus. You don't have to read this damn tripe if it promises boredom. Gawd knows I ain't no pote—only I have the misfortune (for a non-poet) to think & feel in terms of symbols & sensations instead of facts, as poets generally do. A guy with the aesthetic outlook what ain't no demn aesthete, ef ya know wot I mean! Passages in that book "Sirenica" by W. Compton Leith (which I recommended your reading) describe my ineffective type admirably well. Oh, yes—of these 14-line howls one has just been printed: #XXIX— "Nostalgia"—on the Wednesday lit'ry page of the *Prov. Journal.* Please return this bunch some time—tho' they ain't no hurry about it.

And so it goes. See ya later—& meanwhile lemme know about Dacosta.

Yrs for rocks & gaffarel and the open road—
Θεοβάλδος

P.S. Did I tell ya I seen Joe Krutch lectcha on Poe. He just repeated the substance of his book—& made nervous swayings as if he wanted to vault over the desk before him.

My dinosaur bones has came. Several crumbling fragments. Want one for the Museum? Speak up ef ya does, & Grandpa'll bring one along.

P.P.S. Whatcha thinka the NEW PLANET?[1] HOT STUFF!!! It is probably Yuggoth!

Notes

1. Pluto was discovered by C. W. Tombaugh in January 1930, but the discovery was only announced on the front page of the *New York Times* on 14 March. Hence, HPL's p.p.s. was probably written on that day.

[94]   [AHT]

Tiw's Day
[1 April 1930]
All Fools (my patron Saints' day)

Flowing Fountain of Factual Fulgence:—

As for tastes in experience & time-schedules—I see your point of view okay enough in theory, but I have yet to be convinced that the objective world offers sufficient stimuli to produce anything like real contentment in a sensitively organised & disillusioned man; no matter how great may be his capacities for "adjustment to reality"—as Doc Freud terms it. Reality is all right enough so far as it goes—I'm not one of those frantick bozoes who howl that everything is all wrong & poisonous & so on. The only trouble is *that it doesn't go far enough* for a guy with extreme sensitiveness. The faculty of *interest* is a goddam complex thing. It is perfectly true that mild, conventional, & highly respectable people like the average business or professional man can get enough of a kick out of watching the meaningless routine phaenomena of this pimple on the cosmos to warrant their staying alive—but even with them you can see it wears thin now & then, especially in this latest age of standardisation & decreased variety & adventurousness. That's why more & more people kick over the traces & burst out in wild, anti-social vagaries . . . . .

which are just as meaningless as the routine against which they are a protest. And when you leave the amiably respectable class & consider men with individualised imaginations, you can't help seeing that objective phaenomena—endless & predictable repetitions of the same old stuff over & over again—form only the very beginning of what is needed to keep their sense of significance, harmony, & personal adjustment to infinity satisfied. *All* sensitive men have to call in unreality in some form or other or go mad from ennui. That is why religion continues to hang on even when we know it has no foundation in reality. That crazy old half-Tartar bolshevik Lenin stumbled on one snappy mouthful of truth when he said, "Religion is opium for the people."[1] It's just that—& the only reason vast numbers of cultivated men stay cheerful is that they keep doped up on that same obsolete mythology. But that stuff can't last for ever. We know too goddam much about Nature now to have it work. Reaction will try to keep it alive for another generation—we shall see desperate & damn fool movements like "Humanism", neo-popery, Harry Emerson Fosdickism,[2] & so on—but all that will peter out with the dying off of the last generations reared in genuinely subjective religious faith. Read Joseph Wood Krutch's "The Modern Temper" if you want the authentick, expert low-down on all this. Then will come the test of whether man can or can't adequately nourish himself with objective reality alone. I, for one, say he *can't*—& I'm not judging from personal experience alone when I say it. Ol' Art Schopenhauer had the straight goods—however you look at it, there's so goddam much **more** pain than pleasure in any average human life, that it's a losing game unless a guy can pep it up with pure moonshine—either the literal 95-proof pink-snake-evoker, or the churchly hootch of belief in immortality & a benign old gentleman with long whiskers (ah, for the debates of yore!!) & a cosmick purpose . . . or else the Dunsanian conjuration of an illusion of *fantastick & indefinite possibility* as shadow'd forth in certain aesthetick interpretations of selected objective phaenomena, time-sequences, & cosmical & dimensional speculations. Now of these three refuges, I prefer the third by a long shot—because the first is highly unaesthetic in practice & degrading in symbolism, whilst the second is puerile in substance & insulting to the intellect in its outright denial of plain facts & objective probabilities. For—you will notice—I do *not* share the real mystic's *contempt* for facts & objective conditions, even though I fail to find them interesting & satisfying. *On the contrary,* I am forced to *respect* them highly, & allow for them in every system of imaginative refuge I formulate. It gives me no kick at all to emulate the idealist or religionist & invent false conditions & significances which actually deny reality. Like Krutch, I had rather be a man & face reality than be a child & hide my head in a gilded Gothick prie-dieu of absolute pretence. For me, then, is the third course—the consciously artificial manipulation of the theogonist's & myth-maker's privilege in manner of the eighteenth Baron Dunsany . . . . . that is, the deliberate exercise of the human instinct for space, reach, adventure, & cosmic identification through the weaving of fantastick aesthetick impressions *as such*, and *not* as intellectual denials of objective reality. If you get what I mean, I like to *supplement*, rather than *contradict*, reality. I get no kick at all from *postulating what isn't so*, as religionists & idealists do. That leaves me cold—in fact, I have to stop dreaming about an unknown realm (such as Antarctica or Arabia Deserta) as soon as the explorers enter it & discover a set of real conditions which dreams would be forced to contradict. My big kick comes from *taking reality just as it is*—accepting all the limitations of the most orthodox science—& then permitting my symbolising faculty to *build outward* from the existing facts; rearing a structure of *indefinite promise & possibility* whose topless towers are in no cosmos or dimension penetrable by the contradicting-power of the tyrannous & inexorable intellect. But the whole secret of the kick is *that I know damn well it isn't so*. If I let the process interfere with my intellectual perceptions & discriminations in the theistic manner, I'd have no fun at all but merely feel like a damned ass. I'm probably trying to have my cake & eat it at the same time—to get the intoxication of a sense of cosmic contact & significance as the theists do, & yet to avoid the ignorant & ignominious ostrich-act whereby they cripple their vision & secure the desiderate result. But this is wandering from the issue. My point is, *that a highly organised man can't exist endurably without mental expansions beyond objective reality*. I said it before, & I say it still. You yourself get such expansions though your lingering belief in the religious myths of cosmic purpose, values, & governance; myths which you can accept without ignominy because an early theological environment has enabled you actually to imagine that such things are real. I, repudiating the obsolete faiths from the start, can have no such residual illusions—hence if I want to think of the cosmos as a significant thing in which man has no important & symmetrical part, I have to "roll my own". And that's what guys like me & Edward John Moreton Drax Plunkett is doin'! We're only cooking up a passable substitute for a type of delusion which the dying orthodox civilisation of Platonick-Christian speculation took for granted & worked for a kick under the amusing impression that it was reality! And that's that. Every different bimbo to his own brand of gin—& I'll forgive the poor old time-tables if they're the agents which give Providentium an occasional glimpse of your august presence. But even so, they're damned stingy about it!

Thanks for the cutting—you & I know the sort of a place to get born in! No debate there, even if we do differ on subsequent modes of kick-gathering! Speaking of cuttings—here's a couple worth lamping. You set me 'as' summer about the *Chiltern Hundreds*, & I confest ignorance except an *hundred* is an ancient Saxon land unit.[3] Well—here's the rest of the tale from the *Christian Science Monitor*. You can keep this one. The other—to be returned—involves a bit of antient history you may or may not remember. Do you recall a Kalem meeting at 169 Clinton in which we had a hot debate on the authenticity of

highly modern literature, (T. S. Eliot &c.) & I try'd vainly to find a very perti-
nent explanatory article by Edmund Wilson in my files?[4] Think hard! Well—
after five years *I have found it!!* It was in an odd file which I hadn't opened
since leaving 598 Angell—& not in my black walnut cabinet at all! Well—here
it is at last! Now are you convinc'd?

And so it goes. See ya later!

Yrs indefinitely—

ΘΕΟΒΑΛΔΟΣ

Notes

1. Actually, the statement is from Karl Marx (from "Towards a Critique of Hegel's
Philosophy of Right," 1843).
2. Harry Emerson Fosdick (1878–1969), American clergyman and author who attempted to harmonize the findings of modern science with religious belief.
3. The position of Crown Steward and Bailiff of the Chiltern Hundreds is now used
as a procedural device to effect resignation from the House of Commons, as members of the British Parliament are not permitted simply to resign their seats. The legal
anomaly dates to a resolution of the House of Commons of 2 March 1624, when
members of Parliament often were elected to serve against their will.
4. Edmund Wilson, Jr. (1895–1972), a leading American social and literary critic of
the mid-twentieth century. HPL probably refers to his article "Notes on Modern Literature" (*New Republic,* 24 December 1924 and 4 March 1925). Wilson later wrote a
scathing review of HPL's work, "Tales of the Marvellous and the Ridiculous," *New
Yorker* 21, No. 41 (24 November 1945): 100, 103–4, 106.

[95]   [AHT]

Tiw's Day
[15 April 1930]

Pendulum of Peerless Precision:—

Ave, Chronometros! "Friday, April 26th" would be oke for me except
for one trifling detail—namely, that it came in 1929 instead of being due in
1930! Being sensible of the relativity of time as well as of space, I've ransack'd
my memory to see whether I so spent the day that I might sandwich in a future Paterson trip thro' non-Euclidean geometry—but alas! I find that all the
afternoon was consum'd by the latter half of a motor trip with my past &
future hosts, so that I shall be—I mean was—somewhere around Bedford,
N. Y. at the time I ought to be about to be in Paterson. No use—we'll have
to switch the session to 1930 & adhere to the commonplace tri-dimensional
system—according to which the 26th falls on *Saturday.* Is this the day of the
castbroading,[1] or is Friday the 25th the allotted season? It seems to me that
for the 25th my hosts have planned a duplication of that selfsame Apr. 26,
1929 above mention'd, so I hope Saturday the 26th is the auspicious point on

the space-time continuum. But you & Little Belknap can discuss all these mathematical details before Grandpa blows in. It's all one to the old gent so long as you boys suit yourselves!

As for the old dope about cosmick purpose—just refer back to the files for my argument & attitude! How youse guys can still sop up the old hooey is beyond Grandpa Theobald! *Of course* the ultimate construction of the cosmos is unknown & unknowable—didn't Hume & Kant & Spencer get that across a helluva while ago? *But what ground does that give us for concocting unverifiable fairy-tales about it?* The old Koenigsburg Hun[2] only made an ass of himself when he tried the "instinctive category" game—& there's a damn sight *less* excuse for such crap now than there was in the late XVIII century. The whole truth is, that *nobody could possibly hit on such a crazy notion as cosmic consciousness and purpose if governed solely by the evidence available in 1930.* The cosmos, as manifest to us, *suggests only rhythm and pattern and automatic repetition.* No conceivable link or basis exists for trying to explain the whole unknowable outfit in terms of the one local, transient, & insignificant accident which we call purposive consciousness. *Every attempt* at reading this local jumble of gland-and-tissue-reactions into the infinite cosmic mechanism is an obvious heritage from earlier times when men didn't have the knowledge we have. The very fact that neo-theists, with all their scientific opportunities, still believe that the ignorant ancients could discover the truth which baffles even us, is a final knockout blow to their standing as philosophers. Every detail of their psychology proves that their belief is formed not from contemplation of the existing evidence, but from the ignorant heritage of primal days—pounded with crippling force into their susceptible mind & emotions when they were too young to resist. It is significant that all theists try to flatten their children's intellectual foreheads in extreme youth, rather than let them form their own ideas when old enough to judge for themselves. No adult could possibly cook up a delusion like religion today if uncrippled by tradition.

Yrs for exacter clocks & more deities—

Πάππος Θεοβάλδος

Notes

1. JFM was to give a 15-minute talk on the local radio station.
2. I.e., Immanuel Kant.

[96]   [AHT]

Thursday, May 15 1930

Pattern of Predictable Precision:—

God, I swoon! I swoon with the consciousness of compleat & culminant beauty! Iä! Shub-Niggurath! YOG-SOTHOTH!!!! I HAVE SEEN *MAYMONT!!!!!!*

I have your last summer's travelogue so mixt with mine own experiences, that I recall not whether you spoke of visiting Maymont.[1] If you did not, then drop all your rocks this moment & come right down here!! Zounds, Sir, what a world of delirious, unpredictable loveliness & dreamlike enchantment!! Poe's "Domain of Arnheim" and "Island of the Fay" all rolled into one . . . . with mine own "Gardens of Yin"[2] added for good measure! No—I simply *cannot* be awake! And to cap all climaxes, **it was an utter and unpredicted surprise!!!** I stumbled on it yesterday afternoon, *not knowing what I was getting into.* Boy!!! You can bet that today I've come out here to enjoy every minute from eleven a.m. to the closing hour of six! I have my revisory work with me.

You are no doubt sensible, from many observations of mine, that to me the quality of *utter, perfect beauty* assumes *two* supreme incarnations or adumbrations: one, the sight of mystical city towers & roofs outlined against a sunset & glimps'd from a fairly distant balustraded terrace; & the other, the experience of walking (or, as in most of my dreams, aërially floating) thro' aethereal & enchanted gardens of exotick delicacy & opulence, with carved stone bridges, labyrinthine walks, marble fountains, terraces & staircases, strange pagodas, hillside grottos, curious statues, termini, sundials, benches, basins, & lanthorns, lily'd pools of swans & streams with tiers of waterfalls, spreading gingko-trees & drooping, feathery willows, & sun-touched flowers of a bizarre, Klarkash-Tonick pattern never beheld on sea or land . . . . .

Well, by god, Sir, call me an aged liar or not—I vow *I have actually found the garden of my earliest dreams*—& in no other city than Richmond, home of my beloved Poe! Maymont! I shall dream of little else all the few remaining days of my long life!!—

Rapturously thine—

Θεοβάλδος

Notes

1. HPL was exploring Maymont Park in Richmond, VA.
2. Sonnet XVIII of *Fungi from Yuggoth.*

[97]   [AHT]

Home—

June 19, 1930

Highest Hierophant of Horological Helotry:—

Welcome to our city! Just blew in myself, dead broke, & am trying to cope with the piles of accumulated papers & unforwarded mail ingulphing me on every hand. The old town looks pretty damn good—& by an all-around reckoning beats anything I've seen since I left it on the 24th of April. Wish to hell I could move it bodily down to the climate of Charleston—also taking along the meads & groves of the Quinsnicket region, whither I repair each genial afternoon!

Well—as a result of the financial crisis (I had 15¢ in my pocket when I arrived from Athol!) I shall have to make my immediately future wanderings very modest indeed, hence fear desperately that I can't quite make the Westerly jaunt—at least, not if I expect to look in on the Boston convention next month.[1]

Too damn bad your time is so limited—but if you insist on half-living seven or eight lives in one lifetime instead of really living one, (with the ease, leisure, latitude of choice, adventurous uncertainty, & reflective & assimilative enjoyment-pauses necessary to life in the fullest sense) you have to pay the penalty. It may give you a bigger kick to have a dozen irons in the fire than to grasp thoroughly the limited range of impressions & sensations which one man can adequately grasp in the hours & years allotted him. Many are so made, & more are becoming that way under the influence of this overcrowded & overspeeded machine age. But all I have to say is that I can't see the fun of such feverish clock-slavery. Since it is obviously impossible for one man to grasp the absolute *infinity* of impressions in the external world which surrounds him, he might as well give up the idea of omniscience at the very start, & settle down to whatever fraction is the most comfortable. No possible reward exists to compensate for the loss of that freedom & opportunity for full, leisurely assimilation which comes from a rational limitation of activities to such as may be pursued without haste or worry or confining calculation. When all mankind is finally crucified on a rigid & relentless calendar, there will no longer be any reason for a civilised person to remain in existence & suffer the burthen of consciousness. Life will have been stripped of everything which constitutes its legitimate returns. Indeed, I am confident that such future slavery & oppression will produce a widespread group-hysteria & display of abnormal & perverted instinct, finally culminating in a revolt against the monotonising & chafing civilisation responsible for the evil. Complex "civilisation" is asking too much of the human animal as he is made, & is growing less & less worth the trouble of maintaining. Society is growing so abnormal that we may almost consider an anti-social attitude the normal one under present conditions. Or rather—the strictly normal attitude is one opposed to *existing & future* society, though favourable toward the *principle* of social organisation so far as it can *really* promote the freedom, pleasure, & interest-possibility of the individual.

Returning to concrete matters—on account of my brokeness I think I'd better not attempt the airport trip this time; since there is no car line, but only a high-priced 'bus service (the local coaches to Fall River) which would subtract troublesomely from the slim wad I hope to use for our fare to sundry quarries & for Maxfield icecream at Warren. Accordingly I shall turn up at the Crown Monday night at eight p.m.—expecting to find you all cleaned up & gorged, & ready for whatever verbal fighting may naturally suggest itself. Incidentally—I've at last discovered a more hapless slave of the feed-bag than yourself! It is the genial & fantastic Bernard Dwyer, whom I visited in antient Dutch Wiltwyck, up the placid Hudson, & who is now staggering about under a load of 232 pounds. His average dinner is about one & one-half to two times larger than your average, & forms from three to five normal or Theobaldian dinners. I tried to equal him one night, just for the fun of it; but gave out before the end. He knows that he's got to do something about it, & is contemplating a reduced diet plus a boxing course at the Y. M. C. A. He also toys with the idea of paring down & hardening up through a two-year period as a lumberjack in the North woods; in relation to which he has just sought the advice of the well-known poet-professor Lew Sarrett of Northwestern University, who has been a lumberjack in his day.[2] Some day I'll have to get you & Dwyer rounded up at Jake's—for once we could call Jake's bluff & meet his outstanding challenge to the world to consume in one sitting all the hamburg & onions he furnishes for 25¢! Ah, me! How time flies! Upon reflection I've just remembered that I haven't been to Jake's since *September, 1927*, when Talman was here on a reminiscent trip. Hope Jake is still alive!

Just heard from nice old Smithy. He is keeping *Tryout* afloat after all, & has just *shaved off his whiskers* after about half a century. Reborn at seventy-seven!

Well—see ya Monday!

Yr obt

Θεοβάλδος

Notes

1. HPL did in fact attend the NAPA convention in Boston in early July.

2. Lew Sarett [not Sarrett] (1888–1954), author of *The Box of God* (1922) and other poetry volumes. He was professor of speech at Northwestern from 1920 to 1950.

[98]   [AHT]

Sept. 26, 1930

Memory-Mocking Marcher after Melioristick Mirages:—

O Yog-Sothoth, give me strength to play the poltergeist to Paterson! Patience, O High-Priest of petrifick arcana . . . . Grandpa *will* get around to it before the crool snows fall!

It's this way, bozo. I ben staggering under a helluva lotta work what has kep me in most days, & when I get out it's generally to lug home supplies, so that I couldn't tote a wodden box anyhow. Moreover, on the few occasions when I have decamp'd to the antient woods & fields, I have been but ill dispos'd to cut short my afternoons & get around to the box-buying regions before five o'clock closing hours. When I do go, I'll have to mosey around in a dusty cellar for gawd knows how long, trying to hit on a box of the right size, & then tote the damn thing home a mile—a process (though two boxes

were then involv'd) which got me pretty near all in last year. Then the packing
& nailing—& then the peculiarly irritating task of painting a legible address
on the box—& blocking out whatever previous addresses may adorn its rugged surface. And then getting hold of the damn express office, & waiting indoors for the man even tho' the day may be such as to beckon me forth—
Hell! If they like that sort of thing down at the Massasutten, they're welcome
to it!

But I do want to make a decent round of the caves. Yes—I noted that
mysterious & unexplored side-passage, & have thought of using it in fiction.
And as for bodies—trust me to bring in a whole raft of 'em, extending back
to 200,000 B.C. & before . . . . even to the reign of the pre-human Elder
Ones . . . . & with appropriate metal artifacts, plus manuscripts in Atlantean
& Lemurian cylinders.

Oh, say—before I forget it, take a look at this sample of polite insult,
which I have just handed to a goddam dead beat in Chicago, who has owed
me a revision bill dating partly from Feb. 1929 & partly from Sept. 1929. He
has paid no attention whatever to courteous statements, & in the following
words I wash my hands of him & his'n. "Is Chicago a Crime-Ridden City" is
the title of an absurd defence of Chi which I knocked in shape for him a year
& a half ago.

10 Barnes St.,
Providence, R. I.,
Septr. 18, 1930.

Lee Alexander Stone, M. D.,
    Chicago, Illinois

Sir:

In the matter of your persistently unpaid revision bill—concerning
which you so persistently withhold all explanations despite repeated inquiries—I have decided, at the risk of encouraging sharp practices, to
forego the use of a collecting agency & make you a present of the amount
involved.

This is my first encounter with such a hopelessly bad bill, & I believe I may consider the sum ($7.50) as not ill spent in acquiring practi-
cal experience. I needed to be taught caution in accepting unknown* clients without ample** references—especially clients from a strident region which cultivates ostentatious commercial expansion rather than the
honour customary among gentlemen.

Meanwhile I am grateful for so concrete an answer to the popular
question, "Is Chicago a Crime-Ridden City?"

With such consideration as is appropriate to the situation, & trusting that my small gift may prove of financial aid to you, Believe me, Sir,

Yr most obedient hble Servt.
H. P. Lovecraft

* He was Supt. of a branch of Chi. Pub. Health Service during the war!
** Farnsworth Wright was the guy who wished him onto me.

This ought to give the son-of-a-beech-nut a bad quarter of an hour if he isn't wholly pachydermatous!!

Do you follow *Wonder Stories* from month to month? If so, you've noted Klarkash-Ton's presence as a cover-design feature of the Oct. number—& his portrait in the interior pages.[1] You'll also see a picture of "Francis Flagg"—the young *communist* correspondent who got in touch with me through Coates. He is a tubercular sufferer dwelling at Tucson, Arizona—by birth a Canadian of excellent German, English, Scotch, & Irish ancestry, whose real name (which he reserves to sign his poetry with) is Henry George Weiss. In spite of his communistic notions he is a person of keen intelligence & wide erudition—indeed, his very communism is due to a more than commonly keen perception of the existing economic dilemma, which only communism can *ethically* solve. I am a fascist & monarchist instead of a communist because I repudiate the Christian ethics on which the illusion of "justice" is based.

Your fellow-trencherman Bernard Dwyer lately heard from the *W. T.* author Henry S. Whitehead, who says that Wright uniformly rejects his best stories. Very like Wright—whose bland dumbness transcends my utmost limits of comprehension.

And so it goes. Have hope & tolerance . . . them rocks *will* come before the ground freezes!

Yrs for cats & Quebec & caves—
Θεοβάλδος

Notes

1. "Marooned in Andromeda."

[99]   [AHT]

Oct. 24, 1930

The folders has come! Sire, I effuse, I irradiate, I ebull, with febrile & combustible gratitude! And I vow to repay thee in kind, ere another month lapses, by completing that shipment I have been struggling so hard to start making!

But oh, Boy, how kin ah live through the gawdam winter up No'th when places like Savannah & Mobile & St. Augustine & CHARLESTON exist? My imagination, at least, shall revel in these genial regions—thanks to your consideration—whilst my carcass hibernates or freezes or decomposes amidst its objective subarctic milieu.

But cold or no cold, I'm *trying* to devise a *Quebeck* travelogue of some sort, which you shall behold upon its completion.[1] It took more study than I thought to assemble the necessary historick background—so that right now I'm a rival of good old Mac in the matter of early French settlements.

And did I tell you that *W.T.* took my Vermont hell-beater for *350* bucks?[2]

Our young friend Galpinius has just got an exquisite *black kitten* call'd Charles Pierre Baudelaire. Don't I envy him?

More anon.

Yr   obt hble Svt
Θεοβάλδος

Notes

1. *A Description of the Town of Quebeck*, completed January 1931, proved to be HPL's longest single composition. It was published posthumously. See letter 104.
2. I.e., "The Whisperer in Darkness."

[100]   [AHT]

The Hellish Sabbat-Eve
[31 October 1930]

Forward-Facing Fancier of Futile Futurity:—

As to studyin' mineralogy & beginnin' a collection at the rock-mine on my hillside seigniory—Sir, you makes me feel guilty that I ain't matriculated this fall so's to get a cairn started in the middle of the parlor floor! Hell knows I'd be just as ready to furnish such a little accommodation as you'd be if I ast ya to take a cam'ry & git me fotygraffs of all the Dutch colonial houses in Rockland County, N. Y. which represent the second phase of evolution from the original plain steep roof to the familiar curv'd gambrel & porch roof type. That's oke—the only trouble is in gettin' the exact dope about what's wanted, so's not to fill up with all the outstandin' material excep' the rightstuff! As I sez lass June, jest you send me small samples of each kind of stuff you wants, together with written text explainin' details of same, (number'd correspondin' to a sticker on the hunk of rock, to avoid error) & I'll do my best to get out to my habitant's craft & see what he has layin' around—that is, exceptin' in Esquimau weather. I simply ain't got no head for rememberin' this sorta dope—what I sees one day jest goes outa the other eye nex' day. Rocks is rocks to me, jes' like a brimrose at the river's prim. We ain't all encyclopaedias like curatorial folks. But jest be specifick & put your needs in writing, as to one of a mental age under five, & the old man'll see what he can do. Glad to be of service when I know wot constitoots that same. As fer the elusive & intangible quality of *interest*—man, you-all in deep & profoun' piscatological intracutenessess!! Interest! O quest rare, unstable, & unbidden; responding never to a summons, & tarrying never for a plea! What art thou? Whence & wherefore comest thou? Whither & why goest thou? Who hath defin'd & anatomis'd thee? Who explain'd or allocated or predicted thee? Shake thy head, Father Sigmund, at that which thy lore will not cover. Pass glibly, O Doc Jawnbee,[1] over an aether too perverse for thy condition'd reflexes. Do they know aught of its mysteries, who this hellish night burn cosmick beacons on the lonely hills? Cthulhu fhtagn! Cthulhu fhtagn! Iä! Shub-Niggurath! The Goat with a Thousand Young!

No, Sir, I am not insensible of the importance of mineralogy in science; being well aware that the history of the planet & the details of many of its most vivid catastrophes lye hid in the chemical constitution & physical environment of its various sorts of rock. The science of *geology*, that primary branch of learning of which mineralogy is a division, is indeed something in which I might with ease become interested under the proper set of chance conditions; insomuch as it is directly concern'd with that main stream of cosmick pageantry which begins in blank aether and free electrons & ends in the perfection of Nordick man & Georgian architecture. Where mineralogy fails to get a grip on me is in the fact that it is a *secondary* science; an affair mainly of *classification*, with relatively slight *direct* linkage to the dramatick stream of pageantry of elemental conflict & mutation which appeals to the cosmic curiosity or interest-sense of the incurable layman. I am not alone in this—for scores of persons have many times askt me how *anyone* can possibly be interested in so dry a thing as mineralogy. The fact is, I am perhaps *less* anti-mineralogical than the rest of the herd; insomuch as I realise that the trouble is with myself rather than with mineralogy. To the student equipt with a first-rate mind, mineralogy is not dry; because the secondariness of the relationship of its subject-matter to the major stream of cosmic & terrestrial unfolding is lost amidst the easy recognition of that relationship itself. That is, the steps of removal from direct linkage are not emotionally significant to one whose brilliant intellect accepts complexities & tenuities for granted & without effort. But with dreamy, dull-witted plodders like me all is different. We dullards trip on difficulties not even visible to born statisticians & classifiers like you scientists. By the time we've traced the steps of kinship which youse guys lamp Einsteinically from the start as a matter of course, we're all in mentally & imaginatively, with no more pep left to give us a sense of the dramatick pageant whereof the given fraction is a symmetrically adapted part. We're so goddam dizzy counting & analysing trees, that the wood becomes an invisible & unrealisable blur losing all the kick it would pack if we took an eye-shot at it without stopping to examine tree-rings & classify types of foliation. No, bozo, it takes a bigger brain than George D. Layman's to find an epick in a gob of calcite (whatever that is) or a gate to the outer cosmos in some especial form of silicon dioxide. The fault's in us dubs, & not in the CaCO$_3$ or SiO$_2$—but the effect is just the same. It takes something *simpler*— more vivid, direct, and *immediately* dramatic (i.e., allied to the elements of impressive action, conflict human symbolism, or general curiosity)—to knock a row of us mental lightweights into the aisle. Where all you wise bimboes get puzzled, is in your unreadiness to perceive that we poor simps do *not* enjoy *mental exercise for its own sake* as you convex-domed titans do. We don't get even a shadow of a punch from the mental sensation of mastering an intricate complexity *per se,* or coming upon an intricate hidden relationship or distinction in some province remote from daily life or from the foundations of things. All we have wit enough to say or feel in the face of such a thing as that is a languid, "Oh yeah?" Us goofs, in order to be kept from dropping asleep or sucking our thumbs or drinking K. C. N., has gotta be kep' amoozed by something near enough to us to give us a *real* sense of motion, direction, expansion, adventurous uncertainty, novelty, change, rhythm, ego-inflation, expectancy, light, colour, freedom, & all that. There may be sermons in stones,[2] but we want ours on the 'raddio' or in some Bill Sunday's tent. Pep! Jazz! Ackshun! Whoopee! I can get interested in what Harlow Shapley has to say about the size & structure of the universe,[3] or what John Keats has to say about the intimations of hidden, tremulous strangeness & beauty therein; but I'm damned if I have the brains to register any emotional reaction a-tall over the difference betwixt one kind of grey rock & another kind of grey rock. Dumb, of course—but that's me, kid! I gotta have the zip & go of *visible pageantry*—the *historick* element—definite linkage either to cosmick ultimates on the far end, or to Anglo-Saxon mankind on the near end— in order to have a line of dope get acrost wit' me. That is, I ain't got enough brains to spare for any mulling over points that don't pay quick dividends in the kind of historic-pageant-imagery or adventurous expectancy which for me means a genuine emotional wallop. Take a concrete example. Crocodileite doesn't raise my temperature 0.0000001° Centigrade, but *Quebeck* knock'd me so cold that I've been living in another world, imaginatively speaking, ever since I seen it! Looney? Well—what t'ell d'ya' 'speck of a dumb guy?

As for travel matters—it's a lucky devil that kin plan the jaunts you're plannin', even if foreknowledge & calculation do sap 'em of their choicest stimulas! I gotta lamp Nova Scotia myself some day, even tho' I ain't fortunate enough to have any blood-streams reaching thither. The fact is, I respect Nova Scotia more than any other political unit on this terraqueous globe, insomuch as its foundations were laid by the most peculiarly select & noble type of human beings alive—thoughtful New-England gentlemen of the sort who place poetic symmetry & traditional loyalties above wealth & material advantage, and who accordingly relinquish'd all worldly advantage in the

1780's, when the time came to choose betwixt being faithful to their race & heritage & King, at the cost of impoverishment & exile, & being disloyal & hard-headed enough to keep their lands & properties & physical comforts by swearing allegiance to the upstart government of victorious rebels. Rather than enjoy comfort & plenty by foreswearing their traditions & their rightful King, they chose to remain unbroken in their integrity & self-respect, even tho' it robb'd them of all their goods & sent them again as pioneers upon the inhospitable shore of a subarctic wilderness. A false word would have given them slothful ease amidst the rebels. They chose not to say it, but to brave hardship & peril for the sake of honour. And we may well imagine the collective quality of a population assembled through such a principle of selection. All that may be said of New-England as a whole, as a region choicely filled by men whose dominant concernments were with the imponderables, may be doubly said of Nova-Scotia, New-Brunswick, & parts of Ontario—whose founders were, by a new test of the imponderables, selected from a population already select! It is no wonder that, despite its small population, Nova Scotia has ever produced an astonishing proportion of educators, statesmen, clergymen, & men of cultivation & mentality in general. When I think of the loyal gentlemen of that province I blush for my own sloth & lack of spirit in remaining tamely under the rebel flag through a mere love of home soil & hatred of uprooting. God! Was Rhode-Island any the less home soil to the Eastons, Caseys, Bowlers, Vernons, Hazards, Brentons, & so on, who bravely left their native & ancestral scenes in 1779 to enter an unknown icy wilderness? My only excuse is that I have never been asked to take any oath for swearing allegiance to my Sovereign & blood heritage, as they were asked to do. Were I so asked, I have the egotism to believe that I might summon up the manhood to respond as they did, & uproot myself from familiar scenes rather than degrade my honour as a gentleman & an Englishman. In the happily inconceivable event of a war with the United States, I would certainly feel obliged to transfer myself to the territories of the Empire. It would be the rankest of hypocrisy to remain among a people whose cause would mean nothing but the most passionate hatefulness to me, & whose rejoicing & triumphs would mean only my despair. God Save the King!!

Just one thing can make me temporarily forget Charleston—& that is La Vielle Quebec! Oh, boy! No—all spoofin' aside, I don't believe I can ever write a travelogue that anybody'll read; since the place is a veritable rocket-attachment to my imagination, & sends me off on long historical voyagings every time my mind touches it. Think of what it is—the very key & focus of the whole great drama of New-France which forms half the history of this continent! Our own English colonial enterprise had no such *single* keynote—we had our Boston, Newport, New-York, Philadelphia, & Charleston, but the French had just the one centre of all activities; just the one point whither came all their ships from the Old World, & whence departed all their myste-

rious penetrations into the adventurous unknown—traders, Jesuits, warri-
ors—Champlain, Radisson, Groseillier, Joliet, Marquette, Du Lhut, La Salle,
de Tonti, la Vedendraye, Lemoine, d'Iberville, Bienvielle—le grand Dieu,
quels hommes! God, if only I had got this bug in my bean while good old
Mac was alive! I'd have had something to talk with him about by the hour, &
could have cheer'd him up many a time with that show of genuine interest &
like-mindedness which he found so sparingly amongst our more disillusion'd
circle. Then again, reflect that Quebec hath always represented to me the
apex of unattainable sunset mystery ever since I read of our ill-fated New-
England expedition of 1690, under Sir W. Phips, in Cotton Mather's *Magnalia.*
The unscalable cliffs crown'd by the fortalice of the Grand Monarque—that
citadel of mystery whence pour'd the hostile hordes of Frenchmen & Hurons
who descended like daemons on our settlements—Phips's challenge—the
haughty Jacobitical reply of Count Frontenac—our repulse & discouragement—the wreck & winter on hellish Anticosti—. . . . then the repulse of Sir
Hovenden Walker years later . . . . the resolve to conquer or die . . . . delenda
est Carthago . . . . . The immortal WOLFE . . . . the defiant cliffs still frown-
ing . . . . the indomitable resolve of the unconquerable BRITON . . . . The
paths of glory lead but to the grave . . . . GOD SAVE THE KING!! Ours at
last, and *for ever!* Not even the might of the greedy rebel of 1775 could shake
off our Lion & Unicorn. Montgomery slain, Benedict Arnold turn'd back.
Rule Britannia!

And now *I have seen it,* & found just the same beetling cliffs & towering
walls & silver spires & crooked streets that WOLFE glimps'd from afar. . . .
& I have enter'd & trod these streets . . . . walk'd into the magic of the sunset,
& found substance in the gorgeousness of a dream & the pageantry of a fable
. . . Quebec! Can anything else (except Charleston & Providence's antient hill)
ever fill my mind? I started a travelogue last week, but after twenty-four pages
find myself still lingering on the historical background—no farther along than
1689, & with nothing yet about the town as I found it! Yet what would the
town be without its background? Hell! I give it up! I told ya I couldn't write a
travelogue!

I want to see some loyal town that is thoroughly Anglo-Saxon, & not
95% French like Quebec. I think *Halifax* will give me a marvellous kick despite any modern buildings which may deface it. And yet the French aren't so
bad on their own soil. The cursed scum that filter down into our Novanglian
mill villages are the worst of the peasant stock, & no index at all to the general gentle-blooded population of Quebec. The fact is, that urban Quebec has
a fine, conservative type of inhabitant—gentlemen descended from the sei-
gneural class—comparing well with the best blood of Providence or Charleston. The dominance of the popish church is of course an intellectual retarda-
tion, but it is a marvellous social preservative—so that I'm not sure but that
its net effect is actually beneficial. I am certain that if I ever pretended to be-

lieve in any supernatural or teleological mythology at all, I would go the whole way & belong to the only *real* Church in existence—the Holy Catholick Church of St. Peter & his successors, in whose unbroken traditions lie preserved most of the grace & stability of pagan antiquity, plus the mystery of the Orphic, Dionysiac, Apollonian, & Pythagorean cults whose influences combined to create a new mood & a new faith. Pater Noster, Ave Maria, God Save the King! The good point about the French in Quebeck is that they have dwelt immemorially on the same soil amidst the same conditions & traditions. That is what makes a *civilisation!* I'm not at all sure but that they will, in an ironick, deterministic mood of Fate, win by chance much of that New World supremacy which they lost in battle. They cohere & persist—you can't degallicise them. Despite all the English who have enter'd Quebec & settled in the southern part, the province is today more French than it was a century ago—almost as solidly French as it was in 1760. And what's more—the French constantly overflow into New England & Ontario; preserving their institutions wherever they go, whilst we are gradually losing ours amidst the promiscuous floods of cheap vermin from the Old World. Just as the conquer'd Greeks kept their language & manners longer than the all-conquering Romans, so will the French keep theirs long after we are sunk into mongrelisan & mechanisation. They will never be slaves to the melting-pot, the dynamo, & the time-table & for that I respect them, damn 'em! Would that we might learn coherence & conservatism from them—so that we might preserve our triumph over them. No—the French are not bad; & after seeing Quebec I can never again think of Central Falls & Woonsocket & Fall River as wholly foreign. At least, these people have always been part of our history—enemies, perhaps, yet close neighbours & sharers of the 300-year-old New World adventure.

How flat to address a blank with perfectly tranquil emotions:

Observe dull{ ——, whose sluggish mind (if name is trisyllabick)
             { ——, whose unfinisht mind (if name is disyllable)
             { ——, whose microscopick Mind (if name is monosyllable)

Rejects the precepts known to all mankind:
Scorns ev'ry fact, & scours the world to reach
Some height of folly new to human speech:
Begot by b——s, in a bedlam born,
Well-shap'd a gaol or madhouse to adorn;
Void of all things that Art and Virtue praise,
But fashion'd fit for these degen'rate days:
Pattern of all that wakes our honest spleen,
And brother to his own belov'd machine!

I wonder which is best—to find your enemy before writing the satire, or write first & then look for some fellows of your own size?

Well—I'll deliver this batch of rocks before I likewise repudiate responsibilities & beat it for Barbadoes!

Yrs for easy shipping methods—
Θεοβάλδος

Notes

1. The reference is to the American psychologist John B. Watson (1878–1958), founder of behaviorism.
2. Shakespeare, *As You Like It* 2.1.17.
3. Harlow Shapley (1885–1972), American astronomer and director of the Harvard College Observatory (1921–52).

[101]   [AHT]

Reg'lar Dump, 6 November, 1930

Egregious Essence of Explanatory Effulgence:—

Sir, your specifick suggestions are as manna from heaven, & I shall be guided by them in the struggle shortly to take place. If I have not rope & wrapping-paper of suitable tenacity, I will purchase what I think to be most suitable—guided in the case of the former commodity by the samples so thoughtfully enclos'd. And during some future visit I can obtain, under your expert guidance, a fair supply of palliatives for subsequent calamities. Increasing years no doubt make this kind of thing harder & harder for me. It seems more & more of a burthen to do objective things & make purchases involving excursions into the outside world. Like poor old Cook, the manifold claims of diurnal things upon my attention require more & more of my nervous energy to cope with—till finally I shall no doubt emulate him in disappearing without leaving a forwarding address. Rest . . . rest . . . where does one find it? Which reminds me that Cook isn't sure now but that he'll stay up at Coates's for the winter instead of beginning his joint venture with Orton. He speaks of having several times contemplated suicide, tho' in each case postponing the escape. Maybe he & I will fix up some sort of spectacular shuffling-off compact! Oh, yes—and as for quarry-scouring—I'll place your epistle on file for consultation whenever I feel equal to an accumulating session. I can always pretend I can't find it if I want to do some stalling when the collecting season opens. It's so easy for an envelope to fall behind a desk or something . . . . . . And you can do the same if I ask you to study up Dutch colonial architecture & snap me a choice gallery of certain specifick types. . . . .

As for mineralogy—I don't doubt but that the children get excited, for vari-colour'd rocks appeal to the same immature collecting sense that makes 'em rake in marbles & postage stamps & coloured pictures from cigarette packages (if they have that sort of thing nowadays). And apart from that—I conceded most freely that mineralogy must necessarily appeal to adults of a strongly intellectual type, in whose minds the linkage betwixt the actual mineral substances & the cosmic pageantry which formed them is so paramountly visible as not to require a spell-breaking effort for emotional-imaginative realisation. All I said was that for an ordinary dub—a rank layman with no intellectual initiative or surplus of correlative energy—this science must necessarily have less interest-capturing quality than have the primary sciences with the *obvious* & *easily envisaged* relationships to the dramatically dynamic & historically panoramic processes of the universe. Don't get me wrong, bozo, the trouble's with the spectator & not with the science. Of the importance of mineralogy in the slow piecing-together of that vast fabric of fact which forms man's mass'd attack on the question "what is anything?" no unbiass'd observer will be dispos'd to raise the least question. We must simply confess that a devotion to such unspectacular sciences of classification demands a more active & curious intelligence than the average citizen is likely to possess.

No—I hardly fancy'd you wou'd view Nova Scotia thro' my eyes—but damn it all, I wish I could trade a Phillips, Whipple, Casey, Rathbone, Hazard or two for some of your loyal ancestors! God Save the King! But you undoubtedly could *understand* my sentiment if I took the time & energy to explain it. Roughly, I may say that it is based on the simple fact that no one thinks or feels or appreciates or lives a mental-emotional-imaginative life at all, except in terms of the artificial reference-points supply'd him by the enveloping body of race-tradition & heritage into which he is born. We form an emotionally realisable picture of the external world, & an emotionally endurable set of illusions as to values and direction in existence, solely & exclusively through the arbitrary concepts & folkways bequeathed to us through our traditional culture-stream. Without this stream around us we are absolutely adrift in a meaningless & irrelevant chaos which has not the least capacity to give us any satisfaction apart from the trifling animal ones. Pleasure & pain, time & space, relevance & non-relevance, good & evil, interest & non-interest, direction & purpose, beauty & ugliness—all these words, comprising virtually everything within the scope of normal human life, are absolutely blank & without counterparts in the sphere of actual entity save in connexion with the artificial set of reference points provided by cultural heritage. Without our nationality—that is, our culture-grouping—we are merely wretched nuclei of agony & bewilderment in the midst of alien & directionless emptiness. Apart from his race-stream, no human being exists, mentally, as such. He is only one of the hominidae—the raw material of a human being. Therefore a native culture-heritage is the most priceless & indispensable thing any person has—*& he who weakens the grasp of a people upon their inheritance is most nefariously a traitor to the human species.* Of course, our heritage comes in layers of different intensity, each being more vital & potent as it comes closer to our immediate individuality. We have an

Aryan heritage, a Western-European heritage, a Teutono-Celtic heritage, an Anglo-Saxon or English heritage, an Anglo-American heritage, and so on— but we can't detach one layer from another without serious loss—loss of a sense of significance & orientation in the world. America without England is absolutely meaningless to a civilised man of any generation yet grown to maturity. The breaking of the saving tie is leaving these colonies free to build up a repulsive new culture of money, speed, quantity, novelty, & industrial slavery, but that future culture is not ours, & has no meaning for us. Its points of reference & illusions are not any points of reference & illusions which were transmitted to us, & do not form any system of direction & standards which can be emotionally realisable by us. It is as foreign to us as the cultures of the Sumerians, Zimbabweans, and Mayans. Those who will be authentick parts of it are the boys being born right now in the larger & more decadent American cities—they, & those who will be born after them. Possibly the youngest generation already born & mentally active—boys of ten to fifteen—will tend to belong to it, as indeed a widespread shift in their tastes & instincts & loyalties (cf. enc.) would seem to indicate. But to say that all this has anything to do with us is a joke! These boys are the Bedes & Alcuins of a new, encroaching, & apparently inferior culture. We are the Boethii & Symmachi & Cassiodori of an older & perhaps dying culture. It is to our interest to keep our own culture alive as long as we can—& if possible to preserve & defend certain areas against the onslaughts of the enemy. Any means will justify such an end; & since observing the effect of the Catholick Church upon Quebeck, I am half become a Papist in sympathies, tho' not in intellectual belief.

Now as to how all this correlates with my intellectual view of a meaningless cosmos—I truly cannot see where you find inconsistency except through the use of very conventional & non-analytical standards of judgment. It is *because* the cosmos is meaningless that we must secure our individual illusions of values, direction, & interest by upholding the artificial streams which gave us such worlds of salutary illusion. That is—since nothing means anything in itself, we must preserve the proximate & arbitrary background which makes things around us seem as if they did mean something. In other words, we are either Englishmen or nothing whatever. Apart from our inherited network of English ideas, memories, emotions, beliefs, points of view, &c., we are simply bundles of nerve-centres without materials for coherent functioning. Unless there exists an English world for us to live in, our total equipment of interests, perspectives, standards, aspirations, memories, tastes, & so on— everything, in short, that we really live for—at once becomes utterly valueless & meaningless & uncorrelated; a nightmare jumble of unsatisfiable outreachings, without objective linkages or justification, & forming only a source of illimitable misery. Of supreme importance, then, is the secure preservation of an English world around us. Conceivably, of course, an English world might well exist without legal connexion with the government of Great Britain. In

Hellenic times, for example, there was no one Greek nation; but merely a world of Greek culture extending in separate city-states from Massilia in Gaul to the coast of Asia Minor. This arrangement worked because there were no environing influences calculated to break down the culture of any part—yet the disunion was a vast disadvantage, & was instrumental in laying the Greek world open to an external conquest highly injurious to its psychology & morale. Thus in the English world—America has suffered, so far, in only a limited degree; because the forces of ancestral culture have continued to function despite the severance of the political link. But we now have deteriorative agencies—mechanisation, foreigners, &c.—more hostile to continuity than anything which the disunited Hellenic world had to face; so that our ability to preserve a culture of satisfying significance depends greatly on the exact degree of closeness of our linkage to ancestral sources. Nowadays we need more than the mere fact of *being* English in heritage & speech in order to *keep* so. We need the added & positive factors of being *consciously* & *symbolically* so, in order to offer the tangible *resistance* (a vigorous back pull, & not mere inertia) necessary to check decadence. When we fight the ideal of quantity & wealth, we must have the positive English ideal of quality & refinement to pit against it. We must have a rallying point for our emotional life in order to prevent the disorganising influences around us from recrystallising our milieu into definitely hostile & repulsive shapes. It is useless to fight meaningless recrystallisation unless we have a strong hold on the meaningful order behind us, & a solid coördination with the other surviving parts—especially the recognised centre & nucleus—of that order. What little of our past we merely passively harbour, we can lose with tragic ease. We must get a firm & virile grip on it—must recognise & cherish it, & seek solidarity with those parts of the world where it is most strongly entrenched. Possibly you may admit this, yet say that *politial* union is not necessary in order to achieve it. To this one may not reply dogmatically—though one may say that political separation is at least a very evil sort of symbolism, & that in practice it has worked hellish tragedy with the life & standards of the ill-fated, power-&-money-bloated, mongrelised United States . . . . that is, the life & standards of such social or territorial parts as *have* really departed from their inheritance. Of course, vast sections are still English—Vermont, South Carolina, Virginia, the old hill in Providence, & so on. Indeed, I must confess that your mention of Nova Scotia as a *neighbour*—that is, as anything except a continuous & indistinguishable part of the fabric to which we now belong—is almost incomprehensible to me; involving as it does a distinction which I find totally meaningless. I am a part of any region where English people live in an English manner . . . be it R.I., Charleston, Devonshire, Australia, Nova Scotia, or anywhere else. My own position in insisting on unpolluted Englishry is purely selfish & cynical. I want a good time—hence I work for the only environment which can give me a good time. As for the intensity of my emotions about the matter in a cosmos where nothing really counts—I will merely remind you that emotion is not a matter connected with reason. I have the emotions I do, simply because accident has given me a certain sort of glandular system & filled my subconscious mind with a certain set of images and impressions. I hate the rebels of 1775 because they commenced a wreckage which is making their territory unfit for their descendants to live in. God Save the King!

Yrs for Sovereign & Parliament
Theobaldus Anglissimus.

P.S. In connexion with the culture-&-nationality argument—of course, you are not so naive as to suppose that by such symbols as *King* & *England* I mean any more or less than *the continuous stream of English blood & thought & folkways as a whole*—a stream including Ontario as well as Yorkshire, Charleston as well as Melbourne, Marblehead & east side Providence as well as Cape Town & Calcutta & Jamaica. Just as we must *think* in objective terms, so must we *feel* in symbols.

[102]   [AHT]

4 December, 1730

Divine Disposer of Delay'd Dump-Detritus:—

Thank Yuggoth, the damn things is safe at last! But gawd—wotta tragedy that Talman's exterior artistry was lost upon you![1] This is too, too much . . . . he must never, never know. . . . . . And incidentally, his address is 2215 Newkirk Avenue, Brooklyn, N. Y. That's in Flatbush—take the good old BMT & get off at Newkirk Avenue station . . . . some four stops beyond antient Parkside. His telephone is INgersoll—two-1795. Hell, how things change. They never had any such exchange in my day, then only one being honest "Flatbush".

As to where them black diamonds come from—gawd, I'd never a thort ya could forget that, after the helluva time we had findin' it, with everybody tellin' us sumpun different about distances! Oh, well—the taownship was indeed Portsmouth, in & on Rhode-Island, & the commodity originally sought for was indeed combustible carbon. But don't try to burn your specimens. It won't get ya nowhere, no more nor it got the old minin' comp'ny anywhere. Yeah—'graphite from Old Portsmouth "coal" mine' will do elegant for a label. If ya don't use the quotes it ud be a libel—& not talkin' Cockney, nuther!

As for traditions—I still say that for men of our race & age, there is no tradition but the old English one. What the backgroundless upstarts of later generations can get a kick out of is no goddam business of ours. But I did *not* say that the traditions of *any especial period* were necessary. I've before corrected that misapprehension about my general views; a misapprehension based on my *purely personal* & involuntary participation in eighteenth century feeling, which of course has nothing to do with the case. No, indeed—the English tradition which we need to give our lives the illusion of direction & significance is not any mere matter of one century or age. It began when the blood & instincts & habits of Saxon conquerors became fused with the blood & instincts & habits of classically-influenced Norman conquerors, & includes the splendour of Plantagenets & Tudors as well as the taste, elegance, & good-sense of King William, Queen Anne, & the Georges, whom God Save. It involves certain impulses & standards & responses & criteria which have become instinctive with us, & which are for ever antipodally opposed to the degrading fallacies of ochlocracy, speed, quantity, collectivism, regimented regularity, material ostentation, standardisation, &c. &c. which are today punishing these unhappy colonies for their rash & precipitate rebellion against their lawful Sovereign. I have just been saying to a new correspondent that I wish New England could be amputated from the corpse of the dead American U. S. & join'd to the still-loyal Dominion of Canada—of which we would form an admirable & much-needed southerly outlet. Incidentally, I would envy you your coming trip to the present place in *December.* Gawd! I'd better wait for the Dominion to come to me!

As for your rush—you have my sympathy, but you ought not to try to keep so many damn irons in the fire. A few things well done is Grandpa's motto!

And so it goes!

Yr obt
Θεοβάλδος

Notes

1. JFM's assistant had opened the package and discarded the wrapping.

[103] [AHT]

3d Day before the Kalends of Ianuarius
[29 December 1930]

Daedalian Diamond of Dynamick Diversity:—

Well, wot t'ell! So that wa'nt graphite after all! Coal, eh? Fancy coal in a coal mine—who cou'd have expected it? The old boys that started diggin' wa'n't so wrong in theory after all—& who the hell cares for a sordid trifle like utility? If the coal doesn't burn, that's all the more oeconomical. You don't have to replenish your bins each year, & can use the jack to spend the October–April period in Jamaica or Barbadoes! Glad the good o' Eden Musee is all jazzed up with fresh furniture & snappy new exhibits. Nothin' like novelty for a sophisticated audience. When they get fed up on earth-rocks, pep up the show with aerolitick fragments from the vigintillion shatter'd worlds of the fathomless Outer Void.

How t'ell was you to know Arminius was Jonckheer van Talman? Why, Sir, thro' simple historick background-elements of association. You behold the name *Arminius*, & as a theologically inclin'd minister's son at once think of that celebrated Dutch theologian of the Reformation—James Arminius, whose unlatinis'd name was Hermann or something of that sort. Rather famous gink—spawn'd 1560, croak'd 1609. Well—of all us gangsters, who'd be most likely to pick a Latinis'd *Dutch* name to match the sundry Latinisations unofficially represented by Mortonius, Theobaldus, Belnapius, Samuelus, & so on? Why, naturally, our *only Dutch member*—Wilfredus van Talman, scion of Talemas, Blanvelts, Bogards, and all the other contemplative burghers, patroons, & jonckheers of the lower Hudson Valley. Hell! that was clear enough to me the first time I lamped the new-synthetick monicker . . . . . even if I hadn't recognis'd the unmistakable Talmanick script. When, later on, I made idle oral inquiries, I was inform'd that the theologian Arminius was indeed the starting-point of the new nomenclature; tho' overtones involving the Teutonick race-hero Herrmann, or Arminius, chief of the Charusci, who in A. V. C. 760 so tragically annihilated the three legions of P. Quintilius Varus in the Saltus Teutobergiensis, had come to twine themselves around the sonorous appellation. Vare, Vare, legiones redde![1] Well, anyhow, it's a good Dutch handle with a piquant flavour of the Renaissance, & of the Dutch West India Company's Nieuw-Nederland plantation about it. One can be tolerant toward the Dutch, since their province pass'd easily into the hands of the Britannick Maj^ty Charles the Second, whom God Save!

Speaking of His Majesty's American Provinces—I am now on *p. 65* of my history-travelogue of QUEBECK, yet have progress'd no further than the defeat of the rebels under Arnold and Montgomery on Dec. 31, 1775, & their subsequent expulsion from Canada! The theme so ingulphs my imagination—filling it with historick panoramas & sending it off on side-excursions contributory to the general background—that rapid progress or concise compass is impossible. As it is, no one save myself will ever have the patience to read the thing through—a circumstance which does not vastly worry or even interest me. God Save the King! Rule, Britannia! Certainly, it was like a rebirth—or a delay'd first birth—to set foot on soil still loyal to our natural social-political-cultural stream, & I wish to Heaven I might die with the old Union Jack of my fathers floating over me. How I would envy you that Toronto sojourn if it weren't *at this time of year!* I may yet end up in Bermuda, British Honduras, Trinidad, Calcutta, or some place where a decent climate & Britannick supremacy are combin'd!

As for your rush—of course, every mortal mind is differently suited, but I still think you could get a greater total of genuine satisfactions if you would cut down the number & variety of your interests, & take the time for the *full emotional realisation* of a more modest range. Your ease in grasping the *intellec-tual* outlines of a subject in a very brief time has caused you to set up a stan-dard of acquisition based wholly on intellectualism; whereby you deem maximum satisfaction derivable from the crowding of your mind with as many different ideas & surface impressions as possible, & have come to feel a sense of vacancy every moment that you cannot be exercising this mechanical mental-acquisitive function—to such an extent that even rest & food periods must be filled with semblances of the process in the form of popular fiction, the Satevepost, & so on. Now of course it is conceivable that you really couldn't get more pleasure from another regimen—yet I feel quite strongly that you could, once you discarded the purely intellectual ideal which a pre-ternaturally strong & quick mind happened to suggest by accident in the be-ginning. With your regimen, the development of an *inner life of the emotions & imagination* is almost nipped in the bud by the crowding pressure of fresh & emotionally unassimilated ideas; & even the full intellectual digestion & corre-lation of pure ideas is something achieved with the suggestion of grudging—something subconsciously regarded as dull work or duty as contrasted with the sheer delight of raking in new surface fragments. The trouble with all this is that it does not permit the emotions & imagination to expand at any time in that ultimate & unhampered way which (tho' of course at bottom only a vain groping in darkness) gives the illusion of an approximation to *perfect frui-tion*. I don't say that it cuts off *all* perception of emotional-imaginative over-tones, or closes *all* side-avenues of satisfying association-building & visual-imaginative pageantry; but I can't help feeling that it *restricts* these processes to such an extent as to deprive one of more pleasure than is given in compensa-tion by idea-crowding. For example, you need reading or conversation with your meals. Why? What barrier shuts you off from the flood of pleasing & engrossing imaginative associations which the inner life brings up when spe-cific external impressions are withheld? What ultimate extreme of extrover-sion makes necessary a choice betwixt imported ideas & a mere chaos or blank? Under the same circumstances—i.e., a solitary meal—the average per-son has a thousand things to busy him pleasantly. He can be revolving & re-arranging previous mental or imaginative images—or, as is more common in a relaxation-period, he can be giving his imagination free rein to weave fantas-tic associations around the casual objects impinging on his consciousness—the articles of food, the table utensils, any distinctive decorations or personal types that may be present, & so on. The food & silver themselves are enough for an active imagination. Endless chains of fantasy can form themselves around even a spoon. Spoon . . . . silver . . . . pewter . . . . . . Paul Revere . . . . silver-mines . . . . . Mexico . . . . . buried silver plate . . . . . pirates . . . . . shilling . . . argentum . . . . ἄργυρε . . . Pheidon of Ægina . . . . drachma . . . . denarius . . . . the Lydians . . . . Bithynia . . . ΤΙΚΛΑΔΙΟΣ ΚΑΙ ΣΑΡΣΕΒΑΣΤΟ . . . . ΤΙΓΡΑΝΕΣ ΒΑΣΙΛΕΥΣ . . . . silver goblets . . . . silver censers &

cressets . . . . . silver columns . . . . silver domes & spires . . . . the silver spires & belfries of QUEBECK . . . . . flash of sun on bayonets . . . . . WOLFE . . . . God Save the King . . . . . but this is only the tame, narrow start of a real train of associations. And the same with food—coffee . . . . . Arabia . . . . Haroun al Raschid . . . . the Golden Road to Samarcand . . . . . Vathek . . . . . Palace of Eblis . . . . . Sinbad . . . . . the Roc . . . . . the ghouls . . . . . Java . . . . . Malay Priests . . . Angkor . . . . silence & mystery . . . . . the carving that only the moon dares look upon . . . . . . Brazil . . . . . . steaming jungle . . . . . the hieroglyph'd stone that none dares decipher . . . . . Brasil . . . . . Hy-Brasil . . . . . Isles of the Blest . . . . . Druids . . . . Stonehenge . . . . . or take sugar . . . . . waving cane . . . . . Louisiana . . . . . Lafitte . . . . Bienville . . . . . La Salle . . . . Tonty of the Iron Hand . . . . good old Mac² . . . . . . days that were . . . . . gates that seemed to open to farther mysteries of the west . . . . . Cuba . . . . . . Morro Castle . . . . . . John Carter's broadside of 1762, printed at Shakespear's-Head: Morro-Castle taken by Storm . . . . . the *Providence Gazette & Country Journal,* containing the Freshest Advices, Both Foreign & Domestick . . . . Antilles . . . . . . Martinecco . . . . . Obadiah Brown . . . . . . rum, niggers, & molasses . . . . . Lord Timothy Dexter . . . . . warming-pans³ . . . . . Vermont . . . . . . Barbadoes . . . . . Antillia . . . . Atlantis . . . . . Poseidonis . . . . . Lemuria . . . .R'lyeh . . . . . . the temples of orichalch & the columns of chrysoberyl . . . . . chrysoprase . . . . crocodilite . . . . . Cumberlandite . . . . James Ferdinand Plantagenet . . . . . . Paterson . . . . . . William Paterson of N. Jersey . . . . . who killed Billy Patterson⁴ . . . . . . down went McGinty⁵ . . . . . . After the Ball⁶ . . . . Grover Cleveland . . . . . the Yellow Book . . . . . a long way from sugar, but that's what association will do. If you don't believe it, read Ed Poe's introduction to "Murders in the Rue Morgue". Or take beef stew—herds of cattle . . . . . . buffalo . . . . . Sioux . . . . . . Iroquois . . . . . . "What do you hunt?" "We hunt men!" "Ugh! you have found them!" . . . . Count Frontenac . . . . . Phips . . . . . . sacred buffaloes . . . . . steaming, shallow rivers in the sun . . . . . . South Africa . . . . Unknown Zimbabwe . . . . . . Crowns of Upper & Lower Ægyptus . . . . . . Trinacria . . . . . Oxen of Helios . . . . . Apis . . . . . . the immemorial Nile . . . . . . the Cow-Chase . . . . . Maj. John André . . . . . . Cow-Boys . . . . . . Skinners . . . . . . Neutral ground . . . . . . Sir Henry Clinton . . . . the stout Earl of Northumberland . . . . . Tappan . . . . Talman . . . . . the old man killed on his chest of gold . . . . . the lowing herd winds slowly o'er the lea⁷ . . . . common pasturage . . . . . Weybosset Neck . . . . . . wharves keep the homecoming cows from getting ashore on the Towne Streets . . . . . Great Bridge 1771 . . . . Market House 1773 . . . . . Baptist Steeple 1775 . . . . Confound their Politicks . . . . . . Nichols' Dairy . . . . . Borden's Challenge Milk . . . . . . Dryco . . . . . Jake's . . . . hamburg & onions . . . . . Or take roast lamb . . . . . . Charles Lamb . . . . . . Kleiner . . . . . wool . . . . niggers οὐλόθριξ . . . . οὐλοκάρενος . . . . dark curling locks o'erfleec'd his bending head, o'er which a promontory shoulder spread[8] . . . . . . Melanochroic Aryan . . . . . Thyrsis . . . . . sheep on Sicilian slopes . . . . . Where were ye, Nymphs, O where, while Daphnis pin'd? In fair Penëus or in Pindus' glens? For great Anapus' stream was not your haunt, nor Ætna's cliff, nor Acis' sacred rill[9] . . . . . . Tityre, tu patulae recubans sub tegmine fagi[10] . . . . Is wool thy care? let not thy cattle go where bushes are, where burrs & thistles grow[11] . . . . . J. Dryden, Esqr. . . . . Astraea Redux . . . . . God Save the King . . . . . John Clarke & the Charter of 1663 . . . . . sheep on the hills behind Newport . . . . . the Gothick tower . . . . . Jason . . . . Golden Fleece . . . . . . Medea . . . . . . L. Annaeus Seneca . . . . . . Prosperum ac felix scelus virtus vocatur[12] . . . . . Frustrate their knavish Tricks[13] . . . . . Mary had a little lamb . . . . Sterling, in His Maj[ty]'s Province of the Massachusetts Bay . . . . a shepherd boy, he seeks no better name[14] . . . . . on airy downs the shepherd idling lies, & sees tomorrow in the marbled skies[15] . . . . . . the gather'd flocks are in the wattled pen innumerous prest[16] . . . . . . O Jemmy Thomson, Jemmy Thomson O![17] . . . . . . no line which, dying, he cou'd wish to blot[18] . . . . . for we were nurs'd upon the self-same hill, fed the same flock by fountain, shade, & rill[19] . . . . . the jolly shepherd that was of yore is now nor jolly nor shepherd more[20] . . . . . . Kimball's All-Wool Suits, $9.00. Estab. 1857. Give the Boys Fits . . . . fleece . . . . clouds sheep with moist wool, slain by the arrows of the sun . . . . . . Aries, the Ram . . . . . . M. Ulpius Traianus . . . . batter'd gates . . . . . . Amen-Ra . . . . . Neph . . . . . . 𓄿 𓃭 𓏏 𓃀 𓄿 𓃬 . . . . the master ram at last approach'd the gate, charg'd with his wool, & with Ulysses' fate[21] . . . . . . Cyclops . . . . . . Cyclopean masonry . . . . . . Athens . . . . . . Pelasgi . . . . . . Paschal Lamb . . . . . . Ram's Horn . . . . . . Agnus Dei . . . . abroad in the meadows to see the young lambs run sporting about by the side of their dams with fleeces so clean & so white[22] . . . . Epitaphium Viri Venerabilis Dom. N. Mather, carmine lapidario conscriptum[23] . . . . Inter Nov-Anglos theologiae tyrocinia fecit[24] . . . . . . the Lion Bold the lamb doth hold[25] . . . . . the little Lamb doth skip & play, always merry, always gay[26] . . . . . . I love to see the lambs at play, they hop so spry & seem so gay; they nip the grass & then are seen to chase their playmates round the green[27] . . . . . . the Wolf & the Lamb . . . . . . then let him bear away with him the imperishable coverlet, the fleece glittering with tufts of gold[28] . . . . . . Hark! with fresh rage & undiminish'd fire the sweet enthusiast smites the British lyre[29] . . . . . some to the thicket of the forest flock, & some for shelter seek; the hollow rock[30] . . . . my name is Norval; on the Grampian Hills my father feeds his flocks; a frugal swain[31] . . . . Harpalus & eke Corin were herdmen both yfere[32] . . . . & he shall set the sheep on the right hand[33] . . . . . . for they'd left their tails behind them[34] . . . . . . in that Countrie are white Hens without Feathers, but they beare white Woole as Sheepe doe heare[35] . . . . . . 1000 sheep jumping a stone wall . . . . . nor iron bars a sheep-pen[36] . . . . . . Sheepshead Bay . . . . . . Emmons Ave. . . . . . . stink of fish . . . . . Gerritsen tide-mill 1688 . . . . . .

Avenue V .... Neck Road .... Stillwell House ..... Milestone
..... 8¾ miles to Brockland Ferry ...... flat marshlnds, creeks, waving
sedge, flutter of marsh birds ...... curved cottage roofs .... east winds sighing of Old Holland ..... mutton-chop whiskers ..... Victorian aera .....
progress & optimism ..... grow old & on the bum, the worst is yet to
come[37] ..... High on the top the manly corse they lay, & well-fed sheep &
sable oxen slay[38] .... O Gawd! who wants to tote a newspaper to Westermarck-Sailahead's when all this comes out of a sixty-five cent
order of roast lamb? Well, anyhow, you prob'ly get what I mean. The big idea
is that a constant, restless chase after new things prevents one from getting a
kick out of the correlation, rearrangement, juggling, & marshalling of the stuff
already inside the li'l' ol' bean. Why learn when ya ain't got time to enjoy the
dope after ya got it? After all, the purpose of acquiring impressions is to build
up a background of reference-points which shall make one think one under-
stands the cosmos in part, & which does indeed orient one sufficiently to
local phenomena to allow for a very pleasurable ego-projection. But only certain types of impressions contribute to this background—hence the wise guy
tries to see what is merely sterile & superficial (that is, what merely amuses
for the moment without deepening one's inner imaginative resources) in order to cut out such deadwood. Also, he guards against the accumulation of
any sort of material beyond the amount he can *emotionally digest*—i.e., make
part of a subjective pageantry which shall create for him the desiderate sense
of adventurous expectancy and ego-expansion. A smattering of many
things—or even a thorough knowledge of many things if unaccompanied by
the leisure to ruminate on these things & utilise them emotionally—is far less
gratifying than a deeply assimilated knowledge of two or three things. For
example—it is clear from all evidence that the encylopaedic Greek scholars,
like Porson and Jowett,[39] do not even approach the degree of true Hellenism
experienc'd by such a single-track dreamer as John Keats, & that omniscient
historians like H. G. Wells cannot begin to enter into the life of any past period & extract solid enjoyment from it to the extent that relatively ignorant
mediaeval dreamers like Bernard Dwyer, or naive early-Celtick enthusiasts
like Robert E. Howard, can. Certainly, one needs a wide general knowledge
for correlative purpose but this having been gain'd in outline, it is best to specialise in a few things, so that one may not miss the supremely satisfying experience of following up avenues to such a length as to reach opened doors &
participate in the life of previously unattained worlds of recaptured reality or
imaginative expansion. This is the secret of the poet as distinguished from the
prosaicist—the symbol-dreamer & image-singer as distinguish'd from the
chronicler & classifier.

De argumentis—those magazine extracts sure were a mouthful, & I
keenly enjoy'd the perusal of each one of them. I can't say, though, that they
present much which is new. The negrophile article is the usual example of

artful dodging—sedulously avoiding the utterly impartial researches of the really great anthropologists like G. Elliott Smith & Marcelin Boule,[40] (who shew both australoid & negroid stems to be immeasurably ancient variants of homo sapiens, very early differentiated from the main line which produced the Mongol-Nordic-Mediterranean animal, tho' of course not differentiated so early as homo neanderthalensis or rhodesiensis) & refusing to face the really crucial issue—the mental-emotional status & cultural capacity of the African black in his native habitat. Of course, any full survey of the facts would knock all negrophilic arguments into a cocked hat. Research proves the utter inability of the negro to evolve any autochthonous civilisation, or even to assimilate outside civilisations—no matter how long exposed to their influence—until given an infusion of superior blood. The low intellectual content of all native negro art is axiomatic—& a study of African folklore shews infinite depths of chronic simplicity, dulness, & unimaginativeness. We have only to compare African folklore with Amerindian or Polynesian myths in order to appreciate the difference between the undevelopable negroid mind & the imaginatively sensitive & intellectually resourceful mind of the main human stem. Of course the case of the australoid—the Australian blackfellow & (now extinct) Tasmanian is even more emphatic; this race being nearly as far below the negro as the negro is below the full human. Neither of these two variant sub-species has any power or inclination to achieve the more highly-sensitised, conscious, & resource-using level of life which we recognise as civilisation, nor can the infusion of their blood in higher veins act as anything but a drag & a doom to mankind in general. In the article, much is made of a few surface specialisations like hairlessness, in which the negro seems evolved; & an attempt is made to contrast these with the overwhelming preponderance of far more basic (because skeletal & inherent) points in which the Siamian approach is manifest. A word from Smith or Boule on the lack of significance of such isolated points of advanced specialisation (in some ways, certain insects are far more evolved & specialised than humans) would dispose of this argument. Moreover—in citing laboratory comparisons of whites & blacks, the author merely selects a certain assortment of minor results which happen to look favourable to him; wholly overlooking even more numerous & far more weighty tests where Brudder Sambo does not come out so well. Today it is a work of amazing naiveté to drag out poor old Prof. Boas![41] There is no more sense in trying to prove a nigger a white man's equal than in trying to prove a Neanderthal Man's corresponding equality. The only reason that sentimental fanatics have not tried to put over the latter piece of folly is that all the Neanderthals are extinct. We can all think clearly on a purely academic issue; but as soon as it becomes a present problem, mixed up with our artificially trained sentiments & ethical delusions, we at once divide into the two camps of warped emotionalists (who allow their sharp 'is-or-isn't' faculty to be swayed by wishes regarding human importance, destiny, relationships, happiness, &c) & sound realists who don't give a damn for mankind or anything else except a discrimination betwixt what is & what isn't. Now the trickiest catch in the nigger problem is the fact that it is really *twofold*. The black *is* vastly inferior. There can be no question of this among contemporary & unsentimental biologists—eminent Europeans for whom the prejudice-problem does not exist. *But,* it is *also* a fact that there *would be* a very grave & very legitimate problem *even if the negro were the white man's equal.* For the simple fact is, that *two widely dissimilar races, whether equal or not, cannot peaceably coexist in the same territory until they are either uniformly mongrelised or cast in folkways of permanent & traditional personal aloofness.* No normal being feels at ease amidst a population having vast elements radically different from himself in physical aspect & emotional responses. A normal Yankee feels like a fish out of water in a crowd of cultivated Japanese, even though they may be his mental & aesthetic superiors; & the normal Jap feels the same way in a crowd of Yankees. This, of course, implies permanent association. We can all *visit* exotic scenes & like it—& when we are young & unsophisticated we usually think we might continue to like it as a regular thing. But as years pass, the need of old things and usual influences—home faces & home voices—grows stronger & stronger; & we come to see that mongrelism won't work. We require the environing influence of a set of ways & physical types like our own, & will sacrifice anything to get them. Nothing means anything, in the end, except with reference to that continuous immediate fabric of appearances & experiences of which one was originally a part; & if we find ourselves ingulphed by alien & clashing influences, we instinctively fight against them in pursuit of the dominant freeman's average quota of legitimate contentment. Naturally, if a race wants to submit to the fantastic martyrdom of mongrelisation for an agonising period of centuries, there will emerge a new composite race & culture whose members will have attained a new homogeneity—& therefore a new & satisfying equilibrium. But who cares to sacrifice himself for the sake of this hypothetical future race—a race as genuinely foreign & meaningless to him as the Peruvians would have been to the Greeks, or as the Thibetans are to ourselves? All that any living man normally wants—& all that any man worth calling such will stand for—is as stable & pure a perpetuation as possible of the set of forms & appearances to which his value-perceptions are, from the circumstances of moulding, instinctively attuned. That is all there is to life—the preservation of a framework which will render the experience of the individual apparently relevant & significant, & therefore reasonably satisfying. Here we have the normal phenomenon of race-prejudice in a nutshell—the legitimate fight of every virile personality to live in a world where life shall seem to mean something. Nobody gives a damn whether the encroaching diluent element is equal, superior, or inferior—though of course inferiority makes necessary a more drastic policy than might otherwise be followed. When the diluent stock is radically inferior, we must establish an absolute deadline & force all hybrids below in order to preserve the higher stock untainted—just as the Osage Indians kill any member of the tribe who has associated with a nigger, in order to save themselves from the negroid taint affecting & debasing the so-called civilised tribes of Oklahoma—Cherokees, Choctaws, Chickasas, Creeks, & Seminoles—whereas if the stock is equal or superior, we can afford to absorb just as much as we can without peril to our folkways, traditions, & physical type. But in either case we can't allow our institutions, habits, & physical type to be swamped. Superior, equal, or inferior, an alien stock has got to be kept back from such a position as would affect our own chances of living under our normal hereditary influences. This point has not been sufficiently stressed—a very unfortunate circumstance, since it makes the whole issue hinge on a really irrelevant factor; i.e., the question of superiority, equality, or inferiority. It is a waste of time to call attention to the negro's primitiveness, when we know damn well that we'd segregate him just about the same if he were our equal or superior. This is a Nordic country—whether or not the Nordic is superior—& it's a safe bet that we'll keep it so as a general proposition as long as there's any manhood or self-respect in us. These are the things that normal white men fight about—& there's no limit to the fight still left in a decent American when he sees any sort of menace to the environment which means home for him. We've got a hellish enough mess of god damn Dagoes & Poles & Mongoloid kikes on our hands now, but they may be ultimately kept down & partly assimilated to our pattern if we have the rudimentary horse-sense not to let any more wholesale herds of 'em in. The Indian can take care of himself, owing to a general tendency toward geographic localisation. The lid is already on for Chinks & Japs. As for the one element of radical biological inferiority—Rufus Rastus Johnson Brown[42]—it doesn't take any prophet to see that no drop of his blood will ever, with knowledge, reside in the veins of any person accepted as a member of America's recognised dominant class. Just how the black & his tan penumbra can ultimately be adjusted to the American fabric, yet remains to be seen. It is possible that the economic dictatorship of the future can work out a diplomatic plan of separate allocation whereby the blacks may follow a self-contained life of their own, avoiding the keenest hardships of inferiority through a reduced number of points of contact with the whites. This, indeed, is grudgingly & pragmatically seen by the author of your negrophile extract. No one wishes them any intrinsic harm, & all would rejoice if a way were found to ameliorate such difficulties as they have without imperilling the structure of the dominant fabric. It is a fact, however, that sentimentalists exaggerate the woes of the average negro. Millions of them would be perfectly content with a servile status if good physical treatment & amusement could be assured them, & they may yet form a well managed agricultural peasantry. The real problem is the quadroon & octoroon—& still lighter shades. Theirs is a sorry tragedy, but they will have to find a special place. What we can do is to discourage the increase of their numbers by placing the heaviest possible penalties on miscegenation, & arousing as much public sentiment as possible against lax customs & attitudes—especially in the inland South—at present favouring the melancholy & disgusting phenomenon. All told, I think the modern American is pretty well on his guard, at last, against racial & cultural mongrelism. There will be much deterioration, but the Nordic has a fighting chance of coming out on top in the end. I wish we were equally on our guard against the subtler decadence due to economic & mechanical overturns—the shifting & cheapening of standards, & the reduction of life to a crude & colourless quantitative basis, which has come from the impact of science, invention, & organisation upon a group too widely severed from its normal European heritage! Neo-America will probably be Nordic, but it will not be our country in any real sense; since its thread of emotional continuity with us is daily becoming thinner & more merely nominal. The alienage, of course, will not be as great as if the new institutions sprang from foreign blood-impulses & foreign heritages; but it will be sufficiently great to outrage most of our standards & sensibilities, & preclude any feeling of ease or kinship betwixt us & the commercial-mechanical-collectivistic neo-Americans. We shall have to cling to our few coastal strongholds as long as possible—& it will be up to our grandsons to decide whether to go back to England & resume the normal original allegiance, or to go over to the enemy & form part of a turbulent future folk-fabric incomprehensible to us. I wish devoutly that New England could slip out of the mess by getting amicably transferred to the Dominion of Canada. The trade-mad neo-Americans have no liking for us, & love to regard us as decadent & obsolete. Only a month ago a big-business leader urged Connecticut to cut loose from New England & join its social, fiscal, & commercial fortunes to the New-York area. The best thing we could do would be to cede New-York a bit of southwestern Connecticut & put the whole Federal farce of 1789 behind us. Culturally, geographically, & economically we belong with the Dominion of Canada as an extension of the English-speaking maritime provinces. We need Canada as a buttress for our threatened & invaded institutions, & Canada needs us for a thousand economic reasons. As it is, Canada has only one first-class year-round Atlantic port—Halifax—& is forced to use New London & Portland as termini for her transcontinental trunk lines. Canada's tragedy is a semi-uninhabitable climate; & if New England were to join her, our towns would soon be the seat of the choicest English-Canadian life & culture. Boston, Providence, Worcester, Springfield, Hartford, & New Haven would leave Toronto, Winnipeg, & Halifax far behind; & it might be possible to get rid of most of our foreigners by subsidising their emigration to the more highly industrialised area of neo-America. Of course we would be open to French-Canadian invasion—as we are already—but it couldn't be much worse than it is. Tactful governmental measures could check any wholesale descent of Quebec habitants—recognising the St. Lawrence valley as historically & as logically theirs, just as Newfoundland, New-Brunswick, Nova-Scotia, New-England, Ontario, & the Canadian West are historically & logically ours. God! What wouldn't I give to see the old flag go up again over the white belfry of Providence's 1761 Colony-House, whence it was treasonably lower'd on the 4th of May, 1776! God Save the King! An health to His Maj^{ty's} Colony of Rhode-Island & Providence-Plantations!

The article on civilisation & race-mixture is highly interesting, tho' I think the author exaggerates the degree to which most thoughtful persons confuse race- & culture-attributes. Very few, I believe, imagine that any given culture is the inescapable product of one especial biological stream; though the implication is perhaps loosely conveyed by the manner in which one empirically speaks of the partial, flexible, & complex connexion which actually does exist as a matter of practical reality. A culture is the product of many factors— geographical, historical, œconomick, physiological, & so on, of which race is only one. But we must not make the mistake of counting race altogether out. Many features of a culture are determined by the mental, emotional, & physiological characteristics which prior experiences may have fixed in the branch of mankind among whom it arises, so that the given culture will always be better adapted to persons of that type of heredity than to persons of another type—especially a type whose differences are very marked. At this point it must be emphasised that nothing but complete sentimental damn foolishness can possibly underlie any attempt to prove that different races & sub-races do not have differently proportion'd impulses—that is, that each one does not regularly produce a preponderance of a certain physical-emotional-mental type different from the preponderant types of widely different races. Historic conditions tend to encourage the multiplication of some types of persons & the extinction of others; so that if a given race splits in two & spends a thousand or more years under widely different geographic, climatic, economic, social, & political conditions, it will to all intents & purposes have become two separate races—through the fostering of one side of the complex original racial character in once case, & the fostering of a widely different side in another case. To deny this is to go outside adult rationality altogether. Well—it is equally true that each of these two variants will have developed a separate cultural milieu—based originally on the separate environmental conditions encountered, & finally on the modified balance of natural impulses & tendencies in each of the stocks after its modification by natural selection. Clearly, the culture developed by one of the branches will be better adapted to its own members than to the members of the other branch. Of course, a few isolated scions of the other stock, reared from birth in the opposite atmosphere, will be able to mix with their adopted culture on average terms—but this will not be true of any great number. Any pair of representative *groups* chosen from the respective stocks will present substantially differentiated sets of basic impulses; because in each of the stocks the possessors of a certain separate kind of heritable physical temperament will have become more numerous through encouragement, & through the discouragement & elimination of possessors of the opposite physical temperament. Now in dealing with the capacities & adaptabilities of race-stocks, we must always think in mass terms, since it is generally as masses that races figure in national problems. We have no reason to be interested in the chance individual, since individuals do not make a problem. If there were no great masses of blacks in America we would not need to draw a colour-line. What we are interested in is practical reality—the kind of stock, collectively, that an incoming race-element is likely to breed, as compared with the kind which we ourselves breed as a whole. It is perfectly clear that, in the case of the two sub-races cited above, the masses of stock #1 will tend to possess an average physical temperament (on which much of their culture will hinge) decidedly different from the average physical temperament of stock #2; & that, therefore, the introduction of any large element of stock #2 into the compact fabric of stock #1, will produce a deep & serious conflict. Amongst this element, natural moods & circumambient folkways will not coincide; so that the newcomers will either remain on difficult terms as maladjusted outsiders, or else succeed in modifying the existing fabric in their own direction—thus producing a state of intolerable uncongeniality & frustration for the legitimate population of stock #1, & even then not achieving any state really satisfying to themselves. This miserable disturbance of equilibrium will last, of course, until the two elements (racial & cultural alike) are fused into a new homogeneity after an agonising march of wasted generations—there then being evolved a new civilisation unlike either of its predecessors, & not necessarily better or worse than either. Of course, lovers of mongrelism insist that such a bastard culture is miraculously certain to be better than any pure culture—but one need only refer them to history. To call the stabilisation of a relatively pure culture "decay" is simply to invent an artificial & fallacious definition of what cultural excellence is. Of course, all cultures have their eventual senility & death, but there is no reason to think that this cycle is at all accelerated by racial or cultural purity. Both China & Egypt after thousands of years of isolated homogeneity were in an exceedingly healthful condition—& it is only our Western vanity which makes us consider this sort of settled civilisation in any way inferior to our more restless type. Civilisation is merely a matter of comfortable & effective adjustment to the given milieu—in such a way as to give the sensitive individual the best chances for the exploitation of his capacities for enjoyment—& observation seems to indicate that China & Egypt succeeded in the realisation of this condition quite as well as Greece, Italy, & Western Europe. Bertrand Russell, indeed, considers the ancient Chinese civilisation the greatest yet produced on this planet. Fresh cultural impulses are not to be desired until the last dregs of enjoyment have been drained from the old cultures; since the birth-pangs of a new civilisation are so blighting to all the transition-generations, that they cannot be justified by anything save the replacement of a wholly worthless & unsatisfying order by one with a genuine likelihood of being less worthless & unsatisfying. And when a new culture *is* born, it is not always through race-mixture. Race-mixture is *sometimes* a cause, but this is merely because it involves a violent upsetting of traditions & folkways. The real element behind the birth of new cultures is *simply up-heaval*—whether from race-mixture or from other causes. Hellenic culture was probably the result of mixture—the union of hardy Achaian Nordics & of Mediterraneans having a Minoan culture. On the other hand, the Islamic culture of the mediaeval Saracens was due simply to the sudden growth of new modes of thought & feeling within a single race. Destruction—chaos— a shuffle & a fresh deal—this is the kind of thing behind culture-birth. In the present case of neo-America the shuffle is caused less by mongrelisation than by the sudden rise of new ideas about the universe & man's relation to it, plus the sudden changes which mechanisation & collective industry have wrought in our ordinary habits & perspectives of daily life.

Coming back to the hypothetical case of a divided race stream—we have seen that groups of stock #2 cannot exist comfortably in the fabric of stock #1 (& vice versa) by reason of a differentiated physical temperament. It is also true, as we cannot help admitting, that if both stocks (in a state of separation) were to be overwhelmed by some simultaneous cataclysm totally destructive of both cultures; each stock would, upon founding a new culture of its own, develop a set of institutions differing from the other's in ways determined by the age-long differentiation in heritable physical temperament—this wholly irrespective of the fresh environmental conditions. If the two stocks after the cataclysm were subjected to similar environments, the difference would still persist—though of course the comparative paths in later millennia would be just as fruitful in modifying selective influences as were the paths of the pre-cataclysmic millennia. The point is, that a really basic & heritable tendency toward certain ways of life does reside in any stock which has a reasonably long & homogeneous existence under a certain set of conditions—& that it is accordingly both foolish & criminal to mix two such stocks in any considerable quantity with the expectation that either can become assimilated to the other's culture, or that they can fuse—except after agonising & soul-weary generations of useless transition—into any new homogeneous culture satisfying to either component. To this extent we may say that race & culture are connected. They are not indeed synonymous, for historical & environmental conditions are tremendously potent; but they are there just the same. To think that any but Nordics would have made the familiar American fabric which stretches around us, or that any but Nordics can harmoniously enter into it in any substantial quantity, is almost certainly erroneous to a glaring & dangerous degree. We may thank Nature that a certain crude animal instinct toward settled conditions will probably preserve among our healthy & unde-cadent elements an ironclad resistance toward any attempt to effect a farther dilution of our Nordic stock. While scholars argue, healthy Teutono-Celtic manhood asserts itself—& the bars against unassimilable aliens tighten. It is not a question of the equality or inferiority of the invaders—but just a plain question of dissimiliarity. As a matter of fact, though, it *is* mainly the biologically inferior element of the various alien stocks (whose collective average may be, & in some cases undoubtedly is, equal to our own) which has of late years, through principles of selection, been pouring in upon us. The whole question of race-&-culture relationship as connected with environment is pretty well summed up by the historian Freeman in speaking of Hellenism. He says—"Neither the Greeks in any other land, nor any other people in Greece, would have been what the Greeks in Greece actually were."[43] It is likewise true that their cultural evolution depended equally upon the conditions under which each ancestral element occupied the land, the cultural stage of each at the time of fusion, & the historic events attending the occupancy of the land. The Greeks were great as long as they preserved their racial purity. When that was tainted, the decadent Hellenistic age succeeded the Hellenic. As for the difference in biological heritage of different *social classes* in the same racial-cultural fabric; we may say at once that this *may or may not* exist, according to the nature of the social system prevailing, & the nature of the historic factors behind the formation of the original class system. Superior classes—socially, politically, & economically superior, that is—may gain their position in one of many ways, & may hold it in any of several widely different ways. They may spring from the posterity of distinguished individuals early singled out & honoured, but not otherwise different from the general majority; thus holding their advantage through common consent as buttressed by quasi-poetic sentiments of symbolic reverence. In this case—the case of England—marked biological superiority is unlikely, though there is always a natural drift of brighter elements toward the yeoman or middle orders as distinguished from the peasantry & proletariat, on principles of normal selection. Since the aristocracy is hereditarily limited, & accessible only through really unusual displays of natural ability, it follows that much first-rate stock is inevitably kept down on the superior class. Accordingly we may justly assume that an English or typically Teutonic aristocracy of the traditional sort does not imply any superior racial endowment. On the other hand, other aristocracies are differently formed; frequently through the conquest of one race by another, or by the importation of a servile element to stand below a native population. In cases like this, everything depends on the exact nature of the events producing the condition. The conquest and subjection of a predominantly inferior stock produces an inferior lower class—yet when the conquered stock is superior, the master himself must necessarily be at a disadvantage for a time—though eventually the servile conditions of conquest debase even a superior race; weeding out the strong & self-respecting, & producing a fawning, broken race of shrewd, alert, repulsively cowardly cringers, like Jews, or Greeks under the Roman Empire. It is about the same whether the conquered class be a separate nation or an imported slave element—though the debasement is accelerated in the latter case. There is a variant of this general condition when a nation more or less pacifically amalgamates with similar neighbours or admits a fairly equal stock to its boundaries on friendly terms. Then the old dwellers tend to form an aristocracy over the newcomers; though on an easy, non-conquering, & non-debasing plan, in which there is no biological superiority, & which eventually yields to an extension of privilege to the subordinated groups. Rome & its Latin neighbours in early Republican times illustrate this case. An opposite example—shewing the result of a superior race's conquest of inferior stock—is illustrated by the Slavic nations. Here a Nordic aristocracy has subjected a biologically inferior rabble of stupid brachycephalic Alpines—producing a gulf illustrated by the relative endowments of the Conrad-Pulaski-Paderewski[44] type on the one hand, & the swinish Connecticut-Valley factory Polack on the other hand. But the greatest degree of lower-class mental inferiority is found in nominally democratic races where the social boundaries are plastic. In such fabrics, the bright & competent invariably push their way to the posts of privilege; so that after a few generations there are left in the menial & unskilled ranks only such inherently dull individuals as are incapable of mental effort, & unlikely to transmit anything but dulness to their young. This is increasingly the case with America. The rise of good stock may be temporarily checked by economic crises; but in the long run, when the stabilisation of finances has been better approximated by an economic dictatorship, we shall see the ultimate neo-American caste system in all its perfection—the funded proprietor, with ranks constantly swollen from an administrative class, & sending his less competent relatives down into this administrative class—and below this funded-administrative group a graduated series of petty executives & employees, with a bestial proletariat at the bottom. Funded & administrative classes will average the best mentality by a vast margin, & from them will come whatever first-rate intellectual & aesthetic material such a standardised & time-tabled culture can afford. Petty executives will represent a lower & varied mental average—& will furnish the smaller fry of the art-&-learning penumbra. And the menial herd—fortunately smaller than at present because of the multiplicity of machines—will be frankly subnormal in intellect; a well-fed, well-clothed & cheaply amused set of domesticated animals capable of only a few simple quasi-automatic responses to orders. Since class-boundaries will be nominally open, there will of course be many individual shifts of status—fortuitously bright inferiors moving up while decaying superior stock sinks down—yet these connection-currents will be only minor phenomena amidst a largely fixed order. I do not think there will be much active dissatisfaction, since most will probably realise the inevitability of the system—while of course there will be much leisure, personal freedom, & material comfort for all. The sensitive types who suffer from standardisation & untraditionalism will have been eliminated through death, weariness, or return to England. Well—that about finishes my reaction to the race-culture article. My general position on the race question can be summed up by the statement that I consider cultural stability the chief value in all life except life of the most primitive sort. I believe that, for normal civilised persons, virtually all sense of enjoyment—all sense of interest, significance, & direction—all that makes the weary hell of consciousness worth enduring—depends on the preservation of a system of arbitrary reference-points which fit the imagination because of development by similar ancestral types & because of dominance during infantile & formative years. Without this set of reference-points the individual is adrift in a wholly meaningless cosmos, with nothing to live for after the subsidence of youthful adventurousness & animal gusto at the age of thirty or thereabouts. Everything, therefore, depends on the preservation of one's continuous heritage; & absolutely nothing can justify the encouragement of any influence likely to weaken, dilute, or destroy that heritage. Racial admixture—all apart form the question of superiority, equality, or inferiority—is indubitably an influence adverse to cultural & environmental continuity. It weakens everything we really live for, & diminishes all the landmarks of familiarity—moods, accents, thoughts, customs, memories, folklore, perspectives, physiognomical types, &c.—which prevent us from going mad with homesickness, loneliness, & ancestral estrangement. Thus it is the duty of very self-respecting citizen to take a stand against large-scale racial amalgamation—whether with newly invading groups, or with differentiated groups anciently seated amongst us. Of course, I realise that "duty" in the sense of cosmic mandate is a myth—but what I mean is, that this is the course which will be followed by every normal American who wishes to avoid spiritual exile & agony for himself & his descendants, & whose eyes are not blinded by the abstract ethical sentimentalities surviving from a naiver period of our intellectual evolution. My own motto is, 'life in a pure English nation or death'.

The Hergesheimer article[45] is at once amusing and thought-provoking—being as it is the complex product of a mind at once touched with naive, superficial snobbery, and powerful in its attempt to grope for some solution of the problem of values. Poor Joe! The surfaces of economic prosperity & artificially pompous folkways fascinate him, even though he once understood what real hereditary aristocracy is—& yet he keeps an eye open to the genuinely profound question of what really is worth doing, anyway. One has to laugh at his conception of what Newport is—& this from the traditionalist who wrote "Java Head" & "Balisand"! My gawd! Not to know the greatest cultural high spot in New England—the seat of a philosophical society, an artistick life, & an elegant social order at a time when Boston was an overgrown hive of sterile Puritan hypocrites! Hell—the place where his damn'd parvenu Victorians built their ugly rococo monuments of ostentation is where actual Newport people pastur'd cattle & dried fish! He can have his 1870 doghouses & beaches if he wants 'em—but why call 'em Newport? Shades of William Coddington, Nicholas Easton, Christopher Champlin, Godfrey Malbone, & Joseph Wanton, last of His Maj[ty's] loyal governors of the Colony of Rhode-Island and Providence-Plantations! Shades of the Narragansett planters whose gambrel-roof'd town-houses ran along antient Water Street north of Queen's Hithe![46] Shades of Ben Franklin's brother Jim, and the Rhode-Island Almanack! Shades of Sol Southwick & the Newport Mercury! Shades of Gen. Prescott & His Maj[ty's] forces in 1776–79! Shades of those damn'd Frenchmen (tho' officers & noblemen) who tickled rebel society in 1780–81! Ah, me—but that's what rebellion brings. The best blood of Newport went to Halifax & St. Johns in 1783, & now a curst Pennsylvania Dutchman tacks the old town's name on to the cattle runs & fish yards south of the city! May Peter Harrison, Metcalf Bowler, & ol' Bish Berkeley forgive him! God Save the King!

But the boy does shew a true & penetrant thoughtfulness when he adumbrates the perpetual problem of immediate practical values—the problem of how to get the most enjoyment & least suffering out of the wearisome incident of conscious existence—the problem of what in hell to do with oneself apart from the necessities of food, warmth, & lodging. This is really a tremendously deep & significant matter which has not yet received sufficient attention of a truly scholarly sort; a matter quite apart from the objectively scientific & epistemological problem of "what is anything." This separate problem might be summed up in such a query as "What now?" "What of it?" or "Where do we go from here?"—a query asking for information on the relative sense & silliness, emotional profit & empty meaninglessness, of any one possible course of action & manners as compared with any other possible course. What is pleasure? What is interest? What is the least damn foolish thing to do with oneself? To what degree can any one person's pleasure be any other person's—& conversely, to what degree can any one person get pleasure apart from patterns including other persons' ideas of pleasure? Where does the usefulness of convention, with its mercifully devised reference-points & arbitrary illusions of value, begin to be overbalanced by its restrictive & meaningless side? How far can pomp & ceremony be carried in the promotion of one's feeling of significance & adventurous expectancy, without setting up an ironic reaction based on the essential meaningless of all human expression & activity? To what extent can the gestures of superiority be stimulating, when separated from the intellectual & aesthetic actualities on which the concept of superiority is based? Where does elegance leave off being a gateway to contentment & imaginative excitation, & become a matter of affectation, mockery, & even downright ennui & tyranny? What is the boundary betwixt the well-ordered self-expression & proudly non-encroaching reticence which form the natural life of a gentleman, & the devotion to form for form's sake which marks the artificial & meaningless "society person"? What is the least silly & least empty thing to do at any given moment or under any given set of circumstances when economic necessity is not present? To what extent can actual pleasure be derived from a cere-monial assumption of pleasure? To what extent is any pleasure possible without the existence of a ceremonial or at least conventional tradition of what consti-tutes pleasure? What is the real relationship of any given social form to the sub-tle fabric of race-continuity without which we would die or go mad from homesickness? How genuine & satisfying is the ego-exaltation based on artifi-cial & backgroundless social standing; as distinguish'd from the hereditary social standing involving the poetry of historic symbolism & pageantry, or the aes-thetic social standing based on an appreciation of beauty in objects, scenes, forms, relationships, and institutions? Conversely, how far does actual aesthetic status, or ancestral position, satisfy the ego when unsupported by arbitrary dicta? Likewise, how far can social position (real or arbitrary) satisfy one with-out concomitant economic solidity & physical luxury? And how far can wealth & luxury satisfy without good birth, aesthetic cultivation, or arbitrary social recognition? And how far can any one answer to any of these questions be taken as a general truth? Into what groups—or with what individual differ-ences—can people be classified regarding their ego-reactions in these matters? What is solid and what is flimsy for any one person—or is any classification of experience & standards into solid and flimsy categories valid? And does the same person feel the same set of emotional criteria for any considerable period, or under any considerable variety of conditions? To what extent are the stan-dards & pleasure-sources of the present generation more, or less, solidly ra-tional & permanently markable than the standards & pleasure-sources of our—& Hergesheimer's—generation? To what extent has the main stream of Anglo-American culture & socially approved folkways failed to create an atmosphere mentally & emotionally satisfying to the majority of normally brilliant & sensi-tive individuals? To what extent is any possible deficiency related to recently enlarged & rectified perspectives, & recently changed conditions of travel & daily life? To what extent were cultural forms ever satisfying? To what depth does dissatisfaction go? What sort of graph might be plotted to depict our (a) satisfaction & (b) average conformity in cultural matters from 1660 to 1931? What is the real validity, from the standpoint of permanent emotional satisfac-tion, of a retreat from the problem of personal pattern-placement & a quest for ego-expansion through intellectual & aesthetic assimilations & expressions not dependent on group-relationships? To what extent do people differ in their capacity for such non-social satisfactions? What is the real validity from the same emotional standpoint, of social relationships involving individual criteria at variance with the dominant instinctive standards of the group, or the stan-dards based on heredity or intrinsic quality? To what extent does insincere & unsatisfying self-delusion animate such ostensible substitute-placements? To what extent do people differ in their capacity for non-aristocratic or otherwise aesthetically & intellectually inferior social satisfactions? What is the real valid-ity, from the same standpoint, of a retreat from pattern-placement problems to

264 ❋ *Letters to James F. Morton*

simplicity & crudeness, & the erection of a scornful defence mechanism? To what extent can animal satisfactions replace emotional & imaginative satisfactions? Effect of age on replacement-capacity? To what extent can acquisitiveness replace emotional & imaginative satisfactions? As compared with the validity of these escapes & retreats in relation to pattern-placement problems, what is their respective emotional validity in relation to the subtler problems of cosmic futility, unsatisfied mental curiosity, & the ungratifiable yearning for perfect beauty & the fulfilment of adventurous expectancy? How far is the old myth of religious & ethical values able to provide satisfying illusions for intelligent & educated adults? Effect of age on illusion-capacity? Effect of temperament—mental, emotional, aesthetic, and imaginative—or illusion-capacity? What is the permanent gratification-value of mental impression-crowding—hobbies, artificial interests, constant & varied travel, perfunctory reading? Effect of temperament on gratification-capacity? What is the permanent gratification-value of emotional grouping and arranging—as when one links an emotion toward a scene, person, idea, event, or pursuit to another scene, person, idea, event, or pursuit, in order to heighten the gusto of one's emotional enjoyment of either or both? Effect of temperament on gratification-capacity? God, what a mess! I guess cyanide's the most sensible thing after all! But the point is that Joe really gets the big idea that there *is* a problem, which is more than most poor simps do. It gives one pain in the neck to see how even the most studious & well-regarded psychologists glide over this fundamental & perpetual problem of making the boredom of consciousness bearable. Their various modes of over-simplification seem so god damn naive that one wonders how they ever came to make any significant researches at all. One wise old bird reduces all pleasure to the erotic—but doesn't do a curst thing to explain the continued boredom & dissatisfaction of the rounder or potentate who has all the diversified flapper experience he can collect. Another shrewd bimbo reduces the whole business to the sense of superiority, & thinks that a high place (real or subjective) "in the group" is the thing we're all scrambling after. But gawd—what a lot he dodges when he fails to define *what group* (out of an infinite number of conceivable group-images in the subject's mind) he's talking about! A third smart Alec thinks work—expression—fulfilment through creation—is the thing. Oh, yeah? Just *define* the quality & extent of work or expression meant? Not so good? And how about the abject misery of those who have succeeded best in creation & self-expression? It's a great life—& I don't blame Javahead Joe for collecting all the fun he can in his own way, even it that way does seem a bit artificial & superficial to a weary old cynick. At least he senses the complexity of human frustration, bewilderment, & directionlessness, & doesn't try to achieve an optimistic & all-simplifying smirk by affirming a hash of goddam copybook crap that ain't so! Good ol' Joe—let's all drink ourselves happy like Richd Bale, Gent. of Balisand!

As for the final enclosure—"emergent evolution"—I see that dope discuss'd in the *N'Yawk Times* a couple months ago. To be damn frank, I don't think it means very much when ya come right down to cases—any more than the widely advertised suspension of causation due to the quantum theory means much. As sober physicists are shewing, the quantum dope doesn't mean that any conceivable group of specific causes can produce more than one inevitable effect; but merely that we have no possible means of detecting the intra-atomic differences in two or more sets of causes, each set producing one inevitable effect, which are really different but which appear the same to all conceivable analytical methods. The same causes always produce the same one effect—but we can't tell certain types of almost-but-not-quite-identical causes apart, hence can't tell which of several possible sets of antecedents produced it; although (& popular expositors tend to forget this) only one set could really have done so. Well—it's the same way about this "emergent evolution" business, which I'll bet was suggested by the quantum theory. We know damn well that atoms are such complex systems that the union of dissimilar ones produces molecular arrangements whose properties are utterly unrelated to the properties of the molecular arrangements which each kind of constituent atom forms with its own kind. O. K.—but what of it? True, we can't predict the new sort of arrangement from considering the properties of each constituent; but that arrangement is just as inevitable, and just as closely linked to the latent properties of each constituent, as if we *could* so predict it! Only an ostrich could consider causation suspended because we can't *see* it working! And from wide chemical observation, we know about what types of differences between compounds & constituents are customary—know, without finding anything especially new or revolutionary in the knowledge. Who but a naive & sentimental ass bothers about man's crude, meaningless *wishes* in the matter of free-will & significant purpose? Of course, the new & unpredictable constantly appears—but it was all fixed beforehand, whether we knew it or not. Undoubtedly, living protoplasm is such a "new" product in relation to its inorganic antecedents—but what of it? We always realis'd as much with the possible exception of a group of very literal materialists, wholly dominated by Spencer, toward the close of the XIX century!

Yr obt Servt

Θεοβάλδος

P.S. As for the *social* aspects of "emergent evolution"—it need only be pointed out that all attempts to regard society *as an organism* are based on mere *analogy.* Marx & Spengler on the realistic side are just as far off as the "emergents" in this detail. Society consists of separate organisms acting on one another, & is governed by broad apparent probabilities of a different nature from the certainties pertaining to intra-organic action. Nor is it at all certain that the surprises of mass recognisable organic action—i.e., by aridism &c.—are of identical nature with the sharper surprises of intra-molecular chemical action.

Notes

1. The Germanic leader Arminius defeated Roman general P. Quinctilius Varus in the battle of the Teutoberg Forest, in what is now northwest Germany, in the year 9 C.E. A large proportion of three entire legions were lost, and Varus himself committed suicide. According to Suetonius (*Divus Augustus* 23.49), the Emperor Augustus lamented the loss of the legions for years, repeatedly crying, *Quintili Vare, legiones redde!* (Quinctilius Varus, give me back my legions!).

2. Referring to Everett McNeil's book, *Tonty of the Iron Hand* (1925).

3. See letter 70n1. Dexter supposedly had sold bed warming pans in the West Indies as ladles for the molasses industry.

4. "Who struck Billy Patterson?" was a well-known joking enquiry in the U.S. in the nineteenth century, meaning "Who did it? Who was the guilty party?"

5. "Down Went McGinty" (1889) by Joseph Flynn, a humorous stage song.

6. "After the Ball" by Charles K. Harris sold two million pieces of sheet music in 1892 alone.

7. Thomas Gray (1716–1771), *Elegy Written in a Country Church-Yard*, l. 2.

8. *Odyssey* 19.280–81 in the translation of Alexander Pope ("Short woolly curls" for "Dark curling locks" in Pope).

9. Theocritus, *Idyls* 1, in the prose translation of Andrew Lang.

10. Virgil, *Eclogues* 1.1.

11. Virgil, *Georgics* 3.590–91 in the translation of John Dryden.

12. "Prosperum ac felix scelus / Virtus vocatur; sontibus parent boni; / Jus est in armis, opprimit leges timor." (Successful crime is dignified with the name of virtue; the good become the slaves of the impious; might makes right; fear silences the power of the law.) Seneca the Younger, *Hercules Furens* 251–53.

13. From the anthem "God Save the Queen."

14. Alexander Pope, *Pastorals* (1709), Summer, l. 1, used as the epigraph to Robert Bloomfield's *The Farmer's Boy* (London: Vernor & Hood, 1800). HPL owned an edition of 1803 (*LL* 106).

15. Bloomfield, *The Farmer's Boy*, p. 19.

16. James Thomson (1700–1748), *The Seasons* (1726–30), "Summer," ll. 394–95.

17. An anonymous parody of James Thomson's line "O Sophonisba, Sophonisba, O!" from his verse tragedy *Sophonisba* (1730).

18. "Not one immortal, one corrupted thought, / One line which dying he could wish to blot." Lord Lyttelton, "Prologue" to James Thomson's *Coriolanus*, quoted in Samuel Johnson's chapter on James Thomson in *Lives of the English Poets* (1779–81).

19. John Milton, *Lycidias* (1637), ll. 23–24.

20. Edmund Spenser, *The Shepheardes Calender* (1579), "September," ll. 26–27.

21. Homer, *Odyssey* 9.523–24 in the translation of Alexander Pope.

22. Isaac Watts (1674–1748), "Innocent Play," ll. 1–3.

23. The title of a poem by Isaac Watts from *Horae Lyricae* (1706), dedicated to Nathaniel Mather (1669–1688).

24. A line from the above poem ("He established the beginnings of theology among the New Englanders").

25. Verses accompanying the letter L in a children's alphabet book.

26. *The Headless Horseman: A Play.* Based on Washington Irving's "The Legend of Sleepy Hollow." Arranged by C. S. Griffin. Or *Pleasing Toy* by J. H. Butler, another alphabet book for children.

27. Another children's verse: "I love to see the lambs at play; they hop so spry and seem so gay; / They nip the grass and then are seen to chase their playmates on the green."

28. From Pindar's fourth Pythian ode as translated by Ernest Myers (1874).

29. Joseph Warton, "Ode to Mr. West on His Translation of Pindar," ll. 3–4.

30. Hesiod, *Works and Days* 2.213–14 in the translation of Thomas Cooke.

31. From the verse tragedy *Douglas* by John Home (1724–1808).

32. From the ballad "Harpalus" as printed in Thomas Percy's *Reliques of Ancient English Poetry* (1765).

33. Matt. 25:33: "And he shall set the sheep on his right hand, but the goats on the left."

34. From Mother Goose.

35. Sir John Mandeville's *Travels*.

36. John Bunyan (1628–1688), *The Pilgrim's Progress* (1678): "Stone walls do not a prison make, Nor iron bars a cage."

37. A parody of the opening lines of Robert Browning's "Rabbi Ben Ezra": "Grow old with me! / The best is yet to be."

38. Homer, *Iliad* 23.204–5 in the translation of Alexander Pope.

39. Richard Porson (1759–1808), British classical scholar. The Greek typeface Porson was based on his handwriting. Benjamin Jowett (1817–1893), British scholar, classicist, and theologian and Master of Balliol College, Oxford, best known for his translations of Plato's dialogues.

40. Sir Grafton Elliot Smith (1871–1937), Australian anatomist and proponent of the hyperdiffusionist view of prehistory. Marcellin Boule (1861–1942), French palaeontologist who studied and published the first analysis of a complete *Homo neanderthalensis*.

41. Franz Boas (1857–1942), German-American anthropologist, pioneer of modern anthropology, called the "Father of American Anthropology." Boas established that there was no biological "superiority" or "inferiority" in the various human races.

42. "Rufus Rastus Johnson Brown" (1905), words by Andrew B. Sterling, music by Harry Von Tilzer.

43. Edward A. Freeman (1823–1892), "The Practical Bearings of General European History," in *Lectures to American Audiences* (Philadelphia: Porter & Coates, 1882), p. 230.

44. Novelist Joseph Conrad (1857–1924), general and politician Kazimierz Pulaski (1745–1779), and pianist and composer Ignacy Jan Paderewski (1860–1941), all of Polish descent.

45. HPL refers to Joseph Hergesheimer's article "The Golden Littoral," *Saturday Evening Post* (26 July 1930): 3–5, 110, 113, and 115. Hergesheimer (1880–1954) was a well-regarded American novelist.

46. Queen's Hithe (or Queen-Hithe) is the principal wharf in Newport.

[104]   [AHT]

18 Ianuarii, 1931

Pythagorean Pattern of Perspicuous Profundity:—
    Well, Sir, I have the honour to state, that I last Wednesday compleated the following work, design'd solely for my own perusal & for the crystallisation of my recollections, in *136* pages of this crabbed cacography:

A
DESCRIPTION
of the
Town of
QUEBECK, in NEW-FRANCE,
Lately annext to His Britannick Majesty's
DOMINIONS.

——— ——— ———

By H. Lovecraft, Gen[t.]
of
Providence, in New-England.

——————— ——— ———————

Design'd for the Information of the
Curious, & for the Guiding of Travellers
from His Majesty's New-England and other
American Provinces. To which is added, an
historical Account of New-France.

————————————————

The Whole embellish'd with Designs &
Maps Illustrative of the Text.

——————————

CONTENTS:

Providence, in Rhode-Island,
Printed by John Carter, at Shakespear's
Head in Gaol-Lane over-against the Court-
House, and sold by Booksellers and
Stationers generally.
MDCCCCXXXI.

As for occasional controversial topicks—I am acutely sensible that our differences rest upon a divergence in premises, & indeed believe that most profound controversies are similarly animated. That is why, as I have frequently explain'd in some detail, I am so firm an advocate of *ultimate definitions of terms & values* beyond any extent commonly practic'd; & of the abandonment, so far as possible, of all conventional & well-recognised names & terms dealing with entities & processes—it being my conviction, that these latter designations have pick'd up traditional associations & overtones calculated to destroy them for exact use; insomuch as such associations & overtones have references to former conceptions of things (bas'd on the imperfect information of various earlier times, & often in conflict with one another as well as with contemporary perspective and knowledge) which recent discoveries, emotions, and folkways render either wholly or partly irrelevant, or more or less definitely erroneous. It is for this reason that I indulge in what seems like quibbling, or a challenging of the axiomatick, in handling the assertions of an opponent. I am unwilling to have basic aspects of a question obscur'd by *the conventional assumption of agreement where no agreement exists;* hence my invariable question, "What do you mean by that?", when anyone speaks to me of such undefin'd abstractions as "good", "evil", "improvement", "injustice", "morality", "progress", "obligation", "will", "purpose", and so on. Nor is it any spirit of idle contentiousness or empty arrogance which thus impels me to insist upon fundamentals. Rather, I am acutely impress'd by the folly of trying to rear any sort of elaborate superstructure upon foundations not yet tested. It may *sound* odd to place abstractions above concrete matters, but in truth I cannot see how any statements can be made, or judgments form'd, about concrete things, unless there be some glimmering of the system of values whereby such things are rated and classify'd. I do not advance this principle in the nephelocoacygian spirit of one unmindful of practical concerns; indeed, I am specific in my insistence that daily problems be dealt with according to those conservative indications and precepts which empirical experience (in lieu of any more exact knowledge) have shewn to be natural to mankind, and least disagreeable to his inclinations. What I do insist on, is that this conservative balance be not intentionally disturb'd in favour of any new scheme *which is not founded upon something more stable & genuine than the speculations of foundation-shunning & value-inventing idealists.* I do not insist upon basick reality in connexion with anything generally agreeable to normal society, and unsubversive of the equilibrium & freedom needful for artistic culture & individual development in their accustom'd amounts. I insist upon it only when there is a question of upsetting what seems to be natural—or else, of course, where the scientifick question of fact versus non-fact arises as an adjunct of sincere, and theoretically impersonal, philosophick speculation.

Tradition is virtually the only standard, or value, or criterion of interest and direction-purpose illusion, that we have in the world of feeling, action, and art. There it is supreme. But in the world of *thought* & *reality* it is a perfectly meaningless thing; & has no effect except to place obstacles in the way of the discovery of truth. When we wish to obtain any *actual knowledge* of the cosmos and its properties, we must at once put out of our heads all the accumulated notions concerning such things which miscellaneous experience and slipshod inheritance have blindly saddled upon us. "Good", "evil", "duty", "direction", "purpose", "dignity"—applesauce! We must cease to be parts of any system of preconceived bias—Christian, moral, humane, or anything like that—& become simple free inquiring agents, each alone & fearless, facing the varied phenomena of the external world with such processes of cognition & such stores of correlative background-data as repeated former tests may have shewn to be authentick. If *then* we find any of the old traditions verify'd, well & good. But we must not accept anything on any authority save the actual present evidence of the cosmos as judged by the tested information of contemporary science. Real probabilities about the structure & properties of the cosmos, & its relation to living organisms on this planet, can be reach'd only by correlating the findings of all who have competently investigated *both the subject itself, & our mental equipment for approaching & interpreting it*—astronomers, physicists, mathematicians, biologists, psychologists, anthropologists, & so on. The only sensible method is that of assembling all the objective scientifick data of 1931, & forming a fresh chain of partial indications bas'd **exclusively** on that data & on *no conceptions derived from earlier & less ample arrays of data;* meanwhile testing, *by the psychological knowledge of 1931,* the workings & inclinations of our minds in accepting, connecting, & making deductions from data, & **most particularly** *weeding out all tendencies to give more than equal consideration to conceptions which would never have occurred to us had we not formerly harboured provisional & capricious ideas of the universe now conclusively known to be false.* It goes without saying that this realistic principle fully allows for the examination of those irrational feelings & wishes about the universe, upon which idealists so amusingly base their various dogmatick speculations. Psychology handles these glandular phenomena with the utmost exactitude, & traces them with extreme clearness to natural reactions of the uninformed mind when placed in contact with the mysteries, pains, tantalisations, & frustrations of the existing universe. Such illusions of value, purpose, "soul", obligations, "brotherhood" & the like are to be expected in a primitive milieu. Well—it is only this *fundamentalism* (to restore a valuable word from the perverting barbarity of modern jargon) of outlook that I insist upon in an opponent. If he honestly has this, I am prepar'd to view with respect whatever conclusions he may derive from his survey of Nature, no matter how much those conclusions may differ from my own. All that I refuse to respect, is the arbitrary folly of the mystick & the traditional dogmatist, who refuse altogether to employ the outlook & methods of sane reality. I do not think it argues bigotry in me to dismiss these pitiful vestiges of barbarism with only such attention as enables me to recognize their character & realise their remoteness from serious thought. Thus I say frankly that a man like Chesterton is not worth listening to as a thinker, however amusing he may be as a jester; & that people like Bishop Manning[1] are simply quaint intellectual curiosities. But on the other hand, I am prepar'd to listen with the utmost attention & respect to serious quasi-theists like Eddington & Millikan;[2] since, although I deem their teleological views wholly unjustify'd by the phenomena which they cite as a basis, & obviously suggested by the orthodox emotional crippling of their Victorian childhood, I recognise that they do not advance such speculations for any other reason than that they honestly think them suggested by the existing universe. And the same thing goes for the Plantagenistical Meliorism of the Paterson School.

As for the matter of scatter'd interests—of course, each person knows the course which gives him the most pleasure, & I do not doubt but that your many side-lines all knit up somewhere as parts of a world which is coherent & symmetrical in your consciousness—just as with me Quebeck, Arthur Machen, astronomy, Joseph Wood Krutch, sunsets, the Endless Caverns, the Spectator, dinosaurs' eggs, single-truck street-cars with red and green glass in their roofs, stone walls, Georgian doorways, the new Philadelphia parkway and Museum, black cats, certain numbers like 3331, 156, 102, & 416, sonorous Roman names like Cn. Ateius Capito, P. Senecius Herennio, C. Scribonius Libo, &c., &c., the Royal Arms of old ENGLAND, great oaken forests with vast boles & low twisted boughs, the Antarctic continent, the Magellanic clouds, sunken temples, Charleston, Providence, whaling ships, streets & roads that climb uphill & end against the sky, long s's, narrow winding streets with old bookshops near a waterfront amidst which one cannot be sure where one is, dark rivers with many bridges winding betwixt great walls of brick or stone, spires & domes catching the late-afternoon sunlight, hushed hillside meadows at noon, sheep & goats, Egyptian hieroglyphicks, flutes & pipes, cliffs on the sea, certain undefined aromatick odours, certain unidentified strains of musick or kindred sound, ruin'd castles cover'd with ivy, the moon, Orion, observatories, nightmares, daemons, grey jagged mountain-peaks, unknown valleys, Wickford, Marblehead, Fredericksburg, Newburyport, Kingston, railway stations, gambrel roofs, equestrian statues, small farmhouses set against steep rocky hillsides, Vermont, drums, cymbals, & trumpets, the Roman Eagles, SPQR, the Iroquois, Atlantis, Easter Island, Tryout Smithy, Bagdad & Cordova, the West Indies, Japanese gardens, the golden road to Samarcand, the rocky desert of deserts beyond Bodrabain, unicorns, fires on lovely hills, the Milky Way, leagues of level marshland at twilight, Genl. Sir Guy Carleton, Ld Dorchester, Henry St. John, Vis^{ct} Bolingbroke, the Magnalia, Sir W. Phips, K^t, Deerfield, the Unitarian churchyard in Charleston, P. Cornelius Scipio, Caerleon-on-Usk, Iceland, songs and street-scenes of 1895–1900, Confederate uniforms, the Pleiades, meteorites, vast vaulted crypts, thunderstorms, the Boston & Maine Railroad, Angkor, Zimbabwe, the House of Usher, unexpected journeys, the sound of hidden brooks in deeply wooded valleys, the middle Hudson River region, the Wissahickon, encyclopaedias, telescopes, chemical laboratory apparatus, the year 1903, old rag-men with spavined horses & rattling carts calling "raygs, bar-tells . . . . maw-nee fer raygs" in a musical chant, the Dighton Rock,[3] the Seven Golden Cities of Cibola, the Spanish War, Wedgwood pottery, dryads & fauns, high walls of unknown masonry, streets with steps in them, wharves, ship-chandlers' shops, bells heard from a distance & not identified, streets flooded with sunlight from the opposite end, & so on, & so on, all represent facets, ramifications, & association-attributes of one basically coherent ideology & mental-emotional cosmos which my own temperament has evolved in conjunction with the impressions impinging on it; & whose cardinal keynote seems to be the expansion of the ego through the imaginative breaking-down of the laws of time, space, & matter, & the flight of the etherealised personality through a limitless variety of dimensions & cycles. Now the only thing which may justly he said against diffusiveness in general, is that it prevents one from grasping any one thing with sufficient thoroughness to be really master of it. Very few active, bustling, men-of-the-world, it is observ'd, have any philosophick opinions worth considering; insomuch as their perpetual round of affairs has left them too little time to digest any one point of thought with the concentrated leisure necessary for real assimilation & conscious formulation. Thus dutiful little Moe is still a "fundamentalist" Presbyterian, since he drowns reflective thought in a constant turmoil of pedagogy & self-important "usefulness-to-the-community" which turns all his energy to precise, detailed, varied, & unoriginal action. But you, having early insisted on the possession of a coherent & amply buttress'd individual perspective, are naturally not in danger of such stupefying ingulphment; hence do not really need urging toward relaxation except for your own possible pleasure. I think, though, that you wou'd achieve a greater sense of freedom, if you wou'd attempt a *re-definition* of what you consider your linkage to the rest of the organick world; a re-definition which might go deeper than convention & tradition in analysing the tie, and appraising the proportions of reality and illusion in the arbitrary sense of "obligation" which you somehow derive (in common with Puritans generally) from the simple circumstance of being one of an accidental biological type which has likewise evolved several hundred million other individuals of roughly & varyingly similar structure. The real fact is, that the civilisation you inhabit is the work of blind impersonal Nature acting upon the glands & nerves of the different individuals of your species in a way determin'd by chance & their heredity. What each one has done, is merely to respond to external stimuli in the only way he could possibly respond; & the fact that the collective responses of all have happen'd to build up a culture which you relish, is something for which you must thank the bland, purposeless cosmos, & not the puppets through which it has acted. The people who built up your civilisation did not do it for you, but for themselves, as an automatick & inevitable process. They did it because they could not help it; even if a few did vent their egos in the form of Messianick illusion. You owe them absolutely nothing. Each was an unit in himself, and none of them—except a few in your own time—had the least idea that such a person as yourself would ever exist. *No one denies that each of us is 'a human being among other human beings.'* Of course we are all that. **The point is, what the hell of it?** Where do you get the idea that the fact of your being one point externally acted upon among similar points externally acted upon implies any special mystical relationship betwixt these points, apart from a common automatic manner of response to the cosmic environmental forces action on all in common? **What is this quality of "obligation" anyway?** *Where does the conception come from? Where does the emotion come from?* Have you stopped at all to question the source & validity of the impression? Have you not suspected that the smug prevalence of this idea & sentiment is suspiciously connected with the accidental fact of our elder generation's having been artificially steeped (emotionally crippled through the inculcation of artificial delusions in pre-rational infancy) in the theoretic & moralistic hypocrisies of a Christian mythology originated by emotionally warped (ethics-mad & justice-frantic as a result of decadent broken-spiritedness) Orientals? Is there, actually, any meaning whatsoever in the so-called "ethical imperative" or conception of "obligation"? Here is a point which conventional theists & atheists alike ignore to an almost incredible extent—an extent which leaves me appalled at the essential superficiality of mankind. Of well-known living philosophers I can name only two—George

Santayana and Joseph Wood Krutch—who seem to have any power to understand the question of reality here involved. It gets most of the gang miserably
bewildered—but Woodburn Harris (my controversial Vermont correspondent) is beginning to get his eyes opened after months of debate. **What is
"obligation"? Is there such a reality?** No person has any logical right to go
ahead with any philosophical or ethical speculation until he has first coped
with this question in a *really absolute, rational, and untraditional way*. Well, of
course you know what my opinion is—that the notion is traditional bunk, &
that its exaggerated form in the Anglo-Saxon world is an unfortunate accident
due to the saddling of the western world with the misfit Hebraism of the
Christian illusion. The really civilised Hellenick world had a much milder form
of this fallacy—the motivating principle being really that modern enlightened
selfishness which differs so radically from the cheap Semitic Jehovism & cringing before imaginary justice-laws. We in America have the delusion at its
worst, because of the abnormally strong influence of the Old Testament acting
through the Puritans. But it's on the wane—& later generations will find it
hard to understand the nineteenth century idealist. The civilised man's question of what to do with himself does not depend on any "duty" myth. He
knows that the culture wasn't consciously made for his benefit, & he knows
that in the course of natural drift there is no need for him to perform inten-
tional & high-sounding functions of conscious service. The thing for him to do
is simply, in the language of the philosopher Sandusky, **to be himself.** If he is
that, the civilisation will take care of itself—for civilisations are made from the
unconscious sum of the individual self-gratifying activities of all their members.
If you simply enjoy yourself in your own way, you'll be doing all that our ancestors ever did (despite their occasional bluffs, fanaticisms, and sentimental
poses) for the civilisation. But of course I am speaking in a practical & conservative way, & not as a doctrinaire anarchist. To enjoy oneself rationally, one
must have links of continuity with the traditional stream, hence must cultivate
ancestral memories & folkways, & observe sufficient rules of non-
encroachment to make the general survival of such memories & folkways possible. Likewise, he must practice enough compromises and non-encroachments
to make possible the existence of that social order which upholds the enjoy-
ment-giving culture. Don't get me wrong, bozo! I'm not preaching nihilism, but
simply rational Hellenism or Nordick Aryanism. *I'm not attacking the practical
institution of ethics, but merely the myth of mystical cosmic compulsion behind the thoughtless
popular conceptions of ethics.* I have many selfish & ego-expanding impulses of my
own which would, in the long run, work toward the same ultimate cultural end
as the smug conscious-service-impulses of the mystical duty-idealist. For example—I am an Englishman, & for the sake of my ego's own comfort would
fight like hell against any influence opposed to the dominance of English culture. It isn't that I "owe" my race anything, but that my adrenal glands get hot
at the idea of any damn enemy curbing the pattern which means myself. I

don't carry this attitude ponderously, as the idealist carries his self-imposed burden; for I know damn well that our culture can take care of itself most of the time, & that the fussy, self-conscious civic puttering of the layman is always a futile, meaningless thing which does nothing but discharge his own emotions in the guise of noble service. I go my own way & have a good time—but if any chance arises where I *can* be of *real* service to England in time of peril, my ego of course flares up & makes me do what I can to promote the issue necessary to my emotional contentment. God Save the King! The important thing is that England be saved & supreme; not that every individual Englishman contribute an exactly equal amount to the process. Only a naive doctrinaire wastes his time worrying about "whether he is doing his part." If the civilisation is safe—O. K. Some people take naturally to civil administration, so let them run things. The others, by pretending to feel a share in the business of government, simply get in the way of the men who know. And when peril comes, if a man is a real Englishman he won't need any goddam ethical theory to make him take a gun & shoot hell out of any influence that stands in the path of England's glory! If he doesn't feel the impulse, he needn't worry. We'll tell him what to do without any responsibility or obligation on his part. If he wants to come in with us, we'll do his deciding for him. And if he doesn't, we'll see that he doesn't do anybody any harm. Come to think of it, one can sum up nearly the whole of the nineteenth century's smugness, falsetto accent, & unconscious insincerity in the one picture of the average citizen—worrying, amidst the complex & resistless deterministic & financial currents which mould a culture's history, 'whether he is doing his part to serve the race.' O Gawd, O Montreal, O Robert Browning, O Martin Tupper![4] Or—just to be impartial—take the latter half of my own eighteenth century, with its amusing myth, & slogan concerning the "rights" of man. "Rights" of any kind, of course, are an arbitrary & artificial notion with as little basis in objective reality as "obligations". A man is an organic molecular phenomenon accidentally spawned by the processes of Nature and no more distinctive or privileged than a skunk-cabbage, a tree, a rock, or a glacier. There isn't any *ought* about him—he simply *is* . . . just as any chance collocation of electrons, atoms, and molecules is. What will happen to any particular specimen of the breed is simply a matter of chance. Each one will reach out with all its strength for all the gratification-sensations it can get—and the cosmos isn't at all interested in the relative amounts each one secures. Specimens which are strong and have lucky chance on their side will get a good deal. Those which are weak or don't 'get the breaks' won't get very much. What of it? The total amount of energy in the cosmos is unchanged. As an empirical social attitude, it is natural for each individual to favour a system likely to benefit him personally. It is possible to develop a few members of a group to a much higher level of sensitivity & enjoyment-capacity than could possibly be reached by all; this development & stratification being natural & inevitable during the young & vigorous stages of a culture. Amidst this condition the logical attitude of the developed & privileged group is to retain that development & privilege to the utmost feasible extent—& there is no reason why they should not do so. Indeed, it is collectively best for the society that they should—for only such a group can create standards & conditions calculated to make life enjoyable & seemingly significant for high-grade individuals. Real civilisation, & intellectual & aesthetic excellence, spring only from an aristocracy. Meanwhile the logical attitude of the crude & unprivileged rabble—the raw material of personalities rather than personalities—is one of opposition to the existing system, based on a desire for increased gratifications. There is no question of "right" or "wrong". Simply, some have things and some haven't; & those who have hold on, whilst those who haven't, try to grab. This is not an ethical problem, but a study in molecular physics. It is a complex of natural forces, producing an approximate equilibrium & occasionally initiating change. The pressure of the rabble is both individual & collective—that is, isolated members try to climb out of their class, whilst the class as a whole tries to overthrow the system which fixes its position. Both of these factors are eminently normal, & the normal reaction on the part of the superior class is graduated opposition—mild & partial toward the individuals, who eventually succeed in their climb (& without bad results to the culture) after a refining & probationary period, but very determined toward the massed herd—& wisely so, since the welfare of the culture depends on the supremacy of a highly developed class. Eventually, however, there may occur accidents (such as the invention of machinery) which materially shift the balance of power & give the rabble a strength they never had before. It is then natural for the rabble to increase its pressure on the upper class; so that, for the sake of saving the whole culture from destruction, it becomes necessary to grant them certain concessions. This is especially true if conditions so alter as to increase the disadvantages of the rabble, and make their state intolerable enough to drive them to desperation. At this point we behold the growth of a condition roughly describable as "socialistic"—but we must remember that it is a matter of natural forces, and not any outgrowth of non-existent abstractions. The rabble have no "right" to any privileges or even to food and existence—nor have the upper classes themselves. Each simply has what strength & luck gave. And when the rabble gets stronger it can seize more, whilst the upper classes yield because they would be physically overthrown if they did not. All this sounds very shocking & brutal to the nineteenth century idealist—but he must remember that the twentieth century realist makes the statement not because he especially dislikes poetic illusion, but merely *because the facts are what they are*, without any indications of the lace-edged frills envisaged by Victorians. Conversely, it sounds rather ghastly, hollow, mocking, & absurd to the twentieth century realist, to hear the nineteenth century idealist tricking out the stark conflicts of Nature in a pale-pink mythology of false conditions and motivations more suited to the nursery story-hour than to serious adult discussion. To the realist there is something obscenely frivolous in idealism. Note, however, that the two systems are not so far apart. Ethical idealism demands socialism on poetical cosmic grounds involving some mythical linkage of individuals to one another and to the universe—while hard-fact realism is gradually yielding to socialism because that is the only mechanical adjustment of forces which will save our culture-fostering stratified society in the face of a growing revolutionary pressure from increasingly desperate under-men whom mechanisation is gradually forcing into unemployment and starvation. We shall have to pension these under-men by paying them good wages for short-hour work which is not needed at all (because it could easily be done with sparsely manned machinery at full time)—that is, we shall have to organise our governing financial groups in such a way that they will have to disgorge some of their surplus money, & carry on with less profit than they could secure under an unsupervised system. But this will not be done because anybody loves the rabble, or because the rabble has any mystical "right" to things it is powerless to seize. It will be done because the rabble is no longer powerless, but strong & desperate enough to overturn society & set up a communistic barbarism unless soothed with the sop of concessions. As it is, the concessions of the upper classes will really make no great social difference. Money will remain supreme, & the increasingly rapid upward filtering of all the good brains will eventually leave the rabble a stolid, moronic group likely to cause no trouble if well clothed, housed, fed, & amused. Everybody is for himself, & the resultant of all the opposite-pulling forces is the social norm—which changes only as the balance of forces changes. Talk of "great cosmic drifts" is nineteenth century tripe. We know damn well now that accident & circumstance overturn all predictions. There is no cosmic drift toward "democracy". Had not mechanisation come—& it is easy to imagine how the development might have been postponed for thousands of years more—there would be nothing like a permanent social change. A Jacquerie or French Revolution now & then—but what of it? Back to normalcy soon enough! And even now it is clear that democracy has reached its apex and is on the decline. Socialism does not mean democracy, & it is likely that neo-America, with its cut-down fortunes & well-paid workmen, will be one of the most rigidly oligarchical—& eventually aristocratic—countries in the history of the world. Feed the mob, & all is jake!

And about *international relations*, too. Nothing but mischief can be caused by the sentimentalists who try to pretend that different cultures can understand and like one another, or that leaders in different nations will ever coöperate through a common love of mystical (& mythical) cosmic obligations. This is mischievous for two reasons—because it encourages false hopes, & because it tends to make all international arbitration ridiculous in the eyes of men of sense. Woody Wilson's monumental asininity was not so much a matter of *what* he advocated, as a matter of *why* he advocated it & why he expected to be taken seriously. Actually, as Spengler shews, cultures are profoundly rooted, prodigiously unique, & externally hostile things—whose differences are *far greater* than is commonly suspected. We cannot judge cultures, & their deep instinctive attitudes toward one another, by the unctuous amenities of the few internationally-minded aristocrats, intellectuals, & aesthetes who form a cosmopolitan & friendly group because of the common pull of surface manners or special interests. Of course these exotic specimens get on well enough together—but the real peoples as a whole are another matter! Therefore don't let the cause of international equilibrium be made ridiculous by being mixed up with flatulent sentimentalities & pseudo-cosmic bombast. Obligations . . . . human brotherhood . . . . understanding . . . . . . broadmindedness . . . . . . BA-NANA OIL! The tragic trouble with all this goddam crap isn't that it doesn't sound pleasant & poetic, but that it postulates forces & conditions & trends in the universe which do not exist. Now what *are* the realities? Well—the one big reality is simply that every cultural group—that is, every group sufficiently homogeneous to have an unified psychology & differentiated set of folk-ways—is going to grab all it can for itself, exactly as in the past. That's Nature. But it doesn't necessarily mean a literal duplication of all the events & methods of the past—indeed, changed mechanical conditions affecting transportation, commerce, & warfare, make such literal duplication impossible. The primary object of every group, as before, will be to get all it can; but under future conditions the means of getting such a maximum may be different. It is excellent sense to suggest changes in international method when such changes will operate for the benefit of the nation concerned; but rank idiocy to ask a nation to relinquish advantages for the sake of a theoretical and all-inclusive world-civilisation—most of the component nations of which the given nation either hates like hell or regards with indifference. International students may well point out profits to be derived from tariff liberalisations, reciprocal trading agreements, and so on, & may likewise perform real service through efforts to avert needless recourses to arms. The cataclysmically annihilative aspects of future warfare are recognised by all, & it is wholly becoming for men of sense to stress the peril which any nation will share with the rest of civilisation if the next general war is too extensive or too long. Pacificism *as an ethical principle*—the don't-shoot-mamma's-boy sentimentality—is ridiculous, & is recognised as such by the majority. But arguments proving the unprofitability of ultra-modern combat, in view of the almost certain devastations—out of all proportion with those for former wars—equally shared by all participants, are very much in order; & may conceivably have the effect of deterring many nations from precipitating conflicts which would otherwise have occurred. There can never be a guarantee against a war launched by a nation powerful enough to expect a quick victory over all probable opponents; but there almost certainly can be a vast lessening of major conflicts, & an increased disposition of statesmen to try all other means before resorting to a warfare which may bring more loss than gain. The important thing to stress is the *changing nature* of war-fare—whereby among well-equipped nations it ceases to be a genuine battle, in any historically understood sense, & becomes merely a sanguinary nightmare of wholesale mechanical extirpation affecting both military & civilian populations. Once an heroick distinction, it is now an expansive pestilence & calamity like the cyclone or the earthquake. Only among the minor nations can we ever again hope to see wars of the kind that made our arms glorious on the fields of Poitiers, Crecy, & Agincourt—that made William Pepperrell a Baronet at Louisburg, & transferr'd James Wolfe to the Pantheon of Immortals on the Plain of Abraham. But in presenting such an argument to a nation, good sense demands that it be couch'd in *terms of advantage to that nation itself.* Only a fool expects France to limit her army for the sake of an abstract "humanity" including Germany, Italy, bolshevik Russia, and Abyssinia! Encourage among nations the sensible & realistick relationships which must conduce to mutual profit, but don't increase their dislikes by forcibly commanding them to love one another. We may tolerate a Frenchman very well in the abstract—but we begin to hate him as soon as anybody imposes upon us the "obligation" to kiss his perfumed whiskers. Hindoos are splendid in geography books, but not so good when they begin to set up temples in Angell Street—as one "Swami Akilikumda" (or whatever the name is) is doing right now with the aid of a rich, soft-headed widow's money.[5]

Well—that's me, 'bo. If you think I am anti-social, or reluctant to do all that a private citizen needs to do toward maintaining the Anglo-Saxon civilisation, you get me wrong. I've never yet shewn a tendency to break the laws, flout the ancestral folkways, or encourage social, cultural, or political decadence. But I'm a realist, & refuse to let attitudes take the place of actualities, or pretend to be what I'm not. My ideal is maximum pleasure, & I get it by maintaining my own individuality in a way that encroaches on none. My intellectual criterion is simply *truth,* & my one & only guide in taking sides on questions is *whether a thing is or isn't so.* I repudiate idealism not because I despise idealists—indeed, I think they tend to be personally likeable rather than the reverse—but because I see no sense in assuming sets of conditions in the cosmos which have no existence. I have no axes to grind. I don't dislike the hypothetical conditions postulated by idealists, & would be glad to subscribe to a good many of them if they were so. My only objection is that they are not so, & that attempts to read them into the structure of the universe are injurious to the welfare of the only real value in the entire world of ideas—namely, the simple & basic quality of *unadorned truth*—the honest *is-or-isn't criterion.* I don't believe in "right" & "wrong"; but I recognise that some courses are advisable in perpetuating a pleasure-giving milieu whilst some are not. I don't believe in "rights" or "justice"; but I think it is more pleasant to observe the amenities of old tradition, & the symmetries of well-proportion'd emotion, than to torture paupers, incult labourers, snatch candy away from children, or poison urban water-supplies. There is a pleasurable aesthetick value in classical moderation, & the avoidance of those freakish excesses which bespeak the silliness of inadequate or disordered motivation. One of the most pitiful & amusing things about idealism is that it stages its farce of sentimentalities almost for nothing—since after all, the actual line of conduct it enjoins is by no means remote from the ordinary conduct of the civilised pagan & materialist—the man of taste whose only motive force is the Hellenic principle of enlighten'd selfishness. There are certain things that well-bred people naturally do—simply as a matter of aesthetics & social determinism—& it merely makes these things sound hollow & absurd when theorists attempt to bolster up the already-adequate system by tacking on a wholly irrelevant & irrational framework of pseudo-authority, pseudo-correlations, & pseudo-explanations. And so it goes. In the last analysis, I attack the ethical believer not because of what he does or recommends, but because he has—in most cases—committed the logical error of building up a superstructure of cosmic theory without having taken the necessary preliminary step of testing the theory's essential foundation—the existence or non-existence of such a thing as an objectively genuine *obligatory* force in Nature. Whenever he starts out by *honestly tackling* this vital and pivotal ontological point, I prepare myself to attend his discourse with respect and receptiveness.

Oh, by the way—here's something from old California—home of Cosmic Brotherhood, Vedantick Mystick Circles, Surplus Mahatmas, & all such ennobling influences! Our friend Clark Ashton Smith, whose work you appreciate so poignantly, has just got a revision job from a gushing old maid of the New-Thought, Unity, or Swami Mushbah type; whose gifts of expression dangerously rival those of our old standby Dave Bush, & who has just perpetrated a new pome worthy to rank with "Mr. Muling" & "O Suppose".[6] He is frankly stumped this time—& I don't blame him in view of the opening line he quotes—"My soul has the arms of an Octopus". That's all he quotes—but I'm helping him out with a provisional version, spun out of my sympathetick understanding of the Eastern Spirit of Universal Oom. The way Grandpa would dope it out is this—

Unity

My soul has the arms of an octopus
    To cuddle the whole world in;
O'er the cosmick sea, with emotion plus
    I float on a fluttery fin.
For Buddha has bidden my bosom burst
    The collar that cramps us so—
And I sprinkle all space with the love that erst
    Was lavish'd on Limo, O.

Om Mane Kidme On—Gôta Nóbah Nhānās!

As for the race article—the only major fault I find with it is that it spends all its energy attacking a single set of conceptions (i.e., those of biological superiority as a purely Nordic attribute, & of racial mixture as a physical menace) which are by no means those of the enlighten'd & disillusion'd opponent of mongrelism. That is a familiar trick of the pro-mongrelite—to single out a popular superficial attitude as representative of the whole anti-mongrel position, & then declare anti-mongrelism demolish'd because the superficial attitude can be prov'd fallacious. Shrewd—but valueless scientifically & sociologically. No anthropologist of standing insists on the uniformly advanced evolution of the Nordic as compared with that of other Caucasian & Mongolian races. As a matter of fact, it is freely conceded that the Mediterranean race turns out a higher percentage of the aesthetically sensitive, & that the Semitic groups excel in sharp, precise intellection. It may be, too, that the Mongolian excels in aesthetick capacity & normality of philosophical adjustment. What, then, is the secret of pro-Nordicism amongst those who hold these views? Simply this—that ours is a Nordic culture, & that the roots of that culture are so inextricably tangled in the natural standards, perspectives, traditions, memories, instincts, peculiarities, & physical aspects of the Nordic stream that no other influences are fitted to mingle in our fabric. We don't despise the French *in France or Quebeck*, but we don't want them grabbing *our* territory & creating foreign islands like Woonsocket & Fall River. The fact of this *uniqueness* of every separate culture-stream—this dependence of instinctive likes & dislikes, natural methods, unconscious appraisals, &c. &c. on the physical & historic attributes of a single race—is too obvious to be ignored except by empty theorists. I dwelt on that point in my preceding epistle. Now how about us? Well, our stock had a hardy & adventurous history under highly unfavourable sub-arctic conditions, & in conflict with relentless natural enemies. Survival depended on the exaggeration of those glandular reactions tending toward dominance, freedom, boldness, assertiveness, & the retention of a boyhood relentlessness in our attitude toward the external world. Those of us who managed to survive at all, had these qualities in more than the common degree; & of course they became for us the supreme subconscious criterion of human character. It is too late in the day to change this set of feelings, even if there were any reason for change. They are as fixed as our white complexions, tall stature, & other racial attributes. We must simply recognise the fact that, to be congenial for us, a civilisation must be founded on the ideals of unbroken freedom, haughty dominance, executive competence, ("excudent alii spirantia mollis aera", &c.) personal dignity, emotional discipline & economy, & the various other things which historick experience has taught & forced us to cherish above all else. We don't despise art & intellect—indeed, we feel the need for them very acutely & go after them with Nordic determination; but the fact remains, deep down within us, that we don't consider these things such *ut-*

terly essential parts of any tolerable conception of human character as we consider our racial *unbrokenness*. We can *like* a fool or a boor even when we laugh at him. There is nothing *loathsome* or *monstrous* to us in weak thinking or poor taste. But for the cringing, broken, unctuous, subtle type we have a *genuine horror—a sense of outraged Nature*—which excites our deepest nerve-fibres of mental & physical repugnance. Upon this proportioning of instinctive attitudes all our folkways—laws, customs, art, literature, language, sports, working religion, manners, dreams—are exclusively based; so that the inapplicability of these folkways to any group or individual far removed from the Nordic standard is quite self-evident. What we mean by Nordic "superiority" is simply *conformity to those character-expectations which are natural & ineradicable among us.* We are not so naive as to confuse this relative "superiority" (we ought to call it *conformity* or *suitability* instead) with the absolute biological superiority which we recognise in the higher races as a whole as distinguished from the negro, australoid, neanderthal, rhodesian, & other primitive human & humanoid types both living & extinct. We know perfectly well that the Italians excel us in the capacity to savour life & beauty—that their centres of taste are better developed than ours—but they annoy us & fail to fit into our group because their gland-functionings & nerve-reactions do not correspond to what our own heritage has made us expect. We do not call them *inferior*, but simply admit that they are *different* beyond the limits of easy mutual understanding & cultural compatibility. If we wisely kept vast masses of such foreigners out, we could regard them with a more impersonal appreciation. It would be wholly possible, too, to assimilate *a few* to our own fabric. But when we get so damn many of them that a wholesale test of strength betwixt their ideals & ours starts up on our own soil—well, forget your idealism for a second, use your horse-sense, & guess what will happen! It isn't that our unbrokenness & stamina are any more valid a form of "superiority" than the Italian's beauty-sense or the Jew's mental sharpness; but simply that these masculine qualities happen—purely by historic chance—to constitute *our* particular main standard in so deep-seated a way that we cannot help feeling a profound, crawling, physical-emotional aversion toward individuals & groups whose different scales of value-emphases may cause these qualities to be, as we view them, underdeveloped. The plain, honest fact is, that no individuals & groups can live harmoniously together as long as some members are moved by a scale of feelings, standards, & environmental responses radically different from the natural scale of other members. Living side by side with people whose natural impulses & criteria differ widely from ours, gets in time to be an unendurable nightmare. We may continue to respect them in the abstract, but what are we to do when they continue to fail to fulfil our natural conception of personality, meanwhile placing all their own preferential stresses on matters & ideals largely irrelevant & sometimes even repugnant to us? And don't forget that we affect alien groups just as they affect us. Chinamen think our manners are bad, our voices raucous, our odour nauseous, & our white skins and our long noses leprously repulsive. Spaniards think us vulgar, brutal, & gauche. Jews titter & gesture at our mental simplicity, & honestly think we are savage, sadistick, & childishly hypocritical. Well—we think Chinks are slimy jabberers, Spaniards oily, sentimental, treacherous, backward greasers, & Jews cringing whipped curs. What's the answer? *Simply keep the bulk of all these approximately equal & highly developed races as far apart as possible.* Let them study one another as deeply as possible, in the interest of that *intellectual understanding* which makes for appreciation & tolerance. *But don't let them mix too freely, lest the clash of deep & intellectually unreachable emotions upset all the appreciation & tolerance which mental understanding has produced.* And above all, don't get led off on a false trail through observing the easy camaraderie of a few cosmopolitan intellectuals & aristocrats in whom similar manners or special interests have temporarily overriden the deep wells of natural feeling ineradicable from the bulk of each of the divergent race or culture groups represented. One might add whole chapters, too, on the powerful part played by physiognomical dissimilarities. All told, there is no sound policy but that of letting each well-defined group express itself normally, & without the disastrous strain of alien thought-disturbance, within its own accustom'd geographical area. As for loose ends of the article—the author again errs when he assumes that we judge a given race by its degree of dominance or cultural status *at any one period of history.* It is only over long ranges that we form such judgments. We *don't* consider either the original white Hamitick Ægyptians or the Minoans inferior to ourselves. All the evolved races develop superiority when given adequate opportunity. It is only when a race fails to develop *after it has the opportunity* that we draw final adverse conclusions as to its biological status. The negro, for example, had the full run of Africa, including the most favourable climates, & was abundantly exposed to the very earliest Hamitick & Semitick cultures. 8000 or 9000 years ago niggers knew all about civilisation, & were fairly saturated with the influence of the great races in the Nile Valley & down the Red Sea and Indian-Ocean coast. And what good did it do them? Did they carry back any ideas to elevate the mental processes & imaginative sensitivenesses of the free, favourably situated main bulk of their race? Don't be foolish! They were the slaves of all the other races—including the equally black but skeletally & organically different Dravidians—with whom they came in contact, & not a whit more than that. Sambo stands today exactly where he stood when he first scratched for fleas in his native jungle or shovelled manure for Egyptians, Arabs, Carthaginians, Ethiopians, &c., in the adjacent civilised world. When the savage Nordick first struck the Mediterranean world, he conquered a slice of it & founded the glory of Greece. When Chinese culture reached the Mongolian folk of certain islands, we had the splendour of old Japan. When Polynesian ideas hit the Mongoloid Amerindians of the Western World, we had Peru, Mexico, & the Mayas. When Rome conquered barbarous Gaul, the Gauls became the most intelligent of the new imperial-Roman mixture. And then the clumsy Teutons had contact with Romanised Britain, & later with the Norman influence, the result was *us*—like us or not. And all this time the apelike buck nigger is exactly the same animal he was when neolithic Mediterraneans evolved the first Nile culture.* Ho, hum—if any Neanderthaloids had survived, there would doubtless be plenty of idealists to exalt & sentimentalise over them! Poor dears, all they lacked was a chance—just what sort of a chance one doesn't bother to specify.

Yeh—it's damn hard to stop arguing. But you get what I mean—I wanna get down to hard pan & not play around on the surface where nobody knows what either he or the other guy is talking about because both are using *conventional terms* without investigating the relation of these terms to underlying *realities*. For instance—your talk about my 'isolating myself from my fellows' implies a *wholly conventional point of view as to what constitutes one's relationship with his fellows*. I am a complete hermit only by accident—because I don't happen to run across any guys in every-day contacts who have anything to talk about. If I lived where such guys are—as indeed I did live briefly in your general metropolitan zone—I'd be seeing them fairly frequently; in fact, I was constantly in touch with the gang in those days. And as for general social theory—well, by this time I ought to have made it god damn clear how I stand on the question of my place in the Anglo-Saxon fabrick! God Save the King! Rule, Britannia! You mistake my mere unhypocritical selfishness & individualism—a selfishness & individualism involving no hostility toward others, & even including an egotistical solitude for the aggrandisement of the race-&-culture group (what you would, under a different interpretation, call a "civic" sentiment)—for the active & positive misanthropy of a Wandrei or Clark Ashton Smith. What you call my "isolation" is merely my insistence on the absence from cosmic reality of certain mythical conceptions of sentimental obligatory linkage which originated solely in primitive tradition. I simply refuse to swallow meaningless emotional poses without adult anthropological connotations. I am no more isolated than anybody else except by the mere chance of not happening to run across congenial minds in this particular locality. But I simply refuse to pretend an interest in vague assumptions of mystical points of human kinship unrelated to the realities of congenial personality—mystical linkages which have no existence except in the meaningless & sentimental ideology of primitive ignorance & Victorian hypocrisy. I recognise myself as one of a vast number of approximately similar organick entities on this planet, & realise that my mental contentment depends largely on my imaginative adjustment to the pattern form'd by the history & folkways of my group. Does

---

*Acc. to recent estimates, circa 10,000 B.C.

that sound like eccentrick isolation? Rule, Britannia! God Save the King! My only difference from yourself in this respect is that I view the circumstance without traditional trappings, & do not allow the conditions of my imaginative pattern-linkage to impose upon me a needless harness of non-existent, quasi-ritualistic mental inhibitions—the things you recognise as "obligations". I own all *genuine* obligations—that is, I follow such a regimen as will most conduce to (or at least, not detract from) the survival of the pattern promoting my pleasure. But I refuse to emulate the child who plays around with a tiny broom "helping mother sweep"—that is, I refuse to countenance the force of imagining myself an active, conscious, & necessary factor in the drift of our automatic & deterministic culture-unit. I cut out the fairy-tale stuff & face the real facts of the individual's essential automatism & volitional insignificance—being content to "play my part in the civilisation" just as everyone else really does—by living out my own personality in my own way. If my way happened to lie in the direction of public administration, as many people's way does, I'd go in for that sort of thing. Each to his own. But I won't pretend to be what I ain't! Nor is this in the least anti-human, anti-civic, or anti-social. It is merely "anti" a certain hackneyed sentimental illusion about what humanity, civicism, & sociality are. As for my belief that human & inanimate objects, as background-factors, do not essentially differ in essence—what of it? In all truth, many of the inanimate objects which fascinate me (old steeples, Georgian doorways, mysterious ruins, &c.) do so because of symbolick connexion with the stream & drama of human history. It isn't *I* who go in for sterile rocks & mountains!! No—Grandpa's only principle in human affairs *is the casting-off of the fictitious & insincere*. Refusal to *overvalue* people, in the mass, is no indication whatever that one *hates or despises* people. I'm sure I don't.

Well—glad Toronto didn't freeze ya. I had an idea it wasn't anything extra as a repository of the past. I wanna see Halifax & St. John.

—Yr. obt Servt

Θεοβάλδος

P. S. Enclosed is a calendar which you can hang up by your desk to remind you of God's Country.

Parsonage Press plan has gone up the flue, & Cook & Orton blame each other. Another quarrel among the boys for Grandpa to patch up!

Notes

1. William Thomas Manning (1866–1949), British-born American bishop of the Episcopal Church (1921–49). He was generally considered a member of the liberal wing of the church.

2. Both the British astronomer Arthur Stanley Eddington (1882–1944) and the American physicist Robert A. Millikan (1868–1953), winner of the Nobel Prize for physics in 1923, sought to reconcile modern advances in science with religion.

3. Dighton Rock, at Berkley, Massachusetts, is an 11-foot-high "glacial erratic" boulder that once rested on the shore of the Taunton River. It is covered with petroglyphs attributed to sources ranging from Portuguese explorers to Native Americans.

4. Martin Farquhar Tupper (1810–1889), British writer, and poet, and author of *Proverbial Philosophy*, widely derided as a work of banal platitudes.

5. The Vedanta Society, established in 1928 by the Swami Akhilananda at 227 Angell Street, is still a functioning Hindu organization.

6. "War and Dueling Mr. Muling" and "Suppose" are poems in David Van Bush's *Peace Poems and Sausages.*

[105] [AHT]

Antient River-Bank where Old Theobald wander'd
as a brooding youth of 3 in good old 1893, & which is
still unchang'd amidst a world of mechanis'd
decay & putrescent democracy.

Spring!!!!, 1931
[23? March 1931]

Basileus of Brilliancy & Beatitude:—

Well, Sir, as you may see, the Old Man hath bust hibernation at last. The boughs are feathery green, the air is balmy, & the reddening afternoon sun gleaming mystically thro' a tracery of delicate branches. Time is suspended, & mystick yesterdays hang wistfully & alluringly over the wooded slopes & the glassy pool where vivid green rushes shoot up beside the sun's crimson reflection. I am at that ravine-mouth where you & Cook & Munn & Wandrei & I strolled in 1927—when Wandrei darted off to the secluded heights to meditate alone amongst the fauns and dryads. Across the pool, on the heights above, the facade of a Georgian country-seat peeps thro' the trees, with the gable & roof of another far beyond it. At this placid hour there is nothing to remind me that I am not in the past—or in Old England. Ah, me—I trust I may be gather'd to dust before universal decay strips me of such refuges to flee to. As I writ in 1901—

Take heed, Diana, of my humble Plea.
Convey me where my Happiness may last;
Draw me against the tide of Time's rough Sea,
And let my Spirit rest amid the Past![1]

As for this Putnam stuff—I have no confidence that anything will come of it.[2] They merely wish to look over possible sources & see what is potentially available, but in the end I shall doubtless receive a polite note of refusal. Even in the event of publication, financial returns wou'd undoubtedly be very meagre. Wandrei hath just publish'd a volume of verse—"Dark Odyssey"—at his own expence; with phantasticall illustrations by his brother. The poetry is excellent in the manner of the 1890's, & the mechanical form is so sumptuous that my bookplate (the paper stock—*not* Talman's splendid design) looks shabby on the inside cover. Wandrei's brother is a real artist—perhaps even sounder in a technical way than your favourite Klarkash-Ton.

As for controversies—of course I am right, but have it your own way! I am now having a great fight with Sonny over the question of traditionalism—each claims to be more truly old-fashion'd than the other. In a letter mail'd today I think I'm cornering the little imp. About Boas—I did not mean to belittle him unduly, though it did seem to me that he allowed social sentiments to interfere with his impersonality of deduction. What I was *really* laughing at was not Boas himself—whom I freely gave a place among the first-rate anthropologists—but the naive way in which all nigger-lovers turn to him first of all when trying to scrape up a background of scientific support. He is the only first rate living anthropologist to overlook the obvious primitiveness of the negro & the australoid, hence the equalitarian Utopians have to play him up for all he's worth & forget the great bulk of outstanding European opinion—Boule, G. Elliot Smith, Sir Arthur Keith, &c. But anyway, I read of Boas' career with great interest, & am glad that his lifetime of close & diligent research hath been rewarded by the Presidency of the A. A. A. S.[3]

O, dear! Evening chill now! Time for Old Gentlemen to plod homeward across the brooding meads. But 'twas a great afternoon while it lasted. Wish I were in Charleston where there's some really dependable heat that doesn't fade out with the sun!

Best wishes, & hope to see you soon!

Yr obt Servt

Θεοβάλδος

[P.S.] Have just finish'd monstrous 32,000-word antarctic hell-raiser—"At the Mountains of Madness". Gord, but the typing ahead! Left eye rather on the bum of late—hope I shan't have to go back to full-time use of specs.

Florida yet uncertain—trying to collect back debts from all clients.

Notes

1. The fourth and final stanza of "Ode to Selene or Diana," from *Poemata Minora, Volume II* (1902 [not 1901]; *AT* 11).
2. Winfield Shiras of G. P. Putnam's Sons had written HPL, probably at the suggestion of Henry S. Whitehead.

United States.

[106] [AHT]
St. Augustine, in His Maj^{ty's} Province of East-Florida
June 16, 1731
Candescent Corona of Congestedly Catalogued Chronology:—
Well, I'll be damn'd! But I guess I'll see ya O. K. enough, whether in the
real town of Providentium or in that piffling hick region where the post-
master reads the cards and counts the number of words like a tellygraft op-
erator! I'm simply hanging on in a civilis'd climate as long as cash holds out,
& so long as the Greyhound outfit will extend my round trip ticket. I ought
to be in New York betwixt July 10th and 20th—or else in Providence—&
when I hit the decadent cosmopolis I'll kinda arrange my programme to fit
whatever plan you may have plotted out on your highly technologised graph.
   As a whole, *climate* is South Florida's chief asset. It braces the old man up
like a tonick. But the landscape is flat & rotten—swamp or sandy pine bar-
rens—except in spots. Miami's vegetation of the subtropicks doesn't get that
far south, whilst that of the full tropicks does not naturally attain its fullest
development. But *Key West* is the real thing. Vast palms, banyans, & all the
fixings. That's the place for me! Yet it was only founded in 1822, & for all its
distinctiveness has not the utter antique fascination of St. Aug.
   Meanwhile I'll send bulletins and await word—hoping the while that
same happy conjunction can be arrang'd, either in antient Providentium or in
the town of postal priggishness and pusillanimity. Why the hell can't a bimbo
be in two or three places at once? I hope relativity'll conquer that problem
some day!
Expectantly
Θεοβάλδος

[107] [AHT]
Friday Night
[13 November 1931]
Pharaoh-Passing Pinnacle of Petrine Precision:—
   Well, damn it all, I ben out to see our Latin friend[1] at last, & had a nice
social call with him & two of his numberless sons—Ralph, the youth who
drove us into town on one occasion & went back for your lost hammer, &
Carl, who (though I didn't know it before) is the affable young fellow who
runs the steam shovel & has several times spoken to us in the past. Intelligent
chaps, on the whole—Carl is the boy who dealt with your friend Hawkins.

Well, as to the situation—there's absolutely nothing in the quarry itself. Just the same as last July—& Ralph says that they haven't been working the side that yields the varied minerals for some time. I judge that the stuff in the shed is of an earlier vintage—it may even have been there during our last visit.

Now as for the shed stuff—there's only three kinds of assorted rock that you'd care anything about. (a) Pyrite crystals in rock, such as made your mouth water from Bro. Hawkie's description, (b) Talc in good white lumps up to the size of a small ostrich egg, & (c) shredded asbestos in clusters of filaments or fibres perhaps seven or eight inches long & two or three inches broad—not very thick.

The pyrite is probably what you'd want the most. One specimen, to be referred to in subsequent letters as Specimen A, is just about what you describe as having been ferreted out by Hawkshaw the Stony Deteckatiff—a cubical piece of black rock maybe a foot each way, & with one face studded thickly with metallic crystals of large size—several of them easily an inch square. All the Magistres agree that this is about what they sold Hawkins for ten bucks, & they'll let you have it for a similar price—IF (O Tantalus, yuh still got sumpun to learn!) it isn't already preëmpted by a **third** rival in the stony field; one Gordon of some college in His Majesty's Province of Pennsylvania. This bird passed through antient Providentium several months ago, and noted certain specimens that he wanted to think over after he got home. If he wants this prize rock—& Ralph & Carl agree that he was prodigiously taken with it—the Magistres are in honour bound to give it to him; though they'd damn sight rather you had it. An option is an option. They're going to write him at once, & will probably have the straight dope in about a week. If Gordon doesn't speak up, it's yours for a ten-spot. I'm no rockologist, but it looks to me as if this is the sort of stuff you're after. Don't blame me, though, if it ain't. If you have no local representative but a dumbbell layman, that's simply your bad luck. It's a helluva world anyway!

Well—so much for the debatable prize package. Now for something certain. There's just one more good piece of this pyrite rock—with a rich sprinkling of big crystals, one of which is easily an inch square. This is a sort of longish & narrowish affair—something like this: maybe 5 × 5 × 15 inches. If I hadn't seen the other one, I'd have said this was a  regular pip; & even so, it's nothing to get high-hat toward. It would do credit, it seems to me, to any musaeum that couldn't get its big brother. Nobody, so far as I could figure out, has any previous option on this—& I put in an option for you. This is yours for *four* bucks. We will refer to it in future correspondence as Specimen B.

Of the *talc* there is an unlimited amount. Hawkins went for the big lumps, & took several at a dollar each. There are none quite so big now on hand, so any lumps you may wish will be somewhat under one fish per. The Magistres don't know just what to charge, but take as a basis the scale they worked out with Hawkie.

As for the asbestos—there are gallons of it lying around, & I have no idea of how much you want just now. The boys thought that something under a dollar—or at least not over—would be a fair charge for perhaps a derby hat full . . . . say a coupla quarts.

So that's that. Do you want to risk plunging on stones ya ain't seen? I wish to hell you could get up here for a day or two on the museum's jack! Suppose you could swing it? Despite the cold, I'd bundle up & escort you down to Maxfield's! And of course Brother Eddy is open at all hours.

Let me know what ya decide. I'll buy anything you authorise on receipt of cash & authority—& as I said before, the dope about this Gordon reservation ought to be straight in about a week. The pyrite specimens are too heavy for me to lug home—at least, the massive & debatable one is—so if you buy it, don't you think you'd better try to have the Magistres pack it themselves (if they can & will) & ship it to you straight? It would cost less in the end—saving the fee of a local expressman. (Unless, of course, the Magistres would deliver it at #10 in one of their trucks.)

So here's the price-list.

A. Finest Pyrite specimen (salability doubtful)—	$10.00
B. Next-best Pyrite specimen	4.00
Talc—per large lump—not over	1.00
Asbestos—large fibres—2 Quts.—at or under	1.00

The boys seem to be doing most of the active deciding around the quarry these days, & I imagine that Ralph (who, by the way, always makes out my mortgage cheques nowadays) is virtually the head of the business. I think you could write them about any necessary matters without fear of misunderstanding—they are high-school graduates, and talk like any ordinary Anglo-Saxon American. Therefore you might enter in your address-book the following item for future consultation:

Ralph De Magistris,
   Prov. Crushed Stone & Sand Co.,
      647 Manton Ave., Prov., R. I.

And so it goes. The watchword here is "hold everything"—hence the next move is up to you. Gawd, but it was cold out at the quarry! The bleak wind whips relentlessly out of the cryptical westward hills, stinging face & nostrils with an almost purposeful malevolence. I hope to hades we can get this business cleaned up before the damn temperature gets any worse!

Going to hear the astronomer-physicist Willem de Sitter Monday night—he lectures on the size of the universe.[2] Tuesday night a chap has invited me to attend a demonstration of *television*, held under the auspices of the R. I. Engineering Society.

Well—such is which. Hope Paul Pry won't bust open this letter . . . . . & if the says it's overweight he's a goddam liar![3]

Yrs for generous nonchalance—

Θεοβάλδος

Notes

1. Mariano de Magistris.
2. The Dutch mathematician and physicist Willem de Sitter (1872–1934) lectured in Providence on 9 November. HPL mentions him by name in "The Whisperer in Darkness."
3. HPL refers to a postal employee in Paterson, NJ, whom he dubbed "Paul Pry," after a meddlesome fellow consumed with curiosity in the play *Paul Pry* (1825), a farcical comedy by British playwright John Poole (1786–1872).

[108] [AHT]

Decr 3, 1731

Quintessential Quixote of Quarryish Quest:—

Well—it's about time Grandpa made that petrifick report—but I ben simply swamp'd with damn things to attend to. I owe 15-odd epistolae right now—without much prospect of disposin' of 'em.

However—I gotcha rox. Those ingrate serfs wouldn't pack & send 'em . . . . . said they had no gotta de fahcheelities for such procedure, & that any stuff saved for Gordonius woulda hadda ben kep' aroun' till he come for it . . . . . . but Signore Carlo (the pleasant steam shovel guy whom we've talked with in prior ignorance of his identity) brung the junk over here in his shiny & sumptuous limousine free of charge. An' oh, boy, yuh'd orta see Carlo when he's all dolled up in civilian togs. Hotta dog! Some-a swella macaroni!

Hadda spend all of your twelve fish, but I think I got a better value than formerly expected. There was one stupendous piece of talc—which had been there before but which had not been shew'd to me—for which Don Carlos (the only guy about on the occasion I call'd) wanted *four bucks* instead of the solitaire allotted to the talc department. I was pretty sure you'd want it, & was going to have him save it in any case; but thought I'd first try some Semitick tacticks on his second-generation Latinity. So I told him I was sorry, but didn't believe you'd want to pay so much; & asked him how big a piece he would let me have for a one-spot. Oy! vee shood pay it oudt goot maw-nee ven bee-ziness iss badt! But blessa my soul! Carlo heesa gotta beega heart! One a buck? Oh, all right! Taka de beega piece for-a dat! So ya gotta four-fish lump for one, with no extry charge excep' what the additional express or freight'll be next July! The asbestos comes in long strips over a foot from tip to tip unless it crumbles further. I don't know how it rates qualitatively—having only a layman's standards of comparison—but it had orta ho' ya for a while. It's a fair dollar's worth, I guess. But of course the piece de resistance is the big boy with the jumbo cubical pyrites. Yes—the ten-spotter was declar'd available, & I copped it right & proper. Gawd, but what that thing weighs! I don't envy ya next July! The talc isn't as white as some I've seen, but I imagine the main chromatick element is plain, plebeian dirt. Give the thing a bath & it'll reflect credit on the museum!

Hope all is well in idyllick Patersonium, & that the scheduled gang meeting at Little Sonny's will turn out a well-balanc'd success. And whenever you can, run up to antient Providentium for a look at your new stonepile!

> Yrs till the Passaick reverses—
> Θεοβάλδος

[109] [AHT]

> Tiw's Daeg
> [mid-December 1931]

Epoch-Eclipsing Empyrean of Esoteric Energy:—

Hail, Sir Pyrites! This time Grandpa's askin' a favour—tho' come to think of it, it's too tainted with the naive bourgeois pose of altruism to get really into the favour class. But here goes.

Mister, have ya gotta nickel boutcha fra cuppa cawfee? Or more specifically, can you chip into a highly worthy bit of amateur journalistick philanthropy to the extent of one verdant-revers'd portrait of the late Genl. G. Washington, of Mount-Vernon, in Virginia, Esquire?

To define matters more amply—Culinarius Paullus & I are trying to raise a fund of twenty-five bucks to get good old Tryout the new font of type which he so desperately needs, yet which he is so utterly unable to buy. We argue that it's a goddam shame for any such faithful amateur worker to be held back through lack of anything a reasonably modest sum can purchase. We formed the idea right after our Haverhill visit of Octr. 4, but expected to pass it on to the super-competent & ultra-persuasive Leonard E. Tilden, who we thought could milk it out of the Fossils in no time at all. Tilden, however, says he can't attend to it, & flings the buck back to poor old Grandpa Theobald. So it's up to me to bleed as many active arms for a berry each as I can touch—though the hope of getting the jack in time for Yuletide presentation is about up the flue. If we can't scrape up twenty-five, Culinarius & I will try to fill up the gap ourselves. If, on t'other hand, the drive goes over the top, we'll simply shoot the whole works along to honest Smiffkins.

Well—don't make the handout if it means too big a strain on your exchequer, but just keep nice old Smiffkins in mind in case you have a surplus berry. You can send it either to me or to W. P. C. Thanks in advance for whatever ya kin do . . . . Gawd bless yer, guv'nor!

Yr obt Servt

Θεοβάλδος

[110] [AHT]

Day after Candlemas, 1932

[3 February 1932]

Irradiant Incarnation of Infinite Illuminatism:—

Thanks for the puzzle dope—& hope ya have a good time in Philadelphia. I'd like to see the old colonial metropolis myself—it has a never-fading charm for me—& I certainly intend to get another eyeful before many months have fled. As for puzzling—I doubt if I could ever become an enthusiast. I am mildly amused by an isolated charade or anagram now & then, when it comes up by accident, but am bored to tears by any continuous or premeditated session with this amiable form of futility. The reason for my indifference is doubtless closely allied to that behind my total indifference toward games & sports—namely, a lack of excess mental energy, which causes me to resent, unconsciously, the expenditure of any brain-power upon frankly uncorrelated & unprofitable ends. When I put out solid thought & concentration—a visibly exacting process for one never far from the point of nervous exhaustion—I absolutely demand *a tangible return for my pains,* in the form of some gratification of historical, scientifick, or philosophical curiosity, or some aesthetick pleasure to be gain'd thro' the creation, perception, or crystallisation of some symmetrical imaginative picture or impression. Puzzles & games bring not even a faint suggestion of this sort of reward. They reveal no actual secrets of the universe, & help not at all in intensifying or preserving the tantalising moods & elusive dream-vistas of the aesthetick imagination. Aside from exercising the intellect in as dry & artificial a fashion as Cal Coolidge's mechanical horse exercises the body,[1] they are a total loss—except of course for the superficial & childish amusement of seeing a hidden jack-in-the-box pop out, & for the still cheaper egotistical pleasure of beating somebody else & being able to say "what a smart boy I am!" Actually, the sole major pleasure of puzzles for superior persons is the *abstract & intrinsick exercise of the intellect involved;* the delight in the *mere process of tracking something down,* irrespective of the frivolity or futility of the object. Now I do not despise the attitude of those who seek this form of pleasure. On the contrary, I heartily envy anybody with enough excess brains to require such an artificial addition to the normal array of problems confronting the human mind. But I candidly admit I haven't the brains to need this outlet. Just as I haven't such a plethora of physical energy as to make me enjoy walking *for the sake of the exercise,* (as you say you do, whereas I walk for

the sake of the imaginative delights afforded by scenery, architecture, atmosphere. and historick associations) so do I lack that plethora of mental energy
which would make me enjoy pursuing a series of cerebrational steps *for the
sake of the pursuit.* I don't enjoy either exercising or thinking, but I can be
driven to attempt either when enough of a reward is held out. Curiosity
about the actual state of the cosmos is such a reward, but I can't summon up
any corresponding curiosity about an artificial tangle which somebody has
arbitrarily cooked up. I *am* avid to find out what arcane horror lies behind
the sardonic colossi of Easter Island, what process of nature has differentiated men, niggers, & Neanderthalers, & whether the cosmic rays represent
the building-up or breaking-down of matter. These things are real & natural,
& vast drama lies in their solution *because they are connected with obscure primal
laws & not prearranged by any petty human smart aleck.* But I'll be goddamned if I
can work up any avid curiosity over the question of what "my first" plus
"my second" represents, or what common words can be anagrammatically
derived from secura and chesty. What of it? Where's the kick? That is,
where's the kick for him who cares not for processes but for ends? After I
solve the problems—if I do—I don't know a cursed thing more about nature, history, & the universe than I did before. All my solution has not
cleared up any of the myriad points about which I *really am* curious. And as I
said before, I haven't any mental energy to spare on unamusing side-lines.
It's just the same with games. Meaningless spotted pasteboards, carved castles & horses' heads, little balls flying in the air, big balls kicked & grappled
by future bond salesmen & bankers, little balls knocked around with sticks in
the hands of unimaginative manufacturers & senile plutocrats, horses goaded
into foam while describing frantic circles that land them exactly where they
started out . . . . . glory of sport . . . . . rah, rah, rah . . . . . . No, Grandpa ain't
made to relish sech didoes! All these things are, in their superior forms, simply by-products of excess intellectuality—which I haven't the honour to
possess. In their inferior forms they are of course simply avenues of escape
for persons with too poorly proportioned & correlated a perspective to distinguish betwixt the frivolous and the relevant—& my perspective (not thro'
any native intellect of mine, but thro' sheer environmental accident) has not
been suffer'd to remain in that idyllick Arcadian state. Sports of a certain
sort—football, prize-fighting, & the more virile kind generally—may perhaps
have a symbolick value connected with the ceaseless struggle of races & nations for supremacy; but my poetick powers are insufficiently develop'd to
make me take any keen delight in them. I might develop such a taste in time,
but so far I have never seen a football game, bull fight, or sparring mill. In
their day, I shou'd probably have liked gladiatorial sports with real killings.
Habet! habet! Neca, Siphax, neca! Sanguinem bibe![2]

As for hobbies in general—my old head is too tired to take any new
things on! My one aim is to get rid of some of the pressure already upon it.

Hell, but the things that come up each day are beyond my power to cope with. They pile up and up—so that every unexhausted moment of my time is crowded to overflowing. I try to amputate dumbbell branches of my correspondence, but they are like the Hydra's heads. I cut out some reading, but other things crop up. It is literally a fight for breath—& I guess the only way out of it is to disappear and repudiate all obligations as good old Cook did a year ago. But I'll save our your stones, anyhow!

Sunday I went to hear a poetry reading by S. Foster Damon[3] & was damn near knock'd out by the cold. Today ain't so bad, though. Well—good luck!

Θεοβάλδος

Notes

1. President Coolidge had a mechanical horse installed in the White House for the purpose of exercise.

2. "He has him! He has him! Kill, Siphax, kill! Drink his blood!"

3. S[amuel] Foster Damon (1893–1971) was an instructor in the English Department at Harvard. He came to Brown University in 1927 and became associate professor in 1930. He was curator of the Harris Collection of American Poetry and Plays at the John Hay Library.

[111] [AHT]

March 7, 1932

Peak-Passing Pinnacle of Pendulum Prompted Pan-Potentiality:—

By the way—last Saturn's Day Brobst & I went to Bristol by stagecoach, did up all the colonial sights, & stopt at Warren on our way back. After digesting Warren's quiet lanes & doorways we went across the tracks to Aunt Julia's, where we tanked up on twelve different kinds of ice cream—all they're serving at this time of year. The antient gentlewoman, of course, was not there—since (as I wish to gawd I could) she spends all her winters in Florida—but the bimbo in charge was very pleasant, & we got quick service since we were the only customers. Toward the end of the meal the presiding host—overhearing our conversation as it turned upon the famous Wandrei-Plantagenet-Theobald cleanup of MDCCCCXXVII—horned in upon us to tell how well he recalled the celebrated feat of five years agone. It seems that we were remembered better than we realised, & that Aunt Julia shewed our triangularly signed statement year after year to patrons from all over the country—until, alas, she lost it some time last summer. I told the guy that at least two-thirds of the old-time trio had paid him annual visits ever since & would continue to do so; & he replied that he hoped we'd make ourselves known to him the next time we came, since (like me) he very easily forgets faces. I told him, we surely would—if I remembered his face . . . . which I probably shan't, since it's very undistinctive tho' genial. I wonder if he's a grandson of Aunt Julia or just a hired man?

As for the relative sense or folly of this or that pastime or daily regimen, I wou'd be the last to set up any absolute standard. Everything is as Nature happens to shape it in the course of endless kaleidoscopick mutations; & if any pursuit *really does* give pleasure to any representative group of organisms, that is an intrinsick fact which it wou'd be naive & irrelevant to call either absurd or sensible. Criteria of objective value simply do not apply to any natural stimulus-response—since such a thing is merely a case of natural cause & effect; a simple condition, & not a qualitative matter subject to preferential appraisal. The only reason why the good sense of certain pleasures is ever call'd into question, is that the questioner sometimes suspects an element of unconscious insincerity in the advertised joy—believing, perhaps, that the pleasure-seeker is guided by convention & inertia rather than by natural incli-nation, & that his rejoicing is less an actual registry of enjoyment than a con-sciously or at least artificially encouraged attempt to conform to an expected result. The questioner possibly thinks that the subject is losing actual pleasure by following out a conventional course traditionally (& often erroneously) sup-posed to produce pleasure. Of course, there is frequently a kind of mild sec-ondary pleasure in the artificially induced emotion following the performance of some conventionally prescribed programme arbitrarily labelled "pleasant"; but such pleasure is very pale & ineffective as compared with that resulting from the exercise of genuinely natural impulses. Thus the Victorians may have thought they enjoyed the stiff pieties of their Sabbath regimen & of their prim social elaborations; yet in truth they were only whipping themselves up to a pseudo-enjoyment based on what they were told people ought to enjoy. If they had chucked the whole mass & behaved naturally their pleasure would have been increased a thousandfold. Many persons think they enjoy smoking, yet I'll vow that most of the pleasure is feebly artificial—based on what superficial Victorian literary dabblers have maundered about the joy of pipe, gun, dog, & book, or on the cheap "den" pictures of 1902 et circa, with a vacuous youth in a mission morris-chair shewn blandly smirking at visions in up-curling smoke-rings & tagged with the title "Reflections", "Memories" or "Pipe-Dreams". What they experience is not real enjoyment, but merely a soporific sense of staving off some terrible miasma of reality. If they would stop to find a less empty way, they could stave off reality just as effectively & get more real pleasure into the bargain. Still—don't mistake me—I'm not saying that games & sports are necessarily artificial pleasures of this sort, although they certainly are to some who laboriously pursue them. In the main, the very survival of the sporting or competitive principle proves its genuine grounding in the emotions of the majority. All I say in this matter is that *I* don't enjoy these diversions. And in the case of purely intellectual exercises I say it with appropriate hu-miliation—conceding that I haven't enough excess brains to demand their exercise for its own sake. Real pleasure, in general, are those which exercise certain physical instincts in certain ways, which give to the ego a feeling of expansion, freedom, & importance, which satisfy curiosity, & which involve certain rhythms & symmetries of sensory, emotional, & imaginative experience. Naturally, their varieties of concrete form are virtually endless. In the matter of schedule—slavery versus expectant adventurousness, I concede a part of what you claim but do not agree as completely as in the larger question of what forms valid pleasure. So far as my observation of history & human nature extends, I seem to find in mankind a deep & innate longing for freedom of immediate action & for the zest of uncertain vistas which may hold almost any breathless wonder in reserve. In the Aryan this is especially marked. Against this is the natural wish for reasonable security, which causes the individual to relinquish—albeit with reluctance—his immediate latitude of choice & to bind himself to certain steps in advance. But as civilisation grows more complex, this bondage becomes less & less tolerable—till someday a revolt against it will set things back to the start. To love it for its own sake—as some artificially come to do—is not so normal & basic as to hate it. Anticipation is a false lure—because for a keen imagination it is always disappointed.

Well—see ya later!

Πάππος Θεοβάλδος

[112]   [AHT]

Woden's Daeg
[April 1932]

Crowning Cog of Coördinated Chronometry:—

Ah, me—just as one thing clears up, another shuts down! Here the May–June tangle is straightening out . . . . yet lookit wot's struck Grandpa! Teeth, goddamit! A molar that I thought I could jolly along till days of aestival balminess has went bad on me! Ouch! Behold the old man chawin' on one side of his trap . . . . & with the pleasing prospect of probes, burrs, & what the hell else not . . . . . to say nothing of the ensuing bill . . . . . . yawning ahead of him! I've sought an appointment with the local guardian of grinders—but know not how many repetitions it will involve. Eheu! When I would be on the road to Nouvelle-Orleans, La Habana, or where the spirit lists, here I be in the subarctick zone, shadow'd by the crool cold steel & fiscal extortion of the dental chirurgeon! Gawd knows what kind of a trip I'll ever get at!

Well, well—Brother Chang-Hsueh-Liang sure is the chronometrick champeen![1] But in this he surely betrays his ancient cultural tradition, for the cardinal virtue of Asia is its sane and philosophick timelessness. Whenever I contemplate that side of the Oriental nature, with its easy handling of centuries & millennia & its patrician disregard of momentary stirs & bustlings, I am tempted to weep at the futile tail-chasing & clock-grovelling of the hectick west; & to wish that the virile Nordick had never left his homeland in the Hindoo-Koosh to merge his fortunes with the restless, fever'd, machine-driven European chasers after mutable nothingness. Had we stuck to Asia, we might have founded a permanent world-empire of unrivalled splendour & irresistible strength—as mighty & puissant as Rome, & as stable & enduring as antique Ægyptus or deathless Sinae. We might have kill'd off all the slant-eyed yellow folk, & have had long camel-trains of slaves & gold & ivory & strange crystals sent us as tribute by the dark-eyed vassals & cringers of Ind, of Persia, of Africk, of Europa, & of the empires of Cuzco and Uxmal beyond the monstrous River Ocean. Glory to the Æsir! A bullock to golden-bearded Odin, & a fat buck nigger to hammer-wielding Thor! Long life to Astahahn, our capital on the Yann—for here we have fetter'd & manacled Time, who wou'd otherwise slay the gods.[2] Eheu—the things that might have been!

Well—see ya in Iunius or afore . . . & I'll try to get that box & carton stuff if the dentist doesn't lead me to the sepulchre first.

> Yr most obt
>
> Θεοβάλδος

Notes

1. Chang Hsüeh-liang (1901?–2001), Chinese warlord who took control of the province of Manchuria in 1928 upon the murder of his father, Chang Tso-lin. Chang withdrew his forces from the region upon the Japanese invasion of 1931. By "chronometrick champeen," HPL refers to the number of sports and games (including tennis and golf) that Chang attempted to fit into his schedule, along with his military and political duties.
2. From Lord Dunsany's "Idle Days on the Yann" (1910).

[113]   [AHT]

> Woden's-Daeg
>
> [April 1932]

Satient Skyscraper of Saxiscient Sagacity:—

Our different blood heritage would have made us very different from other Asiaticks, though we might well have escap'd the futile tail-chasing of the seething & meaningless Occident. Probably we'd have had more intellectual curiosity than the Chinks—hence would have push'd pure science farther; yet the statick sanity of the East would probably have saved us from wasting this unsullied truth-seeking on the vulgar trivialities of technology & the socially disruptive mistake of widespread mechanisation. In our present decline we are not only going to hell ourselves, but are—because of our vicious meddlesomeness & greed—dragging the otherwise permanent East down with us. I am all sympathy for the Chinks who want us to clear out of the Orient & let 'em alone, & I wish to gawd we'd do it. All we need to do is to see that the East doesn't get united under aggressive Japanese leadership &

form an active menace to the West—or that bolshevik Russia doesn't start exploiting it & turning it against us. Otherwise, I say China for the Chinks. But India's another question. Those damn'd mongrels are wallowing in a genuinely decadent & elastick parody on culture, & if we stepped out they'd merely keep fighting one another till somebody else—Russia or Japan—stepped in.

I'll pass the good word to young Brobst. They're cramming & working him to beat hell just now, so that he hasn't been over here as frequently as in Feby. & March. His worst grind lets up early in June, when his four-months period of probation expires. If a guy can live through that ordeal, he's A-1 material & will probably make good on the rest—though that year at Bellevue would be maddening to anybody who didn't have case-harden'd nerves. It's fortunate some eggs take to that kind of thing. Cripes! I'd faint & go to pieces at some of the sights & duties that Brobst takes as a matter of course, & almost enjoys as a foil to placid ennui. Gord knows I'm no friend of ennui, but I want my kick to come from something other than the gruesomeness of physical & psychological abnormality, pathology, & decay!

And so it goes. See ya later, & regards to the gang. Now off for Bostonium.

Yr obt

Θεοβάλδος

[114]   [AHT]

Tuesday
[5 July 1932]

Dear Jim:—

I appreciated infinitely your sympathetic note of the 2nd, & wish I could say (as indeed I myself irrationally hoped till the very last) that the bad news of last Friday was a premature alarm.

Unfortunately—sudden though it was—it was not; & the most disastrous outcome occurred at one-twenty p.m. Sunday the third.

When I reached here at seven-thirty p.m. Friday my aunt was in a painless semi-coma, & it is doubtful whether she recognised me. Doctor & nurse, however, were leaving nothing undone; & Mrs. Gamwell was coöperating valiantly. General weakening & collapse of the whole organic system, caused by the long strain of arthritic pain & precipitated by an unprecedentedly severe attack, had brought about a sinking from which the doctor gave no hope of recovery. Saturday brought no change, save a period of difficult breathing in the morning which Dr. Brown interpreted as a bad sign—predicting ultimate disaster within twenty-four hours. Sunday the melancholy prediction was fulfilled, & 1932 was irrevocably entered as a black year for this household. The end was so peaceful & unconscious that I could not believe a change had occurred when the nurse declared it final.

Services will be held tomorrow at the Knowles Funeral Chapel on the ancient hill not far from here—& close to where my aunt & Dr. Clark lived in & around 1910. Although Mrs. Clark had no more use for orthodox cant & childish immortality myths than I, the services will be conducted in the ancient Church of England tradition by the Rev. Alfred Johnson, a venerable friend of both Phillips & Clark families who also officiated for my mother in 1921. My aunt would have preferred him, since the poetry of the Anglican ritual is a thing of eternal beauty aside from its hollow meaning, whereas the jargon of the Baptists (her immediate ancestral tradition) & other Evangelicals contains only the hollowness without the beauty. She had no patience, intellectually, with any sects save the Anglican and Unitarian; though she was still technically on the rolls of the old first Baptist Church.

Interment will be in the Clark lot at Swan Point Cemetery—the same cemetery which contains the Phillips lot where I shall be interred. I waived rights in the Lovecraft lot at Woodlawn (N.Y.) a decade ago, since I wish to be permanently merged with Old Providence.

Mrs. Gamwell will appreciate your expressions of sympathy. The present event is, despite its inevitability, a blow of the first magnitude to both survivors—especially to me, since my aunt was the real animating spirit & home-making nucleus of 10 Barnes. The suddenness of the event is both bewildering and merciful—the latter because we cannot yet realise, *subjectively*, that it has actually occurred at all. It would, for example, seem incredibly unnatural to disturb the pillows now arranged for my aunt in the rocker beside my centre-table—her accustomed reading-place each evening. The earlier newspapers piled up during my absence contain interesting annotations in her hand.

Pardon this brief & inadequate note—for amidst the present strain & desolation I skip and tangle everything. Hope I'll have something more coherent (though it couldn't well be more cheerful) to say before your Green Acre address becomes obsolete. I shall hope to see you next month.

Best wishes for the trip.

Yr obt

H.P.L.

[115]   [AHT]

Idibus Sextilis, 1932
[13 August 1932]

Paragon of Pyrite-Picking Profundity:—

Iä! Shub-Niggurath! The Goat With a Thousand Young! So the awful sacrament was not unheard by Them That Wait in Sunken R'lyeh . . . . & That Which Was Sent reach'd the nameless shrine undeteriorated & unintercepted! Thank Yog-Sothoth! And to think things came out *better* than was expected! So the regular guys in the freight game weren't as stickling as that red-tapish old boy up in the attick! I rejoice that ablutions brought to light such hidden glories—& bless the serendipity whereby the stone that the builders rejected become a star bunch of magnetite specimens.[1] It's a great life—& beatify'd be good old Mariano. As for the honest old swain's name & address—here goes:

> Mariano De Magistris,
> Providence Crushed Stone & Sand Co.,
> 647 Manton Ave.,
> Providence, R. I.

I hope to Pete you canna getta heem that-a talca coostomer. Justa do that, an' he damn near geeva you de quarr'!

Glad good old Providentium & Grandpa didn't bore you. It surely was a festive & delectable season for me, & the only lamentable feature of it was the earliness of its termination. Incidentally, I have a fine new fight on my hands—with Hugh B. Cave. He insists on echoing Dr. Johnson's thoughtless dictum, that no man of sense writes but for money,[2] & I am giving him several kinds of argumentative hell. When he returns to R. I. I expect to see him in person—& then I presume the verbal fur will fly!

Trust you'll look favourably on Price's plea for a kind word in the "Eyrie".[3] And while you're about it, why not give young Derleth's "Sheraton Mirror" a boost? He, like Price, has ask'd for 'spontaneous' panegyricks! What a bunch of log-rollers!

And so it goes.

> Yr grovelling & obt Servt
> Θεοβάλδος

P.S. You were right about the cetacean nature of the porpoise. Now I'm wondering where I got the false notion—for this was acquired late in life. All my youth I had the right idea—& then some source I can't place put the error into my head as a "correction".

Notes

1. Cf. Mark 12.10: "The stone which the builders rejected is become the head of the corner:"
2. Samuel Johnson: "No man but a blockhead ever wrote, except for money." Cited in Boswell's *Life of Johnson* (1791), under the year 1776.
3. HPL apparently refers to Price's suggestion that his colleagues write letters to the editor in commendation of his story "The Peacock's Bride" (*WT*, August 1932). Although no letters by HPL's colleagues about the story were actually published, the story was voted the most popular story in that issue, as noted in "The Eyrie" for October 1932.

[116]   [AHT]

Thor's-Daeg, 1932
[late July? 1932]

Imperial Incarnation of Incunabular Inspection:—

As for Hawkesworth[1]—I can well imagine how he felt, for we are now at about the same stage he thought he was at. The major mysteries of the planet have been plumbed—that is, all that seem likely ever to be plumbed—& it is doubtful if any of the devices of the future will have much of a thrill of novelty. There may indeed be strange new things, but these will not be likely to open up any radically fresh vista of knowledge in connexion with matters of common interest. More than that, the abnormal *frequency* of revolutionary discoveries in the past centuries has dulled our imaginations toward *the principle of radical discovery itself;* in other words, we are so *used* to new, strange things that a successful trip to Saturn would not give the average person nearly so great a thrill as the invention of the telephone did in its day. Emotional *freshness* is today denied us. If we have not indeed 'seen it all', we have at least formed *so fatally familiar an idea of what new experiences are like* that novelty will never pack the old-time kick again.

My aunt gets home tomorrow. I'm going over now to put a nice card in her window against that event.

Peace be with you.

Yr obt

Θεοβάλδος

Notes

1. Apparently a reference to John Hawkesworth (1720–1773), British essayist, dramatist, and translator, and friend of Samuel Johnson. HPL may be specifically alluding to Hawkesworth's *Voyages* (1773), a best-selling account of voyages to the South Seas based on the journals of Captain James Cook and others.

[117]   [AHT]

On the Railway Coach in the New-Hampshire
Grants, lately call'd the province of Vermont
Septr. 3, 1932, 3 a.m.

Egregious Epitome of Exalted Eminence:—

O gawd, O Montreal . . . . at last I am bound for the latter & more genuine of the immortal two! But a moving railway carriage is not a distinguish'd aid to the art of calligraphy.

Second start—the train has stopt at Newport (not the one we lately visited), but it's so damn cold that I can hardly guide a pen. Hell, but they ought to heat this beastly carriage! And yet it was hot in Bostonium—eighty-six degrees at noon—so that I felt fine and full of pep but a few short hours ago.

Still—I'll get all pepp'd up again when the train crosses into territory still loyal to our rightful sovereign. Patriotick glow will conquer the chills of the arctick—God Save the King!

Well—the card from me an' Culinarius no doubt appris'd you of our eclipse success. Grandpa is in the two-corona class now—whereas you may get a rainy day in Peru in '37! In Prov. I am told it was rainy. Boston got a good view of its 99% obscuration—but as near as Medford it was half-ruin'd by clouds. I'm hoping that Smithy had as good luck at Haverhill (two sec. totality) as we did at Newburyport.

As for harrowing details—we reached Bossy Gillis's burg long before the eclipse started, & chose an hilltop meadow with a wide view—near the northern end of High Street—as our observatory. The sky was mottled, & naturally we were damn anxious—but the sun came out every little while & gave us long glimpses of the waxing spectacle. The aspect of the landskip did not change in tone until the solar crescent was rather small, & then a kind of sunset vividness became apparent. When the crescent waned to extreme thinness, the scene grew strange & spectral—an almost deathlike quality inhering in the sickly yellowish light. Just about that time the sun went under a cloud, & our expedition commenced cursing in 33 1/3 different languages including Ido.[1] At last, though, the thin thread of the pre-totality glitter emerged into a large patch of absolutely clear sky. The outspread valleys faded into unnatural night—Jupiter came out in the deep-violet heavens—ghoulish shadow-bands raced along the winding white clouds—the last beaded strip of glitter vanished—& the pale corona flicker'd into aureolar radiance around the black disc of the obscuring moon. We were seeing the real show! Though Newburyport was by no means close to the line of maximum duration, the totality lasted for a surprisingly long time—long enough for the impression to sink ineffaceably in. It would have been foolish if we had gone up to the crowded central line in Maine or New Hampshire. The earth was darken'd much more pronouncedly than in our marrow-congealing ordeal of '25, (the coldness of this damn train takes my memory back to that harrowing occasion!) tho' the corona was not so bright. There was a suggestion of a streamer extending above and to the left of the disc, with a shorter corresponding streamer below and to the right. We absorb'd the whole exhibition with open eyes and gaping mouths—I chalking down II whilst Khul-i-N'hari had to be content with I. Too bad about youse poor one-eclipse guys! Finally the beaded crescent reëmerged, the valleys glow'd again in faint, eerie light, & the various partial phases were repeated in reverse order. The marvel was over, & accustom'd things resum'd their wonted sway.

Well—I hopped this freight at eight-forty-five last night, & it was supposed to get to Montreal at eight-ten today—but hades, what delay! I think it's going to camp out at Newport . . . . . maybe they're setting this car in a permanent place as a quick-lunch diner or summer house or something. Here it is five-thirty-five a.m., & Montreal an hundred miles away. Not that I'd kick if they'd only give us some heat. And why the hell couldn't this stalling have occurr'd on His Maj^{ty's} loyal soil, which is but a mineral's trajectory away?

As for the future of discovery—& of human attitudes toward discovery—accurate prediction is naturally impossible, but it's an unobservant guy who doesn't see the growing apathy of the jaded race toward extensions of the frontier. About the only bunch with any feeling of freshness are the goddam bolsheviks—& they'll begin to yawn as soon as they get civilised & lose the novelty of their venture.

As for Wendell P.[2]—he may have had the gift of gab, but I haven't much of an opinion of oratory. It's an amusing accomplishment, but wholly without value as a means of reaching truth. Indeed, it is probably a harmful rather than wholesome influence, since its effect is to move emotion through rhetorical arts irrelevant to truth, & therefore to sway opinion in directions which may conceivably be, & often are, wholly false. In a contest of orators, the most polished & subtle actor—*not* the man with the truest case behind him—is apt to be the winner. The whole process seeks the inculcation of some preconceived & arbitrary opinion, rather than the discovery of *what really is,* irrespective of wishes or consequences. That is why I never feel that I have achieved a real victory when I silence an opponent in an oral argument. The chances are that I may have merely put forth the most showy side of my case & hypnotised him into temporary acquiescence. I don't begin to crow till I have put everything on paper in such a way that he can analyse & reply to my contentions without haste or interruption. No *real* conviction is ever arriv'd at through manner of presentation. Only the *facts themselves,* brought out piecemeal, conscientiously, & without rhetorical flourishes, can be the basis of any legitimate change of opinion. Oratory is for children—it belongs to the naive youth of a race or culture—whilst slow, written scientifick argument is for mature & complexly civilis'd man. God Save the King!

Extry—the damn train is *moving* again! What *can* have happen'd? I'll leave this screed unseal'd & slip in some postcards—safe from Paul Pry—when or if I get to the antient trading post of Hochelaga.[3]

Farewell—& may the saints & the Vargin be with you.

Yr obt Grandsire

Θεοβάλδος

Notes

1. A constructed language that first appeared in 1907, intended to reform perceived flaws in Esperanto that supporters believed to be a hindrance in its propagation as an easy-to-learn second language.

2. Wendell Phillips (1811–1884), American abolitionist and orator.

3. Hochelaga (*beaver dam* or *beaver lake*) was a 16th-century St. Lawrence Iroquoian fortified village at the heart of, or in the immediate vicinity of, Mont Royal in present-day Montreal.

[118]   [AHT]

Septr. 21, 1932

Rex of Rigorous, Recondite, & Rocky Research:—

Good luck on your travels—of which I envy you, geographically, the Philadelphia trip. I fancy that my 1932 wanderings are over—both for financial reasons, & because of the waning temperature. The cold days have taken all the energy out of me, so that the present week has been devoted largely to sick headaches & sleep. Today seems a bit milder, so I may dress & get my dinner down town. Wandrei's visit was delightful, tho' hamper'd by poor weather & by the visitor's bad case of sunburn—which prevented any great pedestrian or other activity. He will be in to see you before he leaves the pest zone for good. Not a bit of change in him since good old 1927—a great boy! My other guest, Carl Ferdinand Strauch—poet & Asst. Librarian of Muhlenberg University (a friend of Brobst's)—was also highly interesting, & very appreciative of the local antiquities & and-wheres. I took both of the children (whose sojourns, unfortunately, did not overlap) to see the famous Harris Collection of American Poetry (finest in the world) at the John Hay Library of Brown University, & they were extremely interested in its contents—which includes Belknap, Loveman, Coates, Goodenough, Pearson, & *David V. Bush* in both "before" & "after" states. Perusal of "Mr. Muling" and "Suppose" convuls'd both young Strauch & the librarian. Wandrei's quest at the collection concerned a very fine but forgotten Massachusetts poet—Frederick Tuckerman—who although writing in the Victorian aera escap'd many of its most absurd characteristicks; also an Harvard youth, Park Barnitz, who killed himself after publishing a remarkable volume of decadent verse (1902) entitled "The Book of Jade" & dedicated to Baudelaire.

As for oratory—I am not insensible that publick speaking has its smoothly pleasing side, or that it forms a graceful decoration for many ceremonial occasions. Indeed, I wou'd be the last to advocate a complete abandonment of instruction in the arts of harmonious address. At the same time, I conceive it to be a very *minor* art, like that of the actor—in fact, it is necessarily even below the actor's art, since it affords less opportunity for the infusion of creative originality. The orator contributes virtually nothing but agreeable sound, & even this is not as closely knit to any really substantial foundation as are the agreeable sounds of musick or poetry. It is an art which can profoundly delight only relatively naive & primitive cultures—or such other cultures as have (like the Greek) been anomalously backward in the single matter of literacy. It is well known that the Greeks were astonishingly late in developing either a written literature or a widespread use of writing—hence the disproportionate emphasis among them of the merely mechanical arts of the smooth oral speaker. Essentially, it cannot be denied that oratory swiftly loses its appeal among a people devoted to rational analysis & generally adult habits of thought. The unctuous intonations, so redolent of *feigned* emotion; the childish *gestures*, so reminiscent of savage gyrations & primitive modes of expression; the exaggerated emphases, so hollow to realistically trained auditors—all these things, & more, militate against the success of oratory among a thoroughly mature & disillusion'd people. Hortensius, & even Cicero, would be laughed out of any modern publick assemblage; & I'd hate to think of what a witty modern columnist would do to poor old spread-eagle Dan Webster![1] The whole psychology behind formal oratory has evaporated. Then, too, it *certainly cannot* be denied that the *chief use* of oratory was always an hortatory one—involving, as I have pointed out before, an attempt to convince without regard to truth. The really sound residue of the art of publick speaking is, as I have just mention'd, that phase which has to do with graceful ceremonial utterances. This differs widely from old-time oratory in its restraint, realistic sincerity, & absence of meretricious tropes & gestures. Publick speaking in legislative bodies has very sensibly withdrawn itself from the oily domain of oratorical rhetorick. The civilised legislator (whenever one manages to get in office under a democracy-feigning plutocracy) does not spout periods, but simply talks facts. The moment that ostentatious feigned emotion appears, the intelligent spectator begins to laugh. Legislation calls for no oratory, but simply for the dry, crisp speech which knows what it is saying.

As for the psychologist's symposium—some of the emotionally tinged replies are amusing. Actually, of course, psychology alone is wholly incapable of judging the inevitability of war. It is only a correlation of psychology, history, & anthropology which proves that war is the inescapable outcome of man's natural ego-assertion under conditions which bring dissimilar groups in contact.

Well—good luck with rocks 'n' everything!

Yr obt

Θεοβάλδος

P. S. Congrats on honours from the puzzlers.

You'll notice I'm trying out an allegedly black ink.

Sir Arthur Keith is presenting new anthropological data tentatively indicating that the human races are separated by *far wider gulfs* than anyone has ever suspected. He now doubts *whether we have any common human ancestor with negroes & australoids*, & believes the Australians are descended from the Java pithecanthropus.

Note the enclosed catalogue from Sonny. The little fool is selling off all

his carefully accumulated books just to get a few immediate cents to spend!
Give him a spanking for me!

Hope the Paterson Puzzlers' convention won't prove too vast a burthen!

Notes

1. Daniel Webster was accused in his day of using "spread-eagle" oratory, or oratory
characterized by bombast and rhetorical figures.

[119]   [AHT]

Tenbarnes—Jany. 12, 1933

Emperor of Esoteric Elusiveness:—

Ecce! Whilst you were in classick Cantabrigia writing Grandpa that you
couldn't get to Providentium, an aged man was sitting in a telephone booth
in the United Cigar Store at the corner of 8th Street & 6th Avenue, Manhattan, calling Sherwood 2-4820, & receiving the dismal news that Curator Morton wou'd not be back on the job till the following Tuesday! Thus does Fate
conspire to keep great souls apart. But what, you may ask, could 8th Street &
6th Avenue have to do with Old Theobald? Well—it's this way. Just before
Christmas I received an invitation from Papa & Mamma Long to drop
around for the holidays and surprise Little Sonny out of a whole year's
moustachelet-growth. Reflecting on the probable mildness of the weather,
the anti-cold protection afforded by the pest zone's subway system, & the
reduced stagecoach fares—eight shillings & four pence—to that noxious
region, I decided to accept—tho' reserving Christmas Day itself for a dinner
& exchange of remembrances with my aunt in a civilised Providence setting.
Behold me, then, on Dec. 26 at two-ten a.m., embarking upon the New Am-
sterdam coach of the New-England Transportation Co.—heavy with the
annual feast consum'd eleven hours previously. The route is somewhat
changed, so that I was whirl'd through Olneyville, North Scituate, Foster,
Danielson, Willimantic, & Hartford before being dropt down to New-Haven
& along the familiar shoar line route. My sentiments were of mingled homesickness at leaving New-England, & of tantalisation at being headed toward
Richmond, Charleston, & St. Augustine without being able to continue
thereto. Dawn came in the neighbourhood of Darien, in His Maj^{ty's} Colony
of Connecticut, & some time later I took my customary glance at the odd
spire of St. Paul's Church in Eastchester—my visit to which was so curiously
deferr'd in bygone days. The coach, having pass'd thro' Fordham, enter'd
New-York by the way of Bloomingdale Road, so that I was set down
squarely at Belknap's door at eight-thirty a.m., without any descent into the
miasmatick reaches of lower Manhattan. The Child was still abed, but Pa &
Ma smuggled the old gentleman into the dining room. When at length Sonny
did toddle drowsily out to breakfast he was properly electrified to see his

Grandpa nodding over the morning *Tribune*—& then & there began a session of arguments on everything from bolshevism to the Iroquois Indians, which lasted till eleven-thirty p.m., Jany. 2. I was provided with a room in the flat next door (where I had one in 1930), so that the visit was very conveniently centralised. At three-thirty p.m. came my *second* Christmas dinner of the year—after which I foreswore the scales until the completion of a suitable reducing programme. The next day I gave Loveman a surprise at Dauber and Pine's, dropt in on Kirk, visited the Whitney Museum, & sent my vain message to Patersonium as chronicled at the outset. I also did some fountain-pen changing at the Waterman office, tho' I am not yet satisfy'd with the result. I simply *cannot* get anything free-flowing enough for my light touch & speed of writing. Wednesday I surprised Talman at his office, and looked Wandrei up in his Greenwich-Village eyrie—84 Horatio Street, Apt. 4-B. The kid is finishing a novel which he began in September, & doesn't seem to want to go home.[1] That night I also met Sonny's hack writer friend Neil Moran[2]—for the first time, though for years we have been *almost* meeting. He seems to be a very pleasant chap—have you met him? I also went over to Loveman's new flat at 17 Middagh Street—where for the first time his various art treasures are adequately display'd. My generous host presented me with two fine museum objects (don't get envious, O Fellow-Curator!)—to wit, a prehistorick stone eikon from Mexico, & an African flint implement, with primitively graven ivory handle; both from the collection of the late Hart Crane, which Crane's mother turned over to him. Thursday Sonny, Wandrei, & I did the Metropolitan Museum, viewing the newly acquired archaick Greek Apollo about which so much has been written. Friday the Child and I argued all day except for a cinema show to which he dragg'd me. Incidentally, I was cinema'd nearly every night—marking my first sight of such performances since last June, when I view'd cinemas under the same auspices. Friday night there was a gang meeting at two-thirty, attended only by Wandrei, Loveman, McGrath, and good old Leeds—who has a job at Coney Island in a place where used correspondence-school courses are sold by mail. Talman and Kirk couldn't come, & Kleiner didn't answer our postcard notice. Orton didn't get our notice till Monday, when he telephoned—too late for a personal meeting. He expects to pass thro' Providence shortly. Saturday Moran, Wandrei, Sonny, & I did the Am. Mus. of Nat. History, & later that night I saw the old year out at Loveman's. Sunday I saw the inside of the new Riverside Church (but Gothick stuff!) for the first time, & did the Brooklyn Museum with Sonny—seeing the new Dutch rooms. On this occasion I had the Child take his first ride on the new 8th Avenue subway—a contraption which I had sampled alone on the preceding Thursday. Monday Sonny & I explored the newly housed Museum of Modern Art—11 West 53d Street—seeing the delightful collection of "American Primitives" on the top floor, & paying our respects to Whistler's famous painting of his mother (lent by the Louvre)[3] . . . . . which Sonny, however, thought a bit bourgeois, Puritanical, & commonplace. That afternoon at three-thirty came *another* gargantuan turkey gorge—my third of the holiday season, & fourth of the fall & winter, counting Thanksgiving. Gawd keep me away from the scales!

Then more argument & cinema . . . . . & finally a session of argument again. At eleven-thirty I departed for the 'bus terminal (return route uncertain*—had to take the thing at the source) & was in ample time for the twelve-ten coach. The route this time was shore line to New-Haven, then up to Middletown, & then across to Willimantic, cutting out Hartford. Dawn came at North-Scituate, in His Majesty's Colony of *Rhode-Island & Providence-Plantations*, and at six-forty-five a.m. I was deposited in the terminal in my native town. God Save the King! I found twenty-two letters awaiting me—besides oceans of piled-up periodicals—& am still wallowing in this accumulation. It's a great life!

But *one* item of that accumulation demands a paragraph by itself—not only a paragraph, but a poem and a paean! It was a package from good old Cook . . . . . . a gift derived from his ruthlessly self-disintegrated library. A three-volume gift printed in 1892 & now out of print . . . . . & something for which I have been pining since 1919. Can I name it without dangerous cardiack palpitations? Behold, Sir—your Grandpa is at last the proud and extatick owner of *MELMOTH, THE WANDERER, by Charles Robert Maturin!*

As for Mr. Hemingway—opinions may well differ on the exact amount of sanguinary virility best fitted for daily life, but these extremist dicta are well worth recording for correlation with the effeminate pacificism & supineness of other extreme schools of thought. Which reminds me—you simply *must* read Prof. Walter B. Pitkin's "History of Human Stupidity", which I read during my visit to Little Belknap. Oh, boy—how he socks your pet notion of nigger equality! He gives the African mind a searching survey that ought to keep the neo-abolitionist element quiet for a while! But as for a philosophick volume of my own—I'm afraid that's rather a large order for a rank layman whose views are really very far from original or unique. Amidst the uncertainties of this age, all prediction is really puerile. A monotonous letdown period—a social revolution & communism—a feudal fascist state—an early general war, complete breakdown, & new barbarism—it's anybody's guess! I heard Prof. J. B. S. Haldane lecture at Brown on the future—& biology's part in it—early last month; & much that he said was true, tho' all long-term prophecies are largely bunk. Enclosed are some cuttings which may be of interest. I'd choose "basick English" to Volapuk[4] any day!

---

*As it turn'd out, the coach left over Central Park West.

And so it goes. Here's hoping you won't be on the move when or if I get around the pest zone during the spring.

Pax vobiscum—

Θεοβάλδος

Notes

1. *Invisible Sun,* a mainstream novel first published in 2011.

2. Neil Moran published chiefly in the detective pulps.

3. James McNeill Whistler (1834–1903), "Arrangement in Grey and Black: Portrait of the Painter's Mother" (popularly known as "Whistler's Mother") (1871), Musée d'Orsay, Paris.

4. Volapük, a constructed international language, created in 1879–80 by Johann Martin Schleyer, a Roman Catholic priest in Baden, Germany. It was largely displaced in the late 19th and early 20th centuries by Esperanto, Ido, and Interlingua.

[120]   [AHT]

Jan. 13, 1933

Have just heard of a rival to Maxfield's—Chauncey E. Green, of Hope Valley, R. I., who offers *137 varieties* of ice cream—though not all are on sale on any one day. Some of the bizarre flavours are *pond lily, pepsin, mango, wild bee honey, dangleberry, manzanita, sweet corn, guava, & snow apple.* Aunt Julia will surely have to go some to lick Chauncey on variety! We'll have to investigate Chauncey. Westerly coaches pass through Hope Valley (so do the New York Greyhounds), but the fare is probably rather formidable. I've never been off the coach there, but it's a delightfully idyllick early-American village which tantalises me every time I whizz through it. I get this dope on Chauncey from a newspaper writeup. Only twelve old reliable staples, the same all the year round, & six exotic brands, changed daily. It would take more than twenty visits to clean up Chauncey's repertoire.

[121]   [AHT]

Theobald Abbey, 1933—Dark of the Moon

Corona of Coruscating Competence:—

As for warfare—with a little common sense it isn't even necessary to call upon the sciences for predictions. We all know from experience that the natural man reaches out for what he wants—& gets if if he has the opportunity & physical strength to do so. We know likewise that no normal & elemental human animal can be cajoled or argued out of wanting what he wants, or of trying to grab it if he has any chance of getting away with it. It is very easy to get people to agree to high-sounding principles—but if their underlying instincts are all set toward a certain goal, they'll forget all about the sonorous theories the first moment they get a chance to snatch what they're really after. All civilisation & all ethical idealism are so flimsily superficial that it is at once pathetic, absurd, & dangerous to base any policy or way of life upon an assumption of their dependable functioning. The law of life is "dog eat dog". Men will listen just so long to owlish & abstract principles—& then kick over the traces & do just as the primal ape within tells them to do! Nor is it likely that more than a few human groups will ever have the patience to listen at all to the preachers of idealistic palliatives & panaceas. As for oratory—as I said before, I don't deny it a place among the pleasing secondary arts. I merely fail to see how it justly deserves the extremely & disproportionately high valuation placed upon it in former times.

Gladda you maybe getta de costoom' for-a Mariano! Hope-a he sells de beeg load of-a talca. You see wotta de beeg science-a man he tella you—no can beata good ol' Providenchia! If I can, I'll try to see what Sig. de Magistris has on hand these days—though I doubt if it can be much. Anyhow, next time I see him I'll tell him who's responsible for the Ward inquiry.

About stamps—I'll try to remember that 11¢ is your new low limit for contemporary regulars. I didn't know you were out for commemoratives, but have been sending all these to good old Tryout!

And so it goes. Any gang meetings lately?

Yrs with forehead to the ground—

Θεοβάλδος

[122]   [AHT]

Tenbarnes—Jany. 26, 1933

Inspir'd Imperator of Investigative Ingenuity:—

Yes—we shine alone among the Melmoth'd! It's damn curious that Culinarius didn't mention his possession of the volumes in past years, for he must have known of my avidity for them. Anyhow, the work's on the Theobald shelves now—& it will certainly take a general cataclysm to get it off 'em! Now may gawd grant me a bit of leisure for reading it through.

As for oeconomy—I may yet beat the records of both your early self & old Sunrise Walker. At Clinton street I occasionally got fodder down to 70¢ per week, although my ignorance of effective laundry methods (for my education in really drastick budgetary limitation did not begin till Jany. 1, 1925) annull'd the good effects of this & brought my bills up to a most unfortunate total. Now my food bill is from two to three dollars weekly, while my laundry has sunk to not more than a dollar a month—less than it used to be per week! You ought to see Grandpa tackle a shirt, or even a soft collar! I do the latter with a toothbrush—which will get off 0.8 of the grime & can get a pseudo-iron'd effect from flat drying. I've also told you of my self-barbering with the device (to hitch on to a Gillette) purchased in 1929 for one dollar. The longer I use it, the better sort of an haircut I can give myself—piecing out with scissors for the graduations around the back of the neck. It is said that the Belgian stratospherist Prof. Piccard[1] cuts his own hair—but when I look at the result in newspaper portraits I feel I am the greater artist! Of course, some of the difference may be due to the dollar machine—but even allowing for that, I have a feeling that M. Auguste's tonsorial taste isn't all it might be. But then—what a rotten stratospherist I'd make!

As for a list of ancestral names—here's the New England dope: Phillips, Place, Rathbone, Whipple, Casey, Perkins, Mathewson, Dyer, Wilcox, Godfrey, Millard, Fish, Ellis, Hazard, Safford, Clemence, Malavery, Dodge, Brownell, West, Newman, Field, Gater.

My interest grows languid & academic as names recede toward the Domesday Book or pre-Renaissance oblivion, since the amount of any one strain of blood I may inherit from such a date is virtually negligible. So long as it isn't nigger or australoid, I don't kick. I hate the Middle Ages so, that I don't take much satisfaction in establishing a linkage with them. If I could only get back to *classical antiquity*, that would be another matter. In imagination I permit myself to fancy that some of the Welshmen in my line may be descended from *Roman* officers in the legions of Cn. Julius Agricola, P. Ostorius Scapula, Q. Lollius Urbicus, & other conquerors or rulers of the Province of Britannia. S. P. Q. R.! God Save the King! Vivant Roma atque Britannia, Imperatrices Mundi & Luces Orbis Terrarum![2] The She-Wolf and the Lion—aeternal and unassailable!

As for Basick English . . . . well, Sir, *I'll* stick to the English of Mr. Addison & Dean Swift! Some day I hope we shall conquer the rest of the world & impose our language upon it—tho' permitting inferior dialects to remain in our curricula as picturesque dead languages. Or else I'm in favor of reviving Latin as the international speech, as it once was. No synthetic dope for Grandpa!

By the way—here's Klarkash-Ton's "Vathek"[3] ending . . . . . which please return at your leisure. Brobst & Strauch find it a bit disappointing, but when I consider the magnitude of the task I cannot feel that the High-Priest of Tsathoggua has done so ill. Much of the Gallick pseudo-Orientalism of Mr. Beckford is very well recaptur'd.

As for lost continents—as I've pointed out, geological & physiographical evidence are against any Atlantick body of land's having existed *since the development of mankind*. In the Pacifick, the most we can say is that the number of islands undoubtedly varies in the course of ages. The Cyclopean ruins on Ponape & Nan-Matal, & the titanick eikons of Easter Island, are probably reliques of a culture which was archipelogick rather than continental, but which may have been instrumental in transmitting certain art forms & folkways from Indo-China to Central America in prehistorick times.

Sometime I may write a compendium of universal philosophy with my favourite cosmos-query "What is Anything?" as a title . . . . but for the present my time & energy are chain'd up by more modest tasks! Incidentally—I chuckle to see many of my views on the displacement of labour by machinery very authoritatively & concretely confirm'd by the investigators of the important (even if capitalistically ridiculed & persecuted) "technocracy" group.

Gladda you maka de sale for-a Signor Mariano's nice-a talca! Gooda rakeoff! I'll finda de way for tella Marian' you helpa heem—den mebbe he feexa you up fina weed rocks for all for-a nawt'n!

And so it goes. Hope we can get together over some of Chauncey's pond lilly & sweet corn ice cream next summer!

   Yr obt Servt

    Θεοβάλδος

Notes

1. Auguste Antoine Piccard (1884–1962), Swiss physicist, inventor, and explorer.
2. "Long live Rome and Britain, empresses of the world and lights of the earth!"
3. "The Third Episode of Vathek," completed from a fragment by William Beckford.

[123] [AHT]

          January over, Thank Yuggoth!,
             [c. 1 February] 1933

Fulgent Finial of Family Fact-Finding:—

So you knew in advance, eh, of the coming of Melmoth? Good old Culinarius! No—I won't tell him of your revelation of foreknowledge. I'm really accumulating a surprising charity library—*six* new volumes (all weird anthologies) from Derleth the other day—discards from his collection. One of them (Bohun Lynch's "Best Ghost Stories") contains Blackwood's "Willows"—hence ecstatic rejoicings on my part. By the way—you're the guy who originally brought Algernon to my notice; a circumstance which earns you my immortal gratitude.

And speaking of charity—these lines are incised with the stylus of another old controversy-pal of yours . . . . . none other than Ernie Edkins of the Halcyon Age. I happened to be discussing fountain-pen woes with him some time ago—mentioning that I can never get a pen to flow freely enough—when lo! he shot me this massive Parker, which he says he can't use because it's *too* free-flowing for him. For *me* the feed is exactly right—but the point is too damn stubby. I may try to see about changing the point—if it can be done without jazzing up the feed. This is the second charity pen I've had—good old Moe having given me a Conklin (left on a desk in his classroom & never claimed) in 1923, when I lost my 1906 Waterman amidst the sands of Marblehead. Easy come, easy go. In March 1926 I lent it to Loveman, & when I made inquiries after returning home from the pest zone in April he couldn't seem to find it. I wonder who'll lose this Parker for me? If all Parkers feed like this, I think I'll shift my loyalty from Watermans. Good old Edkins!

At this point the charity Parker ran dry. Now I'm going to see how it works with Waterman's ink—which I hope won't show any commercial jealousy. This is a bit thinner than the Carter's Kongo Black which (sensible of the proper servile functions of Africk blackness) I've been using since last September. Edkins uses Sheaffer's Skrip (so does my aunt)—which is probably the best of all, although it costs more than the dime-per-2 oz.-bottle Waterman & Kongo. Œconomy always bulks large on the Theobald programme.

As for good English—if anyone can shew any real improvement in structure since Mr. Addison's time, I am willing to consider it; but so far as I can see, most changes since then have been in the direction of affectation & tawdriness. Contemporary prose is especially poor—as was that of the 1780–1850 period. Oddly—much of the prose *syntax* of the Victorian aera (when content was so tawdry) was of almost classical excellence. And as for world conquest—time will tell. I certainly wish we had the virility today which Japan is shewing . . . . . the *bushido* of the samurai is what in better days was the honour of an English gentleman.

I surely hope the more optimistic museum news will prove correct. Too bad the Agassiz castoffs[1] aren't likely to be reasonable in price.

Heard a good poetry reading by Robt. Hillyer[2] Sunday. Next week, Leonard Bacon[3]—& Feby. 19th, T. S. Eliot.

And so it goes.

Yrs. for Hitler & Mussolini & Araki
Θεοβάλδος

Notes

1. Apparently some specimens from the Louis Agassiz Museum of Comparative Zoology at Harvard University, established in 1859 by Swiss palaeontologist Louis Agassiz (1807–1873), professor of zoology and geology at Harvard (1847–73).

2. Robert Hillyer (1895–1961), American poet, essayist, and translator. He won the Pulitzer Prize for his *Collected Verse* (1933).

3. Leonard Bacon (1887–1954), American satirist and poet, winner of the Pulitzer Prize for poetry in 1940 for his book *Sunderland Capture*. His *Lost Buffalo and Other Poems* appeared in 1930. "Although a thorough & ancestral Rhode Islander, he has a wide reputation as an intelligent satirist. I have I [*sic*] always liked his stuff, since to me it seems to have something of the 18th century in it" (HPL to Elizabeth Toldridge, 25 March 1933; ms., JHL). HPL heard him speak on 3 February.

[124] [AHT]

March 9, 1933

Paramount Pinnacle of Progenitorial Pursuit:—

Say—when you go in for a thing you sure *do* go in for it! And I thought *Talman* was a genealogist! No use talking—we Yankees do beat the Dutch!

Old Charley & Norman Bill aren't a bit bad to be descended from—though Saxon Egbert mixes rather harshly with the conquering invader. Better watch out lest your blue corpuscles reënact the Battle of Hastings in your veins! I infer from your account that you're backing Eggie just now. Well—that's all right. I can lick the whole bunch of you—for my Jack Parry claims descent from Owen Gwynedd, Prince of North Wales—the real Cymric stuff, that was paramount & Romanly civilised for centuries before you damn'd Saxons (here, shut up, you Lovecraft & Phillips & Perkins & other strains!) ever knew there was such an island as Britannia! Cna dhy gllyd llnaf lha mynnedd!

Glad your puzzler's convention was a wow. I was cheated of your speech by the hellish cold prevailing on Mr. Hoag's birthday. The mercury was hideously below twenty degrees, & I realised that I could never get over to my aunt's without hiring an hackney-coach, for which I had not the cash.

As for fountain pens—I still can't get a decent point for the Parker Edkins gave me . . . . but shall try again. I'm now dipping a Woolworth pen in Carter's Kongo Black. I'll give Parker's "Quink" a try later on. Just now (in the Waterman at present forming my best pen) I'm using Sheaffer's "Skrip" with very good results. The trouble is that it costs fifteen cents for a bottle much smaller than a dime bottle of Carter's Kongo. That's why—at home—I use Kongo & revert to dipping—saving the Skrip for next summer, when I do my writing on the wooded riverbank away from dipping facilities.

Sympathy on the salary—& congrats that it was no worse! Cook's firm has closed down for an indefinite period, so that he is quite up against it. Campbell is down & out—& with his only ankle broken. Lynch is in desperate straits. Mrs. Miniter is penniless & cannot look ahead—Miss Beebe having had another shock. My own prospects are alarming—may have to give up #10 soon. What a world! John M. Samples—the old-time Silver Clarion—is now a Salvation Army officer & has just been put in charge of a mission at Macon. We'd all better enlist his sympathetic interest!

Hope to see you in August.

Yr obt Servt

Θεοβάλδος

These *oulothrix* Norwegians—so different from the merely wavy-haired Ithacan Greek Eurybates—certainly do present quite a puzzle . . . . altho' frizzy hair does appear sometimes in conclusively non-negroid stocks. The Mongoloid Jewish types of Central Europe abound in frizzly type specimens. The self-barbering quality of this Norse wool ought to make it quite desirable in this tense period—no haircut bills to incur!

Incidentally—the possibility of nigg— (excuse me—*artistically tinted*) blood in Denmark after 1750 or so wouldn't be as slight as in Norway, on account of the Danish West Indies. Whitehead said that the absorption of half-castes into even the Danish nobility was an actual & disconcerting fact.

[125]   [AHT]

March 22, 1933

Immortal Inheritor of Infinite Imperial Insignia:—

Gawdamighty, but how you *can* research once you start researching! Most certainly & seriously, you ought to embody the results of all this in a book—or even several books, each devoted to some especially distinctive line. Such a volume or volumes would have just as much permanent value for later searchers as earlier volumes have had for you in your own quest. Even Talman, whose investigations would appear to be far less profound, has embodied his findings in a book manuscript for whose ultimate publication he hopes. And to think that all this delving is, in a sense, only *preliminary*—to be follow'd by original explorations of the courthouse & the churchyard! I pause aghast & spellbound, in that admiration which cannot aspire to emulation! Your galaxy of royalty quite floors me! Byzantine Emperor, Russian Czar, German Kaiser, Spanish King, Irish King . . . . . & what have you! Why, damn it all, what does the world need of division when all its parts have but one legal Sovereign? To hell with upstarts & pretenders—let every land own the sway of a true English Plantagenet, & submerge its quarrels in one lasting Pax Britannica! Oh, well—there are one or two kings left over for other folks, anyway. Besides Owen Gwynedd I have another Welsh monarch somewhere at the end of a Carew-contributing line, & according to O'Hart's Pedigrees my Caseys are descended from Baudoin Ui Niall (O'Neill), 137th King of Ireland. Begorra, Oi wondther if that's afther makin' mesilf a cousin to the dhrammer-wroiter Eugene O'Neill? But what I want is a real Roman consul of the old respublica—none of your decadent Byzantines! I want to set up the masks of the Fabii, the Cornelii, the Valerii, the Æmilii, the Licinii, the Julii, the Claudii, & so on in my atrium. I feel quite certain that some legatus or centurio of the old stock, settling in Britannia after the conquests of Cn. Julius Agricola, married into the Silures & became one of my remote Welsh progenitors.

Am in a record-breaking turmoil of labour—with the prospect of an 80,000-word novel (for revision at starvation rates) in the offing.[1] May Pegāna's gods have compassion!

Yr grovellingly obeisant Vassal—
Πάππος Θεοβάλδος

Notes

1. HPL alludes to this work in several letters, but never specifies the title or author. The novel probably was not published.

[126]   [AHT]

April 27th, 1933

Canlent Crown of Coelestial Creation:—

Hail, Offspring of Jove! I grovel, with a mortal's humility, before thy thunder-guarded throne! Who am I to dispute supremacy with the seed of antique Ocean, of Ida's (not Haughton!) cloud-piercing crest, of Venus Victrix, & of Pious Æneas? Alas—I have only daemons behind me—my heritage from the black crawling chaos being as follows:

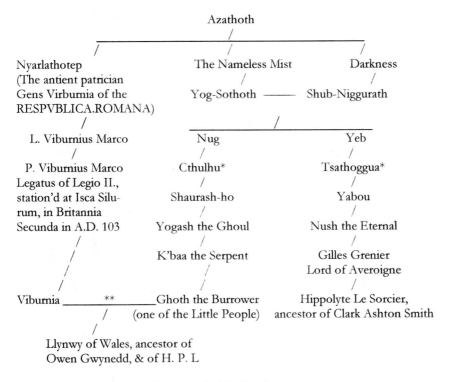

Azathoth
```
                          Azathoth
                             /
          /                  /                      /
Nyarlathotep          The Nameless Mist          Darkness
(The antient patrician        /                      /
Gens Viburnia of the   Yog-Sothoth ——— Shub-Niggurath
RESPVBLICA.ROMANA)
        /                    /
  L. Viburnius Marco        Nug                      Yeb
        /                    /                        /
  P. Viburnius Marco      Cthulhu*              Tsathoggua*
Legatus of Legio II.,       /                        /
station'd at Isca Silu-  Shaurash-ho              Yabou
rum, in Britannia           /                        /
Secunda in A.D. 103   Yogash the Ghoul        Nush the Eternal
        /                    /                        /
        /             K'baa the Serpent         Gilles Grenier
        /                    /                 Lord of Averoigne
        /                    /                        /
Viburnia ____**____  Ghoth the Burrower    Hippolyte Le Sorcier,
        /            (one of the Little People)  ancestor of Clark Ashton Smith
        /
Llynwy of Wales, ancestor of
Owen Gwynedd, & of H. P. L
```

*First of their respective lines to inhabit this planet.
**This union was an hellish & nameless tragedy.

Well—I wish you good luck in your own titanick researches, & hope you get the Smith line all straightened out from the illustrious founder of the gens down to Tryout & Klarkash-Ton! You've certain got Talman licked as a forbear-exhumer; & as I said before, you really ought to publish the result of your labours in book form.

As for me—I stand poised on the brink of Chaos & Ultimate Horror. When you visit these Plantations in the summer you will not cross the familiar threshold of #10, for Grandpa will not be there. Poverty takes its toll; &

as I think I mention'd once before, I shall shortly have to light out for cheaper quarters despite the strong attachment to #10 which seven years of peaceful & congenial residence have bred. Eheu fugaces![1] I don't know whether I shall ever manage to survive the hellish process of uprooting, furniture removal, & re-settlement . . . . . here's hoping your geologist's hammer, knapsack, chisel, & magnets don't get lost in the shuffle. If they do, just file suit against my estate, & the executors will probably fix you up. In all events, gawd help us all! I'm now using up my Sunday-go-to-meetin' stationery in all correspondence, since the central line of its printed inscription will soon be mournfully obsolete; & am also winding up my earthly affairs—getting jobs finished, refusing others, trying to answer all my letters, & in general making my final peace with the world before passing into the long, long, night.

As for a destination—a full decision will not be reach'd till next week. It all depends on whether my aunt & I decide to double up in one cheap flat, or to continue with independent quarters. If the former, we shall probably take

the upper floor of a *real Georgian house* (circa 1800–1810) which lies in a delightfully grassy, secluded, & and-whereish court off College street on the crest of the antient hill beyond the John Hay Library.[2] It is own'd by the college, & heated by steam piped from the library. There are five rooms & a storage attic without cupola—& the *doorway* is a virtual embodiment of my Talman-drawn bookplate! The rent is only forty per month—what I've been paying for my room at #10 alone—which makes my share only twenty—less than a five-spot
per week. It will, if we take it, form the first Georgian house I shall ever have liv'd in—though of course my aunt had a room in the antient Beckwith house (Handicraft Club) a few doors below this grassy court in 1927, as you doubtless recall. I hope this deal goes through—it all depends on how well the interior is able to accommodate our joint furniture, & to provide independent living quarters for what amounts to two separate households with different hours & customs. We shall not be able to inspect the interior till May 1 or 2, since the present tenants do not leave until the former date.

Meanwhile another place—in a neighbourhood not quite so good—is being held in reserve for me in case the households do not merge. This is in the old Victorian Seagrave mansion down the hill in Benefit street, where the well-known astronomer F. E. Seagrave (now located in N.-Scituate) dwelt & had his observatory till 1914.[3] It is three doors north of "The Shunned House" which I embodied in a story, & some distance south of the hidden churchyard & the Mrs. Whitman home. On the ground floor of this joint there is an almost incredible value—a complete little apartment of large living-room, small bedroom, hallway, & bath—for only five bucks a week; & to this I shall turn if the colonial College street joint appears impracticable upon closer inspection. I am completely worn out hunting quarters—though it hath been a liberal education in the architecture of the antient hill. I've probably seen more *interiors* than I ever saw before—some of them tantalisingly colonial.

I suppose that Spring is here—though amidst my present chaos I can but imperfectly appreciate that heartening circumstance. Ora pro nobis. Next week—into the maelstrom!

Thine—

Πάππος Θεοβάλδος

Notes

1. *Eheu fugaces . . . labuntur anni* ("Alas, the fleeing years glide by"). Horace, *Odes* 2.14.1–2.

2. The Samuel B. Mumford house at 66 College Street (moved in 1959 to 65 Prospect Street) was actually built c. 1825.

3. Frank Evans Seagrave (1859–1934). The observatory, headquarters of the Skyscrapers, is now located at 47 Peeptoad Road, North Scituate, RI. Formerly it was located at 119 Benefit Street.

[127]   [AHT]

New Address, effective on and
after May 15: 66 College Street
Providence, Rhode-Island
Cold grey dawn of May 14, 1933

Orthochronous Offspring of Olympian Omnipotence:—

This historick epistle, the last to be writ by me from the time-hallow'd shades of 10 Barnes to any living soul, is to notify you of the new destination which you must seek this summer if you would commune with your hammer, knapsack, magnets, & chisel. Alas for terrestrial mutations! I hate to leave the old spot, & have dismantled as little as possible in view of the advent of the moving man—a stalwart buck nigger with a horse-drawn team—tomorrow. However, there are compensations. You will recall from my preceding bulletin that the choice lay betwixt a joint establishment with my aunt in *a real Georgian house* in a delightful and-where on College Hill, & an apartment for myself alone in the old Seagrave Mansion in Benefit Street. Well—the former won. The house was vacant for inspection May 1ˢᵗ, & it didn't take us three minutes to decide. Boy, what a place! God Save the King! At last—at last— after forty-odd years of wistful worship & avid admiration—Grandpa Theobald will live in a REAL COLONIAL HOUSE. Praise George from whom all blessings flow!!

The new Villa Theobalda—yellow & wooden—is situate on the crest of the antient hill in a quaint grassy court just off College Street—behind & next to the marble John Hay Library of Brown University, about half a mile south of here. It is near the top of the same hill (& on the same side) half-way up which my aunt boarded in 1927 at the Handicraft Club in the old Truman Beckwith house. You doubtless recall that brick edifice & its old-fashion'd terraced garden. It is just possible that I have pointed out the future Domus Theobaldianus to you at one time or another, since one of my aunt's best friends dwells in the lower half. (An antient spinster—a German teacher at the Classical High School,—who was pro-German during the late war, & who tho' the daughter of a Baptist divine hath in latter years been converted to the Popish Church!) My aunt has always had an eye half open for the upper flat whenever it might be vacant. The fine colonial doorway is like my Talman-drawn bookplate come to life, tho' of a slightly later period (circa 1800), with side lights & fan carving instead of a fanlight. Most unfortunately, a Victorian *door* has been inserted—but one can't expect everything. In the rear is a picturesque, village-like, and-whereish garden at a higher level than the front of the house. The upper flat we have taken contains five rooms besides bath & kitchenette nook on the main (second) floor, plus two attick storerooms—one of which is so attractive that I wish I could have it for an extra den! My quarters—a large study & a small bedroom—are on the south side, with my working table under a west window affording a splendid view of some of the lower town's outspread roofs & of the mystical sunsets that flame behind them. The interior is as fascinating as the exterior—with colonial fireplaces, mantels, & chimney cupboards, curving Georgian staircase, wide floor-boards, old-fashion'd latches, small-paned windows, six-panel doors, rear wing with floor at a different level (three steps down), quaint attick stairs, &c.—just like the various old houses open as museums. After admiring such all my life, I find something magical & dreamlike in the notion of *actually living in one* for the first time. To compensate for the built-in alcove shelves at #10, I have purchased three cheap bookcases & a cabinet to file papers in. All this doesn't sound much like an *economy* measure, & yet it is just that. The whole thing—for our two households—costs only what I've been paying for one room & alcove alone at #10. Steam heat & hot water are piped from the adjacent college library—the house being owned by the University.

But gawd, what a job moving will be! I've taken over some of the more fragile bric-a-brac, & have tied my loose papers & magazines into bales for the mover. The real hell will be at the new house, arranging things & re-sorting about 2000 books. May Cthulhu have mercy on me! My aunt isn't going to move in till after I am reasonably settled—if I survive the transitional ordeal.

E. Hoffmann Price is quitting New Orleans & will tarry in the pest zone for a while. I'm advising him to look up the good old gang, & have given him your address together with Talman's, Sonny's, Samuelus's, &c. You'll like him—an alert, voluble chap—highly intelligent, & a West Point graduate. His age is thirty-five.

My "Erich Zann" is just achieving its *5th* sale—this time to a cheap British anthology established by Denis Archer.[1]

Well—here's hoping your hammer, magnets, &c. won't get lost! Now to get my Haldeman-Julius booklets tied together to avoid shuffling.

Yrs from the brink of the Abyss—

Θεοβάλδος

Notes

1. The reprint did not occur, although HPL was paid for it.

[128]   [AHT]

Prospect Terrace on the Antient Hill—94° in the
shade by official reading . . . . . . feeling great
except for a cold wind which cuts through the
warmth. Hope there won't be a thunderstorm.
June 12, 1933

Century-Climbing Caesar of Carolingian Collidity:—

Boy, what a pedigree! I reel! I resign! Even an Irish King to match my Casey royalty . . . . . & a bunch of Castilian potentates to give you a central monicker! And Czars of Muscovy—why not go across & spite Little Sonny by claiming the Kremlin throne & knocking the bolsheviks to hell? And Swedes & Byzantines & Frenchies & Dagoes . . . . . cripes, you start where the League of Nations leaves off! I'm still looking for a Saracen Caliph & a Japanese Mikado amongst the polyglot royalty . . . . Oh, well . . . . wait till I take time to follow up two or three of the long lines on my chart that indicate labyrinthine linkages! I'll send my dollar for your de luxe tables later on.

This is my receiving day for the crown'd heads, for only this morning I heard our Sovereign's voice over the radio opening the oeconomick conference. Delightfully pleasant & musical—& it gave me the greatest kick I've felt since last treading the still-loyal soil of Quebec.

(Leaden clouds to the northwest. Shall I have to cut & run for cover? And yet, considering the Georgian cover I now have, that wouldn't be such a mephitick calamity!)

Well—all the Theobaldi are approximately settled at #66 at last. Gawd, what a joint! Our things fit in unbelievably well, & we're trying to live up to the colonial architecture by soft-pedalling the Victorian bric-a-brac & such. Having two rooms apiece enables us to avoid the flagrant furniture-crowding which existed both at #10 & at #61. Our respective mantels are pretty damn good—appropriate old candlesticks, vases, &c. on both, & suitable paintings above. We have some things from the old house which were long in stor-age—for example, over the staircase will be a huge painting of the rocks at Narragansett Pier by my late elder aunt . . . . who I wish could have survived to see it re-displayed. All told, the layout has some surprising atmospheric resemblances to 454 Angell Street despite its predominant Georgianism. The utter charm & fascination of coming *home* through a carved colonial doorway, & sitting beside a white Georgian mantel gazing out through small-paned windows over a sea of ancient roofs & sun-golden foliage, can scarcely be described without recourse to poesy. The place is so much like a museum that I half expect some guard to shew up & boot me out at five o'clock clos-ing time! Rather good, too, to have a regular domestick environment instead of rooming. Your knapsack et al. *seem* safe so far, & I shall be looking for you about the time July merges into my native August. I've just bought a camp cot to enable me to save occasional guests the expenses of the Crown or its equivalents. What's the use of having space if ya don't make it count?

Price is marooned in a place called Wantagh, N.Y., for lack of cash, hence has so far paid no northern calls. Wandrei, too, is up against it—flat broke, living on credit, & with nothing to clink (to say naught of anything to crackle) in his fray'd & shiny jeans. I doubt if he could raise the price of a Patersonium round trip! Yea, verily, these are days of universal destitution!

Cook & I may very possibly attend the N. Y. convention, hence perhaps I shall see you in the pest zone ere you honour these Plantations. Nothing certain, though. Depends on cash. I'd hate to get as far as N. Y. if I couldn't keep on South at least to Richmond. The pest zone is merely the jumping-off place to somewhere!

Sorry you can't get to your beloved Harvard this year. By the way—would you care for a good picture of your old praeses, Charlie Eliot?[1] My aunt has one which she thinks some real son of the crimson wou'd appreciate more than she. By the way—the enclosed cutting will pain you. Good old Aunt Julia! But I fancy the establishment will live on.

Wish I could get a job on that ghost writers' bureau. Ain't I the bozo that put the specks in spectres of that sort? Which reminds me . . . . . . in over-hauling storage stuff *I have found all my Dave Bush volumes!* They hadn't perish'd after all! They're up in the attick now, but when you blow in we'll have to get 'em down & revive old memories with "Pop" & "Mr. Muling". Mr. Guiter-man's ethnic verses have sprightliness & wit.[2] Just now Friend Adolph is overdoing the selective anthropology a bit, yet there's a damn sight of sense in a lot of his contentions. While of course the demand for more than 0.75 Aryan blood in full citizens is an excessive one except where the diluting blood is biologically inferior—as with negroes & australoids—it remains a fact that many modern nations need to take steps to preserve the integrity of their own native cultures against shrewd & pushing alien influences. One must view such problems realistically—without patriotic sentimentality like

Hitler's on the one hand, & without idealistic sentimentality on the other hand. Certainly, a dash of alien blood of a superior race (among which a large section of Jews as well as Mongols must be included) does not harm another superior stock *so long as the culture is unimpaired.* But that's where the rub comes. When the alien element is strong or shrewd enough to menace the purity of the culture amidst which it parasitically lodges, it is time to do something. So far as Jews are concerned, it wouldn't hurt a nation to absorb a few thousand provided they were not a physiognomically aberrant type & provided they left their culture & folkways behind them so that the new generation would hold no memories except of the dominant racial tradition. Palgrave's Golden Treasury is no less golden because the anthropologist's old man was an ex-Cohen. So far, Hitler is wrong. ***But***—when a clique of sharp, pushing Yids get hold of the professional & cultural life of a nation, become its ostensible mouthpiece, & begin putting across their alien psychology & folkways under the pretence of representing the national-racial culture they prey upon . . . . . then, by god, it's time to forget the fancy principles & do something to re-store control & expression to the real population of the nation concern'd! On that point I'm a red-hot Nazi . . . . . Heil, Hitler! ⤳ !! Deutschland über Alles . . . . . . (until it beings to encroach on Anglo-Saxons, & then to hell with the whole lousy continent & its worn-out attitudes. God Save the King!!!) Well— to make a long story short, I think the Yids had the beginnings of a real strangle-hold on German professional & cultural life, hence I'm glad to see *some* sort of curb applied. The proportion of Jew lawyers in Berlin was a whole epic expressed in simple arithmetic. It was time to weed out the strongly & obviously foreign—even tho' Charlie Chaplin Jr. is going a bit too far. When the legal (or educational or literary or theatrical &c.) machinery of a nation gets concentrated in the hands of a group whose inherited & openly perpetuated system of values & psychological reactions differs perceptibly from that of the nation itself, there is no time for highfalutin babble. Without the least bit of malice, & with no reflections at all on the qualitative status of the aliens concerned, steps must be taken to restore the alienated machinery to people (whether or not of 100% pure blood) who inherit & wish to per-petuate the nation's own traditions & systems of values. It would be silly to assume that Jews & near-Jews like Ludwig[3] &c. really represent the German nation. While it is silly to *suppress* their books, something must be done to emphasise their non-Germanism. And certainly, German natives ought not to be judged in courts where decisions rest with men having non-German in-stincts & sympathies & traditions. So there I pat Handsome Adolf on the back! (His lip-blot is the only really *unforgivable* thing about him . . . oh, if I could only take a Gillette to him & Sonny Belknap!) What this bimbo ought to do is to use a sense of proportion. A man brought up in the real German tradition, with early impressions confirming the virile pagan & Protestant psychology which belongs to the nation & excluding any of the hereditary teachings peculiar to another culture, ought certainly to be a full citizen & potential officeholder even if ¼, ½, or fully Jewish in genealogy. *But no man who inherits Jewish feelings & perspectives ought to hold a pivotal post in any Aryan nation.* That's no insult to intellectual Jews—it's simply common-sense. If the Jews had a nation of their own, (as they *would* if they had our guts & self-respect, god damn 'em!) I'd be the first to insist that it be kept free of Aryan influences. As it is, I honestly regret the Aryan taint (*any* infusion is a "taint" if it's where it *doesn't belong*) in the noble & ancient culture of Japan. Hitler merely applies the wrong test. A real colour-line needs to be drawn only against certain definitely alien physical types—chiefly the biologically underdeveloped black races. Within the truly Caucasian race the test ought to be cultural—depending or each individual's personal history & natural reactions, as determined by proper psychological & other investigations. If any undoubted Caucasian *thinks & feels* like an Aryan, then let him hold office in an Aryan nation. This would not only cut down the unpleasant foreign percentage in power, but would speed up the assimilation of the whole alien element. (Of course, no *new* members of an alien culture ought to be admitted to a nation except in small quantity.) A hideous example of what Hitler is honestly—if crudely—trying to prevent is the stinking Manhattan pest zone. Faugh! Everything gone Yiddish—radical, effeminate psychology dominant—stage & press Jew-ridden—publishing houses (which determine what books shall be publish'd) gobbled by squint-eyed, verminous kikes—books reviewed (which guides publick taste) by flea-whiskered Talmudists—hell! There's an Augean stable for the future Nazis of America! This crime of neglect has spawned a new & degenerate branch of Semitic culture masquerading as a branch of Aryan culture—the international, radical Greenwich-Village-Union-Square sort of thing which today distinguishes New York from America. Decadent—vulgar—cowardly—visionary—anti-American—incomprehensible—feminine—value-destroying . . . . . . & this kind of thing is so gangrenously contagious that it ropes in thousands of Aryans as well. Do you suppose Little Belknap would have gone bolshevik in an American town? I'd like to see Hitler wipe Greater New York clean with poison gas—giving masks to the few remaining people of Aryan culture (even if of Semitic ancestry). The place needs fumigation & a fresh start. (If Harlem didn't get any masks, I'd shed no tears . . . . . & the same goes for the dago slums!) Incidentally—all these newspaper discussions of recent months miss the one great point of the age-long & ineradicable Jew-Aryan line of cleavage. It isn't *religion*—all religion is a negligible factor today. It is only slightly *race*—half the Jews in existence are of very superior stock, as their ability to undermine our culture shews; & only a fraction are more physically repulsive than many races whom we hate less. The real impassible barrier is *cultural.* Our whole system of values differs *utterly & irreconcilably* from the Jewish system, even though (& this is what obscures the real problem) our absurd pretence at harbouring the silly, alien, decadent Jewish by-product called Christianity makes us pretend to endorse the Hebrew slave-psychology. The Jew is a wor-shipper of the sort of intellectual-ethical adjustment which his superstitious ancestors interpreted as cosmic "righteousness". His *supreme* test of value is the degree of perfection of this adjustment—to other things he is relatively indifferent. Now anyone over five years old knows that our pretence at shar-ing this ideal is sheer bullshit. We are Aryan pagans by heritage, & our deep, instinctive code of ultimate values is completely antipodal to the Jew's. Twenty centuries of flabby Christian fakery have not succeeded in changing our real natures one jot. Our code is not that of hair-splitting old slave-women. We are *men*—free men—& *the one sole thing that supremely matters to us is the maintenance of our own unbroken freedom & dominance.* In our hearts—whatever our lips say—our sole definition of a *man* as distinguished from a crawling reptile is a person who possesses a maximum of freedom of action, who lives under the government he *chooses, & who unhesitatingly accepts death in preference to servitude.* If a group of us is weak, it fights until it is either free or dead. It is never *broken* or *cowed*. It may die & vanish, but it never lives to be kicked around. What we can't forgive in the Jew is not the tone of his prayers or the size of his nose, but *the fact that he is willing to survive under the conditions he accepts.* Being *weak* may not have been his fault—but it *is* his fault *that he is alive & not free & dominant.* If we were as weak as he, & could not fight our way to self-respect, we would perish utterly—taunting our foes, virile & unbroken, as the last man fell. *That unbrokenness is all that matters to us.* Now the Jews do not un-derstand our feelings at all. They wonder why we hate them, & point to their oppression by us as if it were a point *for* instead of *against* them in our estima-tion. They cannot see that what we hate is the fact that they have accepted such oppression without fighting to the death. They blame us for mistreating them, & cannot understand that this blame seems very light to people whose only *real* conception of shamefulness is *weakness & servitude.* They think that everyone holds *justice* the supreme good (& we egg them on by *pretending* to live up their notion), whereas we have the wholly different criterion of *freedom, unbrokenness, power, & war-joy.* They have no use for a man who is unjust. We have no use for a man who doesn't relish a good fight or punch an oppressor in the jaw. Those two antipodal, antagonistic, & irreconcilable ideals will per-sist as long as the two cultures exist. Is anyone fool enough to think that Jews & Aryans (culturally such) can live side by side in mutual respect? With such opposite definitions of what forms the essence of manhood, it is likely that many persons of one group will measure up to the other's minimum stan-dards of self-respect? We not only hate the lousy cringer that oppression has made the ghetto-rat—we hate the basic group-psychology which made his ancestors willing to live on in spite of oppression.

Good Jew-Aryan relations can come only after these plain truths are rec-ognised on both sides. In the end, there will have to be a separation of the cultural Jew from the body politic, plus a complete absorption—with abandonment of hereditary traditions—of thousands of other Jews. That will call for concessions on both sides—the Jews will have to realise that they can't drag their folkways into our national patterns, while we will have to abandon the tight race-lines of the Hitlerites. That ought not to be a hardship either way. The Jews are used to subordinate positions, & good governments need impose no hardships on their unassimilable faction. And on the other side— Aryan nations have taken on varying doses of Semitic blood in the past (Spain has oceans of it; England & America since Cromwell's time have absorbed a trickle) without any unfavourable results whatsoever. Give and take. But if any damn Yid expects to produce a permanent dent in our civilisation, he might as well measure his behind for the toe of a well-directed Aryan brogan!

(Goddam! That storm *is* coming! Aryan tho' I am, I fear I shall have to retreat—tho' from an adversary no less mighty than your revered progenitor Jupiter Tonans—or Pluvius . . . . . since it doesn't take a thunderbolt to get a warlike Nordick's pants in such shape that he has to give a cringing Semite a quarter to press 'em. But this trip there'll be plenty of thunderbolts thrown in without extra charge . . . . . . cripes, what a peal! Fare thee well till later— Grandpa hereby folds his tents & beats it for cover . . . . . . the picturesquely Georgian cover of #66.)

Midnight.

Was it a storm . . . . . . or rather, *is* it a storm? You tell 'em, 'bo! Got home just in time—read the paper—beheld a fine clearing & orange-golden sunset—went down to the Waldorf Lunch & returned—& now your celestial forefather is giving old Ma Gaea the works again, with full luminous & acoustick trimmings!

So far, though, no chilling of the air. Boy! Have I been enjoying the warm spell? Ninety degrees Friday, eighty-six degrees Saturday, eighty-six Sunday, ninety-four degrees today . . . . I'll let the oblique-orb'd empyrean know that Grandpa is having his day! Haven't felt so spry since I was in New Orleans—am taking sizeable walks (average twelve miles) each day that the weather isn't doubtful, exploring a delectable rural region north of Providence which I'd never visited before . . . . Smithfield Road, Douglas Pike, Wenscott Reservoir, &c. west of my favourite Quinsnicket stamping-ground. Swell scenery—winding roads, ancient farmsteads, rocky, rolling meadows, mystical, shadowy woods, stone walls, blue lakelets, & splendid prospects whose twilight allurement suggests unrevealed marvels just beyond the horizon's rim. I'm damn glad I never tapped this realm before, since it provides the kick of novelty & unexpectedness for my old age—& right near home. There's still quite a bit of R.I. that I know much less thoroughly than I do Charleston or Natchez or Florida. If only this genial warmth would last! You'd hardly believe how spry the old man can be! But when the mercury drops I'll be as crumpled up as a dish-rag at Jake's. This is my day . . . . let the other guy do his crowing when I'm shivering & hugging the radiator!

Congrats on the rockonomical honours you're pulling down of late. What did I tell ya? Didn't I say them stones of yourn was laid out so swell they'd orta form a goal & model for all live-wire pebbleolatrists? Being chose to deliver words of wisdom to the assembled curatorial sages certainly is worth even such a price as going to Chi at an evil time like this, when the burg is clutter'd up with the magnified hencoops, filling stations, backhouses, petrol tanks, grain-elevators, stationary engines, oil derricks, traffick towers, silos, lunch carts, coal chutes, gallows-trees, & fertiliser factories with which the architectural court-jesters of machine-age barbarism are trying to destroy what little taste the open-mouth'd American booboisie have had since the 1893 fair pulled 'em out of the slough of Victorian chaos & Richardsonian near-Romanesque! Ugh! I don't envy yuh! I wouldn't go near that ash-&-swill-dump of crystallised delirium tremens & apotheosised decadence even it anybody'd pay my fare and throw in a fair salary besides! Of all aesthetick purgatives & structural emeticks . . . . . . Grrr . . . yah!

I perused the article from the *Saddypost* with appropriate melancholy interest, & am grateful for the gruesome glimpse. O gawd—to think that a Pawtucket, R.I. boy like Raymond Mathewson Hood is mixed up in this![4] I shall rub out the Mathewson rectangles on my genealogical chart (no Hoods there, thank heavings!) & omit Pawtucket from my scenick walks. But he'll never put over any of his nonsense in his native state, by god! The *Journal* is gonna build a new edifice downtown here—but it will be pure & traditional Georgian . . . . . God Save the King!

As for this "functional" hash of stalled steam-rollers, capsized Fords, waterfront power-houses, & earthquake ruins . . . . . . I don't think it needs any serious notice from gentlemen . . . . . except so far as zoning-boards may properly legislate against publick nuisances. The whole pox-rotted mess is simply another of those revolts against the unexciting sobriety of decent taste whose last previous example gave us the horrors of Victorianism about a century ago. Ebb & flow . . . systole & diastole . . . . after the Georgian age came 1872 City Halls . . . . . after the good taste of the 1820's came this wave of aesthetic cholera. One might as well call it neo-Victorianism & let it go at that. The Victorians talked just as these puke-producers of the present do . . . . . Hood & his bums could read lots of architectural dicta of 1880 & fancy the old boys were stealing their stuff! In those days, as now, the jigsaw & turret hounds talked about being "original"—"expressing the age & getting away from the past". Their pet word was "eclecticism" instead of "functionalism", but it all amounted to the same thing. What's in a name? That which we call a sewer by any other name would stink as punk![5]

The trouble with this new fad—which may litter up the country with as many eyesores for the next generation to tear down as the "eclectick" fad did—

is that it rests on a theory which *sounds* rather slick when peddled in the abstract. It is all very well to say that buildings should not, as a rule, conspicuously contradict their materials or belie the purposes for which they were made; that their ornaments should not be obtrusive excrescences detracting from natural lines. Fine. But does that precept really explain the boilermakers' nightmares which break out on the landscape under the aegis of modern "functionalism"? Horsefeathers! Cutting out all faddism, nine-tenths of the buildings erected for any given purpose *could not possibly look even remotely like the hashish hells of these addlepated decadents if there were not a deliberate & wholly unmotivated attempt to eliminate every trace of the familiar & the really beautiful.* This is not natural functionalism—it is merely perverse & self-conscious caprice, as artificial in its way as the most hidebound traditionalism. It is just as artificial to go out of the way to avoid a beauty & homelikeness which would otherwise be instinctively followed, as it is to distort & misrepresent a building in order to follow precedent. If modern structures were built without reference to any purpose save the discharge of their respective functions with a minimum of offence to the eye, they would be infinitely more traditional than anything these goddam bolsheviks would tolerate. And that is why their whole line of bull is a cheap fake. They howl that every age ought to have its own forms—to express itself in its own way. All right. But they know damn well that the real expression of an age must be *spontaneous & unlabour'd*—never the fruit of a cut-&-dried propaganda campaign. The riches of the Renaissance & the glory of Gothick were never mapped out in advance & painstakingly pushed on an indifferent or reluctant publick through a ridiculous "Modern Architecture Week" or "Functionality Drive". God in heaven, what cowflap! As if this creaking-jointed, cooked-up scheme of Greenwich-Village dupes had anything in common with the imperceptible mass-movements which form the *real* expression of an age!

Suppose this age "ought" to have a unique expression? Well—then let it go ahead & express! Nobody's stopping it . . . . . if it doesn't express anything new it's very obviously because it hasn't anything new to say. Putting fake words artificially into its mouth won't do any good. Such words aren't the true expression of the age at all—any more than we can say that a dumb man talks when a glib ventriloquist makes words seem to come from him. The pinhead petits-maitres of the Victorian age also thought they'd make their period freely & originally express itself—& look what they did!

What these moon-gazing droolers can't get into their beans is that not every age produces a new art of its own. Contrary to the Marxolaters who assume that every shift of oeconomick balance must necessarily produce a corresponding shift in aestheticks, it is really only once in a long while that a genuinely fresh art emerges. And when such does emerge, it is not in answer to any theorist's summons, or synchronised with any oeconomick development as wheezed in the gags of Carlo Marx! The plain fact is, that an age of science, mechanicks, & commerce is essentially antagonistick to art, & highly unlikely to evoke any new development. Moreover, an art brought to maturity is always more stable than an art in its young & plastick stages. Western civilisation is old. Its recent aspects are not of a sort to inspire fresh aesthetick expression. Nothing has really called forth anything radically new, & there is no reason why any such thing should be called forth. Many of our present forms are distinctly adequate to their purpose, so that they do not call for replacement. Other new forms, evoked through the influence of machinery, can develop most naturally as *branches or modifications* of the existing tradition—with all due allowance for adaptation to function. When anything wholly new is needed, it will appear . . . . but cooking up artificial freaks does nobody any good.

It is utter infantility to claim that the treatment of a mechanically constructed surface with a certain type of harmonious decorative design is "incorrect" merely because the type of design happened to have been evolved in pre-mechanical days. If the design has intrinsic beauty as a stimulus to the eye and a balancer of areas in the composition it is certainly just as correct & effective as any newer type of design, worked out by the modernist gang, could possibly be. No man of sense can study the forms of ornament which the modernists *do* use (for not all of them ignore the deep human instinct for rhythm & pattern flagrantly enough to adopt the functional boiler-factory ideal in all its nitwit purity!) without perceiving that they are certainly no less irrelevant than any traditional form when properly applied. Thus even if we momentarily grant the modernist's contention that pure geometrical form & utilitarian function—wholly divorced from the associational element—are the sole authentick bases of beauty, we must insist that the traditional, whenever it does not belie function or involve irrelevant lines, is *at least equal* in effectiveness to the radically new. Even this point of view disposes of the fallacy that these freakmongers really gain anything by banishing recognised beauty & courting bizarre ugliness.

However, the sensible disputant need not rest here. It is proper for him to call the modernist's bluff on the whole larger question of the *nature of beauty itself.* The modernist's case rests utterly & pathetically on the flimsy faddist assumption that true beauty is a perfectly simple & definite thing—a geometrical property based wholly on abstract arrangements & entirely independent of all associative factors. Only this fantastic assumption can justify the sponsoring of an alleged "art" in which the poignant, potent element of memory-recalling is entirely absent. According to these moderns, art has no business trying to make its spectators feel at home & harmonised with the universe by suggesting previous impressions, recalling previous emotions, or orienting the present with the past. Man, they claim, can be touched just as deeply & richly by totally unaccustomed stimuli as by those familiar & reminiscent stimuli which he can coördinate with his stream of cultural memories & emotional experiences. In a word, the hypothetical modern man is a parvenu bastard without antecedents or memories, & with merely a tabula rasa of abstract receptivities to be formally titillated by mathematical harmonies or 'ideologically propagandised' (as the Little Belknap of 1932–3 would put it) with scientific utilitarianism or social & oeconomick theory. A gas house or motor 'bus can be as beautiful as a temple or a galleon . . . . . a publick library might just as well look like a smallpox hospital as like a library . . . . a house is simply a "living machine" to allow the inhabitants to sleep & feed & keep warm with maximum physiological & oeconomick efficiency, & has nothing to do with satisfying emotional yearnings or pleasing the sense of harmony, continuity, & memory-fulfilment inherent in man.

Well—that's what they say . . . . but any adult who keeps his head level amidst the charlatanic hullabaloo can see what perfect damned crap this whole bolshevik attitude is. All that man is, is the sum of his memories—personal & cultural—& no art could have even a modicum of genuineness or vitality if it did not draw upon the past or find its roots in previous & long-accustomed forms & ways. Every great art tradition which has ever existed—even when most seemingly different from what it superseded—has drawn primarily on antecedent & familiar elements. It may have given these elements a fresh synthesis, but it has never failed to preserve enough to give the emotions a genuine & substantial foothold. Anybody who claims that (for example) the Grecian temple or the Gothick cathedral was as sudden & rootless an architect's dream as the tool-sheds & standpipes of the Chicago Century of Mechanical Tail-Chasing[6] is simply talking through his hat. The whole basis of this radical ballyhoo is as insubstantially windy as the farts of a bean-swilling nigger. To hell with it!

Any race that isn't a promiscuously spawned litter of father-ignorant radicals or church-door foundlings will refuse to live permanently amidst freakish forms which have no relevance to anything it has ever known or heard of or dreamed about. Paste that in your sporty derby, Raymond, & take a look at it when a new generation kicks you back to Pawtucket! This "future" stuff will do on paper—but it isn't the *future* which has shaped our personalities & coloured our imaginations & provided us with all the landmarks & points of reference which we can ever possess. The future is a vague thing which nobody will ever experience—even vicariously—except to an infinitesimally fractional extent. It is a momentary stimulus to youth at a certain stage—a convenient frame on which youth hangs a vaguely roseate but transient curtain of its own irresponsible imaginings—but that is all. As a potent & permanent influence & source of associational images it scarcely counts. And as for the *present*—what is it but a flash . . . . . or a sequel significant only in connexion with the whole time-stream of which the past is the only known & intelligible part? We really live only for the illusion of drama inherent in the correlation of certain vague expectancies with what we remember of the past . . . . . . & yet there are some goddam sonsofbitches who think they can float an aesthetick from which the past is completely omitted! Pretty damn good, if ya asts me—pretty damn good!

An analysis of the assumption-background of these cursed radicals is enough to dispose of them culturally. They freely admit belonging to the alien & usurping machine-culture of deified speed & quantity & impermanence & emptiness instead of to the genuine European civilisation which is now fighting for its life . . . . . the only civilisation which can truly be *ours*. They advocate the aimless, meaningless, & rootless culture of the parvenu who has nothing to remember & no rich heritage with which to correlate himself . . . . . . the parvenu without landmarks or loyalties, who builds his temporary shanty with the intention of shortly tearing it down again! Well—we have seen something of this menacing & usurping barbarism, & know that it is an impoverished, futile growth which merits nothing at our hands save inextinguishable hostility & endless, desperate warfare till we be either victorious or dead to the last man. *Civilisation* means settledness, harmony, leisure, & the preservation of the accumulated heritage of memories which alone gives life the sanity-saving illusions of significance, direction, & interest. It means the enthronement of *permanence & quality*, & the crushing of the speed-quantity-commerce octopus that preys on its vitals. Its natural mood is one of *continuity*, & its natural language is that of an art with roots & memories. Against this real civilisation, & egging on the natural & already dangerous-enough disintegrative forces of utilitarianism & wholesale mechanisation, is arrayed the architectural epilepsy & cultural hysteria of Chicago's Cycle of Shoddy Practicality & Century of post-Antonine Decline. I spit upon it as a friend of civilised mankind & all that civilised mankind has built up in ten thousand years.

Yrs for the old ways

Πάππος Θεοβάλδος

Notes

1. Charles William Eliot (1834–1926), American educator and president of Harvard (1869–1909).

2. Probably Arthur Guiterman (1871–1943), *Ballads of Old New York* (1920).

3. Emil Ludwig (1881–1948), German author of Jewish ancestry (his original name was Emil Cohn) chiefly known for his biographies.

4. Raymond Mathewson Hood (1881–1934) was a celebrated architect born in Pawtucket, RI. The article in question was Forrest Crissey, "Why the Century of Progress Architecture?" *Saturday Evening Post* (10 June 1933): 16–17, about Hood's involvement in the Chicago World's Fair of 1933–34, officially named A Century of Progress International Exposition.

5. A parody of Shakespeare's "What's in a name? That which we call a rose / By any other name would smell as sweet" (*Romeo and Juliet* 2.2.43–44).

6. One of numerous disparaging ways HPL referred to the Chicago World's Fair.

[129]   [AHT]

Abode of Colonial Antiquity—Nones of Quintilis, 1933

[7 July 1933]

Vertex of Vivifying Virtuosity:—

Possibly Culinarius told you of my recent guest—Malik Taus, the Peacock Sultan, otherwise known to fame as Edgar Hoffmann Price. You must know his frequent Orientales in *Weird Tales*. He is visiting in Irvington, New York; & though too busy to do much socialising in N. Y. City, stole four days from his work to give archaick Providentium (which he'd never seen before) the once-over. Young Brobst came over twice during his stay, & made a very congenial third in our literary & philosophical discussions. We had one all-night session—mostly spent in reading & criticising a single story. (By young Strauch of Allentown—Brobst's friend, who visited here last September & will visit again this September.)

Price had his car—a rattletrap 1928 Ford—which enabled me to shew him more of the country than I could otherwise have done. Indeed, his interest & courtesy enabled me to see many inaccessible regions which I had myself never seen before despite a lifetime's residence in these parts. You may recall my mentioning the "Narragansett Country" south of Wickford & west of the bay, otherwise known to fame as the "South County" (actually, King's County, known since the late unfortunate rebellion as Washington County). This is the region where the plantation system existed as in the South—with large estates, many blacks, a Church of England culture, & an agricultural basis centreing in horse-breeding & dairying. In the good old days before the tragedy of 1775–83 Narragansett pacers & Narragansett cheeses were famous in all the world's markets . . . eheu fugaces . . . God Save the King! It was to this region that Newport—across the bay—formed "the town" . . . . indeed, I recall pointing out to you in antient Water Street the town houses of several Narragansett planters. About one-third of my ancestry comes from the Narragansett country—Phillips, Place, Hazard, Wilcox, Casey, Dyer, &c. It had long irked me that I had never seen the choicest spots of this territory, yet the non-possession of a coach & a reluctance to impose on others led me to postpone my explorations—there being no publick conveyances penetrating these fastnesses of the past. We saw the *edge* of the South County at Wickford—but the core remained untouch'd.

Well—Price unlock'd for me the long-wish'd wonderland. And what a land it is! Nowhere else have I beheld scenery so idyllick, or rusticity so unspoil'd. Winding roads, stone walls, verdant slopes & meads, shadowy woods, embower'd cots & villages & steeples, shimmering streams & azure meres, stately mansions, venerable water-mills, breath-taking prospects—all the loveliness & wholesomeness of a real civilisation as contrasted with the offal & miasma of mechanised, quantitative, democratick modernity. We visited the antient snuff-mill where the late eminent painter, Gilbert Stuart, Esq., was born, &

spent some time at the great Rowland Robinson house (1705) amidst its gigantick willows, where a country-gentleman of vast urbanity shew'd us the
interior as well as the exterior. The Robinsons are an offshoot of the Hazards, & so value the connexion that they have always had over the door the
heraldick escallop of the Hazard arms . . . . . a thing which, I may reflect with
satisfaction, belongs to me as much as to them. The Robinson house is the
last unchanged example of our South-County plantation-houses—a type
which did not emulate the plantation architecture of any part of the South,
but which employ'd the true New-England gambrel form on an unprecedentedly large scale. Another place we visited was the glebe—long-deserted rec-
tory of Dr. MacSparran, who presided over that white church in Wickford
(mov'd up from a rural spot five miles below) which I shew'd you some years
ago. Its dank, shadowy courtyards, lushly overgrown with vines & briars, have
a spectral & almost sinister aspect. On the hill above it is Hannah Robinson's
Rock (about which a story clings), commanding the finest rural prospect I
have anywhere seen—miles of coiling river, mead & forest, distant white
church on a headland, shining, mystical, far-off sea . . . . . oh, boy! you'll have
to hire a bicycle or tin lizzie & see it some day! But the climax was Kingston
village—a veritable inland Marblehead, dizzying in its unspoiled colonial
beauty, & *never before seen* by me. On the way back I blew Price to a typical
R. I. clam dinner at antient Pawtuxet . . . . . & later stopt at a Waldorf to tank
up myself.

As for the subjects of recent comment—I freely concede that a nation
may sometimes advantageously pick up occasional points from an outside
group, but insist that any decided hybridisation of the culture-stream is un-
qualifiedly bad. So with modernity. Admittedly all civilisation is fluid, & subject to slow normal changes. It does not follow, however, that *every* change is
good, or even possessed of a slight element of good. Some shifts are unquali-
fiedly bad—& among these must be reckon'd all imagination-impoverishing
breaks with the background which shaped the race's basic thought & feeling.

Yrs for the past—

Θεοβάλδος

P.S. Enclos'd is a circular of Klarkash-Ton's new brochure.[1] It's great stuff—
you ought to get it. It would awake you to a new appreciation of a powerfully
phantastick mind.

Notes

1. *The Double Shadow and Other Fantasies* (1933).

[130] [AHT]

The Antient River-Bank—July 18, 1933

Topless Tower of Terrestrial Truth-Tracing:—

I was interested in Jonckheer Wilfredus's golf controversy—a ramification of which (here enclos'd) in the *Sunday Times*. He is determin'd to annex to the Netherlands everything worth annexing! What a pity—from his angle—that your Dutch strain of blood prov'd a bum steer. Had that pann'd out, W. B. T. would have a ready reason for all your eminent qualities!

As for modern architecture, &c.—I'd like to have the honour of setting off the first blast when they clear away the rubbish of that Century of Misdirected Effort!

Blessings—

Θεοβάλδος

P.S. Pardon my script if it's bummer than usual. It's getting dark—eight-thirty p.m.—& the mosquito air fleet is busy!

[131] [AHT]

The Ancient Hill
August 26, 1933

Lanthorn of Limitless Learnedness:—

Have started a new hell-raiser—"The Thing on the Doorstep".[1] Am hoping to snatch time to experiment with more fiction now that additional markets are appearing.

And so it goes. Welcome home, & don't get the rocks & ancestors mixed up!

Yr obt Servt

Θεοβάλδος

P.S. I've read an interesting life of Daniel Webster—with a good deal of interesting N. E. antiquarian background—by Fuess, the present headmaster of Phillips Andover.

Notes

1. According to the ms., HPL wrote the story on 21–24 August. Either the date of the letter is erroneous or he was still tinkering with the text.

[132]   [AHT]

The Antient Hill—Sept. 20, 1933

Heav'n-High Hierarch of Hereditary Harvesting:—

Alas that I cou'd not have been in on that historick triangular meeting whose tantalising bulletin greeted me upon my return from antient Quebec! Glowing reports reach me, not only from Little Sonny but from the Peacock Sultan as well—the latter dignitary, after an eventful run including tree-climbing, cow-butting, burned-out engines, & the like, & a pause at St. Augustine, being once more establish'd at 1416 Josephine Street in New-France's southernmost outpost. There's a boy for you! No cut-&-dried schedules for him! His last plan—as outlined to me late in August—was to hibernate in *Miami* . . . . . yet my new communication from him bears the good old Nouvelle-Orleans postmark. Charm of the unexpected . . . . . who the hell wants to know what lies around the corner? We don't know where we're going, but we're on our way! Consider & draw a lesson therefrom! I'm glad to see that you & Sultan Malik took to each other—he devotes nearly half a page to your enthusiastick praise, having obviously been heavily impress'd. He'll be around again, never fear! Even now he is congratulating himself that enough of the Juggernaut is left to take him to Chicago, California, & Cross Plains, Texas. Gone today, here tomorrow! That's the way to squeeze the savour out of life's brief & meaningless flash—although I, personally, wouldn't enjoy itinerancy unless I had a fully settled home with books & familiar objects to return to. He is the complete bird of passage—but I am merely the restless navigator who explores far shores only to return to Devon's ancient lanes & abbey towers in the end. I got a card from St. Augustine—where I wish to gawd I could be until the middle of next June!

Glad to hear the Sonnykins is expanding & trying to get a really and truly grown-up line on the surrounding world! Hope he can succeed in re-regularising the meetings, & in importing enough suitable new material to freshen & amplify them a bit. That friend of his—Neil Moran—wouldn't be a bad acquisition—& possibly some of your Paterson literati might fit in well. Anything that can mature & de-communise the child is all to the good—& I wish you luck in your missionary work! No—I certainly won't discourage any contacts or pursuits which can help to draw the little imp out of his nephelo-coccysia of abstraction, artificiality, & uncorrelated book-l'arnin'! The Blue Pencil bunch might be a useful antidote for his exoticism—their domestick commonplaceness being a pull in the right direction, away from Baudclaircian decadence, Briffaultian[1] freakishness, & general overbookishness as distinguish'd from experience. Single-taxery would certainly form a vast improvement over Stalinism—& even mineralogy compares favourably with Marxism. I wonder if the young rascal will ever be making trips to Providence to inspect honest Mariano's quarry? Well—do your best, & the old gentleman will back you up! There's a lot of great material buried in that infant, & the bimbo who brings it out will certainly be performing a valuable service! The first point is to get him interested in something beside the sterile juggling of social ideas on paper.

Well—my aunt has made real progress these days, being now all around the house on crutches or with cane.[2] In order to make things practicable when I'm not available (the nurse went a fortnight ago), we've installed an electrical dingus which kicks the front door open by pressing a button upstairs . . . . . . one of the very few mitigating advantages of the machine age. (Irony: if we'd had it last June 14 my aunt wouldn't have fallen at all!) Meals come in from the boarding-house across the back garden. I hope the patient can manage to get a little open-air diversion before the congealing hell of winter sets in.

Speaking of travels—I hope that maternal grandson of a dog Paul Pry condescended to pass along the bulletins of my recent Quebec jaunt! The trip was a welcome surprise—I didn't think I could make it till a few days before—& turned out to be a brilliant success. On the outbound trip I look'd up the antient Deane Winthrop house in Winthrop—built in 1637, & one of the oldest edifices in the colonies. It is a simple farmhouse, but very solidly built. In the base of the colossal brick chimney is a secret room—of a sort very common in seventeenth century Massachusetts houses. A society maintains the place. That evening I call'd on Culinarius—as you know from our joint card if that copper-squeezer at the village post-office didn't hold it up. Then the long train ride—spent in reading & drowsing, & unusually pleasant because there were no roystering alcohol-seekers aboard as in '30 & '32. The return of King Gambrinus to the States has its compensations![3] Most of the passengers were honest, simple French peasants bent on visiting ancestral soil or on grovelling at the popish shrine of La Bonne Ste. Anne de Beaupré. And at last—after a post-auroral dash through the increasingly picturesque provincial countryside—came the mighty fortress of the North itself . . . . . the rockbound stronghold which defy'd the fleet of Phips & form'd the Carthage of Cotton Mather's minatory thunderings! To enter Quebec—something that Phips couldn't do, & that Wolfe could do only at the cost of his life! Most inspiring of all was the sight of our Old Flag—the time-hallow'd Union Jack which ought to be floating at this moment over the 1761 Colony-House on Providence's antient hill—fluttering from the lofty citadel & the towers of the Houses of Parliament. God Save the King!

I had four days—all delectably hot & sunny—in Quebec, & certainly made the most of them. Boy, what a town! Old grey walls, majestick citadel, dizzying cliffs, silver spires, antient red roofs, mazes of winding ways, constant musick of mellow chimes & clopping hooves over century'd cobblestones, throngs of cassock'd, shovel-hatted priests, robed nuns, & tonsured barefoot friars, vistas of huddled chimney-pots, broad blue river far below, vivid verdant countryside, & the dim, distant line of the purple Laurentians . . . . . I also took some suburban trips—a walk to Sillery, up the river (whose

headland church is such an universal landmark), & a trolley ride to the upper
level of the Montmorency Falls, where stands Kent House (enlarged & vilely
defaced as an hotel), the Georgian mansion inhabited in the 1790's by the
Duke of Kent, Queen Victoria's father. I loaf'd, read, & wrote in all the parks
& on the citadel embankment, & look'd up the exact spot of Wolfe's ascent
of the cliff—not an easy quest, since it is unmark'd, & since the local Gauls
aren't a bit eager to point out the route of the guy who lick'd the breeches off
'em! One of the things about Quebec that always strikes me forcibly is the
sky—the odd cloud formations peculiar to northerly latitudes & virtually unknown in southern New-England. Mist & vapour assume phantastick & por-
tentous aspects, & at sunset on Labour Day I saw one of the most impressive
phaenomena imaginable from a vantage-point on the antient citadel overlooking the river & the Levis cliffs beyond. The evening was predominantly clear;
but some strange refractive quality gave the dying solar rays an abnormal redness, whilst from the zenith to the southeastern horizon stretch'd an almost
black funnel of churning nimbus clouds—the small end meeting the earth at
some inland point beyond Levis. From a place midway in this cloud-funnel,
zigzag streaks of lightning would occasionally dart toward the ground, with
faint rumbles of thunder following tardily after. Finally—while the blood-red
sun still bathed the river & cliffs & housetops in a supernal light—a pallid arc
of rainbow sprang into sight above the distant Isle d'Orleans; its upper end
lost in the great funnel cloud. I have never seen such a phaenomenon before,
& doubt if it cou'd occur as far south as Providence. Another striking thing is
the almost perpetual mist which spectrally hovers about the mountains &
valleys near Lake Memphramagog, at the Vermont-Quebec line. With such
bizarre skies, I do not wonder that the virile northern races excel the decadent Latins of the south in phantastick imagination. My ride back to the
States was extremely delightful—an apocalyptick sunset over a grotesquely
steepled hilltop village, & a great round moon flooding strange plains with an
eery radiance. Dawn came in a New-Hampshire lake-&-mountain region of
uncommon beauty, & I glimps'd Webster's early home (now an orphanage)
from the train south of Franklin. Boston at nine a.m.—& then good old Salem & Marblehead! In Salem I came some interesting new things . . . . getting
inside the fine old Richard Derby house (1762) for the first time. One high
spot was the perfect reproduction of a gabled house of 1650 lately built on
the grounds of the Pequot Mills. Every detail of seventeenth century work is
duplicated with scholarly fidelity, & I could hardly believe it was a modern
fac-simile. But the climax was the splendid reproduction of the pioneer Salem
settlement of 1626 et seq., carefully constructed & laid out in Forest River
Park. This was supervised by the eminent George Francis Dow, & consists of
a generous plot of ground at the harbour's edge, painstakingly landscaped &
covered with absolutely perfect duplicates of the very earliest huts &
houses—dwellings of a sort which has utterly vanish'd. All the early industries

are also reproduced—there being such things as the antient saw-pit, black-smith shop, salt-works, brick-plant, fish-drying outfit, & so on. Nothing else that I have ever seen gives one so good a picture of the rough pioneer life led during the first decade of Novanglian colonisation. Marblehead possess'd its accustom'd charm—tho' my inspection was broken by several showers. I finally got utterly drench'd in Bostonium as I darted from the N. station to pay a call on Culinarius.[4]

On my return I struck a season of lousy weather—rain & cold—& nearly froze with the premature autumnal chill. Only the good old oil heater kept me alive! Monday & yesterday, however, were fair & warm; so that I did quite a bit of writing outdoors. Indeed—I spent Monday amidst rural scenes—in & around the good old Quinsnicket woods!

Have found a new cheap eatery at the foot of the hill which gives splendid dinners for a quarter or thirty cents—complete with coffee & dessert. Dago joint call'd "Al's Lunch". So far it has kept clear of Jakish extremes in the matter of clientele.

I'll remember you to Brobst—who always has a standing set of regards to be sent to you. Next month he goes to the Boston City Hospital for a year's study & service.

Don't let the old grind press too hard on you! Life is something to be savour'd slowly & leisurely.

Regards, blessings, & compliments.

Yr obt hble Servt

Πάππος Θεοβάλδος

Notes

1. HPL refers to social anthropologist Robert Briffault (1876–1948), author of *Breakdown: The Collapse of Traditional Civilization* (1932) and other works.

2. Shortly after moving into 66 College St., Annie E. P. Gamwell had broken her ankle when she fell down the stairs.

3. Although the 18th Amendment was not officially repealed until 6 December 1933, President Roosevelt had signed an amendment to the Volstead Act on 23 March 1933 allowing the manufacture of beer with 3.2% alcohol. Gambrinus was a legendary king of Flanders and the patron saint of beer.

4. Cook vividly recounts HPL's visit following an exhausting trip to and from Quebec, which Cook elected not to go on, in *In Memoriam: Howard Phillips Lovecraft* . . . (*LR* 130–31).

[133] [AHT]

Octr. 6, 1933

Defeatless Diviner of Dynastick Derivations:—

Incidentally—my aunt is making great progress these days—going across the back garden to the boarding-house each day for lunch, & taking short walks as far as the college grounds. A single cane is now the mechanical aid to loco-motion. A week ago a friend took us for a motor ride to antient *Wickford* (three guesses as to polite suggester of destination), which form'd my aunt's first defi-nite outing since the mishap. Despite the autumnal season the day was tolerable in temperature, & glamourous & golden as to sun. The countryside wore its most pleasing aspect, with the first-fruits of harvest-time mix'd with the declin-ing *vestigia* of the summer. Wickford display'd all the accustom'd fascination, with white gables & venerable gardens gorgeous in the mystical late-afternoon radiance. We drove down the great street of elms to the waterfront, around by the antient Narragansett church (1705), & all thro' the village generally. Nothing has chang'd since you beheld it three years ago—for time & vandalism are un-known in Wickford. In such a place I would like to dwell tho' I have no com-plaint to make of the felicitous and-where in which I am now situate! There is an added fascination now in visiting antient houses—knowing what it is to an-other of them that I shall be going back in the evening.

One thing I like about this place is the refined & sedate club of felidae on the roof of a shed across the garden, in plain sight of my study windows. There are seldom fewer than one or two sleek old Toms at the "clubhouse", & occasionally as many as five or six or seven. Four of them belong to the antient gentlewoman residing two doors below here. In view of the preva-lence of fraternity-houses in the neighbourhood, I am calling this pleasing sodality the Kappa Alpha Tau—which stands for Κομποον Αιλουρον Ταξις.[1] The President (with whom I am become such good friends that he rolls over & kicks & purrs like a kitten upon my approach) is a huge, handsome black-&-white gentleman of antient lineage. The Vice-President is a gigantick tiger of prodigious dignity. The Secretary is a great Maltese with white spots. There is one very sprightly young fellow (also a Maltese), smaller than the rest of the boys, who is undergoing initiation.

Yrs for stones 'n' ancestors 'n' everything—

Πάππος Θεοβάλδος

Notes

1. Band of elegant or well-dressed cats.

[134]   [AHT]

Antient Woodland of Quinsnicket—
Shivering amidst autumnal splendour.
[October 1933]

Imam of Investigative Invincibility:—

Well, well! The old man's still out in the open! But though it's quite oke for brisk walking, it ain't so good for settin' down & writin'. Hard work guiding the muscles of my pen hand, for I doubt if the thermometer is over sixty-eight degrees. Glorious autumnal scenery. I've spent the last week tramping over archaick rustick landskips, searching out areas still unspoil'd by modernity. One or two disappointments—like that road we travers'd last August—but other discoveries make up for 'em. I shall introduce you to some of these regions next year—though, come to think of it, you *have* seen a good deal of the best of 'em (around Lime Rock) during the intensive quarry-combing of 1927–29. Yesterday some distant relatives gave my aunt & me a motor ride, & oh, boy! Was it an event? Over the new Boston road (south of the old Post Road) to Dedham, & then back via Westwood, Medfield, W. Medway, Franklin, & Woonsocket—a route of which three-fourths was utterly unfamiliar to me, & most of which was of marvellous scenick attractiveness. Some of these inland villages are ineffably beautiful & unspoil'd. Hell! I didn't know what a hinterland lay just back of the familiar scenes of my long lifetime!

Getting too cold to write—this is like trying to engrave the Lord's Prayer on the head of a pin amidst a fit of palsy!

Yrs for orthodoxy—

Θεοβάλδος

[135]   [AHT]

All-Hallows', 1933

Star-Surpassing Summit of Systematick Searching:—

Yes—I ought to know R. I. a bit before I quit. As for hitch-hiking—I have no prejudice either for or against, if the lifts come naturally & unsolicited. A gentleman never asks favours, but never hesitates to accept them when they are proffered. If a coach with a friendly driver happens to come along during an unpicturesque stretch, it is only the part of good sense to accept a ride until the landskip again becomes sightly enough to demand walking. Drivers vary in different parts of the colonies. The hard, suspicious, & largely foreign population of the North generally ignores the pedestrian. In the American & open-handed South, however, offers of transportation are universal—& so insistent in Florida that it is almost impossible to take a walk of any distance along a main highway without expending endless ergs of tact in declining courtesies. I *never* walked the full distance between Dunedin and Clearwater in all my long stay in Pinellas County—the commonplace nature of the scenery making the feat rather futile. And yet I have *asked* for a ride only once in a long lifetime—on Tuesday, May 14, 1929, when I was in Hurley N. Y. & missed the last stage-coach which would get me back to Kingston in time for the noon coach for New Paltz—missing which latter I would have to stay over in Ulster County another day. On that occasion I waved my hand at the first driver I saw—a genial giant on a Standard Oil truck—& was granted the desiderate boon despite a "No riders" sign . . . the g. g. perfunctorily warning me that Jawn D.

wouldn't compensate heirs if the damn thing blew up and sprinkled the wild domed hills with Theobaldian disjecta membra. I *did* catch the N. P. coach—by a hair's breadth—& had a great afternoon despite a rain which soaked all of me & most of my new-bought guide-book. That night I slept in Albany, & the next day made my only trip through the Hoosac Tunnel—to Athol—the Mohawk Trail coaches not having begun operations for the summer. Ah, me—life's vicissitudes! And my rain-soaked suit was press'd by Goodman J. Jasius, in Exchange street over-against the Transcript office, whilst I writ a letter in a borrow'd pair of pantaloons. Those quaint old pre-depression days!

Speaking of Athol & its fixtures—did I mention in my last that good old Culinarius has left old Beacon Hill flat & skipped to the paternal hearth of Walter John Coates, in North Mont-polar, Vermont? Of all nut stunts, when he had a perfectly good job—but nerves is nerves! Starting life anew beneath the aurora . . . . brrr!!! recent postal reports a temperature of twelve degrees and a twelve inch fall of snow . . . . . chacon a son gustibus non disputation, & all that! Brobst—now at the Boston City Hospital for a year—knock'd at #7 in vain. The bird had flew. Well—I hope the arctic waste will satisfy him, & aid in that process of intellectual vegetation to which he told Sonny the residue of his misspent existence wou'd be devoted!

As for commerce—of course, some equivalent of it is more or less of a necessary evil. The objection is the psychology it breeds. He who has to calculate & match wits for his subsistence, develops a kind of unlovely caution & suspicious parsimony not possessed by the gentleman of estate, or the man who works for a salary, tills the soil, or exercises a profession primarily for its own sake. The trading & financial mind is the most repellent of all types—& it breeds a noxious & pervasive set of standards based on such false, artificial values as wealth for its own sake, industry as an end in itself, solvency as the supreme virtue, & so on. Its whole atmosphere is of pettiness, low cunning, greed, & bourgeois callousness to life's real values. The prevalence of this scheming pedlar's attitude is responsible for certain ugly qualities in the close Northern as distinguished from the generous (agricultural-patriarchal-aristocratick) Southern mind, & likewise for the whole disgusting speed-&-quantity barbarism which is striving to replace civilisation on this continent. All of New England's real glory consists in a reaction against this insidious cancer—for thank heaven its paralysing effect was not universal. However—I'm not blaming individuals for their occupation; & if your John had a shop, so also did more than one chart-rectangle behind me. God's blood—my own great-grandfather Capt. Jeremiah Phillips ran a mill for profit, & was killed in its machinery Monday, Nov. 20, 1848 . . . . . jedgment o' heaven! And still nearer kin have, with less condign punishment, exercised the profit motive . . . . . Hell, no—it isn't that commerce is other than a natural anthropological phase intervening betwixt the stages of pure feudalism & social control of industry. Merchants had to be, & even the cancerous spread of the trading ideal was an unavoidable episode in the haphazard growth of these colonies. Nobody is to *blame*. But one hates to think of the whole thing & its set of motivations. If only the romance of Yankee brigs had been part of a collective government enterprise, with pure adventure & wonder—instead of the belittling hope of gain—motivating the daring captains & crews! That's one reason I'm so red-hot for fascism. Anything that can stop the snivelling, crawling profit-motive & calculative psychology out of a people, helps to raise that people in the scale of absolute human values. When people no longer waste themselves on "rugged individualism" in mere *industry*, they will be ripe for a truer individualism as rational & aesthetick beings. Viva Mussolini! God speed a planned, aristocratick state before things blow up into the planned proletarian state of Little Sonny's dreams!

Hope you have rich digging in Room 328.

Yrs for Hitler & Mustapha Kemal[1]—

Θεοβάλδος

Notes

1. Mustafa Kemal Atatürk (1881–1938), revolutionary statesman, writer, founder of the Republic of Turkey, and the first Turkish President.

[136]   [AHT]

Novr. 13, 1933

Vaticinative Vertex of Vivifying Vision:—

I note your precise attitude in the matter of hitch-hiking, & fancy I tend to react somewhat similarly. Whatever involves the element of mendicancy, imposition, & encroachment is indisputably in bad taste. Congratulations on your *absolutely* immaculate record! Query—would it still be immac if you had been stranded in a town with just about twenty minutes to catch a 'bus three miles away, & with a certainty of wasting a full afternoon & having to stay over night (@ $1.50) where you didn't want to stay if you miss'd the damn 'bus? Foremost of all, I am a realist!

Culinarius certainly has me puzzled! But I presume, after all, the metropolitanism of Boston began to get his goat just as that of the Noveboracense pest zone began to get mine. It would take an expert to dive down & fathom the well-springs of his impulses—but the keynote of his psychology seems to be a sort of *bitterness* regarding the whole external world . . . . an attitude which seems odd to me, since I recognise the bland impersonality of all cosmic processes, & the consequent silliness of expecting anything to be other than as it is. Last year he emphasised his abandonment of all literary standards, & his complete devotion to "action" stories & to such spectacles as prize-fights—which he followed assiduously at the Boston Garden & other local arenas. Then this year he told Little Belknap that he was resolved to "vegetate intellectually" henceforward. To Cole not long ago he expressed a complete reversal of his old attitude regarding the meaninglessness of material success—averring that he had come to see the folly of any standard of achievement save money-making, & holding up the rugged Mr. A. M. Adams—reputed to have made a fortune through some astute commercial transaction—as an ideal. And all the while he is publishing in *Driftwind* a series of savagely socialistic "pomes" (that is, irregular lines of prose) under his "Crossman" pseudonym[1]—amiably expressing the belief that the vicious capitalistic class desires to have all workers slaughtered by means of an opportune war before they rebel from starvation. Well—here's hoping a quiet vegetative period in the arctic will impart tranquillity & reflective poise. Coates will prove a good soothing influence.

As for commerce—the Greeks of the classick aera thought as I do; deeming mercantile transactions unbecoming to real citizens, & leaving such pursuits to aliens—largely Phoenicians. The profit-motive always leaves a trail of smallness & ignominy. What did I tell ya? Not only did divine vengeance overtake my mill-owning great-grandsire, but even your Jawn Cogan had to get pizen'd! The old Harry seizes his own! It would certainly be picturesque if you could sport a snappy murderess on your ancestral parchments!

I'll be all eyes when you trot out them fluorescent minerals; for the principle of natural philosophy involv'd—the absorption of radiant energy & re-emission at a lower wave-length—has strongly interested me. I think I've seen luminous fluor-spar in my youth, though probably no such gallery of wonders as your description suggests.

Enclosed is that Dutch-New England article I told you about—please return.[2] I assume that Jonckheer Wilfredus didn't give you one. I find that very few laymen know anything about that Dutch hold on the Maine Coast 1674–6.

Gawd be with you!

Πάππος Θεοβάλδος

Notes

1. Cook published these pieces in various booklets of limited distribution. The socialist pieces are collected, in part, in *W. Paul Cook: The Wandering Life of a Yankee Printer* (2007). Cook's other Crossman pieces are gathered in *Willis T. Crossman's Vermont: Stories by W. Paul Cook* (2005). Both books are edited by Sean Donnelly.

2. "Some Dutch Footprints in New England."

[137]   [AHT]

Novr. 21, 1933

Crown of CONSOBRINAL Clarification:—

All Hail! Welcome to the family circle! Blood is thicker than 3.2% beer! I thought there must be a link somewhere betwixt two such unbeatable ice-cream champeens! Just one happy household . . . . . which includes, come to think of it, the doc that set my aunt's ankle (a grandson, in several great-nesses, of Steve Place & Marthy Perkins) . . . . . . as well as a soulful poetess friend of my aunt's—Miss Ada Perkins—who lives only a block from here & was over last week, calling up ancestral data on both her John Perkins & Rev. Chad Brown sides. Well—we'll simply have to start a collection for a monu-ment to our revered common ancestor of Newent & Ipswich[1] . . . . . . let's see . . . . . where shall we locate it? In Newent? In Ipswich? In Providence? In Paterson? I scarcely need express the pride which I feel at discovering so no-ble a fruit of the ancient tree. The Perkinses have justify'd their existence . . . . for the first time I realise how great a calamity to posterity it wou'd have been, had the stout ship *Lyon* fallen victim to the treacherous deep!

Naturally, I've just raked up all my available Perkins notes, which form a fortunately stapled-together item amidst the chaos of that big bundle which I undid & shew'd you last August. Oddly enough, however, my primary addi-tion to your data will not come from this source, but from a new genealogical dictionary (which I'll look up again & cite by name if you wish) added to the Provpublibe within the past year & a half. This book—alone of all sources known to me, & probably because of the results of recent research—gives the *surname* of old John o' Newent's wife, though it adds nothing else to the facts concerning her. Be prepared, then (unless you are too cautious to endorse a single-book statement) to record on your charts as *our* common multiple-great-grandma the name of *Judith Gater.* GATER . . . . a name I never encoun-ter'd elsewhere, but which your exhaustless acumen may be able to trace to Bill the Conk, Charley Maine, Ivan the Terrible, Richard Coeur de Lion, Con-stantinus Palaeologus, Louis XI, Brian Boru, Haroun al Raschid, Cn. Pom-peius Magnus, Philip of Macedon, Tut-Ankh-Amen, Deucalion, Uranus, & a lot of them other ginks as figure on your vary'd heraldick scrolls.

A bit of good luck in yesterday's mail—Wright has finally accepted the joint tale by Price & me that he turned down a coupla months ago.[2] One hundred forty bucks. How Sultan Malik & I will split it (if we ever get it) re-mains to be seen.

I have a guest today—a lively younger tiger gentleman who last August was just a single handful. Is he playful & purr-ful? Boy! He's asleep just now, or I'd make him sign with a paw-print.

Yr obt Cousin

Θεοβάλδος Ρέρκινς

Notes

1. Newent is a small town in the Forest of Dean in Gloucestershire, England. The Ipswich HPL refers to is probably not the town in Massachusetts (cited in "The Shadow over Innsmouth") but the town in Suffolk, England.
2. "Through the Gates of the Silver Key."

[138] [AHT]

Dec. 19, 1933

Emperor of Etherick Education:—

Old Plymouth . . . . . Almost *313* years of continuous settlement, & the air of eighteenth century still hanging thick about it! God Save the King! I haven't a drop of its blood (any more than I have of Quebec's or Charleston's!), but it gives me a whale of a kick for all that. Your forest preserve—Morton Park—is a nifty slice of nature, very like my own Quinsnicket. It encloses a fine little pond, & borders on the shore of a larger lake (the source of the Town Brook) called "Billington Sea." As I told Jonckheer Talman, I'll bet my breeches that use of "Sea" for a small land-locked bit of water is one of those many Dutch tricks of speech which the Pilgrims pick'd up in Leyden. You get the analogy—Zuyder Zee, Tappan Zee, &c. 1620–1933 . . . . . . what a stretch! In 1620 the pathless black woods stretched indefinitely to the west. Northward, only the cursed Frenchman with towns at Quebec, Tadoussac, & Port Royal, & a garrison at Pentagoët. Southward, a few Dutchmen on Manhattan Island, & then only the wilderness till our Dominion of Virginia, with the straggling roofs of Jamestown, was reached. Then more wilderness—desolate marshy creeks—a few crumbling Huguenot ruins—and finally the damned Spaniard at San Augustin—a town fifty-five years old & having some houses which still survive. And what a future lay ahead—a great civilisation in the eighteenth century, & then a decline to a coarse democratical barbarism & speed-&-quantity worship not much to be preferr'd to the culture of the Wampanoags & Narragansetts! Aye—but these colonies have been lovely in their day.

The Kappa Alpha Tau has several new members—a fine all-black fellow, a curious grey piebald chap, a rather pale tiger, a black-&-white boy who I am sure must be Pres. Randall's son, a fat pale-yellow gentleman, & a trim tiger much like Vice-Pres. Osterberg. The black boy & the piebald display combative tendencies promising considerable entertainment. But there is bad news, too. Little Galpin—last July's handful of wobbly grey fur who grew to be such a friendly, sportive, & vociferously purr-ful visitor—has not been seen at his home for a week. I can't believe he has met with an accident, for he has never braved the streets outside our placid island of semi-rural and-whereness. Rather do I fancy he was stolen. I hope he has a good home.

Aunt increasingly active. We've seen several art exhibits, & last Sunday took in a classy lecture on stained glass at the museum—by the well-known Boston designer Joe Reynolds, who hails from our R. I. *Wickford*.[1]

Well—here's wishing you a riotous Yule!

Yr obt kinsman & hble Servt
Theobaldus Percinus.

Notes

1. Joseph G. Reynolds (1886–1972), stained glass artist and designer. He was a partner in the stained glass studio of Reynolds, Francis & Rohnstock, Boston.

[139]   [AHT]

230, West-97th St., cor. of the
Bloomingdale Road, over-against Stryker's Bay.
Bloomingdale, in His Maj^{ty's} Province of New-York.
Dec. 29, 1933

Parallelless Praeses of Picaresque Peregrinations:—

Have been hectically rush'd ever since I struck this damned burg. Over at Loveman's Christmas—& he gave me a real Egyptian *ushabti*—a thing I've wanted for years. Wait till you see how I've combined it with another gift from Sonny. At Wandrei's Wednesday, & met his brother—a *marvellous* fantastic artist. Also met Desmond Hall, Editor of *Astounding*. You'll see Wandrei Monday—he'll be here for dinner.

Well—I had a great Yule at home before hopping the midnight stage for putrescent megalopolis. Fixed up the sitting-room hearth with greens & surprised my aunt—& borrowed a cat for the occasion. Heard carol-singing in the early evening in the quaint cobblestoned courtyard of the Georgian Beckwith mansion (where my aunt was in 1927) half way down the ancient hill. Old Providence . . . . . and where! Glorious world of traditional continuity . . . . & to think that supposedly sane people live *voluntarily* in this lousy rat-warren which now seethes around me!

Well—see ya Monday.

Yr dutiful cousin & obt. Servt
Περκινος Θεοβάλδος

[140]   [AHT]

Perkins Manor
March 6, 1934

Cadent Convert to Connubial Cotenation:—

Congratulations upon the startling news retail'd in your just-receiv'd epistle!¹ Hail, noble captive! May your fetters prove both felicitous & permanent, & may the verdant awakening slopes of Parnassus resound with gay & tuneful epithalamia! When enter'd upon with analytical insight & mature calculation of future trends of temperament & aspiration, the antient institution of matrimony has much to recommend it; & I feel confident that the present venture contains all those elements of well-advisedness which conduce to stability & success. The gifts & excellences of the bride need no reiteration to one of the amateur circle, whilst the genius of the groom shines with its own radiance. Pray convey my compliments & felicitations to Mrs. Morton, & extend to her on my behalf an hearty welcome into the antient Perkins gens. Talassë! Talassë![2] Incidentally, I hope the Ridgewood parsonage was a colonial one, adjacent to a Georgian-steepled fane.

Regarding this WODA outfit—the trouble must be something deeper than any mere change of schedule, for the usual wave-length number raised *another station altogether*—some damn'd Newark affair. Or am I to understand that Paterson does not use the aether *every day*? Never before to my recollection has the given number fail'd to summon up the good old bombycine metropolis, hence I imagin'd it was as constant in its output as Providentium's three wave-factories. But of course I may have been wrong. Well—so long as the headliner ain't on, I don't give a damn whether the joint altogether canned, or put on part time, or merely given another pitch in the vibratory gamut. Tip me off when the spread of enlightenment is resum'd.

Climate hath certainly been throwing its most extreme fits hereabouts! On Feby. 9th all local records for frigid horror were shatter'd by an hydrargyral reading of *seventeen below*—whilst reports from Culinarius in Vermont are simply beyond transcription! On Feby. 26 a terrifick niveous infliction paralysed Novanglian traffick—but at last the hyemal malefice appears to be spent. Yesterday Mijnheer Fahrenheit's gleaming column climb'd almost to seventy degrees—& I accordingly broke hibernation by indulging in the season's first rural ramble—sloshing with caoutchouc-clad dawgs over the awakening meads and woodlands of antient Quinsnicket, where the mystical aura of Pan's rousing was manifest in melting snows, swollen streams, & a vague, elusive aroma of stirring earth. Never in my life have I beheld the brooks & ponds at an higher level, & when I cross'd the Blackstone betwixt Lonsdale & Valley Falls I saw that it had flooded its banks up to the very slopes of the gorge—so that great trees & many buildings arose like Atlantean reliques from out a broad aqueous expanse. I see by tonight's paper that some apprehension is felt regarding floods—though 'tis not likely that any damage as extensive as that of 1927 will occur. May Pegāna protect the cover'd bridges of Vermont!

I lately read the celebrated "Anthony Adverse"[3] (lent by Dwyer)—taking five days to plough my leisurely course through its 1224 pages. I presume it might have taken you all of three hours to cover that much ground. The thing gives a picture of the late eighteenth & early nineteenth centuries, tho' it is indubitably overrated. A bit mawkish, & heavy with bald philosophick speculation. Other recent items on my calendar are Dunsany's new book—"The Curse of the Wise Woman"—Weigall's "Wanderings in Roman Britain", & A. Merritt's old yarn "The Metal Monster",[4] which I had never read before because Eddy told me it was dull. The damn'd fool! (nephew—not our late bibliophilick friend) Actually, the book contains the most remarkable presentation of the *utterly alien & non-human* that I have ever seen. I don't wonder that Merritt calls it his "best & worst" production. The human characters are commonplace & wooden—just pulp hokum—but the *scenes & phaenomena* . . . . oh, boy! By the way—can you now claim A. M. as a kinsman-in-law?

Don't let your deferr'd honeymoon interfere with your Providence trip next summer—why not bring the bride for a belated wedding gorge at Aunt Julia's in Warren?

Blessings—

L. Percinius Theobaldus

Notes

1. JFM had announced his impending marriage to the amateur journalist Pearl K. Merritt.

2. Apparently Greek for "Endure!" or "Persevere!"

3. A best-selling historical novel, set largely in the eighteenth century, by Hervey Allen.

4. HPL read the serialization in the *Argosy* (7 August–25 September 1920; rpt. Hippocampus Press, 2002); it was lent to him by R. H. Barlow. It was the first of three versions of the novel: there was a revised version in *Science and Invention* (October 1927–September 1928; as *The Metal Emperor*) and a book version (Avon, 1946).

[141]   [AHT]

March 28, 1734

Beacon-Bright Basker in Befitting Bulletining:—

Again congrats! This time on your front-cover fame as one of the country's leading mineralogists. I'll say you're that! Ask Mariano if ya don't believe me! Coast to coast—New-Jersey to Oregon Territory! I enjoy'd the article greatly, & can find no pretext on which to differ from its conclusions.[1] Good work! And say—that magazine is quite a neat little proposition as a whole. I never realis'd that mineralogy was such a widespread popular institution as to command a chatty, sociable, non-technical press of its own. My idea of a rockological publication was a ponderous sort of sheet full of jawbreaking disquisitions on crocodileite & Cumberlandite that nobody cou'd possibly understand! To those with the right kind of taste, mineral-collecting must be almost as much fun as tropical fish!

Now as to the Big Bozo's fictional pipe-dream—help! help![2] What the hell do I know about such popular detective-formula dope as this . . . . . me what ain't read a detec story in these twenty or twenty-five years? Naturally you realise that this is a one hundred percent artificial formula proposition—absolute cheap-pulp tripe in conception & design. Damn it all, this old boy must have actual genius to be able to cook up a list of characters so completely devoid of all characteristicks save those of cut-&-dry'd detectkatiff con-

vention. A triumph of elimination, ef ya ast me! And people actually *read* this
stuff! Ho, hum . . . by Nature's kindly law . . . . . Well—I can believe His Nibs
when he tells ya he don't read nothin' but stoneocracy & Nick Carter. He
didn't need to say it—the synopsis tells its own tale!

Actually, though, I don't see why a trained detec pulpist couldn't make
quite a thing out of this idea of doing sherlocking through abstruse petro-
glyphical clues. Naturally, every science which involves strange & intricate
identifications & proofs of things is capable of clever use by the facile
vandiner[3]—so why not mineralogy? And I can easily believe that a well-
concocted series of this sort—if freed from Doc Dake's hilarious crudities,
tritenesses, & naivete—would go over big with the devotees of the especial
science involv'd. No spoofing, I advise ya to try it. With your joint equipment
of genuine literary taste & an exhaustive knowledge of the detective-fiction
field, you ought to be able to make something of this idea if anybody could.
And by the way—if you need any technical tips on the raciest way to sling the
formula, the boy to ask is our friend Malik Taus, the Peacock Sultan—now,
as you know, to be address'd at 10 Whiting Apts., Pawhuska, Okla. Sleuth
stuff is his one long suit nowadays. I, on the other hand, am all at sea where
artificial devices of this sort are concern'd.

As to Doc's dope—to begin with, I can't but vociferate the opinion that
the saddling of the lay-figures with rockological names is a lousily cheap trick.
Nothing makes a tale so hollow & unconvincing as punning, allegorical, eccentric, or excessively put nomenclature. See how asinine poor old Dickens's
grotesque concoctions appear today—& how pompous and stilted even the
names of my eighteenth century—Peregrine Pickle, Anthony Absolute, Sir
Lucius O'Trigger,[4] &c.—are. For gawd's sake don't have puppets like Sir
Stoneham Pyrites, Capt. Magnetite de Magistris, Prof. Boulder B. Traprock,
&c. &c. cluttering up your pages! But as for Doc's general ideas—some of
'em ain't bad. It ought to be quite interesting to have the technical spieling of
mineralogy unwound snappily in the course of unravelling some clue or tracking down some rock-greedy fiend in human form. For instance—you could
have a great mineralogical curator from Paterson murdered by some spy of
the American Museum—the latter institution being jealous of having its peb-
ble section surpass'd. Later it could be discover'd that the assassin had left his
photograph imprinted on some obscurely sensitive stone (if none exists, invent one!) that yields up its secrets only under a blend of infra-mauve light
from a special fur-lined vacuum tube. Then, when the murderer has explain'd
this away by saying he left the image on some other visit, in stalks Old King
Brady the Petrological Pinkerton with a radio-active kind of feldspar or
sparkill or solidified argon which restores the life-vibrations of the murder'd
man. Up sits the great curator on his bier, & points his finger at the dastard
from 79th street. "He done it!" "He done it!" But since the victim ain't dead
no more, the murderer is left off on probation . . . . tho' the American Mu-

seum is forced to transfer most of its treasures to the enlarged marble palace at Summer Street & Broadway. Everybody happy—all's well that ends well. In our next issue, Curator Plantagenet-Perkins & Old King Brady Dake foil the miscreants who plan to mine gold from the sun in space-ships & put the world off the gold standard. I fancy your idea of canning the serial stuff & having a series of independent shorts is by far the best one. You could vary your locale & incidents magnificently; having unknown minerals found in crypts under aeon-old deserted cities in the African jungle, & all that. Then there are hellish stony secrets filtering down from the forgotten elder world—think of the Eye of Tsathoggua, hinted at in the Livre d'Eibon, & of the carved primal monstrosity in lavender pyrojadeite caught in a Kanaka fisherman's net off the coast of Ponape![5] God! Suppose the world *knew why* Curator Konbifhashi Taximeto of the Wiggiwaga Museum in Kyoto committed hara-kiri after examining the fluorescent emanations of this unholy blasphemy through the differential spectroheliograph.

Well—as for Doc Dake's current outline . . . . I guess you can tactfully get rid of it before you really start to work. These alleged authors are pretty easy to handle—discard their dope little by little & substitute your own, & in the end they not only swallow it but honestly believe they wrote it themselves! Thus some of my revision clients congratulate *themselves* when the readers of *Weird Tales* praise stories (like "The Last Test", "The Curse of Yig", "The Horror in the Museum", "Winged Death", &c) that *I* wrote.[6] Jolly the old boy along. It would be hard, I fancy, to find a tamer & flatter hash of stock situations than the worthy Oregonite has mapped out. The end appears to be a more or less climaxless let down—the nature of the crime, when found, being commonplace & without human interest or dramatic possibilities. Instead of suggesting the hand of cryptic priests of forgotten Thibetan gods *at first*, & then trickling down to some prosaic local Al Capone with a mineralogical slant, the thing to do is to suggest the ordinary things first & *then* have some really vivid angle develop. Planting an Oriental unmotivatedly—having him actually only the emissary of a white man—is a bit clumsy. Some real plot with interest—& with an adequate final wallop—is needed. Less rambling technology & more story. Whatever minerals are stolen ought to be stolen *for some unusual & dramatic reason* (to appear at the climax), or else the circumstances of the tracking-down & solution of the crime ought to include some powerful climactic incident of human drama. The interest of a mere mathematical solution leading to the exposure of a common thief under circumstances of no especial vividness, is certainly not sufficient to float a story. Try to invent some reason why a certain man's or group's desire for a certain mineral is of a strange, astonishing, & sinister nature not to be suspected from the identity of the mineral itself. When the Eagle-Eyed Sleuth begins to suspect the possibility of such a reason, he at last knows to what previously unlikely quarter to turn his search. The reader isn't let in on the dope till the climax—but then it all comes out with a bang. If you wanted to make the stuff more serious, you could have the climax hinge on some delicate human situation—the involvement of some tremendous dignitary & the resultant psychological dilemma, or anything of that sort. I'm not very good at thinking up twists of that sort, but Price could give you dozens of suggestions. Better try him—let him see Doc Dake's verbal comic strip & explain what you want to do.

Speaking of deteckatiff dope—the enclosed Dickybird stamp[7] on its envelope (which I have been instructed to pass along to you) is a reminder of a case on which Inspectors Smiffkins & Theobald-Perkins of Scotland Yard are now working. On the 10th of March, 1934, I receiv'd from Groveland Grange an epistle containing a request that I pass the envelope & stamp along to you. Well—the stamp was only a common three cent Washington of the current series, so instead of blindly obeying, I put it to one side & asked my correspondent if he hadn't made some mistake. Incidentally, I noted (& mention'd) that the envelope bore a "Returned for postage" stamping—over which the stamp was affixed—& a double Haverhill postmark . . . one *March 9, 10:30 a.m.* & the other *March 9, 11:30 a.m.* Well—honest Tryout reply'd by return mail, outlining the following facts & venturing the following conclusion:

(a) The letter had been mailed with a Dickybird—hence the request to shoot along to Paterson.

(b) It *had not* been returned to Groveland Grange for postage.

(c) Smiffkins *has never used or possessed* (except, I suppose, for one in his collection) a three cent Washington stamp, such as the envelope bore. *Conclusion:* Some damn'd thieving clerk in the Haverhill P.O. peeled off & swiped the valuable Dickybird & substituted a common stamp after affixing a false "Returned for postage" legend to explain the removal of the Dicky.

Well—Inspector Theobald-Perkins now haul'd out the offending envelope & put it under the fluorescent lens. Sure enough, the paper bore marks of the peeling off of a long Dicky prior to the affixing of the common Georgiwash. *Natural* peeling would not cause this roughness. Besides, if the letter had *really* been found stampless it would either have *really* been sent back to Smiffkins or (in case the evidence of former stamp presence was unmistakable) have been sent ahead to me without any stamp. I've had 'em come that way. No ordinary postal clerk gives away three-centers thro' sheer philanthropy. Just why the elaborate "Returned for postage" dodge was used is not quite clear to me, unless it was to still curiosity of some sort at the Providence office. Perhaps, though, since the theft occurred after cancellation (I know it did from the state of the postmark); the robber didn't wish to risk either an *obviously artificially peeled* stampless envelope or an obviously interpolated common stamp. But he sent the letter on with amusing speed only an hour betwixt postmarks! I noticed this myself before hearing Tryout's explanation, & wonder'd how any ordinary postman could ever have got the letter back to 408 & ahead to the P.O. again in a single hour! So, after due use of his massive eye & eagle brain, Inspector

Theobald-Perkins decided that the suspicions of Smiffkins were indeed justify'd. Tryout has suspected local clarks of such malefactions before, & the pusillanimousness of that damn'd rat Paul Pry in your own office proves what low fellows occasionally get into the postal personnel! The envelope of evidence has now gone back to Inspector Tryout-Smith, & the next act in the drama will be his confrontation of a dismay'd post office force with the damning clue. I have as yet receiv'd no report of this, but am daily awaiting bulletins. The eye of justice never sleeps! Meanwhile Smiffkins, resolv'd that you shou'd not be an innocent sufferer from the iniquity of the Merrimack Valley, sent along another Dicky for you—which actually got through this time, & which I herewith transmit. Here's hoping to gawd it gets past Paul Pry—it would be like that bird to use ultra-red light on the envelope, detect the treasure within, & abstract it through a fake tear—subsequently patching up the envelope with one of these "Received in Bad Condition" stickers. Yes—& it would be like his damn'd insolence to add insult to injury by tacking on a postage-due stamp into the bargain, & mulcting you of three or six or nine hard-earn'd denarii! When Sonny & I get the Soviets to working, we'll clean all these shifty vermin out of the postal service, substituting social-minded comrades with Marxian idealism!

Well—gawd be with you! Don't let old Dake drag down your lit'ry ideels!

Yr. obt.—

Grandpa Theobald-Perkins.

Notes

1. *Rocks and Minerals* 8, No. 3 (September 1933).
2. Evidently a colleague of JFM suggested that they collaborate on a series of detective stories with a mineralogical theme.
3. S. S. Van Dine was the pseudonym of Willard Huntington Wright (1888–1939), art critic and author, who created the popular fictional detective Philo Vance, who first appeared in books in the 1920s, then in movies and on the radio.
4. The first-named is a character in Tobias Smollett's novel *Peregrine Pickle* (1751); the second and third are in Richard Brinsley Sheridan's play *The Rivals* (1775).
5. Cf. an early note in HPL's *Commonplace Book:* [60] "Fisherman casts his net into the sea by moonlight—what he finds."
6. HPL refers to Adolphe de Castro ("The Last Test"), Zealia Bishop ("The Curse of Yig"), and Hazel Heald ("The Horror in the Museum" and "Winged Death"), among others.
7. HPL refers to a flat plate engraved souvenir stamp designed by Victor S. McCloskey, Jr., issued on 10 February 1934 to commemorate the second Antarctic expedition of Richard E. Byrd (1888–1957).

[142]   [AHT]

Home again—but on a bench in a park in a
strange part of the city, which I've never visited
more than 2 or 3 times before in my life.
July 19, 1934

Adonei-anointed Acme of Arctic Acuteness:—

Yours of the 3ᵈ & 7ᵗʰ duly awaited me upon my shivering return to my ice-bound native shoars. The menace of coming autumn is in the air, & I shrink from the thought of early frosts, falling leaves, & the subtle melancholy of harvest-time. But I sure have had a damn fine trip—over whose pleasures I can ponder as I crouch half-paralysed before the blazing hearth!

You last heard from me, I conceive, in antient Charleston; where I announc'd with melancholy my inability to pause in the pest zone. After two days there, I reluctantly moved north to Richmond—where I got a dollar room with running water only half a block from the site of the old Allan mansion where Poe grew up. Only a day there—spend in exquisite Maymont Park & among the Poe reliques. Then on to Fredericksburg, where I wandered through Georgian lanes & dreamed on Meditation Rock. Then Washington—where I stopped two days & did the following things I had never done before: (a) explored interior of capitol, (b) ditto Pan-American Union, (c) ascended the Washington Monument (what a view!), (d) visited Rock Creek Park, & (e) inspected the furnish'd interior of Arlington mansion on the heights across the Potomack. This last-named item gave me a big kick. I had been through the house before it was furnished—but now it is re-born as a typical plantation home of early-XIX-century Virginia . . . a fragment of the greatest civilisation which has ever existed on this continent. It was with reluctance that I left it behind to take the coach for the bourgeois, trade-ridden North.

But Philadelphia had its compensations. I wondered through some of the choicest ancient areas, visited old Germantown & the lordly Wissahickon, & took a look at the well-housed Fossil Library in the new Franklin Institute.[1] And as a climax I visited the neat brick cottage at N. 7ᵗʰ & Spring Garden Streets where Poe dwelt from 1842 to 1844—now restored & opened as a publick museum. It is set amidst a garden in the rear of a larger house, & looks just as it did in Poe's day. The furniture is of the 'forties, & includes a couple of pieces (chair & desk) which actually belonged to the bard. The rooms are small, but their arrangement is pleasing; & it is not difficult to imagine Poe as on the premises & ready to welcome his guests. In the adjacent larger house is an excellent collection of reliques, including magazines containing the first appearance of most of the tales & poems. This cottage was open'd to the publick only a few months ago—I heard the exercises (with speeches by William Lyon Phelps[2] et al.) over the radio.

When I hit the pest zone I found Sonny about to depart with papa &
mamma for Asbury Park & Ocean Grove, in your own present common-
wealth; & at their cordial invitation I went along with them. Boardwalk dull as
hell—but had the usual interesting arguments with the Child to the rhythm of
the icy Atlantick. On getting back to New York I could stop only a couple of
nights—& couldn't look up anybody save Fra Samuelus. He—lavish soul—
quite overwhelmed me by presenting me with that slim, conventionalised bird
of carved, lacquered horn which you must have noticed around his dump
during the past few years. It is—as you doubtless know—a typical specimen
of the carving of Yankee sailors in the India trade a century ago . . . made
under the influence of Sino-Japanese craftsmanship traditions. It stands as if
poised for flight thro' gulphs beyond the galaxy—& I have always called it
(borrowing a title from an old weird tale) "The Bird of Space".[3] I have admired it for years, & it certainly gives me a kick to be its actual possessor. If
Loveman keeps this up, it'll be my museum instead of his'n which will rival
your'n!

Well—I came home on the midnight coach July 9–10th, & struck the first
disconcertingly cold weather since last May. Damn the Yankee climate! Dawn
came near the R. I. line, & it was surely good to see once more the rolling
hills, stone walls, great elms, & white village steeples of my native sod. God
Save the King! Then there loom'd up before me a distant prospect of the
spires & domes of antient PROVIDENCE, all golden in the morning light.
Home! Found my aunt in splendid health—going everywhere without a cane.
And at the boarding-house across the back garden I found something else of
infinite interest & grace—something small & coal-black & furry, that is still a
bit wobbly on its little legs, tho' already beginning to be playful. Just a double-
handful with great eyes undecided whether to turn green or yellow . . . .
Mrs. Spotty's latest child, born last month & known as Samuel Perkins. You'll
see the young devil next month . . . . . . & I leave to your imagination the
amount of borrowing I have done. Yesterday young Mr. Perkins spent a couple of hours at #66, crawling all over his Grandpa, chewing the old gentleman's fingers & coat-lapels, & finally dropping off to sleep whilst Grandpa
read the *Evening Bulletin*. He hasn't begun to purr yet, but probably will
shortly—since his development is of almost Galpininan precosity. Grandpa's
little nigger-man! He looks like a bear-cub of paperweight size—& I certainly
must get a photograph of him soon. He's surely slated to spend a lot of time
over at Grandpa's. When he grows up he'll doubtless join the Kappa Alpha
Tau on the shed roof beyond the side garden. Incidentally—Mrs. Spotty's
remaining February child—Betsey Perkins, an almost precise black & white
duplicate of herself—is getting to be quite as big as mamma, tho' she still
seeks nourishment from the maternal bosom along with little brother Sam.
And so it goes. But the worst thing is the pile of unread periodicals, undone
jobs, & unanswered mail that I found awaiting me. Ædepol! I'm still in the

midst of it, without a second's breathing space . . . . . indeed, my valise isn't fully unpack'd yet! However—I palliate things by doing as much as possible in the open air . . . . . . parks & countryside & andwheres. At present I'm in a strange, semi-shew park behind the Y. M. C. A. off Broad Street . . . . dividing attention betwixt my correspondence and a daylight band concert.

Your participation in the Royal birthday celebration[4] is a stroke of luck which I most venomously envy you. Damn it all, it ain't fair! . . . . to waste such a boon on a misguided rebel & roundhead. How I would have eaten these festivities up! The King—supreme symbolick focus of our race & civilisation . . . . . Rule, Britannia!! And there surely was an added attraction for your Caledonian acquaintance! Well—I had many chances to salute the Old Flag in St. Augustine, where most of the historick houses bear it, together with the Spanish & rebel flags, in commemoration of the various governments under which the antient town has existed. God Save the King!!

Just read "Pete Ashley"—the novel of old Charleston life by Du Bose Heyward. Great antiquarian stuff, though a bit wooden & romantic as a transcript of reality. Did I mention meeting, in Charleston, an extremely gifted gentlewoman who is chairman of the Charleston Art Commission & author of the standard history of the eighteenth century Charleston stage? A Miss Eola Willis, who dwells in her centuried hereditary mansion in Tradd street. Her book & anecdotes confirm my belief that the culture of Charleston is the finest that ever flowered in North America. You ought to see the literary tone of the *South-Carolina Gazette* in the 1730's, when the North was atrophied in theological delusion! The more I learn of the South, the more my Confederate bias is strengthened.

Well—I guess I'll ring off & move up closer to the band, which not long ago play'd the Royal anthem whose local popularity your grandsire so considerably extended.

> Hoping to see you soon—
> Theobaldus Perkins.

Notes

1. The Library of Amateur Journalism, now at the University of Wisconsin Special Collections Library, is an immense collection of amateur journals assembled and maintained by the Fossils, the alumni organization of amateur journalists.
2. William Lyon Phelps (1865–1943), a leading American literary critic and academician (Lampson Professor of English at Yale, 1901–33) of the period.
3. Everil Worrell, "The Bird of Space" (*WT*, September 1926).
4. King George V of England celebrated his 69th birthday on 3 June 1934.

[143]   [AHT]

Home—driven indoors by the cold.

July 24, 1934.

Knowledge-Knitting Knight of Kendallick Kinship:—

Evoë! The keys of the antient city will be on hand, accompany'd by a suitable brass band & fife & drum corps, at the Crown Tavern on Thor's-Daeg, The Second of Sextilis, at nine of the morning or shortly thereafter.

Nine days to August 2—see ya then!

With obeisant dust-rubbings—

Theobaldus Perkins, Gent.

[144]   [AHT]

Prospect Terrace—Sunset—August 8, 1934

Peerless Peak of Parentage-Pursuit:—

Both cards duly received—& the view of Portland arouses a proper envy within me. I saw Portland only once—in 1927. Glad you've had smooth sailing, & that the Onset jaunt came off properly. Do you share Little Sonny's enthusiasm for Onset? That, by the way, is the scene of my solitary aëroplane ascent in 1929.

Shiveringly thy slave—

Theobaldus Perkins

[145]   [AHT]

Crouched before the oil stove with a blanket around me

August 22, 1934

Feat-fecund Ferreter of Fulgent Forbears:—

Congrats on the ten new fish in your net! Ædepol! You have so many forefathers now that you could sell or give away a dozen without feeling the difference!

See ya sometime if I don't congeal.

Yrs betwixt shivers—

Theobaldus Perkins

[146]   [AHT]

Septr. 24, 1934

Paramount Pattern of Peter-prying Persistence:—

Well—I guess I told you of what an interesting outing I had last month. Doubtless you received the cards signed by Cook, Cole, Smiffkins, Lynch, &c. Good old Tryout looked just the same as of yore—he hasn't aged a bit since I first saw him in 1921. Eighty-two on Oct 24. Cole had one of his nervous smashes & had to go home prematurely. Too damn bad—both city & country seem to get him. *Now* he's all up in arms against the lone open spaces—says he wants to go to New York (ugh!) & live 'among the radicals below Fourteenth Street'!!! God in heaven, what an environment for the erstwhile Athol sage! The young radicals of West 97th are bad enough! I guess I told you that I was at the Myers joint in Cambridge one evening, & saw young Peter, now seventeen.[1] He was a toddler of six when I last previously beheld him, but Jove, what a young aesthete he's grown to be! An antiquarian, too . . . as fond of the 1840 period as I am of the eighteenth century. He's bought a costume of the period—frock coat, stovepipe hat, &c.—& wears it all he can . . . . . sometimes even around the neighbourhood after dark. In many ways he reminds me of Sonny Belknap—just now he is a great aristocrat & conservative. "The older I grow," he gravely remarked at dinner, "the more conservative do I tend to become in my basic social, political, aesthetic, & religious philosophy!" Religious? Oh, Boy! Not satisfied with Sonny's erstwhile popery, he goes The Child one better & is a devotee of the *Orthodox Greek Church* . . . whose doctrine, ritual, & music he expounds learnedly & at length. Some kid—& bright as a whole stack of gold eagles! When he goes bolshevik he'll probably out-bolshevik Sonny! I guess I also mention'd that Cole & his family brought me home Aug. 26, & that my aunt & I took 'em down to Aunt Julia's. They simply aren't in the running with us as to quantity—which reminds me that Dwyer says ice-cream *is* one of his specialties! Two historick battles of the century certainly loom ahead—the Morton-Theobald preliminary contest, & finally the epoch-making clash betwixt Battling Bernie & the winner of the prelim! Well—on the night of the 26th I merely used #66 as an inn. Without having unpack'd my valise I moved on the next day to antient NANTUCKET!

And boy! did ah have a time at old Sherburne? Dun't esk it a foolish question a'ready! What a place! What a place! I've forgotten how much I told you of my week's stay. Had a room at the old Overlook (formerly Verandah House) in Step Lane near the North Church . . . . a former colonial mansion with small-paned windows, wide floor-boards, &c. On the third floor, with a swell sweep of town, harbour, & sea. When not freezing to death I did the town from A to Z—all the old houses (Coffin, Coleman, &c.) & museums, all the old church interiors (every one has galleries & box pews), the 1746 windmill, the Maria Mitchell Observatory (had a great glimpse of Saturn one night), &c. &c. Took Cap'n Folger's sightseeing trip around the whole island—which allow'd fifteen minutes for strolling through the quaint lanes of "S'conset". And did the suburbs of Nantucket Town on a *hired bicycle*—the first time in twenty years that I'd been on a wheel. Riding was just as easy & familiar as if I had last dismounted only the day before—& the effect of this revived process was infinitely exhilarating & rejuvenating. It brought the old 1900 period back with ineffable poignancy, till I felt as if I ought to be hurrying home in time for the opening of Hope Street High School! I wish to gawd it weren't conspicuous for an old geezer to ride a bike around Providence! Didn't get fatigued at all, & must have made twenty-five miles an hour when the wind was favourable. Passed two horseless carriages on one stretch! At times I did some historick reading at the old Nantucket Athenaeum—though it was so damn cold I could scarcely take legible pencil notes! Well—on the whole, Nantucket has to go down on the records as one of the premier high spots![2]—along with CHARLESTON, Quebec, Marblehead, & Newburyport. It is amusing to think that I was never there before—a place only ninety miles away! I'll have to get there again—tho' for *climate* I prefer St. Augustine!

Home Sept. 3—& on the 4th my aunt set out for a fortnight in Ogunquit, Maine, where she had a very congenial time. Meanwhile I was knock'd flat with piled-up work—& on the 12th was bowled over with a hellish siege of indigestion. In bed a week—or dragging betwixt there & kitchen & bathroom—but fortunately I was all stocked up with supplies.

By the time my aunt came home I was able to be dressed & un-alarming in aspect. Pain all gone now, though I'm feeling none too rugged, & am still pretty damn careful what kind of stuff I dump into the old belly. Couldn't do any reading or writing to speak of during the worst of the trouble, so that I'm simply knocked down and out now. Shall have to send a form letter to my fifty-two-odd correspondents—or something!

But the saddest news is yet to come. Alas—how can I impart it unmov'd? Little Sam Perkins, the tiny ball of black fur whom you saw in August, is no more! He was ill then—but fully recover'd & was quite his usual dynamick little self. As late as Sept. 7 he spent the day with Grandpa—tearing about the place, shuffling the papers on the old gentleman's desk, & finally stretching out like a little ebony stick in the semicircular chair, sound asleep. On the morning of the 10th, however, he was found peacefully lifeless in the garden—& from no apparent cause. Now he sleeps beneath the shrubbery amidst which he play'd in life. Blessed little piece of the Night! He liv'd but from June to September, & will never know what the winter's hellish cold is like. The Kappa Alpha Tau is in deep mourning, & President Randall often news in elegiack numbers—

> The ancient garden seems tonight
> A deeper gloom to bear,
> As if some silent shadow's blight
> Were hov'ring in the air.

> With hidden griefs the grasses sway,
> Unable quite to word them—
> Remembering from yesterday
> The little paws that stirr'd them.

During his later days Master Perkins was fully inducted into the K.A.T.—appearing frequently on the clubhouse roof. Eheu—the old place is not the same without him!

And so it goes.

> Yrs for bigger & better forefathers
> —Theobaldus Perkins, Gent.

Notes

1. Mr. and Mrs. Denys P. Myers, whom HPL described as "old-time amateurs," and their son Peter.
2. See "The Unknown City in the Ocean," *Perspective Review*, Winter 1934 (Fourth Anniversary Number): 7–8. In *CE* 4.

[147]   [AHT]

The Georgian Citadel
Feby. 13, 1935

Supreme Sultan of Scintillance-Spreading Smith-Seekers:—

That Kalem meeting surely was a winner.[1] It totalled 15, counting a pair (Loveman's friend Dean Phillips & a pal of his'n) who blew in after the original bunch had begun to scatter. Had you cast gloom over the assemblage by your departure before these youths blew in? This was the first meeting in recent years when *every invited guest* (& more, at that!) shew'd up. Did that young rascal Talman send you the snaps he took of us with that patent Nazi camera when we weren't looking? I came out as the most absurd clown of all. He caught me as I was looking up & saying something—& my mouth was screw'd up as if I were about to launch a parabola of tobacco-juice toward a remote cuspidor![2]

The rest of the visit was pretty fair. The day after the meeting Sonny, Bobby Barlow, & I went over to Koenig's Electrical Testing Laboratories & were shewn all over the place. Full of weird devices suggestive of spaceships, ray-projectors, & such like—for the purpose of gauging the safety & durability of every sort of household electrical device. Some of the ways in which common forms of wear & tear are duplicated & intensified for testing purposes are genuine triumphs of ingenuity. Koenig is really a great chap. He flashed some artificial lightning for us—of the sort Charles P. Steinmetz invented some years ago. We did & re-did the Met-Mus, & haunted the art department of the Pub Libe. Bobby also sunk a young fortune in art materials—dry point apparatus, copper plates, &c. If Belknap & I hadn't kept a close watch on him, he'd probably have squander'd his return fare to Washington! We picked up some genuine book bargains, though—little Barlow got George W. M. Reynold's "Wagner, the Wehr-Wolf" for fifteen cents in a Fourth Avenue joint (fine old edition of the 1850's), whilst Grandpa got "The Monk" (same 1924 reprint that you have) for one smacker. Amusingly enough, we stumbled into good old Arturo's joint without knowing it. We were doing the dives on the east side of Fourth Avenue one after the other, & as we enter'd one—as perfect strangers—an unexpectedly familiar voice sang out from the shadowy rear—"Hey, youse guys!" It was during the impromptu semi-Kalem meeting that follow'd, that I pickt up "The Monk." To cap the climax, I *later* learn'd that this was the same shop which Kirk established with that ratty little Kamin person[3] a decade ago, in pre-Chelsea days. Lord almighty—didn't Sonny & I help fix up that joint—accompanying Georgius as he carted the contents of a lately deceas'd gentleman's library thither in two taximeter hackney-coaches? Old memories! Well—on another occasion quite a bunch congregated at Loveman's & were regaled by the sight of almost four hundred Clark Ashton Smith drawings (I can see your mouth water!) lately brought from Cleveland. I had seen this array in Cleveland in '22, but they were wholly new to Sonny, little Barlow, & the Wandrei boys. Bobby almost went into convulsions over them! Well—the festivities began to die down on Jan. 7. Barlow took a morning coach back to Washington, but Grandpa hung on till midnight—when the Wandreis saw me off. They have quite a joint in decadent Greenwich—155 W. 10—over a sort of cross between a barroom & a 'Bohemian' beanery called "Julius's".

I reach'd Providentium's antient hill in the grey foggy dawn, & have been immers'd in labours ever since. Of the hellish snowstorm of Jany. 23–4 I need not speak. Gawd! And it was down around zero for more'n a whole damn week—so that I couldn't get outa the house for eight days runnin'. This winter surely is an hellish mess—even tho' 'taint quite so lousy as its unmentionable predecessor.

And so it goes.

Benedictions—

Theobaldus Perkins.

Notes

1. HPL refers to a gathering of the Kalems on 2 January 1935.

2. See the cover photograph of Kenneth W. Faig, Jr., *The Unknown Lovecraft* (New York: Hippocampus Press, 2009).

3. Martin Kamin, an erstwhile colleague of George Kirk.

[148]   [AHT]

IV Ante Nones Aprilis

[1 April 1935]

Premier Pursuer of Proaval Particulars:—

Nope—Grandpa ain't getting sporty! On the other hand, this yaller journalism is really the essence of conservatism . . . involving the using-up of some bargain stationery purchased in the year 1910—just a quarter-century ago—& brought to light during the course of some file-sorting involving the unpacking of long-neglected boxes! Kin ya beat it? When, as a youth of twenty, I laid in these ochraceous pads, did I ever think a grey-headed old has-been of almost forty-five would be scrawling on 'em in the virtually fabulous future of year of *1935?* 1935 . . . . . even today it has an unreal, far-ahead sound! Can *I* be living in a year whose numeral seems as fantastically remote as 2000 or 2500 or 5000? Where *have* all the intervening twelvemonths gone to? Even 1910 is fantastic enough to one whose sense of existence is somehow curiously oriented to *1903*. And can it be that the world of 1910 will in turn give place to something as different as 1910 is from 1450? Is there to be a war . . . a breakdown of capitalism & democratick illusion . . . an emergence from millennial attitudes & folkways . . . . . a rise of nightmare "modernism" in architecture . . . & a discovery by me of something called "amateur journalism"? Bless my soul, but such predictions sound fantastick! King Edward has just died, but I dare say the Prince of Wales (or I should call him George V now!) will be an even better-liked focus for our racial-cultural loyalty. In this local region, President Taft is something of a disappointment—but I hope we'll have T. R. back in 1912. Hope Premier Asquith can head off the disgusting radical schemes of that wretched little Welshman Lloyd-George . . . . there's actually some talk about subtracting power from the House of Lords!

Ah, me! Ah, me! And yet that grotesque alleged calendar above my desk *does* say *1935* . . . . but here's the same yellow pad & the same old man & the same (or perhaps worse) undecipherable hieroglyphs![1]

The file-upheaval, by the way, springs from that cabinet-purchase of Jany. 21 which I mention'd to you, & from its equally spectacular sequel of March 22. On the latter day I supplemented my original purchase with a set of 6 small papier-maché-and-wood-frame cabinets secured at a bargain sale for a dollar each, & so small (22 × 13 × 9½″) that they can be tucked into odd corners without disturbing in the least the general furnishing plan of this antient study. They are four-drawer affairs, in imitation brown grained wood finish. Together with the two wooden cabinets, they provide *thirty-four* new drawers to accomodate my scatter'd pamphlets, cuttings, old letters, & the like. Well—I spent forty-eight hours without a break readjusting my files, & at last I have things in better order than they've been in since the long-departed year of this pad! Boy—was it a job? And yet even now a helluva lotta things remain piled upon open shelves or stack'd in perishable cardboard boxes. The wooden cabinets contain my antiquarian files (in part), my collection of family photographs (transferr'd from the upper drawer of the library table, which now accomodates the overflow of the *Farmer's Almanack* file in the lower drawer (where it has been since 1870)), & the few amateur journals which exceed 7 × 10. Two of the small cabinets—set side by side to make one at the far end of the library table—hold the bulk of my amateur collection—now in easily consultable shape for the first time in history. Another (tucked beside the ebony table in front of the fire-place) holds stray Americana. A fourth—beside my desk—holds current miscellany & poetic & bibliophilic odds & ends. The two residual ones (one under my desk, t'other beside the typewriter table) provisionally accomodate old letters. Hell of an upheaval—but worth it!

Decently early spring for this lousy latitude. Guess I told you about the

Hokusai & Soviet Art lectures & the poetry readings in February. Well—on March 2–3 young Bobby Moe shew'd up[2]—& believe me, he's some kid! I don't wonder old Deacon Mocrates is proud of him! I hadn't seen him since 1923, when he was a little towhead of eleven. Now he's twenty-two, & two years out of the University of Wisconsin—fine, manly chap . . . courteous, attractive, & with hair-trigger intellect. Has none of his pa's naive belief in the supernatural. He's already looked up Koenig (a fellow-electrical engineer) in N. Y. & may get out to Paterson before long. You'll like him. He came in his faithful 1928 Ford (which he parked in one of the and-wheres betwixt Angell & Waterman streets), & slept on a camp cot in the sitting-room here.

Well—this host business prov'd only the first of my outings. On March 6th the mercury was up to sixty-five degrees, so that I took the first pedestrian jaunt of the season, walking twelve miles . . . to & from my favourite Quinsnicket region. Vernal suggestions in the air despite bare boughs o'erhead and slush underfoot—& at evening the thin crescent moon & glowing Venus made a magnificent picture in the west. A later walk (March 20th) cover'd eight miles. But all the same, I wish I were in good old Charleston! Heard good lectures lately—one on the recently uncover'd mosaicks in the great church of Hagia Sophia in Constantinoplis . . . by Thomas Whittemore, the guy that uncover'd 'em . . . & t'other on the cosmick rays by Prof. W. F. G. Swann of the Franklin Institute.[3]

Read Augie Derleth's new detec novel—"Three Who Dy'd"—& guess'd the outcome in full on page 145 (out of 252). A cleverer book than its predecessor.[4] Also lapp'd up Gustav Meyrink's "The Golem", lent me by little Bobby Barlow. The most magnificent weird thing I've come across in aeons! The cinema of identical title in 1921 was a mere substitute using the name—with nothing of the novel in it. Yuggoth, what a study in subtle fear, brooding hints of magick, & driftings to & fro across the borderline betwixt dream & waking! There are no overt monsters or miracles—just symbols & suggestions. As a study in lurking, insidious *regional* horror it has scarcely a peer—doing for the antient, crumbling Prague ghetto what I unsuccessfully strove to do for rotting Newburyport in "The Shadow over Innsmouth". Have you read it? If ya ain't, ya missed sumpum!

Pick'd up a damn useful item t'other day—the new 1-volume *Modern Encyclopaedia*, now issued by Grosset & Dunlap for only *$1.95*. I needed this badly—my latest other one being of 1914. This chronicles events as recent as *last November*. I was tempted by the original $3.00 edition in '33—but now I'm glad I waited.

Hope the Fossils can stop their whisker-pulling at the coming reunion. This has been a great year for warfare, with *every* existing organisation sporting a lively free-for-all. By the way—I learn with mild amusement that a quondam opponent of mine has begun to fade from publick recollection . . . at least, so far as his features are concern'd. Not long ago Edwin Hadley Smith sent me for identification a snapshot of the 1921 convention, shewing two grinning simps lined up against the brass rail of the Brunswick's steps. It came from you—& although you had managed to identify Grandpa Theobald, you were in doubt about the other smirking nitwit. Indeed—you went far enough to suggest that it might be little Wisecrack Sandy. Oh, boy! Is fame such? How couldst thou! Hast so soon forgot that this was the famous reconciliation-photograph of the THEOBALD-DOWDELL scrapping duo? Another version (for at least three kodaks immortalised the scene . . . I had Kleiner snap it with mine!) was published in the *National Tribute* of the Honble George St. Julian Houtain. And today the great William J. Dowdell is mistaken for good ol' Bozo Al! You may recall that on July 6, 1921 . . . the day the state of war betwixt the U.S. & Germany *legally* ceased . . . Bill Dowdell & Grandpa met in person for the first time—& proceeded to shake hands instead of mashing each other's maps to a sanguinary pulp! Old days . . . old days . . . . I suppose Dowdell & I wouldn't know each other by sight if we were to meet on the street now!

And so it goes. Hope the rock industry is still prospering, & that you get to see some of the gang now & then.

Yrs for memories of 1910
—Theobaldus Perkins.

April 2, 1935

P.S. In the course of my exhumations (vide infra) I came upon the remains of old composition books which I used in 1905 and 1906. One of them (according to the cover) contain'd a story (which I've completely forgotten) called "Gone, But Whither?" I'll bet it was a hellraiser! Written Dec. 1905. Well—*thirty years later* the remaining blank sheets of the same book may go into another story (probably just as lousy) by the same still-surviving relique! Tempus, tempus! Quid es?[5] Another book was "A Brief Course in Astronomy; Descriptive, Practical, & Observational; For Beginners & General Readers" (1906). That got as far as the typed stage—tho' all manuscripts are long ago thrown away! Dies alteri! Dies alteri! Non sum qualis eram![6] Eheu fugaces!

Notes

1. Similar images and concepts may be found in HPL's "The Shadow out of Time," recently completed.

2. Robert Ellis Moe, son of Maurice W. Moe.

3. Thomas Whittemore (1871–1950), American archaeologist who devoted himself chiefly to Byzantine and Coptic art. William Francis Gray Swann (1884–1962), British physicist and director of the Franklin Institute in Philadelphia (1927–59).

4. *Murder Stalks the Wakely Family* (1934).

5. "Time, time! What are you?"

6. "Other days! Other days! I am not what I once was." The last sentence is taken from Horace's *Odes* 4.1.3 and was used as the title of a celebrated poem by Ernest Dowson.

[149] [AHT]

Freya's Daeg, 1935
[10 May 1935]

Aidenn-Assisted Acme of Accumulative Arcanosophy:—

Bad news—though I knew it was coming. R. I. School of Design to erect
its new building very shortly on the College Street site now occupied by that
quaint Georgian row. Gordamnation!!!

Kid Moe's second visit was quite a travel event. He blew in on the morning of Saturday, April 27, in his faithful 1928 Ford—& we certainly put in a
strenuous two days in that venerable vehicle. Saturday we visited antient
Newport—going by the way of Fall River (ugh!) to avoid the piratical toll of
the Mt. Hope Bridge. We descended the Island by the East Road, and had a
splendid close-up of one of the century'd *windmills* . . . atop a knoll with
crumbling farm buildings, stone walls, & a flock of sheep with small lambkins
in the best pastoral tradition. Then down to ol' Bish Berkeley's "Whitehall"—
which I beheld for the second time in my life. These horseless kerridges do
git ya 'roun'! Next the Hanging Rocks & Purgatory—then the cliffs & forty-
steps (where I slipp'd on the rocks & got soaked whilst trying to peer into a
sea-cave I never noticed before!), & then the venerable town itself.

Went all over the 1739 colony house—which is all fixed up since we explored it with Wandrei in '27. Now just as it was in the good old days. Also
trod the standard rounds—having parked the Ford near the Colony-House.
We didn't miss much—& ended up with a chop-suey & chow-mein feed at a
Chink joint in Broadway . . . . for it seems that young Bob is as much of a
gastronomick Sinophile as you are. I'll hafta head ya to this place next August.
Then back to #66—where we parked the kid on a camp cot in the manner of
last March. It was a glorious hot day—one of the few decent occasions during the present alleged "spring". Eighty-two degrees in Providence—though
not so good in sea-chill'd Newport.

The next day—Sunday the 28th—we hit the pike for antient New Bedford . . . going to Fall River (ugh) by way of Warren, Swansea Village & the
now-little-used fragments of the old road (which was the *main* road back in
'26, when we made that coach trip). When we got to N. B. we found the
whaling museum closed—but had a good enough time mopping up Johnny-
cake Hill (with its Seaman's Bethel & Mariner's Home mention'd in "Moby
Dick") & the crumbling & picturesque waterfront. After this we set off
southward to sample something still better—something I had long wish'd
ardently to see, tho' I never dared ask Sonny's papa (the only motorist with
whom I've ever ridden thro' N. B.) to detour that far. There's no publick
transportation. I allude to the Round Hills estate of Col. E. H. R. Green (old
Hetty's boy) in South Dartmouth, where the old whaling barque *Charles W.
Morgan* (built in 1841) is preserv'd at a realistick-looking wharf—but solidly
embedded in concrete as a permanent exhibit. We went all over the vessel—

which is tremendously fascinating—& Bob snapped dozens of pictures of it
. . . inside & out. On the Green estate is also an antient windmill mov'd from
Rhode-Island. They have to come to us of the good things!

We subsequently explor'd a region—where S. Mass. adjoins S. E. Rhode-
Island—which I had never seen before in my life. Splendid unspoil'd countryside with rambling stone walls & idyllick white-steepled villages of the old New
England type. Of the latter the two best specimens—Adamsville & Little
Compton Commons—are both in Rhode-Island. Adamsville contains the
world's only known monument to an *hen*—perpetuating the fame of the
Rhode-Island Red, a breed evolv'd in that village from East-Indian & Chinese
gallinaceous forbears. At Little Compton Commons can be found the home &
grave of Elizabeth Alden Pabodie—daught of the fam'd John Alden & Priscilla
Mullins of Plymouth, & first white woman born in New-England. This region
was once the seat of the Seaconnet Indians—whose squaw-sachem Awashanks
was persuaded by the noted old Warrior Capt. Benjamin Church not to join
King Philip's conspiracy in 1675. It was settled from Plymouth about 1673, &
(like Barrington, Warren, & Bristol) came into the Bay in 1691 & into Rhode-
Island (when a boundary dispute was settled by His Maj^{ty} George II) in 1747.
Capt. Church lyes bury'd not far from Little Compton Commons.

Well—at last we turn'd north thro' Tiverton, where on our left we had
some marvellous vistas of low-lying fields & blue water. We could see St.
George's Gothick tower crowning its Newport knoll across the Seaconnet
River. Here, too, we pass'd the home of Capt. Robert Gray, the navigator who
in 1792 discover'd the Columbia River in the far-off Oregon country—naming
it after his stout Rhode-Island barque. Then back home via Fall River & antient
Warren—at which latter place we tanked up at Aunt Julia's on a full ice-cream
dinner. The repertoire is badly cut down this year—only about a dozen flavours, all fairly common. Bob was easily defeated on quantity—three rounds
being his limit. Programme as follows: (Moe: chocolate chip, coffee, caramel,
banana, ginger, pistachio. Grandpa: chocolate chip, coffee, caramel, banana,
lemon, & strawberry. None of my favourite grape!) Finally back to the and-
wheres—after which I regretfully guided the guest out of town & took a four-
mile walk before returning home. Quite a session. Here are some of the pictures I took—which I'll ask you to return at your convenience.

May 3–4–5 I visited Cole in Wollaston, but lousy cold weather queered
the sightseeing. We did get a bit of antient *Marblehead*, though. Saturday evening Mr. & Mrs. Myers were over at the Carbonaceous dump, & quite a few
amateur reminiscences were exchang'd. Sunday I was return'd to #66 in the
family Chevrolet.

Cook is wavering betwixt Campbell's St. Louis bait & a proposition of
Orton's in Western Vermont. We shall see what will happen.

As for me, I'm damn near frozen (or rather, radiator-chain'd), & hope to
gawd the Florida trip can be managed. What in hell *is* the g. d. matter with

this g. d. arctic climate?

Yrs for palmettoes & live-oaks—
Theobaldus Perkins.

[150]   [AHT]

c/o R. H. Barlow Box 88, De Land, Fla.
July 21, 1935

Dauntless Disciple of Drastick Denudation:—

The visit somewhat parallels last year's, except that Little Bobby's papa is now at home. His elder brother Wayne—a second Leftenant at Ft. Sam Houston—was here on a furlough during the early weeks, & proved a delightful companion, but the expiration of his leave hath now snatch'd him away. Of the felidae, old Doodlebug & High have vanish'd, whilst Jack flourishes with a neck only slightly awry from last year's snake bite. Low has been given to a grocery store in Eustis, but her two kittens Henry Clay (yellow) & Alfred A. Knopf (tiger) remain as permanent additions to the flock. And besides all these there are two lordly & pamper'd Persians—Cyrus & Darius— whom Bobby brought down from Washington.

As for the duration of the visit—so insistent is the super-hospitality of the Barlovii that I'm damn'd if I know whether I'm a guest or a prisoner! Every time try to speak of a getaway, the household makes me feel that I'd be practicing croolty to children by leaving little Bobby to a grandfatherless monotony . . . . indeed, the latest plea is *that I stay down all winter.* This I really would hate to do, since I am lost without my books & files & familiar home things after a certain length of time. I shall have to find a tactful way of breaking loose before the north gets hellish with autumn—for it would wreck me to plunge out of this earthly paradise into the viciousness of a northern September or October.

Yrs. for clothes & less activism—
Theobaldus Perkins.

[151]   [AHT]

The Genial Tropicks
August 1, 1735

Avid Assimilator of Arctick Asparities:—

Well—just a last word befo' you-all takes off for Novanglia's frozen steppes! I'm still amongst the palms & live-oaks, & feeling like a sixteen-year-old—tho' I surely will have to pull up stakes before this month is out.

Glad you're feeling better these days. I know how it is to perk up after one is about all in. That's the way with me last June. The arctick winter had me down & out—limp as a dishrag—but the minute I hit the genial live-oak belt around CHARLESTON I began to brace up as if in response to a swig of hootch . . . & was ready to fight any guy under 175 pounds by the time I struck Floriday. Right now I betcha I could stay ten rounds in a bout with Talman or Koenig, & mop the floor up with a pair of Belknaps—one in each horny fist. You'd orta see me cut scrub palmettos or weed the cacti outa the lawn! Just now, though, I'm relaxing—on a bench in the landscape garden with little Alfred A. Knopf (tiger) alternately purring & drowsing beside me.

And so it goes. Have a good time, & don't get friz. Cook may not go to St. Louis after all.

Benedictions—

Theobaldus Perkins.

[152]   [AHT]

San Augustin
19 de Augusto

Fulgent Frequenter of Frozen Fastnesses:—

Brrrr . . . back to the arctick! Your bulletin from the Statler reach'd me just as I was about to hop off for the Barren Waste. It sure has been a great visit, & has set Grandpa up physically to a surprising extent. But soon enough, alas, the cold nights of the north will have me flabbily languishing again! The Barlovii have also lit out—going for a fortnight to Daytona Beach—so that only an empty house now marks the scene of a festive visit of two months & nine days.

By the way—on August 14th at eight p.m. I beheld a phenomenon which, though I had always known of it from books, I had never seen before in the course of a long lifetime. No one else present had ever seen it before either— although the company included persons up to the age of sixty-six. I refer to a lunar rainbow—a clear, complete bow in the northwestern sky opposite the rising full moon. Bob claimed he could detect *colours* in it—especially red on the outer edge—though to me it appear'd of an uniform greyness—faint tho' distinct. Having beheld two total solar eclipses & now a lunar rainbow, I feel myself quite a connoisseur of odd phenomena! The moon is a great sight down here—rising beyond the grotesque pines which border the lake, & being reflected picturesquely in the latter's glassy surface.

Oh, yes—about meeting in the pest zone . . . . . it all depends on finances. You'll probably be back by the time I pass through—but the question is whether or not I shall be so utterly strapp'd that I'll have to shoot right through to #66 without so much as seeing anybody. Here's hoping for the best—but I don't want to write home for funds if I can help it. I shall cut my eating down to twenty-five cents per day—but even so rent eats up one's pile in no time. Thank Yuggoth my ticket home is safe!

Price wants me to make a trip to California to collaborate with him—but I shall want a lot of definite data for it. Just now, #66 College is the place I want to linger at!

Well—be see 'n' ya!
Θεοβάλδος Περκινς

[153]   [AHT]

The Antient Hill at Last
—Septr. 16, MDCCCCXXXV

Ave, Apotheosis of Ancestral Archaeology!

Bad news must come first. Brace yourself for the worst . . . or rather, the near-worst, since so far as I know, Aunt Julia's still exists. JAKE'S HAS FAILED!

I look'd up at the long-familiar facade, & beheld only emptiness & a "For Rent" sign. Sic transit gloria mundi! After all these years . . . . & only this spring, when I took young Moe there, it seemed to be flourishing as of yore! With this added to the demolition of the antient College hill row, Providentium certainly has become the merest shadow of itself! It is a sad thing to see the world crumble to pieces before one's eyes! Talman will surely weep when he receives the melancholy tidings!

But just to balance that which the past hath devoured, guess what the past has this moment vomited forth . . . out of the immeasurable abyss of time? Don't laugh . . . . . but believe it or not, I've just had a letter from DAVE BUSH! Speaking of the devil . . . . our reminiscent conversation of the other night must have set some psychick current working, for upon my return I found a message from the damn'd old reprobate awaiting me. First word in nearly a decade. The cuss is now in San Francisco, & wants some more doggerel doctor'd. Heigho, but this is certainly like the old days! I'm telling him the usual rates still hold good . . . wonder what will come of the matter? Davy, Davy, Davy!

Kappa Alpha Tau fraternity prospers. Old President Randall welcomed me by purring & rolling over, & "little" Johnny Perkins—now a huge warrior—spends most of his time over here. Johnny is even now snoozing in a neighbouring chair.

And so it goes.

Pax vobiscum . . . . .
Theobaldus Perkins.

[154]   [AHT]

Boston, Mass.
Oct. 17, 1935

Hail, Prince of Progenitor-Probers!

Lookit the Kalem meeting back in antient Bostonium! Guard of honour landed in Providentium Wednseday at six a.m.—& now the whole delegation is Hubbing among books, museums, & antiquities. Decent weather so far. Home Friday night—when, alas, the pilgrim has to embark for the pest zone.

Wish we could get to Concord, Salem, or some such place—but conditions don't look favourable.

On account of Spencer's delay, I am stirring up critical reports myself[1]— with his permission. Hope we get report in the Dec. *N. A.*[2]

Well, I must leave space so that the Traveller's message won't overlap Paul Pry's limits!

Benedictions—

Theobaldus Perkins.

Notes

1. Truman J. Spencer, chairman of the Bureau of Critics of the NAPA. HPL wrote many criticisms of amateur verse for the "Bureau of Critics" column in the *National Amateur* from 1931 to 1936.
2. The issue contained HPL's "Some Current Amateur Verse."

[155]   [AHT]

New Haven, Conn.

Oct. 18, 1935

Hail, Searchlight of Stony Scintillance!

Look at the old man in antient New Haven—digging up Sonny's ancestors from the churchyards. Aunt & I got a ride here in a friend's car, & she visited some old dame here while I had seven & one-half hours free for exploration. Not so much colonial architecture as Providence, but the endless labyrinths of Yale quadrangles—Gothick & Georgian—forms the most glamourous & enchanting sight I've seen in aeons—a perfect old-world picture! Have seen all of these magical quadrangles & most of the museums also. Pretty full programme. I must get here again!

Spent Sept. 20–23 with Cole, & we took many trips in rural Massachusetts. Saw Nahant & Marblehead, & went to the majestick hills of Wilbraham to deposit the ashes of Mrs. Dowe at her native soil.[1] Also toured Cape Cod & layed on the sands of Chatham. There's a chance that I may accompany Cole over the Mohawk Trail & into Vermont when the autumn foliage is at its height. His Chevrolet is *heated!*

Pax vobiscum—

Theo: Perkins.

Notes

1. Jennie E. T. Dowe (1840–1919), amateur journalist and mother of Edith Miniter.

[156]   [AHT]

The Antient Hill
Dec. 29, 1935

Long-Lost Lanthorn of Learned Luminiscence:—

I visited antient Connecticut Hall (1752—oldest Yale College building, where the rebel Nathan Hale of the Class of 1773 room'd), old Centre Church on the enormous green (1812—with an interesting crypt containing the grave of Benedict Arnold's first wife), the Pierpont house (1767—now Yale Faculty Club), the historical, art, & natural history musaea, the Farnum & Marsh botanick gardens, & various other points of interest—crowding as much as possible into the limited time available. Fact is, I don't see how the hell I *did* take in so much!

Well—the high spot—or spots—were perhaps the great new quadrangles of the University—each an absolutely faithful reproduction of old-time architecture & atmosphere, & forming a self-contain'd little world in itself. The Gothick courtyards transport one in fancy to mediaeval Oxford or Cambridge—spires, oriels, painted arches, mullion'd windows, arcades with groin'd roofs, climbing ivy, sundials, lawns, gardens, vine-clad walls and flagstoned walks—everything to give the young occupants that mass'd impression of their accumulated cultural heritage which they might obtain in OLD ENGLAND itself. To stroll thro' these cloister'd quadrangles in the golden light of late afternoon; at dusk, when the candles behind the diamond-pan'd casements flicker up one by one; or in the beams of a mellow Hunter's moon; is to walk bodily into an enchanted region of dream. It is the past & the antient Mother Land brought magically to the present time & place. GOD SAVE THE KING! The choicest of these Gothick quadrangles is Calhoun College—nam'd for the great Carolinian (whose grave in St. Philip's churchyard CHARLESTON, I had visited scarce two months before), who was a graduate of Yale.

Nor are the Georgian quadrangles less glamourous—each being a magical summoning-up of the world of two centuries ago. Many distinct styles of Georgian architecture are represented, & the guildings & landscaping alike reflect the finest taste which European civilisation hath yet evolv'd or is ever likely to evolve. Lucky (tho' probably callously unappreciative at the time) is the youth whose formative years are spent amid such scenes! I wander'd for hours thro' this limitless labyrinth of unexpected elder microcosms, & mourn'd the lack of further time. Certainly, I must stop off at New Haven again in some aestival season, since many of its treasures would require weeks for proper inspection appreciation.

Meanwhile the antient buildings at the bottom of College Hill are all down (except the bottom one, which is to be preserv'd & restor'd), & a new Georgian edifice is about to rise on the site. Thank God nothing modernistick will insult the eye!

Leedle Meestah Stoiling—the precocious and erudite seedling from the

stock of Shem whom you met at Sonny's last September—has been in town
for the past week, & has been frequently to see the Old Gent. Shew'd him
[   ] thro' my batter'd old telescope last night. The archaick wreck
(not me—the telescope) will do pretty well under a power of forty-five, but
with one hundred it ain't so hot. Leedle Meestah Stoiling's papa is still in
Providence a good deal, & I've seen him quite a few times during the autumn
& winter. A damn nice chap—as cultivated as an Aryan. Harvard '12. Brobst
& his new wife were over the other day, & he enquir'd especially for you.
John Perkins is now a veritable mountain of black fur, but he still comes over
frequently to see his Grandpa. He knows the old gentleman who gives him
catnip! He'll be a year old on the Ides of Februarius.

Had a good Yule—a tree again, all lit up (not me—the tree), & a fairish
semicircle of modest gifts around its base. Dinner with my aunt at a place
down the hill—a Georgian edifice in Benefit Street, of about the same date as
#66. Damn good turkey.

And now I'm about to hop a stage-coach for Bloomingdale to visit little
Sonny a week. Hope I'll see you during that all too crowded interval—how
about it—has the Child plann'd a gang meeting? He tells me something about
some lecture of yours, but I can't be sure whether he's spoofing or not. Hope
also to see Kleiner, Talman, Arturo, the Wandrei boys, Samuelus, G. Willard,
& all the rest. And may Yuggoth keep the thermometer up! Down around
twenty-four degrees now—but I guess I can get to the station without the use
of a taximeter hackney-coach. Stage leaves at one a.m., & draws into the stable at 33d Street around 7:45 a.m.

See ya later.

Your obt Grandsire—
Theobaldus Perkins.

[157]   [AHT]

The Antient Hill
Feby. 23, 1936

Ultimate Upland of Universal Unriddling:—

Hope ya had a good time at the Puzzlers' Convention. I suppose it takes
superfluous brains to make one enjoy such things. Me, I ain't got enough to
spare from the simple tasks of satisfying my curiosity about things that jest
come nacherel in the cosmos. I think only under compulsion—when the rewards are great, or the penalties of non-thinking extreme. That goes for chess,
too. An ancient & picturesque game, which I'd be sorry to see vanish from the
stream of western tradition . . . but I'm no good at it & can't keep awake over it.
I've learned & forgotten the rules three separate times . . . . . & wouldn't have
tried at all if I hadn't inherited a set (two sets, in fact) of ivory chessmen which I
thought I ought to live up to for tradition's sake. A gentleman must play (or

have play'd) chess, just as he must fence & ride (or have fenc'd & ridden. I didn't get around to these, except with wooden swords & on a hike, so I ain't no gent) & know (or have known) Latin & Greek. Well—congrats to your household on its collective progress in these intellectual trimmings!

And so Ed Baird is still alive! Bless my soul! There's a bimbo as never rejected a manuscript of mine, & once accepted seven all in a bunch! Just my ideal editorial type . . . . . . except where the financial end is concern'd. Hope ya kin get your *Black Cat* file. I used to buy that reg'lar-like, & recall the swell weird stuff it had. That & the old *All-Story* were the first sources of contemporary weird material I ever stumbled on!

My "Mountains of Madness" running in *Astounding*—Feb.–Mar.–April. Some misprints, but cou'd be worse. Illustrations damn good—the bozo who drew those Elder Things had certainly read the text!

Sir, Yr obsequious & ever-grovelling foot-scraper
Πάππος Θεοβάλδος

[158]   [AHT]

The Antient Hill
May 9, 1936

Luminous Lanthorn of Lithological Lucidity:—

Yuggoth, what a year! 1936 is just about blotted out for Grandpa! Not merely completely sunk, but tunnelling a mile under the sea-bottom! Letters since February unanswer'd—borrow'd books piled ceiling high unread— N. A. P. A. duties shoved on Kleiner—revision jobs return'd unperform'd—in short, general hell & damnation! My aunt's illness[1] proved severe & protracted, so that she was at the Jane Brown Hospital March 17th to April 7th. From April 7th to 21st she was at a convalescent home, but now she is back at #66 & well on the road to recovery. She still, however, requires considerable coöperation in household administration. My own grippe attack concluded in early February, but cold weather & the strain of recent events have kept my energies at a low ebb. I am about 'all in' nervously, & have so little power of concentration that it takes me an hour to do what I could ordinarily do in about five minutes. Some good hot weather, though, will help to set me on my feet at least tolerably— that, & some uninterrupted leisure free from responsibility. Barlow has invited me to De Land again, but I greatly doubt my ability to accept. As for my general programme of activities—it is an utter mess, & will never he cleaned up save through the relentless exercise of neglect & repudiation.

Concerning recent climatick conditions—I have no language at my command which can express my opinion of them. After a year in the Marine Corps, or among the stevedores of South Water Street, I might possess a store of adjectives & metaphors capable of embodying my sentiments . . . . but lacking such educational opportunities, I can no more than choke & sputter & clench a futile fist. In March I *thought* there was going to be some spring—& then came the return engagement of January which the calendar ironically call'd "April". 'Oh, to be in CHARLESTON, now that April's here . . .'[2] But alas, no CHARLESTON for Grandpa! Well—the sun slowly swung north after the long arctick night. The grass grew green, the boughs budded, the flavous forsythias flower'd—& on April 28th came a day warm enough to go out! Open water in the Yukon! Since then there have been several tolerable days, & I can now walk up the hill without exhaustion or cardiack thumpings. On three occasions I have taken my work out to Prospect Terrace, tho' the cold usually drives me in before sunset. Meanwhile the trees have gain'd a generous leafage, whilst many a shrub is bright with blooms. Visually, antient Providentium is indeed a thing of beauty! I have not as yet attempted any rural walks, but on April 30th my aunt & I were treated to a motor ride thro' the awakening countryside to the maritime village of Westport-Point, in the Province of the Massachusetts-Bay. This journey included some very pleasing landskips of the traditional New-England sort, the section travers'd being especially rich in stone walls. A midway point was the idyllick metropolis of *Fall-River* . . . . & on this occasion we pass'd thro' a residential part, on the heights above the dingy commercial section, which truly contradicted the impression convey'd by the city as a whole. Fall-River the Beautiful . . . . perchance some of the amateurs, passing thro' it on the way to a New-Bedford convention in 1937 (shou'd such occur), will become so struck with its charms that they will nominate it for the 1938 assemblage!

On Monday last there open'd in this town the Tercentenary observances in honour of Rhode-Island's founding. Commencing the event was a parade in antient costumes from the College gate down the hill—past #66's alley—to the Market-House, where the column was join'd by a coach (a real survivor of the eighteenth century) & four, bearing His Excellency, Theodore Francis Green, Esq., Governor of the Colony. The augmented detachment (led by a military company in the rebel uniform of the late war of 1775–83) then proceeded down the Town Street to the Colony-House (1761), where was conducted a mock-session of the legislature of May 4, 1776, that treasonable occasion upon which the colony disavow'd the rightful authority of our Sovereign & Parliament. In this mock-session, the part of each of the old-time legislators was taken by a lineal descendant; Governor Green representing his ancestor Col. Arnold, who presented to the deputies the first draught of the seditious resolution adopted. Since the minutes of the meeting are extant, the speeches of the present imitators were correct; & I may add that they acquitted themselves with surprising histrionick ability. Their costumes were of greater correctness & better fit than is common in civick pageantry, & the general effect was one of fascinating convincingness. The room, of course, was the same as that in which the real session was held one hundred sixty years ago; & so excellent was the spectacle, that one might with ease imagine the calendar to have been truly turn'd back. There was but little space for spectators, but I had the good fortune to get in & secure a very tolerable vantage-point. Mov'd by the verisimilitude of the occasion, I found it difficult to keep from hissing the advocates of treason, & from applauding those loyal deputies who urg'd a proper arbitration of current difficulties (in the manner of a New Deal as oppos'd to the sort of upheaval Belknap wou'd propose) within the lawful limits of His Majesty's government. However, the minions of Satan won, as on the occasion when the Arch-Fiend rous'd his allies with those words writ down by Mr. Milton:

> "We may with more successful Hope resolve
> To wage, by Force or Guile, eternal War,
> Irreconcilable to our grand Foe . . . ."[3]

As they concluded their session, the legislators utter'd the new formula "God Save the United Colonies"—whilst I, with unbroken loyalty to our past & our race, chanted as always the rightful words GOD SAVE THE KING!

At a later session held in the new marble State-House (which I did not attend) the visiting Governor of His Majesty's Province of the Massachusetts-Bay—the Rt. Honble James Michael Curley, Gent.—presented to Governor Green of this Colony a copy of that resolution lately adopted by the Bay's General-Court, repealing the banishment impos'd upon Mr. R. Williams at session in Newton (afterwards Cambridge) in October, 1635. After 300½ years, I have no doubt but that Mr. Williams is deeply sensible of this delicate mark of consideration. Another event connected with the Tercentenary celebration is a highly interesting loan exhibit of antient furniture & household objects in the modest abode (1742) of Stephen Hopkins, Esq., only two squares from #66 on the antient hill. My aunt & I visited this on May 1st, & accounted ourselves well repaid for the long journey. Further attractions will be the opening to the publick of two of the great mansions on the hill south of here—the John Brown house (1786—call'd by John Quincy Adams, Esq. "the finest private mansion on this continent"), & the Edward Carrington house (1809).[4] The former opening is only temporary, but the Carrington house has been given outright to the R. I. School of Design—together with all its antient contents—as a permanent musaeum. You have seen the exteriors of both of these houses, & I trust you will find their interiors accessible when next you honour this town with your presence. On April 25th my aunt (on her first walk of any distance since her illness) & I visited the still-clos'd Carrington House & explor'd the curious cobblestoned courtyard leading to the extensive stables—a sequester'd world of 1809 in the midst of modern decadence. I had not before enter'd the grounds of this place, since up to last year it was still tenanted by the descendants of Genl Carrington.

By the way—on March 10th *another* of this southerly group of mansions (the Joseph Nightingale house—1792—now tenanted by John Nicholas Brown, Esq.) was enter'd by a member (or semi-member or ex-member) of our learned circle; none other than *Edw: Lazare, Esq.*, who had been sent thither from the pest zone to appraise (for insurance purposes) the library of Mr. Brown. I had not seen this sprightly youth since April 17, 1929 (at a Wednesday night meeting in Kirk's basement in West 11th Street . . . the *last* meeting poor old Mac ever attended. You were there, & we were all a bit alarm'd by Mac's *dazed* demeanour. Six days later Talman heard of his seizure, & Sonny, Wandrei, Talman, & I went over to St. John's Hospital in Queens to visit him.), & would scarcely have recognis'd him on the street. He seems *darker* than in bygone years, tho' he does not appear sensibly *older*. Lazare call'd upon me as soon as his duties permitted, & we had dinner at the good old spaghetti place. (VIVAT . MVSSOLINVS . AETHIOPIA . DEVICTA .)⁵ It was surely curious & pleasing to behold the emergence of a familiar figure from the idealising mists of the past. Quaint old 1929! As remote—sociologically & psychologically—as that year of 1792 in which the Nightingale-Brown mansion was built!

Recent lectures of interest have been on Plato's Republick, modern art, Gilbert Stuart, Rhode Island silversmiths, archaick Greek art, Philosophy and Poetry, early classical sculpture, Mayan ruins, & the Michelson-Morley experiment. The last-named, deliver'd at the college Monday night, was by Prof. Dayton C. Miller,⁶ former colleague of Morley & present continuer of the experiment. He furnish'd startlingly convincing proof that the *real* results of the experiment did *not* shew that *total* absence of effect of the observer's motion on the speed of light which forms the underlying assumption of the Einstein theory. Instead, there is merely a lack of the *full* difference which the observer's motion ought (according to the old theory of time & space) to make. Prof. Miller very pertinently asks whether Einstein—& Eddington & Jeans & all the rest—ought to assume (& base a whole theory of cosmick entity on that assumption) that the Michelson-Morley experiment always gives *zero* (reckoning any difference from that as *error*), *when in truth it always gives a fairly constant difference from zero; in the direction that the earth's motion (in orbit, & in cosmick space with the sun) wou'd indicate (according to the old pre-Einstein concept), tho' not of the amount demanded by that motion* (in the absence of unknown complicating factors). Miller himself offers no dogmatic solution, but suggests that *a drift in the luminiferous aether* (assuming, contrary to Einstein, that such exists) in the direction of the Earth's motion would account—on the basis of *the old pre-Einstein universe of non-relativity*—for the fact that the observer's change of place in space gives *some* of the effect demanded by the old concept, but not *all* of the required amount. If Miller is right, the whole fabrick of relativity collapses, & we have once more the absolute dimensions & real time which we had before 1905. Just how his experiments—of incredible care, elaborateness, frequency, & repetition under every conceivable change of conditions—are regarded by the bulk of recent physicists & mathematicians, I do not know—but his explanation of them seemed to indicate a more serious challenge to Einstein than any previously offer'd by other non-relativitists. I shall be eager to learn what the disciples of relativity have to say of him & his work. Prof. Miller's lecture was illustrated, & was mark'd by a singular & felicitous clearness of expression. Of the laymen who attended it, most departed with a better idea of the famous experiment than they ever had before.

Turning to puzzles of a more artificial sort—I surely recognise the unaffected enthusiasm with which many persons pursue them. Of the *fact* there can be no doubt. That which is—in itself—a puzzle to me is the *reason*. I am of course sensible of the current explanation that puzzles form (a) an intrinsick exercise for the mental faculties, and (b) an escape from reality which surpasses any *idle* or *easy* diversion in potency by reason of its *totally engrossing* those faculties which wou'd otherwise be dwelling on wearisome or unpleasant facts. That artificial puzzles *can* be both of these things I have no doubt. What amazes me is their ability to captivate mankind *when much superior exponents of both functions exist in readily accessible form.* By such superior exponents I mean, of course, *problems in genuine knowledge* of a sort outside the habitual pursuits of the given follower. I term such problems superior because they not only discharge *both* functions of the artificial puzzle—affording cerebral gymnasticks & engrossing the consciousness in a pleasantly impersonal way—but *in addition* provide their pursuer with a sense of *genuine adventure* (the zest of pushing ahead into *real* territory hitherto unoccupied), of gratify'd curiosity (about *actual* things in his environment, in the past, & in the cosmos which had before been seal'd mysteries), of substantial conquest (the mastering of obstacles *of importance & genuineness,* instead of the mere mental boon-doggling incident to the overcoming of needless & artificial straw-men & set-ups), of improved adjustment to life & the universe (resulting from a better understanding of more & more regions of the *real* external world, & a lessening of the groping, fragmentary mental life of the herd, which is a mere ignorant drift down a dark river with unseen banks), & of a generally heighten'd status in the cosmos (as of one whose range of vision & of comprehension constantly increases, whose sense of *real* values is constantly exercised & whetted, & whose feeling of *power* is augmented by the steady acquisition of *important* & *genuine* information & by the subtle consciousness of having great *actual* resources.). Now all these *added* advantages involve no sacrifice of any of the advantages of artificial puzzles. The *mental exercise* is there, & the *escape* is there if one takes care to expand his horizon in directions remote from his usual work. What more *variety* in intellectual exercise may a man ask, than that afforded (for example) by a breathless chase after the secrets of the Dark Ages in Italy and elsewhere (when did Latin give place to the vulgar tongue in common speech—when did Greek gain ascendancy in the border provinces of the Eastern Empire—to what extent did Roman institutions persist in Britain between the fall of the southeastern parts (ending with Anderida (Pevensey) in A. D. 491) & the final defeat of "Candidan" or Aurelius Candidanus at Durham in A. D. 582—&c. &c. &c.); an attempt to grasp the doctrine of relativity & to appraise the Michelson-Morley experiment as in ol' Dayt

Miller's recent lecture; a tracing of archaic Greek cultural influences (independent of the Minoan) from Assyria through Phoenicia, Cyprus, & Rhodes by means of ivory artifacts which incidentally prove the existence of *elephants* (whether African or Indian nobody knows) in Syria; a quest for knowledge of the general condition of the other planets of our system; a probing of the rocks of our planet (this had orta hit you!) for evidence as to its evolution; a survey of the mysterious processes of human life, as in a reading of Wells's "Science of Life" & cognate works; an adventurous glance into man's unknown past—such as Sonny used to take before he went bolshevik-businessman; an intensive glance at the growth and folkways of any region (Charleston, St. Augustine, New Orleans, Newport) for the sake of the drama and pageantry involv'd; a *correlated* survey of world history in order to get oriented to surroundings & preceding influences; vicarious adventure in far lands of mystery (page good ol' Arturo) like Thibet & Borneo & Rhodesia; a conquest of new lands in the empire of taste—musick (still ahead of *me*, alas!), painting, sculpture, architecture; efforts to understand the spirit & literature of some alien culture; a glance at philosophy to try to uncover that galling eternal question "what is anything"?; a realistick & disinterested attack on the problems of social institutions & oeconomicks to see what extremists at both ends like Sonny & Let 'em Starve Hoover are really driving at; fling at genealogy to chase down some actual genes and chromosomes; a guess at the megalithick secrets of Easter Island; a study of the sources of familiar words (what connexion is there betwixt the god Æolus and the Greek name—αιλυρος—for a nice kittie?); chilling speculations on the Witch-Cult in Western Europe;[7] delvings into the origins of folklore; tracing of physical & mathematical laws thro' interesting & adventurous chains of facts & deductions; plunges into literature & recaptures of lost moods & attitudes whose surviving vestigia have always proved puzzling; explorations of myths & conjectures as to their origins in nature . . . . &c. &c. &c. Why, hell's bells, what greater refreshment can any tired mind want than a fling at one or more things like these . . . things that *really have a meaning* instead of being cardboard & tinsel set-ups, & that can differ just as much from one's regular mental activities as any rebus in the *Sunday Journal* or charade in the old *Farmer's Almanack?* How in thunder can anybody—with the millionfold questions of the *real* cosmos pressing in upon his curiosity & mocking the tragically short instant he has for their solution—waste his few brief years in chewing pencils over framed-up anagrams & synthetick word-squares & puppet acrosticks? Bridge, golf, baseball, & puzzles . . . . . & this is what the neo-Americans call a civilisation! Well—that's what a pack of acquisitive tradesmen *would* turn to! And the deadly clock ticks on, & another generation go down into the dust without ever having comprehended the world around them or the past behind them. No wonder the bewildered bastards vacillate around between blind Hoovers & blind Hueys, & grovel before either myth-peddling popes or thought-castrating Methodist shamans & medicine-men. However, this is not criticism of your own choice circle of riddle-riders. Youse guys keep puzzles in their place, & don't let 'em become a dominant interest. My attitude is one of sheer *curiosity*—as to why a person habitually given to the mental exploration of realities in one field, chooses as his diversion a duplication of the same mental process in a purely *artificial* field—where all the obstacles are needless, all the triumphs empty, & all the discoveries cut-&-dried things that somebody cooked up before—instead of in *another natural field*, where there would be just as much variety & refreshment & exercise, plus a sense of *real* adventure & achievement (plunging into fresh discoveries of things *which exist & have meaning*, & adding to one's mental treasury new visions & comprehensions of the existing environment which increase one's orientation & sense of power), & a relieving & spirit-expanding gratification of that burning, harassing *curiosity* which is ever provoked by the down-pressing black clouds of the unknown. What new horizon did any word-square ever bring? What mystery did any rebus ever light up? What sense of placement & direction in the seething, bewildering cosmos did any charade ever promote? What *do* the puzzlers get out of their toils except the relatively minor titillation of exercise & escape *for their own sakes*—a mere matter of *means* without *ends*? Does not puzzling tend to exalt *process* over *object*? I can understand a keen mind's wanting exercise, but I can't understand its preferring a form which is *only exercise*, when there is also available such a piquant, interesting, & insistent variety of forms which contain *no less exercise, but which, in addition, lead somewhere.* Even if a person knows virtually everything there is to know about the cosmos (like Galpin or the little Sterling boy you met last January), I should think his diversions would be the increased acquisition of detail'd impressions in some real but unaccustom'd field (of which, even for the profoundest scholars, an infinity must necessarily remain to provoke curiosity & invite conquest) rather than the idle setting-up of meaningless hurdles to jump over. How can a man bear to die without having done *all in his power* to learn where he stands in space & time & the historick stream? How can he spend *laborious, brain-fatiguing, energy-consuming hours* figuring out empty & unrevealing artificialities, & yet go to his grave (as many brilliant men have done) with half his horizons clogged with vagueness, ignorance, illusion, & unsatisfy'd curiosity? Gawd knows I know little enough, but I go as far as my peanut brain allows! When I want to show off my rudimentary 2 + 2 faculty to myself, I want something *real* as well as the feeble ego-titillation of a mere *demonstration.* I am a miser of my low-flickering energies. When I have to exercise reason, I want it to take me somewhere—to alleviate some of the cosmic curiosities & historick bewilderments which assail me on every hand. I am oppressed by not knowing how thousands of things came to be—by not knowing what actual forces & linkages lie beyond familiar appearances—by not knowing what larger relationships bind the apparently isolated trends & phaenomena around and behind me—by not grasping the drama & pageantry of a million unread epics of age-long historick evolution—by all those lacunae which the shortness of existence

& the fatigue of my not-so-hot cerebrum conspire to leave in my scroll of comprehension. So when I feel like stretching the scant grey matter a bit, I'm damn'd if I want to do it in vacuo! When I want a tough nut to chew on, I don't choose a wooden one carved to order by a Connecticut craftsman. Instead, I merely turn to one of those *real* puzzles in nature which are always tormenting me. Just what basis for emotion there is in the diagonal of a word-square, I can't say. I only know such things leave me cold. But as you can see, I **am** burningly interested in trying to solve the tough psychological puzzle—a genuine, inherent mystery of the external world—of why some people *do* go 'rah-rah' over the diagonals of word-squares. *That's* what *I* call a puzzle for the pleasurable exercise of human ingenuity (ingenuity in assembling & correlating data, & testing by actual cases) & this escape from accustom'd (literary, historical, architectural, &c.) mental ruts & muscle strainings.

Whether I shall ever solve this real-life rebus I can't say. Perhaps I shall—for at times I believe there is a whole school of philosophy which exalts mere *means* & *processes* over *actual rewards,* & which builds a deeply-ingrain'd ideology (no harm in using The Child's pet word when it comes in handy!) upon the timeworn psychological exaggeration that 'it's the struggle that counts'. This is a philosophy which seems to me false, wasteful, & unscientifick, but it must exist to some extent in order to account for the survival & tolerance of competitive commercial "civilisations", the curious persistence & popularity of sports, & various other odd anthropological manifestations. Probably it develops originally from the over-predominance of certain primitive instincts of high survival-value in early tribal life—later rationalising itself, obtaining mytholgical backing, & spreading to elements other than those among whom it arose. In most cases it appears allied with another vestigial stigma of of dawn-man—that direct, unsubtilised ego-exaltation forming the common instinct of rivalry, jealousy, & competition. This composite *process-exalting* & *rivalry-fostering* philosophy is found mostly as an ingredient of other & more complex philosophies extending all the way up the scale from the back house-pit of "rugged individualism" to the subtle rationalism with which John Dewey has salvaged the sinking pragmatism of William James. Perhaps an expanded & collectivised trace of it—in the form of pride in *national* (not personal) strength, & the determination to keep one's race or nation dominant among its contemporaries (S. P. Q. R.! Alala! Rule, Britannia! Viva Il Duce! Avanti! Banzai! Heil, Hitler! A South Carolinian, Sir, can lick ten damn'd Yankees with one flick of his riding whip! &c.), is essential to the survival in unbroken form of any social group. Well—somewhere out of this vague, elusive, often unrecognised, & sometimes self-contradictory mix'd philosophy, the ideals of *sport* & of *artificial puzzling* must have been born. They do not essentially clash with our biological heritage—being indeed outgrowths of one part of it—& they become widely popularised thro' tradition & convention. I suppose their existence is no more remarkable than that of belief in religion & other forms of magick. My aunt en-

joys the First Baptist Church—so why shouldn't the late Hank Whitehead enjoy a boxing-match, or another light of learning enjoy a problem in chess or
cryptography? Eddie Poe was a puzzle-hound, so that an old Poëlater[8] like
Grandpa Theobald hadn't orta take no lofty pose as a supercilious critick! The
fact is, I wouldn't be surpris'd if the hidden factor (not so much the *origin &*
existence of the puzzling instinct as the *spread & survival & intensity* of it) were one
which is complimentary to the puzzlers & uncomplimentary to me . . . . . that is,
the factor of *surplus mental vigour* on the puzzlers' part, & of limited mental vigour on my own. The puzzler has so much excess brain power conceivably, that
he does not feel the spending of mental energy. Nothing is wasted except time,
because he has more energy than he could exhaust even if he spent *all* his waking hours in (suitably rotated) hard cerebral labour. This bears out the contention of Freud & others that "brain fog" is only an illusion or mis-direction of
emotion—& that true mental fatigue *cannot exist* in a first-rate brain. Perhaps the
puzzler & chess-addict is like the batteries of some horseless carriages—which
commonly get overcharged thro' the continuous generation of energy, & force
the driver to turn on the lights in the daytime to reduce things to normal. This,
however, leaves unanswer'd the question of why he doesn't choose to spend his
time in some *equally brain-excercising* pursuit which *also* brings other pleasures &
advantages . . . why he doesn't get an interferometer & study the borderline
problems of radiant energy (a fascinating & tantalising mystery held out by the
cosmos) instead of moving carv'd pieces of wood or ivory over painted squares,
or finding seventy-five letter words which mean a carnivorous earthworm of
Jugoslavia. But is an answer to this beyond possibility? How about the easy
saturation of the human pleasure-faculty? Has not many a person become so
absorbed in a plate of Aunt Julia's ice-cream that he has linger'd in Warren till
dusk & thus cheated himself of (or perhaps merely ceased to wish for) a daylight ride through the stone-wall'd landskip beyond? It may be that for a certain
type of mind the *sheer sensation of cerebral action* is so intrinsically pleasurable as to
leave for the moment no room for other desires. That is, the subject is so
keenly titillated by the mechanical motion of his own brain-cells, that he cannot
for the nonce feel curiosity or the longing for expanded horizons. This is at
least a working theory to explain an observ'd condition, that it does not bring
up the question of the relative *wisdom* of the narrower as oppos'd to the more
inclusive gratification. Indeed, that question involves a very profound dilemma
in philosophy—that is, whether the possession & satisfaction of a wide range
of sensitivities & desires has any advantage over the possession & satisfaction
of a very small range; or in other words, whether *satisfaction per se* is always the
same in pleasure-content, or whether the expenditure of a quantitatively greater
store of cell-energy in the opposite processes of desire (volition, curiosity, sensitivity, &c.) & satisfaction produces more pleasurable sensation than the attainment of an equal satisfaction-equilibrium through the expenditure of a lesser
store of cell-energy. This general dilemma I believe to be still unsettled—nor

am I certain that the conditions are the same in *all* phases of human desire & activity. My own opinion has tended to vacillate. Some fifteen years ago I recall saying that a contented cat is better off than a philosopher.[9] Today I am not so sure. Being neither—despite my close friendship for Mr. John Perkins, who sits comfortably curl'd up in the green-cushion'd semicircular chair beside me & occasionally emits a drowsy purr—I can afford to be neutral!

Speaking of forefathers—a new acquaintance of mine, one Frederick J. Pabody of Cleveland tells me you're doing a damn good job digging his up for him. He comes of a Little Compton, Rhode-Island line—as you doubtless know even more detailedly than I do. This bird—of whose existence I had not the faintest idea until Feby. 27, 1936—wrote me in care of Street & Smith after noticing my mention of a "Prof. Pabodie" in the "Mountains of Madness". He thought I might have taken the name from real life somewhere, & that I could possibly give him a few stray tips on his great-grands. Actually, I merely chose Pabodie at random as a monicker typical of good old New England stock. In answering Fred J. I recalled you have a Peabody line, & thought you might be able to slip him some useful dates & data. Accordingly I suggested that he get in touch with you. He misread my script rendering of your name as WARTON (he musta ben studying the eighteenth century potes!), & wrote you on that assumption . . . . . & that damn fool Paul Pry at the village Post Office didn't have the common sense to deduce who a " ' "rton, Paterson Museum" would naturally be! (He spends all his time reading the pustkyards & racketeering for spare pennies.) Eventually I set Pabody right—& the result is a satisfy'd client. Fred J. seems to be rather a nice chap—& it seems that he has at various times entertain'd ambitions regarding the composition of weird & science fiction. Congratulations on your new-found cousin! I've never had it straight before just how the Essex County *Peabodys* & the Little Compton (& later Providence) *Pabodies* were connected. I see your Frank & Fred's Bill were scions of the same brood.

Hell, I was an old-timer thirty years ago! I printed papers by hand in pencil in 1899 & probably before—& I began hectographing the *Rhode-Island Journal of Astronomy* early in 1905.[10] I even have duplicates of this last which I could flash on my fellow-greybeards if they demand documentary proof. I didn't learn of organised *amateur* journalism until late in life—1914 (March)—but I'm told that *any* amateur publishing, organised or otherwise, is enough to let a real, honest-to-gawd gerontocrat in. Being in the Alumni Association already, I haven't been anxious to increase my annual dues—obligations—but in time I certainly must line up with the main old-geezer division. Cole got in last year. By the way—why the hell doesn't E. H. C. merge the Alumni Association into the Fossils? I should think the old-timers ought to pool their energies & resources instead of scattering them . . . . . . just as the youngsters really ought to get together & fuse the National with the Erford pseudo-United.

1936 seems to be a year of trouble for others as well as for myself. Leedle

Meestah Stoiling has had a very close call—abscess of lower colon, operation, blood transfusion, intra-venous nourishment, &c. He is pulling around again now, though, & tutoring like the devil to see if he can still get into Harvard next fall at the age of sixteen. Wandrei has been more or less under the weather, & relays the information that both of Sonny's parents have had grippe. Bobby Barlow has had bad trouble with his throat, & Klarkash-Ton is in a frightful dilemma—with his father in feeble health, & only himself to attend to the chores—which include tending forty hens & fetching water from a well nearly one-fourth mile away. No word from Cook.

Have had a change of company since beginning this epistle. Mr. Perkins expressed a wish to return home (or at least to rove in the sunlit garden), but I have since caught his little brother—Gilbert John Murray Kynymond Elliot, fourth Earl of Minto[11]—who is black on top & white on the bottom. Lord Minto was born last October, & will be a pretty big boy when you see him in September. He is now purring in the Morris-Chair in the corner—which is his favourite, just as the green-cushion'd semicircular chair is Mr. Perkins's favourite.

Well—I'm glad all goes well at Summer Street & Broadway.

> Yr obt Servt
> Theobaldus Perkins

Notes

1. HPL wrote to his correspondents that his aunt Annie E. P. Gamwell was suffering a severe case of "grippe," but in fact she had breast cancer and was undergoing a mastectomy.

2. Robert Browning (1812–1889), "Home-Thoughts, from Abroad" (1845), ll. 1–2, but read "England" for "Charleston."

3. *Paradise Lost* 1.120–22.

4. HPL refers to the John Brown house (1786–88) at 52 Power Street and the Edward Carrington house (1810, 1812) at 66 Williams Street.

5. "Long live Mussolini, now that Ethiopia is defeated." The Italian army had invaded Ethiopia in October 1935 and defeated the Ethiopian army in May 1936. Ethiopia was liberated by Allied forces in late 1941.

6. Dayton C. Miller (1866–1941), American physicist and astronomer and opponent of Einstein's theory of relativity.

7. See Margaret A. Murray's *The Witch-Cult in Western Europe* (Oxford: Clarendon Press, 1921).

8. I.e., a devotee of Edgar Allan Poe.

9. See "Nietzscheism and Realism" (1922): "It is good to be a cynic—it is better to be a contented cat—and it is best not to exist at all" (*CE* 5.71).

10. The first issue of the *Rhode Island Journal of Astronomy* dates to 2 August 1903.

11. John Murray Kynynmond, 4th Earl of Minto (1845–1914), Governor-General of Canada (1898–1904) and Viceroy of India (1905–10).

[159]   [AHT]

What, again?
May 12, 1736

Daemon of Deciphering Determination:—

Now I hope to gawd you won't tell me that this pedigree of the Providence settler has been exploded by subsequent research! It was—in 1900—accepted not only by the author of the book but by the eminent local historian Edward Field (a descendant), whose standard Rhode-Island History I possess. It would be tragick if I had learn'd, late in life, something which ain't so!

John Field (the astronomer ——— Jane Amys
1520?–1587   ?–Aug. 30, 1609
                                    /
             William Feild————————Jane (Sotwell) Burdett
             (note odd spelling)   d. Oct. 21, 1623
             ?–1623
        /
John Field————————? d. 1686
(Providence Settler)
d. 1686
        /
        Hannah Field————————James Mathewson
        d. 1703   d. Dec. 3, 1682
      /   /   /
Ruth Mathewson—Benjamin Whipple   James Mathewson Jr.   John Mathewson
d. 1704   d. 1704   1666–1737   1668–1716
                                  m. Eliz. Clemence   m. Deliverance Melevery
                                  1673–1736   1673–1716
        /   /   /
Benjamin Whipple Jr.*   James Mathewson 3d_m._Elizabeth Mathewson
1687–1786   b. 1702   b. 1706
m. Esther Millard
        /   /
Benedict Whipple _____m_____Elizabeth Mathewson
1739–1819   1736–1802
            /
        Esther Whipple————————Asaph Phillips
        1767–1842   1764–1829
                /
            Jeremiah Phillips————————Rhoby Rathbone
            1800–1848   1797–1898
                /
            Whipple Phillips————————Rhoby Place
            1833–1904   1827–1896
            /
        Sarah Phillips————————Winfield Lovecraft
        1857–1921   1853–1898
                /
            H. P. L
            1890–1936?

*This is, save for the centenarian Mary (Brownell)-Hazard, the longest-lived known ancestor I possess. Well toward the 100-mark, but couldn't quite make it! Poor Ben, to be cut off in youth!

The following table traces the lineage of John Field of Providence, & the descent of the compiler, H. P. Lovecraft, from him:

I. (1)   *Roger del Feld,* born Sowerby 1240.

II. (3)   *Thomas del Feld,* born Sowerby 1278. Juror at Sowerby 1307. In Wakefield rolls 1314 and 1322.

III. (5)   *John del Feld,* born Sowerby 1300. Named in rolls 1326 et seq.

IV. (8)   *Thomas del Feld,* born Sowerby 1330. m. Annabell _____. Named in rolls 1364. Constable of Sowerby 1365. Went to Bradford. d. 1391.

V. (13)   *Thomas del Felde de Bolton* of Bradford, 1360–1429. Married Isabel _____. Left lands, tenants, &c.

VI. (21)   *William Feld,* born (prob.) Bradford. Res. Bradford parish. Married Katherine _____. Died April, 1480.

VII. (30)   *William Feld,* born Bradford. Removed to East Ardsley.

VIII. (35)   *Richard Feld* of East Ardsley. Husbandman of parish of Ardeslowe. Married Elizabeth _____. Will made Aug. 19, 1542, proved Dec. 8, 1542.

IX. (42)   *John Field* of East Ardlsey. Born between 1515 & 1525; died May, 1587. Married Jane Amyas, who died August 30, 1609. (She was daughter of John Amyas of Aredeslow, of a Yorkshire house extending back to time of Edward I, with seat near Ardsley.) John Field was called "The Proto-Copernican of England", since his Ephemeris (1557) was the first English account of the motions of the heavenly bodies. Claimed as an Oxonian. Spent much time abroad, especially in Germany. Information concerning him to be found in *Gentleman's Magazine* for May, 1834, & November, 1862. John Field secured an official confirmation of the ancient Field *arms* (vide supra), together with the granting of the following new *crest,* evidently in commemoration of his astronomical services: *A dexter arm issuing out of clouds fesseways proper, habited gules, holding in the hand, also proper, a sphere or.* (This ought to be the crest of the Providence branch. I'll have to ask Talman to draw it out for me.)[1]

X. (67)   *William Feild* (note spelling) born Ardsley. Died 1623. Married Mrs. Jane (Sotwell) Burdett, widow of George Burdett of Carhead, Thurnscoe. She was buried Oct. 21, 1623, in Silkstone Parish. (She was daughter of Rev. John Sotwell, vicar of Peniston.)

XI. (121) *JOHN FIELD*, born Thurnscoe. Settler & home lot proprietor Providence, R. I. Numerous civic distinctions mentioned in standard American genealogies. Died Providence, 1686.

XII. *Hannah Field* died 1703. Married James Mathewson of Providence. (Died Dec. 3, 1682.)

XIII. *Ruth Mathewson* died 1704. Married Benjamin Whipple Sr. (1654–1704).

James Mathewson, Jr., 1666–1737. Married Elizabeth Clemence (1673–1736).

John Mathewson, 1668–1716. Married Deliverance Melevery (1673–1716).

XIV. *Benjamin Whipple*, Jr. 1687–1786. Son of Ruth Mathewson. Married Esther Millard.

James Mathewson, 3d, born 1702. Son of James Mathewson Jr. Married his cousin Elizabeth Mathewson (born 1706).

Eizabeth Mathewson, born 1706. Daughter of John Mathewson. Married her cousin James Mathewson, 3d. (born 1702)

XV. *Benedict Whipple*, 1739–1819. Son of Benjamin Whipple, Jr. Married his second cousin (herself child of first cousin) Elizabeth Mathewson, second. (1736–1802)

Elizabeth Mathewson, 1736–1802. Daughter of James 3d & Elizabeth Mathewson. Married her second cousin Benedict Whipple (1739–1819).

XVI. *Esther Whipple*, 1767–1842. Daughter of Benedict Whipple & Elizabath Mathewson, second, (1736–1802). Married Asaph Phillips (1764–1829).

XVII. *Jeremiah Phillips*, 1800–1848. Son of Asaph Phillips & Esther Whipple. Married Roby Rathbone (1797–1848).

XVIII. *Whipple V. Phillips*, 1833–1904. Son of Jeremiah. Married Rhoby Alzada Place (1827–1896).

XIX. *Sarah Susan Phillips*, 1857–1921. Daughter of Whipple, married Winfield S. Lovecraft (1853–1898).

XX. *Howard Phillips Lovecraft*, 1890–1936. (If many more tasks pile up on him!) Son of W. S. Lovecraft & Sarah Phillips.

By the way—did you notice in one of the Oakland amateur papers the news that savage old Ida C. Haughton, my deadly foe in the early 1920's, was burned to death a year ago through the igniting of her clothing at a fireplace? Poor old gal! I'm surely sorry to hear it! I wished her a lot of things, but nothing quite as drastic as that!

No progress in cleaning up my programme as yet. I suppose I was a damn fool to spend a whole afternoon on this Field hunt when I might have got all the dope later in predigested & easily copyable form. The family grey matter seems to have petered out since The Proto-Copernican's day!

Vacuously & drivellingly thine—
Theobaldus Perkins-Field.

Notes

1. See Kenneth W. Faig, Jr., "Quae Amamus Tuemur: Ancestors in Lovecraft's Life and Fiction," in *The Unknown Lovecraft*, n. 42 (pp. 45–46).

[160]   [AHT]

The Antient Hill
July 25, 1936

Dauntless Defender of Devious Deciphering:—

Turning to melancholy matters—mourning prevails in Kappa Alpha Tau circles. Alas—my best friends are no more! A month ago both Mr. John Perkins (born February 1935—coal black save for a tiny white cravat) & his younger brother the Earl of Minto (born October 1935—black & white) succumb'd to some malady which is afflicting all the local felidae—a thing which may be an obscure epidemick, yet which may reflect the malign activities of some contemptible poisoner. The sad end of the brothers seem'd connected with some digestive disorder, & recall'd the equally sad fate of their bygone black bother . . . . little Sam Perkins, whom you met . . . . . . in September, 1934. If this *is* the mark of some wretched neo-Borgia, I hope to gawd somebody feeds him a slow pizen a thousandfold more painful than that with which he has subtly supply'd his innocent furry victims! For a time it looked as if there'd be no more kittens at the house across the garden, since a coupla months ago the white-&-black matriarch of the clan was given away to the psychological laboratory of Brown University, where it was expected she would round out her days in ease & luxury, being used (in conjunction with other felidae, canidae, &c.) in tests of instinct, intelligence, perception, & what-the-hell for the benefit of successive generations of students. Since the tragedy, however, old lady Perkins has been recalled from her academick career, & once more roams her accustom'd and-where—serenaded by all the gallant swains of the Kappa Alpha Tau, including the night-black, rangy Mr. Perkins Sr. She call'd here t'other day, & was duly regaled with catnip purchas'd for younger mouths!

Tom Angell has a whole raft of descendants around these parts—indeed, we've known many bearing the surname. I believe I told you that my grandmother had a seat beside James Burrill Angell (late president of the University of Michigan and father of Yale's present president)[1] at the old Smithville Seminary in Scituate in the forties. I ain't got no Angell blood—only what one might pick up by induction or seepage by living thirty-four years in Angell Street.

As to puzzles & puzzlers—I won't start any new argument, since the anthropological phenomenon is a visible fact for all to observe & analyse. It's all right for you Master Minds—but I still think it would be a kindly service to dubs of my level if their few faint cerebral throbs could be turn'd into useful channels. The more I observe the abysmal, inspissated *ignorance* of the bulk of allegedly cultivated people—folks who think a lot of themselves & their position, & who conclude a vast quota of university graduates—the more I believe that something is radically wrong with conventional education & tradition. These pompous, self-complacent "best people" with their blind spots, delusions, prejudices, & callousness—poor devils who have no conception of their orientation to human history & to the cosmos—are the victims of some ingrained fallacy regarding the development & direction of cerebral energy. They don't lack brains, but have never been taught how to get the full benefit of what they have. They squander energy on the vapid & meaningless intricacies of bridge & whist, yet gape like bewildered yokels at the historical & sociological changes taking place around them. They potter around with crossword and jigsaw puzzles, yet look upon the vestigia of the past with no more comprehension than that provided by flashy guidebooks & superficial (& biassed) history courses. They mull over the technicalities of football, yet lay aside only half-understood the *Harpers* to which they subscribe. They memorise useless gossip about families as commonplace as themselves, yet know no more about atoms, nebulae, & genes than a stevedore—& no more about *minerals* than *I* do! They grope blindly through a world whose landmarks are hidden from them—throwing the beams of their lanthorns on some trivial object or objects pulled out of their pockets, instead of letting those beams shine on the terrain around, behind, and ahead. They are more ridiculous than the peasants and coal-heavers they despise—for instead of merely pure ignorance they possess the hypocritical combination of ignorance plus baseless pride & complacency. As I survey the existing state of society, I am inclin'd to be more and more sympathetick with the view of such radicals as Sonny Belknap & Briffault, that the very basis of western culture—its "ideology", as the Child wou'd say—needs some sort of overhauling & rationalisation to bring it into line with what is now known of the universe, of the trends & and values in human life & organisation, & of the structure & processes of human thought & emotion. An ignorantly drifting race needs to be taught what to do with itself & its potentialities. Not that I wou'd recommend quite the *same* sort of upheaval which Belknap & Briffault advocate. They are such systematick uprooters that they wou'd like to throw overboard the useful & still-valid along with the useless & fallacious, just for the fun of throwing. Moreover, they advocate violent & sudden methods likely to cause as much avoidable harm as good. My idea wou'd be simply a sharper attention to the subject of human values & current knowledge, a systematick educational campaign among teachers & academic authorities, & a breaking-away from conventional smugness, complacency, acquiescence, & supine worldliness on the part of the essayists, journalists, & commentators who play so vast yet quiet a part in the moulding of publick opinion. However, I recognise with Belknap & Briffault that all rational improvement is vastly hampered by the prevalence of the profit-motive. Commercial aims & ideals are the death of rationality & beauty in human life. As I advance in years & reflect in a more & more impersonal way, I realise that *socialism* of some kind is essential to any genuine, profound, & humane civilisation. I do not think that Marxian communism is the right sort, since it involves as many fresh fallacies as remedies. But certainly competitive plutocracy must be dethroned somehow. The only decent government is one which keeps oeconomick affairs within its control; assuring a livelihood to all, & preventing the waste & duplication of competitive effort. It ought to be administered by a small board of highly trained executives with centralised power, of the same race & background as those of the nation as a whole, & chosen (after psychological & educational tests necessary for candidacy) by the vote of such citizens as can pass a certain reasonable set of mental, scholastic, & cultural examinations. Whether such a kind of government can ever be attained by any existing Aryan nation, we cannot say. All that we know is that it is the only kind of government worth working toward. Our generation can never hope to see it—but we can at least favour every slight feasible change which lead toward it, & oppose every slogan-inspired force of reaction which leads away from it. I'm not for Earl Browder's Communist Party[2] but for the New Deal—yet, after all, my cleavage form the basic ideals of Belknap & Briffault is probably not as great as my cleavage from those of Hoover & Landon & Ogden Mills & J. P. Morgan.[3] The only points where I line up with the Republican-plutocratick corpses & racketeers against the Marxists & Calvertonians are (1) my insistence on a general preservation of the main stream of western culture, & (2) my repudiation of widespread social revolution as a short cut to a rational political & oeconomick order. Just what will really happen, we cannot tell. Northern Europe will probably make the needed transitions in an orderly way; Southern Europe with bloodshed & suffering. Russia has had her ordeal, & will probably retrograde successfully toward a rational norm. Japan may achieve a curious blend of feudal agrarianism & socialism, based on military power, which will have a long stability. The United States is a puzzle. It may experiment with individualistic reaction, have another depression worse than the present one, & fall tumultuously into communism. Or it may stick to the New Deal, experiment intelligently, & strike a rational & orderly collectivism in the gradual North-European way. The problem would be simpler if immigrant ideas & heritages were absent—but even so, the sound English spirit may triumph. As times of crisis draw near, the criminal folly of separation from the Empire & its wholesome influence in 1783 becomes more & more apparent. God Save the King! But I was talking of puzzles—& I digress!

The loss of good ol' Two-Gun Bob sure is a hell of a knockout.[4] Sultan Malik—the only one of us who ever met Two-Gun in person—says he feels "clubbed over the head" . . . . . & I can fully comprehend the sensation. The shock to poor old Dr. Howard must be appalling—wife & splendid child gone at one stroke—but he is carrying on like a true Texas pioneer. He has presented Robert's library to the latter's alma mater—Howard Payne College at Brownwood—as the nucleus of a Robert E. Howard Memorial Collection. Now he wants Price to come to Cross Plains to straighten out Two-Gun's papers & manuscripts—but the Sultan isn't sure whether he can or not. Poor Two-Gun! Tough, hairy-chested, go-to-hell, eat-'em-alive as he seem'd to be, he must have been morbidly emotional at bottom. Most of us, despite the strongest filial ties, recognise the grim inevitability of the elder generation's passing & accept such bereavements philosophically. We shall see many obituaries in both "fan" & professional magazines (a long one by me will appear in Schwartz's *FM*)—& Barlow has prepared a fine elegiack sonnet which Wright has accepted. This is little Bobby's first professional placement—& it is tragick that his debut should have to have so melancholy a background. The *suddenness* of the event makes it all the more devastating. Price & Wollheim had cheerful cards from R. E. H. as late as June 3, & I had a long normal letter written May 13. My answer to that letter—32 pages of argument—reached Cross Plains too late to be read. Without question, Two-Gun Bob had the last word in our six-year-long debate—an advantage I won't begrudge him, poor chap, under the circumstances! Requiescat in victoria!

This is the worst blow weird magazine fiction has had since the passing of good old Whitehead in '32. Nobody else in the gang had quite the driving zest & spontaneity of Two-Gun. It is hard to say just what made his stories stand out so, but the real secret is that *he was in every one of them himself.* Even when he made outward concessions to commercial criticks & Mammon-guided editors he had an inner force & sincerity which broke through the surface & put the imprint of his personality on everything he wrote. He was really even more gifted than appears from his publish'd work; being an encyclopaedick student of southwestern history, & having a truly epical power of capturing the colour & repeating the annals of his beloved native region. His long, essay-like letters—with their fragments of bygone strife, their exaltations of barbarick life, & their tirades against civilisation—ought some day to see the light of print. Had he liv'd longer—he was thirty last January—he wou'd almost undoubtedly have made his mark in serious literature as a regional author. But even his existing stories were distinctive enough. Never again will the pulps get anything with such force & colour. Eheu fugaces! Two-Gun Bob lived in & near Texas all his life, & was passionately devoted to its history & folkways. He came of old planter stock—largely Scotch-Irish—from Georgia & North Carolina. Celtick antiquities & antient history in general claim'd much of his attention—& no one cou'd excel him in tales of barbarick or prehistorick life. He saw many phases of the vanishing frontier—from open-range cow-punching to oil-drilling—& knocked about among the types of Tejanos. His first story was written at the age of fifteen, & his first placement was with *Weird Tales* in 1924, at the age of eighteen. "Wolfshead", in the April '26 issue of *Weird Tales,* was the tale which first brought him general notice. It had the cover design, & I can recall reading it on a prematurely warm day on a bench in Brooklyn's Prospect Park just before my return to civilisation. Later came the "Solomon Kane", "Bran Mak Morn", "King Kull", & Conan" yarns—plus the Oriental battle-tales, prize-fight stories, & humorously realistick "westerns" in other magazines. Two-Gun was nearly six feet tall, with the massive build of a pugilist. He was very dark save for Celtick blue eyes. A hearty lion & heavy drinker, he always toted a revolver (alas, to find so tragick a final use!) & seem'd a veritable em-bodiment of the wild west. Toward the last he changed a bit in appearance—getting stout & round-faced, & growing a fierce pair of moustachios which (in conjunction with a ten-gallon hat) made him look almost like a western cinema sheriff. 1936 surely has taken heavy toll! Doubtless you know of the deaths of M. R. James at seventy-three & of George Allan England at fifty-nine.

And so it goes. Benedictions—& hope to see ya before the worst chill of autumn closes in!

Yr obt Servt
Θεοβάλδος Περκινς

Notes

1. Angell (1829–1916) was president of Brown University (1868–77). HPL owned a copy of his *Reminiscences* (1912; *LL* 30). He was the father of James Rowland Angell (1869–1949), president of Yale (1921–37).
2, Earl Russell Browder (1891–1973) founded the Communist Party of America in 1919. He served as its general secretary from 1930 to 1945.
3. HPL refers to President Herbert Hoover; Alf Landon (1887–1987), governor of Kansas and Republican candidate for president in 1936; Ogden Mills (1884–1937), American businessman and secretary of the treasury under Hoover; and J. P. Morgan (1937–1913), American financier.
4. Robert E. Howard committed suicide on 11 June 1936.

[161]   [AHT]

The Antient Hill
August 18, 1936

August Antagonist of Ambulatory Answering:—

[. . .] We have discover'd ourselves to be *sixth cousins* by virtue of the fol-lowing descent from a common forbear:

John Rathbone—born 1658

John Rathbone—born 1693	Rev. Joshua Rathbone—born 1696
John Rathbone—born 1720	Rev. Valentine Rathbone—born 1724
John Rathbone—born 1750	Hannah Rathbone
Sarah Rathbone Rhoby Rathbone	Eliza Jane Hayward
Rhoby Place Whipple Phillips	Ellen Maria Stowell
Sarah Phillips	E. D. Barlow Jr.
H. P. L.	R. H. B.

It is curious that Bob & I are both descended from old John in just seven generations, although Bob is young enough to be my son.

Well—don't bother to answer this, but herald your advent with a timely card.

Regards to the Missus.

—Grandpa

[162]   [AHT]

[H. P. Lovecraft's last letter, unfinished, found on his desk after he had been taken to the hospital, where the end came to him; also his memos for the letter & an intended enclosure.

Hadley N. A. P. A. donations to self & R. K.
Goodenough
Edkins
Cook
Californian
Kleiner criticism
Floods
Recent *Weird Tale* issues:
Finlay & C. A. S. verses
         Derleth
         Leiber (odd about Sp. stencil work) & Fischer
         Kuttner & de Castro
         Innsmouth
         Chivers
         Surrealism (?)
         Winterset & Mids. N.D.][1]

The Antient Hill
[December 1936?–February? 1937]
Pinnacled Pharos of Petrological Profundity:—

Continuing the chronicle of Theobaldian vegetativeness from Sept. 13's train-time onward, we find no extremely striking landmarks to record . . . . . unless the abysmal foot swelling & damned intestinal grippe of recent weeks form an item of biographical interest. Cripes, but I'm about all in—with the strength of an eviscerated dishrag!

Following your too-soon-terminated sojourn, the next social event of the dying season was a visit from young Moe Sept. 19–20, which included some sight-seeing in his 1928 Ford. Meanwhile I plugged along with that damned Renshaw job[2]—being unable to persuade the author to reproportion those familiar allusions or to let me doctor the whole thing up into something definite. Time got rushed toward the last, so that I had to work sixty hours without sleep in order to make the deadline. Cooking up a good reading course was a helluva job. In the end everything was cut down ruthlessly—though the result is a very neat little cloth-bound volume. I read the proofs three times, reducing errors to a minimum.

October 9th I attended a meeting of the local organisation of amateur astronomers—"The Skyscrapers", which functions more or less under the auspices of Brown University—& was astonished at its degree of development. Some of the members are really serious scientific observers, & the society has recently purchased a well-known private observatory (that of the late F. E. Seagrave[3]—whom Charles A. A. Parker once knew—with an 8" refracting telescope) in the western part of the state. It has separate meteor, variable star, planet, &c. sections, which hold meetings of their own & report as units, & enjoys the use of the college observatory. At the recent meeting there was an address on early Rhode-Island astronomy, & the reflecting telescope of Joseph Brown—used to observe the transit of Venus here on June 3, 1769 & owned by the college since 1780—was exhibited. Oddly enough, that meeting proved a prelude to another & wholly unrelated revival of my old astronomical interests. Down in De Land my friend Charles B. Johnston has become connected with Stetson University & its astronomical society, & asked me for a series of elementary articles on the heavens for the local paper. I had an old series— published twenty-two years ago—which seemed of about the right sort; but when I got them out, their obsoleteness completely bowled me over.[4] The progress of the science in the last twenty or thirty years had left me utterly behind, & I saw that I'd have to do a helluva lot of brushing up if I ever expected to bridge the last decades & give the ancient articles an intelligent revision to date. Well—I decided to try it, hence began an intermittent reading course with which I'm still busy. Our public library has some excellent new books on the subject—the textbook by J. C. Duncan & the layman's manuals by Bartky & Stokeley [*sic*] being apparently the best short cuts for the non-mathematical amateur. Curious how one's early interests crop up again in one's sunset years. I used to be an ardent amateur chemist as well as astronomer—& the other day I learned that one of the youths of the fantasy fan group is likewise a chemical enthusiast—having assembled a really impressive laboratory besides organising an Organic Chemists' Correspondence Club.

Also in October I came into touch with a rather quaint egg in San Francisco—one Stuart Morton (relative o' yourn?) Boland, who seems to possess occult leanings. He is a librarian of some sort, has travelled extensively, & claims to have seen many real-life prototypes of the *Necronomicon*. He most generously presented me with a fine book on primal American civilisations,[5] plus some of his photographs of Aztec ruins (largely in Teotihuacán) taken on a recent Mexican trip.

As for outings—of course I kept in the open most of the time until the hellish chill of autumn finally began to shut down. Even after that I managed to take occasional trips to the woods & fields throughout October & just over the line into November. The unique feature of my autumnal explorations was that I succeeded in discovering several splendid rural regions within a three-mile radius of here *which I had never seen before*. One is a wooded hill—Neutaconkanut—on the western rim of the town (much south of Friend Mariano), whence a series of marvellous views of the outspread city & adjacent countryside may be obtained. I had often ascended it before, but the exquisitely mystical sylvan scenery beyond the crest—curious mounds, hummocked pastures, & hushed, hidden valleys—was wholly new to me. On October 28th I explored this region still further—including the country west of Neutaconkanut & the western slopes of that eminence itself. At certain stages of this ramble I penetrated a terrain which took me half a mile from any spot I had ever trod before in the course of a long life. I followed a road which branches north & west from the Plainfield Pike, ascending a low rise which skirts Neutaconkanut's western foot & which commands an utterly idyllic vista of rolling meadows, ancient stone walls, hoary groves, & distant cottage roofs to the west & south. Only two or three miles from the city's heart, & yet in the primal rural New England of the first colonists! Just before sunset I ascended the hill by a precipitous cart-path bordering an ancient wood, & from the dizzy crest obtained an almost stupefying prospect of unfolded leagues of farmsteads & champaigns, gleaming rivulets & far-off forests, & mystical orange sky with a great solar disc sinking redly amidst bars of stratus clouds. Entering the wood, 1 saw the actual sunset through the trees, & then turned east to cross the hill to that more familiar cityward slope which I have always known. Never before had I realised the great extent of Neutaconkanut's surface. It is really a miniature plateau or table-land, with valleys, ridges, & summits of its own, rather than a simple hill. From some of its hidden interior meadows—remote from every sign of nearby human life—I secured truly marvellous glimpses of the remote urban skyline—a dream of enchanted pinnacles & domes half-floating in air, & with an obscure aura of mystery around them. The upper windows of some of the taller towers held the fire of the sun after I had lost it, affording a spectacle of cryptic & curious glamour. Then I saw the great yellow disc of the Hunter's Moon (two days before full) floating above the belfries & minarets, while in the orange-glowing west Venus & Jupiter commenced to twinkle. My route across the plateau was varied—sometimes through the interior, but now & then getting toward the wooded edge where dark valleys slope down to the plain below, & huge balanced boulders on rocky heights impart a spectral, druidic effect as they stand out against the twilight. I did not begin to cover the full extent of the plateau, & can see that I have a field for several voyages of discovery when warm days return. Finally I came to more familiar ground—where the grassy ridge of an old buried aqueduct gives the illusion of one of those vestigial Roman roads in Machen's Caermaen country—& stood once more on the well-known eastward crest which I have gazed at since infancy. The outspread city was rapidly lighting up, & lay like a constellation in the deepening dusk. The moon poured down increasing floods of pale gold, & the glow of Venus & Jupiter in the fading west grew intense. Then down the steep hillside to the car line (too cold for enjoyable walking without scenery to compensate for shivers) & back to the prosaic haunts of man.

October 20 & 21 were phenomenally warm, & I utilised them in exploring a hitherto untapped region down the east shore of Narragansett Bay where the Barrington Parkway winds along the lofty bluff above the water. It is, in general, the area to the right of our usual route to Aunt Julia's. I found a highly fascinating forest called the Squantum Woods—where there are great oaks & birches, steep slopes & rock ledges, & breath-taking westward vistas beyond the trees. On both occasions there was a fine sunset—then glimpses of the crescent moon, Venus, & Jupiter . . . & the lights of far-off Providence from high places along the parkway. On my expedition of the 20th a particularly congenial bodyguard or retinue attended me through the sunlit arcades of the grove—in the persons of *two tiny kittens*, one gray & one tortoise-shell, who appeared out of nowhere in the midst of the sylvan solitudes. Blithe spirits of the ancient wood—furry faunlets of the shadowy vale! I wonder where their mother was? Judging by their diminutiveness, they could scarce have been fully graduated from her as a source of nourishment. Probably they appertained to an hospital whose grounds are contiguous with the mystical forest. Both were at first very timid, & reluctant to let Grandpa catch them; but eventually the little grey fellow became very purr-ful & amicable—climbing over the old gentleman, playing with twigs & with Grandpa's watch-charm, & eventually curling up & going to sleep in the grandpaternal lap. But Little Brother remained suspicious & aloof—clawing & spitting with surprising vehemence on the one occasion when Grandpa caught him. He hung around, however, because he didn't want to lose his brother! Not wishing to wake my new friend, I carried him about when I continued my ramble—Little Tortoise-Shell Brother tagging along reluctantly & dubiously at a discreet distance in the rear. When the grey faunlet awaked, he requested to be set down; but proceeded to trot companionably after Grandpa—sometimes getting under the old gentleman's feet & considerably retarding progress. Thus I roamed the venerable forest aisles for an hour & a half—till the ruddy disc of the sun vanished behind the farther hills. As I emerged from the wood, I feared that my faithful retinue might follow me on to the broad parkway & incur the perils of motor traffic—and was considering expedients (such as putting Little Grey Boy a short distance up a tree) for discouraging their further attendance—but discovered that they were not without native caution. Or perhaps they were wholly genii loci, without real existence apart from their dim nemorense habitat. At any rate, Little Grey Boy paused at the edge of the grove with a mewed farewell—& naturally Little Tortoise-Shell had no great eagerness to follow. I bade them a regretful & ceremonious adieu—& on the next day looked for them in vain.

As a whole, our autumn was notably lacking in visual splendour. Not as prematurely cold as I had feared, but with the dullest October foliage within my memory. Half the trees were swept bare by heavy rains as soon at they began to turn, whilst the other half remained green for an anomalous length of time—the leaves then falling almost as soon as they did turn. *Red* hues were especially rare. The result was a tremendous loss of glamour—although we heard of gorgeous woodlands at points not many miles distant, while the Vermont & New-Hampshire leafage is said to have been of unparalleled magnificence. Derleth also told of riotous autumn colours in Wisconsin.

By the way—another event of that genial October 20th was my first sight of President Roosevelt, who was in town in the morning & who spoke from the terrace of our marble state-house. Despite the crowds, I obtained several close & excellent glimpses of the distinguished visitor whose coming triumph was so obvious—my third sight of a chief executive; T. R. & Big Bill Taft constituting the others.

As for the November election—I expected a brilliant victory, but the *extent* of the landslide surprised & delighted me. Late in October I attended a highly interesting New Deal rally, with the eminent Rabbi Wise of New York as principal speaker.[6] He sized up the inevitable awakening of the public mind with phenomenal penetration & wit, & exposed the putrescent deadness & irrelevance of the obsolete slogans & artificial basic premises in which the reactionaries based their pitiful appeal. I can well imagine the Wall Street Nazis of Hoover & Ogden Mills cursing him as a dangerous non-Aryan intellectual! On the eve of the election I did—for the second time in a long life—what I did on the night of November 7–8th, 1916, when the fortunes of Hughes & Wilson hung in the balance ("he kep' us outa war") . . . went to a late cinema show where election returns were announced. The national results were early manifest, but the state & city figures (a clean Democratic sweep) took longer to settle. By the time the performance closed—two-forty-five a. m.—there was no danger of any contrary report next day as there was twenty years ago.[7] On that occasion, you will recall, the nation retired believing Hughes elected, but had that belief shattered the next day. All in all, the recent triumph is pretty significant in what it implies. The feeble arguments, obvious hokum, absurd accusations, & occasionally underhanded tactics of the enemy reacted against them, while some obscure instinct of common sense seemed to hold the extreme radicals to the Popular Front & keep them from wasting their votes on obviously hopeless tickets. It amuses me to see the woebegone state of the staid reactionary reliques with whom I am surrounded—the Providence old-family clique away from whose past-drugged ideology it is impossible to pull my aunt. Around election time I came damn near having a family feud on my hands! Poor old ostriches! Trembling for the republic's safety, they actually thought their beloved Langston or Langhorne or Lemke (or whatever his name was) had a chance![8] However, the intelligent university element was not so blind. Indeed, one of the professors said just before the election that his idea of a rotten sport was a man who would actually *take* one of the pro-Lansdowne (or whatever his name was) bets offered by the walrus-moustached constitution-savers of the Hope Club easy-chairs. Well—even the most stubborn must some day learn that the tide of social evolution cannot be checked forever. The shade of old King Canute will again speak his famed command to the waves, & teach the economic royalists of this age the lesson he taught the courtiers of his own.

With the coming of hibernation there came also a few compensating events in the form of lectures—on subjects as varied as the Williamsburg restoration, the relation of poetry to philosophy, Peruvian antiquities, Italian Romanesque architecture, & Greek astronomical hypotheses. The last-named formed a very timely coincidence in view of my recent researches—and included the exhibition of Christopher Clavius's celebrated volume with its defence & explanation of the Ptolemaic system.[9]

I trust that your Yule was duly festive. Ours here was commendably cheerful—including a turkey dinner at the boarding-house across the garden, with a congenial cat meandering among the tables & finally jumping up on the windowseat for a nap. We had a tree by the living-room fireplace—its verdant boughs thickly festooned with a tinsel imitation of Florida's best Spanish moss, & its outlines emphasised by a not ungraceful lighting system. Around its base were ranged the modest Saturnalian gifts—which included (on my side) a hassock tall enough to let me reach the top shelves of my bookcases, & (on my aunt's side) a cabinet of drawers for odds & ends, not unlike my own filing cabinets, but of more ladylike arrangement & aspect. Of outside gifts the most distinctive was perhaps that which came quite unexpectedly from one of the kid fantasy fan group (Willis Conover, Jun. of Cambridge, Md.)—for lo! when I had removed numberless layers of corrugated paper & excelsior, what should I find before me but the yellowed & crumbling fragments of *a long-interred human skull!* Verily, a fitting gift from a youthful ghoul to one of the hoary elders of the necropolitan clan! This sightlessly staring monument of mortality came from an Indian mound not far from the sender's home on the Maryland eastern shore—a place distinguished by many archaeological exploits on the part of Conover & his young friends. Its condition is such as to make its reassembling a somewhat ticklish task—so that I may reserve it for the ministrations of some expert mender like Bobby Barlow upon the occasion of a future visit. Viewing this shattered yield of the ossuary, the reflective fancy strives to evoke the image of him to whom it once belonged. Was it some feathered chieftain who in his day oft ululated in triumph as he counted the tufted scalps sliced from coppery or colonist foes? Or some crafty medicine-man who with mask & drum called forth from the Great Abyss those shadowy things which were better left uncalled? This we this we may never know—unless perchance some incantation droned out from the pages of the *Necronomicon* will have power to draw strange emanations from the lifeless & centuried clay, & raise up amidst the cobwebs of my ancient study a shimmering mist not without power to speak. In such a case, the revelation might be such that no man hearing it could any longer live save as one of those hapless entities 'who laugh, but smile no more'![10]

Since Yuletide, my annals are largely the quiet chronicles of infirmity. Despite the general mildness of the winter, I was caught in the cold two or three times in early December—& as a result have had some of my old-time foot & ankle swelling, which occasionally forces me to wear an old pair of cut & stretched shoes. This won't wholly go until I've had a week or two of eighty degree weather to be outdoors & active in. And on top of this came the pervasive & enervating malady (probably some sort of intestinal grippe) which has forced me on a diet & sapped my strength to a minimum. My programme, as you may well imagine, has greatly suffered—but so far I haven't been forced wholly off my feet. Indeed, on warm days I totter forth in the afternoon for air & exercise. Were the winter so cold as to prevent these modest airings, I should be much worse off.

By the way, I was glad to learn of your enjoyable year's-end pilgrimage as related in your Cincinnati card. Glad the floods didn't catch you, as they might have done a little later!

I've lacked the time & energy to read recent *Weird Tale* issues systematically, but have merely glanced at such tales as have been mentioned in my correspondence. Among these is "The Headless Miller of Kobold's Keep", which I enjoyed very much despite certain obvious crudities.[11] This story—of whose author I never heard before—has a peculiar atmospheric quality which makes for convincingness. I liked the Finlay illustrations to my two tales—indeed, I believe Finlay is the best all-around artist *Weird Tales* has ever had.

His drawing for the "Doorstep" was really an imaginative masterpiece. Wright has generously presented me with the originals of both "Haunter" & "Doorstep" pictures—& they far transcend the mechanical reproductions. I am now in epistolary touch with Finlay, & find him a most remarkable youth—a poet as well as artist. He is only twenty-two, & a native & resident of Rochester, New York. His cover-design is good, though lacking his typical genius. Not long ago, Finlay was expressing regret at the decline of the old-time custom of writing verses on appreciated works of art, so I turned out the following specimen just to shew him that Grandpa still adheres to the ancient tradition:

> To Mr. Finlay, upon his Drawing for
> Mr. Bloch's Tale, "The Faceless God."
>
> In dim abysses pulse the shapes of night,
>   Hungry and hideous, with strange mitres crown'd;
> Black pinions beating in fantastic flight
>   From orb to orb thro' sunless voids profound.
> None dares to name the cosmos whence they course,
>   Or guess the look on each amorphous face,
> Or speak the words that with resistless force
>   Would draw them from the hells of outer space.
>
> Yet here upon a page our frighten'd glance
>   Finds monstrous forms no human eye should see;
> Hints of those blasphemies whose countenance
>   Spreads death & madness thro' infinity.
> What limner he who braves black gulfs alone
>   And lives to make their alien horrors known?

The original of this drawing—Finlay's acknowledged masterpiece to date—hangs framed upon the walls of Wright's office. The model for the quasi-feline faces was the cherished Finlay cat "Tammany", who has since departed this life amidst universal lamentation. But having writ these lines upon the work of a new-found genius, I could not forbear writing some more upon the products of one well-tested by time . . . hence the following to a tried & true colleague of fifteen years, whose greatness not even the underestimation of certain eminent critics can obscure. Which reminds me that Klarkash-Ton is now having an exhibition of his grotesque sculptures at the Crocker Art Gallery in Sacramento. He is now experimenting—with increasing success—in the making of moulds & casts of certain pieces; so that each sculptural effort will not be limited to one lone specimen. I am eager to behold the fruits of this process. But here is the tribute:

To Clark Ashton Smith, Esq., upon his
Fantastic Tales, Verses, Pictures, & Sculptures:

A time-black tower against dim banks of cloud;
  Around its base the pathless, pressing wood.
Shadows & silence, moss & mould, enshroud
  Grey, age-fell'd slabs that once as cromlechs stood.
No fall of foot, no song of bird awakes
  The lethal aisles of sempiternal night,
Tho' oft with stir of wings the dense air shakes,
  As in the tower there glows a pallid light.

For here, apart, dwells one whose hands have wrought
  Strange eidola that chill the world with fear;
Whose graven runes in tones of dread have taught
  What things beyond the star-gulfs lurk & leer.
Dark Lord of Averoigne—whose windows stare
  On pits of dream no other gaze could bear!

On the whole, recent *Weird Tale* issues perpetuate the usual qualitative average. Two-Gun Bob shines posthumously in December—his description of the ancient ruins holding a very striking quality. Bloch's Haitian tale has good touches, & Kuttner's story is excellent—with a real punch for a climax. I didn't care much for "The Album" (despite a certain atmospheric effectiveness) because of the anachronisms—the tacit assumption that successful photography existed in the eighteenth century (actually, nothing like a permanent photograph existed before Niepce's classic achievement of 1814),[12] & the absurd gibberish supposed (judging from the date the book began to work, as indicated by its captures) to represent the English of the late eighteenth century. Tsathoggua! but what sort of insanity gets hold of some of these birds (W. H. Hodgson is the classic & memorable offender, & Seabury Quinn has likewise pulled some choice boners in this line) when they try to represent the diction of an age which after all is, historically speaking, essentially modern? Haven't they ever read Goldsmith & Fielding & Johnson & Gibbon & Sterne & Smollett & dozens of other prose writers of that fairly recent yesterday? What in Yuggoth's name causes them to drag down from the remoter reaches of antiquity a cobwebbed jargon more Chaucerian or Elizabethan than anything else, & serve it up as contemporary with Burke's speeches & the seditious Declaration of Independence? Actually—assuming a date around 1780—the message in the book (in "The Album") would have run something like this:

To Whomsoever May Open This Book:
This is set down as a Warning to you, Sir or Madam, that you are not to open this Book beyond the Place mark'd by a red Riband. It wou'd be better for you to throw the whole Book unopen'd into the Fire; but being unable to do so myself, I cannot hope that you will. I do nevertheless adjure you to look nowhere in it beyond the Riband, lest you lose yourself to this World, Body & Soul; for truly, it is a Tomb for the Living.

But instead of such a straight eighteenth century text, see what a mess of quasi-Tudor bunk the author had . . . "booke", "worlde", "bodie & soule" . . . Hell! "Portrait of a Murderer" is poor, & "The Theatre Upstairs" (by a friend of Talman's) does not live up to its atmospheric possibilities. Comte d'Erlette's offering is just another pot-boiler, & Sultan Malik's collaborated dime novel has just a touch of redeeming mystery & suspense. "Out of the Sun" is incredibly bad—even for pulp "scientifiction".[13] The January issue—which I've read only in part—has a good professional debut by young Rimel,[14] as well as the interesting "Kobold's Keep". I've only just dipped into the February issue, but note a powerful (even if a bit hackneyed) tale by Two-Gun, & a very good attempt by Little Augie to give the old "beast with five fingers" plot a new twist.[15] By the way—Little Augie's first continuous serious novel is just appearing under Scribner auspices. It is a Wisconsin historical tale—the first of a long cycle—entitled "Still Is the Summer Night".

Descending to the ridiculous—Hill-Billy Crawford has at last issued my "Innsmouth" as a lousily misprinted & sloppily bound book. The printed errata slip doesn't cover half the mistakes—but I'll send you a full list if you ever get the damn thing. The one redeeming feature is the set of four Utpatel illustrations.

Wright informs me that "Pickman's Model" is about to be reprinted again—in a Special Coronation Omnibus of the "Not at Night" series. The material reward will be only £1 sterling—but it will gratify me to be connected in any way with the enthronement of our new Sovereign. God Save the King!

By the way—to let an association of ideas start me off at a tangent—here's a remarkable case of coincidence or "small world" stuff or what-the-hell. You've probably heard me spout more than a dozen times those favourite lines of mine from the close of "King John", which make me swell with a kind of exaltation every time I even think if them:

> This England never did, nor never shall,
> Lie at the proud Foot of a Conqueror,
> But when it first did help to wound itself.
> Now these her Princes are come home again,
> Come the three Corners of the World in Arms,

> And we shall shock them. Naught shall make us rue
> If England to itself do rest but true![16]

I had the privilege of hearing these lines on the actual boards a quarter of a century ago when Robert Mantell's[17] repertory company played Providence, & ever afterward associated them with the extremely gifted young actor who spoke them in the part of the bastard Faulconbridge—a chap named Fritz Leiber,[18] who handled all such secondary roles as Horatio, Mercutio, Iago, Macduff, Richmond, Edgar, Bassanio, Antony, & so on. I used to think that Leiber was really better than Mantell himself—for the latter was getting egotistical, self-conscious, & stagey. Well—I lately had occasion to revive those ancient memories, when I received (through *Astounding Stories*) a communication from *Fritz Leiber's son & namesake*—a fanatical & scholarly devotee of weird fiction & the aesthetic, psychological, & philosophical background behind it. Young Fritz (twenty-five, a University of Chicago graduate, & entering his father's profession) has one of the keenest minds I have ever encountered, & in the interval since last November has become one of the star correspondents on my desperately crowded list. His understanding of the profound emotions behind the groping for cosmic concepts surpasses that of almost anyone else with whom I've discussed the matter; & his own tales & poems, while not without marks of the beginner, shew infinite insight & promise. Papa's genius certainly reached the second generation in this case— for whether or not Fritz Jun. equals his sire on the boards, he'll certainly get somewhere in literature if he keeps on at his present rate. He has had classic thespian experience—having played in his father's companies (which have never visited Providence) in recent years those selfsame roles (Edgar, Iago, &c.) which in my day old Fritz himself played in Mantell's companies. Incidentally, I saw old Fritz in two cinemas last year the Pasteur opera—& "Anthony Adverse".[19] Young Fritz has a momentary bit in the current "Camille" film—which I have not seen.[20] Pater et filius reside together (though young Fritz has a wife) in Beverly Hills, California—the same town with young Henry Kuttner. Young Fritz resembles his parent—who, by the way, is an amateur sculptor of much talent, with some remarkable Shakespearian busts to his credit. The son's artistic ability is manifest in something he sent me for Christmas—a series of strangely potent & macabre illustrations for some of my tales. These designs were produced by a novel & original process which the artist-inventor calls "splatter-stencil work", & they convey surprisingly vivid effects in a semi-futuristic way. The best is probably one shewing the earthward flight of certain winged entities from nighted Yuggoth—illustrating "The Whisperer in Darkness". There will shortly be circulated among the gang (you can be on the list if you like) a remarkable unpublished novelette by young Leiber—"Adept's Gambit", rejected by Wright & now under revision according to my suggestions. It is a very brilliant piece of fantastic imagination—with suggestions of Cabell, Beckford, Dunsany, & even Two-Gun Bob—& ought to see publication some day. Being wholly out of the cheap tradesman tradition, it has small chance of early magazine placement—hence the idea of circulation amongst the members of the circle. This novelette is part of a very unusual myth-cycle spontaneously evolved in the correspondence of young Leiber & his closest friend—Harry O. Fischer of lately-inundated Louisville.[21] Fischer has also come within my congested epistolary circle, & is in some ways even more remarkable than Leiber—he has more imaginative fertility, though less concentrated emotional power & philosophic thought. Their myth-cycle, originally started by Fischer, involves my own pantheon of Yog-Sothoth, Cthulhu, &c., & revolves round the adventures of two roving characters (Fafhrd the Viking, modelled after Leiber (who is six feet four) & the Grey Mouser, modelled after the diminutive Fischer) in a vague congeries of fabulous & half-fabulous worlds of the remote past. Fischer's parts if this cycle are vivid but unformulated & disjointed, so that at present Leiber—the better craftsman—is the only publicly visible author of the pair. "Adept's Gambit" is laid in the Syria of the earlier Hellenistic period, but soon moves away from Tyre & Ephesus to a fabulous mountain realm of inland Asia. Fischer's wife is an accomplished artist, & has made several very effective pastel drawings of some of the inconceivable entities in the Fafhrd-Mouser cycle.

Oh—by the way. You may recall my having mentioned that old de Castro, when here last August, discovered that he had known the father of young Henry Kuttner a generation ago. Kuttner Sr. is long dead, but the other day the youthful heir announced that old 'Dolph had crossed the continent & blown in on him! Hope he doesn't bore the kid to death with his tales of departed grandeur . . . "how I made William H. Taft & Warren G. Harding president" & all that! If you've ever seen the popular syndicated cartoon-series featuring "Judge Puffle", you have Old Dolph to the life![22]

Not much energy for reading these days, but some of my political-minded colleagues are bullying me into digesting Strachey's "Nature of Capitalist Crisis" & R. P. Dutt's "Fascism & Social Revolution". A more voluntary piece of recent reading is the very excellent life of Thomas Holley Chivers by my next-door neighbour (literally, since his field of endeavour is in the marble library adjacent to #66) Prof. S. Foster Damon, & I have emerged from it with a new respect for the powers & genius of Poe's eccentric friend, rival, & imaginative kinsman. I should never have let myself be prejudiced by the absurd and ineffable slop which he sometimes perpetrated. Like Blackwood, he was undisciplined & uneven—& suppose one tried to judge brother Algy by something like "The Extra Day" or "The Garden of Survival"? Setting aside his junk, we may see him as the possessor of a rich cosmic imagination, an occasionally inspired command of pictorial symbols, & a metrical sense which in musical value and sensitiveness to new, bizarre, & obscure harmonies was not inferior to Poe's own. He & Poe undoubtedly borrowed ideas, phrases, & metres from each other, yet in every case the borrowing was attended with such distinctive individual development that charges of plagiarism are absurd. Chivers was injudicious & irresponsible in making occasional charges of plagiarism (which never, however, involved any diminution of his general esteem or his desire to refute Griswoldian & other libels) against Poe after the latter's death. Prof. Damon (formerly of your alma mater) is one if the two leading authorities on Chivers, & The Harris Collection of American Poetry (housed in the John Hay next door), of which he is curator, contains the largest existing array of the poet's works. All Chivers scholars come to Providence & the ancient hill in order to consult material & among those who have done so is Prof. Lewis Chase of North Carolina, the other leading authority on the bard.[23] Chase lived here a year or two, going over Chivers material & collaborating with Damon. The two of them will eventually issue a complete annotated edition of Chivers' works.[24] Our friend Samuelus, as you are doubtless aware, is an old-time Chivers enthusiast. That poem on Chivers in the Caxton "Herm" was originally published in my *Conservative* in '23.[25]

Speaking of American poetry (& you can let that apply to either Chivers or S. L.!)—I saw the cinema of the recent drama "Winterset", & found it impressively good despite the absurdly slipped-in happy ending. I had heard great accounts of it, but was prepared to be disappointed because of the presumable conflict betwixt a modern setting, & the poetic, conventionalised, consciously exaggerated & coincidence-ridden nature of the play. Actually, the effect was truly powerful. Great care in arrangements & scenic effects removed the whole episode from the realm of the distance-lent glamour which 1936 will have in eyes of 2436 or so. The slum settings in the shadow of Brooklyn Bridge— against a background of ceaseless rain—reminded me of the misty, half-unreal Dublin of "The Informer". And the acting, too, was very adequate. The one other cinema I've seen this winter is "A Midsummer Night's Dream"—& it was certainly no disappointment.[26] The delivery of the lines was in nearly every case excellent; & though there were some cuts in the text which I lamented, these did not amount to more than the excisions common to all acting versions from the Restoration down. The music blended effectively with setting & dialogue, & the pageantry was excellently managed. Some of the elusively weird photographic effects connected with the haunted wood were incomparably fine. As the animating spirit of the grove, that little elf who played Puck certainly scored a triumph. In aspect & voice & demeanour he represented with utter perfection the bland, mischievous *indifferentism* of the traditional sylvan deity, while that shrill, eery, alienly-motivated mirth of his was the most convincing thing of its kind that I've ever seen.

During the past few months so many of my correspondents in the pest zone have been writing me about that display of fantastic & surrealistic painting at the Museum of Modern Art that I'm hoping its travelling residue will include ancient Providence on its route. The group of elder sources—pictorial fantaisistes as far back at El Greco & Hell-Fire Bosch—would have especially fascinated me . . . but I fear it won't be included in the migratory aftermath. In general, though, I am not a surrealistic enthusiast, for I think the practitioners of the school give their subconscious impressions too much automatic leeway. Not that the impressions are not potentially valuable, but that they tend to become trivial & meaningless except when more or less guided by some coherent imaginative concept. A thing like Señor Dali's humorously-dubbed "Wet Watches"[27] tends to become a reductio ad absurdum of the fantastic principle, & to exemplify the aesthetic decadence so manifest in many phases of our moribund & socially transitional era. However, I surely concede that this form of expression should be adequately recognised; since many of its products undoubtedly do possess a powerful imaginative reach & freshness, whilst the whole movement cannot but make important & revivifying contributions to the main stream of art. There is no drawing a line betwixt what is to be called extreme fantasy of a traditional type & what is to be called surrealism; & I have no doubt but that the nightmare landscapes of some of the surrealists correspond, as well as any actual creations could, to the iconographic horrors attributed by sundry fictioneers to mad or daemon-haunted artists. If there were a real Richard Upton Pickman or Felix Ebbonly,[28] I am sure he would have been represented in the recent exhibition by several blasphemous & abhorrent canvases! Better than the surrealists, though, is good old Nick Roerich, whose joint at Riverside Drive & 103rd Street is one of my shrines in the pest zone.[29] There is something in his handling of perspective & atmosphere which to me suggests other dimensions & alien orders of being—or at least, the gateways leading to such. Those fantastic carven stones in lonely upland deserts—those ominous, almost sentient, lines of jagged pinnacles—& above all, those curious cubical edifices clinging to precipitous slopes & edging upward to forbidden needle-like peaks!

[Unfinished.]

Notes

1. The notation is by August Derleth. Derleth dated the letter to March 1937, but it is very unlikely that it was written so late as that, as by that time HPL was too ill to write. He probably worked on the letter for several months, beginning as early as December 1936.

2. I.e., *Well Bred Speech* (1936) by Anne Tillery Renshaw. Much of HPL's work (including the essay now known as "Suggestions for a Reading Guide") was excised from the final work. Cf. *SL* 5.421–22.

3. Frank E. Seagrave (1860–1934), Rhode Island astronomer. In 1878 he erected an astronomical observatory at his home on Benefit Street, but around 1914 he moved the observatory to a house in North Scituate.

4. Charles Blackburn Johnston, the Barlows' handyman in DeLand, had asked HPL for a series of "elementary articles on the heavens for the local paper" (see *SL* 5.422). HPL unearthed his series, "Mysteries of the Heavens" (1915), for that purpose, but never revised the articles.

5. Possibly Herbert J. Spinden, *Ancient Civilizations of Mexico and Central America* (New York: American Museum of Natural History, 1917, 1922, or 1928); *LL* 829.

6. Rabbi Stephen Wise (1874–1949), a leading figure in more than a dozen Jewish organizations, probably the most influential and well-respected American Jew of his generation.

7. In the election of 1916, many citizens on the East Coast retired on election night thinking that the Republican candidate Charles Evans Hughes had won the election, but late returns from California and other western states allowed the Democrat Woodrow Wilson to be reelected.

8. The reference is both to Alf Landon, the orthodox Republican candidate for president, and to William Lemke, a third-party candidate supported by the radical political activists Charles E. Coughlin and Francis E. Townsend.

9. Christoph Clavius (1538–1612), German Jesuit mathematician and astronomer, and the main architect of the modern Gregorian calendar. HPL refers to *In Sphaeram Ioannis de Sacro Bosco Commentarius* (1581), a book that defended the Ptolemaic system and attacked Copernicus.

10. Poe, "The Haunted Palace," l. 48.

11. G. Garnet [pseud. of Irvin Ashkenazy], "The Headless Miller of Kobold's Keep" (*WT*, January 1937).

12. Joseph Nicéphore Niépce (1765–1833), French inventor and a pioneer in photography. HPL appears to be wrong about the date: his earliest known photoetching (non-extant) dates to 1822, and his earliest surviving photograph dates to 1825.

13. Robert E. Howard, "The Fire of Asshurbanipal"; Robert Bloch, "Mother of Serpents"; Henry Kuttner, "It Walks by Night"; Amelia Reynolds Long, "The Album"; Otis Adelbert Kline and E. Hoffmann Price, "The Cyclops of Xoatl"; John Russell Fearn, "Portrait of a Murderer"; August W. Derleth and Mark Schorer, "The Woman at Loon Point"; Manly Wade Wellman, "The Theater Upstairs"; and Granville S. Hoss, "Out of the Sun," all in *WT*, December 1936.

14. Duane Rimel, "The Disinterment" (*WT*, January 1937).

15. Robert E. Howard, "Dig Me No Grave"; August Derleth, "Glory Hand," both in *WT*, February 1937.

16. Shakespeare, *King John* 5.7.112–18.

17. Robert B. Mantell (1854–1928), Scottish actor and producer. The Robert Mantell Repertoire was active from 1904 to 1918.

18. HPL refers to Fritz Leiber, Sr. (1882–1949), stage and film actor.

19. *The Story of Louis Pasteur* (Warner Bros., 1935), directed by William Dieterle; starring Paul Muni, Josephine Hutchinson, and Anita Louise. *Anthony Adverse* (Warner Bros., 1936), produced by Hal B. Walls and Jack L. Warner, directed by Mervyn LeRoy; starring Fredric March, Olivia de Havilland, Donald Wood, and Anita Louise. Based on the novel by Hervey Allen.

20. *Camille* (MGM, 1936), directed by George Cukor, starring Greta Garbo, Lionel Barrymore, and Robert Taylor. Based on the novel and play *La Dame aud camélias* by Alexandre Dumas fils.

21. Harry Otto Fischer (1910–1986), friend of Fritz Leiber who collaborated with him on some of the early Fafhrd and Gray Mouser tales. The mention of "lately-inundated Louisville" refers to the flooding of the Ohio River in January and February 1937. At one point 70 percent of the city was under water.

22. Gene Ahern wrote and drew *Room & Board*, starring Judge Puffle, a cartoon strip created (not by Ahern) in 1936. Judge Puffle was a character very similar to Major Hoople in his own strip, *Our Boarding House*.

23. Lewis Nathaniel Chase (1873–1937), professor of English at Duke University (1929–37) and author of *Thomas Holley Chivers: A Selection* (1929).

24. The edition never materialized. One volume only of Chivers's *Complete Works* (Providence: Brown University Press, 1957), an edition of Chivers's correspondence from 1838 to 1858, appeared under the editorship of E. L. Chase and L. F. Parks.

25. "Thomas Holley Chivers (Buried at Decatur, Georgia)."

26. *Winterset* (RKO, 1936), produced by Pandro S. Berman, directed by Alfred Santell; starring Burgess Meredith, Margo Ciannelli, and Eduardo Ciannelli. Based on the play by Maxwell Anderson. *The Informer* (RKO, 1935), produced and directed by John Ford; starring Victor McLaglen, Heather Angel, and Preston Foster. Based on the novel by Liam O'Flaherty. *A Midsummer Night's Dream* (Warner Bros., 1935), directed by William Dieterle and Max Reinhardt; starring Ian Hunter, Dick Powell, James Cagney, Olivia de Havilland.

27. *The Persistence of Memory* (1931) (*La persistencia de la memoria*), known by some as "Melting Clocks" or "Wet Watches," is the most famous painting by Salvador Dalí (1904–1989).

28. Fictitious artists in, respectively, HPL's "Pickman's Model" and Clark Ashton Smith's "The City of the Singing Flame."

29. HPL frequently visited the Nicholas Roerich Museum (in his day at 103rd Street and Riverside Drive in Manhattan, now at 317 West 107th Street), devoted to the Russian painter Roerich (1874–1947). Roerich is mentioned six times in *At the Mountains of Madness*, as HPL suggests that the city of the Old Ones is reminiscent of Roerich's paintings of Himalayan monasteries.

Appendix

Lovecraft and Morton

"Conservatism" Gone Mad

James F. Morton

For the true conservative one must always have a large measure of respect. He represents the desirable and indeed necessary social influence which restrains the more radical among us from proceeding with excessive haste in our anxiety to cure that which is awry in conditions as they exist. Evolution proceeds by gradual, often imperceptible changes, and does not favor short cuts, save under exceptional conditions. Revolutions are frequently inevitable, but they are usually followed by periods of reaction, so that the net gain is but small. In its many thousand years of experience, the race has learned certain lessons, which are not to be lightly tossed away. Many changes must be brought about; and no idea, custom or institution is too sacred to admit of challenge, but the burden of proof remains with the innovator, and there is always danger of "throwing out the baby with the bath." Besides, a recognition of the need of reform does not always imply that the correct application of the reform has yet been discovered.

As a representative of somewhat extreme radicalism I cheerfully admit the foregoing principles, and would not abolish the sane conservative even if I could do so. The radical is necessary to insure progress and prevent stagnation, and the conservative is needed to keep the balance and to save the principle of orderliness in the midst of the necessary transition from the old to the new. The radical may become fanatical and destructive, and the conservative may become a bigot and a reactionary. I presume that Mr. H. P. Lovecraft, who chooses to label himself "The Conservative" par excellence, is a rather young man who will at some future day smile at the amusing dogmatism with which he now assumes to lay down the law. By the courtesy of Mr. Isaacson I have the opportunity to see the July issue of the Lovecraftian publication. The editor takes himself more seriously than he is fully warranted in doing. His knowledge and appreciation of literature seem to stop with the poets of the seventeenth and eighteenth centuries, for whom nobody has a greater respect than I. At the same time, Mr. Lovecraft would gain a deeper insight into the more subtle essence of the creative imagination by a more sympathetic study of the modern movements, from which he so brusquely turns aside. Great English poets do not come among us every day; but the general average of the poetic work of our own day gives no indication of a decadence. Even among the Imagists, erratic though an Ezra Pound or an Amy Lowell may be in spots, there is wholesome work of its own kind, which has a legitimate place in the literary field. The ancient laws of metre are no more decisive in settling the position of a modern poet than the still older creed of the three unities in determining the value of a dramatic production. *"Tempora mutantur, et nos mutamur in illis."* Mr. Lovecraft will scarcely, I trust, deny to the author of "Invictus" the power to write in perfect metrical form; yet in work which more experienced critics than our amateur "Conservative" hail as among his best, Henley has again and again adopted the flowing free rhythm, and he stands by no means alone among poets of high rank in passing readily from the older to the newer forms of verse. Mr. Lovecraft's conservatism, in this as in some other matters, smacks not so much of loyalty to present accepted truths or even still current habits of thought, as of reversion to the outgrown partial and restricted views of a past age. It is in large measure reaction, rather than conservatism.

The very tone of his attempt to pass judgment on Mr. Isaacson at once betrays him. It is inconceivable to him that the radical should have any recognized position, however, or should be even tolerated. He begs the whole question from the beginning by using radicalism as in itself a term of reproach. Mr. Isaacson's very moderate progressivism is stigmatized as "astonishing," and as certain to "arouse an overwhelming chorus of opposition from the saner (!) elements in amateur journalism."[1] Thus far the "overwhelming chorus" consists solely of Mr. Lovecraft. Really sane thinkers meet new ideas with argument if not convinced by the first presentation. They do not hold up their hands in holy horror at the presumption of the rash mortal who ventures to imply that all wisdom is not interred with the past. The manner assumed by Mr. Lovecraft puts him out of court at the start from the standpoint of fair criticism. His ejaculations bespeak something other than a clearcut vision.

The rabid attack, in prose and verse, on Walt Whitman was to have been expected. In the main it answers itself. There was a day when such a diatribe might have served its turn, and have found a general echo among the more superficial and ill informed readers of modern poetry. Fortunately, Whitman is today better known and better understood. Too many of the masters of criticism in America, England, France and Germany have penetrated to the heart of his message, and have borne enthusiastic witness to his greatness and nobility for his memory to suffer injury from any amount of mudslinging by one whose literary judgment is colored and distorted by the fact that he is a pronounced *laudator temporis acti*. It is hard to believe that Mr. Lovecraft even read Whitman at first hand and impossible to believe his reading of the great bard proceeded beyond the handful of poems included in the small section entitled "Children of Adam." No person who has read and assimilated "Song

---

1. [HPL], "In a Major Key," *Conservative* 1, No. 2 (July 1915): 11; rpt *CE* 1.56.

of the Universal," "Pioneers, O Pioneers," "Song of the Open Road," "Out of the Cradle Endlessly Rocking," "When Lilacs Last in the Dooryard Bloomed," or any of a hundred other masterpieces of transcendent rhythm and lofty thought could pen or endorse the extraordinary lines in which Mr. Lovecraft so completely distorts the nature and significance of Whitman's work. The spirit which could win the laudation of an Emerson, the style which won the impassioned admiration of so fine an artist as John Addington Symonds may well endure the reproaches of a Lovecraft.

It is not surprising to find a "conservative" of Mr. Lovecraft's type unashamed to advocate the base passion of race prejudice. Here again dogmatism is made to do duty for argument. As an enemy of democracy, Mr. Lovecraft holds that a mere accident of birth should determine for all time the social status of an individual; that the color of the skin should count for more than the quality of the brain or the character. That he gives no reasons for the reactionary assertions is not surprising. Race prejudice is not defensible by reason. The rightful charge against "The Birth of a Nation" is not that its history is false in detail, but that it places the relations between the white and the colored Americans in a false perspective, grouping and massing its incidents in such a manner as to make isolated occurrences appear as typical, and to incite bad blood between the races. Mr. Lovecraft has no scientific warrant for the pretence that race prejudice is more "a gift of Nature" or an essential factor in social evolution than any other prejudice whatever. It is the product of specific historic causes, and does not strike its roots deep in the foundations of human nature. Like other vices it can be readily overcome by individuals capable of rising to a rational view of existence.

As to the assault on Mr. Isaacson's extreme pacifism, the subject is one on which legitimate differences of opinion exist. The one thing certain, however, is that Mr. Lovecraft passes the bounds of decent criticism in the language employed. When writing as a superheated American patriot, one should take care not to stultify himself by denying the fundamental principles of Americanism, one of the chief among which is freedom of speech. When he declares that the expression of an opinion of which he disapproves "would be deserving of severe legal punishment" he brands himself as false to the spirit of liberty and democracy. One who is not even loyal to the Bill of Rights contained in our National Constitution is hardly in a position to set himself up as an authority on patriotism. Mr. Isaacson's attitude may be never so mistaken as a matter of fact; he or any other person has a right to the expression of any honest opinion without being "deserving of severe punishment," and without the need of being patronizingly "excused" by anybody. Mr. Lovecraft's incidental ignorance of the fact that Anarchism and Socialism are not identical and interchangeable terms, and of the further fact that many radicals and progressive thinkers of many shades of opinion have no connection whatever with either Anarchy or Socialism, need only be mentioned in passing.

From the sample afforded in the paper under discussion it is evident that Mr. Lovecraft needs to serve a long and humble apprenticeship before he will become qualified to sit in the master's seat and to thunder forth *ex cathedra* judgments. The one thing in his favor is his evident sincerity. Let him once come to realize the value of appreciating the many points of view shared by persons as sincere as he and better informed in certain particulars, and he will become less narrow and intolerant. His vigor of style, when wedded to clearer conceptions based on a wider comprehension, will make him a writer of power.

The Isaacsonio-Mortoniad

H. P. Lovecraft

Composed in a Major Key

"Arma virosque cano."

Wake, Heav'nly Muse! to hear the tuneless yell
Of Infidelity and Israel:
Mortonian mists th' embattled field befog,
Whilst Carlo barks from shelt'ring synagogue.
Beware, *Conservative*, the hostile two;
The learned atheist and the vengeful Jew.
With frothing mouth and fact-destroying lance,
Observe the radicals in pomp advance.
Their thoughts, their speech, and e'en their press are free
(For folly oft appears as liberty).
With Whitman's word their soaring sails they fire,
And cast upon the foe their native mire.
Impetuous Isaacson, in roaring rage,
Mixes the marks of ev'ry previous age.
The quaint Dan Chaucer and the good Queen Bess,
To his blind hate an equal age confess,
While heedless Raleigh nods to Handel's chords,
As Lovelace, from his prison-cell, applauds;
Melodious Herrick's ghost, with boundless scope,
Lives on and wears the periwig of Pope.
Nurs'd thus in Chaos, it were vain to dream
That captious Charles could pen a scholar's theme;
His sneering "Honi soit qui mal y pense"
He fathers on the cynic court of France!
Yet let us not at his crude scribbling smile,
When he but boasts of his unfashion'd style;
He laughs at learning, and leads on the day
When scholarship will earn the name of play!

Drunk with his freedom, worldly he indites,
And now "abeisance" for "obeisance" writes!
Since art and letters have no pow'r to please,
In politics his nerves he seeks to ease:
Here is his Oriental fancy daz'd,
With din a thousand demagogues have rais'd.
Amid the noise the loudest shrieks he heeds,
And gobbles, hook and line, the rabble's creeds.
"All men are equal! Let us have no kings!"
(How tritely thus the well-worn sentence rings.)
"All races are alike! Despite their hues
Raise hook-nos'd octaroons and woolly Jews!
Let Afric ape with Aryan combine,
And sink the white man in a mongrel line!"
Thus the mad Isaacson, whose rabid pace
Would plunge a mighty nation in disgrace.
His empty freedom and his negro lore
He seeks to lay at fair Columbia's door;
But let him not our dignity degrade:
Columbia was by sturdy Saxons made!
Whilst the brave Semite loud of freedom cants,
Against this freedom he, forgetful, rants:
Eternal licence for himself he pleads,
Yet seeks restraint for his opponents' deeds;
With the same force that at oppression rails,
He'd bar *The Jeffersonian* from the mails!
When outrag'd Georgia from the law breaks free,
And hangs some murd'rer from a friendly tree,
Should not our hero with his praises fill
The echoing air, and sing the people's will?
Blush, sweet Consistency! Judaea's child,
With hot hysteria, waxes monstrous wild;
Apes Don Quixote with his fuming mind,
Whilst Goodwin, like poor Sancho, rides behind.
One vile assassin and his proper fate,
To Isaacson can damn a sovereign state!
But tho' with fury fill'd, his valour shrinks,
When on the sterner side of life he thinks.
However natural, whate'er their cause,
With sobbing sigh he mourns the wicked wars.
Careless of honour, void of saving sense,
He begs the land to banish its defence:
Like Christian saint to turn the other cheek,

And injuries from bolder neighbours seek.
Too proud to fight, he hopes for war to cease,
And welcomes insult as the price of peace!
From peace to luxury the step is slight,
And Venus reigns when Mars withdraws his might.
Thus the soft Isaacson, to war oppos'd,
Finds wondrous charms in Paphian lines disclos'd;
Tho' duly shock'd by riotous Vanbrugh,
He reads the artful Whitman thro' and thro';
And when the sober try his taste to cure,
He shouts that vice, if unasham'd, is pure!
When crafty Whitman admiration draws
With loftier flights, and rugged, conscious flaws,
The willing Charles dilates his eager throat,
And swallows at a gulp each faulty note:
He thrives on discord, and the witless lay
To him grows great if form be cast away.
Thus did old Walt the force of folly see,
And gilded brazen trash with novelty!
So vanish, Isaacson! Declaim no more,
But turn thy fancy to rabbinic lore.
Sound now the trumpets, and awake the drums,
For matchless Morton in his chariot comes!
The Dean of Darkness, wrecker of the church,
Crowing with scorn from his exalted perch!
Great Antichrist! The friend of Reason's rule,
Who looks for reason in the churlish fool;
Who fondly dreams a rabble can be sway'd
By fine abstractions saints have disobey'd!
But search not Morton for the vulgar fault,
Nor scan his page for awkward phrase or halt:
Whate'er your talent, and howe'er you feel,
He forms a foeman worthy of your steel.
His steps, tho' wild, a subtle charm attends,
And art to him unnumber'd graces lends.
When he insults, his polish soothes the pain,
And victims, undisturb'd, as friends remain.
Thus privileged, great Morton's force is spent
On those who favour, while they still dissent.
He lauds the negro, and the negro shines
As long as we sit rapt o'er Morton's lines;
When the stern rays of Truth our minds awake,
We weep that such a sage should e'er mistake.

So venerated Morton rules the skies,
And pleases when he means to patronise!
Shall we complain when such a pen appears
To shake our doctrines or excite our fears?
Shall Morton's thunder rouse vindictive ire,
Or shall we smile, uninjur'd, and admire?
Thus from the window, undisturb'd and warm,
We safely view the grandeur of the storm:
The raging blast, sent earthward to destroy,
Is watch'd and study'd with artistic joy.
Loud-thund'ring Morton, shaking land and sea,
Parts Socialism from raging anarchy.
In dumb discretion we his word admit;
One's but the brink; the other is the pit!
If such dark regions tyranny could own,
Well might they seat King Morton on their throne!
And now farewell! With unconfounded mien
We watch the mighty atheist quit the scene.
Soon will his shafts to other targets fly,
As some evangelist attracts his eye.
Tho' like a bull at us he plunges one day,
Tomorrow he'll be goring Billy Sunday!

Save the Old Brick Row

To the Editor of the Sunday Journal: [1]

For the past few months I have been astonished and grieved to hear from correspondents in Providence, where I am an appreciative annual visitor, that plans have been prepared for the destruction of that incomparably fine row of old brick warehouses in South Water Street, whose simple lines and perfect adaptation to the waterfront scene make them such a notable architectural asset to your lovely Georgian seaport. It increases my amazement to be told that this destruction is not planned for the usual commercial reasons, but in the interest of a "more beautiful" approach to the new courthouse in South Main Street; as if any sort of artificial landscape or monumental beauty could match the unstudied and spontaneous exquisiteness of the present arrangement; whereby the artistically grouped neo-colonial gables of the court house are seen rising gracefully out of the splendid line of really old slant roofs which the threatened warehouses form.

---

1. Text is from HPL's typescript (ms, JHL). Published as "Praises Beauty of 'Old Brick Row': Removal of Ancient Warehouses Along South Water Street Would Mean Needless Destruction of Notable Architectural Asset That Should Be Prevented," *Providence Sunday Journal* (22 December 1929): Section A, p. 5.

Cannot something be done to open the eyes of the "powers that be" to the real aesthetic merits of the situation? That the architecture of a city ought to sum up its spirit and history is a truth evidently well known in Providence; since a number of splendid new Georgian buildings—including the great courthouse itself—attest the local determination to preserve the Georgian tradition. Should it not then be obvious that this ancient and graceful row forms exactly the setting demanded by an old New England waterfront where history revolves around brave, glamorous memories of ships and cargoes and the Indies? Rows of warehouses like this are the most vivid of all symbols of the glorious maritime days which laid the foundations of New England's prosperity. They stretched along the wharves of all the great seaports—Portland, Portsmouth, Newburyport, Salem, Boston, New Bedford, and so on—and are still to be found in many of these cities. Providence, in view of its size and activity, is unusually lucky to have so magnificently intact a row of them; and it would be an act of peculiarly myopic vandalism to sacrifice this rare and harmonious heritage for the sake of a raw, "synthetic" beauty of more formal and coldly statuesque character. As one of New England ancestry, birth, and education, I may be pardoned for feeling very strongly in this matter.

That I am not alone in my opinion has been amply demonstrated to me by the fondness of artists for the old brick row as a subject, by various statements, and by several letters clipped from the Journal. I am told that many persons of the highest taste in Providence, including that eminent architectural authority Norman M. Isham and the late Henry A. Barker, have strongly regretted the threatened doom of these artistic buildings; and that several European visitors of aesthetic distinction—John Drinkwater, James Stephens, and Padraic Colum among others—have given warm praise to their seasoned exquisiteness, and to the quiet way in which they carry on the picturesque seaport traditions of the old world. Not long ago, too, I saw them praised in a current novel—where it was said that the "mellow redness . . . brings with it a glamour."[1]

But what has impressed me most of all in the printed pleas for the row's retention is the suggestion that the buildings be carefully restored and given a new fireproof interior in order to serve as the city's much-needed Hall of Records. This has a very personal interest for me, insomuch as I happen to be writing these lines in just such a restored brick building—the Municipal Museum of Paterson, New Jersey, of which I have the honor to be Curator.

Indeed, I noticed with pleasure that one of the letters in the Journal expressly cited the Paterson Museum as a case of successful restoration. This museum, established only five years ago, was allotted one of the city's older brick buildings as its initial unit; and at once proceeded to use the splendidly solid and graceful walls as the shell of a new interior. The result, as I think every visitor must agree, has been eminently satisfactory; for the retention of

---

1. Percy Marks (1891–1956), *A Dead Man Dies* (New York: Century Co., 1929), p. 222.

the massive old walls has in no way interfered with the modern arrangement
and effectiveness of the hundred-per-cent-fireproof stories installed within.
The economy of such a course is naturally very great—in fact, it is seldom
that the most disinterested demands of art so exactly coincide with the most
practical interests of municipal finance.

Pictures of the old brick row in the recent Netopian—receipt of which
has called forth this eleventh-hour plea—increase the sense of sadness that
one cannot help entertaining at the thought of Providence's losing this find
and eurhythmic legacy of its adventurous past. It will seem strange to visit the
city next spring and find a barren waste where I have been used to seeing this
delicious bit of New England congruity, and I fervently hope that some determined and vigorous move on the part of local citizens and art-lovers may
spare me such a painful experience.

JAMES F. MORTON.

Paterson Museum,
Paterson, N. J.,
Dec. 17, 1929.

[Christmas Greetings to James F. Morton]

As Saturnalian garlands wreathe
    The pillars of each pagan door,
Let one unalter'd Roman breathe
    His annual Yuletide wish once more![1]

From mines celestial Santa digs a gem
To deck your proud Museum's diadem;
A common stone, yet worthy of a place
In some dark alcove, or inferior case:
'Tis Christmas cheer—swell'd livelier and greater
By him who bears it to a sage Curator!

Whilst cheaper souls extatick bark,
    And slop effusive o'er each page,
To milder purrs I bid thee hark,
    As feline Theobald greets a Sage.

When by the happy Yuletide fire
    There soars the Ave and Te Deum,
May Jersey's choicest cats conspire
    To fix their mews in thy Musaeum!

---

1. To James F. Morton, Samuel Loveman, and Annie E. P. Gamwell.

God rest thee, merry Gentleman, may naught
Intrude this Yuletide to dismay thy thought;
May woe in seven letters, clos'd with E,
Lie horizontal, and remote from thee,
Whilst thy sure fame, in vast museums stor'd,
Mounts vertical to join the heav'nly horde!

Correspondence with William L. Bryant

[1] [A.Ms., JHL]

10 Barnes St.,
Providence, R.I.,
April 25, 1927

William Bryant, Esq.,
Curator, Park Museum,
Providence, R.I.,

My dear Sir:—

You will probably recall my visit of last August to the Museum in company with Mr. James F. Morton, Curator of the new Museum at Paterson, New Jersey. Mr. Morton was highly grateful for the many courtesies extended him, & intends at no distant date to forward you the assortment of New Jersey minerals which he promised.

I am once more imposing on your consideration in his behalf in an effort to learn the exact location & conditions surrounding several local mineral beds which he is anxious to visit on his coming trip here. His time will be exceedingly limited, & he has left to me the task of ascertaining the details about certain quarries mentioned in a recent article in *The American Mineralogist*.[1] Knowing that deposits are sometimes exhausted, & that rich localities are often privately owned & closed to the public, he is especially anxious not to follow any false leads during his crowded sojourn; hence asks me to discover particulars in these directions in order that he may attempt only feasible trips. He also wishes to be very sure in the matter of reaching the respective deposits, since there is no time to lose in mistakes.

Now my own knowledge of mineral conditions is absolutely *nil*, & even my geography is by no means equal to the task of identifying the various regions & quarries named in the quoted article. Clearly, I must have expert & specialised advice—& I know of no source more likely to yield definite results than your-

---

1. Lloyd W. Fisher and Edwin K. Gedney, "Notes on Mineral Localities of Rhode Island: 1. Providence County," *American Mineralogist* 11, no. 12 (December 1926): 334–40.

self. I am aware how great an imposition it seems to burden you with such a long & detailed set of questions, & can only plead in palliation that it is all in the cause of science—Mr. Morton being assuredly a highly worthy upholder of that honourable cause! I am endeavouring to make the answering as easy as possible by drawing a sort of crude questionnaire, which you will find enclosed, together with a self-addressed stamped envelope. Let me add that if this forms too great a demand on your time, I shall be equally grateful for merely the name & address of someone else likely to furnish the needed data. I believe that the Brown professor of Geology lives only a block or two from my own door, but not knowing him personally, I hesitate to bombard him with inquiries. Your own former favours to Mr. Morton have singled you out as a first victim!

With sincere thanks in advance for anything you can do to set me on the track of the data which Mr. Morton needs, & with renewed apologies for troubling you, I am

Very truly yours,
H. P. Lovecraft

P.S. I am not certain of the exact date of Mr. Morton's visit, but when he is in the city he will in all probability call upon you.

[2] [T.Ms., JHL]

April 27, 1927

Mr. H. P. Lovecraft
10 Barn [*sic*] Street
Providence, Rhode Island

My Dear Mr. Lovecraft:

I have inclosed your questionnaire with the letter to Dr. Fisher of Brown University with a request that he fill it out and return it to me. As soon as I get it, I will send it on to you.

Dr. Fisher no doubt has all the information you wish as he told me he has been visiting most of the localities and knows far more about them than I do as yet. I have only lived here two years and have not had a chance to see many of the outcrops.

With kind regards,
Yours very truly,
William L. Bryant
Director of the Museum.

[3] [A.Ms., JHL]

10 Barnes St.,
Providence, R.I.,
May 18, 1927

Dear Mr. Bryant:—

When I communicated the very kind favours of yourself & Mr. Fisher to Mr. Morton, his gratitude was extreme; & he has now written particulars concerning the first of his spring-&-summer visits to these parts.

If all goes well, he will reach here late in the afternoon of June 6th, staying over night & devoting the following day—Tuesday, June 7th—to the mineralogical excursion. On that occasion he will probably have to be at the New York Boat by 6:30 p.m. or thereabouts; but even so, there will be a reasonably decent period of time for rock-gathering on a modest scale. Mr. Morton's preference—as determined wholly by what he has read & heard—is for Cumberland as a field of action; but he holds himself very ready to defer to the judgment of yourself & Mr. Fisher in mapping out his itinerary.

If you & Mr. Fisher have the leisure to guide & accompany the Morton expedition on this particular date, it is needless to say how gladly & gratefully your participation will be hailed. In such a fortunate eventuality you might let me know, as far as possible in advance, of the exact conditions involved—time & place of meeting, & so on. The almost three weeks intervening will no doubt give you & Mr. Fisher time to decide or arrange details without inconvenience. If the trip will be unfeasible for you, I would also appreciate hearing—& am enclosing a self-addressed envelope for reply in any case. This will probably form the first of three New England visits made by Mr. Morton during the coming season, hence there need not be too great disappointment if good arrangements cannot be hit upon for June 7th.

Thanking you again for your courtesies, & hoping that conditions may turn out auspiciously for the full-strength expedition,

I remain
Most sincerely & cordially yours,
H. P. Lovecraft

Writings by James F. Morton

Fragments of a Mental Autobiography

I

I remarked to "Doc" Swift the other day that I had some rather odd ideas on a certain subject. "Jim," said he, "if there is anything odd, you will be sure to have it." I am afraid the genial Doctor is not alone in his notion of oddity. For, consider the matter a moment. It will take but little observation to discern the fact that few of mankind are really *thinkers*. The mass drift along lazily, allowing a few leaders to do all their thinking for them. They accept established creeds, customs and institutions, not because these are reasonable, but because they are old. The prevalence of mob consciousness, as distinguished from individual initiative, is one of the most lamentable symptoms of the imperfection of our present civilization. Instances are innumerable, from the hideous lynching mobs to the idiots who crowd around to see a street fight, or stand thirty deep before a store window to watch a man put a collar button on and off. The morbid, vulgar curiosity which causes women of imaginary decency to strip the church in which has occurred one of those acts of legalized prostitution called a fashionable wedding—a mere swap of money for title, rehearsed beforehand like a circus performance—to secure souvenirs of the disgraceful affair, has its counterpart in a thousand acts to be observed every day.

Take the existence of the thing we call fashion. The love of beauty is one of the fine endowments of the human race; but the eagerness to render prompt and servile obedience to the insolent dictates of a gang of shallow-minded "society leaders" or a set of Paris dressmakers has no relation to the aesthetic element in life. It is a mere proof of flunkeyism, which shows that our democracy is as yet little more than a sham. Even now it is declared that the modern Juggernaut has this year commanded that our women shall commit an inexcusable crime against nature by murdering themselves with tight corsets. Why? No one on earth can give a reason which will stand a moment's analysis. The wasp waist is not even beautiful, but the grossest monstrosity that can be conceived. And yet, women who pretend to consider themselves possessed of ordinary intelligence will descend to this infamy; for an insult to the elementary principles of health is no less than infamous. Our national worship of wealth and of titled loafers should make every American blush for shame. It is even a good business proposition to flaunt our dishonor in our face. At this moment, an advertisement is conspicuously displayed on New York billboards, exhibiting a vapid-looking woman cooing: "Everybody is good to me, because I wear lots of jewels and look rich," concluding with a notice of jewelry on the installment plan. Another advertiser, a wine merchant, displays this legend: "Since the visit of the King of Spain to England, sherry is the proper drink," assuming that Americans are such confirmed lick-spittle toadies that such an announcement will naturally appeal to them. These are but a few of the many straws showing the anti-democratic tendency of the prevailing wind.

To assume that the majority is right, is to take an extraordinarily superficial view of history. The majority simply does not think at all. It is tossed about by the prevailing current, and is right or wrong purely by accident. The prevalence of a given belief does not even tend to establish its truth. We know better than our fathers in a host of matters; and our children will go as

far beyond us. In refusing to listen to a new idea, we commit the old, old error of the ages. Even the wisest thinkers cannot always or even usually escape
the contagion of popular prejudice. Blackstone, as keen and clear a reasoner
as England has produced, could not see the slightest flaw in the common law
of England, and even applauded its monstrous reduction of married women
to the position of mere chattels. Hugh Miller, Agassiz and Virchow, by their
strange incapacity to appreciate the truths of evolution, added years of life to
the ignorant prejudice which so long retarded the full realization of the value
of Darwin's demonstrations. Gladstone could not comprehend the degree to
which scientific criticism had shattered the authority of the Mosaic books;
and Newman—but let us draw the veil in pity of the weakness of a great man.
In the light of these striking instances, before proceeding further with the
argument, I will ask the reader to pause and consider whether it is safe to
predicate infallibility of any doctrine, merely because it is current, and unques-
tioningly accepted by many great and good men and women.

II

In my former installment, I referred briefly to the well known fact that great
names can be cited on behalf of every belief, no matter how preposterous,
and that the most absurd and puerile superstitions have received the reverent
support of some of the greatest thinkers in history. It is now a mere platitude
to declare that every generation has persecuted and derided the noblest of its
sons and daughters, simply because they were ahead of their times. Socrates
drinking the hemlock, Bruno at the stake, Algernon Sidney on the scaffold,
Thomas Paine reaping a heritage of the vilest ingratitude from the nation
whose independence he was the first to declare, Garrison dragged through
Boston streets with a rope around his neck, show the spirit of conservatism
in every age. Yet we are totally blind to the palpable fact that our own era is
no exception to the general rule; and we ourselves exhibit the same mean
intolerance to the unpopular side of all great questions that we condemn in
our ancestors. A new idea is not necessarily right, because it is new; but it has
an even chance of being right, and is entitled to a fair hearing and to a candid
weighing of the arguments adduced in its favor. Why are we so afraid of
learning something? Why do we prefer to stick forever in the mud of old
dogmas, and to let our minds be "ruled by the tomb"?

The prevalence of sectional beliefs, of doctrines devoutly maintained by
all who happen to be born in a certain section, is a striking instance of extreme shallowness. There is one chance in a hundred that such doctrines may
be sound; but few things are more unlikely. Of course, where the entire population of a given locality is composed of calm philosophers and close analytic
reasoners, something may be said for its peculiar notions. But where the people are warmblooded and emotional, the prospect that by some unnatural
circumstance the exact truth has been revealed only to them, is practically out

of the question. The prejudice against a particular race, for example, being a mere offshoot of local conditions in each instance, would be too senseless and contemptible even to consider, were it not that it is pregnant with such huge evils that it must be fought, instead of ignored.

A priori, then, it is at least equally probable that a new idea, soberly advanced by a person of average reasoning power, is superior to the current belief, as that it is not. The probability becomes still greater, when the arguments brought forward to support it are met by sneers, vituperation, and persecution, instead of by calm and deliberate refutation. A fallacy can always be upset by logic, and a lie exposed by letting in the light. The suppression of free speech is pretty clear evidence that the suppressors have a sneaking fear of the weakness of their own cause. If the heretic is wrong, burning him at the stake is the worst way to silence his error. Even a bad cause wins sympathy through martyrdom. A vicious doctrine is most dangerous to society, when it is stealthily whispered from ear to ear, instead of being openly proclaimed where it can be publicly confuted.

It is true that multitudes of cranks arise in every age, whose novelties are less rational than the creeds they seek to displace. It is also true that many of our present customs and institutions are still beneficial to the race, and will be needed for hundreds of years to come, and that among the many doctrines loosely accepted by the popular mind are not a few which are so demonstrably true as to stand the test of all criticism. Not all the old is false; not all the novel is true. But all the old is rightfully subject to criticism, and deserves respect only in proportion as it can meet the issue; and all the novel is entitled to be heard, and merits acceptance in proportion as it can prove its claims to the mind which is large enough to be impartial.

In proceeding, in future installments, to sketch some phases of my own mental history, I ask that the general position taken in this and the preceding number be clearly borne in mind, as giving a clue to the whole. While it has been my lot to uphold many unpopular beliefs, I have sought only to approach truth as nearly as possible, and have no more love for extravagance or oddity than for blind and shallow conformity.

III

It was that red hair which began it! So, at least, I have often chosen to imagine. Doubtless, however, the fundamental cause lay farther back. By every hereditary law I should have remained, as I began, a staunch conservative. With clerical ancestors on both sides of the house, distinguished for scholarship, and on one side for notable literary achievement, I was born into what Oliver Wendell Holmes has termed "the Brahmin caste of New England." My family were all Baptists, although my father and sister preceded me in the direction of Liberalism; and my brothers have followed. Most of them have stopped in the halfway house of Unitarianism. It need scarcely be said that my early training was along strict and religious lines. This, however, was in no way repulsive to me. My parents did not belong to the sour-faced, kill-joy order; and my home-life was not of the harsh and unlovely nature which often drives high spirited youth to rebellion. There were some clouds and shadows, as in every household; but its members were closely welded together in a deep affection, which has persisted through all the changes of the passing years and the radical differences of belief that have come to exist between us. Nor was religion itself presented in so stern and unpleasing an aspect as to cause a later revulsion against it. On the contrary, our church was composed of persons of above the average intelligence and culture, and signally favored in the quality of her successive pastorates. One of the best theological seminaries in the country overshadowed us, maintaining an exceptionally high intellectual standard in the promulgation of orthodox doctrines. When I left the church it was with the kindest feelings toward all connected with it, and in simple obedience to the higher call of truth.

I have anticipated a little, in order to repel the common and superficial charge that the radical is merely a soured and disgusted conservative, led by indignant impulse, rather than sober reflection. Now as to the real beginning of the series of changes which have led my mind to a position so far from its starting-point. Let it be borne in mind that the account is but fragmentary, and that autobiographical details not directly connected with the formation of my mental attitudes are rigorously excluded.

At the period of my earliest recollections, I was a bashful boy, awkward because self-conscious, ambitious for public activities, exceedingly timid in social life, sensitive to the verge of morbidity, with a strong inherited bent for literature and taste for study, endowed with a somewhat inflexible Puritanic conscience, yet fond of outdoor sports, particularly baseball, fishing, swimming, diving and walking, particularly excelling my companions in the two last named exercises. Unfortunately for myself, I was no fighter; and an appeal to force usually resulted disastrously to me. I gained some little ground, however, by being a fair wrestler, but not enough to hold my own in the schoolboy world.

These, then, were the circumstances under which the persistent bullying of my fistic superiors, coupled with unending taunts concerning my red hair, first bred in my boyish mind the germs which were later to fructify into a realization of the extreme fallibility of public opinion. Where a born scrapper would have fought it out, and thought no more of it, I brooded bitterly over the injustice, and was driven to seek solace in my books, whereof I was a precocious and omnivorous devourer, to find triumph in excelling my persecutors in school honors and compelling their unwilling respect, and to begin the formulation of serious—if immature—opinions on social questions. Whereto all this led, may appear in the sequel.

IV

Outside ordinary childish pursuits, my earliest interests were of a religious nature. The altruistic ideals of primitive Christianity appealed to me with resistless force; and I could not understand the relative indifference of my companions, even after they had professed to have undergone a religious experience. It was all intensely real to me; and I was sufficiently unsophisticated not to comprehend the impassable gulf that lies between the teachings of Jesus and the dogmas and practice of the churches today. Hence I became an extremely active worker in the church, being baptized on "confession of faith" at the mature age of ten. I took the whole matter very seriously, being constantly engaged in the study of the Bible and of Biblical commentaries and other theological works. Even later, in my choice of college courses, I insisted on including Hebrew as well as Greek, and have read and studied practically all the New Testament and much of the Old, in the original languages. But I was independent in many ways, even in my religious activities. Thus I was prompt to adopt the Revised Version, including the more radical changes of the American Committee, and felt something like contempt for those who were content with anything less than the most perfect possible translation of the message they professed to revere as divine. I did not then realize that the conservatism which clings to the King James version, crammed full of errors and direct perversions of the supposed "inspired" original, was simply the same spirit which in all things prefers custom to truth, and imagines that age and long acceptance can turn a lie into anything different from what it was in the beginning. I was prayer meeting leader, Sunday School teacher and even superintendent of a little mission school for a time. Until well along in my college course, few doubts of the truth of orthodox Christianity obtruded themselves upon me.

I cannot recall the first serious awakening to the debatability of the creed of my boyhood. My mental evolution has not been characterized by a series of shocks, but by a gradual progress from one attitude to another. Before accepting new ideas, I have tried them by every test known to me, and still remain always ready to abandon them, and return to the old standpoint, or pass on to some different position, if a more enlightened reason should seem to require, or if a fair trial should clearly demonstrate their practical deficiency. Later on, I may give some illustrations of this.

If my memory serves me correctly, it was the study of Plato that first impressed me with the suggestion of a broader idealistic philosophy than that of orthodoxy. The tribalism and anthropomorphism of the Bible could not hold their own against the larger cosmic conceptions; and I gradually began to look further. Like all who really study the subject, I was of course compelled to admit the unescapable truths of modern science, established by Darwin and his successors, and with them that of the true history of the human race, as distinguished from theological myths. This, however, was a history of the outward processes; and the power back of the evolutionary forces remained unrevealed by science. So I set myself to the search, as thousands of greater minds had done in the past. How I sped, is next to be shown.

V

The primary tendency of my philosophical speculations lay in the direction of idealism. Behind the phenomenal universe, there seemed to me to lurk mysteries which no materialistic conceptions could satisfactorily explain. At first, I endeavored to hold firmly to the idea of a personal God, eliminating the anthropomorphic features of the Jewish and Christian myths. But this theistic position proved untenable, raising new difficulties to take the place of the old. The origin of such a being was as unaccountable as the origin of a self-existent universe. As the most promising hypothesis, though not altogether free from questionable features, I came to lean to the pantheistic position, accepting a form of idealistic monism. The unity of being and its transcendental source in infinite consciousness seemed to be as near as the human mind could approach to the fundamental basis of the universe.

When my speculations had reached this point, my attention was drawn to the Theosophical philosophy and movement. Its metaphysical system appealed to me very strongly; and I soon identified myself with the Society. On the division that took place in its ranks, I remained loyal to the wing headed by William Q. Judge, and later by Katharine Tingley. Both these leaders, whom I have met personally, were indeed remarkable personages. There may have been, probably was, some charlatanry in connection with the establishment of the Theosophical Society, and with the meteoric career of Helena P. Blavatsky; but the movement as a whole still presents itself to me as fundamentally sincere and aimed at the attainment of high ideals. Even now that I have recognized the inadequacy of the evidence on which many of the Theosophical tenets rest, its general point of view is in many respects attractive to me; and its basic attitude possesses at least a strong speculative value. Modern science supplies us with conclusive proof of the processes by which the activities of the universe are carried on. To question the truth of evolution, in the light of actual present knowledge, is like disputing the proposition that two and two make four. But to the query what force sets these processes in motion, and what ultimate reality underlies the varied manifestations of the universe, science confesses itself unable to return an answer. In this avowal there is no humiliation, since the questions to which science is able to reply are those of most vital practical concern to humanity. Nevertheless, the mind refuses to remain content with its incapacity to solve the deeper mysteries. The religions of the world are proven inadequate, by their self-stultifying inconsistency with known facts. The errors of the

Bible are as glaring and fundamental as those of the Koran or the Avesta; and as a body of philosophy it is in many respects inferior to the Vedas or the collected teachings of Buddha and of Confucius, although occasionally reaching heights of sublimity and depths of truth but dimly shadowed forth in the other sacred books of the world. The character of Jesus, as portrayed more or less truthfully in the Gospels, has but one equal or superior in all history. It is likely that absolute impartiality would rank Buddha in the first place; while Zoroaster and Socrates, Lao Tse and Confucius, reach almost the same exalted station among the world's supreme prophets. The moral grandeur of these men, however, far from marking them as beings from a different sphere, simply demonstrates the ideal development possible to all men by the same resolute cultivation of their own highest individuality. In making gods or infallible guides of them, we utterly lose the real value of their example.

My Intellectual Evolution

My "spiritual and intellectual evolution" has been too complex to be briefly summed up. My mind has ever been a restless one, and has led me afar in the search for evidence. I have passed through more phases than many good persons ever heard of, and have delved into more theories and cults than are commonly realized as existing. There are few phases of religious thought which I have not probed as deeply as my measure of intellectuality rendered possible. I have been afraid to overlook any, lest haply the truth might lurk in some unsuspected and seemingly unpromising quarter. While I presume this symposium is necessarily confined to religious experience and conclusions, I may add that I have undergone a parallel and equally elaborate evolution in the study of economics, social and political theories, arriving at a pronounced belief in a basic democracy founded on equality of fundamental opportunities and the abrogation of special privilege, and that my acceptance of the Single Tax as the most vital step in economic and social progress came only after many years of close study of counter-theories.

I was born in a family of Baptists, of the old "Brahmin caste" of New England. My father and both grandfathers were Baptist preachers; and one of my uncles is still a missionary of the Baptist faith in Burma. I was reared in Newton Center, Mass., the seat of one of the leading Baptist theological seminaries; and hardly more than a stone's throw from my home was a home for the children of the same sect. Accordingly, I drank in the teachings of the Baptist denomination at one of the chief fountain-heads, and received them not in a crude and repellant form, but in the best phases of presentation. At the mature age of ten, I was received into the church on profession of faith; and I was indeed an ardent believer. I took an active part in young people's and later in general prayer-meetings, taught a Sunday School class for some years, and was for two years superintendent of a mission Sunday School in the vicinity. At college, I studied Hebrew and Greek, the latter for many reasons, the former to be able to read the Old Testament in the original language. I have so read a portion of it, and have read the whole New Testament in its original Greek, besides studying intensively with the aid of commentators of all schools and "Bible helps" of every kind; while the number of the theological books read by me would be much larger than the average private library.

During my college course, my faith began to be shaken, not so much by direct arguments from the "higher critics" as by the study of Plato and other exponents of a broad philosophy, by the side of which anthropomorphic doctrines appeared pitifully narrow. My growing disbelief led me in time to withdraw formally from church membership. I then made a close investigation of Spiritualism, at one time becoming strongly inclined toward it, but ultimately becoming convinced that its evidences were inadequate. For a much longer period, I clung to Theosophy; and for a number of years engaged in the exploration of different aspects of what is called Occultism. Of course, I had long since given exhaustive study to the claims of the Protestant and Catholic sects of Christianity, orthodox and liberal, and found them all lacking in the same manner as the Baptist faith of my youth. The various types of "New Thought" and numerous cults of diverse degrees of "queerness" all interested me.

The final outcome of my studies was a passing over to complete Agnosticism. I never liked to call myself an Atheist, since that term seemed to me to presuppose too much certainty of a negative character. For about twenty years, however, my real belief differed from absolute Atheism by little more than a shade. It was during this period that I became aggressively active in the national and international Freethought movement, in which at times I have played a role of considerable prominence.

A few years ago, I became acquainted with the Bahai movement. At first, I regarded it with amused interest, as one of many little cults; but gradually I found myself drawn into closer and closer relation with it. There was a wideness in its attitude which I had not found elsewhere. It held place for what was best in Christianity, Judaism, Mohammedanism, Buddhism, Freethought and all the rest, warring with none of these, but finding each of them definitely serviceable to the larger spiritual plan of the universe. It is the great reconciler and harmonizer. I have discovered in it an abiding-place which I had sought in vain for many restless years. It increases, rather than decreases, my eagerness to continue the investigation of truth without bias, and to labor energetically in all branches of human service. I have no fault to find with the differing conclusions of other truth-lovers, and am ready to work with them all as occasion offers.

A Few Memories

My personal sense of loss in the passing of Howard Lovecraft is still far too acute to permit me to gather my recollections of him and to write of them with any degree of calmness. Howard was a person absolutely unforgettable by any who came within range of his influence. I have never known any human being approximating his totally unique characteristics. Great and lasting as were his services to amateur journalism, they formed but a tiny percentage of those activities which brought him into close contact with the most intimate circle of his friends. To this belonged primarily a group of his fellow writers of weird and exotic fiction, with a very small number of amateur journalists and still fewer outside both these ranks. With this intimate circle he kept in constant touch through correspondence and, where possible, through personal contact. Certain of his closest friends he had never even seen. This did not mean quite so much to him as it would to most of us, for correspondence was almost the breath of life to him. He said to me one day that, no matter how long he had known a man, and how often he had met him on the most friendly terms, he never felt that he really knew him until he had corresponded for some time with him. Howard himself was most at home with pen in hand. I think of him as the last of the great classical letter-writers, and as almost single-handedly saving correspondence from being a lost art. He hated the typewriter and used it only to meet the demands of editors. He said that interposition of a mechanical device impeded the flow of thought. Hence in all his private correspondence he wrote unweariedly page after page in his well-known fine script. His letters were lengthy almost beyond belief; and he loved to devote numberless pages to detailed accounts of the places which he visited, and still more to endless arguments on all conceivable subjects, in which he delighted beyond measure. A letter of thirty or more closely written pages was by no means an isolated phenomenon with him.

Howard liked to consider himself a man of the eighteenth century, in which, he maintained, the true race pattern of the Anglo-Saxon people had most effectively culminated. He was inordinately devoted to Georgian architecture, and held that it afforded the only correct model for the homes and public buildings of those who would show the best taste. His utmost scorn was reserved for structures and interiors showing any trace of Victorian influence. He held firmly to the spelling, punctuation, capitalization, and vocabulary of the eighteenth century, whenever and wherever it was possible to do so. He was probably the only twentieth-century person in either England or America who actually talked, without the faintest effort or affectation, after the manner of Dr. Samuel Johnson, and followed the same practice in his letters. There was no posing in this, which was to him an absolutely natural mode of expression. In his light moments, he delighted in playfully indulging himself in modern slang, and thus going to the opposite pole from his nor-

428   ❋   *Letters to James F. Morton*

mal method; and when he did so, he did it well and showed complete mastery of his linguistic material. But he knew no resting-place between the two extremes. He tried valiantly, at least until a late period in his life, to uphold the artificial Popean verse as what the best poetry should be. But his own keen sense and powers of humor could not be denied. I remember that I once told him frankly that some of his particularly extreme justification and admiration of the eighteenth century was palpably a pose. He laughed and answered: "But isn't it an artistic pose?" I could never overcome the feeling that his tongue was often in his cheek when he persisted in claiming that he regarded himself as still a loyal subject of the king of Great Britain and condemned the American Revolution as a great error or worse. He meant this in part, but only in part, as it formed an element in his general somewhat top-heavy theory. But his solitary adhesion to the spirit of any age long since left behind in the evolution of our race only endeared him the more to his friends, though we argued with him ferociously and at immense length in our endless correspondence.

Howard always insisted on taking the attitude of an arch-materialist, and declared that all conceptions of right and wrong were simply amusing delusions. Nevertheless, he was himself the most rigid Puritan on earth, both theoretically and practically. His mode of maintaining his standards was to pronounce as inartistic and contrary to a gentleman's code the things of which he disapproved; but the result was all that could be demanded by the most strict ethicist.

Howard was always, above all else, the perfect gentleman. No matter how much he was provoked, it seemed impossible for him to lose his temper. If bitterly angered, he showed the fact only by a growing coolness of demeanor and an exaggerated formal politeness. To strangers and casual acquaintances his manner was that of a calm courtesy; to his friends, one of indescribable and gentle graciousness, rarely marked by anything approaching exuberance. He did not believe in enthusiasm, though sometimes a pastoral scene or an unusually fine example of a colonial doorway would elicit a strong outcry of admiration or delight. He declared that the only correct attitude toward life was that of a quiet and amused philosophical detachment, and that when life ceased to be amusing, it was time to retire from it.

But to write in any thorough way regarding one who was in many respects the most remarkable character I have ever known would require volumes. These little snatches of impressions garnered through years of close friendship may suffice for the present as indications of a very limited number of the more salient aspects under which Howard Lovecraft was seen and known by those who were nearest to him in sympathy and understanding.

Writings about James F. Morton

[James F. Morton in *Who's Who*]

MORTON, James Ferdinand, curator: *b.* Littleton, Mass., Oct. 18, 1870; *s.* James Ferdinand and Caroline Edwards (Smith) M.; A.B., A.M., Harvard, 1892; speaker's diploma, Sch. of Expression, 1894; unmarried. Field sec. N.Y. State Single Tax League, 1916–18, for N.Y. State Farmers' Nat. Single Tax League, 1917–18; sec. Common Commercial Language Com. 1919–24; curator Paterson (N.J.) Mus. since 1925. Originator of intercollegiate debates; lectures on social and lit. topics; former mem. Home Colony, Wash., and editor The Demonstrator. Ex-pres. Nat. Amateur Press Assn.; ex-chmn. exec. com. and ex-councilor Esperanto Assn. N. America; ex-pres. Thos. Paine Nat. History Assn.; mem. Mineral. Soc. America, Science League America, Am. Assn. Museum, Am. Forestry Assn., Henry George Foundation, Passaic County Hist. Soc., Nat. Assn. for Advancement of Colored People, New York Esperanto Soc., Harmonio, Voluntary Parenthood League, N.Y. Pub. Lecture Assn., League of Nations Non-Partisan Assn., A.A.A.S., Universal Esperanto Assn., Rocks and Minerals Assn., Alumni Assn. of Curry School of Expression, National Puzzlers' League, Am. Cryptogram Assn., Phi Beta Kappa Alumni of New York (also Alpha of Mass.). *Clubs:* Manhattan Single Tax, Blue Pencil, Torch, The Fossils, Manuscript, The Riddlers, Interstate Hiking, Nat. Travel, Kalem, New York Mineralogical Club. *Author:* The Curse of Race Prejudice, 1906; and numerous pamphlets, poems and mag. articles; on revision staff Larned's History for Ready Reference, 1919–21. *Home:* 334 Summer St. *Address:* Paterson Museum, Paterson, N.J.

Memorial of James F. Morton

O. Ivan Lee, *Jersey City, New Jersey*

James F. Morton, Curator of the Paterson Museum since 1925, died at St. Joseph's Hospital in that city early on the morning of October 7, 1941, from injuries received the previous evening in near-by Totowa Borough, where he was struck by an automobile. His tragic death was a shock to his own community and to the metropolitan area where he had many friends and acquaintances due to his activity in civic, social, literary and scientific circles.

He was a direct descendant of an old American family which has lived here since the landing of the Pilgrims in the year 1620. Mr. Morton's grandfather, Rev. Samuel Francis Smith (1808-1895) was the author of the words of the song "America." Born in Littleton, Massachusetts, on October 18, 1870, Mr. Morton was the son of the late James Ferdinand Morton and Caroline Edwards (Smith) Morton. His father was at one time the principal of Phillips Academy in Exeter, New Hampshire.

He received his Bachelor of Arts and Master of Arts degrees from Harvard from which University he was graduated with "cum laude" in 1892. He was an outstanding student while in college. He was a member of Phi Beta Kappa Alumni of New York and was largely responsible for the establishment of inter-collegiate debate. Later he became a member of the New York and Massachusetts bars.

Mr. Morton also attended and graduated from the Curry School of Expression. For several years he traveled extensively and gained considerable prominence as a lecturer speaking on various social and literary topics. During his youth he also spent considerable time in France which enabled him to use the French language fluently.

The exceptionally wide scope of his interests is evidenced by his being a member of the National Amateur Press Association, of which he was a former president; former vice-president of the Esperanto Association of North America (a group which seeks to establish a universal language); a former president of the Thomas Paine National History Association; and a leader in the American Association of Museums, American Forestry Association, and the Science League of America.

Mr. Morton was an ardent advocate of the single tax plan, and the author of the two books on the subject, "The Philosophy of the Single Tax" and "Single Tax Review." In another book entitled "The Curse of Race Prejudice" he championed Negro rights. He was a member of many societies and clubs including: The Harvard Club, Blue Pencil Club, Institute of American Genealogy, Genealogical Society of New Jersey, League of Nations Non-Partisan Association, Paterson Manuscript Club, Rocks and Minerals Association, and others. His love of natural science and history developed a deep appreciation for minerals. For many years he was a Fellow of The Mineralogical Society of America, and a highly esteemed member of The New York Mineralogical Club. Although nearly 71 years of age, he was remarkably active and energetic and very fond of walking and visiting mineral localities far and near. His accounts of the results of these excursions were always characterized by great factual clarity and by the refreshing enthusiasm of a born collector.

As Curator of the collections under his care, he had expanded them until the Paterson Museum had attained an enviable national reputation. When the International Geological Congress met in Washington in 1933, its members signified their desire to visit three museums possessing mineralogical specimens of special interest to them—the Smithsonian Institution, the American Museum of Natural History, and the Paterson Museum. Three hundred delegates made the pilgrimage and were amazed at the richness and scope of the mineralogical exhibits. A group of specimens from Franklin especially impressed them, while the Paterson minerals, of which Mr. Morton had listed more than 57 species, were deemed of surpassing interest.

In years to come, many visiting mineralogists will study the Museum collection with pleasure and profit, and marvel at and admire the splendid specimens there assembled and displayed, but the genial charm and the quiet cultured discourse of its late custodian will be sadly missed but long remembered by those who were privileged to know him best.

Mr. Morton is survived by his wife, the former Pearl K. Merritt, as well as by two brothers, Frank, of South Sudbury, Massachusetts, Nelson, of Melrose Highland, Massachusetts, and one sister, Mrs. Mary Ziegler of Gates Mills, Ohio.

James Ferdinand Morton, Jr.

Edward H. Cole

The two following articles by Edward H. Cole, published twenty-three years apart, are especially interesting because Cole had completely forgotten the first article when he prepared the second, and yet his viewpoint remained nearly the same after many more years of friendship. In spite of certain duplications, we are reprinting both articles in full. The first was published in the National Amateur *for November, 1918, while Morton lived, of course, and the second in the* National Amateur *for December, 1941, as an obituary. No record or memorial of Morton would be complete without these articles.*

No. One—1918

No less great and deep is the love for amateur journalism which James F. Morton, Jr., bears. Although he has been an amateur journalist rather fewer years than has his very good friend, Dr. Swift, no one who beholds the light that glows in his eyes at amateur conventions or who knows the readiness and the fervor with which he expounds amateur journalism on any occasion can doubt the part that amateur journalism plays in Jim Morton's life. One cannot turn many pages of amateur history of the past thirty years without discovering the very important part that Morton has played in its work.

James F. Morton, Jr., is the most eminent representative of one of the very first families in amateur journalism. "First families" is not figurative language; for indeed every member of the family of James S. Morton, Sr., has, I believe, been an amateur journalist of more or less fame. Besides James F., Jr., there has been Mary White Morton, a poetess of talent, who married John Ziegler of Cleveland, erstwhile publisher of an exquisite amateur paper; there is Nelson Glazier Morton, president of the National in 1900–1901, and as devoted to its interests always as his elder brother is; there was Frank Morton, who published many numbers of a delightful *Reverie* and was a loved member of the Hub Club for several years; and then James F. Morton, Sr., and his wife joined with their children in issuing a family amateur journal, *Mortonia.* Frank Morton's wife wrote occasionally for amateur papers and was also a member of the Hub Club. The first meeting of that venerable organization I ever attended, in November, 1905, was at their home in Melrose. Nelson

Morton's wife, Nellie Morton, has also written for amateur papers and is likewise affiliated with the Hub Club. Now their little girl, Dorothy, has within the twelvemonth made her way into the ranks of amateur journalists. The virus of amateur journalism must be in the blood of the Mortons.

It must be fully thirty years since James F. Morton, Jr., loomed on the amateur horizon. There are multitudes of stories about him in those early years; and he himself has given a picture of himself in his reminiscences published several years ago as "Fragments of a Mental Autobiography." It is not wholly irrelevant here to mention that Edwin Hadley Smith had the levity to refer to that somewhat remarkable series of introspections as the "Autobiography of a Mental Fragment." Morton has the type of brain that is so great that to the common man on the street he seems "touched." His acquaintances have reason to believe him demented, for there is hardly a fad or a fancy, especially of advanced and free thought, which Morton has not championed. No other amateur journalist and only rare men probably have broader interests or a more gifted brain. Unfortunately, as is apt to be characteristic of such persons, there is in his nature an impracticableness that has undoubtedly kept his light very much hidden under the world's bushel. Other similarly endowed men with harder heads for business are in the seats of the mighty among the nation's elect.

James Morton has never done himself justice as publisher of an amateur paper. Wealth never came to him in any degree equal to his brains. Likewise he was never, I believe, a printer. He has had to depend upon his contributions to the papers of more fortunate amateur journalists to make his reputation. There are not many of the foremost magazines issued since 1889 to which he has not been a contributor. What papers he has published have been small in number of pages and generally 6 × 9 inches. To do himself credit, he should have had the facilities of a Spencer or a Cook.

Morton's contributions to the amateur press have been of infinite variety. He is a prolific writer, an energetic and a profound thinker, a man of unconfined interests. Accordingly, his Collected Works would undoubtedly be a truly amazing series of essays and editorials and poems upon almost every topic of importance in the history of the past three decades. There would also be a mass of articles upon intellectual and academic subjects. James' brother, Nelson (himself no narrow reader), says that he knows of no one with a like capacity to James' for devouring books. It would be absurd, of course, to claim that there is nothing he has not read; but it is unquestionable that many a Carnegie Library does not contain either the variety or the quantity of the books he can intimately discuss. I have heard him discourse at first hand upon the silliness of the *Elsie* books for girls and upon the beauties of Fitzgerald's *Omar Khayyam* and the intricacies of Browning. His papers in the amateur press reveal even more intellectual accomplishments.

I venture to state, however, that the Jimmie Morton whom so many persons love to remember could never be conceived of from his published writings. Of course, the intellectuality of the man is only a part of his personality. Morton is far from being only the brave, fearless, ponderous Black-Knight errant of intellectualism that in print he appears to be. True, he is as ready on the platform as in the journalistic forum to champion losing causes, misunderstood movements of whatever sort, or the issue of honor and justice. If anything, he is too willing a champion and, although he contributes obvious fervor and indubitable common sense to the debate, becomes wearisome. I have known persons to hold their heads when James Morton was again granted the floor. Nevertheless, it is only by beholding the ardent honesty of his motives and his unfailing readiness to unfurl the Oriflame to fight for Right that a true conception is obtained of his personality.

An honester man never trod the earth. His life has exemplified his belief in high principles of conduct and his frequent martyrdom has proved that with him precept and practice are one. Independence of judgment has led him to adopt many ideas as yet considered advanced. Free Love, the Single Tax, the universal language Esperanto are among the movements which he has given his energies to advance. He joined the colony at Home, Washington,[1] I understand; but never indulged in the excesses that brought a raid from the authorities. His conduct on that occasion, however, was typical of the man's love of justice, for he was reported by the newspapers as having harangued the officials and urged them to arrest him, too, as his offence in abetting was as great as that of the others in acting the principles of the colony. He has, I hear, ceased to advocate free love, though he believes that the modern marriage ceremony, if not the whole code of which it is a part, is absurd. Esperanto and the Single Tax are now his professional hobbies. He is a prominent member of the Esperantists and was the American delegate to the great international congress held abroad before the war. The past few years he has been a lecturer upon the principles of the Single Tax, an occupation which has delighted both his friends and him, for it has seemed at last that Jimmie Morton had entered exactly the sort of life work that suited him and that was remunerative. It has suited him so perfectly that he has continued it even though it has not of late been remunerative. But that act is also characteristic of the man.

Judged by the motto of our common Alma Mater, *Veritas*, James Morton should be—and I know he is—a well-beloved son. He is not only a searcher after Truth, but he is a pioneer torchbearer of Truth. What I have written in the preceding paragraph is conclusive evidence of this fact. Morton's truth-seeking, nevertheless, is not at all confined to the paths of the future little trod; he fights valiantly to uproot the superstitions that still endure out of an unthinking past. He is a member not only of the famous Sunrise Club but also of the Thirteen Club.

---

1. Around the turn of the twentieth century, Home, Washington, was considered a model, utopian community of anarchists. [*Ed.*]

All this is not Jimmie Morton the amateur journalist; but it is the background of the man himself which must be understood in order to know him as an amateur. For James is quite an amazing person to meet if one doesn't know what to expect. His very appearance is out of the ordinary. He has—or used to have—decidedly red curly hair. Of late years, the brick red has paled and now there are stray locks of silver that indicate that the ultimate effect will be as striking, even though more becoming his years, as was the original hue. His complexion is also ruddy. His eyes are exceedingly deep set. Frequently his features are tinged with melancholy; but when he engages in conversation or debate, the animation of his countenance eradicates all trace of this quality. In his younger days, he was rather thin and inclined to be rawboned and gawky; but the past decade has endowed him with ample flesh and his appearance has become impressive and at times distinguished.

Morton is an inveterate talker as well as an insatiable reader. Even though he is an excellent after-dinner speaker and an able debater and a practiced orator, he is most enjoyable as a conversationalist. There are few limits to the range of his conversational abilities. His knowledge is both extensive and intensive. Because he is a profound thinker, conversation with him is a rare privilege.

One of the perversities of human nature is that such a man should have moments of pettiness and childishness. It is only fair to say that those occasions are relatively rare with Morton. Perhaps they stand out the more clearly for that very reason. I shall but mention the fact in order not to leave my characterization incomplete.

What has been Morton's contribution to amateur journalism? Well, he has made no mean gift of himself; and amateur journalism will never be poverty-stricken so long as in its ranks are men of such rich and extraordinary intellect as James Morton. He has managed several important campaigns, notably those of Doctor Swift in 1892 and Mrs. Miniter in 1909. At conventions he has always been an important figure; his counsel has resulted in the sane settlement of a multitude of perplexing questions. He is no mean parliamentarian and has helped untangle many difficult knots of procedure. He has contributed wisely to the laws of the association; not a few of the most important paragraphs in the constitution are of his making. James F. Morton, Jr., is a man whose place in the senate of notables of amateur journalism is secure.

No. Two—1941

Putting into words those feelings and remembrances that in themselves create a fitting memorial:

To write of Jim Morton as gone connotes in a personal way all that depth of sorrow and that sense of ineffable tragedy that the Latin Virgil expressed so simply in "Ilium fuit." A man of true greatness of mind and soul has departed from among us. We have lost a Nestor. Words are indeed a meagre medium through which to tell the grief and the sense of unutterable bereavement that his passing has left in the hearts of those who were blessed with his friendship.

As I look back over the thirty-five years of my acquaintance with Jim, I find it impossible to understand what the National Amateur Press Association will be without his fervent loyalty and judicious counsel. Our conventions have lost one of our most faithful attendants, one of our wisest advisors, one whose voice was ever raised in fervent advocacy of fairness and justice, of moderation and toleration. Long years of experience had tempered his judgments; his words were always to be considered and weighed before action was final. The long-standing policy of the National in recognizing the right of competing associations to their separate existence and in seeking amicable co-operation in furthering the best interests of our institution was largely of his making. He never failed to move for the sending of fraternal greetings to other conventions; and he was the constant ambassador of good will between the National Amateur Press Association and the Esperantists, of whom he was likewise a most distinguished member. And can those who have heard his fervid and deeply sincere and moving words commending our hobby or speaking in heartfelt recollection of its great advocates ever forget the enthusiasm of his spirit and the felicity and power of his expression? One who was indeed a mighty fortress of our association, a pillar of strength and substance, has gone from us and has left an ever empty space against the sky.

Those same qualities marked, too, his affiliation with The Fossils, the association of elder amateur journalists. Among them he rose likewise to the highest position, and in retirement he was a Cincinnatus among them. No member was ever more loyal, more concerned about the welfare of The Amateur Journalists of the Past. Among them, likewise, his counsels were ever toward toleration and moderation. His position for many years as chairman of the Necrology Committee was marked by constantly felicitous and moving tributes to comrades of other years that will not soon be forgotten by those who heard them. Now it will fall to other hands as skillfully to express the common sorrow for him who so aptly phrased the hearts of others for a multitude of their fellows. How difficult and how heavy the task will be!

It is not needful here to enumerate the numerous activities and the multitudinous affiliations that were but the many facets in the jewel of Jim Morton's life. Harvard graduate and president of his class, which will celebrate the fiftieth anniversary of its graduation in 1942, he entered upon a life of service to his fellow men with a determination to fight for many reforms that would make the world a better place in which to live. He was in many respects a Radical. He did not live to see many of the reforms which he advocated become the practice of society, and he himself became somewhat the Conservative as the years marched on, even though he did not materially alter his personal views. He joined the colony at Home, Washington. One of the anecdotes about him that I heard in my early years concerned the occasion when the colony was raided and the Law took into its toils many of the leaders of the community. Morton is said to have assailed the officers verbally for not having arrested him, too. He declared, so the story runs, that his "crimes" had been as great as those who had been seized; why shouldn't he be taken into custody likewise? Though the story came to me second-hand, it is plausible. It does truly give evidence of the sense of fair play and justice that marked his whole life. Another reform to which he devoted much of his energy was Henry George's Single Tax. Indeed, he is the author of one of the best books on the subject; and only last year he spoke feelingly to me of the utter desirability of the idea. He was ever an advocate of fair play for the negro. He devoted vastly of his time and energy toward overcoming the unconscionable treatment of the black man that the United States has accorded. The effort bespeaks the greatness of soul that Jim Morton possessed, the tolerance and love of justice that marked his life. Everyone is familiar with his advocacy of Esperanto, the universal tongue. He never failed to attend the annual meeting of the Esperantist Society; and he looked upon the language as a step toward the brotherhood of man.

Those who were acquainted with his early years and his "impractical" following of "lost causes" beheld with wonder and amusement the conservatism of his later years. After what approached a lifetime of apparent improvidence and accompanying hardship, he settled down to the curatorship of the Paterson Museum. The position was steady and conservative; many doubted that he would find it congenial or had it in his nature to abide in one place and position for long. That he made of the Museum one of the most remarkable local institutions in America is a tribute to the genius and the originality of the man. That he succeeded in manœuvering through the difficulties of a municipal position and in winning the co-operation and the esteem of the public officials is but the last amazing achievement of a distinctly astounding man His funeral was attended by one of the largest groups of mourners from all walks, races, and creeds of men that has ever assembled on such an occasion.

Jim Morton's mind was extraordinary for its grasp, its retentiveness, and its broad range of knowledge. No subject was too intricate for him to penetrate its mazes. Literature of all nations, languages of wide variety, religion, philosophy, law, puzzledom,—all, and many more, fell captive to his brain. Many years ago he was reputed to have a repertory of over five thousand selections of prose and verse which he could deliver at will. He fell completely into the mood of each, when he obliged those who eagerly begged him to recite, and would deliver the piece with unforgettable oratorical and elocutionary skill.

In earlier years Jim was inclined to be deeply serious and somewhat morose. It used to be a game at convention to bait him, simply because the vigor and the vocabulary of his peevishness were so in excess of what the occasion demanded that he was truly funny. The sending of postcards to absent members and the incessant autographing of souvenir menus and convention programs were especially irritating to him. He would sign, but under voluminous protest and with much coaxing. Of recent years his spirit was noticeably more equable. Humor marked his conversation frequently and the lighter side of life met with his frequent approval. And at late conventions I have several times twitted him for inevitably hauling forth a stack of postcards to be sent to the absent and insisting that I affix my name!

In conversation, Jim was a tremendous asset to any gathering. My recollections of early years are rich with memories of the times when Jim Morton and Edith Miniter and Will Murphy would make an evening sparkle with wit and give me a burden of wisdom to carry home. When Howard Lovecraft was among us, his mind alone was capable of meeting Jim Morton's on the same plane, and an evening in their presence was hours with the gods. I regret that I never had the pleasure of meeting with the group that foregathered during the years when Lovecraft was in New York. It would have been memorable throughout a lifetime to have exchanged thoughts with Lovecraft, Morton, Kleiner, Loveman, and the other kindred spirits and fine minds that were there assembled.

As my spirit seeks so futilely to interpret the man Morton, I can best [come] to conclusion with the recollection of his noble capacity for friendship. He loved his fellow men; he cherished those whom time had made worthy of his esteem. To meet Jim Morton anew, to behold the glad smile of greeting that filled his countenance with geniality and warmth, and to hear his voice, vibrant with genuine happiness and warm welcome, was to feel to the fullest the fraternalism and the humanness that binds the hearts of amateur journalists with hoops of steel. His feelings were never superficial; they were from the heart. He and I often differed in opinion; we fought many a battle. More often our minds met in accord. With Jim I could always speak my mind and be certain of a generous hearing and a fair appraisal. We respected each other's views, and we honored each other's right to an opinion. I have never known a fairer opponent; I can never have a more honored friend.

Mortonius

E. Hoffmann Price

When I met him in June, 1933, he was sixty-three; a big man, with a great shock of snow white hair, and generous white moustache, trimmed perfectly to the line of his mouth. As nearly as I can recollect first impressions, it seems that squareness and massiveness distinguished both head and face. An anthropologist could express this accurately, but then, I'd be driven to a dictionary, and so might some of you!

Then call the effect squarish, and permit me that horribly overworked and rarely justified word, "leonine;" for James Morton's hair, though neatly trimmed and neatly kept as his bachelor apartment, nevertheless suggested Leo's mane. And his voice was deep, and resonant. Or do I have this impression only because, very early during the visit, he recited so impressively and well from Mallory's *Morte d'Arthur,* "He . . . the gentlest knight" etc., and added that that was his favorite epic.

Blue eyes, bright and keen and deep set, were canopied by white brows. I didn't know at the time what his age was, and aside from the hair, and the maturity of the face, there was no evidence of his years; the voice, the alertness of manner and gesture, the keen enthusiasms he showed us, me and Frank Belknap Long, Jr., who guided me to Paterson and the municipal museum, made him ageless.

"Don't order beer," Long cautioned, when Morton suggested that we eat. "He belongs to a temperance society."

"Good guy anyway," I stage-whispered, and decided, then and there, and in keeping with the Lovecraft tradition, on Latinizing our host's name; or had HPL conferred the "Iacobus Ferdinandus Mortonius"? Makes no difference; within the hour, the curator of Paterson Museum became Mortonius, *par excellence.*

He belonged to a temperance association. which I forgave.

He belonged to a mineralogical society, which impressed me.

He belonged to a genealogical society, which intrigued me.

He belonged to a puzzle and cryptogram club, which baffled me.

He belonged to the, or an Esperanto society, which made me wonder what he did with his spare time.

He belonged to an association of curators, which convinced me that he did at times find time for the museum business.

I beg pardon of Allah, and of Mrs. Morton, and of all the Morton kinfolk, if I have omitted one or two or five or ten other learned societies to which he belonged.

Wait! He was deeply interested in the Bahai Movement, which led me to suspect that Mortonius was a man with whom almost anyone would have *something* in common. God knows, I was not cramped because tact forbade me to lecture on outstanding *soleras* of Spanish sherry, or the peculiar flavor Panay rum acquires from its cooperage. Putting it another way, it is difficult for me to picture any man whose specialty Mortonius could not discuss, and appreciate.

I hope that I do not give the picture of a parader of learning or of achievements. The man was too busy doing to have ever any time for anything as passive as a cataloging of deeds. Within the hour, I recognized him as one with the truly grasping intellect; slave driver whipping and scourging to its utmost production every captured idea and talent, and at the same time, relentlessly seeking new serfs. An enormous zest, and in this respect, Mortonius reminded me of Lovecraft, albeit there was no outward resemblance.

Stimulating—Lord, how that word is bandied about!—but Mortonius *was* stimulating. I believe that a totem pole would presently have responded to the man's enthusiasm and eagerness. I do not believe he had the capacity for being bored. It would have taken an exceedingly cunning and subtle man to have found a subject or an endeavor which Mortonius either had not mastered, or would not attempt to master.

I must except the very obvious vices, as he called them, and as they doubtless are, of (A)—the art and science of drinking, and (B)—the appreciation of tobacco's diverse forms. Yet I must add this: he was no bigot. He told me, some six years later, that the intolerance and bigotry had done more harm to the cause of temperance than any other force, and that as far as he was concerned, the limit of his crusading was to inform and enlighten any person requesting his, Morton's, views on the matter. This attitude gives hint as to the basis for my immediate respect and admiration of him.

Mind you, we two, Long and I, were at the time some thirty years his junior; but we weren't in the company of an "old man", respectfully bored and tolerant. Nor did he act the sage talking down to half-baked youth. It was man to man, the chronology of things being of no account.

His whimsy was delightful. I urged him to hold forth on genealogy, its methods, and the like. He did so, and at last announced, very solemnly, that his own lineage was remarkable; that he was descended from a god, a river, and a mountain. I went poker faced and granted that my ancestry was neither divine nor geographical, that any one of those origins was striking, and that all three seemed over-generous, and would he kindly name the one human ancestor, male or female, and explain the linkage, as there were sundry combinations possible.

He got the chart. And only then did the eye-twinkle betray the solemn buffoonery. He had started off so seriously that one almost believed him, at first!

That day was more than thirteen years ago. We three sat in his quarters until late. I can't describe the place except in the broadest terms: it seems to me now that it was dark, perhaps from panelling; there were many book shelves; a stark, severe, unadorned place, with a tiny kitchen for home snacks when studies made it inconvenient to eat out. And this kitchen, like all else, was battle ship neat and unadorned.

My professional writing had hit an all time low, though Mortonius always marvelled that anyone could write fiction which would sell, and mourned his own stupidity; he didn't say he lacked the time for fiction, he bluntly said he simply could not, and felt low about his abysmal awkwardness. He never mentioned the several non-fiction works he'd published. Anyway, I was thinking of the museum he'd showed us, after visitors' hours, and of the several Oriental rugs displayed, though the exhibits were predominantly geological. So I asked him if, in the event that it became necessary, he'd take my collection of Persian carpets as a loan until I either had to sell them, or else could afford a place large enough to use them.

He agreed, but hoped no such emergency arose. I felt better. The collection, though modest, would not have been out of place in the Paterson Museum; I could see a gleam in his eye, the fight between good will to me, and the hope for a rounding out of his almost non-existent Oriental textile section.

Thus it began: one afternoon, and one evening, colorful and rich, so that as I booted my Ford back to Manhattan, the thanks I gave Long were from the heart.

Morton's obituary notices give all vital statistics, and his background, and his lineage, scholastic honors, profession, and the like; these I do not know, and need not know, for I pretend to no more than to recording impressions. My memory may be faulty in various details; in which case, while I am sorry, I beg no one's pardon. I repeat, this is what *I* remember, and the peace upon you!

Pearl K. Morton—I never had the pleasure of paying my respects to the wife he married so late in life, in 1938, as I remember it—wrote me, saying in response to my expressions of condolence, "You do seem to have become pretty well acquainted with him in those three days. I think it was his brief stay with you, that he spoke about with so much enthusiasm on his return from his Pacific Coast trip. Going through his files, I find quite a few letters from you, and wondered at the 'Mortonius'. (*N.B.—this would make it seem that I, not HPL or anyone else, owns the patent-rights on the Latinization.—EHP.*) He must have saved all your letters. That is not usual, as every year he had a 'clearing out' and a very great deal went into the wastebasket.

"James' death was so very unnecessary that I still begrudge the means of his passing, though I would have missed him as much in any event. The automobile which fatally injured him was going down a hill in a rather infrequented suburban part of Paterson, and a parked truck put him on the wrong side of the road just as James was on it too. There were no witnesses. James made no statement at the police station which was fortunately right on the corner, or he would have bled to death before I could have reached him. Even the surgeon thought he had a fighting chance but the injury to his spine, which was not discovered until the autopsy, was the real cause of his death, and he did not wake up from his sleep that night. He would have lost his leg in any event, though the surgeon put it in a cast. This was around midnight. Practically his last words were, 'Have I an hour?' He knew too much about medicine not to realize the seriousness of the symptoms which both doctors thought were from severe shock. Yet he went to sleep thinking he had a fighting chance. I shall always be glad of that, and also that he did not know he would not wake up again.

"He had so many collections, minerals, books, etc., that I would have found it much easier if I had known what he wanted done. The museum of course has another curator. James' own mineral collection of some 2500 specimens I am keeping as he had them, until after the war, when I hope to place them as a whole, with some museum. . . . One of the Ketcham genealogists has all his Ketcham data, and hopes to get it out in published form eventually I have been extremely busy in my employment, and that has helped a lot. Even after a year, I would still not be at all surprised to hear his key in the lock again."

This is Pearl K. Morton's account. It speaks for itself. It makes me regret keenly the necessities—let me rather say, the accumulated past stupidities whose ultimate effect was a necessity that forbade my driving on from my winter in New Orleans to visit Mortonius and his wife in the spring of 1941. He died, October 5, 1941, en route to a meeting of the Chaucer Club; and I note from the just discovered *Brooklynite* that he was president of the Blue Pencil Club. I did not hear of his death until July of 1942; I think W. Paul Cook passed on the word, or did I, digging up long neglected correspondence, send Mortonius further genealogical data, not knowing he had returned to his ancestors, the God, the River, and the Mountain?

Well: I have now disposed of the death, so that I can now cut back, back to July of 1939, when he came to the west coast to attend a curator's convention, and collect mineralogical specimens, and have a glimpse of Los Angeles, and spend a few days with me in Redwood City, and only Allah, the Knower, could say what multitude of other things this energetic person planned. Mind you, he was now seventy; just getting his second wind, and doubtless buckling down to make up for the idleness the allotted span which he had exceeded.

I met him at the St. Francis Hotel in San Francisco. Robert H. Barlow was there with him. Mortonius *had* aged. He was not quite as square and upright, his eyes had not quite that intense gleam, and while his voice was far from senile, it seemed to me it had not quite that one time deepness. But after just a moment of feeling that I had to moderate my nervous stride to his slower cadence, that impression passed.

Odd: he'd been so young at sixty-three that that which might have been largely the fatigue of a week or more of travelling made me feel he'd aged. But he quickly set me aright. He got that second wind before we completed the thirty mile drive to Redwood City. And that evening, we settled down to planning for the two days he could spare; and when I heard his overall plan, I wondered how he could give me even a day!

It was appalling, that schedule.

In the morning, we set out for Pinnacles, a peculiar genealogical [*sic*] formation some miles beyond Hollister. This was his choice, after methodical analysis of all the geological debaucheries I listed as being within driving range.

"Mmm . . . Mt. Lassen, quiescent volcano, fumaroles, sulphur subliming at the 8000 foot level, and forming in a pumice matrix . . . you tempt me, tempt me sorely . . . 325 miles each way—you're sure you can do 325 miles in six hours?"

"Easily. Standing on my head. Straight wide road, you can make around 75 up the central valley, and 60 over half way to Mineral; thereafter, it is slow, but you're almost there. And you can do the volcano and accessories in, say, six hours after passing Mineral."

He checked it over, fought the temptation, conquered it.

I relaxed. "You're a benefactor, Mortonius. I *could* have done it, I really wanted to do it, but it is terrific punishment. And climbing the trail from the parking place at the foot, to the crater's 10,500 foot height is fatiguing, the elevation buckles one's legs. I said a total of eighteen hours, but—"

Hmmm . . . more like twenty four.

And so we dismissed that, and became practical.

We skipped Lick Observatory, though it was only twenty miles (with more than 300 hairpin curves in 4000 foot rise) off our route; we did however stop in Sunnyvale to look at the exhibit of a well known local mineralogist; we stopped for a quick look at Alum Rock Park, and Mortonius crowded every second to the bursting point. Sight seeing stimulated him; I began to see why he never drank. It'd been a sheer waste of rum! And as we rode, he planned, discoursed, argued, discussed. Leaving Pinnacles, he wondered if we couldn't swing such and such a way, for a look at Monterey Bay.

Well, I had had a full and complete day. Winding roads; not the race track stretches of the Mt. Lassen trip. We'd crawled hundreds of feet through caverns. We'd geologized. Barlow and I gaped like fools, and so did my wife; but I saved the California delegation by muttering, gravely, "As a guess, that formation is conglomerate."

He agreed from a distance that it might well be, and after a closer look said that it assuredly was. I said, "I am very happy. *Conglomerate* is the only geological term I know. It lends a touch of erudition. I've never before visited it on a geologist. But from now on—"

Well, that's a sample of the froth we batted back for hours. But there were solid phases, too.

I talked him out of going from Pinnacles to Monterey by suggesting an alternative: a detour to the New Almaden quicksilver mine, for some years shut down.

Before we got to New Almaden, Mortonius began to show signs of fatigue. His eagerness had been a bit in excess of his endurance. But we younger ones were proportionately as whipped down as he.

The next day, we left my wife at home; Barlow and Mortonius and I drove up into the Mt. Saint Helena region, where, I believe, Robert Louis

Stevenson once spent some time. Mortonius was in search of quicksilver mines, and we found an abandoned one.

I can still see him, putting on his rubber soled sneakers, getting his haversack and his hammer, and then scrambling about like a lizard. He had put on a bit of weight since 1933, and it showed at the waistline—but a geologist's hammer somehow affected him as a fire gong is traditionally claimed to have affected a retired fire-horse. He moved like a cat.

Barlow and I, working under broad instructions, picked up this and that. Some bits we got from the mine dump were discarded, others were retained; whether from tact, or from real interest, I do not know. Mortonius sized up every man as a potential deputy-geologist; and so, on this our first attempt, he might not have wished to be too sternly discouraging. He hadn't lived his years for nothing!

That mine sacked, he consulted his note book. I got out my map. "We've made remarkable time, I never imagined you'd get us here so quickly. Now, since it's early, could you—"

I sized up the mileage. "Christ, yes! Standing on my head."

"Ah . . . why not remain sitting behind the wheel, and we'll have more time for work?"

We ribbed each other, and regularly. Every so often, he'd give me a gentle knifing for my profanity. I am aware that its use detracts from the force of an utterance rather than otherwise, but it's an old 15th United States Regular Cavalry tradition, and holiday exuberance, pleasure at Mortonius' presence, and the exhilaration of booting the throttle kept my speech highly colored with cavalry language. Finally, I got my revenge for his reproofs:

"You didn't check that last one, Mortonius!"

"Which one?"

"*Puta-'ng-na-mo!* It's Tagalog with a tinge of Spanish. And then you overlooked a blend of Chinese and Igorrote. You are inconsistent. When disciplining the young, or admonishing them, one must crack down on each offense."

So he laughed and held it was unethical for me to take advantage of an illiterate Puritan; and I, sensing that my guest had a genuine aversion to profanity, and one deeper than his mild protest would suggest, met him half way and ceased "speaking with tongues". He was, as I said, moderate in all things, even in the expression of firm convictions.

No, he was not moderate in *all* things!

I told him I'd get him to the next station in jig time, but the map fooled me. The side road was damnable, frightful, and I am used to savage roads, at home and in jungle Mexico. What his notebook led me into was a nightmare so narrow that I had my choice between barging into the bank, or dropping off the shoulder and into a ravine. The rust was a foot deep. The pull was heavy, and the curves were sharp, with the result that where mules carrying loads of ore could manage nicely, a car of 142 inch wheelbase would skip and skid and loop almost as badly as though it had been navigating ice-covered curves. This was July third, smouldering and smoking hot, with not a breath of air; the temperature gauge read 210, and momentarily I expected to see steam gushing from the radiator. When they start boiling on such a pull, the loss of a drop causes the loss of further drops, and in geometrical ratio. The day was wearing on, the road became worse, the skidding and whipping became more dangerous, and my hands were blistering from grappling the wheel; and finally, all indications pointed to a dead-end—

To attempt retracing these miles in reverse, for there were no turn-out spaces, might cool the engine, but would be downright dangerous. And I'd told him it was a cinch!

It got so bad I was good and dam . . . er, darn worried.

I literally sweated it out.

Finally, the crest. Not a dead end, but better road. Below us, a lovely valley. I pulled up.

This interrupted an earnest discussion of H. P. Lovecraft.

I said, devoutly, "Thank God, we're out of it."

"Ah—out of what—" Then Mortonius saw the valley, the vista, and said, "You did well to halt here, I'd not have missed this for anything, this is splendid!"

"My dear sir, I pulled up because I was ready to collapse from sheer relief." Then, with exquisite irony, "Or perhaps you didn't observe what we've been driving through?"

"A road of some sort, doubtless, I hope I didn't miss anything as charming—"

"No, God damn it, you missed the fact that our necks were on the block for the past ten miles."

"You seemed quite at ease, quite competent. Well—" deep sigh. "I am afraid we over-shot that quicksilver mine. Now, we could turn here and go back, but our first mine really sufficed."

Once more, that energetic man let reason prevail.

So he moved to the front seat, leaving Barlow to meditate, and Mortonius and I chatted our way home.

We spoke, I think, of Lovecraft. His death was then newly upon us. Barlow, barely twenty; I, more than twice as old; and the "Venerable Mortonius", little short of three-score and ten; our day was bound into a unit by a common taste for things time-exempt, yet most of all by our desire to speak to others who had known HPL.

In two days, we burned a fifty five gallon barrel of gas. (Archeological note: I bought it in bulk, those days, literally by the barrel, and carried spare cans in the trunk, it was cheaper.) Mortonius regretted that the day had been too short for a detour to see Clark Ashton Smith, in Auburn; an extra hundred miles would have done it, but he felt that one shouldn't overtax one's self. Considerate cuss, what?

We classified specimens that night.

The following day, while Barlow recovered from clambering over rock piles, Mortonius and I hiked in the hills about Emerald Lake. He found the sandstone outcroppings on Handley Trail quite interesting; he lectured on "pot holes", and explained how the sea had once lapped the top of a hill now some hundreds of feet above sea level. Then he proposed scaling the rocks.

Heights make me dizzy, but I couldn't back down. He led the way, wearing his rubber soled sneakers, and he was agile, handy, relaxed; I gritted my teeth.

But once on the smooth, curved top, we sat there, looking out over the lower extremity of San Francisco Bay, and northward to Mt. Diabolo. "Satan," I said, "has taken me to a high place, but I am not tempted."

He chuckled at the blasphemy and said that flattering two people at one stroke was deft indeed.

We sat there for perhaps two hours. I listened, while he filled in the picture I had got from my two meetings with Lovecraft. He rounded out aspects I had no more than surmised. He hoped that the next trip out, we could drive to Mt. Lassen; he envied me my several climbs to the crater and into it. He acted as though he had the assurance of another half century. Or, did he have some vague foreknowledge, or was it the man's wisdom telling him how the odds stack up, each time another year is chalked up, so that he had to squeeze all the savor, all the richness, all the beauty out of every minute of his travelling time?

Mortonius makes it very clear why Cato, at the age of eighty, began to study Greek. Mortonius had more plans than any boy could have had; and they were well ordered.

I managed to climb down after him, and without falling; the descent is always the most trying. Then we revived Barlow, and I drove them to the bus station. That is the last time I saw Mortonius. An exchange of friendly malice, a handclasp, and then, "Peaceful journeying!"

Later that year, I drove to Lassen, and violated a Federal law prohibiting the taking of geological specimens; I sent Mortonius sublimed sulfur in a pumice matrix. I ribbed him, in the whimsically pompous phrasing he himself loved to use, and maliciously told him that in view of his love of law and order, he'd doubtless have to return the specimens, or report me to the Secretary of the Interior, under whose jurisdiction was the volcano and its by-products. I tabulated other Federal laws I'd violated, and made him, finally, an accessory before the fact, in this final outrage. (Drinking bootleg liquor, as Mortonius saw it, was far worse than the mere partaking of alcohol, as such.)

His retort was a masterpiece of foolery and quasi-legalism. In the first place, since one can not give too much credence to a confessed law breaker, he was not compelled to believe that the specimen had actually come from

Mt. Lassen; in the second place, I had no witnesses to prove that I had violated the law; and in the third place, the Secretary of the Interior probably hadn't missed the chunks anyway. We had a lot of fun bandying nonsense, and burlesquing erudition.

I hope that the illegally acquired specimen actually did interest him. I hope that that chunk of lava I took from the Pedregal, some miles from Mexico City, did give him some pleasure for its own sake. I am sorry I did not know, in 1939, that within three miles of the house there is a deposit of cinnabar, and evidence of lava flow. It would have been good to watch him with his hammer, darting, clambering, agile as a cat, picking up, scrutinizing under the glass, discarding one specimen, putting another into his haversack.

I remember him somewhat as the curator whose demonstration of fluorescence in minerals subjected to ultra-violet rays gave me a story idea; I remember him somewhat also as a man who loved to recite *Morte d'Arthur;* but I think I remember him most of all as a geologist and sight-seer, all aglow with enthusiasm, seeing all things, and finding interesting everything he saw, and making those things vividly interesting to whoever had the wit to listen to him.

His widow, as you remember, says that his last words were, "Have I an hour?" For the man could think, and feel, and appreciate so much in one hour, that an hour had greater value to him than to other people. Or maybe he wondered if he had an hour in which to plan, for the utmost efficiency and richness, his final excursion; properly to take leave of her, and then to visualize the road ahead, so that he could reach his destination on time, and yet have picked up a lot of specimens along the way.

For Mortonius could not go empty handed to his ancestors, a God, a Mountain, and a River.

May they be pleased with him, and with the collected things he offered them, and with the tale of his intense years.

Comments on Mr. Price's Article

Pearl K. Morton

Reading over Mr. Price's article on Mortonius it is a temptation to make comments paragraph by paragraph. He kept the "generous white moustache" because in his early boyhood he fell out of a tree cutting his lip so badly there was a permanent scar. Once a year he had the moustache shaved and at the same time—usually in midsummer—had as close a haircut as he could persuade the barber to give him. He always warned me before going through this ceremony. The change was almost ghastly. One of his admiring friends asked me indignantly why I let him do a thing like that, and I replied to her derisively, "Let him? Did you say LET him?"

True, James did not believe in indulging in intoxicating liquor of any kind, but he believed too strongly in individual liberty to be a prohibitionist so-called. I can not find any temperance society in his list of clubs, nor did I ever hear him try to persuade a person not to drink. I attended many convention dinners and house parties with him where drinking took place and I not only did not notice any disapproval on his part but I admired the courteous way he refused a proffered drink, with so much ease yet firmness that there was no argument about it. When I later commented on it, he replied, "There are ways of doing things." I myself always found it difficult to refuse a drink or a cigarette without arousing some form of antagonism. James never did. Yet he disapproved thoroughly of drinking. For that matter he disapproved thoroughly of women using cosmetics, and we had many arguments on that point for years. I tried to convince him that it was the misuse of cosmetics which was his real objection. For a time, when he admired a good looking woman, I would tell him exactly what cosmetics that woman had used, adding that she knew exactly how much and what kind to use. He always replied that the woman in question was good looking enough so that she did not need to use cosmetics. Here too his belief in personal liberty and his natural courtesy kept him from making personal comments unless the other person brought up the subject.

As curator of the Paterson Museum, he put in a full time day's work, and he built up the mineral collection from practically nothing. Starting out at first with the conscientious idea of earning his salary, he became more and more enthusiastic and really put in more labor and time than was necessary. I sadly realized that way back in his early youth he should have known that he was a scientist by nature, and have trained himself for the scientific field. I say "sadly" because I myself, knowing him since 1915 and sensing that he was hunting hopelessly for something that would hold his interest, did not recognize the fact that he was a scientist. "Why," I asked him, "didn't your teachers know that you had the mind of a scientist and have you take the proper subjects? Surely in college you should have taken a bachelor of science course?" He replied that he had done too well in the subjects he had taken up, his marks were too good in languages, literature etc.

While he gave so much time to the museum, he did not like to give up his other interests. Years before I married him I worried about his spells of utter exhaustion and demanded that each time he joined a new club or took up a new interest he drop a club or an interest. This was very hard for him to do, but when I married him in March 1934 I put my foot down and every time he got interested in some club or movement in Paterson he would regretfully give up something else. As the club meeting he gave up was usually held in New York, that saved a lot of tiresome traveling. He would never have done this however had he not himself known that he was overtaxing his apparently unlimited strength and vitality.

Referring to the "intellectual" conversation, I found by accident just how far that could go. James and Mr. Gabelle and I were coming back on the train

448 ❀ *Letters to James F. Morton*

to Paterson. I had a window seat and leaning against the glass, went off to sleep. Awakening slightly, I realized both men were talking at full speed, and keeping my eyes closed, I listened. I have a college degree but I couldn't grasp what those two were talking about. They were having a wonderful time! Thinking over that incident, I asked James why he didn't invite a few friends for an evening, cook one of his specialties for the main dish, and I'd simply stay in town—in other words, an intimate little intellectual party, all men. The idea intrigued him and he worked out all the details himself. A party of four, including himself, a simple meal all his own—at that time he was enthusiastic about new recipes—and an evening of effortless discussion. I did get up early enough to set the table before I left for work, and I made sure staples were on hand, but James planned his own menu, cooked and served the dinner. I believe escalloped oysters was the main dish for the first dinner, with hot rolls. The men had a thoroughly good time, I did not return until the party was over—we had a signal—and one of the men liked the idea so well, he had a similar party of his own. Some months later James invited three poets.

His interest in cooking came about when I suggested that we eat all our meals including dinners at home. I had wearied of restaurant meals. As we had both lived in furnished rooms so much, the possession of a real stove and an electric refrigerator seemed almost a miracle. I came home one night to find James carefully boiling sugar to make lemonade. I was interested as the idea was new to me. He had found the recipe in a cookbook. Boiling the sugar made it possible to have good lemonade with a minimum of sugar, which was impor- tant as James' doctor had told him to go slow on sweets and very slow on salt. With lots of lemon juice and very little sugar, James was able to have all the cold lemonade he wanted in hot weather. On hot nights he would get up and go for the lemonade jug. "It's so refreshing" he would mutter as he went back to sleep. I asked him why he had not had a refrigerator when he first took his apartment, but manlike he had thought it would be too much trouble. I sug- gested that he write a pamphlet on how a bachelor could be comfortable in his own apartment and while the idea intrigued him, he thought he did not know the subject well enough. Another night I came home to find him struggling with chestnuts. He liked to look in the cookbook and find a recipe that sounded interesting to try. One recipe had about every ingredient that existed and we decided it was too much work to make so little of it so we doubled the amounts, even the mustard. I did have sense enough not to double the salt. The result was delicious except that the mustard flavor predominated strongly. I forget now what was in that dish, but I do remember that mustard. As the food got a little less hot it tasted all the more of mustard. James asked me wistfully what was I going to do with what was left? We had worked so long and care- fully on it! The next day as an experiment I stirred in a can of beans as that was about the only food we hadn't put in, and the result was very good. The mus- tard taste was just about medium.

I had encouraged James' interest in cooking both so he would want to eat at home, and because it was the only unintellectual hobby he had and I thought it would rest him However there was too much he wanted to accomplish, and he came to begrudge the time it took. Gradually he gave it up entirely though he was always interested in finding new foods in cans that were especially good. Six common-day vegetables he would never touch, beets, cabbage, onions, turnips, carrots and cauliflower. He never could resist gadgets and was always bringing some home, and actually brought home two for scraping carrots and cabbage primarily.

James liked to talk so much that no one thought he sometimes had to stop. I remember one mineral trip lasting some days when he lectured on minerals during the day and played intellectual games all evening I recognized the signs of exhaustion and told him we both had to have an evening of peace and quiet. But it was hard. The others were perfectly willing for me to sleep off a headache, but they wanted James. He finally told them firmly that we had plans for that evening. "We'll go to the movie with you!" they chorused. James told them we weren't going to a movie. They were puzzled, but we couldn't tell them their company was not wanted, and the next morning we could not tell them how we had spent the long hours of that evening. "We know you didn't go to bed because we saw your light at eleven o'clock!" How could we tell them that their beloved Intellectual had spent five solid hours slumped peacefully in the one good chair the room afforded reading one detective magazine after another, not saying one single word. I was stretched out on the bed with all the pillows, likewise reading and not talking. Our room was quiet, it was peaceful outside, and no one bothered us. It was a most delightful evening.

I used to think it was James' legal training which made him want to be so clear in his lecturing. This was all right for students but when he talked at club meetings or dinners and brought his remarks to a perfect finish and then went back and explained all over again, his audience rebelled. I knew later that it was the scientist in him which made him want to be so exact. He was at his best in the favorite three minute and five minute speeches which were so popular at anniversary and club dinners. He could pack more into a short space of time than any one I knew, and he could talk fast and still be easily understood. Once at a Walt Whitman dinner, the radicals got in control and many of the listeners squirmed in their seats, wishing they could speak clearly the thoughts that were in their minds. James' friends remembered with relief that he was the last speaker. He would tell them! He did too. Unfortunately I was not present, but to this day I keep hearing about that dinner and how in his brief speech James brought the meeting back to sanity, and to the real object of their coming together—Walt Whitman. The first year I met James, at the N.A.P.A. convention at New York in 1915, I also heard him lecture for the first time. The delegates were led on a tour of New York streets and we came to Union Square. Several speakers were holding forth on boxes to brief audiences. We told James he had to make a speech and he willingly complied. (He had his lecturer's license.) His voice could be heard from one end of the Square to the other and we gleefully gathered around as the audiences of all the other speakers came over to hear what this new man was saying. One of the other speakers recognizing defeat, brought over his soapbox and suggested that James climb on it, which he willingly did.

Some one wrote that James was the sponsor of lost causes. He worked hard in behalf of the Single Tax, giving his services as a lecturer free for his expenses en route only, and writing several pamphlets on that subject himself. He attended a gathering of the Nudist Club one Sunday in the early summer because he believed in what they were trying to accomplish, and he got a terrific attack of sunburn as a reward. He planned to go at least once a year, just as he tried to go into New York for Esperanto meetings upon occasion "just to let them know I believe in them." Perhaps the memories of his agonizing sunburn had something to do with it, but he never did go again. He realized how difficult it was for the average person to understand the beliefs of the true nudist. In fact the more trouble a new movement he believed in was having, the more anxious he was to help. I suspect he was a few generations ahead of his time himself.

Mr. Price's statement, "Heights make me dizzy, but I couldn't back down . . . I gritted my teeth", brings back memories of my own struggle with heights. Once James realized that my fear of heights was something I could not control, and after watching me climb down in absolute panic an easy path where I had to see the heights below, he was careful in selecting his routes when I was with him. Once James and his brother Nelson tried to scale a rocky hill at Andover, N. H., where there was no path, just climbing straight up. This was many years ago, but Nelson still remembers it and remarked that having climbed just so far they simply had to go on as they could not climb down. "We never thought we'd make it!" he finished. James showed me that hill, and it did look like a possible though arduous climb.

James loved exploring new places and traveling to new sites, so much so that I told him once he must have been an unwanted baby. "My mother did too want me!" he exploded indignantly.

Jim Morton

W. Paul Cook

Would that at least a dozen different people could give us as living a picture of Jim Morton in as many activities as Hoffmann Price has in his sketch of the mineralogist!

It would seem to be destined that James should be more of a legend in his life than after he had left it. Nearly fifty years ago when I first encountered amateur journalism, James Ferdinand Morton Jr. was a legendary character, though intensely active and personally known. Beginning with his brilliant but erratic studentship at Harvard, stories were current everywhere of his equally erratic if not equally brilliant career after he left college.

But after he "settled down" at last in Paterson he really and truly settled down, and, while his interests were as varied as ever (as, with his mind, they had to be) the erraticism largely if not wholly disappeared, the radical effervescent spirit was calmed, and the tales began to be forgotten as those who had known him well dropped out. He was still the great liberal (so liberal that, as some one said, he "leaned over backward") but there came a solidity, a sense of responsibility to himself and to his "job", that had been wholly lacking. After sixty years of following will-o'-the-wisps, and living as precariously as that indicates, he became a "substantial citizen." Instead of being the friend of Emma Goldman and the rest of the "Paterson Reds" when they were red and not a confused pink, and presiding at a meeting at which Emma spoke in New York which caused several riot squads to be called out, James disappeared from the more livid news items, and was mentioned only in the reports of meetings of literary and learned societies and in *Who's Who*. The balance wheel, the gyroscopic device which he had always possessed somewhere, had started turning. But who am I to talk of balance wheels!

One sentence at least in Hoffmann Price's article will cause a smile from those who knew James in his younger days: "He was moderate in all things, even in the expression of firm convictions." I can imagine a few whom I could name crying, "What a change, what a 'settling down' indeed!" (There is the story of the new straw hat: For year after year Jim appeared at conventions with the same straw hat, which was getting browner and browner with the years until another shade would make it black. One year, I fear not entirely from charitable motives, a number of the boys took up a collection, bought a new hat, and presented it to James with due ceremony. For once Jim was speechless. He took that new hat, slammed it on the floor, and jumped on it.)

There was a change, indeed, from the fiery red-headed radical of the Paterson Reds era to white-haired Curator of the Paterson Museum, but not such a change in that exploring mind as it would seem.

There is even a connection or something between the GHOST and Morton. Just as I was preparing to issue the first number, James told me that his collection of school readers, on which he had been working for years (I had seen him add to it in Eddy's in Providence and at Day's and Colesworthy's on Cornhill) was as complete as it ever could be made I at once commissioned him to write an article on it, which he promised to do. But as far as I know the article had not been started when he died.

Three pictures of James remain, curiously, with me. The first, a slender young man with an ancient straw skimmer perched on top of a shock of red hair. Next, a rather more portly (but never fat), genial and suave white-haired scientist demonstrating with delight the fluorescence of minerals. Then, during an evening spent at my room in Boston (the last time I saw him, I think), saying "Paul, why don't you tell me to remove my coat? It's hot here." And my saying, "Migawd, James, I didn't know you were such a stickler for etiquette. Am I supposed to help you off with it?" At this same meeting he had a paroxysm of stifling and coughing, at which I was alarmed. "It is nothing," said James, "I have made a study of the condition, and while incurable, it will never kill me." And it didn't.

As to everything being "ship-shape" in Jim's bachelor kitchen, I can only say that Ed Price visited the place on a different day from that on which I saw it!, although it was probably the same year, within a few weeks, and possibly within a few days or even hours.

While in the Paterson Museum I purposely called him "Dr. Morton", in which way he had been introduced on a radio broadcast, only to be rebuked for the formality, and assured that he had no Doctor's degree anyway—had never regarded the title worth going after.

The real calibre of the Morton mind had perhaps its best demonstration when he performed the feat that made him the Curator and "settled him down."

Now this story came originally from Lovecraft, but was later verified by James when I asked him about it. "How in the world did you do it, Jim?" I asked. "Oh," said he, "anyone can do anything under the spur of necessity and if they become interested. It was not as difficult as it looked!"

There was a reorganization planned of the Paterson Municipal Museum and a Curator was needed. Friends told Morton about it and urged that he apply for the position. It was a competitive examination, it being necessary that the new Curator have a definite program and show ability to carry it out. Hitherto there had been only a loose organization of the Museum and no set plan by which it was run. James at the time was at loose ends and looked over the possibilities. He decided that the Museum should specialize in minerals. Paterson lies at the centre of a very interesting country, mineralogically, but the Museum's mineral collection was small and poorly displayed and arranged. Morton told the group they would not see him for three weeks. He shut himself up in his room with a library. At the end of the three weeks he appeared and announced that he was ready for the examination. He presented his plan to the Museum board, underwent a stiff examination by experts, and was appointed Curator. In other words, in three weeks James had taken a several years' course in mineralogy. He at once became widely known in that science. I doubt if such a feat was ever duplicated.

It was in connection with his minerals that James told me a story that he said was such a series of coincidences it could never be used in fiction. There was one mineral the museum did not have and it was to be found only in one place in the East, a quarry located in Providence, Rhode Island. James knew but one person in Providence, that being Howard Lovecraft. The owner of the quarry was a "foreigner," not of a benign disposition and suspicious of everyone. There was one mortgage, and one only, held on the quarry. That mortgage was part of the small estate owned by Lovecraft. The owner thawed and aided Morton in securing what he wanted.

As one result of this mineralizing expedition to Rhode Island there was piled in the corner of Lovecraft's room for over a year a ton or so of rocks left there by Morton. When I suggested that each chunk be carefully wrapped in tissue paper and the collection packed in boxes and shipped to Morton to get them out of the way, Lovecraft treated the suggestion with a snort. They were going to stay right there until Jim came for them. He eventually did.

James Morton

Rheinhart Kleiner

The following comprises Chapter IV of Recreations of an Amateur Journalist, *by Rheinhart Kleiner, a lengthy manuscript which is scheduled for publication in the far distant future if all concerned live long enough. Chapter IV, dealing entirely with James Morton, fits into this issue of the Ghost so nicely it is torn out of its context and given advance publication.*

James F. Morton died in Paterson, N. J., in 1941 at the age of seventy. Cremation took place in accordance with his wish, and Pearl K. Morton, his widow, consigned the ashes to Ernest A. Dench, who was to arrange to have them thrown from some hilltop in Northern New Jersey's countryside. A year or more passed, and hearing no more of it I visited Dench one day and asked him when Morton's wishes were to be carried out. One thing or another, it seemed, had intervened, but I could hope to be advised when the ashes were scattered. I received more or less sudden notice, in the latter part of 1945, that this was finally to be done—furthermore, the ashes were to be scattered in Chester and I was to do the scattering.

On Sunday, February 10, 1946, a group of Woodland Trail Walkers, headed by Ernest A. Dench, came down to my house, in the hollow of the Chester hills, and Dench handed me the little package he carried. I had previously arranged with a friend and neighbor, who owned a house and a number of acres just under the Chester ridge, to let me do the scattering from a hilly elevation some distance behind the house. So Dench, with all his hikers, clad in their winter outdoor gear, and Ruth Pietchman and myself, leaped into a few cars and proceeded to the place agreed upon—no more than ten minutes away. We paused for hot coffee at the camp site immediately behind the house, and I unwrapped the package. It was a fair-sized container of circular form and bore James F. Morton's name and dates in typewritten characters an the outside.

It was a somewhat peculiar experience to pry off the cover and to realize that these white ashes were all that remained of a man who had so recently been alive and moving among us. Ruth Pietchman, who had wept at his passing a few years before, looked ready to weep again, but the time had come to start. I might say that all but four members of that group were utter strangers to James F. Morton. Only Ernest A. Dench, Paul H. Schubert—a former Paterson Rambler—Ruth Pietchman and myself had known him in life. Dench, by marrying Iva Rae Merritt—Pearl K. Morton's sister—had become a brother-in-law of Morton, but had had a previous long and intimate acquaintance with him as a fellow Blue Penciller and follower of the trails. Paul H. Schubert, as I have said, had become a friend in the Paterson Rambling Club, as had Ruth Pietchman, but Miss Pietchman had later joined the Blue Pencil Club and, with her sister Esther, had been numbered among Morton's favorites. My own acquaintance and friendship with him had closely paralleled Dench's—amateur journalism, and the hiking activities we shared together, had been the bond between us.

We started up a somewhat steep incline, and with a sinking heart, I suddenly realized that I was doing what I had been expressly forbidden to do. I knew it because of what was happening in my wrists, my arms and my chest. But the objective of our climb was not so far off, and I felt sure I could hold out that long, as proved to be the case. I reached our goal at the tail-end of the procession, but the precious container was still under my arm and, after standing for a few moments, I felt normal again.

I could imagine how Morton would have conducted such an occasion, with his love of the dramatic and his fondness for forensic display. I smiled a bit wryly when I thought of the poor, incompetent hands into which the occasion of which he was the center, had fallen.

But there was nothing else to do but go ahead with it. A stiff breeze—with a bitter edge—seemed suddenly to whip up, but it had probably been blowing all the while without my noticing it. The hikers, with Dench and Schubert among them, had ranged themselves a little at one side. A few, Ruth Pietchman among them, were on the other side.

I removed my hat, and immediately Dench, Schubert and all the male hikers did so. I had expected to be panic-stricken, but it seemed very natural to speak a few words in explanation of the scene, in praise of the departed, and in the hope that his ashes might find the dispersal which James Morton had wished. I put my fingers in the container, and drawing out a handful of ashes, cast it forth, symbolically, upon the breeze. Some of the fine, white substance, sped away immediately to the south, as it seemed to me. Some of it seemed to fall, but only for a moment, upon the dried and withered grasses. Then this, too, was suddenly whipped away, and I could not see where it had gone. Passing the container before the hikers, I suggested that those who wished might also throw a handful to the winds. All of them did so.

It has since seemed a curious circumstance to me, that I, who was not one of Morton's closest or oldest friends, should have found myself performing this last office for him. It is true that I cannot even remember when that footing which made it possible for me to call him friend, was established. I had marked him, long ago, at one of my first Blue Pencil meetings, as he spoke on various topics and, at this particular gathering, quoted long stretches of Tennyson. After that, I heard him talk very often, and recite very often, and we met again and again. I had admired him from the beginning, but what made him think that I was worthy of his attention?

If I have the least inkling of what it was, it must have been at a Blue Pencil dinner when Morton sat at one end of a long table and I at the other. When he rose to speak, I could see him plainly because he faced toward me, and I know that I was fully in his view. Why did his eye, as he spoke, keep running down toward me so often? Did he feel a quick understanding, even an eager sympathy, in the comparatively unknown youth who listened to him so intently? I hope so. But I cannot even be sure that that was the occasion when he gave me more than a passing thought.

But somehow or other, we did draw together a little more closely at our meetings, our picnics and our rambles. Dench was also included in this little special group—possibly even Otto Knack. No doubt our New England ramble had had a tendency to draw Morton, Dench and myself together, years before. But now, in the early 1920's, James Morton had become curator of the Paterson Museum, had moved all his household effects to Paterson, and had even joined the Paterson Rambling Club. Dench lived in the Sheepshead Bay locality at that time, and I was still in the Bushwick section of Brooklyn. James Morton invited Dench and myself to Paterson for a Sunday ramble with his newly discovered club. We need only try it once, said Morton; and we were willing to do so, at least once. But from that time on, Dench and I appeared every Sunday—barring special private ventures—at Paterson City Hall, where the ramblers assembled and where they boarded the special bus. It marked the beginning of a wonderful experience, not only for me, but for everyone who joined us. Not Morton, nor Dench, nor myself, would have cared to miss a single one of our all-year schedule of outdoor events.

Morton finally proposed a week in the Kittatinneys, just walking all day, and sleeping outdoors wherever we happened to find ourselves at night. Dench, for some reason, could not go, and so Morton and I took the trip alone. Now that twenty years have passed, I cannot begin to recall half our experiences, and should probably prove a bore if I did so.

But I do remember our walking along the topmost ridge of the Kittatinneys, with a dense wilderness on every side below us. We were in rattle-snake country and this was the sort of terrain they loved—berry bushes, rocks lying about in profusion, and practically no visitors. Our guide book even told us of a man who lived in Colesville, below us, who came up here at certain times to hunt the rattlers. This venturesome person practically wrapped himself in burlap before coming up here. But all I can say of our own experience, is that we made a fire for our lunch, sat around in the sun for a while, and then moved on, with the day, toward twilight. We saw no rattlers.

Those who have never gone on a hike, may be interested in what we wore. The styles may have changed among hikers since those days, but everything we wore was khaki-colored. I wore army breeches, as did many other followers of the trail, but Morton and a few similarly conservative individuals preferred long trousers, albeit of the prevailing color. I wore wrap leggings and heavy shoes, but heavy shoes were all that Morton required. I had a lightweight coat, with no unusual equipment of pockets, but Morton had a fairly heavy hunting coat with pockets in every imaginable place. In addition, we each carried a shoulder-pack, or knapsack, and lugged about thirty-five or forty pounds of food in each one. This quantity was reduced so rapidly that only the first day's weight was anything to be afraid of. Sometimes we wore caps, and sometimes not, but each of us always bore an alpenstock, or hiking stick, in his hand. I carried a few items of supply for which Morton had no need—a generous quantity of tobacco and three pipes.

On this particular trip, I half trotted—or so it must have seemed to Morton—up a preliminary slope which was really just a gradual ascent. Morton plugged along at some distance behind me, his face of a lobster red, and frequently he mopped his brow, for it was a hot day in July. I finally paused and sat on a rock until he came up to me. He arrived and, wringing out his handkerchief, remarked, "Ye Gods, what a pace you set, Rheinhart!" I emitted a few deprecatory puffs of pipe-smoke, but said nothing. Inwardly I chuckled, however, at the recollection of Morton's doubt, long ago, as to whether a "lounge lizard" could really stand the rigors of outdoor life! By this time, in fact, Morton and Dench—when I went out with the latter—were depending upon me to build the fire and prepare the meals at suitable intervals during a day's hike. Both Morton and Dench, at that time, were somewhat incapable of such effort, although Dench, who has continued his hiking activities up to the present day, has probably advanced considerably in the matter of outdoor fire-building and cooking.

It was at some time during this trip that I made a passing thrust with my stick at a wasp's nest, hanging from a tree. Nothing happened, and I tried it again. This time, more than enough happened, for the air suddenly filled with enraged wasps, and I decided to make a precipitate departure. Morton was already a little ahead of me, but somewhat lower on the hillside, and I took some rapid leaps in his direction. Seeing the reason for my action, he immediately increased his own speed and urged me to run in another direction. This was reasonable advice, but a pricking in my right thumb and a sharp sting in front of my left ear, seemed to retard my thought processes but not the speed of my flight. So with Morton galloping ahead, and I at his heels, we reached the valley. Morton, I am glad to say, had not been touched, and the effect of my own pricking and stingings soon passed off. I knew myself to have been at fault and bore Morton's reproaches meekly.

We decided to spend one night on top of the highest elevation in the region, and this meant a somewhat arduous climb of a few hours. For the last thirty feet or so, we had to crawl on our hands and knees, over shale and gravel. Then we found one or two large table rocks, adequate for sleeping, and there we had our evening meal as the sun gradually sank. A flat rock, even though quite free of knobs and protuberances, may seem an uncomfortable roost, and from some points of view, it is just that, I should be inclined to say that youth can find any cot endurable, but Morton was twenty years older than myself, and he did not mind the accommodations, either. Maybe there is something in one's attitude toward life and experience which makes it possible to sleep on a rock without protest! I suppose we have all known individuals who were somewhat on the "fussy" side, and these are the ones who could not be expected to find sport in physical exposure to the elements, in primitive accommodations for eating and sleeping, or in general hardship and discomfort all around!

Our hope of spending the night on our lofty perch was short-lived, however. An extremely cold wind blew up in the small hours of the morning, and we packed up under the stars to seek a more sheltered place farther down. After an hour's scrambling, falling and feeling about in an unfamiliar world—and decidedly by accident and not design—we found a rude shack, in the center of which stood a rough but fairly large table. Without further ado, we threw our blankets on it, and climbed up ourselves. In no time at all, we had resumed our interrupted slumbers.

Much of this area has since become a state park, some excellent motor roads wind through it, and from the top to which we crawled on our hands and knees, a lofty stone observation tower now rises.

At another time, we slept on a hillside, with the usual expanse of heavily wooded territory below us. Usually before going to sleep, we played a game of "quotations," in which one repeated a couplet or quatrain and the other had to identify it. Morton was likely to quote something fairly impressive from Bailey's *Festus*, or Wordsworth's *Prelude*, or even *Percy's Reliques,* but I need not say that his acquaintance with English poetry was much wider! Henley was a special favorite of his, but as I happened to be an admirer of him, too, Morton had to be careful of what he chose for quoting. Many a time—although not in our games—had I heard him recite:

> *The nightingale has a lyre of gold;*
> *The lark's is a clarion call,*
> *And the blackbird plays but a box-wood flute*
> *But I love him best of all.*

I was more likely to come out with something like this:

> *Not, Celia, that I juster am*
> *Or better than the rest!*
> *For I would change each hour like them,*
> *Were not my heart at rest.*

After a while, however, we had acquired such familiarity with each other's stock of poetical standbys, that the game languished.

The final quotation, on the evening of which I speak, was accompanied by a comparatively feeble flash of lightning from the darkening sky, and it was followed by a distant rumble of thunder. Then we fell back on our blankets and dozed off.

Not long thereafter it began to rain, and fairly soon it began to pour. The first shock of the falling rain awakened us, but our army ponchos were of no use in affording protection. On thinking it over, we decided to remain where we were, and take it, rather than scurry down through the slanting rain to the woods below us. When morning broke, with early sunlight, everything we owned and everything we wore was wringing wet. We could not even find a dry match to light a fire, and what we both ardently desired was a cup of hot coffee. But way down among the trees I could espy a wisp of smoke—a wisp, it was true, but still substantial enough to mean more than a campfire. I decided to locate the place from which it came, and bidding Morton be of good cheer, I started down toward it. To make short of the matter, I found a humble shack with the door open, and plainly in sight on the stove was what looked and smelled exactly like a pot of coffee—which it was beyond question. The elderly foreign woman to whom I spoke could not understand, nor could her aging husband, sitting nearby with a pipe in his mouth. Taking a coin from my pocket, I slapped it on the table, picked up the coffee-pot and fled hastily. Morton raised his head somewhat wanly when I came back, and regarded my coffee-pot a little incredulously. Then, after he had taken a swallow, he murmured, "Rheinhart, you're a daisy!"

James F. Morton was a well-disposed man, mentally. He hoped and expected the best from society and the individual. He might have been termed an optimist, as, in fact, he regarded himself. It used to seem to me that he made a mistake in expecting the world to be ruled by logical considerations, or what seemed such to him, and the frequent proofs he must have found of man's failure or, inability to live in accordance with logic sometimes ruffled him. That was when he may have seemed short-tempered, unreasonable or testy to an unsympathetic observer.

Morton, dining in a restaurant, could never understand why items no longer available had not been crossed off the menu. Nor could he understand how a right-minded company of people could listen with roars of laughter to the reminiscences of a former Tammany ward heeler. Tammany was politically reprehensible and he saw no reason for slapping a former adherent of such an organization on the back.

During my active period in the N.A.P.A., he wrote very little. One or two smaller ventures of his were published, but they were not especially important and received little attention. In my own day, at least, he was not regarded as one of our leading amateur writers, but rather as a power at conventions and in the political conclaves of the association. When he wrote, however, it always seemed to me that few could surpass him in sheer lucidity and in that charm which inheres in the masterly assembling of various factual details for purposes of discussion.

He was a mainstay of the Blue Pencil Club for many years, and it was his influence, when he moved to Paterson, which finally brought the club across the river. This was not the result of deliberate action on his part, but if one man's influence counted it was that of James Morton. His entry into the competitive examination for curator of the Paterson Museum came about largely as the result of coincidence. The Blue Pencil Club had been spending week-ends at a small New Jersey resort called Echo Lake, which was conducted by the wife of the then librarian of Paterson. The librarian met Morton, and after various conversations with him, urged him to take the examination. Up to that time, the museum had been a part of the library, and its removal into a separate building required the setting up of a special administration. So James Morton, who had had no regular connection for years, took the test and won. His Harvard background, his degree of Master of Arts from that institution, and his long career as a lecturer and public speaker now began to yield results. Some of Morton's most useful and happy years followed upon his appointment to the post of curator.

The rooms of his apartment were lined with books, for the most part, and among the bookcases stood a large cabinet, full of mineral specimens—the latter consisting of selections from the large accumulations he had been instrumental in bringing to the shelves of the museum. The region of Paterson is noted, at least among eastern communities, for the number and variety of the minerals to be found there. Morton's efforts had placed the Paterson Museum in a commanding position with its fine collection of such rarities.

He had always possessed a fine literary taste, and seemed more and more inclined toward our older authors as the years passed. *Percy's Reliques* was one of the first books I ever heard him mention, and this undoubtedly led him into the field of ancient English and Scotch ballads as it has been opened and developed by modern scholarship. This interest led him back to Beowulf and Langland and the really ancient eddas and sagas which are not easily found in the average bookstore. Malory's *Morte d'Arthur,* Burton's *Thousand and One Nights,* and Doughty's *Arabia Deserta* were the sort of thing he relished. Then, of course, there were the old English dramatists; and such well-nigh forgotten classics as *Gammer Gurton's Needle*, *Ralph Roister*, and others of their time, struck a responsive fiber within him.

For relaxation of another sort, he turned to "pulp" magazines which contained detective stories, tales of the weird, and what not. I have at times been astounded at the heaps of such literature which gathered on his desk. I have read that Woodrow Wilson, Justice Oliver Wendell Holmes, and national figures of equal weight, were given to the same discursive exercises. So be it! I, a much lesser man, seem to have a long way to go yet before I shall be ready to return to the literary interests of my boyhood!

Morton revealed the Yankee in him by his preoccupation with gadgets—especially those having to do with kitchen operations. The inside of his closet door was hung from top to bottom with gadgets of every imaginable size, shape and use.

I did not see much of him in the last year or two of his life. Before his marriage to Pearl K. Merritt, when he lived alone in Paterson, I was accustomed to spending the final hours of a Sunday evening in his room, following a hike. Here, he sometimes showed me old scrapbooks and old trophies of his activities as an amateur journalist, a Harvard student, a lecturer, and as a specialist in minerals. I was particularly, interested in a scrapbook containing his early attempts at versification, and could see that Morton's final mastery of metrics had not been easily arrived at. He was aware of his early defects, and must have striven mightily to overcome them, as I know he finally did, since during the time I knew him he won the poet laureateship of the National.

It used to be a matter of wonder to me that he did not concentrate upon a verse-form somewhat like that of Whitman's—a poet of whom he was an ardent admirer—but I think he found the form, at least, too easy—so easy, in fact, that the spirit might well escape while the poet was wrestling with the form. So he confined himself within the conventional patterns set by tradition and did well with them.

And since one of my own measures of a man's capacity—a thoroughly ridiculous and unreasonable measure, I admit!—is whether or not he has shown skill as a letter-writer, I suppose I must admit that seldom, indeed, did I ever get a letter from James Morton! No future biographer will ever come to me for evidences of Morton's prowess as a follower of Walpole, Fitzgerald, Lamb or Stevenson! That he wrote letters, I know, and those I have seen were long affairs which were intended to prove someone else wrong or himself right, in an argument. Such letters did not awaken a genial glow of admiration in the recipient, although judging by the one or two which were shown to me, they contained absolutely nothing that was extraneous to the argument and never dealt in personalities. Their infuriating effect upon the recipient was due chiefly to the fact that they proved him, with unanswerable logic, to be hopelessly and completely in the wrong.

But I never had any weighty arguments with him. and felt quite sure that he would shortly have tied me into a knot if I had. My chief weapon against him—but never, as I have said, in a real argument—was a sudden and direct conversational thrust which set him back on his heels for a moment. James Morton even admitted that, agile and resourceful as his mind was, he could sometimes be caught without defenses.

*   *   *

The foregoing paragraphs have been, at best, but a scanty presentation of my contacts and relations with James Morton. I might have told more of his activities in the Blue Pencil Club, and I might have gone into further detail about our hikes. But I feel that enough has been told to indicate, at least in part, what manner of man he was. His influence in my own life was incalculable. Only H. P. Lovecraft came anywhere near him in his effect upon my life and thoughts. This may seem of the least importance, but both of them confirmed me in my boyhood passion for books, for one thing, but from Morton I derived the special advantage of frequent personal contact and, albeit indirectly, of word of mouth precept. I am sure he never knew, and I, myself, did not suspect at the time, how valuable his conversation was to me. I know that my own life was enriched by his personality and his culture, and it is now forever poorer since he has gone.

Years ago I read a poem by Thomas Love Peacock entitled *Three Times Three,* and I thought the last stanza not unapplicable to James Morton. I offer that stanza to the reader as, in the main, an adequate summing up of the virtues of the genial man I knew—albeit over-stated and over-expansive in some details:

> *He kept at true good humor's mark*
> *The social flow of pleasure's tide;*
> *He never made a brow look dark,*
> *Nor caused a tear, but when he died.*
> *No sorrow round his tomb should dwell:*
> *More pleased his gay old ghost would be,*
> *For funeral song and passing bell,*
> *To hear no sound but three times three.*

Glossary of Frequently Mentioned Names

Adams, Hazel Pratt (d. 1927), wife of A. M. Adams, both amateur journalists. Upon her death, HPL wrote the elegy "The Absent Leader."

Bacon, Victor E. (1905–1997), amateur journalist and editor of *Bacon's Essays*, which published work by HPL and Clark Ashton Smith, and Official Editor of the United Amateur Press Association (1925–26).

Baird, Edwin (1886–1957), first editor of *Weird Tales* (Mar. 1923–Apr. 1924), who accepted HPL's first submissions to the magazine. Also editor of *Real Detective Stories*.

Barlow, R[obert] H[ayward] (1918–1951), author and collector. As a teenager he corresponded with HPL and acted as his host during two long visits in the summers of 1934 and 1935. In the 1930s he wrote several works of weird and fantasy fiction, some in collaboration with HPL. HPL appointed him his literary executor. He assisted August Derleth and Donald Wandrei in preparing the early HPL volumes for Arkham House. In the 1940s he went to Mexico and became a distinguished anthropologist. He died by suicide. HPL's letters to Barlow have been published as *O Fortunate Floridian* (Tampa: University of Tampa Press, 2007).

Beebe, Evanore (1858–1935), friend of Edith Miniter who shared her home in Wilbraham, MA.

Blackwood, Algernon (1869–1951), prolific British author of weird and fantasy tales whose work HPL greatly admired when he read it in 1924.

Bloch, Robert (1917–1994), author of weird and suspense fiction who came into correspondence with HPL in 1933. HPL tutored him in the craft of writing during their four-year association.

Brobst, Harry K[ern] (1909–2010), late associate of HPL who moved to Providence in 1932 and saw HPL regularly thereafter.

Bullen, John Ravenor (1886–1927), amateur poet from Canada. HPL edited his poems, *White Fire* (1927), for posthumous publication.

Bush, (Rev.) David Van (1882–1959), prolific author of inspirational verse and popular psychology manuals, many of them revised by HPL.

Campbell, Paul J., amateur journalist and editor of the *Liberal* and other amateur papers.

Cave, Hugh B[arnett] (1910–2004), prolific author of stories for the pulp magazines. Lived near HPL in Pawtuxet, RI. They corresponded briefly but never met.

Clark, Lillian D[elora] (1856–1932), HPL's maternal aunt. She married Dr. Franklin Chase Clark in 1902. From 1926 to her death she shared quarters with HPL at 10 Barnes Street.

Coates, Walter J[ohn] (1880–1941), friend of W. Paul Cook and editor of *Driftwind*.

Cole, Edward H[arold] (1892–1966), longtime amateur associate of HPL, living in the Boston area. Editor of the *Olympian*.

Conover, Willis (1921–1996), weird fiction fan who edited *Science-Fantasy Correspondent* (1936–37) and was a late correspondent of HPL.

Cook, W. Paul (1881–1948), publisher of the *Monadnock Monthly*, the *Vagrant*, and other amateur journals; a longtime amateur journalist, printer, and life-long friend of HPL. He first visited HPL in 1917, and it was he who urged HPL to resume writing fiction after a hiatus of nine years. In 1927 Cook published the *Recluse*, with HPL's "Supernatural Horror in Literature."

Crane, Hart (1899–1932), eminent American poet who met HPL sporadi-cally in Cleveland (1922) and New York (1924–26, 1930). HPL admired his work, especially *The Bridge* (1930), on which HPL saw him at work in 1924. He died by suicide.

Crawford, William L[evy] (1911–1984), editor of *Marvel Tales* and *Unusual Stories* and publisher of the Visionary Publishing Company, which issued HPL's *The Shadow over Innsmouth* (1936).

de Castro, Adolphe (Danziger) (1859–1959), author, co-translator with Ambrose Bierce of Richard Voss's *The Monk and the Hangman's Daughter*, and correspondent of HPL. HPL revised his "The Last Test" and "The Electric Executioner."

Daas, Edward F. (1879–1962), amateur journalist who recruited HPL into the movement in 1914.

Davis, Edgar J., young amateur journalist with whom HPL explored New-buryport and other locales in New England.

de Magistris, Mariano, HPL's tenant who operated a rock quarry in west-ern Rhode Island owned by HPL's family.

Dench, Ernest A[lfred], British-born Brooklyn amateur, author of *Making the Movies* (1915) and other books about the cinema.

Derleth, August W[illiam] (1909–1971), author of weird tales and also a long series of regional and historical works set in his native Wisconsin. Af-ter HPL's death, he and Donald Wandrei founded the publishing firm of Arkham House to preserve HPL's work in book form.

Dowdell, William J. (1898–1953), amateur journalist who abruptly resigned as president of the NAPA in late 1922, leading the executive judges to ap-point HPL as interim president.

Dunsany, Lord (Edward John Moreton Drax Plunkett) (1878–1957), Irish writer of fantasy tales whose work notably influenced HPL after HPL read it in 1919.

Dwyer, Bernard Austin (1897–1943), weird fiction fan and would-be writer and artist, living in West Shokan, NY; correspondent of HPL.

Eddy, Clifford M[artin] (1896–1967), pulp fiction writer for whom HPL revised several stories in 1923–24 and who also worked with HPL on ghostwriting work for Harry Houdini in 1926.

Edkins, Ernest A[rthur] (1867–1946), amateur journalist associated with the "halcyon days" of the NAPA (1885–95). He came in touch with HPL in 1932.

Finlay, Virgil (1914–1971), one of the great weird artists of his time and a prolific contributor of artwork to the pulps; late correspondent of HPL.

Galpin, Alfred (1901–1983), amateur journalist, French scholar, composer, and protégé, then longtime friend, of HPL. He lived in Appleton, WI.

Gamwell, Annie E[meline] P[hillips] (1866–1941), HPL's younger aunt, living with him at 66 College Street (1933–37). She had been married (1897–1936) to Edward F[rancis] Gamwell (1869–1936).

Goodenough, Arthur H[enry] (1871–1936), amateur poet who resided in Brattleboro, VT. HPL visited him there on several occasions.

Haggerty, Vincent B., amateur journalist associated with the NAPA in the 1920s and 1930s.

Haughton, Ida C. (d. 1935?), amateur journalist with whom HPL had a bitter feud in the early 1920s. He directed the pungent satirical poem "Medusa: A Portrait" (1922) at her.

Henneberger, J[acob] C[lark] (1890–1969), founder of *College Humor* (1922f.) and the original publisher of *Weird Tales*.

Hoag, Jonathan E[than] (1831–1927), amateur poet for whom HPL regularly wrote birthday poems from 1918 to 1927; upon Hoag's death he wrote the elegy "Ave atque Vale." HPL was the chief editor of *The Poetical Works of Jonathan E. Hoag* (1923).

Hodgson, William Hope (1877–1918), British author of weird fiction whose work had fallen into obscurity until it was rediscovered in the 1930s.

Houdini, Harry (stage name of Ehrich Weiss, 1874–1926), celebrated escape artist and opponent of spiritualism for whom HPL ghostwrote the story "Under the Pyramids" (1924; published as "Imprisoned with the Pharaohs") and for whom he did other revisory work in 1926, just prior to Houdini's death.

Houtain, George Julian (1884–1945), amateur journalist who established the semi-professional humor magazine *Home Brew*, for which he commissioned HPL to write "Herbert West—Reanimator" (1921–22) and "The Lurking Fear" (1922).

Howard, Robert E[rvin] (1906–1936), prolific Texas author of weird and adventure tales for *Weird Tales* and other pulp magazines; creator of the adventure hero Conan of Cimmeria. He and HPL corresponded voluminously from 1930 to 1936. He committed suicide when he heard of his mother's impending death.

Kirk, George [Willard] (1898–1962), member of the Kalem Club. He published *Twenty-one Letters of Ambrose Bierce* (1922) and ran the Chelsea Bookshop in New York.

Kleiner, Rheinhart (1892–1949), amateur poet and longtime friend of HPL. He visited HPL in Providence in 1918, 1919, and 1920, and met him frequently during the heyday of the Kalem Club (1924–26).

Kline, Otis Adelbert (1891–1946), prolific writer for *Weird Tales* and other pulp magazines; also a literary agent for Robert E. Howard and others.

Koenig, H[erman] C[harles] (1893–1959), late associate of HPL who spearheaded the rediscovery of the work of William Hope Hodgson.

Kuttner, Henry (1915–1958), prolific author of science fiction and horror tales for the pulps and a late correspondent of HPL (1936–37). HPL introduced him to C[atherine] L[ucile] Moore (1911–1987), whom he would later marry.

Lawson, Horace L., amateur journalist and editor of the *Wolverine*, which published several of HPL's stories and also some installments of the pseudonymous column "The Vivisector" (as by "Zoilus").

Leeds, Arthur (1882–1952?), an associate of HPL in New York and member of the Kalem Club. He was the author (with J. Berg Esenwein) of *Writing the Photoplay* (Springfield, MA: The Home Correspondence School, 1913; rev. ed. 1919).

Leiber, Fritz, Jr. (1910–1992), late associate of HPL who became one of the leading figures in science fiction and fantasy. For a time both he and his wife Jonquil corresponded separately with HPL.

Long, Frank Belknap (1901–1994), fiction writer and poet and one of HPL's closest friends and correspondents. Late in life he wrote the memoir, *Howard Phillips Lovecraft: Dreamer on the Nightside* (1975).

Loveman, Samuel E. (1887–1976), poet and longtime friend of HPL and Hart Crane, and associate of Ambrose Bierce, Hart Crane, George Sterling, and Clark Ashton Smith. He wrote *The Hermaphrodite* (1926) and other works.

Lynch, Joseph Bernard (1879–1952), amateur journalist and member of the Hub Club.

Machen, Arthur (1863–1947), Welsh author of weird fiction whose work influenced HPL significantly after he read it in 1923.

Martin, Harry E., amateur journalist and official editor of the NAPA during the period of HPL's interim presidency (1922–23).

McNeil, Everett (1862–1929), author of historical and adventure novels for boys; member of the Kalem Club.

Merritt, A[braham] (1884–1943), writer of fantasy and horror tales for the pulps. His work was much admired by HPL in spite of its concessions to pulp formulae. His late novel, *Dwellers in the Mirage* (1932), may have been influenced by HPL.

Miniter, Edith (1867–1934), amateur author who also professionally published a novel, *Our Natupski Neighbors* (1916) and many short stories. HPL was guest at her home in Wilbraham, Massachusetts, in the summer of 1928.

Moe, Maurice W[inter] (1882–1940), amateur journalist, English teacher, and longtime friend and correspondent of HPL. He lived successively in Appleton and Milwaukee, WI.

Munn, H[arold] Warner (1903–1981), contributor to the pulp magazines, living near W. Paul Cook in Athol, MA.

Orton, Vrest (1897–1986), a late member of the Kalem Club. He was for a time an editor at the *Saturday Review* and later the founder of the Vermont Country Store. He compiled an early bibliography of Theodore Dreiser, *Dreiserana* (1929).

Parker, Charles A. A. (1880–1965), amateur journalist and editor of the little magazine *L'Alouette*, chiefly devoted to poetry.

Pearson, James Larkin (1879–1981), amateur journalist and author of several volumes of poetry.

Phillips, Whipple Van Buren (1833–1904), HPL's maternal grandfather. A wealthy industrialist, he established the Owyhee Land and Irrigation Company in Idaho. He provided strong guidance to HPL in the absence of HPL's father. His death in 1904 and the subsequent mismanagement of his estate forced HPL and his mother to move from 454 Angell Street to smaller quarters at 598 Angell Street.

Poe, Edgar Allan (1809–1849), pioneering American author of weird fiction.

Price, E[dgar] Hoffmann (1898–1988), prolific pulp writer of weird and adventure tales. HPL met him in New Orleans in 1932 and corresponded extensively with him thereafter.

Quinn, Seabury (1889–1969), prolific author of weird and detective tales to the pulps, notably a series of tales involving the psychic detective Jules de Grandin.

Renshaw, Anne Tillery, prolific amateur journalist and professor. She met HPL during the latter's visit to Washington, DC, in April 1925. In 1936 she commissioned HPL to revise a textbook of English usage, *Well-Bred Speech* (1936), although much of the work HPL did for it was excised and remains unpublished.

Rimel, Duane W[eldon] (1915–1996), weird fiction fan and late associate of HPL, who revised some of his early tales.

Sandusky, Albert A. (d. 1934?), amateur journalist whose use of slang captivated HPL. HPL met him frequently during trips to the Boston area.

Schwartz, Julius (1915–2004), editor of *Fantasy Magazine* who acted as HPL's agent in marketing *At the Mountains of Madness* to *Astounding Stories.*

Sechrist, Edward Lloyd (1873–1953), amateur journalist and beekeeper. HPL met him on several occasions, especially during visits to Washington, DC.

Smith, Charles W. ("Tryout") (1852–1948), longtime amateur journalist, editor of the *Tryout,* and friend and correspondent of HPL.

Smith, Clark Ashton (1893–1961), prolific California poet and writer of fantasy tales. He received a "fan" letter from HPL in 1922 and corresponded with him until HPL's death.

Smith, Edwin Hadley (1869–1944), a leading amateur journalist of the period, chiefly associated with the NAPA.

Sterling, Kenneth (1920–1995), young science fiction fan who came into contact with HPL in 1934. They collaborated on the science fiction story "In the Walls of Eryx" (1935). Sterling later became a distinguished physician.

Strauch, Carl Ferdinand (1908–1989), friend of Harry Brobst and correspondent of HPL. He later became a distinguished professor and critic.

Talman, Wilfred Blanch (1904–1986), correspondent of HPL and late member of the Kalem Club. HPL assisted Talman on his story "Two Black Bottles" (1926) and wrote "Some Dutch Footprints in New England" for Talman to publish in *De Halve Maen,* the journal of the Holland Society of New York. Late in life he wrote the memoir *The Normal Lovecraft* (1973).

Tucker, Gertrude E., editor of the Reading Lamp, evidently a literary agency. She also edited the *Reading Lamp,* a literary journal for which HPL wrote at least one review (not located).

Utpatel, Frank (1908–1980), artist friend of August Derleth who illustrated some of Derleth's work for *Weird Tales* and later did many jackets and interiors (primarily woodcuts) for Arkham House; late correspondent of HPL.

Wandrei, Donald (1908–1987), poet and author of weird fiction, science fiction, and detective tales. He corresponded with HPL from 1926 to 1937, visited HPL in Providence in 1927 and 1932, and met HPL occasionally in New York during the 1930s. He helped HPL get "The Shadow out of Time" published in *Astounding Stories*. After HPL's death he and August Derleth founded the publishing firm Arkham House to preserve HPL's work. For their joint correspondence, see *Mysteries of Time and Spirit*.

Wandrei, Howard (1909–1956), younger brother of Donald Wandrei, premier weird artist and prolific author of weird fiction, science fiction, and detective stories; correspondent of HPL.

Weiss, Henry George (1898–1946), Canadian-born poet and essayist who wrote weird fiction under the pseudonym "Francis Flagg." He came in touch with HPL in 1930; his communist leanings may have influenced HPL's leftward political shift in the 1930s.

Whitehead, Henry S[t. Clair] (1882–1932), author of weird and adventure tales, many of them set in the Virgin Islands. HPL corresponded with him and visited him in Florida in 1931. HPL wrote a brief eulogy of Whitehead for *Weird Tales*.

Wollheim, Donald A[llen] (1914–1990), editor of the *Phantagraph* and *Fanciful Tales* and prolific author and editor in the science fiction field.

Wright, Farnsworth (1888–1940), editor of *Weird Tales* (1924–40). He rejected some of HPL's best work of the 1930s, only to publish it after HPL's death upon submittal by August Derleth.

Bibliography

A. Works by H. P. Lovecraft

Books

The *Ancient Track: Complete Poetical Works*. Edited by S. T. Joshi. San Francisco: Night Shade Books, 2001.

The *Annotated Supernatural Horror in Literature*. Edited by S. T. Joshi. New York: Hippocampus Press, 2000.

At the Mountains of Madness and Other Novels. Edited by S. T. Joshi. Sauk City, WI: Arkham House, [1985]. [*MM*]

Collected Essays. Edited by S. T. Joshi. New York: Hippocampus Press, 2004–06. 5 vols. [*CE*]

Commonplace Book. Edited by David E. Schultz. West Warwick, RI: Necronomicon Press, 1987; also in *Miscellaneous Writings* and *Collected Essays*.

Dagon and Other Macabre Tales. Edited by S. T. Joshi. Sauk City, WI: Arkham House, [1986]. [*D*]

The Dunwich Horror and Others. Edited by S. T. Joshi. Sauk City, WI: Arkham House, [1984]. [*DH*]

Essential Solitude: The Letters of H. P. Lovecraft and August Derleth. Edited by David E. Schultz and S. T. Joshi. New York: Hippocampus Press, 2008.

The Horror in the Museum and Other Revisions. Edited by S. T. Joshi. Sauk City, WI: Arkham House, [1989]. [*HM*]

Letters from New York. Edited by S. T. Joshi and David E. Schultz. San Francisco: Night Shade Books, 2005.

Letters to Rheinhart Kleiner. Edited by S. T. Joshi and David E. Schultz. New York: Hippocampus Press, 2005.

Lord of a Visible World: An Autobiography in Letters. Edited by S. T. Joshi and David E. Schultz. Athens: Ohio University Press, 2000.

A Means to Freedom: The Letters of H. P. Lovecraft and Robert E. Howard. Edited by S. T. Joshi, David E. Schultz, and Rusty Burke. New York: Hippocampus Press, 2009.

Miscellaneous Writings. Edited by S. T. Joshi. Sauk City, WI: Arkham House, 1995.

Mysteries of Time and Spirit: The Letters of H. P. Lovecraft and Donald Wandrei. Edited by S. T. Joshi and David E. Schultz. San Francisco: Night Shade Books, 2002.

Selected Letters. Edited by August Derleth, Donald Wandrei, and James Turner. Sauk City, WI: Arkham House, 1965–76. 5 vols. [*SL*]

The Shadow over Innsmouth. Everett, PA: Visionary Publishing Co., 1936.

The Shunned House. Athol, MA: Recluse Press, 1928 (printed but not bound or distributed until 1959–61). In *MM*.

Stories

At the Mountains of Madness. *Astounding Stories* 16, No. 6 (February 1936): 8–32; 17, No. 1 (March 1936): 125–55; 17, No. 2 (April 1936): 132–50. In *MM*.

The Case of Charles Dexter Ward. *WT* 35, No. 9 (May 1941): 8–40; 35, No. 10 (July 1941): 84–121 (abridged). In *MM*.

"The Cats of Ulthar." *Tryout* 6, No. 11 (November 1920): [3–9]. *WT* 7, No. 2 (February 1926): 252–54. *WT* 21, No. 2 (February 1933): 259–61.

"The Colour out of Space." *Amazing Stories* 2, No. 6 (Sept. 1927): 557–67. In *DH*.

"Dagon." *Vagrant* No. 11 (Nov. 1919): 23–29. *WT* 2, No. 3 (Oct. 1923): 23–25. In *D*.

The Dream-Quest of Unknown Kadath. First published in *Beyond the Wall of Sleep*. Sauk City, WI: Arkham House, 1943. In *MM*.

"The Dunwich Horror." *WT* 13, No. 4 (Apr. 1929): 481–508. In *DH*.

"Facts concerning the Late Arthur Jermyn and His Family." *Wolverine* No. 9 (Mar. 1921): 3–11. *WT* 3, No. 4 (April 1924): 15–18 (as "The White Ape"). *WT* 25, No. 5 (May 1935): 642–48 (as "Arthur Jermyn"). In *D*.

"The Festival." *WT* 5, No. 1 (Jan. 1925): 169–74. *WT* 22, No. 4 (Oct. 1933): 519–20, 522–28. In *D*.

"The Haunter of the Dark." *WT* 28, No. 5 (Dec. 1936): 538–53. In *DH*.

"The Hound." *WT* 3, No. 2 (Feb. 1924): 50–52, 78. *WT* 14, No. 3 (Sept. 1929): 421–25, 432. In *D*.

"The Music of Erich Zann." *National Amateur* 44, No. 4 (Mar. 1922): 38–40. *WT* 5, No. 5 (May 1925): 219–34. In *Creeps by Night: Chills and Thrills*, ed. Dashiell Hammett. New York: John Day Co., 1931, pp. 347–63. In *Modern Tales of Horror*, ed. Dashiell Hammett. London: Victor Gollancz, 1932, pp. 301–17. *Evening Standard* (London) (24 October 1932): 20–21. *WT* 24, No. 5 (November 1934): 644–48, 655–56. In *DH*.

"Pickman's Model." *WT* 10, No. 4 (October 1927): 505–14. In *The "Not at Night" Omnibus*, ed. Christine Campbell Thomson. London: Selwyn & Blount, [1937], pp. 119–31. In *DH*.

"The Rats in the Walls." *WT* 3, No. 3 (March 1924): 25–31. *WT* 15, No. 6 (June 1930): 841–53. In *Switch On the Light*, ed. Christine Campbell Thomson. London: Selwyn & Blount, 1931, pp. 141–65. In *DH*.

"The Statement of Randolph Carter." *Vagrant* No. 13 (May 1920): 41–48. *WT* 5, No. 2 (Feb. 1925): 149–53. In *MM*.

"The Thing on the Doorstep." *WT* 29, No. 1 (Jan. 1937): 52–70. In *DH*.

"The Tomb." *Vagrant* no. 14 (March 1922): 50–64. *WT* 7, no. 1 (January 1926): 117–23. In *D*.

"The Unnamable." *WT* 6, no. 1 (July 1925): 78–82. In *D*.

Revisions and Collaborations

Bishop, Zealia Brown Reed. "The Curse of Yig." *WT* 14, No. 5 (November 1929): 625–36. In *HM*.

de Castro, Adolphe. "The Electric Executioner." *WT* 16, No. 2 (August 1930): 223–36. In *HM*.

———. "The Last Test." *WT* 12, No. 5 (November 1928): 625–56. In *HM*.

Eddy, C. M. "Ashes." *WT* 3, No. 3 (March 1924): 22–24. In *HM*.

———. "The Ghost-Eater." *WT* 3, No. 4 (April 1924): 72–75.

———. "The Loved Dead." *WT* 4, No. 2 (May–June–July 1924): 54–57. In *HM*.

Greene, Sonia. "The Horror at Martin's Beach." *WT* 2, No. 4 (November 1923): 75–76, 83 (as "The Invisible Monster"). In *HM*.

Heald, Hazel. "The Horror in the Museum." *WT* 22, No. 1 (July 1933): 49–68. In *HM*.

———. "Winged Death." *WT* 23, No. 3 (March 1934): 299–315. In *HM*.

Houdini, Harry. "Under the Pyramids." *WT* 4, No. 2 (May–June–July 1924): 3–12 (as "Imprisoned with the Pharaohs"; as by "Houdini"). In *D*.

Price, E. Hoffmann. "Through the Gates of the Silver Key." *WT* 24, No. 1 (July 1934): 60–85. In *MM*.

Talman, Wilfred Blanch. "Two Black Bottles." *WT* 10, No. 2 (August 1927): 251–58.

Essays

"Cats and Dogs." *Leaves* No. 1 (Summer 1937): 25–34 (as by "Lewis Theobald, Jun."). In *CE* 5.

A Description of the Town of Quebeck, in New-France. In *CE* 4.

"In Memoriam: Robert Ervin Howard." *Fantasy Magazine* No. 38 (September 1936): 29–31. In *CE* 5.

"Preface." In *White Fire* by John Ravenor Bullen. Athol, MA: Recluse Press, 1927 [actually January 1928], pp. 7–13. In *CE* 2.

"Observations on Several Parts of America." In *CE* 4.

"Save the Old Brick Row." (As by James F. Morton.) *Providence Sunday Journal* (22 December 129): Section A, p. 5.

"Sleepy Hollow To-day." In *Junior Literature: Book Two*, ed. Sterling A. Leonard and Harold Y. Moffett. New York:: Macmillan, 1930, 1935, pp. 545–46 (extract from "Observations on Several Parts of America"). In *CE* 4.

"Some Current Amateur Verse." *National Amateur* 58, No. 2 (December 1935): 14–15 (signed "H. P. L.").

"Some Dutch Footprints in New England." *De Halve Maen* 9, No. 1 (18 October 1933): 2, 4.

"Supernatural Horror in Literature." *Recluse* No. 1 (1927): 23–59. Rev. ed. in *Fantasy Fan* (October 1933–February 1935). In *D*, *CE* 2.

"Travels in the Provinces of America." In *CE* 4.

Poems [all poems are in *AT*]

"The Adventures of Ulysses; or, The New Odyssey."

"The Ancient Track." *WT* 15, No. 3 (Mar. 1930): 300.

"Ave atque Vale: To Jonathan E. Hoag, Esq.: February 10, 1831–October 17th, 1927." *Tryout*, 11, No. 10 (December 1927): [3–4].

"The East India Brick Row." *Providence Journal* 102, No. 7 (8 January 1930): 13.

"An Epistle to the Rt. Honble Maurice Winter Moe, Esq. of Zythopolis, in the Northwest Territory of HIS MAJESTY'S American Dominion."

"In Memoriam: J. E. T. D." *Tryout* 5, No. 3 (March 1919): [6] (as by "Ward Phillips"). In *In Memoriam: Jennie E. T. Dowe*, ed. Michael White. Dorchester, MA: [W. Paul Cook,] September 1921, p. 56.

"The Isaacsonio-Mortoniad."

[On a Scene in Rural Rhode Island.]

[On J. F. Roy Erford.]

"The Outpost." *Bacon's Essays* 3, No. 1 (Spring 1930): 7. *Fantasy Magazine* 3, No. 3 (May 1934): 24–25. *O-Wash-Ta-Nong* 3, No. 1 (January 1938): 1.

Poemata Minora, Volume II (1902).

"Prologue" to "Fragments from an Hour of Inspiration" by Jonathan E. Hoag. *Tryout* 3, No. 8 (July 1917): [17]. In Jonathan E. Hoag. *The Poetical Works of Jonathan E. Hoag*. New York: [Privately printed,] 1923, p. 41 (as "Prologue" to "Amid Inspiring Scenes").

"Recapture." *WT* 15, No. 5 (May 1930): 693. (Later sonnet XXXIV of *Fungi from Yuggoth*.)

"To Clark Ashton Smith, Esq., upon his Fantastic Tales, Verses, Pictures, & Sculptures." *Weird Tales* 31, No. 4 (April 1938): 392 (as "To Clark Ashton Smith").

"To Endymion: (Frank Belknap Long, Jr.): Upon His Coming of Age, April 27, 1923." *Tryout* 8, No. 10 (September 1923): [15–16] (as by "L. Theobald, Jun.").

"To Mr. Finlay, upon his Drawing for Mr. Bloch's Tale, 'The Faceless God.'" *Phantagraph* 6, No. 1 (May 1937). *Weird Tales* 30, No. 1 (July 1937): 17.

"To Mr. Hoag upon His 93rd Birthday, February 10, 1924." *Troy* [NY] *Times* (9 February 1924). *Pegasus* [3] (July 1924): 33.

"To Rheinhart Kleiner, Esq., upon His Town Fables and Elegies." *Tryout* 8, No. 7 (April 1923): [11–14] (as by "Lewis Theobald, Jun.").

[Untitled: "MADAM, what thankful Raptures rouse my Breast,"].

B. Select Works by James F. Morton

Books

The *American Secular Union: Its Aims and Plans and the Basis of its Appeal to All True Americans*. Philadelphia, 1910.

Another Blow to Royalty. San Francisco: Free Society, 1900.

Better Than Socialism. New York: The Single Tax Review?, 191-?

The *Case of Billy Sunday: His Arraignment on Serious Charges and Self-Conviction of Guilt*. New York: Truth Seeker Co., 1915.

The Curse of Race Prejudice. 1906.

Do You Want Free Speech? Home, WA: [The Author], 1902.

Exempting the Churches. New York: The Truth Seeker Co., 1916.

The Philosophy of the Single Tax. New York, 19–.

The Truth About Francisco Ferrer. New York: The Truth Seeker, 1913.

Periodicals

The Beacon.

Demonstrator: A Weekly Periodical of Fact, Thought and Comment.

Libra.

Loyal Citizen Sovereignty.

The Stray One: An Occasional Amateur Publication.

Essays

"Another Free Speech Case." *The Agitator* 1, No. 24 (November 1, 1911).

"C. L. James." *Mother Earth* 6, No. 6 (August 1911).

"Come, Let Us Reason Together." *The Stray One* 3 (June 1911): 1–2.

"Concerning Amateur Matters." *The Stray One* [1] (March 1909): 7–9.

"Concerning John W. Smith." *The Stray One* [1] (March 1909): 10–11.

"Concerning the Warren Convention." *Brooklynite* 17, No. 1 (February 1927): 2–4.

"'Conservatism' Gone Mad." *In a Minor Key* No. 2 [1915]: [15–16].

"Do You Want Free Speech?" *Demonstrator* 2 (March 18, 1903)–9 (May 6, 1903).

"Dr. Swift on the Negro." *The Stray One* [1] (March 1909): 6-7.

"Ernest Adams." *Brooklynite* 23, No. 3 (December 1934): 2.

"A Few Memories." *Olympian* No. 35 (Autumn 1940): 24–28.

"For the Good of the Cause." *The Stray One* 2 (June 1909): 2.

"Fossiliferous Folly." *The Stray One* 3 (June 1911): 4–6.

"Fragments of a Mental Autobiography." I, *Libra* 1, No. 2 (April 1907): [1–2]; II, *Libra* 1, No. 3 (June 1907): [1–2]; III, *Libra* 1, No. 4 (August 1907): [1]; IV, *Libra* 1, No. 5 (October 1907): [1]; V, *Libra* 1, No. 6 (December 1907): [1–2].

"Freedom of Expression." *Demonstrator* 1 (March 11, 1903).

"Historian's Report, 1924–25." *Brooklynite* 15, No. 3 (July 1925): 6–7.

"How I Like to Spend My Evenings." *Brooklynite* 23, No. 3 (December 1933): 2.

"I Say." *The Stray One* 3 (June 1911): 2–4.

"If I Could Take My Ideal Vacation." *Brooklynite* 20, No. 2 (September 1930): 1.

"In the Balance." *Libra* 1, No. 5 (October 1907): [2–4]; 1, No. 6 (December 1907): [2–4].

"Is It All a Dream?" *Free Society Library* 5 (June 1900).

"The Latest Press Outrage." *Clothed with the Sun* 2, No. 10 (November 1901).

"Leaders." *Brooklynite* 25, No. 2 (September 1935): 1.

"Man's Strongest Motive." *Brooklynite* 27, No. 2 (September 1937): 1–2.

"The Many Roads to Freedom." *The Agitator* 1, no. 7 (February 15, 1911).

"Memorizing Literature." *National Amateur* 41, No. 6 (July 1919): 249–51.

"Miscellanea." *The Stray One* [1] (March 1909): 11–12; 2 (June 1909): 3

"Misrepresenters of Anarchy." *Demonstrator* 11 (May 20, 1903)–13 (June 3, 1903).

"A Modern Adventure?" *Brooklynite* 28, No. 1 (June 1938): 2.

"A Monumental Defence of Free Speech." *Mother Earth* 6, No. 10 (December 1911).

"More on the Religious Question." *The Stray One* [1] (March 1909): 4–5.

"My Funniest Experience." *Brooklynite* 14, No. 1 (January 1924): 5–6.

"My Intellectual Evolution." *Liberal* 1, No. 3 (February 1923): 11–13.

"One of My Pet Theories." *Brooklynite* 25, No. 4 (March 1936): 1–2.

"The Origin and Working of the Comstock Laws." *Birth Control Review*

"Our Next President." *The Stray One* 2 (June 1909): 1–2.

"Our Position." *Demonstrator* 15 (June 17, 1903).

"Parks." *Brooklynite* 26, No. 4 (March 1937): 1.

"Phobias." *Brooklynite* 21, No. 3 (January 1932): 1, 4.

"The Point of View." *The Stray One* [1] (March 1909): [1].

"The Political Situation." *The Stray One* [1] (March 1909): 2–3.

"Prevention of Conception as a Duty." In William Josephus Robinson, ed. *Fewer and Better Babies; or, The Limitation of Offspring by the Prevention of Conception.* New York: The Critic and Guide Company (1916): 195–204.

"Reformers and Ethics." *Altruria* 2, No. 5 (November 1907).

"Smoke Screens." *Brooklynite* 26, No. 2 (September 1936): 1.

"Some Church and State Items." *The Stray One* [1] (March 1909): 7.

"Some Fruits of Race Prejudice." *The Stray One* [1] (March 1909): 9–10.

"Some Notes on Monarchs." *The Stray One* [1] (March 1909): 5–6.

"Stepping Out." *Brooklynite* 22, No. 2 (September 1932): 2.

"The Political Situation." *The Stray One* [1] (March 1909): 2–3.

"Southern Barbarism." *Lucifer, the Light Bearer* 775 (August 19, 1899).

"The Unevenness of Justice." *The Stray One* [1] (March 1909): 3–4.

"What of the Amendments." *The Stray One* 2 (June 1909): 3.

"Why Were They Martyrs?" *Demonstrator* 32 (November 11, 1903).
"Wife and Prostitute." *Lucifer, the Light Bearer* 748 (February 4, 1899).

Poems

"Castles in the Air." *Brooklynite* 19, No. 5 (March 1930): 8.
"Christmas Spirit." *Brooklynite* 18, No. 1 (February 1928): 4.
"Design in Living." *Brooklynite* 24, No. 4 (March 1935): 1.
"Dreams." *Brooklynite* 19, No. 2 (June 1929): 1.
"Fashion Bondage." *Brooklynite* 17, No. 1 (February 1927): 2.
"Fate." *Brooklynite* 18, No. 3 (September 1928): 7.
"Fause Murdoch." *Conservative* No. 13 (July 1923): 12–16.
"Forbidden Fruit." *Brooklynite* 25, No. 3 (December 1935): 2.
"Friends and Enemies." *Brooklynite* 19, No. 1 (March 1929): 1.
"A Hallowe'en Ballad." *Brooklynite* 16, No. 3 (October 1926): 4.
"Haunted Houses." *Weird Tales* 3, No. 3 (March 1924): 84 (with JFM's letter
    to the editor, as printed in "The Eyrie").
"Humor." *Brooklynite* 20, No. 4 (March 1931): 1.
"Idealism." *Brooklynite* 19, No. 4 (December 1929): 8.
"If I Had Lived A Hundred Years Ago." *Brooklynite* 19, No. 5 (March 1930): 4–5.
"Intelligence Tests." *Brooklynite* 19, No. 5 (March 1930): 5.
"Lest We Forget: To the Chicago Martyrs." *Clothed with the Sun* 2. No. 11 (De-
    cember 1901).
"Looking Backward." *Brooklynite* 19, No. 3 (September 1929): 5.
"A Mid-Summer Episode." *Brooklynite* 19, No. 5 (March 1930): 6–7.
"A Narrow Squeak." *Brooklynite* 27, No. 4 (March 1938): 2.
"My Most Cherished Illusion." *Brooklynite* 19, No. 5 (March 1930): 3–4.
"One Christmas I Remember." *Brooklynite* 19, No. 5 (March 1930): 2–3.
"The Path I Did not Take." *Brooklynite* 19, No. 5 (March 1930): 8.
"The Penalties of Intelligence." *Brooklynite* 19, No. 5 (March 1930): 8.
"Price Tags." *Brooklynite* 18, No. 3 (September 1928): 2.
"Something I'd Like to Forget." *Brooklynite* 19, No. 5 (March 1930): 7–8.
"Spring for Me." *Brooklynite* 12, No. 2 (April 1922): 4.
"Subway Conversations and Observations." *Brooklynite* 13, No. 3 (July 1923): 7.
"Suppressed Desires." *Brooklynite* 19, No. 5 (March 1930): 6.
"Thoughts on Marriage." *Brooklynite* 23, No. 4 (March 1934): 1.
"To G.W.K. on His 27th Birthday." In *Lovecraft's New York Circle: The Kalem
    Club, 1924–1927*, ed. Mara Kirk Hart and S. T. Joshi. New York: Hippo-
    campus Press, p. 210.
"To Howard." Unpublished quatrain, ms. JHL.
"The Weather." *Brooklynite* 22, No. 4 (March 1933): 4.
"What I Like to Eat, and Why." *Brooklynite* 12, No. 4 (October 1922): 2.
"What Price Civilization?" *Brooklynite* 21, No. 2 (October 1931): 1.
"What Will People Say?" *Brooklynite* 18, No. 4 (December 1928): 1.

"When I Have Time." *Brooklynite* 19, No. 5 (March 1930): 5.
"When Ships Come In." *Brooklynite* 17, No. 4 (November 1927): 4.

C. Works by Others

Dates in angular brackets indicate first publication.

Allen, Hervey (1889–1949). *Anthony Adverse.* New York: Farrar & Rinehart, 1933.

Bartky, Walter (1901–?). *Highlights of Astronomy.* Chicago: University of Chicago Press, 1935.

Barlow, R. H. (1918–1951). "R. E. H." *WT* 28, No. 3 (October 1936): 353.

Beckford, William (1759–1844). *Vathek.* <1786> Introduction by Ben Ray Redman, illustrated by Mahlon Blaine. New York: John Day Co., 1928. (*LL* 75)

———. *The Episodes of Vathek.* Translated from the French by Sir Frank T. Marzials. <1912> Boston: Small, Maynard & Co., [1922?] or [1924?]. (*LL* 73)

Bierce, Ambrose (1842–1914?). *Twenty-one Letters of Ambrose Bierce.* Edited with a Note by Samuel Loveman. Cleveland: George Kirk, 1922. (*LL* 89)

Blackwood, Algernon (1869–1951). *The Extra Day.* London: Macmillan, 1915.

———. *The Garden of Survival.* London: Macmillan, 1918.

Bregenzer, Don, and Samuel Loveman (1887–1976), ed. *A Round-Table in Poictesme: A Symposium.* Cleveland: Colophon Club, 1924. (*LL* 117)

Brontë, Emily. *Wuthering Heights.* See Mitford.

Buchan, John (1875–1940). *Midwinter.* New York: George H. Doran, 1923.

Bush, David Van (1882–1959). *Peace Poems and Sausages.* [Webster, SD: Reporter & Farmer Print, 1915.]

———. *"Pike's Peak or Bust"; or, The Possibilities of the Will.* [Webster, SD: The Reporter & Farmer, 1916.]

———. *Soul Poems and Love Lyrics.* St Louis: David Van Bush, [1916].

Cole, Edward H. "James Ferdinand Morton, Jr." *Ghost* No. 5 (July 1947): 11–15.

Cook, W. Paul. "Jim Morton." *Ghost* No. 5 (July 1947): 9–11.

Crawford, F. Marion (1854–1909). *Wandering Ghosts.* New York: Macmillan, 1911. London: T. Fisher Unwin, 1911 (as *Uncanny Tales*). [Contains: "The Upper Berth," "For the Blood Is the Life," and "The Dead Smile."]

Derleth, August (1909–1971). "The Sheraton Mirror." *Weird Tales* (September 1932).

———. *Still Is the Summer Night.* New York: Charles Scribner's Sons, 1937.

———. *Three Who Died.* New York: Loring & Mussey, 1935. (*LL* 237)

Duncan, John Charles (1882–?). *Astronomy.* New York: Harper & Brothers, 1926; 3rd ed. 1935.

Dunsany, Lord (1878–1957). *The Curse of the Wise Woman.* London: Heinemann, 1933.

————. *The Lost Silk Hat.* In *Five Plays.* London: Grant Richards, 1914. (*LL* 275)

Dutt, R. Palme (1896–1974). *Fascism and Social Revolution.* New York: International Publishers, 1934.

Eddy, C. M., Jr. (1896–1967). "Black Noon." In Eddy's *Exit into Eternity.* Providence, RI: Oxford Press, 1973.

Flecker, James Elroy (1884–1915). *Hassan: The Story of Hassan of Baghdad and How He Came to Make the Golden Journey to Samarkand.* New York: Alfred A. Knopf, 1922.

Fuess, Claude Moore (1885–1963). *Daniel Webster.* Boston: Little, Brown, 1930. 2 vols.

Hart, Mara Kirk, and S. T. Joshi, ed. *Lovecraft's New York Circle: The Kalem Club, 1924–1927.* New York: Hippocampus Press, 2006.

Hergesheimer, Joseph (1880–1954). *Balisand.* New York: Knopf, 1924.

————. *Java Head.* New York: Knopf, 1918.

Heyward, DuBose (1885–1940). *Peter Ashley.* New York: Farrar & Rinehart, 1932.

Hylton, J[ohn] Dunbar (1837–1893). *The Bride of Gettysburg: An Episode of 1863, in Three Parts.* Palmyra, NJ, 1878.

Kittredge, George Lyman (1860–1941). *The Old Farmer and His Almanack.* Boston: W. Ware & Co., 1904. (*LL* 504)

Kleiner, Rheinhart. "James Morton." *Ghost* No. 5 (July 1947): 15–20.

Krutch, Joseph Wood (1893–1970). *The Modern Temper. A Study and a Confession.* New York: Harcourt, Brace, 1929.

Lederer, Charles (1856–1925). *Drawing Made Easy: A Book That Can Teach You How to Draw.* Chicago: Hall & McCreary, 1927. (*LL* 520)

Leiber, Fritz (1910–1991). "Adept's Gambit." In Leiber's *Night's Black Agents.* Sauk City, WI: Arkham House, 1950.

Leith, W. Compton (pseud. of O. M. Dalton, 1866–1945). *Sirenica.* <1913> With an Introduction by William Marion Reedy. Portland, ME: Thomas Bird Mosher, 1927. (*LL* 523)

Lewis, Matthew Gregory (1775–1818). *The Monk.* <1796> London: Brentano's, [1924]. 3 vols. in 1. (*LL* 531)

Long, Frank Belknap (1901–1994). *A Man from Genoa and Other Poems.* Athol, MA: W. Paul Cook, 1926.

Longa, Ernesto A. *Anarchist Periodicals in English Published in the United States (1833–1955): An Annotated Guide.* Toronto: Scarecrow Press, 2010.

————. "An American Humorist." *Conservative* No. 12 (March 1923): 2–5.

Loveman, Samuel (1887–1976). *The Hermaphrodite: A Poem.* Athol, MA: W. Paul Cook, 1926. (*LL* 549)

————. *The Hermaphrodite and Other Poems.* Caldwell, ID: The Caxton Printers, 1936. (*LL* 550)

————. *Out of the Immortal Night: Selected Works by Samuel Loveman.* Ed. S. T. Joshi and David E. Schultz. New York: Hippocampus Press, 2004.

Lynch, John Gilbert Bohun (1884–1928), ed. *The Best Ghost Stories.* Boston: Small, Maynard & Co., [1924]. (*LL* 558)

Machen, Arthur. (1863–1947). *Hieroglyphics: A Note upon Ecstasy in Literature.* London: Grant Richards, 1902. (*LL* 571)

———. *The Hill of Dreams.* London: E. Grant Richards, 1907. (*LL* 572)

———. *The House of Souls.* <1906> New York: Alfred A. Knopf, 1923. (*LL* 573) [Contains: "The White People."]

———. *The Terror.* London: Duckworth, 1917.

Marsh, Richard (1857–1915). *The Beetle.* London: Skeffington, 1897. (*LL* 595)

Mather, Cotton (1663–1728). *Magnalia Christi Americana.* London: Printed for T. Parkhurst, 1702. (*LL* 598)

Maturin, Charles Robert (1782?–1824). *Melmoth the Wanderer.* <1820> London: Richard Bentley & Son, 1892. 3 vols. (*LL* 599)

Merritt, A. (1884–1943). *The Metal Monster. Argosy* (7 August–25 September 1920). Rpt. New York: Hippocampus Press, 2002.

Merritt, Pearl K. "Comments on Mr. Price's Article." *Ghost* No. 5 (July 1947): 6–9.

Meyrink, Gustav (1868–1932). *The Golem.* <1915> Tr. Madge Pemberton. London: Gollancz; Boston: Houghton Mifflin, 1928.

Mitford, Mary Russell (1797–1855). *Our Village.* <1832> Brontë, Emily (1818–1848). *Wuthering Heights.* <1847> New York: Century Co., 1906. (*LL* 611)

The Modern Encyclopedia: A New Library of World Knowledge. Ed. A. H. McDannald. New York: Grosset & Dunlap, 1935. (*LL* 613) First published by W. H. Wise & Co. (New York), 1933 (rev. 1935).

O'Brien, Edward J. (1890–1941). *The Dance of the Machines: The American Short Story and the Industrial Age.* New York: Macaulay Co., 1929. (*LL* 651)

———, ed. *The Best Short Stories of 1928 and the Yearbook of the American Short Story.* New York: Dodd, Mead, 1928. (*LL* 650)

Orton, Vrest (1897–1986). *Dreiserana: A Book about His Books.* New York: [Stratford Press,] 1929. Rpt. New York: Haskell House, 1973. (*LL* 655)

Palgrave, Francis T. (1824–1897), ed. *The Golden Treasury: Selected from the Best Songs and Lyrical Poems in the English Language.* London: Macmillan, 1861. (*LL* 671)

Pendergast, P[atrick] J[ames] (1850–?). *Selected Gems.* [Jamaica Plain, MA: Angel Guardian Press, 1917.]

Pitkin, Walter B. (1878–1953). *A Short Introduction to the History of Human Stupidity.* New York: Simon & Schuster, 1932.

Price, E. Hoffman[n]. "Mortonius." *Ghost* No. 5 (July 1947): 1–6.

Quinn, Seabury (1889–1969). "The Phantom Farmhouse." *WT* (October 1923).

Radcliffe, Ann (1764–1823). *The Italian; or, The Confessional of the Black Penitents.* London: T. Cadell & W. Davies, 1797.

Reeve, Clara (1729–1807). *The Old English Baron: A Gothic Story.* London: Colchester, 1777 (as *The Champion of Virtue*). (*LL* 724)

Reynolds, George W. M. (1814–1879). *Faust: A Romance of the Secret Tribunals.* London: G. Vickers, 1847.

———. *Wagner the Wehr-Wolf.* London: J. Dicks, 1848, 1857, 1872.

Saintsbury, George (1843–1933), ed. *Tales of Mystery.* New York: Macmillan, 1891. [Containing extracts from Ann Radcliffe, *The Mysteries of Udolpho;* Matthew Gregory Lewis, *The Monk;* and Charles Robert Maturin, *Melmoth the Wanderer.*] (*LL* 755)

Scott, Sir Walter (1771–1832). *Letters on Demonology and Witchcraft.* <1830> London: George Routledge & Sons, 1884. (*LL* 771)

Smith, Clark Ashton. (1893–1961). *The Double Shadow and Other Fantasies.* [Auburn, CA: Auburn Journal Press, 1933.] (*LL* 810)

———. "The End of the Story." *WT* 15, No. 5 (May 1930): 637–48.

———. "Marooned in Andromeda." *Wonder Stories* 2, No. 5 (October 1930): 390–401, 465.

———. "A Night in Malnéant." In *The Double Shadow and Other Fantasies.*

———. "The Tale of Satampra Zeiros." *WT* 18, No. 4 (November 1931): 491–99.

——— (with William Beckford). "The Third Episode of Vathek." *Leaves* No. 1 (Summer 1937): 1–24.

Spengler, Oswald (1880–1936). *Der Untergang des Abendlandes.* <1918–22> Tr. by Charles Francis Atkinson as *The Decline of the West.* London: George Allen & Unwin, 1922–26. 2 vols.

Stoker, Bram (1847–1912). *The Jewel of Seven Stars.* London: Heinemann, 1903. London: William Rider & Son, 1912, 1919.

Stokley, James (1900–?). *Stars and Telescopes.* New York: Harper & Brothers, 1936.

Stormonth, James (1824–1882). *A Dictionary of the English Language.* <1871> New York: Harper & Brothers, 1885. (*LL* 850)

Strachey, John (1901–1963). *The Nature of Capitalist Crisis.* London: Gollancz, 1935.

Suter, J. Paul. "Beyond the Door." *WT* 1, No. 2 (April 1923).

Tarkington, Booth (1869–1946). *Alice Adams.* Garden City, NY: Doubleday, Page, 1921.

Thomson, Christine Campbell (1897–1985), ed. *Not at Night.* London: Selwyn & Blount, 1925. (*LL* 879)

———, ed. *More Not at Night.* London: Selwyn & Blount, 1926.

Walpole, Horace (1717–1797). *The Castle of Otranto.* London: Printed for Thos. Lownds, 1764. (*LL* 916)

Wandrei, Donald (1908–1987). *Dark Odyssey.* St. Paul, MN: Webb Publishing Co., [1931]. (*LL* 917)

————.*Dead Titans, Waken! and Invisible Sun*. Lakewood, CO: Centipede Press, 2011.

————. "The Red Brain." *WT* 10, No. 4 (October 1927): 531–37. *WT* 27, No. 5 (May 1936): 626–28, 630–33.

Wells, H. G. (1866–1946), Julian Huxley, and G. P. Wells. *The Science of Life: A Summary of Contemporary Knowledge about Life and Its Possibilities*. London: Amalgamated Press, 1930 (2 vols.). Garden City, NY: Doubleday, Doran, 1931 (4 vols.).

Weigall, Arthur (1880–1934). *Wanderings in Roman Britain*. London: Butterworth, 1926. (*LL* 933)

Whitman, Sarah Helen Power (1803–1878). *Poems*. 2nd ed. Providence: Preston & Rounds, 1894. (*LL* 951)

Willis, Eola (1856–1952). *The Charleston Stage in the XVIII Century, with Social Settings of the Time*. Columbia, SC: The State Co., 1924.

Index

Adams, A. M. 54, 343
Adams, Hazel Pratt 27, 35n9
Adams, Henry 56
Adams, John Quincy 374
Addison, Joseph 38n9, 312, 314
"Adept's Gambit" (Leiber) 401–2
"Adventures of Ulysses, The." *See*
    "Poem of Ulysses, The"
Aeneid (Virgil) 160
"After the Ball" 266n6
Agassiz, Louis 314
Agricola, Cn. Julius 316
Ainsworth, William Harrison 91
Akhilinanda, Swami 279
"Album, The" (Long) 399–400
Alcott, Louisa May 45
Alice Adams (Tarkington) 61
All-Story Weekly 40, 372
Allan, John 177
Alouette, L' 13, 63n1
"Amateur Humorist, An" (Long) 51
American Mineralogist 416
"Ancient Track, The" 200–201, 205
Angell, James Burrill 386
Anthony Adverse (Allen) 347
Anthony Adverse (film) 401
Arminius, James 247
Arnold, Benedict 103, 239, 370
"Arthur Jermyn." *See* "Facts concerning the
    Late Arthur Jermyn and His Family"
Asbury, Herbert 171–72
"Ashes" (Lovecraft-Eddy) 57
Associated Press 207, 208
Astounding Stories 346, 372, 401
At the Mountains of Madness 14, 287, 372,
    381, 406n29
Augustus (Emperor of Rome) 266n1
Avare, L' (Molière) 47

Bacon, Leonard 314
Bacon, Victor E. 141
Baird, Edwin 40, 43, 44, 46–47, 49, 54,
    57, 61, 65, 66, 67, 68, 145, 372
Balch, Allan C. 36, 39
Balderston, John 152n1
Balisand (Hergesheimer) 261

"Ballade of the City of New London,
    The" 143
Barker, Henry A. 414
Barlow, R. H. 16, 164n2, 359, 360, 362,
    366, 367, 372, 382, 389, 390–91, 397,
    441–44
Barlow, Wayne 366
Barnitz, Park 305
Barrow, J. E. 177
Bartram, John 102
Beckford, William 312, 402
Beebe, Evanore 315
Beetle, The (Marsh) 49
Bennis, Mr. and Mrs. 119–20
Bergson, Henri 197
Berkeley, George 364
Best Ghost Stories (Lynch) 313
"Beyond the Door" (Suter) 40
Bierce, Ambrose 161
Bicknell, Thomas W. 135n2
"Bird of Space, The" 354
Birth of a Nation, The (film) 409
Bishop, Zealia Brown Reed 139n1
Black Cat 13, 40, 372
Black Mask 13, 35n4, 40
Blackwood, Algernon 161, 313, 402
Blavatsky, Helena P. 424
Bloch, Robert 398, 399
Bloomfield, Robert 266nn14–15
Blue Pencil Club 33, 68, 75, 82, 83, 93,
    124, 157, 208, 335, 441, 455, 459, 461
Boas, Franz 252, 287
Boland, Stuart Morton 393
Bolitho, William 218–19
Bond, Frederick Bligh 132
Book of Jade, The (Barnitz) 305
Bookfellow Anthology, A (Seymour) 82
Boston Transcript 170, 206
Boule, Pierre Marcelin 252
Bride of Gettysburg, The (Hylton) 83, 179
"Bride of Osiris, The" (Kline) 145
Brief Course in Astronomy, A 363
Briffault, Robert 335, 387, 388
Brobst, Harry 295, 299, 305, 312, 332,
    338, 341, 371

483

CPSIA information can be obtained at www.ICGtesting.com
Printed in the USA
BVOW07s1212051213

338136BV00010B/306/P